The Feminist Film Philosophy Reader

The Feminist Film Philosophy Reader

Edited by Lucy Bolton

BLOOMSBURY ACADEMIC
LONDON • NEW YORK • OXFORD • NEW DELHI • SYDNEY

BLOOMSBURY ACADEMIC
Bloomsbury Publishing Plc, 50 Bedford Square, London, WC1B 3DP, UK
Bloomsbury Publishing Inc, 1359 Broadway, New York, NY 10018, USA
Bloomsbury Publishing Ireland, 29 Earlsfort Terrace, Dublin 2, D02 AY28, Ireland

BLOOMSBURY, BLOOMSBURY ACADEMIC and the Diana logo are
trademarks of Bloomsbury Publishing Plc

First published in Great Britain 2026

Cover design: Ben Anslow
Cover image: *Out of Blue* (2018), dir. Carol Morley (Image courtesy of the artist)

A catalogue record for this book is available from the British Library.

A catalog record for this book is available from the Library of Congress.

ISBN: HB: 978-1-8390-2657-7
         PB: 978-1-8390-2656-0
       ePDF: 978-1-8390-2659-1
      eBook: 978-1-8390-2658-4

Typeset by Integra Software Services Pvt. Ltd.
Printed and bound in India

For product safety related questions contact productsafety@bloomsbury.com.

To find out more about our authors and books visit www.bloomsbury.com
and sign up for our newsletters.

This anthology is dedicated to the students on my Film Philosophy and Feminist Film Philosophy modules over the past fifteen years, and also those to come in the future.

For Jessica, Phoebe and Martha, with love always.

Contents

Figures

Permissions

Part 1 Thinking for a Feminist Philosophy of Cinema

'The Cinema', Virginia Woolf, originally published in *The Nation and Athenaeum*, 3 July 1926, pp 381–3.

'The Male Gift', Christine Battersby, from *Gender and Genius: Towards a Female Aesthetic* by Christine Battersby, 1994, Women's Press. © Christine Battersby. This work is subject to copyright. All digital English language rights are held under licence by Bloomsbury Publishing PLC for as long as the whole of the digitised format of the English-language text of *Gender and Genius* is included in the online platform called Bloomsbury Philosophy Library. This includes the right to copy, distribute and make available through any and all means now known or hereafter invented, the digitised English language text of Chapter 4, excerpted here. All other rights, including translation rights and rights to the digitised text in languages other than English, are held by Christine Battersby as author and publisher of all hardback and paperback editions. Christine Battersby can be contacted via The Philosophy Department, University of Warwick, Coventry, CV4 7AL, UK. Bloomsbury Publishing PLC is located at 50 Bedford Square, London, WC1B 3DP.

'A Note on Anger', Marilyn Frye, from *Politics of Reality: Essays In Feminist Theory* by Marilyn Frye. © 1983 by Marilyn Frye. Used by permission of Crossing Press, an imprint of Random House, a division of Penguin Random House LLC. All rights reserved.

'The Sensory Celebration (I)', Anne Dufourmantelle, from *Power of Gentleness: Meditations on the Risk of Living* by Anne Dufourmantelle. Used with permission of Fordham University Press, © 2018; permission conveyed through Copyright Clearance Center, Inc.

Part 2 Film Aesthetics

'Vision and Choice in Morality', Iris Murdoch, originally published in *Proceedings of the Aristotelian Society, Supplementary Volume, Dreams and Self-Knowledge*, Vol. 30, (1956), pp 32–58. By permission of the Curtis Brown Group on behalf of the Estate of Iris Murdoch. © Iris Murdoch, 1956.

'The Language of Film', Katherine Thomson-Jones, from *Aesthetics and Film* by Katherine Thomson-Jones. © Katherine Thomson-Jones 2008, Continuum, an imprint of Bloomsbury Publishing Plc.

'Back to the Future? Contemporary Cinema and the Challenges for Theorists', Sylvie Magerstädt, from *Philosophy, Myth and Epic Cinema: Beyond Mere Illusions* by Sylvie Magerstädt. © 2015 by Sylvie Magerstädt. Reproduced with permission of the Licensor through PLSclear.

'Horrorism; or, On Violence Against the Helpless', Adriana Cavarero, from *Horrorism: Naming Contemporary Violence* by Adriana Cavarero, translated by William McCuaig. Copyright © 2009 Columbia University Press. Reprinted with permission of Columbia University Press.

Part 3 Film Phenomenology and Bodies

Part 4 Film and the Time Machine

Part 5 Film's Political Power

Part 6 Changing the Dominant Imaginary

Acknowledgements

My first thanks go to the editors that I have worked with at Bloomsbury throughout this project. Anna Coatman helped me get the proposal off the ground, Camilla Erskine helped me improve it, Rebecca Barden helped me with the budget and Barbara Cohen Bastos saw me through to submission. Rex Cleaver was calmness personified. Thanks to you all, and everyone involved in the production process.

Richard Menzies has helped and supported me at every stage of this book. Reading, copy-editing, proofreading, discovering and chasing copyright holders: he really deserves an editorial credit.

On 18 June 2019, I held a meeting in the Queen Mary Chapel yurt on campus, for the most inspirational gathering of women. Using flip chart paper and pens, and drinking lots of tea, they helped me compile a list of women philosophers whose work I should consider for this Reader. They also convinced me – and I hope I them – of the need for this book, and it was a truly unforgettable, inspirational and generative event. (I have kept all the notes, of course.) Thanks to chaplain Ella Sharples for the use of the yurt and Kiera Vaclavik for approving the research funds to make it happen. Thanks to all who came on the day and also those who contributed from a distance: Anna Backman Rogers, Jenny Chamarette, Anna Coatman, Catherine Constable, Sarah Cooper, Matilda Mroz, Alice Pember, Anat Pick, Hollie Price, Davina Quinlivan, Libby Saxton, Emma Wilson and Catherine Wheatley.

My friends and family have contributed and helped as always, and I know how lucky I am to have such brilliant people around me. Thank you Jean Bolton, Bela Kapur, Gabby Nemeth, Lindsey Smith and Laura Wykes.

This book reflects all my work since my re-entry into academia in 2004, and the communities in which I have been lucky enough to carry it out. I have fantastic colleagues in the Film Department at Queen Mary University of London, and an incredible network of film philosophers through the *Film-Philosophy* journal and conferences. Special thanks to Kelli Fuery, Janet Harbord, Alasdair King, John Ó Maoilearca, Anat Pick, Richard Rushton, Libby Saxton, David Sorfa and Catherine Wheatley. Thank you to the brilliant feminist scholarship, collegiality and friendship of Hannah Hamad, Tanya Horeck, Deborah Jermyn, Julie Lobalzo Wright, Marjorie Rosen, Aparna Sharma and Melanie Williams. Students on my Film Philosophy and Feminist Film Philosophy modules have enabled this project more than they can possibly realise, as have PhD students and friends. Particular thanks to Hollie Price and Sebastian Antti Juhana Mylly for their help with getting on top of copyright in the early days. Thank you to the brilliant PhD students who I have had the privilege of supervising whilst working on this book: Georgia Brown, Jade Evans, Cathy Lomax, Alice Pember, Giulia Rainoldi, Giulia Rho and Yue Liu.

Curating these works and obtaining permissions to reproduce them has been an extraordinary experience, taxing at times, but also a priceless opportunity to communicate with some of the philosophers featured. Thank you to Christine Battersby, Rosi Braidotti, Patricia Hill Collins, Marilyn Frye, Siri Hustvedt and Elaine Scarry, for your generosity and support. Thanks to all the philosophers and rights holders who agreed to my use of the essays and images in this volume, particularly Breast Cancer Prevention Partners, Donnelly/Colt, Marc Tyler Nobleman, Matuschka and Toronto Metropolitan University's The Image Centre. I have made great efforts to obtain permission to reproduce the copyrighted material in this book. If appropriate acknowledgement has not been made, we will be happy to rectify this in subsequent reprints.

In the course of curating and editing this book, my dear friend and colleague Geetha Ramanathan has passed away. Geetha's work has been a longstanding inspiration for me and it was a huge honour when she wrote a volume on Kathleen Collins for *Visionaries*, the book series I co-edit with Richard Rushton. Geetha was excited about *The Feminist Film Philosophy Reader* and wrote a characteristically brilliant and generous endorsement for the original proposal in 2022. I want to acknowledge her role in making this book happen and thank her deeply and sincerely.

Finally, huge thanks to Carol Morley and Cairo Cannon for permission to use Detective Mike Hoolihan on the cover, and for your continuing support and generosity.

Lucy Bolton
May, 2025

Note on the Texts

There are twenty-seven articles, essays and book chapters reproduced in *The Feminist Film Philosophy Reader*, ranging from 1926 to 2020. Each is reproduced faithfully, as it appears in its original publication, without alteration of style or content, save for the removal of some epigraphs for copyright reasons and the correction of some obvious typographical errors.

General Introduction

In *Showing Up*, directed by Kelly Reichardt in 2022, the complicated and occasionally fraught relationship between Lizzy (Michelle Williams) and Jo (Hong Chau) is mediated by a wounded pigeon. Lizzy's cat, Ricky, caught the pigeon, and Lizzy discovered it and unceremoniously put it out of her window. Jo then finds the wounded pigeon and shares the incident with Lizzy, who does not reveal Ricky's, and her, role in the pigeon's situation. Through their shared care of the pigeon, including bandaging its wounded wing (Figure 0.1), Lizzy and Jo each have a focus other than themselves, enabling them to communicate: this despite the ongoing problems with a lack of hot water that Lizzy, as Jo's tenant, is angry and increasingly impatient about, and the fact that both women are artists consumed with the creation of work for their upcoming shows. The film creates rounded characters who have very different personalities and lifestyles. Jo is calm, sociable and sexual; Lizzy is grumpy, solitary and heavily involved with her challenging family. By the end of the film, both of their shows have been successful, and the pigeon is released from its bandages and flies away. The final moments of the film feature Jo and Lizzy walking together, looking out for the pigeon in an easy-going way.

Figure 0.1 Lizzy and Jo bandage the pigeon (*Showing Up*).

This lyrical, unhurried and delicate film can be understood from several philosophical perspectives.[1] A reading inspired by Luce Irigaray's notions of 'women speaking together' and 'refusing to go to market' (Irigaray [1977] 1985) might see the pigeon as enabling Lizzy and Jo to enter into a 'horizon between women' (Irigaray 1986). Mary Midgley's work on 'mixed communities', including domestic animals, might open up the film to consideration in terms of environmental ethics (1983). The way in which Jo and Lizzy nurse the pigeon invites a consideration of a feminist ethics of care (Donovan and Adams 2007), and understanding their very different styles of making art would benefit from the perspectives of feminist aesthetics (Eaton 2021).

This brief evaluation of the concepts prompted by *Showing Up* is indicative of the feminist film philosophical approach that this book is designed to support. *The Feminist Film Philosophy Reader* is a selection of works by women that I propose prompt reflection on cinema, shine light on women within films, and offer a range of departure points for feminist film philosophy. In 1986, Ursula Le Guin proposed the carrier bag theory of fiction. Thinking in terms of novels, Le Guin argued that:

> the natural, proper, fitting shape of the novel might be that of a sack, a bag. A book holds words. Words hold things. They bear meanings. A novel is a medicine bundle, holding things in a particular, powerful relation to one another and to us. ([1986] 2019: 34)

In *The Feminist Film Philosophy Reader*, I aspire to create a similar collection, or carrier bag, but perhaps it is more like a sturdy rucksack. It is a collection of writings that I intend to be a resource for those of us who study, teach and write about feminism, film and philosophy. It is not chronological, nor does it tell a linear story, or provide a comprehensive collection. (This is far too vast a field for any collection to claim to be that.)

I have brought together these essays, chapters and papers, in a loose assemblage, because they are insightful and they offer multiple perspectives on philosophical thinking about the world, how it appears and how we look at it. As Le Guin explains, in relation to the genre of science-fiction,

> If, however, one avoids the linear, progressive, Time's-(killing)-arrow mode of the Techno-Heroic, and redefines technology and science as primarily cultural carrier bag rather than weapon of domination, one pleasant side effect is that science fiction can be seen as a far less rigid, narrow field, not necessarily Promethean or apocalyptic at all, and in fact less a mythological genre that a realistic one. ([1986] 2019: 36)

This idea of resisting the domination of linearity and embracing instead a more complex development of contributions from a broad, flexible and occasionally unruly community, underpins this anthology. The conventional definitions of 'feminist', 'film' and 'philosophy' may not be rigidly adhered to in every selected piece, but, overall, the collection presents a broad array of richly conceived and dazzlingly written arguments about the ways of our visual worlds.

What is Philosophy?

The Feminist Film Philosophy Reader is inclined to agree with Mary Midgley's comparison of philosophy with plumbing (1996). For Midgley,

> Plumbing and philosophy are both activities that arise because elaborate cultures like ours have, beneath their surface, a fairly complex system which is usually unnoticed, but which sometimes goes wrong. In both cases, this can have serious consequences. Each system supplies vital needs for those who live above it. Each is hard to repair when it does go wrong, because neither of them was ever consciously planned as a whole. (1996: 1)

As Midgley observes, there is a problem with people accepting the need for philosophy, whereas few would dispute the need for plumbing. The problem with the perception of philosophy might be because, 'when the concepts we are living by work badly, they don't usually drip audibly through the ceiling or swamp the kitchen floor. They just quietly distort and obstruct our thinking' (1996: 2). And Midgley believes that all our thinking works through images (1996: 12). Whether or not it is new ideas occurring to us as images, and expressed as metaphors, 'We think as whole people, not as disembodied minds, not as computers' (1996: 12), and this means that we have to be nimble and flexible to work out where interesting images and ideas take us. Everybody, Midgley believes, 'must start from where they are' (1996: 12).

This approach to philosophy, as being imbricated within our daily lives, makes sense of our relationship with film philosophy as it is an art form about people and their worlds. Even if a film takes place in a film world where the rules of our world do not apply, we usually have a connection with how that world is structured, what the moral landscape is and the value of life forms. But, most importantly, there is no straightforward progress or linearity of films in the same way that there isn't one in philosophy. Film philosophy has to be able to adapt, and to adjust nimbly to understanding each film world, just as philosophy, in Midgley's assessment, 'has to manoeuvre somewhat unpredictably to meet the varying emergencies of a changing pattern of life' (2018: 5). This is the requirement that I am trying to begin to tackle with this volume: it is about the potential of the selected works to be helpful, insightful and constructive when we are reflecting on moving images and their philosophical natures.

Where is Feminist Film Philosophy?

There are no collections of feminist film philosophy, or philosophy by women about film. There are feminist film theory monographs, edited collections and anthologies, dating back to the 1980s and 1990s, and these books are still being published and are greatly valued, but the field of feminist film philosophy is as yet unconsolidated. There is no overview of women's philosophy on film, which has resulted to some extent in the slow growth of the work of women philosophers in this now established sub-discipline (Sorfa 2016). The field of film philosophy has been dominated by particular male philosophical voices, such as Gilles Deleuze, Stanley Cavell and Nöel Carroll, and there is still a great deal of ongoing work devoted to developing their ideas in numerous directions and contexts. There are very few books about film philosophy based on the work of specific female philosophers, which leads to the perpetuation of the dominance of the white male voices in research, scholarship and teaching.

It is stating the obvious to say that there is limitless philosophical work by women on concepts, notions and analyses that are relevant to and insightful about images, sounds, moving images and stories. There may not be a list reaching back over the twentieth century of women academic philosophers who focused on film, as many were occupied with the fundamental tenets of feminism and women's liberation, but the ideas are there, if only they were more high profile and received attention. This book will be a valuable resource of such work for scholars to teach, learn and develop in keeping with the film philosophical approach; in other words, some of the texts will focus on film, and specific films, but others will talk about images, representations and reflections that can be brought into conversation with cinema and used to develop new film philosophical thinking. I have included, in the Appendix to this book, an outline of suggested topics and resources in order to indicate how this material could be used to teach a feminist film philosophy module.

This book is not a collection of feminist film theory. There are already many brilliant such anthologies: a few examples include *Feminism and Film*, edited by E. Ann Kaplan (2000); *Feminisms*, edited by Laura

Mulvey and Anna Backman Rogers (2015) and *Film Feminisms: A Global Introduction*, by Kristin Lené Hole and Dijana Jelača (2018). In 2016, So Mayer's *Political Animals* made a significant intervention in the field of feminist film studies, arguing that their conclusion is the place where they say 'over to you' (Mayer 2016: 189). Mayer considers feminist film to be an open letter, and curation of the films, the filmmakers and their histories, to be an act of care (Mayer 2016: 192). My view of *The Feminist Film Philosophy Reader* is that it is similarly a call to action, and that care is at the heart of the project: care for the philosophical work of women in this field, as well as for the scholars now working on film philosophy and perhaps searching for some feminist inspiration.

There are a few compendiums of film philosophy that have brought together a wide range of scholars to cover particular topics in their specific essays. Feminist film philosophy, however, receives scant attention. *Film, Theory and Philosophy*, edited by Felicity Colman (2009) features three chapters on the work of women out of thirty-two thinkers. *The Palgrave Handbook of the Philosophy of Film and Motion Pictures* (Carroll et al. 2019) features one chapter, out of forty-two, on feminist philosophy of film. *The Routledge Companion to Philosophy and Film* (Livingstone 2011) has sixty chapters, with one on gender. There is an urgent need to consider the work of women in this field, and to bring them into conversation with each other, across time, as needed: their voices must not feature as an optional outlier anymore.

There are many books in the now well-established field of film philosophy that discuss what film philosophy is. The foundational debates about whether films simply illustrate philosophical ideas or are capable of being philosophical texts themselves were rehearsed and refined by scholars such as Christopher Falzon (2002), Steven Mulhall (2002) and Thomas Wartenberg (2007).[2] There are multiple edited collections that examine a range of approaches and engagements between philosophy and film, such as those by Wartenberg and Curran (2005), Freeland and Wartenberg (1995) and Carel and Tuck (2011). Film philosophy has developed into some more specific areas, such as ethics (Downing and Saxton 2009; Wheatley 2009; Choi and Frey 2014; Sinnerbrink 2016; Bolton, Martin-Jones and Sinnerbrink 2023), aesthetics (Thomson-Jones 2008; Klevan 2018) and, inevitably, the analytic/continental divide (Currie 1995; Allen and Smith 1997; Slugan 2019). The field of feminist film philosophy continues to grow as more scholars turn to the work of women philosophers and unleash their film philosophical potential (Constable 2005; Bolton 2011; Ince 2017; Bolton 2019; Fuery 2022; Dalton and Tyrer 2024). The work of women filmmakers is the subject of the book series *Visionaries*, where each volume takes a philosophical approach to the world view and the preoccupations of particular directors.[3] As the conversations with women thinkers and filmmakers from the past and the present are beginning to thrive, so do the connections and the possibilities for a more diverse and intersectional feminist future.

Making the Choices

The rationale for my choices of what to include in this collection has been mainly focused on the potential of each piece to inspire creative and innovative film philosophy. These essays, chapters and articles are drawn from work by women across a century of writing about film, but also about feminist politics and cultural critique. Each text offers the opportunity for film thinkers to run with the ideas, images and philosophies, as each has enormous relevance to contemporary work about film and visual culture.

There were, inevitably, pieces of work that I had to leave out of this book. Sometimes, the impediment was cost, if the price charged by rights-holders was prohibitive. But also, there were some cases where the work is readily available and already has the attention of film philosophers, whereas I felt some lesser known – but equally striking – contributions would be more in keeping with my project to diversify the field.

There were also some pieces of work that, although absolutely wonderful and inspirational, did not strike quite so many notes of contemporary relevance as others.

Of the pieces I had to leave out, these are perhaps the most noteworthy. Michèle Le Dœuff's 'Long Hair, Short Ideas', in *The Philosophical Imaginary*, is a striking and significant challenge to the masculinity of the philosophical tradition and an evocatively visual polemic (1989). Kara Keeling's brilliant work in *The Witch's Flight: The Cinematic, the Black Femme, and the Image of Common Sense* (2007) and *Queer Times, Black Futures* (2019) has taken Deleuzian thought and film philosophy more broadly into the realms of race, sexuality and gender in cinema, and constitutes a significant and influential body of work. Susan Sontag's writing on film (1967) and photography (1977) is inspirational and vigorous, and needs to be brought into film philosophy discussions far more frequently.

This book can be used at all levels of research and scholarship: from A-Level to doctoral, post-doctoral and professional academic research. My hope is that students will find this book stimulating and game-changing, and that academics in the field will read it to see who they could be working on. It is not, of course, an attempt at a canon of any kind. It is an open offering, in response to what Midgley described as 'the whole reductive, scientist, mechanistic, fantasy-ridden creed which still constantly distorts the world-view of our age' (2018: 188). To that litany, add technocratic, misogynistic, racist, ableist and auto-cratic, and it is clear that critical, creative, feminist work is needed as a matter of urgency. *The Feminist Film Philosophy Reader* should therefore be seen as unfinished, and as Alix Beeston and Stefan Solomon argue in their ingenious collection about the feminist potential of the unfinished film, the 'focus on the unfinished allows for the recovery of projects and practitioners marginalized within film industries and scholarship alike' (2023, 11). In that vein, this anthology is a starting point. It is my hope that the work in this book, the philosophers and critics, the films and other artworks they write about, and the interconnections between the various arguments, will prompt new directions in feminist film philosophy, and populate the conversations with numerous voices (Lennard 2019). Let's now immerse ourselves in some radical thinking, and be energized by the possibilities these writings offer for film, and driven to follow up leads and expand the collection: as Le Guin ([1986] 2019) observed, 'Still there are seeds to be gathered, and room in the bag for stars.'

Notes

1. I am grateful to Anat Pick and her as yet unpublished writing on *Showing Up*, 'Kelly Reichardt's Multispecies Comedy of Care'.
2. For an overview of the development of the discipline of film philosophy, see Sinnorbrink (2011).
3. *Visionaries: the Work of Women Filmmakers*, is a series co-edited by Lucy Bolton and Richard Rushton at Edinburgh University Press. See https://edinburghuniversitypress.com/series-visionaries-the-work-of-women-filmmakers (accessed 3 May 2025).

References

Allen, R. and M. Smith (1997), *Film Theory and Philosophy*, Oxford: Clarendon.
Beeston, A. and S. Solomon (2023), *Incomplete: the Feminist Possibilities of the Unfinished Film*, California: University of California Press.
Bolton, L. (2011), *Film and Female Consciousness: Irigaray, Cinema and Thinking Women*, Basingstoke: Palgrave.
Bolton, L. (2019), *Contemporary Cinema and the Philosophy of Iris Murdoch*, Edinburgh: Edinburgh University Press.

Bolton, L., D. Martin-Jones and R. Sinnerbrink, eds (2023), *Contemporary Screen Ethics: Absences, Identities, Belonging, Looking Anew*, Edinburgh: Edinburgh University Press.

Carel, H. and G. Tuck, eds (2011), *New Takes in Film-Philosophy*, Basingstoke: Palgrave Macmillan.

Carroll, N., L. T. Di Summa and S. Loht, eds (2019), *The Palgrave Handbook of the Philosophy of Film and Motion Pictures*, Basingstoke: Palgrave Macmillan.

Choi, J. and M. Frey, eds (2014), *Cine-ethics: Ethical Dimensions of Film Theory, Practice and Spectatorship*, New York and London: Routledge.

Colman, F. (2009), *Film, Theory and Philosophy: The Key Thinkers*. London and New York: Routledge.

Constable, C. (2005), *Thinking in Images: Film Theory, Feminist Philosophy and Marlene Dietrich*, London: BFI.

Currie, G. (1995), *Image and Mind: Film, Philosophy and Cognitive Science*, Cambridge: Cambridge University Press.

Dalton, B. and B. Tyrer, eds (2024), 'Catherine Malabou, Plasticity and Film', *Film-Philosophy*, 28 (3): 413–27.

Donovan, J. and C. Adams (2007), *The Feminist Care Tradition in Animal Ethics*, New York and Chichester: Columbia University Press.

Downing, L. and L. Saxton (2009), *Film and Ethics: Foreclosed Encounters*, London: Routledge.

Eaton, A. W. (2021), 'Feminist Aesthetics', in Ásta and K. Q. Hall (eds), *The Oxford Handbook of Feminist Philosophy*, 295–311, Oxford: Oxford University Press.

Falzon, C. (2002), *Philosophy Goes to the Movies: An Introduction to Philosophy*, New York and London: Routledge.

Freeland, C. and T. E. Wartenberg (1995), *Philosophy and Film*, New York and London: Routledge.

Fuery, K. (2022), *Ambiguous Cinema: From Simone de Beauvoir to Feminist Film-Phenomenology*, Edinburgh: Edinburgh University Press.

Hole, K. L. and D. Jelača, eds (2018), *Film Feminisms: A Global Introduction*, London: Routledge.

Ince, K. (2017), *The Body and the Screen: Female Subjectivities in Contemporary Women's Cinema*, New York: Bloomsbury Academic.

Irigaray, L. ([1977] 1985), *This Sex which is Not One*, trans. C. Porter with C. Burke, Ithaca and New York: Cornell University Press.

Irigaray, L. (1986), *Divine Women*, trans. S. Muecke, Occasional Papers 8, Sydney: Local Consumption Publications.

Kaplan, E. A. (2000), *Feminism and Film*, Oxford: Oxford University Press.

Keeling, K. (2007), *The Witch's Flight: The Cinematic, the Black Femme, and the Image of Common Sense*, Durham, NC: Duke University Press.

Keeling, K. (2019), *Queer Times, Black Futures*, New York: New York University Press.

Klevan, A. (2018), *Aesthetic Evaluation and Film*, Manchester: Manchester University Press.

Le Dœuff, M. (1989), 'Long Hair, Short Ideas', in M. Le Dœuff, *The Philosophical Imaginary*, 100–28, London: Athlone.

Le Guin, U. K. ([1986] 2019), *The Carrier Bag Theory of Fiction*, London: Ignota.

Lennard, N. (2019), *Being Numerous: Essays on a Non-Fascist Life*, London and New York: Verso.

Livingstone, P., ed. (2011), *The Routledge Companion to Philosophy and Film* (Routledge Philosophy Companions), London and New York: Routledge.

Mayer, S. (2016), *Political Animals: The New Feminist Cinema*, London: I.B. Tauris.

Midgley, M. (1983), *Animals and Why They Matter*, Harmondsworth: Penguin.

Midgley, M. (1996), *Utopias, Dolphins and Computers*, London and New York: Routledge.

Midgley, M. (2018), *What is Philosophy For?*, London: Bloomsbury Academic.

Mulhall, S. (2002), *On Film: Thinking in Action*, London and New York: Routledge.

Mulvey, L. and A. Backman Rogers (2015), *Feminisms: Diversity, Difference and Multiplicity in Contemporary Film Cultures*, Amsterdam: Amsterdam University Press.

Sinnerbrink, R. (2011), *New Philosophies of Film: Thinking Images*, London: Continuum.

Sinnerbrink, R. (2016), *Cinematic Ethics: Exploring Ethical Experience Through Film*, London: Routledge.

Slugan, M. (2019), *Noël Carroll on Film: A Philosophy of Art and Popular Culture*, London: Bloomsbury Academic.

Sontag, S. (1967), *Against Interpretation and Other Essays*, London: Eyre & Spottiswoode.

Sontag, S. (1977), *On Photography*, New York: Farrar, Straus and Giroux.

Sorfa, D. (2016), 'What Is Film-Philosophy?', *Film-Philosophy*, 20 (1): 1–5.

Thomson-Jones, K. (2008), *Aesthetics and Film*, London: Continuum.

Wartenberg, T. E. (2007), *Thinking on Screen: Film as Philosophy*, London: Routledge.

Wartenberg, T. E. and A. Curran, eds (2005), *The Philosophy of Film: Introductory Text and Readings*, Malden, MA and Oxford: Blackwell Publishing.

Wheatley, C. (2009), *Michael Haneke's Cinema: The Ethic of the Image*, New York and Oxford: Berghan Books.

Part 1 Thinking for a Feminist Philosophy of Cinema

Introduction

In 2022, Chantal Akerman's *Jeanne Dielman, 23, quai du Commerce, 1080 Bruxelles* topped the *Sight & Sound* ten-yearly poll, crowning the film as the greatest film of all time. The feminist film, so relentless in its depiction of domestic drudgery and so surprising with its sex work and killing, is also a contemplative collection of a woman's idiosyncrasies. In a pair of charming but slightly melancholy scenes, Jeanne goes to her favourite café, where she has her preferred waitress and seat of choice (Figure P1.1). Jeanne looks relaxed and seems to mindfully enjoy her cup of coffee. When she returns, however, the elements of the treasured experience are all wrong: another woman is sitting in her favourite seat, and the waitress is a different one who does not know her order. The level of detail of Jeanne's life that the film portrays, and Delphine Seyrig's outstandingly nuanced performance, convey psychological depth and emotional precarity through commanding our attention to watch her. We *see*, and understand, her experience: we are *told* very little.

Virginia Woolf's iconic essay on the cinema shows how she was intrigued and challenged by film in 1926. In what can be considered early film phenomenology, Woolf observes that we need to allow cinema to do what it can do, which is to convey thought by shape more effectively than by words. In response to the strange accidental shadow that spread across the screen when she watched *The Cabinet of Dr Caligari*, Woolf observed that 'the monstrous quivering tadpole seemed to be fear itself, and not the statement "I am afraid"'. This perceptive and intuitive response prefigures the work of film phenomenologists such as Vivian Sobchack (1992; 2004) and Laura U. Marks (1999; 2002), and succeeds in specifying what Woolf calls the enormous riches that the filmmaker has at his (*sic*) command. Perhaps Woolf would have said that the sight of Jeanne Dielman polishing her son's shoes, kneading a meatloaf or unfolding and re-folding the sofa bed, is 'boredom itself, and not the statement "I am bored"'. The film clearly resonates with Simone de Beauvoir's discussion of reproductive labour and the distraction of women's time away from more creative pursuits ([1953] 1997: 470–8).

Christine Battersby's work in *Gender and Genius* (1989) and *The Phenomenal Woman* (1998) is a treasure trove of feminist analyses of the concepts and notions of male philosophers, from Aristotle to Lacan and Kant to Deleuze and Guattari. In 'The Male Gift', Battersby shines a brilliant light on the preening misogyny of the writer who thinks himself a genius, and the phallic imaginary of the male artist. 'The Male Gift' pinions iconic and canonical men, and lays bare their failure to include women in their professed pantheon of greatness, alongside their elevation of their natural skills and aptitudes. It is only right, then, to follow Battersby's scrutiny with Marilyn Frye's 'A Note on Anger', which tackles the frustrations and disrespect at the root of women's anger and the experience of its dismissal. Frye's essay, from 1983, feels urgent, not just relevant,

Figure P1.1 Jeanne enjoys her solitary coffee in her favourite seat (*Jeanne Dielman 23, quai du Commerce, 1080 Bruxelles*).

in her demonstration of the nuances of the acceptance and rejection of women's anger and its relationship to claiming space.[1]

Taking the fury down more than a few notches, 'The Sensory Celebration' by Anne Dufourmantelle is an appeal for gentleness as a slower, more careful and sensorial way of being. As well as the state of being, Dufourmantelle describes images such as the joining of sky and sea, the halo of lamps at night, or the belly of an animal. This mode of being and of attending resonates with the type of attention that feminist film phenomenology calls for: the visual descriptions of where gentleness can be found and what it can look like constitute what Dufourmantelle describes as a 'continual invitation to become infected by it'. This beautiful, serene, short essay is an inducement to us to work at cultivating what Iris Murdoch called 'a just and loving gaze'(1971: 33).[2]

This Part is an indication to the reader about the project of this book as a whole, which will challenge received thinking about the form and meaning of film and philosophy, and will indicate where feminist philosophical approaches can be found.

Notes

1. It is useful to compare Frye's essay with that of Helen Wood on 'an intersectional politics of irreverent rage' (2019).
2. Iris Murdoch discusses her understanding of the concept of attention, which she says she has borrowed from Simone Weil, as being 'a just and loving gaze directed upon an individual reality', which she believes to be 'the characteristic and proper mark of the active moral agent' (1971: 33). It is here where she draws upon the image

of a hovering kestrel as an example of a sight that draws us out of our own egoistic fantasies. In Bolton (2019) I examined these Murdochian ideas.

References

Battersby, C. (1989), *Gender and Genius: Towards a Feminist Aesthetics*, London: The Women's Press.

Battersby, C. (1998), *The Phenomenal Woman: Feminist Metaphysics and the Patterns of Identity*, Oxford: Polity.

Beauvoir, S. de ([1953] 1997), *The Second Sex*, trans. H. M. Parshley, London: Jonathan Cape.

Bolton, L. (2019), *Contemporary Cinema and the Philosophy of Iris Murdoch*, Edinburgh: Edinburgh University Press.

Marks, L. U. (1999), *The Skin of the Film: Intercultural Cinema, Embodiment, and the Senses*, Durham, NC: Duke University Press.

Marks, L. U. (2002), *Touch: Sensuous Theory and Multisensory Media*, Minneapolis: University of Minnesota Press.

Murdoch, I. (1971), *The Sovereignty of Good*, London: Routledge and Kegan Paul.

Sobchack, V. (1992), *The Address of the Eye: A Phenomenology of Film Experience*, Princeton, NJ and Oxford: Princeton University Press.

Sobchack, V. (2004), *Carnal Thoughts: Embodiment and Moving Image Culture*, Berkeley, CA and London: University of California Press.

Wood, H. (2019), 'Fuck the Patriarchy: Towards an Intersectional Politics of Irreverent Rage', *Feminist Media Studies*, 19 (4): 609–15.

1 The Cinema

VIRGINIA WOOLF

People say that the savage no longer exists in us, that we are at the fag-end of civilisation, that everything has been said already, and that it is too late to be ambitious. But these philosophers have presumably forgotten the movies. They have never seen the savages of the twentieth century watching the pictures. They have never sat themselves in front of the screen and thought how, for all the clothes on their backs and the carpets at their feet, no great distance separates them from those bright-eyed, naked men who knocked two bars of iron together and heard in that clangour a foretaste of the music of Mozart.

The bars in this case, of course, are so highly wrought and so covered over with accretions of alien matter that it is extremely difficult to hear anything distinctly. All is hubble-bubble, swarm, and chaos. We are peering over the edge of a cauldron in which fragments of all shapes and savours seem to simmer; now and again some vast form heaves itself up, and seems about to haul itself out of chaos. Yet, at first sight, the art of the cinema seems simple, even stupid. There is the King shaking hands with a football team; there is Sir Thomas Lipton's yacht; there is Jack Horner winning the Grand National. The eye licks it all up instantaneously, and the brain, agreeably titillated, settles down to watch things happening without bestirring itself to think. For the ordinary eye, the English unaesthetic eye, is a simple mechanism, which takes care that the body does not fall down coal-holes, provides the brain with toys and sweetmeats to keep it quiet, and can be trusted to go on behaving like a competent nursemaid until the brain comes to the conclusion that it is time to wake up. What is its surprise, then, to be roused suddenly in the midst of its agreeable somnolence and asked for help? The eye is in difficulties. The eye wants help. The eye says to the brain, "Something is happening which I do not in the least understand. You are needed." Together they look at the King, the boat, the horse, and the brain sees at once that they have taken on a quality which does not belong to the simple photograph of real life. They have become not more beautiful, in the sense in which pictures are beautiful, but shall we call it (our vocabulary is miserably insufficient) more real, or real with a different reality from that which we perceive in daily life? We behold them as they are when we are not there. We see life as it is when we have no part in it. As we gaze we seem to be removed from the pettiness of actual existence. The horse will not knock us down. The King will not grasp our hands. The wave will not wet our feet. From this point of vantage, as we watch the antics of our kind, we have time to feel pity and amusement, to generalize, to endow one man with the attributes of the race. Watching the boat sail and the wave break, we have time to open our minds wide to beauty and register on top of it the queer sensation—this beauty will continue, and this beauty will flourish whether we behold it or not. Further, all this happened ten years ago, we are told. We are beholding a world which has gone beneath the waves. Brides are emerging from the Abbey—they are now mothers; ushers are ardent—they are now silent; mothers are tearful; guests are joyful; this has been won and that has been lost, and it is over and done with. The war sprung its chasm at the feet of all this innocence and ignorance, but it was thus that we danced and pirouetted, toiled and desired, thus that the sun shone and the clouds scudded up to the very end.

But the picture-makers seem dissatisfied with such obvious sources of interest as the passage of time and the suggestiveness of reality. They despise the flights of gulls, ships on the Thames, the Prince of Wales, the Mile End Road, Piccadilly Circus. They want to be improving, altering, making an art of their own—naturally, for so much seems to be within their scope. So many arts seemed to stand by ready to offer their help. For example, there was literature. All the famous novels of the world, with their well-known characters, and their famous scenes, only asked, it seemed, to be put on the films. What could be easier and simpler? The cinema fell upon its prey with immense rapacity, and to this moment largely subsists upon the body of its unfortunate victim. But the results are disastrous to both. The alliance is unnatural. Eye and brain are torn asunder ruthlessly as they try vainly to work in couples. The eye says: "Here is Anna Karenina." A voluptuous lady in black velvet wearing pearls comes before us. But the brain says: "That is no more Anna Karenina than it is Queen Victoria." For the brain knows Anna almost entirely by the inside of her mind—her charm, her passion, her despair. All the emphasis is laid by the cinema upon her teeth, her pearls, and her velvet. Then "Anna falls in love with Vronsky"—that is to say, the lady in black velvet falls into the arms of a gentleman in uniform, and they kiss with enormous succulence, great deliberation, and infinite gesticulation on a sofa in an extremely well-appointed library, while a gardener incidentally mows the lawn. So we lurch and lumber through the most famous novels of the world. So we spell them out in words of one syllable written, too, in the scrawl of an illiterate schoolboy. A kiss is love. A broken cup is jealousy. A grin is happiness. Death is a hearse. None of these things has the least connection with the novel that Tolstoy wrote, and it is only when we give up trying to connect the pictures with the book that we guess from some accidental scene—like the gardener mowing the lawn—what the cinema might do if it were left to its own devices.

But what, then, are its devices? If it ceased to be a parasite, how would it walk erect? At present it is only from hints that one can frame any conjecture. For instance, at a performance of *Dr. Caligari* the other day, a shadow shaped like a tadpole suddenly appeared at one corner of the screen. It swelled to an immense size, quivered, bulged, and sank back again into nonentity. For a moment it seemed to embody some monstrous, diseased imagination of the lunatic's brain. For a moment it seemed as if thought could be conveyed by shape more effectively than by words. The monstrous, quivering tadpole seemed to be fear itself, and not the statement, "I am afraid." In fact, the shadow was accidental, and the effect unintentional. But if a shadow at a certain moment can suggest so much more than the actual gestures and words of men and women in a state of fear, it seems plain that the cinema has within its grasp innumerable symbols for emotions that have so far failed to find expression. Terror has, besides its ordinary forms, the shape of a tadpole; it burgeons, bulges, quivers, disappears. Anger is not merely rant and rhetoric, red faces and clenched fists. It is perhaps a black line wriggling upon a white sheet. Anna and Vronsky need no longer scowl and grimace. They have at their command—but what? Is there, we ask, some secret language which we feel and see, but never speak, and, if so, could this be made visible to the eye? Is there any characteristic which thought possesses that can be rendered visible without the help of words? It has speed and lowness; dartlike directness and vaporous circumlocution. But it has also, especially in moments of emotion, the picture-making power, the need to lift its burden to another bearer; to let an image run side by side along with it. The likeness of the thought is, for some reason, more beautiful, more comprehensible, more available than the thought itself. As everybody knows, in Shakespeare the most complex ideas form chains of images through which we mount, changing and turning, until we reach the light of day. But, obviously, the images of a poet are not to be cast in bronze, or traced by pencil. They are compact of a thousand suggestions of which the visual is only the most obvious or the uppermost. Even the simplest image: "My luve's like a red, red rose, that's newly sprung in June," presents us with impressions of moisture and warmth and the glow of crimson and the softness of petals inextricably mixed and strung upon the lilt of a rhythm which is itself the voice of the passion and hesitation of the lover. All this, which is accessible to words, and to words alone, the cinema must avoid.

Yet if so much of our thinking and feeling is connected with seeing, some residue of visual emotion which is of no use either to painter or to poet may still await the cinema. That such symbols will be quite unlike the real objects which we see before us seems highly probable. Something abstract, something which moves with controlled or conscious art, something which calls for the very slightest help from words or music to make itself intelligible, yet justly uses them subserviently—of such movements and abstractions the films may, in time to come, be composed. Then, indeed, when some new symbol for expressing thought is found, the film-maker has enormous riches at his command. The exactitude of reality and its surprising power of suggestion are to be had for the asking. Annas and Vronskys—there they are in the flesh. If into this reality he could breathe emotion, could animate the perfect form with thought, then his booty could be hauled in hand over hand. Then, as smoke pours from Vesuvius, we should be able to see thought in its wildness, in its beauty, in its oddity, pouring from men with their elbows on a table; from women with their little handbags slipping to the floor. We should see these emotions mingling together and affecting each other.

We should see violent changes of emotion produced by their collision. The most fantastic contrasts could be flashed before us with a speed which the writer can only toil after in vain; the dream architecture of arches and battlements, of cascades falling and fountains rising, which sometimes visits us in sleep or shapes itself in half-darkened rooms, could be realized before our waking eyes. No fantasy could be too far-fetched or insubstantial. The past could be unrolled, distances annihilated, and the gulfs which dislocate novels (when, for instance, Tolstoy has to pass from Levin to Anna, and in so doing jars his story and wrenches and arrests our sympathies) could, by the sameness of the background, by the repetition of some scene, be smoothed away.

How all this is to be attempted, much less achieved, no one at the moment can tell us. We get intimations only in the chaos of the streets, perhaps, when some momentary assemble of colour, sound, movement suggests that here is a scene waiting a new art to be transfixed. And sometimes at the cinema, in the midst of its immense dexterity and enormous technical proficiency, the curtain parts and we behold, far off, some unknown and unexpected beauty. But it is for a moment only. For a strange thing has happened—while all the other arts were born naked, this, the youngest, has been born fully clothed. It can say everything before it has anything to say. It is as if the savage tribe, instead of finding two bars of iron to play with, had found, scattering the sea shore, fiddles, flutes, saxophones, grand pianos by Erard and Bechstein, and had begun with incredible energy, but without knowing a note of music, to hammer and thump upon them all at the same time.

Originally published in *The Nation and Athenaeum*, 3 July 1926, pp. 381–3.

2 The Male Gift

CHRISTINE BATTERSBY

The Renaissance artist had aimed to *mirror* a universal truth that existed independently of his own self, and subjectivity was therefore a barrier rather than an aid to artistic invention. But for the Romantics individuality and particularity were no longer handicaps to artistic production. The artist offered his own inner landscape as one of the poles against which others could align the compasses of their own minds. Coleridge theorised the new aesthetics in *Biographia Literaria* [1817]; but the changes in taste that embraced artistic idiosyncrasy pre-dated him, and occurred during the closing years of the eighteenth century. Thus Jean-Jacques Rousseau's autobiographical *Confessions* [1781] opens with a boast that a Renaissance author or artist would have scorned to make:

> I have resolved on an enterprise which has no precedent, and which, once complete, will have no imitator. My purpose is to display to my kind a portrait in every way true to nature, and the man I shall portray will be myself.

> Simply myself. I know my own heart and understand my fellow man. But I am made unlike anyone I have ever met; I will even venture to say that I am like no one in the whole world. I may be no better, but at least I am different.

These words of Rousseau's symbolise the new attitudes to the self: as an author he is proud of his uniqueness; he preens himself on his originality. His aim is to 'tell the truth' – sincerely, if not always accurately – by faithfully portraying his own (very individual) soul, and the desires and needs of his own (very inadequate) body. Rousseau paints himself as a naïve, vain, impetuous, obsessive, fickle, fanciful, childlike creature – swayed more by strong emotions and sympathies than by reason. He is a charming monster: sometimes bafflingly pure, but with a tendency to disease and madness. Rousseau projects himself, in other words, in very much the way that the Renaissance caricatured woman: as locked into his own very subjective and sexually disturbed psyche. Later, for the nineteenth-century Romantics, Rousseau's defence of the common man – his attack on the institutional privileges of property, Church and urban society – came to symbolise the (lost) potential of revolutionary France ... when all men had been declared equals and brothers in freedom. But Rousseau also symbolises the way that Romanticism made women Others rather than brothers. The free, imperfect man whose abasement and unique individuality was glorified remained a *hero* ... heroines had, at best, a supportive role.

The 'feminine' Rousseau was anti-female ... at least, anti-educated and creative females. In his *Letter to Mr d'Alembert* (1758), women are even denied the appropriate feelings to *appreciate* art properly, let alone *produce* it:

> Women, in general, possess no artistic sensibility ... nor genius. They can acquire a knowledge ... of anything through hard work. But the celestial fire that emblazens and ignites the soul, the inspiration that

consumes and devours …, these sublime ecstasies that reside in the depths of the heart are always lacking in women's writings. These creations are as cold and pretty as women; they have an abundance of spirit but lack soul; they are a hundred times more reasoned than impassioned. [Quoted and trans. Citron, 1986, p. 225]

In the Renaissance, it was males who possessed judgement and *ingenium* … and women who had too much in the way of feelings, too little in the way of reason to be real artists. For Rousseau the equations are reversed: woman has too much judgement, too little emotion. In the older tradition, fire was a physiological reality that was essentially bound up with the vital forces of male sexuality … and women were, in general, too cold to be great artists. By the time that Rousseau was writing, this physiology was out of date. But Rousseau's woman remains cold: still lacking the fires of sublime ecstasy and of divine inspiration. The accounts of maleness and femaleness have changed; but the old misogynistic vocabulary remains – reinterpreted in such a way as to represent women as metaphorically frigid and hence as creatively sterile.

Rousseau was by no means alone in maintaining this link between creative power and the psychic 'heat' of the heroic male. One of the most famous eighteenth-century descriptions of poetic genius was that of Shaftesbury: 'a poet is indeed a second *Maker*; a just Prometheus under Jove' [1711, i, p. 136]. The idea that the genius is a Prometheus, who has stolen fire from the gods and brought it to earth as a gift to male-kind, is one that we find in many Romantic writings. In Percy Bysshe Shelley's 'Prometheus Unbound' (1820), for example, speech, civilisation and poetry are all gifts of Prometheus to mankind. Prometheus allies himself with Saturn – said by Shelley to be the true god of energy and power – rebels against Jupiter (Saturn's upstart son) and, through his heroic daring and extreme suffering, produces a revolution that makes all men (= males) quasi-divine.

When Shelley wrote about Prometheus, he did not go on to spell out the misogynistic implications of a mythology that made Woman (Pandora) part of the punishment meted out to male-kind for Prometheus's presumption in stealing fire from the gods. In a way appropriate to Mary Wollstonecraft's son-in-law, Shelley (quite consciously) tried to distance himself from the gender-stereotyping of his time – and especially of his great hero, Rousseau. Shelley was revolutionary enough to dream of extending freedom and equality to women. But, as McNiece remarks – thinking that this proves Shelley makes men and women 'transcendently equal' – for Shelley the heroine is always 'the beloved counterpart, shadow, other self, and ideal support of the hero' [1969, p. 180]. She has instinctive knowledge of the truth … and her beauty (of spirit, as well as body) inspires the poetic hero to effective action. It is, however, always a *male* task to shape this truth into verse and, by so doing, to act as a charismatic leader of mankind.

As in the Galenic account of procreation, females could provide the matter – and assist the males in a kind of subsidiary way with the processes of (re)production – but it was a primarily *male* task to form that matter into art. The Romantics' muddling of the old categories of 'female', 'feminine' and 'male' did not fundamentally disturb the old sexual hierarchies – and produced, at best, a male ambivalence towards female authorship. On a personal level, for example, Shelley encouraged Mary Wollstonecraft Shelley to write … but also (apparently) found her writing threatening. We can see this in the original 'Preface' to *Frankenstein* [1818] which Percy wrote himself, assuming his wife's voice to explain the story's genesis in an informal competition set up in 1816 between Byron, himself and Mary (still, at that time, his wife-to-be). The idea, it seems, was to emulate the German ghost-stories that the three friends read to each other during wet evenings spent around Byron's Swiss fireside.

Percy's 'Preface' places the two male authors centre-stage – and not in the manner implied by the novel itself, as the models for Frankenstein's dream of divine omnipotence … and consequent monstrosity.

Instead, Percy's voice presents Byron and himself as Mary's authorial rivals: they, too, had supernatural stories to recount. 'The weather, however, suddenly became serene', and the two men set off on a comradely trek through the Alps, where they 'lost, in the magnificent scenes … all memory of their ghostly visions'. The sun-lit visions of the males in the mountains were so vivid that they effaced the fictions of the fire-lit darkness. Percy's 'Preface' implicitly ranks the natural sublimities of the two men's day-time world (which produced poetry) above the hallucinations of Mary ('a most humble novelist') [pp. 58, 57]. The men transcend the enclosed space – and the horrors of domesticity – which trap the woman in a world of shadows. In the Myth of the Cave in Plato's *Republic* (one of Percy's favourite texts), sunlight represents Truth, whilst firelight only creates a ghostly imitation of reality for those imprisoned down below, inside the Cave of Illusion. Appropriating Plato's imagery and the voice of female modesty, Percy puts Mary in her authorial place. Ghost stories are for women; Poetic Truth for men.

Shelley's anxieties about female authorship are further illustrated by one of his own 'ghostly visions' during the weeks when Frankenstein was born. We know from Byron's mistress and doctor – also full (writing) members of the Gothic house-party, despite Shelley's version of events – that during one of the recitations, Percy retired, screaming … traumatised by a vision of Mary's body with nipples transformed to eyes. Medical expertise was required before the poet could recover his equilibrium.[1] Since the Romantic author creates the world anew in the way that it presents itself to his own, unique angle of view, Shelley's 'fit of phantasy' is symptomatic of a general male unease. As Gilbert and Gubar show in the brilliant opening chapter of *The Madwoman in the Attic* [1979], throughout the nineteenth century – and even today – the pen has been represented as a metaphorical penis. The writer's watching eyes belong with penises … not with female breasts.

In a letter to R. W. Dixon dated 1886, Gerard Manley Hopkins pithily summarises this phallic view of art. For him the Artist's 'most essential quality' is

> masterly execution, which is a kind of male gift, and especially marks off men from women, the begetting of one's thoughts on paper, on verse, or whatever the matter is … [T]he mastery I speak of is not so much in the mind as a puberty in the life of that quality. The male quality is the creative gift. [*Madwoman*, p. 3]

The Jesuit poet has dressed in Victorian majesty the rather bathetic view of Timon, one of Rochester's characters: 'I … never Rhym'd, but for my Pintle's [penis's] sake' [quoted ibid., p. 6]. The sexually chaste nineteenth-century Christian and the notorious seventeenth-century rake unite in making the poet's pen an extension of the male sexual organ.

We can find a similar perspective in twentieth-century poetics, after Romanticism has merged into Modernism. In 'The Figure of the Youth as Virile Poet' [1943], for example, Wallace Stevens remarked that 'The centuries have a way of being male', and says that this maleness comes 'in part, from their philosophers and poets' [p. 52]. For Stevens this is appropriate, since 'There can be no poetry without the personality of the poet', and the definition of poetry has to start with character-sketches [p. 46]. The sketch he offers us is that of 'the genius, or, rather, the youth as virile poet' [p. 66]. Stevens even denies that the Muse is female:

> *No longer do I believe that there is a mystic muse, sister of the Minotaur. This is another of the monsters I had for nurse, whom I have wasted. I am myself a part of what is real, and it is my own speech and the strength of it, this only, that I hear or ever shall.* [p. 60, original in italics]

All the poet's energies come from his own strong self, and that self is necessarily male. The poet, he claims, should write a poetry that 'satisfies both the reason and the imagination' [p. 42].

With the Muse (the imagination) incorporated within the male body, the poet remains male, virile and powerful. But

> if, for the poet, the imagination is paramount, and if he dwells apart in his imagination, as the philosopher dwells in his reason, and as the priest dwells in his belief, the masculine nature that we propose for one that must be the master of our lives will be lost as, for example, in the folds of the garments of the ghost or ghosts of Aristotle. [pp. 66–67]

Steven's poet is a male androgyne. Imagination is the feminine side of his mind; this is the Muse that must be incorporated into his virile male body. Stevens denies woman reason – and creativity. The final evocation of the ghost of Aristotle seems to suggest that he is aware of the sources of his beliefs. But whatever the metaphysical wrappings of this masculine poetics, Stevens seems to be agreeing with the anonymous eighteenth-century objector to Aphra Behn, who wrote in 1702:

> What a Pox have the Women to do with the Muses? I grant you the Poets call the Nine Muses by the Names of Women, but why so? not because the Sex had any thing to do with Poetry, but because in that Sex they're much fitter for prostitution. [Lock, 1976, p. 26]

The paintbrush and sculptor's chisel are also phallic signifiers. Renoir, for example, is alleged to have said 'that he painted his paintings with his prick' [quoted *Madwoman*, p.6]. He most certainly wrote that

> women are monsters who are authors, lawyers and politicians, like George Sand, Madame Adam, and other bores who are nothing more than five-legged beasts. The woman who is an artist is merely ridiculous, but I feel that it is acceptable for a woman to be a singer or a dancer. In Antiquity and among simple people, women sing and dance and they do not therefore become less feminine. Gracefulness is a woman's domain and even her duty. [White, 1972, p. 171]

This is a common form of artistic misogyny. But in the fine arts there is another logic of sexual exclusion that is more prevalent than Renoir's … or even that underlying Ruskin's pronouncements about male and female roles in *Sesame and Lilies* (1867):

> Now their separate characters are these. The man's power is active, progressive and defensive. He is eminently the doer, the creator, the discoverer. His intellect is for invention and speculation. But the woman's intellect is not for invention or creation but sweet ordering, arrangement and decision. Her great function is praise. [Parker and Pollock, 1981, p. 9]

For Renoir, woman's status as a beautiful object confines her to social roles that involve artistic *display*, rather than artistic *invention*. By contrast, Ruskin's woman is a born housekeeper. She tidies the house of art while man exercises his inventive muscles, and she applauds when he brings home the creative bacon. But many of the examples provided by Parker and Pollock in *Old Mistresses* [1981] provide a further position in the pornographic gymnastics of sexualised art criticism. Writing in 1871, John Jackson Jarves provides an illustration. He divides 'feminine' from non-feminine fields of art, suggesting that women '*Naturally*' pick artistic fields that involve 'the least expenditure of mental capital'. Crafts that appeal to women's 'nice feeling for form, quick perceptions' and 'mobile fancy' are allocated to the 'feminine'. He gives clay-modelling as his example, but adds that when women venture into the more masculine genre of sculpture, 'women by *nature* are likewise prompted … to motives of fancy and sentiment rather than realistic portraiture or absolute creative imagination' [ibid., p. 10, Parker and Pollock's emphases].

Male cultural supremacy is secured by such territorial divisions. Unlike Renoir and Ruskin, Jarves allows women inventive capacities – but only of inferior kinds. Absolute creative imagination is limited to certain sub-sections of subject-matter in certain privileged genres: such as realistic sculptures, oil paintings of (nude) human beings, group portraits or history paintings. Since women were deemed 'unsexed' by skill in these exclusively male fields of art, there could be no temptations to the truly 'feminine' psyche. Thus, although the 'feminine' is not consistently downgraded in phallic criticism, in these modes of *territorial* apartheid, 'feminine' and 'masculine' are synonymous with 'female' and 'male', and 'genius' becomes a kind of psychic beard – a secondary sexual characteristic of mature (European) males. In the words of Léon Legrange (1860):

> Male genius has nothing to fear from female taste. Let men of genius conceive of great architectural projects, monumental sculpture, and elevated forms of painting. In a word, let men busy themselves with all that has to do with great art. Let women occupy themselves with those types of art they have always preferred, such as pastels, portraits or miniatures. Or the painting of flowers, those prodigies of grace and freshness which alone can compete with the grace and freshness of women themselves. [Trans. from French and quoted ibid., p. 13]

Such gendering of creative territories is much more common in the fine arts than in literature. But there are, of course, examples in literary criticism, too. Indeed, we saw Shelley implicitly gendering the ghost-story as female. And in Chapter 2 we observed Anthony Burgess employing similar devices to downgrade female novelists. Burgess (a novelist himself) is supercilious about novel-writing: this female genre does not represent True Art. It is an inferior form of literature … and literature itself is inferior to musical composition … an activity, apparently, that requires *male* sexuality. Significantly, in *The Independent* of 23 May 1988 Anthony Burgess reveals that he thinks of himself as 'primarily a composer' … which explains why he can use music as a truss to protect his own creative balls. But, of course, few male novelists view themselves as essentially musicians, and as such have had to opt for more subtle means of guarding their manhood. Historically, the novel has been less easy to marginalise from High Art than flower-painting, clay-modelling, watercolour landscapes and other 'crafts'. Male novelists have had to find ways of reassuring themselves of their virility whilst still recognising that 'feminine' qualities such as sensitivity, passivity, emotionality and introspective self-consciousness are also expected of them.

The Virility School of Creativity seems to have been particularly important in the middle years of this century. Its sires include Picasso, Jackson Pollock, and in literature Hemingway, Henry Miller and Mailer. It was by no means a cohesive school … but rather a variety of gut reactions to an ideology that credited a creator with a male sexual drive but a feminine psyche. It encompasses a variety of machismo stances. Jackson Pollock and Henry Miller, for example, stressed their maleness precisely in order to compensate for the essentially intuitive and passive nature of their own working methods. Pollock's famous 'drip' paintings started by liquid simply falling on to the huge unstretched canvases laid out on floors or walls: and then (he claimed) the paintings 'contacted' him as he walked round and 'in' them, and revealed to him the shapes that he must form [O'Hara, 1959, p. 32]. Scale, size, aggression – and picture-titles drawn from the mythologies of patriarchal power – were employed to masculinise these 'drip' techniques into 'Action Painting'. Analogously, Henry Miller idealised authors as radio 'antennae', picking up currents and ideas from the pervading atmosphere [Plimpton, 1963, pp. 172–3]. But Miller's prose is frantically insistent that the author is *not-female*: hence the excessively violent (and monotonous) details of sexual exploits with the Otherness of cunts.

The typical Hemingway hero, on the other hand, was very different: full of machismo, but sexually impotent. As Peter Schwenger notes in his analysis of a group of these Virile Novelists, in every case 'Beneath the blatant *machismo* one finds considerable ambivalence towards the traditional masculine role' [1984, p.14]. In his subsequent chapters, Schwenger expresses his puzzlement in reconciling feminist theory (with its analysis of the way the pen has been represented as a penis) with his own observations that the buddies of the Virility School are only too aware that it is 'sissy' to write novels. Like the feminist critics whose writings he cites, Schwenger fails to make a clear distinction between the 'feminine' and the 'female'. Indeed, the novelists he examines also seem confused. Their texts stress maleness to counterbalance the effeminacy expected from members of their profession.

A kind of vulgar Freudianism was used to portray all creative activity as sublimated sexual libido … and as Freud himself indicated that only males could be really said to have libidos, Freudianism was very reassuring [see Chapter 14, below]. Via Freud the figure of the talented male melancholic (who transcends his melancholic madness) was transposed into that of the virile but neurotic artist (who sublimates his neurosis). Metaphors of male lust and male sexual sickness are thus scattered liberally through George Plimpton's third compilation of Paris Review Interviews, *Writers at Work* [1967]. There James Jones talks about the writer's 'desire for self-exposure'. The writer wants to 'impose [his] personality upon the world', and the simile that follows excludes the woman writer. The author is 'like one of those guys who has a compulsion to take his thing out and show it on the street' [p. 250].

Cocteau, by contrast, seems to have male masturbation in mind when he asks. 'This sickness, to express oneself. What is it?' The query follows on from a remark that seems to resemble Rousseau's in excluding women from having even good taste in art. 'Appreciation of art is a moral erection; otherwise mere dilettantism. I believe sexuality is the basis of all friendship' [ibid., p. 81]. For Norman Mailer, on the other hand, his own act of writing is like the desire of a man 'to perform the sexual act under every kind of condition, emotion, and mood available to him' [ibid., p. 275]. The sexual performance fantasised must surely be that of a sexual bully … not the raped or sexually degraded victim! But just how mentally sick *is* Mailer? He would feel happier – more male – if he could persuade us that he is potentially very sick indeed, but has redirected his sickness into literature instead of deeds. As he famously brags elsewhere, 'a good novelist can do with everything but the remnant of his balls' [1961, p. 387].

Even contemporary male novelists who present themselves as sympathetic to feminism, like John Fowles, find themselves trapped within the spiritual pornography of the School of Virility. And I am not just thinking here of *Mantissa* [1982], Fowles 'comic' excursus into soft porn. This parody of male fantasies about women functions as just one more male fantasy, in which (between acting dirty) the male narrator talks dirty with a (sometimes feminist) Muse [Woodcock, 1984]. Fowles caricatures feminism; but he has not simply grown more conservative with age. Throughout his fiction, his alliance with the 'feminine' always co-existed with a double *male* perspective on women. On the one hand, his heroines are cyphers objectified by male desire. On the other hand, they are represented as having wants and needs which must be respected: otherwise female allure will be lost [*The Collector*, 1963]; male happiness and the fabric of a patriarchal society will be threatened [*The French Lieutenant's Woman*, 1969]; and men will be trapped in delusory fantasies about muses, goddesses and love [*The Magus*, 1966].

Fowles recognises that there never was a time in which males could simply treat women as objects, and that this is a superficial conception of a male utopia. He tries to maintain authorial distance from the fetish that makes 'MOUSE' the signifier for Woman – 'the letter M and then, after a space' (in which 'an O-shaped vulva' is inserted) 'the letters U, S, E' [1974, pp. 81–2]. But what gives Fowles's fiction its power is his own attraction towards that zero: that mysterious O(therness) that completes the male creator and the male procreator. Like the narrator of 'The Ebony Tower' [1974], Fowles feels nostalgia for the old aesthetics of virility, that made great art emerge from '"Balls. Spunk. Any spunk. Even Hitler's spunk. Or nothing"', and which consigns the abstraction and intellectualisation of modern art to the '"Triumph of the bloody eunuch"'. What is needed instead is '"Cock. Not fundamentals. Fundaments … Pair of tits and a cunt. All that goes with them. That's reality"' [pp. 45–46]. Although in Fowles's story there is a female creator (nicknamed 'Mouse') – and self-conscious echoes of Gwen John (and Rodin) – the woman's creativity emerges out of sexual perversion: 'the real repression must be of a normal sexuality, a femaleness that cried out for … ' [p. 93]. Fowles clings to the tradition that makes great creators male.[2] Like the other members of the Virility School, he makes art *dis*placed male sexuality … but *mis*placed female sexuality.

From *Gender and Genius: Towards a Female Aesthetic* by
Christine Battersby, 1994, Women's Press. © Christine Battersby.

Notes

1.   For the diary entries of Dr Polidori and Claire Clairmont (Mary's step-sister, as well as Byron's mistress), see Cameron [1974], pp. 92, 586. In her own 'Introduction' to *Frankenstein*, written for the 1831 edition, Mary denies that she was ever in competition with Byron and her (dead) husband [1817, p. 53]. This has been interpreted by Poovey as a part of Mary's unwillingness to measure herself against her two intimidating male companions, and as an indication of her 'wholehearted acceptance of an essentially subordinate and passive role' [1984, pp. 141, 142]. But such a reading is suspect. We know that Percy Bysshe Shelley invented several details of the occasion: that the writing was an exclusively night-time activity, and that it involved only the three authors. Why should we accept his account of the rest of the story? By refusing to slot herself into her dead husband's mythologising of authorial competition – a mythologising that, in Mary's words, shows the two men downgrading 'the platitude of prose' – Mary resisted the males' claim to superiority of vision. As Poovey shows, Mary did herself internalise the social denigration of female authorship; but this does not make her a thorough-going conservative… even in later life. [See also Chapter 10, below.]
2.   It is not just in his fiction that John Fowles associates great art with maleness. In one of his critical pieces, 'Hardy and the Hag' (1977), psychoanalytic theory is employed to rationalise the gendering of creativity. See Bruce Woodcock [1984], p. 21.

References

Dates in square brackets refer to the first appearance, publication or relevant edition of the work, not to the date of the text consulted.

Cameron, Kenneth Neill, *Shelley: The Golden Years*, Harvard University Press, 1974.
Citron, Marcia J., 'Women and the Lied, 1775–1850', in *Women Making Music: The Western Art Tradition, 1150–1950*, eds. Jane Bowers and Judith Tick, London: Macmillan, 1986, pp. 224–48.
Coleridge, Samuel Taylor, *Biographia Literaria* [1817], Introduction by Arthur Symons, London: Dent, Everyman ed., n.d.
Fowles, John [1969], *The French Lieutenant's Woman*, London: Pan, 1987.
Fowles, John [1974], 'The Ebony Tower', in *The Ebony Tower*, London: New York: Panther, 1975.
Fritz, Paul and Morton, Richard (eds), *Woman in the Eighteenth Century and Other Essays*, Toronto: Hakkert, 1976.
Gilbert, Sandra M. and Gubar, Susan. *The Madwoman in the Attic: The Woman Writer and the Nineteenth-Century Literary Imagination*, Yale University Press, 1979.
Lock, F.P., 'Astraea's "Vacant Throne": The Successors of Aphra Behn', in Fritz and Morton [1976], pp. 25–36.
McNiece, Gerald, *Shelley and the Revolutionary Idea*, Harvard University Press, 1969.
Mailer, Norman, *Advertisements for Myself* [1961], London: Panther, 1968.
O'Hara, Frank, *Jackson Pollock*, New York: George Braziller, Great American Artists Series, 1959.
Parker, Rozsika and Griselda Pollock [1981], *Old Mistresses: Women, Art and Ideology*, London: Routledge, 1981.

Plimpton, George [1963] (ed.), *Writers at Work: The Paris Review Interviews*, Harmondsworth: Penguin, 2nd series, 1977.

Plimpton, George [1967], *Writers at Work: The Paris Review Interviews* Harmondsworth: Penguin, 3rd series, 1977.

Poovey, Mary, *The Proper Lady and the Woman Writer: Ideology as Style in the Works of Mary Wollstonecraft, Mary Shelley, and Jane Austen* [1984], University of Chicago Press, p.b. ed., 1985.

Rousseau, Jean-Jacques, *The Confessions* [1781], trans. J.M. Cohen, Harmondsworth: Penguin, 1953.

Schwenger, Peter, *Phallic Critiques: Masculinity and Twentieth-Century Literature*, London: Routledge, 1984.

Shaftesbury, Anthony Ashley Cooper, Third Earl of, *Characteristics of Men, Manners, Opinions, Times* [1711], ed. John M. Robertson, Indianapolis: Bobbs-Merrill, 1964.

Shelley, Mary [1818], *Frankenstein; or, The Modern Prometheus*, containing P.B. Shelley's 1818 'Preface' and the author's 1831 'Introduction', ed. Maurice Hindle, Harmondsworth: Penguin, 1985.

Shelley, Percy Bysshe, 'Preface' to *Frankenstein* [1818], in Shelley, Mary [1818].

Stevens, Wallace, 'The Figure of the Youth as Virile Poet' [1943], reprinted in his *The Necessary Angel: Essays on Reality and the Imagination*, New York: Alfred A. Knopf Inc., Vintage ed. 1951.

White, Barbara Ehrlich, 'Renoir's Sensuous Women' [1972], in *Woman as Sex Object*, eds. Thomas B. Hess and Linda Nochlin, London: Allen Lane, 1973, pp. 166–81.

Woodcock, Bruce, *Male Mythologies, John Fowles and Masculinity*, Brighton: Harvester; New Jersey: Barnes and Noble, 1984.

3 A Note on Anger

MARILYN FRYE

It is a tiresome truth of women's experience that our anger is generally not well-received. Men (and sometimes women) ignore it, see it as our being "upset" or "hysterical," or see it as craziness. Attention is turned not to what we are angry about but to the project of calming us down and to the topic of our "mental stability." It is as common as dirty socks. Every woman knows it, has lived it. Men receive women's anger as incongruous and irrational and in many cases they are simply unable to improvise any way to cope with it: they strike out physically, slapping or beating the angry woman, or they retreat, covering their incompetence with something like "I can't deal with you when you're like this."[1]

I don't read men's misreading of women's anger and their inability to respond appropriately to it as wholly or always willful and malicious, as always simply a pretense put up just to frustrate the anger and avoid acting on the matter the anger is about. It has often not felt to me like simple perversity in the situations I have experienced, and this judgment is supported also by my experience on the other side of oppression's barriers, as a white woman encountering the anger of women of color. The anger is in fact sane and sound, but its *seeming* crazy and bizarre to the receiver is also real. In many situations men really do experience women's anger as some sort of unnatural and baffling event that has no intelligible place in the causal order unless the man can see the woman as "out of order."

Though it is correct to deplore and denounce this odd combination of ignorance and incompetence as sexist (or racist), that is neither intellectually nor politically sufficient. We can, if we will, learn something from this phenomenon.

Anger seems to be a reaction to being thwarted, frustrated or harmed. It comes when your momentum is dispersed or deflected. You are going along living your life, tending your business, pursuing your project, and then you are stopped; a bureaucratic tangle, someone's unwillingness to lend reasonable assistance, the breakdown of a car. The energy that was moving you along your course cannot flow; it is blocked, it becomes turbulent. In some cases you feel frustrated, irritated, disoriented or depressed; in some cases you become angry.

The frustrating situations which generate anger, as opposed to those which merely make you displeased or depressed, are those in which you see yourself not simply as obstructed or hindered, but as wronged. You become angry when you see the obstruction or hindrance as unjust or unfair, or when you see it as due to someone's malice or inexcusable incompetence. Most of us, if we are kept from going to the concert or the ball game by the weather, are disappointed, maybe grouchy, perhaps depressed; but if we are kept from going because our partner lost the tickets, we are more likely to be angry. If a person does shake a fist at the sky in anger about the weather, she is either ridiculous or she is pretending or even believing

---

I am indebted to C. S. for valuable criticism of earlier drafts of this essay.

that there is some sort of agent up there whose responsibility in this matter makes the snowstorm a wrong rather than a misfortune. Anger implies not only that the inhibition or obstruction was distressing, but that it was an offense.

To be or be perceived as wronged, you have to be or be perceived as right. Anger is always righteous. To be angry you have to have some sense of the rightness or propriety of your position and your interest in whatever has been hindered, interfered with or harmed, and anger implies a claim to such rightness or propriety. When you are not "right" or "in the right," anger is inappropriate, or impossible.[2] Suppose that in the midst of cooking something you realize you need mushrooms. You've seen an ad in the paper that says a particular store has a special on mushrooms. You dash off to that store but find that they don't have any mushrooms, at any price. You may be angry. But if it turns out that you misremembered the ad, and it was actually another store's ad, that will take the wind out of your sails. If you are not right in your expectation, you are not wronged in its disappointment.

There are many kinds and senses of presence, propriety, position and place, many kinds of "being in the right." I do not mean here to speak just of "rights" in some strict political or legal sense. I mean to speak of something which is the logical mate of respect.[3]

When a person is harmlessly about her business, pursuing her interests as she sees fit, employing means and using resources which are properly hers to employ, respect dictates that you permit her actions, and the objects and conditions these require, to be under her control or to happen as felicitously as the fates will allow. If she is engaged in building bookshelves, respect dictates that you not saunter up and take the hammer without bothering to ask her if she's finished with it (unless, of course, you need it to defend both your lives by braining a dangerous intruder). Whether or not the hammer is, in a legal sense, her property, it is in her domain and associated with her by the web of connections her purposive behavior weaves. If you walk off with it (in the absence of some overriding factor like the intruder), your act implies that you do not acknowledge that it is "rightful" that the hammer be in her domain: for instance, that you think she does not have a right to use it because she stole it; or she ought not be making bookshelves on company time; or she's botched it up so badly she shouldn't bother continuing anyway; or you simply don't think she or her project is worth minimal recognition and consideration. If you think any of these things, then there is something about her and/or her project which you are not respecting.

The domain one acknowledges in respecting a person, a project or act is not simply physical, encompassing physical objects. Acknowledgement of right may dictate refraining from making conversation which would distract a person, or it might dictate encouraging her or not discouraging her. Her attention, her confidence, her sense of well-being, her freedom to speak her mind, her access to knowledge and skills, are all matters within her domain.

Anger implies a claim to domain—a claim that one is a being whose purposes and activities require and create a web of objects, spaces, attitudes and interests that is worthy of respect, and that the topic of this anger is a matter rightly within that web. You walk off with my hammer and I angrily demand that you bring it back. Implicitly, I claim that my project is worthy, that I am within my rights to be doing it, that the web of connections it weaves rightly encompasses that hammer. Or you wantonly criticize my work, without invitation, and I angrily tell you to mind your own business. Implicitly, I claim the right to do this work, the propriety of relying only on my own judgment if I wish, and the sanctity of whatever confidence I have in my abilities and the success of the project. There is something I demand that you respect.[4]

Being angry is usefully understood on analogy with acts the philosopher J. L. Austin called "speech acts."[5] When you say something like "I promise" or "I apologize," you do not just assert or report something about yourself, you also reorient yourself and another person to each other. You become committed, another comes to count on you; you undo a debt, an imbalance of good and ill will is repaired. This alteration of relations requires and involves a certain cooperation from the second party. You can say, "I promise I'll write you," but also the other must take herself to be someone to whom you are obligated and must count on your doing what you said you'd do. If the second party's "uptake" is not forthcoming, the relation between the two does not take the intended shape, and the "promise" collapses. Your speech just hangs there— embarrassed, unconsummated.

Being angry at someone is somewhat like a speech act in that it has a certain conventional force whereby it sets people up in a certain sort of orientation to each other; and like a speech act, it cannot "come off" if it does not get uptake.

One woman told of this experience: She had gone to some trouble to adjust the carburetor on her car and shortly thereafter an attendant at a gas station started monkeying with it. She was dismayed and sharply told him to stop.[6] He became very agitated and yelled at her, calling her a crazy bitch.

Other responses might have been forthcoming from the attendant. He might have demanded to know why he shouldn't touch it; he might have defensively claimed he was only looking at it and wasn't going to touch it; he might have tried to persuade her that it was indeed the right thing to do, to try changing its adjustment. All of these responses take the anger on by directly responding to the claims implicit in it: accepting them or challenging them, accepting or defending himself against the implicit charge or accusation. He did not meet the anger and its claims. He moved to a different level. What he did was irrelevant. He changed the subject—from the matter of his actions and the carburetor to the matter of her character and sanity. He did not give her anger uptake.

Deprived of uptake, the woman's anger is left as just a burst of expression of individual feeling. As a social act, an act of communication, it just doesn't happen. It is, as Austin would have said, "non-played."

The sort of uncooperativeness displayed by the gas station attendant is a rejection of anger's claims. It rejects them not simply as arguably false or unjustified, but as claims so wildly and obviously off the mark as to confound response. It rejects them as claims only someone in an abnormal state—hysterical or mad— could make; as implying accusations so obviously fantastic that they could be motivated only by a fevered and indiscriminate malice. The claimant can only be a crazy bitch.

One's anger presupposes certain things about what sort of being one is and what sorts of relations are possible between oneself and another. The patterns of claims someone can and cannot countenance, of the acts one can and cannot give uptake to, is a partial map of one's world view. It reveals something of one's understanding of the essential natures and relations of things.

You say the movie is at 7:30 and I disagree, saying it is at 7:00. I am puzzled by your getting it wrong, since I think you must have phoned the theater, just as I did. But we are still in the same world of belief and discourse. Another day, you say you are the messiah and I should worship you. This situation is rather different. I don't know how to argue with you about that (assuming I am satisfied that we mean the same things by these words). I have certain understandings of what a messiah would be if there were one, of what worship is, and of the circumstances under which worship might be appropriate. These are enmeshed far more deeply in my basic understanding of the world than is my confidence in the health of any one particular human being I may encounter. As I understand this world, human individuals run amok far more often than messiahs appear, if they ever do. If I am convinced that you are serious, I can only suppose there is, in some sense, something wrong with you.

To get angry is to claim implicitly that one is a certain sort of being, a being which can (and in this case does) stand in a certain relation and position *a propos* the being one is angry at. One claims that one is in certain ways and dimensions *respectable*. One makes claims upon respect. For any woman to presuppose any such thing of herself is at best potentially problematic and at worst incomprehensible in the world of male-supremacy where women are Women and men are Men. A man's concept of Woman and of Man, and his understanding of what sorts of relations and connections are possible between beings of these sorts, to a great extent determine the range of his capacity to comprehend these claims, and hence of his capacity to give uptake to women's anger.

In some cases women can get angry without much risk of being thought crazy, hushed up or beaten up. Usually, women can get angry at children, or in behalf of children. A woman may get away with being angry at some oaf who slammed a door and thus ruined her souffle, or at another who disarranged the pages of a report she has typed and is collating. On the other hand, she is not likely to get away with being angry at the oaf who maladjusts her carburetor. The pattern is obvious. Kids, homemaking and secretarial service belong to women; cars belong to men. So long as a woman is operating squarely within a realm which is generally recognized as a woman's realm, labeled as such by stereotypes of women and of certain activities, her anger will quite likely be tolerated, at least not thought crazy. It seems to me that in general, if a woman's purposive behavior and the web of interests and authority it weaves can be seen as falling within the place and functions of Mother/Caretaker/Conserver/Helpmate, her claim to authority, interest, presence and place will make sense to relevant others. It is likely to accord well enough with their concept of Woman.[7]

We are indebted to women of the nineteenth century for extending the range of tolerance of women's anger. The struggles and victories of abolitionists, suffragists, prohibitionists and other reformers made it relatively safe for women to get angry, publicly, in behalf of great moral causes. Generally speaking, women can get angry about such things as nuclear energy and arms, pollution, war, starving children or drunken driving. (This does not mean, still, that we are so likely to be taken very seriously. Our anger is likely to be perceived as "understandable, but ill-informed.")

This extension, hard won as it was, represents only a relatively small shift in the concept of Woman. Historically and logically it was an extension of our "right" to mother. We can be relatively easily perceived as mothers to our nations or to our peoples (which in some cases are imaged in dominant mythology as childlike), or to the species. By virtue of this, we can be understood if we claim legitimate interest and some degree of authority in the matter of their protection and preservation.[8] Also, as an extension of mothering into matters of public welfare, it still permits women's anger only *in behalf of others*, not in our own behalves.

A woman's anger on another's behalf is far more likely to get uptake, and even acceptance, than her anger in her own behalf. This is why it is easier for a woman to be passionately anti-abortion than passionately "pro-choice." One is within the bounds of concepts of Woman which are more widely shared and more warmly sanctioned when one's passion is in defense of others (especially if the others can plausibly be presented as "innocent" and as "children" or "babies"). For the same sorts of reasons, women's claims to some sort of propriety and authority in our interest in "peace" and "the survival of humanity" are generally more credible in this culture than women's claims to a like propriety and authority in our interests in our own skins, genitals or wombs. Hence it is safer to get angry about nuclear power than about one's own rape; the former is more likely to be intelligible, to get uptake.

To expand the scope of one's intelligible anger is to change one's place in the universe, to change another's concept of what one is, to become something different in that social and collective scheme which determines the limits of the intelligible. Nineteenth century women succeeded in expanding the concept of Woman, that is, really, the concept of Mother, to the point where a woman could express anger in a public matter and be found intelligible. Contemporary feminists have taken on the more radical project of expanding the concept of Woman to the point where a woman can assert herself and make demands upon respect, in public or private, simply in her own behalf. Not, that is, as any kind or degree of Mother, but simply as a being, herself, worthy of respect.

Not all anger is justified, and as long as we have concepts of ourselves, others and the relations amongst us, some anger will sometimes be unintelligible. And of course others' concepts of us are not always objectionable. Different men, and indeed different women, differ in detail in what concept they have of Woman, and what they would or could perceive as "a woman going about her business, pursuing her interests, by means and using resources which are properly hers to employ." Some men, for instance, think all affairs pertaining to birth control are entirely "female" concerns and virtue requires of men who engage sexually with women only that they let women take care of it. But also, some husbands think a wife's fecundity is entirely the husband's to control and manage. The first sort of man would be baffled by a woman's anger at his not taking any responsibility; the second sort would be baffled by his wife's anger at his getting her pregnant. In both cases, the discovery of what baffles is the discovery of some aspect of what the man thinks a woman is.

No two women live, in a daily and detailed way, in identical spaces created by identical ranges of concepts of Woman. Some of us, indeed, have consciously constructed situations for ourselves in which we will be shaped by chosen and wholesome concepts of Woman. For better or for worse though, in each of our lives, others' concepts of us are revealed by the limits of the intelligibility of our anger. Anger can be an instrument of cartography. By determining where, with whom, about what and in what circumstances one can get angry and get uptake, one can map others' concepts of who and what one is.

One woman took this thought home with her and tried it out. She walked about the apartment she shared, not unhappily, with her young husband, testing in imagination for the viability of her anger—in what situations it would "work," would get uptake. She discovered the pattern was very simple and clear. It went with the floor plan. She could get angry quite freely in the kitchen and somewhat less freely and about a more limited range of things in the living room. She could not get angry in the bedroom.

Anger. Domain. Respect.

Notes

1. See "Getting Angry," by Susi Kaplow, and "Men and Violence," a transcript of a taped consciousness-raising session, in *Radical Feminism*, edited by Anne Koedt, Ellen Levine and Anita Rapone (Quadrangle, New York, 1973).

2. Some people are surely careless and irresponsible in their anger and don't pay much attention to whether they are right or not, not caring much about whether their anger is appropriate or not. But I suspect that such people think they are right to get their way whether or not they are the right person, in the right circumstance, with the right expectations, etc.

3. See "Rape and Respect," by Carolyn Shafer and Marilyn Frye, in *Feminism and Philosophy*, edited by Mary Vetterling-Braggin, Frederick A. Elliston and Jane English (Littlefield, Adams & Co., Totowa, New Jersey, 1977).

4.   I use examples of one person angry at one other person about one thing because they are simple paradigms. Of course one can get angry at oneself, or at many others, and a group can be angry. The picture presented here can be extended to these sorts of cases, but it is not my purpose to do that in this sketch.

5.   J. L. Austin, *How To Do Things With Words* (Oxford University Press, 1962).

6.   For those who do not know about carburetors: This organ of the gasoline engine mixes gasoline and air (oxygen) in just the right proportions to enable the gasoline to ignite and to burn efficiently. Getting it properly adjusted is a delicate and often frustrating job, and its maladjustment causes all sorts of trouble. When you've got it right, you don't touch it; and even when you suspect it is not right, it is the last thing you experiment with in your diagnostic efforts.

7.   Often a woman's anger, even when she is within this range of social places, will not be taken particularly seriously, but that is because all that belongs in this range of social places is likely to be thought trivial. Not being taken seriously is not quite the same as being thought mad. Still, if the woman insists persistently enough on her anger being taken seriously, she may begin to seem mad, for she will seem to have her values all mixed up and distorted.

8.   I have considerable respect for mothering and believe that the attitudes and practices of good mothering can make a very valuable contribution to the conduct of things in the sphere of public politics and morality. Things will have changed more, and more for the better, when we can mother as appropriate without being seen as Mothers, and can, as women, do a great deal else as well.

4 The Sensory Celebration (I)

ANNE DUFOURMANTELLE

Nothing but stillness can remain when hearts are full
Of their own sweetness, bodies of their loveliness.

W. B. Yeats

Gentleness is an occasion for sensory celebration. Tact and the tactile, touch, taste, perfumes, sounds, all opening access. If it can instill violence in fragility, be beautiful, erotic, enter into a sacred dance with the desired body of the other, it is not without secret. That is to say, without freedom until the last moment.

Gentleness has many affinities to light. Its radiation, its intensity, its transformations, its night. If it had to be pictured in space it would be a moving curve, however miniscule. Music being the most direct translation perhaps, along with touch. The contrasting melodic lines harmonize with the rhythm, the voice, and the instrument. The andantes of Mozart's 21st and 24th concertos are not only perfect, they weave a cathedral of sounds. A perfect balance. In the music of the Renaissance and of the Middle Ages we actually hear the sacred and sensitive tessitura. When Anne Azema sings the *lais* of the troubadours or the lament of Isolde, gentleness is elevated to its most passionate.

The image is another entrance into gentleness. The painting *The Return of the Prodigal Son* by Rembrandt at the Hermitage in Saint Petersburg is a wonderful example of this.

Tact, the intelligence of touch, is an accelerator of life that halts madness. During psychotic episodes gentleness is frightening. It is the mortal disparity between the real and its shadow projected within the psyche. Each sensation foretells a possible danger.

Refinement coincides with gentleness, particularly in craftsmanship. It is the way wood is carved, worked, the subtlety of its color, the unfolding of a curve in the late Baroque period. Gentleness seems to be inlaid with the gesture, joined to it within the material. Five thousand coats of lacquer were required in order to make a piece of furniture for the royal court in Beijing. In accounts, the touch was said to have been like the gentleness of rain and the fineness of a child's hair. The softness [*douceur*] of silk, polished glass, spun silver, the texture of velvet, of the skin that it covers, of the eye beholding them.

Hieratic figures made by Giotto. The illuminated fixed in a simplicity that gives them, like that of the convent cells painted by Fra Angelico, a sweetness without weakness or mannerism. Their gentleness invites the viewer to participate in a scene that cannot help but ensure distance. It holds at bay the gaze where it alights.

Gentleness joining sky and sea in Venice. Gentleness of summer skies, of atmospheres, of clouds. Delicacy in these non-closed edges—interior and exterior, liquid and ethereal.

Gentleness of lamps at night. The halo and its limitation. Their preciseness, often on stage. Cutting a naked body. The cutout of an alcove. The high flame. All these edges of light that darkness defines and in a way protects.

There is no limit to gentleness, rather a continual invitation to become infected by it—and that invitation can be broken in an instant.

The values that agree with gentleness are sometimes grueling, they require an etiquette above and beyond what is encouraged as a mere sweetener to our lives. They require keeping watch.

Is gentleness only obvious when it deserts us, and when it returns? When suffering ends, when the rolling of the wave leaves foam on the sand as gentle as air, or is it rather a singular essence savored only for its own sake?

An animal's belly. The throbbing of a vein that surfaces from under the skin. Very aged skin like a translucent pebble. The skin of a very young child, his or her cheek still covered in an invisible fuzz. The calm of breathing, of what contains and protects life. And of what offers itself through touch.

Gentleness is also harmony. The manner in which the orchestra harmonizes, or in which two of Rothko's flat planes will interact along a red horizon. It is the proportion of a face.

The sweetness of the ineffable. Beauty of what doesn't appear in the given appearance of things and phenomena, of what can only be touched in a face, of what loosens its grip entirely. Gentleness reveals the gap between what is there and what escapes. The carnal and the spiritual, but not only the gaps, the ellipses—in language, in the visible, in the baroque spiral, in the lines of anamorphosis.

From *Power of Gentleness: Meditations on the Risk of Living* by Anne Dufourmantelle.
Used with permission of Fordham University Press, © 2018; permission
conveyed through Copyright Clearance Center, Inc.

Part 2 Film Aesthetics

Introduction

The film *Innocence* (directed by Lucile Hadžihalilović, 2004) begins with an overhead shot of a box of some kind, with a star-shaped panel on top, trundling along on a journey somewhere. It is a coffin, which we next see on the floor of a girls' school dormitory. A group of girls surrounds the coffin, shot from the waist down, showing only very short white pleated skirts, pale legs, ankle socks and chunky boots. The eldest girl arrives with a key, unlocks the coffin and lifts its lid. Inside is a young girl, sleeping, resembling a corpse. She opens her eyes and looks up at those surrounding her coffin. She sits up, and we see more of the group of girls: they are of varying heights and ages, differentiated by the colour of their hair ribbons, and they silently study the new arrival. One asks the child's name, and she replies 'Iris' (Zoé Auclair), and the eldest girl, Bianca (Bérangère Haubruge), introduces them all. Iris is naked apart from her knickers, and appears stunned yet compliant. The sight of a naked child, arising from the coffin in which she has just arrived, and surrounded by these subdued, wraith-like girls, is chilling and perplexing, beautiful and horrifying (see Figure P2.1).

The film is enigmatically called *Innocence*, and takes place in a girls' school where they are all dressed in white and lessons appear just to focus on evolution and ballet. The visual style of the film, however, creates a realm of unease through the girls' clothes being that bit too short, the shots of them undressing and swimming seeming prurient, and the school has hidden rooms, basements and elderly ladies who remain sidelined and silent. The ballet classes and performances reveal that the girls are being groomed for a sexualized money-making spectacle, and the competition for a place at ballet school subjects the finalists to ruthless assessment of their physical flaws. The soundscape features forest sounds and rumbling noises emanating through grills in the ground, behind doors and along tunnels that are not explained. The music that the girls dance and play to may be popular classical music (Prokoviev and Janáček) but tunes are rendered menacing by echoing piano renditions. As the camera weaves around the group of girls playing in a forest glade, their hula hoops, clapping games, and swings seem to epitomize the 'specific positive style of feminine body comportment and movement, which is learned as the girl comes to understand that she is a girl', as described by Iris Marion Young ([1990] 2005: 43). The film's beauty is sinister, and the costumes, actions and characters are menacing. In one scene, a disgruntled member of Iris's group, usurped by her arrival, whips Iris with reeds, wipes her finger over the bleeding scratches she has caused on Iris's legs, and puts her bloody finger into her mouth to taste. This is not innocent child's play, and indeed the film asks whether the trappings of girlhood are innocent in any way as they are prepared for the exploitation and vulnerability of female adolescence (Rushton 2007; Quinlivan 2009; Wilson 2012). One of the reasons that this film is so fascinating and unsettling is that we are able to see images that we believe *should* be

Figure P2.1 Iris arrives at the school in a coffin (*Innocence*).

innocent, but feel their dangers, and suspect the girls are unaware of their destiny. This knowing subversion of the apparent innocence of the clothing and physical activity of young girls is an example of devastating feminist aesthetics.

In this Part, each essay reframes ways of thinking about what we see on screen. In Iris Murdoch's paper, 'Vision and Choice in Morality', given in 1956, she is responding to a paper by Ronald W. Hepburn at a symposium of the Aristotelian Society. In typically meticulous fashion, Murdoch positions her arguments within the philosophical tradition of behaviourist ethics and takes issue with the idea that morality is about definitions and words, recommendations and prohibitions. Murdoch calls for us to consider our 'inner life' and what our moral vision might look like. Murdoch observes that 'we differ not only because we select different objects out of the same world but because we see different worlds'. Her investigation of the notion of moral vision, and the inadequacy of linguistic moral philosophy, invites the consideration of stories as inspiration for moral thinking, and indeed 'philosophical pictures of morality' (Bolton 2017). These words support the idea that film might be a potentially transformative moral experience: and perhaps cinema more broadly than the individual film.

Analytic philosopher Katherine Thomson-Jones is interested in the debate about film as language, and whether there is a language of film images. Considering frames, images, montage and semiotics, Thomson-Jones's resistance to the idea of film as a language resonates with Woolf's separation of word and image in her 1926 essay. The difficulties with the film-language analogy only serve to emphasis the particular significance of the moving image. Sylvie Magerstädt tackles the aesthetics of digital cinema and questions of realism and spectacle. Engaging with several influential film philosophy voices, Magerstädt raises the question of belief in the connection between CGI Visual Effects and our world, and assesses the notion of the creation of possible worlds.

In her unflinching chapter, Adriana Cavarero coins the term 'horrorism' for scenes of contemporary violence, invoking the concepts of terrorism and horror. She harks back to Medea and Medusa as icons of this particular form of violence that exceeds killing, and that seemingly relishes the interstitial realm of torture and the tearing to pieces of the vulnerable human body. Cavarero cites repugnance as a response to this destruction, which she sees in the actions of a suicide bomber who explodes themselves as well as defenceless others. These ideas, pertaining to a particular kind of violence and cruelty, remind us of gruesome on-screen violence. Cavarero's horror at this real or imagined enemy, who threatens more than death, begs questions about the justification for these characters and their actions featuring in cinematic incarnations, and how we relate them to our perception of dangers in the world.

A similarly contemporary use of words to describe film images is Eliza Steinbock's term 'shimmering' for a character 'slipping in and out of shadows' and who 'moves into and out of the light, becoming a shimmer of a body, difficult to grasp perceptually'. Steinbock's proposal is that trans cultural producers have reintroduced shimmering into our line of vision, which is where trans people can be seen. Embedded in a history of imagery and film writing, Steinbock demonstrates non-binary thinking within phantasmagoric visual culture. There are links here with Elizabeth Freeman's queer historical concept of 'temporal drag' (in Part 4), and the 'pull of the deep past on the present'. The ability of Cavarero and Steinbock to mine cinema's past and differentiate the present results in innovative feminist philosophy that meets some of the needs of contemporary film aesthetics.

Several of these essays and chapters could feature in more than one Part, and the final one here by Siri Hustvedt could certainly be at home in the Parts on time and phenomenology. Hustvedt considers our memory of art, and is included here because she writes so compellingly about the complexity of our remembering of images. Memory is a popular topic for filmmakers who like to destabilize our reliance on it – both that of the characters and our own – but it is also intriguing to consider how we remember films. We cannot possibly remember the whole film from pre-credit producer acknowledgements to the final line of end credits, so we inevitably remember moments and moving images. And these memories are rooted in our bodies and our emotions: our relationship to visual art is a form of intersubjectivity. Perhaps we remember what we see and hear, along with how we felt, and so the post-viewing, unconscious selection of film memories arises out of our own very particular positionality.

There were many other pieces that I wanted to include in this Part, including 'Bathsheba or the Interior Bible' by Hélène Cixous (1993), where her close analysis of a nude Bathsheba bathing by Rembrandt (1654) and his The Slaughtered Ox (1655), resonates with Hustvedt's comparison of Artemisia Gentileschi's painting of Judith's decapitation of Holofernes (1614–20) with Caravaggio's of the same scene. The analysis of violence and beauty, and the deep-rooted strictures of gender, in all these paintings, prompt reflection on the cinematic depictions of such matters. Susan Sontag's essay on 'The Imagination of Disaster' ([1965] 2009) addresses similar matters to Cavarero's on horrorism, but in the realm of science fiction. Sontag describes how films can provide something novels never can, which is 'sensuous elaboration'. She writes, 'in the films it is by means of images and sounds, not words that have to be translated by the imagination, that one can participate in the fantasy of living through one's own death and more, the death of cities, the destruction of humanity itself' ([1965] 2009: 212). These 'aesthetics of destruction' (213) may be similar to those found in horror films and monster movies, but Sontag argues that contemporary reality has 'greatly enlarged the imagination of disaster' and that the protagonists 'no longer seem wholly innocent' (215). Sontag's work on cinema is so valuable and thoughtful, and I cannot do justice to it here by citing from one essay. But her conclusion, that the collective nightmares we see in films is now too close to our reality, is surely even more relevant now than it was when she wrote this in 1965.

References

Bolton, L. (2017), 'Murdoch and *Margaret*: Learning a Moral Life', *Film-Philosophy*, 21 (3): 265–80.

Cixous, H. (1993), 'Bathsheba or the Interior Bible', *New Literary History*, 24 (4): 820–36.

Quinlivan, D. (2009), 'Material Hauntings: The Kinaesthesia of Sound in *Innocence*', *Studies in French Cinema* 9 (3): 215–24.

Rushton, R. (2007), 'Three Modes of Terror: Transcendence, Submission, Incorporation', *Nottingham French Studies*, 45 (3): 109–20.

Sontag, S. ([1965] 2009), 'The Imagination of Disaster', reproduced in *Against Interpretation and Other Essays* by S. Sontag, 209–25, London: Penguin.

Wilson, E. (2012), 'Girlhood in *Innocence*', in *Existentialism and Contemporary Cinema, A Beauvoirian Perspective*, edited by Jean-Pierre Boulé and Ursula Tidd, 17–32, New York and Oxford: Berghahn Books.

Young, I. M. ([1990] 2005), 'Throwing Like a Girl: A Phenomenology of Feminine Body Comportment, Motility, and Spatiality', in *On Female Body Experience: 'Throwing Like a Girl' and Other Essays in Feminist Philosophy and Social Theory* by I. M. Young, 27–45, Oxford: Oxford University Press.

5   Vision and Choice in Morality

IRIS MURDOCH

I agree very much with the general direction of Mr. Hepburn's argument. My main criticism will be that he has not made enough of his case. He wishes to draw our attention to certain aspects of our life as moral beings which have been neglected in the models offered by philosophers; he argues that "fables" and "patterns", rather than rules, are for many people the form which their morality most naturally takes, and that there are familiar ways of appraising the claims of these fables to act as moral guides. Mr. Hepburn asks himself whether the inclusion of such phenomena under the heading of "the moral" would conflict with current views either of "the mind" or of moral judgment itself, and decides that there is no conflict. The inclusion of the new material is therefore neither morally nor philosophically objectionable. He concludes by indicating a contrast between the "subjective" moral fable and the "objective" religious story.

I want to begin by discussing the type of argument which is appropriate to the kind of investigation on which Mr. Hepburn has embarked. It is a peculiarity of ethics that the initial segregation of the items to be studied is less easy than in other branches of philosophy. Mr. Hepburn himself moves, quite frankly, between moralising and philosophising in his paper, and at one point, when considering different modes of appraising fables, says that "theories can be confirmed or upset by such tests". By this I take him to mean that if it should turn out on investigation that fable-making was something which we always judged to be detrimental to morality, then we should have to exclude it from the field of study of the moral philosopher. Now it has been assumed, roughly since Moore, that we can distinguish two questions: "What is my morality?" and "What is morality as such?" After an initial period of excitement over this distinction, ethics is moving in the direction of finding it less simple. When we survey the feuds of our recent ancestors who are not in the linguistic tradition, for instance, the differences of opinion of Joseph, Taylor, Ross, Prichard, it is easy to see that these philosophers had very different interests and attitudes to the world, and were concerned accordingly to display different aspects of the moral life. Can it be safely assumed that linguistic philosophers are immune from such partiality, being able to derive from the study of language some sort of initial definition and subsequent analysis of morality which shall have the prestige and neutrality of logic? Here it is especially important to attend to the initial delineation of the field of study, observing where and in what way moral judgments may be involved, and then to consider the relations between the selected phenomena and the philosophical technique used to describe them. A narrow or partial selection of phenomena may suggest certain particular techniques which will in turn seem to lend support to that particular selection; and then a circle is formed out of which it may be hard to break. It is therefore advisable to return frequently to an initial survey of "the moral" so as to reconsider, in the light of a primary apprehension of what morality is, what our technical devices actually *do* for us. Why do we do moral philosophy anyway? For the sake of "completeness"? It is the great merit of Mr. Hepburn's paper to redirect our attention to a particular, perhaps neglected, group of these original phenomena.

What impact such a study should have upon current views is not immediately clear. Hepburn speaks of his fables as an alternative "model". Strictly speaking, they do not constitute a philosophical model at all in the sense of a "logical picture", valid irrespective of the content of the morality or the consciousness in question. They are ideas which are consciously entertained as an aid to, or as a part of, morality; nor is it immediately clear that they can be regarded as forms or vehicles fit to receive all and any moral content. Whether a comprehensive and clear distinction between form and content can at all be made in morality is precisely one of the questions which, it seems to me, is raised by consideration of Mr. Hepburn's new material. This material, furthermore, is extremely rich and various, and an important distinction is made at the very end of the paper. I shall attempt to proceed by dividing and classifying further the phenomena in question and trying as I do so to make clear the implications for current philosophical techniques of the inclusion of these phenomena within the field of "the moral".

I shall begin by outlining the view with which I want to bring our fresh evidence into relation, and perhaps into conflict, emphasising its main points of interest and attraction. It may be that no one individual completely adheres to this position, but I think that it will sound familiar and may pass as a summary of what has quite lately been maintained and not authoritatively or as a whole displaced. I shall call it, with apologies to those who do not hold it, the "current view". The remote ancestors of this view are Hume, Kant, and Mill; its more immediate determinants are Rylean behaviourism and the view of meaning, together with its anti-metaphysical corollaries, which we connect with the "verification principle", but which also has its background in the works of Russell and the British empiricists. On this view, the moral life of the individual is a series of overt choices which take place in a series of specifiable situations. The individual's "stream of consciousness" is of comparatively little importance, partly because it is often not there at all (having been thought to be continuous for wrong reasons), and more pertinently because it is and can only be through overt acts that we can characterise another person, or ourselves, mentally or morally. Further, a moral judgment, as opposed to a whim or taste preference, is one which is supported by reasons held by the agent to be valid for all others placed as he, and which would involve the objective specification of the situation in terms of facts available to disinterested scrutiny. Moral *words* come into the picture because we not only make choices, but also guide choices by verbal recommendations. This group of words have their meaning, in accordance with the situation outlined above, through the two elements of recommendation and specification (evaluative and descriptive meaning). The specification (of good-making criteria) will differ according to the moral code of the agent, while the element of recommendation will remain constant. A moral concept then will be roughly an objective definition of a certain area of activity plus a recommendation or prohibition.

The charms of this view are obvious. It displays the moral agent as rational and responsible and also as free; he moves unhindered against a background of facts and can alter the descriptive meaning of his moral words at will. The view thus combines the philosophical insight of Hume (we live in a world of disconnected facts) with that of Kant (morality is rational and seeks universally valid reasons), while more surreptitiously it embodies the morality of Mill ("a creed learnt by heart is paganism"). All this is achieved, moreover, by a "linguistic" method which provides a meaning for moral words which eschews earlier errors and construes these words as nearly as possible on the model of empirical terms, giving them definite factual criteria of application, and without reference to transcendent entities or states of consciousness. Morality can then be shown to be rational after its own fashion,[1] while at the same time a method is provided whereby we can analyse any morality, reflective or unreflective, our own or someone else's. This neatly reconciles the opposite ways in which Hume and Kant reached the same conclusion about heteronomy of the will. The points in this, I am afraid very condensed, account which I should like to emphasise for future reference are these: the behaviouristic treatment of the "inner life", the view of moral concepts as factual specifications plus recommendations, the universalisability of the moral judgment, and the accompanying picture of moral freedom. Of these points, the first and third are explicitly raised by Mr. Hepburn, and the last is, I think, implicitly raised by the conclusion of his paper.

I have suggested that Mr. Hepburn's initial argument, whereby he draws our attention to a certain range of moral phenomena, needs further consideration in that the phenomena indicated are rather various. I want now to begin to sort out these phenomena and bring them into relation with the current view. In a philosophical analysis of morality what place should be given to the "inner life"? Mr. Hepburn apparently does not wish to dissent from the current treatment of the inner, but wishes merely to show the importance of the "fable" in the moral life of certain kinds of imaginative people. He suggests that these people have a "less usual way of looking at life"; he also implies that a fable *ought* to be comprehensive and coherent, as in the examples which he cites. This seems, however, to be an arbitrary and unnecessary limitation of the field. To begin with, why insist that a fable be comprehensive? There may be brief fables (stories which order small segments of our lives); there may, on the other hand, be highly integrated and comprehensive systems of rules, either held consciously (as in a legalistic morality) or unconsciously (in a habitual morality). What doubtless lies behind Mr. Hepburn's view here is a moral judgment to the effect that if one is going to understand one's life imaginatively one must aim at completeness. But the point is rather (and this Mr. Hepburn also says) that we know how to assess these fables from a moral point of view; and we do not in practice think that completeness must be had at any price. In fact, and this is to turn to the other point, are these ways of looking at life really so unusual? If we drop the insistence that fables must be highly coherent and comprehensive, is not fable-making a fairly natural and ordinary activity of human beings and is it not continuous with our most everyday methods of reflecting on and understanding our lives? Here one may distinguish a number of different but similar things which merge into each other. There is the highly reflective and imaginative personal fable (which is what Mr. Hepburn mainly has in mind), the "story of one's life", of which, whether kept privately or displayed to others, most people have formed some conception, more ephemeral and disconnected stories and shapings of particular incidents or periods, metaphors explanatory of situations or changes, miscellaneous personal attitudes and visions which may show dramatically in special modes of description or in a more diffused manner in the selection of explanatory concepts. This indicates, of course, a region much wider than that with which Mr. Hepburn was concerned: a region in which the "personal visions" in question may be overt or secret, more or less pictorial, and, in the ordinary sense of the word, imaginative or unimaginative. This, however, is the variegated region to which we must attend if we are to meet the problems raised by Mr. Hepburn's fables, which are themselves a section quite arbitrarily, as it seems to me, isolated.

Now if we ask how this region is treated on the current view, the answer is complex and it is at once necessary to make a distinction. What must here be clearly separated is the notion of inner or private psychological phenomena, open to introspection, and the notion of private or personal vision which may find expression overtly or inwardly. There has, I think, been some tendency for the discrediting of the "inner" in the former sense to involve the neglect of the "inner" in the latter sense. Recent philosophy has concentrated upon the task of resolving "the mind" into sets of identifiable activities, where the problem is first, how to isolate and identify such of these activities as are purely introspectible ones, and second, how to assess the importance of these inner proceedings as criteria for the application of words descriptive of the mind. The arguments on both these points are familiar. Introspectible entities present difficulties of identification; however, it may be conceded that "mental events" exist, in the sense that there are mental images, speeches uttered to oneself, and perhaps more obscure occurrences which ask for metaphorical descriptions. (See Professor Ryle in *Aristotelian Society*, *Supplementary Volume*, 1951.) These events, however, are in no way privileged, either as being causes of more outward activity or as being the hidden core or essence of individual minds. The concepts which we use to comprehend and describe the mind depend almost entirely on overt criteria.

How does this affect ethics? On the one hand, in a legitimate way through the elimination of hypostatised and non-observable "qualities", "sentiments" or "acts of will" which might have been thought to be bearers of moral value. On the other hand, our by now fairly modified mental behaviourism has tended, in the field of ethics, to lend support to a more rigid moral behaviourism, which has much more extensive implications; this is partly because, as we have constantly seen, modern ethics lags behind other branches of philosophy and assimilates their findings at first in a crude form, and partly because of more or less conscious *moral* attitudes which favour a behaviouristic picture. That is, it has been readily assumed that in assembling the data (initial definition) for the moral philosopher to work on, we can safely leave aside not only the inner monologue and its like, but also overt manifestations of personal attitudes, speculations, or visions of life such as might find expression in talk not immediately directed to the solution of specific moral problems. In short, the material which the philosopher is to work on is simply (under the heading of behaviour) acts and choices, and (under the heading of language) choice-guiding words together with the arguments which display the descriptive meaning of these words. Here two philosophical conceptions reach out towards each other and, in a hazy region, seem to meet. On the one hand, there is no inner life, and moral concepts too must have meaning through definite external criteria. On the other hand, morality is choice, and moral language guides choice through factual specification. The result is a picture, which seems to have the authority of the modern view of the mind, of the essence of the moral life as sets of external choices backed up by arguments which appeal to facts. The picture is simple, behaviouristic, anti-metaphysical, and leaves no place for commerce with "the transcendent". It gathers force too from the evaluation which it implicitly contains and which may be put in the form of an appeal to "the moral life as we know it": surely we see that morality is essentially behaviour. "If we were to ask of a person 'what are his moral principles?' the way in which we could be most sure of a true answer would be by studying what he *did*." (Mr. R. M. Hare, *The Language of Morals*, p. 1.)

Now clearly, as a piece of moral advice it might be wise to tell somebody: don't speculate, just concentrate on *this* state of affairs and see what is to be done. It is an important fact that our lives occur temporally in the way that they do, and that we tend, for purposes of getting on to the next thing, to construct them into a series of situations. However, if one is, as a moral philosopher, exclusively interested in this fact one will miss certain important aspects of morals. I suggested earlier that care must be taken in the initial assembly of data, as this may affect the subsequent techniques which will in turn seem to endorse the data. I shall now briefly discuss the area in question (the "inner life" in the sense of personal attitudes and visions which do not obviously take the form of choice-guiding arguments) from the point of view of its claim to form part of the data of ethics; and I shall then go on to discuss the compatibility of these data with current techniques.

Ethics need not have any quarrel with the argument against the inner in its most modified form. At any rate, I do not at this point wish to propose any quarrel. The data in question are all "events" and "activities" which are either overt (conversation, story-telling) or if introspectible are identifiable and in principle exposable (private stories, images, inner monologue). Now activities of this kind certainly constitute an important part of what, in the ordinary sense, a person "is like". When we apprehend and assess other people we do not consider only their solutions to specifiable practical problems, we consider something more elusive which may be called their total vision of life, as shown in their mode of speech or silence, their choice of words, their assessments of others, their conception of their own lives, what they think attractive or praise-worthy, what they think funny: in short the configurations of their thought which show continually in their reactions and conversation. These things, which may be overtly and comprehensibly displayed or inwardly elaborated and guessed at, constitute what, making different points in the two metaphors, one may call the texture of a man's being or the nature of his personal vision. Now with regard to this area various attitudes may be adopted by the moral philosopher. It may be held that these elusive activities are irrelevant to morality which concerns definite moral choices and the reasons therefor. It may be held that these activities are of interest in so far as they make choices and their reasons more comprehensible. It may be held that these activities can be regarded as being themselves moral acts resulting from responsible choices and requiring reasons. All these three positions would be in different ways compatible with the current view. Or finally, it may be held that these activities are themselves direct expressions of a person's "moral nature" or "moral being" and demand a type of description which is not limited to the choice and argument model.

It may be said at once (in answer to the first of the four views mentioned above) that we do to a considerable extent include the area in question in our moral assessments of others and indeed of ourselves, and we usually know very well in practice how to balance definite performance against apprehended "being" in our judgments. The question is, what technique is suitable to the analysis of such material. It is proposed on the current view that we regard moral differences as differences of choice, given a discussable background of facts. Moral arguments will be possible where people have similar criteria of application (share descriptive meanings of moral terms) and differ about what exactly the facts are. Moral arguments will be difficult or impossible where the differences are differences of criteria. This picture seems plausible if we take as the centre of "the moral" the situation of a man making a definite choice (such as whether to join a political party) and defending it by reasons containing reference to facts. It seems less plausible when we attend to the notion of "moral being" as self-reflection or complex attitudes to life which are continuously displayed and elaborated in overt and inward speech but are not separable temporally into situations. Here moral differences look less like differences of choice, given the same facts, and more like differences of vision. In other words, a moral concept seems less like a movable and extensible ring laid down to cover a certain area of fact, and more like a total difference of *Gestalt*. We differ not only because we select different objects out of the same world but because we see different worlds.

I take it that it is part of Mr. Hepburn's purpose to suggest that morality is understanding, interpretation and reflection as well as "choice". Mr. Hepburn is cautious, however, in that he seems content to regard these as merely preliminaries to choice. Whereas I would argue that we cannot accommodate this aspect of morals without modifying our view of "concepts" and "meaning"; and when we do this the idea of choice becomes more problematic. In construing meaning for purposes of ethics, philosophers have been anxious to keep as near as possible to a model suitable for simple empirical terms. "Good" is to have meaning in the same way as "red", except that the factual criteria may vary and a recommendation is added. This is one result of assuming that moral philosophy can be made linguistic simply by putting "good" into inverted commas. That this is insufficient may be overlooked so long as we construe the moral life behaviouristically as strings of choices and recommendations backed up by reference to facts. In such a world "good" and "right" *could* be the only "moral words". But if we attend to the more complex regions which lie outside "actions" and "choices" we see moral differences as differences of understanding (and after all, to view them so is as old as moral philosophy itself), more or less extensive and important, which may show openly or privately as differences of story or metaphor or as differences of moral vocabulary betokening different ranges and ramifications of moral concept. Here communication of a new moral concept cannot necessarily be achieved by specification of factual criteria open to any observer ("Approve of *this* area!") but may involve the communication of a completely new, possibly far-reaching and coherent, vision; and it is surely true that we cannot always *understand* other people's moral concepts.[2] If we take the view that moral differences are in this sense "conceptual" and not exclusively behaviouristic we shall also be able to see moral philosophy itself as a more systematic and reflective extension of what ordinary moral agents are continually doing, and as able in its turn to influence morality. Great philosophers coin new moral concepts and communicate new moral visions and modes of understanding.[3]

It is not difficult to see why such a view of morals and of moral philosophy is regarded in some quarters with suspicion. Briefly, there are at least three reasons, two of them predominantly moral, and one more philosophical. First, it is felt to be dangerous to regard morality as insight (or understanding or sensibility) rather than as action plus argument closely related to action. This view is partly perhaps a reaction against emotivism, which tended to confuse insight with emotion; mainly, however, it represents a determination to value action as against understanding or meditation. Notice with what passion philosophers hastened to correct the error of Moore, who separated insight from action. Here, all I can say is that in this complicated matter most moral agents know how to proceed. Moral insight, as communicable vision or as quality of being, *is* something separable from definitive performance, and we do not always, though doubtless we do usually, require performance as, or allow performance to be, the test of the vision or of the person who holds it. The second point concerns freedom. On the current view the moral agent is free to withdraw, survey the facts, and choose again. There is, moreover, an open field for argument of an empirical fact-investigating kind among those who have similar principles. This view is Kantian in atmosphere: moral beings, or those of them who can communicate, live in the same world. It is also Humian: only carelessness and inattention, that is habitual and traditional attitudes, separate us from "the facts". Argument or tradition may then be stressed, according to taste. If, however, we hold that a man's morality is not only his choices but his vision, then this may be deep, ramified, hard to change and not easily open to argument. It is also less realistic to say that it is itself something which we choose; and then it may seem that our conception of moral freedom is in danger. Here it may be said that those who think that freedom is absolute in the "withdraw and reflect" sense confuse the wish with the fact—and that in any case there is no need to equate the freedom needed to ensure morality with a complete independence of deep conceptual attitudes. It may be argued that we *ought* always to assume that perfect communication and *disinterested* reflection about facts can precede moral judgment, and it is true that such an attitude may often be desirable. But this is itself a Liberal ideal. Finally, the notion that moral differences are conceptual (in the sense of being differences of vision) and must be studied as such is unpopular in so far as it makes impossible the reduction of ethics to logic, since it suggests that morality must, to some extent at any rate, be studied historically. This does not of course imply abandoning the linguistic method, it rather implies taking it seriously.

So far I have been attempting to bring certain moral data, covering a rather wider field than that originally indicated by Mr. Hepburn, into conflict with two related dogmas: moral behaviourism and the descriptive-evaluative view of moral concepts. I shall now go on to the cases, which Mr. Hepburn took as the centre of his argument, of more coherent personal fables, and attempt to bring this data into conflict with certain current views about universal rules. I shall want here to distinguish the personal fable as such from "personal vision" or "moral being", on the one hand, which I have just been discussing, where differences may be conceptual without being uniquely personal or pictorial, and from theological structures on the other hand, which may be thought of as "transcendent realities", and which I shall be discussing later. Here my first argument will be brief and negative: why insist on forcing moral attitudes into the "universality" model when this is contrary to appearances? My second argument will be to the effect that certain moralities make use, positively, of a quite different model.

Mr. Hepburn says readily that a fable will imply rules of conduct. Now clearly any fable, if it is connected with practice, and is not merely a private film show *à la* Walter Mitty, will imply rules since a discipline is required to put any plan into action. The question which we need to answer in order to relate this phenomenon to the current view is whether a morally important fable will always imply universal rules. It has been powerfully argued, especially by Mr. Hare (*P.A.S.* [*Proceedings of the Aristotelian Society*] 1954–55) that a *moral* decision is one which is supportable by reasons which are universalisable. Here we may get the full force of what is meant by a philosophical model. We are being asked to conceive of a structure of would-be universal reasoning as lying at the core of any activity which could properly be called moral.

How do we decide whether a fable is morally important? If my argument (which forms an internally connected edifice, just as the current view does) is accepted so far, then it will be conceded that a considerable area of personal reflection is morally important in the sense of constituting a person's general conceptual attitude and day-to-day "being", which will in turn connect in complex ways with his more obviously moral "acts". And here must be included a man's meditation upon the conception of his own life, with its selective and dramatic emphases and implications of direction. Again, we have in practice ways of distinguishing fables which are morally relevant from those which are more purely decorative,[4] and it suffices for the argument if fables are sometimes of the former kind. Such fables may be more or less closely and more or less obviously connected with "action" and "choice".

For purposes of the present question let us consider the cases where fables are fairly closely related to action. Now clearly a fable may very well have practical implications which *can* be regarded as universal rules. This will be so especially when the fable expresses some sort of generally accepted and comprehensible social pattern. Parables of widely held religions, which have the concreteness of personal fables, may have universalisable implications for similar reasons. Such will, however, not so obviously be the case, either where the fable is elaborately personal, or where the fable includes the conception that the individual is unique. If one is Napoleon one does not think that everyone should do as one does oneself. Let us consider these cases.

A man may penetrate his life with reflection, seeing it as having a certain meaning and a certain kind of movement. Alternatively, and in fact the alternatives can shade into each other, a man may regard himself as set apart from others, by a superiority which brings special responsibilities, or by a curse, or some other unique destiny. Both these fables may issue in practical judgments, possibly of great importance. Now, does the question whether these are moral decisions really depend on the answer to the question: would you wish anyone else so placed to act similarly? If faced with this somewhat surprising query the fable-makers might reply, "yes, I suppose so"; or possibly they might reply (in the first case), "But nobody could be in *this* position without being *me*", or (in the second case), "No, for nobody else has *my* destiny". It will then also be so that, when asked for reasons for their actions, the first man will answer, "You wouldn't understand", and the second man will give reasons which will only be cogent if one agrees that he is unique. My point is that here the "universal rules" model simply no longer describes the situation. One can force the situation into the model if one pleases, but whatever is the point of doing so? To do so is to blur a real difference, the difference between moral attitudes which have this sort of personal background and these which do not. Whether such attitudes seem to us desirable or praiseworthy is quite another question.

I leave my negative argument here and go on to the second argument. It is at this point that one may raise the question, touched on by Mr. Hepburn, of the contrast between art and morals. I agree here with Mr. Hepburn's criticisms of Mr. Hampshire, but again would wish to carry the matter further. Some people stress the dissimilarity between art and morals because they want to insist that morality is rational, in the sense of legislating for repeatable situations by specification of morally relevant facts. Other people stress the similarity between art and morals because they want to insist that morality is imaginative and creative and not limited to duties of special obligation. Is there a conflict here? Let us consider the latter case. In the paper already mentioned (*P.A.S.* 1954–55) Mr. Hare excellently emphasises the importance of distinguishing the pair general and specific from the pair universal and particular. Accepting this distinction, one may say that a moral agent may explore a situation imaginatively and in detail and frame a highly specific maxim to cover it, which may nevertheless be offered as a universal rule. This would seem to reconcile the two parties mentioned above; and I think that this would also be the position that Mr. Hepburn would take up.

I have already argued that there are kinds of moral outlook which it seems pointless to crush at all costs into the universal rules formula. I want now to consider whether there are not positive and radical moral conceptions which are unconnected with the view that morality is essentially universal rules. I have in mind moral attitudes which emphasise the inexhaustible detail of the world, the endlessness of the task of understanding, the importance of not assuming that one has got individuals and situations "taped", the connection of knowledge with love and of spiritual insight with apprehension of the unique. Such a description would in fact roughly fit types of moral attitude in other ways very dissimilar; certain idealist views, certain existentialist views, certain Catholic views.[5]

Now it may be argued that one may well meditate upon the mysteriousness and inexhaustibility of the world, but meanwhile one has continually to make judgments on the basis of what one thinks one knows, and these, if moral, will claim to be universal. Here again, let us pause and consider what after all a philosophical model is for. If we give in here and agree that somebody whose belief and moral inspiration was of the kind mentioned above would of course, when he acts, wish others so placed to act as he does, what does it profit us? We have won a similarity, but we have lost a much more important and interesting difference. There are people whose fundamental moral belief is that we all live in the same empirical and rationally comprehensible world and that morality is the adoption of universal and openly defensible rules of conduct. There are other people whose fundamental belief is that we live in a world whose mystery transcends us and that morality is the exploration of that mystery in so far as it concerns each individual. It is only by sharpening the universality model to a point of extreme abstraction that it can be made to cover both views.

One may suspect, in fact, that much of the charm of "universality" is borrowed surreptitiously from "generality". Mr. Hampshire,[6] for instance, who does not explicitly make Mr. Hare's distinction, emphasises the repeatability of moral situations; and Mr. Hare himself says "we steer a middle course" between the "hidebound inflexibility" of the man who never adjusts rules to situations, and the "neurotic indetermination" of the man who always hesitates because he fears he has not understood. (*P.A.S.* 1954–55, p. 310.) But who steers this middle course? To select the middle course is itself a moral choice: the choice which, transformed into a description of morality, Mr. Hare wishes us to make true by definition. We do continually have to make choices—but why should we blot out as irrelevant the different background of these choices, whether they are made confidently on the basis of a clear specification of the situation, or tentatively, with no confidence of having sufficiently explored the details? Why should attention to detail, or belief in its inexhaustibility, necessarily bring paralysis, rather than, say, inducing humility and being an expression of love?

Mr. Hare and Mr. Gellner (also in *P.A.S.* 1954–55) caricature a person whom they call an "existentialist" who seems to have nothing to say for himself except that he thinks he has a duty to do a certain action, but has no views on whether anyone else so placed should act similarly. With no further explanation this view seems absurd, especially when we contrast it with everyday ideas of morality as rules which are not only universal but also general. However, no real existentialist is so tongue-tied. Any attitude may be made to look absurd if its conceptual background is removed. A morality, if I am right, is a ramification of concepts, and this only appears, in current writings, not to be so because on the one hand the key concepts of our general social morality (freedom, tolerance, factual arguments, etc.) have become practically unconscious and are taken for granted, and on the other hand because the concepts are what they are (insistence on specification of generally observable facts, etc.) whereas, a man who hesitated, always acted with an air of doubt, thought it meaningless to legislate for others, and so on, might well be able to explain his conduct rationally in terms of different concepts.

Here again, it is not difficult to see why such views are met with hostility and why the current model is defended with passion. Doubtless "everyday morality", in our society at any rate, is of the kind currently described, where rules are universal, fairly general without being too general, and where clear and above-board factual reasoning is required to justify choices. It is felt (Mr. Gellner obviously feels)[7] that other attitudes will tend to be non-rational and possibly non-democratic; whereas Hare would perhaps suspect that a refusal to accept his picture constituted a sort of moral evasion, an attempt to avoid responsibility by pretending that everything is too difficult: and clearly there are views and attitudes which would justify both fears. However, on the one hand, even a disreputable view may still be a moral view,[8] and on the other hand, if we look with understanding, these alternative views are not by any means so sinister or so unusual. Let us consider in more detail some of the reasons for mistrust.

It may be held that views which emphasise "particularity" and "inexhaustibility" will involve inability to describe and specify and hence breakdown of communication, and it may be felt that this will at best condone slackness and at worst encourage violence. Mr. Hare says briskly that individuals (and doubtless situations) "can be described as fully and precisely as we wish". Now, with the best will in the world, this is not always so. There are situations which are obscure and people who are incomprehensible, and the moral agent, as well as the artist, may find himself unable to describe something which in some sense he apprehends. Language has limitations and there are moments when, if it is to serve us, it has to be used creatively, and the effort may fail. When we consider here the role of language in illuminating situations, how insufficient seems the notion of linguistic moral philosophy as the elaboration of the evaluative-descriptive formula. From here we may see that the task of moral philosophers has been to extend, as poets may extend, the limits of the language, and enable it to illuminate regions of reality which were formerly dark. Where the attempt fails, and one has to choose without having understood, the virtues of faith and hope have their place. It is very well to say that one should always attempt a full understanding and a precise description, but to say that one can always be confident that one has understood seems plainly unrealistic. There are even moments when understanding *ought* to be withheld.

The insistence that morality is essentially rules may be seen as an attempt to secure us against the ambiguity of the world. Rules may be ambiguous in that we have to decide how to apply them, but at least in attempting an ever more detailed specification one is moving in the direction of complete clarity. If I am right, however, this cannot properly be taken as the only structural model of morality. There are times when it is proper to stress, not the comprehensibility of the world, but its incomprehensibility, and there are types of morality which emphasise this more than is customary in utilitarian Liberal moralities. We may consider here the importance of parables and stories as moral guides. Mr. Hepburn says that parables will imply maxims, but rightly adds that "one parable is never logically equivalent to the expression of one maxim". How ambiguous a parable appears to be will depend on the coherence of the moral world in which it is being used. Certain parables or stories undoubtedly owe their power to the fact that they incarnate a moral truth which is paradoxical, infinitely suggestive and open to continual reinterpretation. (For instance, the story in the New Testament about the woman who broke the alabaster box of very precious ointment, or the parable of the prodigal son.) Such stories provide, precisely through their concreteness and consequent ambiguity, sources of moral inspiration which highly specific rules could not give.[9] Consider too the adaptability which a religion may gain from having as its centre a person and not a set of rules. (For a determined rejection of such "concrete" guidance, see Kant's remarks about Christ in the *Grundlegung*.) It may be said, that a moral attitude which lays emphasis on ambiguity and paradox is not for everyday consumption. There are, however, moments when situations are unclear and what is needed is not a renewed attempt to specify the facts, but a fresh vision which may be derived from a "story" or from some sustaining concept which is able to deal with what is obstinately obscure, and represents a "mode of understanding" of an alternative type. Such concepts are, of course, not necessarily recondite or sophisticated; "hope" and "love" are the names of two of them. And there are doubtless some people who direct their whole lives in the latter way. The "moral" dangers of such attitudes are plain. All that can be said is that we know roughly how to deal with these dangers and part of the moral life is dealing with them.[10]

I come now at the end of my paper to a matter of great importance which must, however, be dealt with briefly. What I have attempted to do so far is, by appeal to a certain range of "moral data", to suggest that the current model illuminates and describes only a certain type or area of moral life, and that if we attempt to construe all moral activities in terms of it we are led to ignore important differences. In order properly to analyse these differences, I argued, it was necessary to think of morality not solely as choice and fact-specifying argument, but as differences between sets of concepts—where an exclusive emphasis on choice and argument would be itself one conceptual attitude among others. What I have said so far has been said without raising the question of naturalism.

I think that a good deal of the power of the current view derives from a feeling that it constitutes a defence against the fallacy of naturalism; and it does appear to do this, since patently no argument can proceed directly from fact to value if it has to go *via* the agent's choice of good-making criteria. Let us, however, see how the position is affected by the alternative view I have outlined above. Is there in fact a knockdown argument against naturalism? The argument against it may be divided, I suggest, into the following components. (1) An argument against metaphysical entities. This may come in a strong form which claims that all concepts of metaphysical entities are empty, or in a weak form which merely holds that the existence of such entities cannot be philosophically established. (2) A closely related dogma concerning meaning, which I have discussed above, to the effect that empirical terms have meaning *via* fixed specification of empirical criteria, and moral terms have meaning *via* movable specification of empirical criteria, plus recommendation. This will imply that a moral term cannot be defined by a non-moral term. (3) The use of these insights to point out that any argument which professes to move directly from fact to value contains a concealed evaluative major premise. (4) A *moral* argument or recommendation of a Liberal type: don't be dogmatic, always reflect and argue, respect the attitudes of others. Behind the first two points lie the assumptions of British empiricism, and behind the fourth lie the moral attitudes of Protestantism and Liberalism.

The total argument has sometimes been presented as if it were the exposure of a quasi-logical mistake; if we dismember it, however, we can see that only (3) has a strictly logical air. We can also more coolly decide which parts are acceptable and what it is able to prove. For myself, I accept the weak form of (1). (For instance: there are no philosophical proofs of the existence of God, but it is not senseless to believe in God.) Where (2) is concerned I have attempted to offer an alternative view of moral concepts which shows moral differences as differences of vision not of choice. What effect does a modified acceptance of (1) and a rejection of (2) have upon one's view of alleged arguments from fact to value? Such arguments, it would be currently held, can be faulty either because they involve a definition of moral terms in non-moral terms (the case dealt with by (2)) or because they are elliptical (the case dealt with by (3)). These alleged mistakes are closely related but not identical. Someone who says "Statistics show that people constantly do this, so it must be all right" (pattern of certain familiar arguments) should have it pointed out that he is concealing the premiss "What is customary is right." He must also realise (it would be argued) that "What is customary is right" is a moral judgment freely endorsed by himself and not a definition of "right". The notion that "customary" defines "right" may be the psychological cause of, or the would-be reason for, the curtailing of the argument, but it is not the same thing as the curtailing of the argument. The man may publicise his premiss, still insisting on the definition. In many cases, of course, the exposure of the premiss destroys the appeal of the argument, which may depend (as in the example above) upon the hearer's imagining that he has got to accept the conclusion or deny the plain facts; and I would certainly want to endorse many arguments of type (3) whose purpose is solely to achieve such an exposure. I turn now to the other contention, which is the more interesting one.

Why can moral terms not be defined in non-moral terms? The answer to this question is given by the world picture which goes with the current view, and whose purpose at this point is to safeguard a certain conception of freedom. The descriptive-evaluative distinction is simply another way of saying that moral terms cannot be *defined* in non-moral terms because the agent *freely* selects the criteria. The moral word cannot *mean* the empirical state of affairs it commends since it can be used to commend others without change of essential meaning. This can be plausibly illustrated in the case of "good". If, however, we do not accept the current view of moral concepts as commendations of neutral areas, and consider rather the way in which a moral outlook is shown in ramifications of more specialised concepts which themselves determine a vision of the world, then the prohibition on defining value in terms of fact loses much of its point. It is, of course, the case that moral arguments may proceed by appeal to facts; but what may be lost to view, especially if we consider only simple utilitarian arguments, is that such arguments take place within a moral attitude where some sovereign concept decides the relevance of the facts and may, indeed, render them observable. The too rigid affirmation of a link between certain facts and an evaluation could appear here either as a *moral* error or as a *linguistic* error. The moral error could be, for instance, "lack of realism" (lack of a suitably wide and reflective attitude to facts) and would be judged as such in the light of a rival moral attitude concerning what was morally relevant. The linguistic error could be, for instance, a failure to understand the customary degree of generality of a moral word; although here one might need further information before deciding whether an unusual use of a word represented a linguistic misunderstanding rather than a moral difference. My point is that if we regard the current view, not as a final truth about the separability of fact and value, but as itself representing a type of moral attitude, then we shall not think that there is a *philosophical* error which consists in merging fact and value. On the alternative view which I have suggested fact and value merge in a quite innocuous way. There would, indeed, scarcely be an objection to saying that there were "moral facts" in the sense of moral interpretations of situations where the moral concept in question determines what the situation is, and if the concept is withdrawn we are not left with the same situation or the same facts. In short, if moral concepts are regarded as deep moral configurations of the world, rather than as lines drawn round separable factual areas, then there will be no facts "behind them" for them to be erroneously defined in terms of. There is nothing sinister about this view; freedom here will consist, not in being able to lift the concept off the otherwise unaltered facts and lay it down elsewhere, but in being able to "deepen" or "reorganise" the concept or change it for another one.[11] On such a view, it may be noted, moral freedom looks more like a mode of reflection which we may have to achieve, and less like a capacity to vary our choices which we have by definition. I hardly think this a disadvantage.

It is from here that we can see what the problem of naturalism really is. We have noted the anti-metaphysical argument (1), the argument against concealment of premises (3), and the dogma about the essential separability of fact and value (2). There remains a question which is fundamentally an evaluative one concerning how we picture morality and its source. I think that much of the impetus of the argument against naturalism comes from its connection with, and its tendency to safeguard, a Liberal evaluation (4). It is felt to be important that morality should be flexible and argumentative, centred upon the individual, and that no alleged transcendent metaphysical realities, such as God, or History, or the Church, should be allowed to overshadow the moral life. But, and this is the point to which I have been wanting to get, if I am right in accepting the weaker version of (1) and in rejecting (2), then there is nothing in the so-called argument against naturalism to prove that *belief* in the transcendent can form no point of a system of morality.

We may now turn back to the real world and consider with an open mind what part such belief does play in morals. There is surely an important and philosophically interesting difference between the man who believes that moral values are modes of empirically describable activity which he endorses and commends and the man who believes that moral values are visions, inspirations or powers which emanate from a transcendent source concerning which he is called on to make discoveries and may at present know little. Whether such deep differences of outlook correlate with obvious differences of moral procedure will depend on further details of the beliefs and society in question. It has been possible to ignore such differences in England partly because the Protestant Christian and the Liberal atheist have, for historical reasons, so much in common. If, however, we interest ourselves in the conceptual background of choice, and the "vision" and "moral being" of the chooser, we shall see naturalism not as a fallacy but as a different system of concepts. The current model, so far from refuting naturalism, merely summarises a non-naturalistic moral attitude. The true naturalist (the Marxist, for instance, or certain kinds of Christian) is one who *believes* that as moral beings we are immersed in a reality which transcends us and that moral progress consists in awareness of this reality and submission to its purposes.

The defender of the current view may maintain that in so far as the naturalist's arguments are not erroneous philosophical ones (which we have already excluded) they are mere blind appeals to non-rational conceptions and cannot be called proper moral reasons. Here I can only reply that I do not accept the implied definition of "rational" and "moral" and have already argued this at length. Whether a particular argument is rational or (in some sense of "seriously offered") moral is something which we decide, in ways which are hard to summarise, by considering the weight and coherence of the total attitude—and we may assess in this way arguments which conform to the current pattern just as much as those which do not.

The final argument of the defender of the current view will be the deep one that whatever set of concepts incarnate a man's morality, that man has *chosen* those concepts, and so at one remove the familiar pattern can re-emerge. It may be felt that this argument at least is inescapable; Mr. Hepburn apparently thinks so, since he says that it is a truth of logic that the will is autonomous. Here one can only come back again to the question: what is a philosophical model for? The Liberal wants all the time to draw attention to the *point of discontinuity* between the choosing agent and the world. He sees the agent as central, solitary, responsible, displaying his values in his selection of acts and attitudes. The naturalist on the other hand, differs from the Liberal precisely in *not* seeing the moral agent in this way; and whereas the Liberal thinks that the naturalist has certain erroneous beliefs and fails to realise the responsibility which he nevertheless has, the naturalist thinks that the Liberal fails to understand the truth about the universe and wrongly imagines himself to be the source of all value. (Remember Belloc's remark about the lady who decided to give the universe a piece of her mind.) Different conceptions of moral freedom, which would need to be explained at length, go with these two views. Why should they be planed down and assimilated to each other?

It was Mr. Hepburn's intention to lead us back from abstract philosophical formulae to the patterns and models which are really used by moral agents. I have argued, I hope, in the spirit of that intention. I have wished to deny the claim of the current view to picture morality as such. The current view pictures a type of morality. Philosophers have been misled, not only by a rationalistic desire for unity, but also by certain simplified and generalised moral attitudes current in our society, into seeking a single philosophical definition of morality. If, however, we go back again to the data we see that there are fundamentally different moral pictures which different individuals use or which the same individual may use at different times. Why should philosophy be less various, where the differences in what it attempts to analyse are so important? Wittgenstein says (*Untersuchungen* 226e) that "What has to be accepted, the given, is—so one could say—*forms of life*." For purposes of analysis moral philosophy should remain at the level of the differences, taking the moral forms of life as given, and not try to *get behind them* to a single form.

I suggested above that ethics had in the past, in one of its aspects, been continuous with the efforts of ordinary moral agents to conceptualise their situations. This kind of imaginative exploration of the moral life is being practised by contemporary continental philosophers, often without special metaphysical pretensions; and there is no reason why such exploration should be combined with erroneous philosophical arguments. It has been largely abandoned in this country since philosophers have been under the impression that ethics must be neutral analysis or nothing. I have argued that in so far as ethics sets out to be analysis rather than exploration it can attain only a precarious neutrality, like that of history, and not the pure neutrality of logic. This will also imply that ethics is in certain important respects discontinuous with the rest of philosophy, as political philosophy, with its more detailed historical implications, is usually conceded to be. Ethics surely is in fact, as it has always *mutatis mutandis* been, both exploration and analysis; nor can we assume that even if we try explicitly to separate these two activities we shall necessarily be successful.

Here, if we abandon the notion of a pure formula, we shall be able once again to see how deeply moral attitudes influence philosophical pictures of morality. (This present writing is doubtless no conception [*sic*].) There is perhaps in the end no peace between those who think that morality is complex and various, and those who think it is simple and unitary, or between those who think that other people are usually hard to understand and those who think they are usually easy to understand. All one can do is try to lay one's cards on the table.

Originally published in *Proceedings of the Aristotelian Society, Supplementary Volume, Dreams and Self-Knowledge*, Vol. 30, (1956), pp. 32–58. By permission of the Curtis Brown Group on behalf of the Estate of Iris Murdoch. © Iris Murdoch, 1956.

Notes

1. Those who prefer Burke to Mill may find the "unconscious" version of the model more attractive, wherein morality appears as habit, and moral remarks are rules for beginners.
2. On this and related topics see Mrs. Foot's excellent paper in *Aristotelian Society, Supplementary Volume*, 1954.
3. We may reflect here upon the attitude which certain modern philosophers take up toward their predecessors. Mr. Weldon (*Vocabulary of Politics*) argues that most political philosophies are tautologous conceptual structures surrounding empirical recommendations. Mr. Hare (*Proceedings of the Aristotelian Society,* 1954-55) speaks of "the oldest and most ineradicable vice of moralists—the unwillingness to make moral decisions". (Hence the search for Golden Rules and other such simplifications.) It is easy to see how both these attitudes arise from the current view of morality as surveying the facts and making a choice. But great moral and political philosophers offer us new concepts with which to interpret the world, and they simplify because they are philosophers. What these linguistic analysts mistrust is precisely language.
4. There are forms of unity in life stories which can safely be said to be purely of aesthetic interest. Vladimir Nabokov, for instance, in his autobiography, *Speak, Memory*, tells how General Kuropatkin, who once played with matches with him as a child, was recognised by his father years later, when disguised and fleeing from the Bolsheviks, by a flaring match light. Nabokov adds, "The following of such thematic designs through one's life should be, I think, the true purpose of autobiography." The king of this region is Proust.
5. I regret mentioning without expounding, but to elaborate these themes here would take too long. Miscellaneous examples of the kind of view I have in mind, may be found in Nedoncelle, *Vers une Philosophie de l'Amour*; Marcel, *Etre et Avoir*, Rousselot, "Synthèse aperceptive et philosophie de l'amour", *Revue de Philosophie*, 1910. Behind the current view lies British empiricism. Behind these views lie idealism and perhaps certain aspects of Thomism. See Marcel on his debt to Bradley in the *Journal Métaphysique*. It is Kierkegaard who most specifically,

though in some ways tiresomely, displays the transformation of an idealist philosophy into a phenomenology of individual moral struggle.

6. His article "Logic and Appreciation" in *Aesthetics and Language*, edited by William Elton.

7. Mr. Gellner contrasts U-type evaluations (which claim universality) with E-type ones (which do not), and connects the former with rational argument, and the latter with disreputable things such as the *Fuehrerprinzip, credo quia absurdum,* and romantic love.

8. It may be noted that Mr. Gellner regards both the systems which he describes as "moralities", and admits that he does not see "by what standard external to both one could choose between them".

9. Mr. Hare says that it is odd that existentialists like to discuss moral questions by writing novels since "no work of fiction can be about a concrete individual" (*P.A.S.* 1954–55, p. 310). This seems a strange view. We *imagine* fictitious characters as concrete individuals and although it is true that the information which we have about them is limited, this may be so also in the case of real people, and anyway the information is endlessly open to reinterpretation. In fact, we may, in the course of time, alter our assessment of a fictitious character. We do not see the same Stavrogin or the same Charlus at forty that we saw at twenty. Why existentialists like writing novels is plain. A novelist can readily *represent* a situation in which the agent is immersed, which he only partly understands, and whose solution may involve a clash of irreconcilable moral viewpoints. Whether and in what circumstances such a "representation" constitutes an "explanation" is, of course, another question.

10. If time and space permitted it would be tempting to digress here on the subject of "symbols". Symbols ("the language of the unconscious") may play, in ways which are still largely obscure, a spiritually liberating role. Jung (*Answer to Job*, p. 172) contrasts the maternal attitude of the Catholic church, which "gives the archetypal symbolisms the necessary freedom and space in which to develop" with the paternal attitude of Protestantism with its more rationalistic rule-conscious viewpoint. Whether or not one cares for Jung's general attitude (which seems to make absolute some rather dubious concept of "psychic vitality") there is a contrast here and an interesting one. A deeper realisation of the rôle of symbols in morality need not involve (as certain critics seem to fear) any overthrow of reason. Reason must, however, especially in this region, appear in her other *persona* as imagination.

11. In certain cases, whether we speak of deepening or of changing a concept will be a, not necessarily unimportant, question of words. When we deepen our concept of "love" or "courage" we may or may not want to retain the same word.

6 The Language of Film

KATHERINE THOMSON-JONES

The influence of a literary paradigm is felt, not only in the debate about film authorship, but also in another debate that bridges classical and psycho-semiotic film theory. This is the debate about whether there is a language of film and, consequently, whether we understand and appreciate a film in fundamentally the same way as we understand and appreciate a literary work. Given that languages have to be learnt by grasping the conventions that govern the meaning of words and the operations of grammar, the possibility that film functions like a language has serious implications for its claim to realism. As we learnt in Chapter 2, the realism of film is often explained in terms of our seemingly natural ability to recognize on the film screen what was filmed. But if we are 'reading' film like a language, then this recognitional capacity is not natural, after all, but conventional, and the accessibility of film images cannot be taken as a sign of their realism. If we wish, therefore, to settle on a coherent picture of the nature of film, particularly in its traditional medium, we must take up the debate about film and language.

In the heyday of psycho-semiotic film theory, it was quite common for scholars to talk about the 'grammar' of the film or the shot,[1] and even today, it is common for scholars to talk about 'reading' a film or film genre.[2] In most of these instances, however, language terms are only being used metaphorically, and without any ontological commitments, to refer to different modes of film analysis and interpretation. This reflects a broader tendency in the arts to use language terms to suggest the seriousness and rigor of a particular mode of analysis or the elevated status of a certain art form or genre – as when art historians identify a mature style of painting or architecture in terms of its distinctive 'grammar'. But in relation to art in general, language terms are not only used metaphorically. Nelson Goodman, for example, does not call his seminal work in aesthetics, *Languages of Art*,[3] just because it sounds serious and intriguing. Rather, he uses this title because his work contains a theory about the language-like conventionality of artistic representation. Similarly, when film theorist Christian Metz uses language terms, it is not merely for rhetorical flourish. In his case, it is because he is applying the general semiotics of the Swiss linguist Ferdinand de Saussure to film. Since Saussure prioritized language as the paradigmatic semiotic system, it is not surprising that Metz refers to 'cinematographic language,' and aims 'to study the orderings and functionings of the main signifying units used in the cinematic message'.[4]

When language terms are used literally in relation to film, the philosopher naturally pricks her ears. Now we have a genuinely philosophical question to consider concerning the nature of film. The question of whether there is a language of film is not the question of whether films involve language – say with dialogue or text, but whether there is a language of film images. The images in a film are the individual shots, traditionally animated as a succession of frames passing before the projector beam, and then combined into sequences through editing. Thus the question of whether there is a language of film images is the question of whether individual shots and their combinations constitute a language. In other words, it is either the question of whether individual shots function like words or sentences, or it is the question of whether the combination of individual shots occurs in the same way as the combination of words and sentences. Furthermore, the question of whether shots function as words or sentences concerns whether they acquire their literal or intrinsic meaning in the same way as words and sentences. This means that the starting question, whether there is a language of film, tends to reduce to the question of whether we understand film as a language. When the focus is on narrative film, this question becomes even more focused: Do we understand the story in a film in the same way that we understand a story in a novel, say, which is written out in a familiar language?

Even though there may be no definition of language, we can agree on a range of uncontroversial examples like English, French and Arabic. These and other natural languages are the subject of linguistics, and the aim for many film theorists in defending the language-like nature of film is to qualify film for the rigours of linguistic analysis. Metz sums up this aim when he suggests that the precise, analytical methods of linguistics 'provide the semiotics of the cinema with a constant and precious aid in establishing units that, though they are still approximate, are liable over time (and, one hopes, through the work of many scholars) to become progressively refined'.[5] Given that the purpose of the film-language analogy is to qualify film for linguistic analysis, the best way to test the analogy is by comparing film to a language like English that already qualifies for such analysis.

In an initial comparison, we immediately see that the 'language' of film images is more limited than English in its modes of transmission and representation. Whereas English is available through all our senses – through sight in its written form, through hearing in its spoken form, through touch in Braille, and at least in principle through taste and smell in coded forms, film 'language' is only available to us through sight. Furthermore, in the written form of English, the wide variety of fonts and styles of handwriting suggest a degree of flexibility in exactly how we represent a natural language. But with a film image, there is no such flexibility: Any modification to how the image looks changes its meaning.[6] These differences raise interesting questions about whether film 'language' can be translated in the way that all natural languages can be translated into one another (albeit with some loss in shades of meaning). The Russian silent-film-maker and theorist, Vsevolod Pudovkin, argued that the task of the film director is to translate a fully written-out scenario, word-by-word, into images that are then edited together just as the words of the scenario are combined into sentences and phrases.[7] This might strike one as a highly idiosyncratic view of film-making, however. If it does, the underlying reason may have to do with further differences between language and film that we shall discuss in this chapter.

If you are already suspicious of the film-language analogy, you may want to consider a weaker claim: Not that film is a language, but that film belongs to a larger category which also includes languages. This is the category of semiotic systems or systems of signs. Other things that have been called semiotic systems include the natural languages, traffic signs, ships' signalling systems, the gestures of Trappist monks, semaphore, conventions of dress or costume, and even myths. Semiotics is the study of systems of signs and specifically the codes that determine the meaning of signs. Film semiotics, in particular, reduces the task of the film theorist and critic to one of 'de-coding' films, thereby determining, not just what every shot and sequence means, but how every shot and sequence means what it means – by what cultural, artistic or cinematic convention.

The questions whether film is a system of signs to be de-coded and whether film is a language are intertwined in psycho-semiotic film theory. Nevertheless, there are several concerns specific to the first question that we shall consider. These have to do with the implications of using key terms like 'code' and 'sign' in equivocal and ambiguous ways, as well as with the prospects for substantial theoretical results in the mere classification of conventions. Ultimately, however, our goal in this chapter is to see whether our understanding of the nature and value of film art is deepened or merely obfuscated by the comparison to language and other sign-systems.

Film, Language and Montage

Even though the film-language analogy is most fully developed in psycho-semiotic film theory, it is first made much earlier, during the era of silent film, by those Soviet film-makers and theorists, particularly Pudovkin and Sergei Eisenstein, who take editing or montage to be the defining feature of film art. Both Pudovkin and Eisenstein are interested in how the meaning of a film *qua* work of art, and not just the depictive meaning of its individual shots, is created in context through the process of montage. In order to emphasize the importance of montage for creating meaning and artistic value, Pudovkin makes a comparison between film and literature. In a literary work, he suggests, it is not the literal meaning of individual words that matters aesthetically but instead how the writer combines those words to create rich images and associations. The example Pudovkin uses involves the initial selection of the word, 'beech,' which, on its own, 'is only the raw skeleton of a meaning, so to speak, a concept without essence or precision'. When this word is combined in a phrase like, '"the tender green of a young beech,"' it is no longer 'merely a bare suggestion'. Rather, it 'has become part of a definite, literary form. The dead word has been waked to life through art'.[8] Pudovkin goes on to suggest that the individual words of a literary work are equivalent to the individual shots of a film. Thus in the same way, what those shots literally mean in terms of what they show is not aesthetically relevant, and the accumulated literal meaning of the shots is not equivalent to the meaning of the film. Rather, the creative combination of shots through editing yields the only meaning that matters for evaluating and interpreting a film.

One problem with this account is that in both the case of literature and the case of film, even though context is important for interpretation, literal meaning still matters. Thus to use Pudovkin's own example, it matters what the word 'beech' literally means in the phrase, 'the tender green of a young beech', even though it is only the phrase as a whole that gives us an image of this particular beech tree. It would make a difference to the connotative meaning of the line if, for example, the poet had written 'willow' or 'bicycle' instead of 'beech'. This problem reflects the limitations of the exclusive emphasis on editing among Soviet film-makers. Whereas it is undoubtedly true that editing adds meaning and value to a film, it is also true that a well-composed and expressive shot can have the same kind of meaning and value.

Another problem with Pudovkin's account is that words and shots resist comparison. As Metz will later point out, even a close-up shot of a single object – say a revolver – cannot be translated as the single word, 'revolver', 'but at the very least, and without speaking of the connotations, it signifies "Here is a revolver!"'.[9] Metz goes on to suggest that the shot is not even equivalent to a sentence, since it contains 'a quantity of undefined information'. All the detail contained in a shot of a landscape, say, could be expressed in a multitude of ways, in a multitude of sentences. Thus, Metz concludes, a shot is only equivalent to 'the complex statement of undefined length'.[10] This is also because a shot, like a statement and unlike a sentence, is always asserted – as indicated by Metz's translation of the close-up shot of a revolver as '*Here is* a revolver'. At this point one might be tempted to give up on the analogy between the shot and any part of language. We will return to this possibility a little further ahead. For now, it is enough to note that the word-shot analogy on which Pudovkin relies is problematic.

Like Pudovkin, Eisenstein is interested in the way that editing creates connotative meaning. But he seeks to avoid some of Pudovkin's difficulties by using a different language analogy: Instead of comparing film with literature, Eisenstein compares film, and specifically shot combinations, with a kind of character in

Japanese writing, derived from Chinese writing, that he calls an ideogram. This kind of character refers to an abstract idea by means of combining and modifying pictographic characters that depict, in a stylized way, non-abstract objects associated with the idea. The Chinese character for 'bright', for example, combines the pictograms that represent the sun and the moon, and the Chinese character for 'good' combines the pictograms that represent a woman and a child. As Eisenstein describes the way such characters function, '[b]y the combination of two "depictables" is achieved the representation of something that is graphically undepictable'. Then he claims that this exact same process occurs in film. In virtue of editing, shots 'that are *depictive*, single in meaning, neutral in content' are combined 'into *intellectual* contexts and series'.[11]

Eisenstein's own films were the testing ground for his theory of 'intellectual montage'. In *October: Ten Days that Shook the World* (1927), a commemorative dramatization of the Bolshevik Revolution of October 1917, there is a famous sequence that juxtaposes a Baroque image of Jesus with images of Hindu deities, the Buddha, Aztec gods, and finally a primitive idol, in order to suggest the sameness of all religions. The idol is then compared with military regalia to suggest the linking of patriotism and religious fervour. In another sequence, shots of Alexander Kerensky, head of the pre-revolutionary Provisional Government, are interspersed with shots of a preening mechanical peacock, to suggest, quite clearly, the leader's vanity and decadence.

The fact that these shot sequences are so distinctive immediately raises doubts about the utility of Eisenstein's theory as a general account of the meaning of a film. Sometimes – perhaps most of the time, there is no conceptual meaning generated by a certain combination of images. When a fight scene in a Kung Fu movie is edited so that we see only the most salient moments of action, the meaning of the sequence depends upon the literal meaning of the individual shots, each depicting part of the action. In other words, the ordering of shots may not have any meaning beyond the meaning that it has for the action. Moreover, this case is not unusual, since we are often meant to pay attention, first and foremost, to what is shown, rather than what is merely suggested, on screen.

Film Semiotics

Motivated by a commitment to Bazinian realism, the next generation of theorists interested in film language are highly critical of Eisenstein's account. Metz, in particular, seems to think that the montagists overemphasized symbolic meaning in film at the expense of depictive meaning. As a result, they failed to recognize the natural tendency of the film medium towards narrative – just by joining meaningful images together, a film tells a story. Thus according to Metz, '[g]oing from one image to two images, is to go from image to language'.[12]

Christian Metz has been called the most important film theorist since Bazin. Indeed, Alfred Guzzetti characterizes Metz's importance in terms of a dialogue between Metz and Bazin: With the title of his main work of film theory, Bazin asks, What is Cinema?, and Metz replies, 'cinema is a language'. Even if Metz is not the first film theorist to think of film in terms of language, Guzzetti insists that Metz is the first theorist to inform this way of thinking with a sophisticated understanding of linguistics, particularly the linguistics of Saussure.[13]

In fact, however, Metz's answer to Bazin's question is not so simple, precisely because he was working within the technical framework of Saussurian linguistics. On Metz's account, film is not just a language but a language without a system. This qualification reflects Saussure's distinction between *langue* and *parole*, or language and language system. *Langue* is the system of rules and conventions or codes that make up a language, independently of its use on particular occasions. *Parole* is an instance of language use. Saussure was most interested in *langue*, or the language system, and he might have said that every individual film is the *parole* of an underlying film *langue*. But Metz, based on his close study of film, argues that there is no underlying system of which individual films represent particular applications. There is just the film language being created as it is used in every film.

The language analogy holds for Metz insofar as film is fundamentally communicative – each film has a message for its viewers. But the analogy only goes so far because a film's message is available to us directly and naturally, and not by means of convention, given our ability to recognize what an image depicts. At some points in Metz's account, this seems to mean that the message of a particular film is not heavily coded. But Metz retreats from this claim in suggesting that the standard combination and organization of the natural signs of film images, particularly in the creation of a narrative, creates a cinematic code that it is the task of film semioticians[14] to analyse.

Metz is most interested in codes that are specific to the film medium, which include conventions of film punctuation like the fade in and out, and the dissolve, as well as conventions of montage for presenting the depictive material. According to Metz, a film is made up of basic units of meaning that he calls 'syntagmas'. In his analysis of narrative film, Metz arrives at a taxonomy of eight different kinds of syntagma. A series of shots that alternate between two events might constitute an 'alternate syntagma' insofar as it shows two events occurring simultaneously. Moreover, a series of shots showing a landscape might constitute a 'descriptive syntagma' insofar as it shows what the landscape is like rather than events unfolding over time. The reason that the syntagmas constitute codes is that they determine meaning conventionally, according to standard practices of montage. Thus, for example, even if the depicted content of individual shots in an alternating sequence is naturally available to us, we have to learn that the alternating sequence itself indicates simultaneity.

Metz assumes that the codes of film punctuation and montage concern denotation in film, or what the images in a film literally show us. But there are also codes that govern connotation in film, or the symbolic and expressive meaning that a shot or a series of shots acquires. For example, an American Gangster film might give an impression of foreboding in the way that it presents a scene of deserted wharves. While it is important to figure out the conventions governing the creation of such an impression, Metz gives priority to figuring out conventions governing denotation. In fact, however, it is not clear that Metz's distinction between denotation and connotation in a film can be upheld, since, as Gilbert Harman suggests, we figure out the plot of a film by referring both to what is shown and the way it is shown in context.[15] But even if the distinction could be upheld, another film semiotician, Peter Wollen, argues that Metz has his priorities wrong. It is connotative meaning and not denotative meaning that is the proper subject of film aesthetics and criticism. More generally, Wollen argues that Metz's analysis of cinematic codes and meaning is limited by Metz's adherence to the language analogy. For Wollen, since language is simply one kind of sign system among many, we must analyse film, not in terms of language, but just as another sign system.

For this kind of analysis, Wollen relies on a theory of signs given by the philosopher Charles Pierce who, along with Saussure, is considered to be a co-founder of semiotics. According to Pierce, a sign can function in three ways – as an icon, as an index, and as a symbol. According to Wollen, the film image can combine all three aspects of the sign. Insofar as a film image resembles its subject, it functions as an icon; insofar as a film image is causally related to its subject, it functions as an index; and, insofar as a film image bears connotative meaning as a result of context and convention, it functions as a symbol. A great film-maker is someone who can manipulate all three aspects of the sign, so that his films have 'pictorial beauty' (due to the iconic function), 'documentary truth' (due to the indexical function), and 'conceptual meaning' (due to the symbolic function). Wollen cites French New Wave director, Jean-Luc Godard, as an example of a film-maker who is great in this respect.[16]

By appealing to a general theory of signs, Wollen moves away from the linguistic analogy. Part of the reason that he is not tied to this analogy in the same way as Metz is that Wollen does not assume that film is essentially communicative and that every film carries a message. As works of art, films explore the implications of signs rather than simply using them to communicate. However, there are still codes for the film semiotician to study, which are the means by which we interpret the signs making up a film. According to Wollen, works of art 'exploit and call attention to various codes. The greatest works "interrogate" their own codes by pitting them against each other'.[17]

Despite their differences, then, Metz and Wollen agree that film theory and criticism is largely concerned with identifying, organizing and deciphering cinematic codes. But what, exactly, *is* a cinematic code? In ordinary language use, 'code' can mean either a cipher – in the sense of de-coding a message, or a convention or style – in the sense of codes of dress and military behaviour. The difficulty, according to Harman, is that film semioticians fail to mark this distinction in their use of the term. Thus, it is unclear whether Metz's syntagma taxonomy is an exercise in de-coding in the sense of explicating how a film has a meaning or in the sense of identifying structural features of a film. Similarly, when Wollen refers to the importance of iconography in film, and the codes of symbolic meaning on which it depends, he seems to be talking about style, expression, thematic material, and symbolism all at the same time. This leads Harman to accuse film semioticians of 'cheating' with their broad and loose use of the term 'code'. This usage, he argues, 'disguises the fact that much of aesthetics and criticism is properly concerned with something other than the significance of signs'.[18]

Remember, as well, that the ultimate purpose of both the language analogy and broader semiotic analysis in film theory is to help us account for the way that films acquire meaning, particularly story meaning, and thus how we understand them. But it is not clear that the work of film semioticians so far has contributed to an account of film interpretation. Take, once again, Metz's syntagma taxonomy: It may be satisfying to be able to identify and label the various standard relationships between edited shots. But being able to identify *when* I understand an alternating sequence as indicating simultaneity hardly explains *why* I understand the sequence in this way or what significance this has for my understanding of the story or film as a whole. And, in general, taxonomies of cinematic codes do not substitute for a theory of meaning or close contextual analysis of a particular film's narrative and narration.

Let's Face it: Film is *Not* a Language!

These concerns about the efficacy and breadth of semiotic and language-based theoretical approaches to film are shared by the philosopher Gregory Currie. His interest in understanding how language works in terms of communication leads him to confirm many of Metz's own worries about the weakness of the analogy between language and film. Ultimately, in showing just how different film is from language, Currie quashes Metz's hope of using linguistics to understand film. Currie goes further, however, to claim that, even if film could be compared to a language, this would not provide a method for interpreting the story of a film. This is because, in order to figure out what particular images mean for the story, we have to pay attention to context, or how the images fit with other images as well as with dialogue and other sound cues.

In setting up a comparison between film and language, Currie focuses on five features of a natural language like English that are 'salient in terms of communication,' and the logical relations between these features. English is both (1) productive and (2) conventional, and as a result, it is (3) recursive, (4) molecular and (5) acontextual. As we shall learn, film is also productive and many film language advocates have insisted on its conventionality. But film is not recursive, molecular and acontextual. Since these three features simply follow from the combination of productivity and conventionality, the fact that film does not have them is a decisive indicator of just how different film must be from language.

English is productive because an unlimited number of English sentences can be uttered and understood. We can use and understand sentences we have never heard before or that have never even been used before. As well, English is conventional because the meaning of its words and sentences is determined by how we use its words and sentences in certain standard ways in order to communicate with each other. Whereas, in principle, any word could have been used to designate the animal that we call a horse, we all stick to calling this animal a horse so that we can understand one another. As a result of its conventionality, language has to be learnt – we have to learn what members of a certain language community happen to call things, since there is no natural and universal way that words and sentences have to mean. Since language is productive, however, it cannot be the case that we learn English sentence by sentence. (Otherwise how could we understand new sentences as soon as we encounter them?) Instead, we must learn English recursively: We acquire a set of conventions that assign meanings to a finite stock of words and a set of rules for the combination of these words into an infinite number of sentences. In turn, this means that English is molecular – its sentences are built up from independently meaningful units – words or 'meaning atoms' – by rules that make the meaning of sentences depend on the meaning of their parts. And finally, since the meaning of a word is determined by convention and the meaning of a sentence is determined by the meanings of the words in it, literal meaning in our language is acontextual[19] – so the word 'horse' is always going to refer to the same kind of four-legged animal even if it acquires further connotations in specific linguistic contexts.

The next step is to consider whether film images possess these five interconnected, communicative features of a language. Since there is an unlimited number of things that can be conveyed by film images, advocates of film language are going to want to claim that film 'language' is productive. They also tend to emphasize its conventionality, though some more than others. Whereas Metz recognized that the depictive meaning of individual shots is natural and only insisted on denotative conventions for narrative meaning, another leading semiotician, Umberto Eco, insists that the conventions go all the way down, so to speak, determining the literal meaning of a single shot.[20] This is because even the most realistic and character- istic shot of an object does not reproduce the object exactly – three-dimensionality is lost, for example, on the screen. Therefore, for the viewer to recognize the object in the shot requires her to already know which features of an object are salient for its representation. And, according to Eco, we can only know this according to some kind of internalized convention. At this point, however, a problem arises. If we insist on the conventionality of film language along with its productivity, we are automatically committed to claiming that film language is recursive, molecular and acontextual. Unfortunately, this claim is false, which means that film images just don't work like a language.

There are no atoms of meaning for film images, since it is not the case that we understand a film image by understanding its parts and the rules according to which they are combined. A part of an image – say, a uniformly sandy part of an image of the Sahara in *Lawrence of Arabia* (1962) – just has meaning as a part and not independently of the whole. Although one could take parts of several images and combine them to make a new image, we surely do not want to say that every image is a collage or a composite in this way. Moreover, the parts of a composite image would still be parts of the original images from which they were extracted in the sense that they would not convey anything new in their new context – if we included the sandy image-part from *Lawrence of Arabia* in our composite image, that part of the new image would still just show sand. Thus image-parts are clearly not meaning atoms. But without meaning atoms, there is nothing to build up, according to rules, into a whole that is therefore meaningful both recursively and acontextually.

Insofar as we understand film images, it cannot be a result of our having acquired a lexicon of image-parts and having mastered rules for their grammatical combination. While we may not understand the dialogue in a Korean or a Turkish film without subtitles, we have no trouble making out the image track (assuming the images are in-focus and properly lit) even if what we make out includes unrecognizable objects and unfamiliar landscapes. What this suggests is that meaning in film, despite the standardization of film practice, is not conventional after all. For how could film language be productive, such that we recognize images we have never seen before, and still be conventional, given that we do not recognize new images as the result of their being built out of independently meaningful units according to rules? Currie argues that the productivity of film images has to be explained, not in terms of conventionality, but in terms of natural generativity. This notion is connected to Currie's argument for film realism that we discussed in Chapter 2. Just as with other kinds of picture, film images are understood insofar as we recognize what they depict in the same way as we would in real life. Thus we can understand new images insofar as we automatically and naturally recognize everything they show us.

Even if the meaning of film images is not determined conventionally, it can still be influenced by convention. After all, a filmed scene will look the way it does as a result of various conventions of dress, décor, and decorum. Objects within the filmed scene may have symbolic meaning – for instance, a crucifix, or a conventionally determined function – for instance, money. But none of these conventional influences mean that the image itself – like the word, 'horse,' is conventional. The problem, Currie suggests, with much of the semiotic theorizing about film, is that its conclusions about film language depend on glossing over this distinction and using the term 'convention' just as loosely and ambiguously as the term 'code'.

Given that film images lack important communicative features of language, Currie concludes that there is no language of film. This conclusion seems to foreclose the possibility of using linguistic analysis to solve the problem of film interpretation. However, it may be that this was never a real possibility in the first place. For, as Currie then goes on to suggest, even if there were a language of film, this would not wholly explain how we understand the story told by a film. Even though both words and images may have an acontextual, literal meaning, the former conventionally and the latter naturally, when either words or images are combined to make a narrative, context suddenly becomes highly important.

This is analogous to the importance of context in determining the meaning of utterances as opposed to the literal meaning of the words uttered. When you exclaim, 'I can't believe that this is happening to me!' or, 'My life sucks!', I have to know more than the literal meaning of the words you utter in order to know what you're talking about. I have to understand both the literal meaning of the words and the context in which you utter them – so, for example, I have to know what 'this' is that is happening to you or how your life can 'suck' but not in any literal way. Arguably, this is still a matter of literal meaning, but then we need a distinction between the literal meaning of the utterance, which depends on context, and the literal meaning of the string of words uttered, which does not. In literary works, context is even more important for understanding. For as well as understanding the context for particular utterances made by the characters or the narrator, we have to understand the narrative context of particular events so that we can figure out what is happening to the characters. Say we have a literary description of the heroine sipping some soup prepared by her jealous cousin immediately followed by a description of the heroine falling ill. We have to figure out whether the soup is the cause of her illness by making reference to what we already know about the story, especially the characters' motives.

The importance of context for narrative understanding is no less with film than with literature. If a shot of the heroine sipping her cousin's soup were immediately followed by a shot or sequence of the heroine falling ill, we would also have to figure out the relation between the depicted events by way of context. Recognizing what is depicted in the shots is only part of the process by which I come to understand the story. Thus a theory about how I come to recognize what is depicted in the shots will provide at best a partial explanation of narrative interpretation. In Chapter 6, we will examine more fully how film interpretation works. For now, it is enough to note that it is not just that there are problems with the analogy between film and language; there are also problems with the motivation for this analogy which is a solution to the problem of interpretation.

There may still be one final way to save the film-language analogy, however. What about the claim, not that film images themselves have a language-like structure, but that film images combine with one another in language-like ways? Is the meaning of certain standard shot combinations determined conventionally in just the same way as with sentential connectives? Take, as an example, the sentential connective, 'because'. When we join together two sentences, P and Q, with 'because,' there is a convention determining a literal meaning – that P is in some way a result of Q. But there is no analogous convention for determining that the event depicted in one shot is caused by the event depicted in the preceding shot. Rather, as with the example of the poisoned soup, we have to infer from the narrative context whether a particular pairing of shots indicates a causal relationship.

However, you might reply that even if there is no convention for signalling causation in a film, there are other conventions of editing that function like conventions determining the meaning of sentential connectives. Take, for example, shot/reverse-shot editing that combines a face-on shot of a character with a second shot from that character's point of view.[21] Given the frequent and standard use of this combination, is there a convention determining that any shot following a face-on shot of a character is from that character's point of view? No. In many instances, face-on character shots are not followed by point-of-view shots. But how, then, do we just seem to know when a shot following a face-on character shot is from that character's point of view?

It helps that shot/reverse-shot editing is used frequently in mainstream film. But, ultimately, we have to be paying attention to contextual cues. Perhaps, for example, the shot/reverse-shot combination is preceded by a medium-long shot of the character facing a certain scene, so that after the face-on shot, we know that the next shot showing the same scene from the character's perspective is a point-of-view shot. Or perhaps the shot/reverse-shot combination is part of a sequence that depicts two characters in conversation such that it is the dialogue that primarily cues the viewer to recognize a point of view. Whatever the particular contextual cues may be, the point is that we rely on such cues to understand the literal significance of an edited sequence in a way that we do not to understand the literal significance of sentential connectives.

Once again, therefore, film fails to exhibit a key feature of language – in this case, the acontextuality of the literal meaning of words. The example of shot/reverse-shot editing does not, however, suggest the complete absence of conventions governing the meaning of shot combinations in film. Metz's syntagmas and cases of film punctuation, like the fade in and out to indicate a significant passage of time, may still involve conventions. But even if there are a few conventions in film, they cannot function without individual shots already having a literal, natural meaning. Given the natural generativity of film images, we just don't need as many conventions to determine meaning in film except at the level of the ordering of images. At this level, conventions help constrain the interpretation of the film, which, Currie suggests, is the only way in which film conventions resemble language conventions.[22] But interpretation is a subject for another chapter.

Conclusions

In this chapter, we have examined the dangerous move from a metaphorical to a literal use of language terms in relation to film. Here is what we have covered:

1. Pudovkin's analogy between the shot and the word in terms of connotative meaning.

2. Eisenstein's analogy between a shot combination and an ideogram in terms of conceptual meaning.

3. Metz, Wollen and Eco's reduction of film analysis to a mysterious process of de-coding.

4. Currie's argument to show that film lacks the essential and interconnected communicative features of a natural language.

5. The further claim that, even if film were a language, this would not be enough to explain interpretation.

At this point, we might just content ourselves with saying that film is *like* a language in several ways – for example, in the way that some conventions play a role in constraining interpretation or in the way that film images are productive. But film is probably like a lot of other things in this same kind of loose and partial way. Ultimately, then, this kind of likeness is not enough to give us insight into the nature of film art.

From *Aesthetics and Film* by Katherine Thomson-Jones. © Katherine Thomson-Jones 2008, Continuum, an imprint of Bloomsbury Publishing Plc.

Notes

1. As with the following examples: Spottiswoode (1950); and, Arijon (1976).
2. As with the following examples: Monaco (2000); and, McDonald (2005).
3. Goodman (1976).
4. Metz (1974b: 92).
5. Ibid., 107.
6. Currie (1995a: 117–18).
7. Pudovkin (1958: 121).
8. Ibid., 24.
9. Metz (1974a: 67).
10. Metz (1974c: 115).
11. Eisenstein (1957: 29–30).
12. Metz (1974a: 46).
13. Guzzetti (1985: 177–93).
14. Semiotic theorists can be called semiologists, semioticists, or semioticians. Given that 'semiologist' is often reserved for theorists working strictly in the tradition of Saussure, and given that 'semioticist' is the least common of the three terms, I prefer 'semiotician'.
15. Harman (1999: 92–93).
16. Wollen (1972b: 155).
17. Quoted by Harman in his (1999: 95).
18. Ibid., 96.
19. Currie (1995a: 121–22).
20. See, for example, Eco (1985).
21. The comparison between sentential connectives and shot/reverse-shot editing is made by Currie in his (2006: 97–98).
22. Currie (1995a: 135–36).

References

Arijon, D. (1976), *Grammar of the Film Language* (London and Boston: Focal Press).

Currie, G. (1995a), *Image and Mind: Film, Philosophy, and Cognitive Science* (New York: Cambridge University Press).

Currie, G. (2006), 'The Long Goodbye: The Imaginary Language of Film', in N. Carroll and J. Choi (eds), *Philosophy of Film and Motion Pictures: An Anthology* (pp. 91–99) (Malden, MA: Blackwell).

Eco, U. (1985), 'On the Contribution of Film to Semiotics', in G. Mast and M. Cohen (eds.), *Film Theory and Criticism: Introductory Readings*, Third edition (pp. 194–214) (New York and Oxford: Oxford University Press).

Eisenstein, S. (1957), 'The Cinematic Principle and the Ideogram', *Film Form and Film Sense*, ed. and tr. J. Leyda (pp. 28–44) (New York: Meridian).

Goodman, N. (1976), *Languages of Art* (Indianapolis: Hackett).

Guzzetti, A. (1985), 'Christian Metz and the Semiology of the Cinema', in G. Mast and M. Cohen, *Film Theory and Criticism: Introductory Readings*, Third edition (pp. 177–93) (New York and Oxford: Oxford University Press).

Harman, G. (1999) 'Semiotics and the Cinema: Metz and Wollen', in L. Braudy and M. Cohen (eds), *Film Theory and Criticism: Introductory Readings*, Fifth edition (pp. 90–8) (New York and Oxford: Oxford University Press).

McDonald, K. (2005), *Reading A Japanese Film: Cinema in Context* (Honolulu: University of Hawaii Press).

Metz, C. (1974a), 'The Cinema: Language or Language System?', in *Film Language: A Semiotics of the Cinema*, tr. M. Taylor (pp. 31–91) (New York: Oxford University Press).

Metz, C. (1974b), 'Some Points in the Semiotics of the Cinema,' in *Film Language: A Semiotics of the Cinema*, tr. M. Taylor (pp. 92–107) (New York: Oxford University Press).

Metz, C. (1974c), 'Problems of Detonation in the Fiction Film', in *Film Language: A Semiotics of the Cinema*, tr. M. Taylor (pp. 108–46) (New York: Oxford University Press).

Monaco, J. (2000), *How to Read A Film: The World of Movies*, *Media, Multimedia*: *Language, History, Theory*, Third edition (New York: Oxford University Press).

Pudovkin, V. I. (1958), *Film Technique and Film Acting*, tr. and ed. I. Montagu (New York, Grover Press).

Spottiswoode, R. (1950), *A Grammar of the Film: An Analysis of Film Technique* (Berkeley: University of California Press).

Wollen, P. (1972b), 'The Semiology of the Cinema', in *Signs and Meaning in the Cinema* (pp. 116–55) (Bloomington: Indiana University Press).

7 Back to the Future? Contemporary Cinema and the Challenges for Theorists

SYLVIE MAGERSTÄDT

Brave New Worlds: Living Dinosaurs, CGI and a New Aesthetics

Following from this discussion of Deleuze, I would like to propose three key themes when looking at digital cinema and the concepts applied to it: the apparent conflict between a realist (mainstream) cinema that aims at truthfulness and a creative will to art that is more experimental both in terms of visual representation and storytelling; the notion of the revival of the spectacular and the appearance of new spiritual automata; and finally the question of belief that connects contemporary cinema to the world.

In one of the earliest articles discussing the aesthetic consequences of CGI—'Film Theory for the Digital World'—John Andrew Berton Jr. (1990) revisits classical texts from the early stages of film theory. This approach is grounded in the argument that the arrival of digital technologies can be compared to the arrival of cinema as a new medium, a claim that has also been made by a number of other scholars.[1] Berton points out that Kuleshov had put great emphasis on the ability of filmmakers to control the *organization* of images in order to enable the audience to easily and efficiently understand the film. Here, digital cinema seems to deliver exactly what Kuleshov had anticipated almost one hundred years ago. Yet, Kuleshov did not want to use this control in order to create something magical, but in order to achieve a level of realism that allows the audience to be drawn into the film rather than distracted by insignificant details that might be part of a 'real' (i.e., photo-realistic) shot. These elements do not naturally exist in digital cinema, because a digital image only entails those elements that are specifically and individually *created* to be in this image. However, as Berton argues, digital artists in practice often include these 'meaningless' elements, often simply because they are technologically available and can thus flaunt the technology. Nevertheless, there might be more to this than just an attempt at showing off computer skills. When Berton discusses André Bazin's concept of cinematic realism, he seems to focus on Bazin's apparent emphasis on cinema's ability to recreate reality accurately with a minimum of reinterpretation. Yet he also suggests that Bazin's notion of realism is based on complex connections between the objects and the world within an image, as well as other images. I would argue that this complexity of actual reality is in part also constituted by the above-mentioned 'insignificant' or meaningless elements, so that their inclusion in digital cinema can also mean an enrichment of digital worlds beyond a mere demonstration of technology. Berton (1990, 9) is nevertheless right when he states that the challenge for contemporary digital filmmakers lies in 'embracing the highest possible technology in image generation without allowing the technology itself to rule the work'. The clue to creating believable worlds seems to be the combination of convincing technology and coherent storytelling. The 'computer makes the viewer believe that an object exists, but the artist must make the viewer believe that the object's existence has meaning' (Berton 1990, 9). The suggestion is therefore to shift the focus of debate from the production processes behind the images to the way in which these images create new, complex worlds.

In conclusion, Berton suggests that the improvement in technologies might reduce the artist's concern with basic aspects of filmmaking by allowing him to fully focus on the *content* and *aesthetic concepts* used to realize his cinematic vision and thus liberates him creatively. The abilities of digital cinema could therefore be facilitating a greater level of realism in terms of convincing digital worlds *as well as* a new level of creative power that is unrestrained by the limits of technical development. Yet, if technology no longer defines the boundaries in which we create stories, we will need some other form of anchoring that prevents (at least mainstream) cinema from becoming a purely abstract speculation without context and meaning. The importance of anchoring had already been emphasized by Michael Heim (1993) when examining virtual realities. He suggested that we always 'need some sense of metaphysical anchoring … A virtual world can be virtual only as long as we can contrast it with the real (anchored) world. Virtual worlds can then maintain an aura of imaginary reality, a multiplicity that is playful rather than maddening' (Heim 1993, 133).

The notion of anchorage with regard to what we describe as 'real' is also discussed by Stephen Prince (1996, 28) who suggests—drawing on *Jurassic Park* (dir. S. Spielberg, 1993)—that it might be primarily film theorists that struggle with analysing phenomena such as watching 'moving, breathing, and chomping dinosaurs, images which have no basis in any photographable reality but which nevertheless seemed realistic'. Audiences on the other hand seem much more willing to accept these images as 'real'. With regard to his now widely discussed concept of 'perceptual realism', Prince acknowledges that despite the fact that computer-generated images do not always have a (living) reference in reality, they still have *certain references* to physical reality. This means that the individual elements of the image, such as lighting, surface texture, movements and so on provide the audience with clues that are familiar to them, so that they are easily able to refer the 'unreal' images to their own physical world space. Digital creatures are convincing when they provide these anchors. The notion of anchorage can be extended to the appearances of the medium itself. Several writers have pointed out that particularly early digital cinema aimed at imitating the effects of the medium—such as lens flare, motion blur, film grain—just as much as the elements of the actual world. As King (2000, 55) pointed out, the aim 'was to make the dinosaurs achieve the same level of reality as the rest of the film, as much as any exterior reference point of "reality", to integrate them seamlessly into the fictional fabric'. Against writers like Michelle Pierson (1999a), who claimed that the focus of these early CGI creatures was on spectacle that disrupted narrative, King (2000, 55) argues that these effects that mimic the medium itself 'aspire to the status of naturalistic "invisibility"'. Likewise, Prince (1996, 32) suggests that we should focus on 'the kinds of linkages that connect the represented fictionalized reality of a given film to the visual and social coordinates of our own three-dimensional world, and this can be done for both "realist" and "fantasy" films alike'. The new images appear to look 'natural', maybe even more natural in the way they help us 'understand' the images as related to the narrative, in contrast, for example, to the use of wireframe models and other cinematic tricks of classical cinema that always felt somewhat disjointed from the rest of the film.

Deleuze had argued that in mainstream cinema, the overarching story is part of what creates the unity of the images. Based on this, I will argue that rather than a decline of narrative, as many writers claim to see in digital mainstream cinema, the importance of universal stories—*myths*—in creating coherent and accessible fictional universes is more important than ever. However, this does not mean that the way these stories are told hasn't changed. Warren Buckland (1999) argues that the composition of images as well as the choice of shots and perspectives available in digital cinema is fully within the concept of realism developed by Bazin. Mainstream Hollywood cinema thus creates its unique 'illusionist realism' even more so within modern CGI films. Even though these images may not be realistic in a strict ontological sense, Buckland argues, like Prince, that the audience does not usually make a high ontological commitment to the reality of cinematic objects, but neither does it simply regard them as purely imaginary during the film experience. However, this was true before as well as after the arrival of digital technologies in cinema. Even though scenes in contemporary digital and 3D films may look spectacular and show off the technology as said above, this is not necessarily the sole motivation. Discussing a jungle scene from Cameron's recent 3D blockbuster *Avatar* (2009) Jockenhövel (2011) argues that an attempt at realism, at creating a believable world, rather than just visual spectacle was the main motivation behind this scene. 'As Jack runs through the forest on the thick branches of giant trees, the camera constantly gazes downwards, accenting the tallness of the trees and the danger of the height, 3D offers exciting visuals but also reinforces the hazardous and thrilling situation of the protagonists, thus serving a narrative purpose as well' (Jockenhövel 2011, 9). This example illustrates that visual, artistic aspects and narrative demands do not necessarily counteract each other, but that elements of digital cinema can fulfil a dual purpose in this respect and as a consequence enhance the impact of the story.

In a later article on CGI, Pierson focuses more on editing and the way it is influenced by digital technologies. Here, she argues that today the 'editing of Hollywood films is much less obviously motivated by the desire to maintain visual and narrative continuity than it was even a decade ago' (Pierson 1999b, 34), an argument that we will try to substantiate when looking at specific film examples in Part II. She also suggests that digital technologies in postproduction allow and demand for new concepts of montage that create new modes of enchantment. A combination of her previous theories on contemplative scenes in combination with new styles of montage that can create a sense of reenchantment seems to be pointing back to the time-image and its impact on the contemporary movement-image.

This also brings us to the second aspect that relates Deleuze's theories to contemporary digital cinema. This is what he called the 'Catholic quality' of the movement-image. In his *History of Christianity*, Diarmaid MacCulloch (2009, 681–2) outlines how the Catholic Church discovered the visual aspects of splendour and scale as its unique selling point after the Reformation and this relates to what Deleuze describes here. The return of grand scale mise-en-scène and epic storytelling is closely connected to the creative possibilities initiated by new technologies. This new dimension is illustrated by Jane Shadbolt's comparison between the 1933 and the 2005 versions of *King Kong*:

> From 1933, the miniature physicality of O'Brien's animated rabbit-fur and foam puppets as they wrestle in their tiny toy-like forest, … and the need for shots made of separate elements [make the scenes look] static and locked off. … But in the twenty-first century Kong, the swooping virtual cameras revolve around him in his new incarnation as a giant life-like silverback grappling with the invented V-Rex dinosaurs. Here he exists in an endless, virtual CGI space where the camera, and thus audience, are swept into the action to travel with him. (Shadbolt 2013)

The notion of 'being drawn in' and 'swept away' occurs frequently in discussions of contemporary blockbuster cinema and although there is an aspect of realism in this, it also hints at a certain 'larger than life' experience that points beyond an experience of our world. In his essay, 'Le réel, c'est l'impossible: The Sublime Time of Special Effects', Sean Cubitt (1999) discusses the use of special effects in connection with philosophical notions of the sublime and the spectacle. Like some of the aforementioned film scholars, he also compares digital technology to tendencies in early cinema, especially Méliès and his cinema of attractions. According to Cubitt (1999, 128), the sublime 'points towards a time beyond the mundane, a post-mortem time, or a time of the gods. The different temporality which the special effect occupies vis-à-vis the time of narrative indicates its extra-historical, extra-temporal status'. Cubitt applies this primarily to CGI effects that in his view 'interrupt' the narrative, a phenomenon that has also been described by Pierson, who argued that the 'sequences featuring CGI commonly exhibit a mode of spectatorial address that—with its tableau-style framing, longer takes, and strategic intercutting between shots of the computer-generated object and reaction shots of characters—solicits a contemplative viewing of the computer-generated image' (Pierson 1999a: 169). Yet, she also acknowledges that not every appearance of a computer-generated image is exposed in this way. Usually, there are various modes of presentation of digital special effects in one film, as otherwise the event of first appearance would lose its uniqueness. I want to argue that this notion of the sublime can also be applied to more recent digital cinema despite the fact that the novelty effect has arguably worn off. In films such as LOTR [*The Lord of the Rings* trilogy] and *Wrath* [*Wrath of the Titans*] in particular, we are frequently confronted with digital shots that use grand digital mise-en-scène to illustrate, for example, the sheer vastness of the territory covered and emphasize the smallness of the characters in relation to the task at hand. Similarly, shots that signify the grandeur of buildings beyond human comprehension aim to incite the same awe in us that people in the middle-ages must have felt when entering Gothic cathedrals. It is no longer the individual CGI creature, but the environment itself that becomes the subject of sublime time. Although these scenes clearly mark a break in the action and are in that sense positioned outside or beyond the 'ordinary' narration, they nevertheless have an important function in driving the story. Cubitt describes these scenes as being illusionistic rather than representational with a unique temporality that differs from the rest of the film. I would like to suggest that these 'illusionist' scenes allow for an element of awe and contemplation (a feature of the time-image) to enter the movement-images of mainstream cinema. As we will see, this notion of the sublime is also particularly important for an understanding of the distinction between the film version and its literary predecessor when looking at LOTR.

King (2000) draws on Slater's article on the *Spectacle of 'Natural Magic'* (1995) when he suggests that a modernity, which follows the notion of 'seeing is believing' has a problem as 'it must constantly generate visual spectacles which inspire belief' (Slater 1995, 220, as cited in King 2000, 56). This notion of belief brings us to the third aspect that connects Deleuze to digital cinema. In *Filmosophy*, Frampton (2006) envisions film as a form of thinking, a system of thoughts, ideas and memories. Frampton claims that cinema 'believes in its objects just as we have a belief about our past. Film can thus possibly help us understand our own forms of memory and recollection' (Frampton 2006, 19). Yet Frampton insists that he does not simply use film to illustrate thought processes, but that cinema itself *is* a form of thinking. There are several problems with understanding this theory, especially since Frampton proceeds by saying that the basic and most obvious elements that show us thought processes in film are metaphors and illustrations, whereas he simultaneously criticizes theorists who use cinema as illustration for philosophical concepts. The more interesting argument is that Frampton suggests that a simple analogy between film and thinking is far too limiting. Similar to Martin and Ostwalt's notion in chapter 1, he objects that theorists do not 'seem confident enough to allow "thinking" into the plainest of films. The reason most writers hold this view is that they are not able to get past the idea of thinking as "obvious" or "ostensibly intentional"' (Frampton 2006, 32). He argues that it is well worth taking mainstream cinema into account when talking about film and thinking, and I would like to add that this applies even more so when we talk about cinema and belief. Frampton argues that by claiming that cinema reinstates our belief in the world, Deleuze promotes a unique filmic thinking about our world. This thinking interprets and changes our world, creating a film-world to which we relate not only rationally but intuitively and emotionally. Frampton points out that especially the latest developments in cinema demand new concepts of thinking as new technologies of image creation liberate narration from traditional concepts of referentiality and authorship, a point that we have discussed above. He emphasizes that cinema has always created its own world and the audience has always been prepared to accept the world cinema creates. With contemporary digital cinema we are leaving the last connections to physical laws and photo-real references behind, while creating worlds that are as compelling and realistic as never before. Frampton suggests that what we see in a film is not only an image or a character, but also the film's own 'belief' in and about this image or character.

Frampton further argues that the audience does not want the film to explain itself, but to provide the rhetoric tools that allow it to experience and engage with the film, both consciously and subconsciously. He writes that audiences want 'to believe the film, want to be swept into the film, want to engage with the drama as fully as possible. They want the horror to scare us, the comedy to make us laugh, the drama to make us cry' (Frampton 2006, 154). Frampton points out that our engagement with a film might be a conscious process when we start watching the film, but as soon the film develops we rather *feel* the film directly. Especially recent cinema, that seamlessly mixes digital and photo-real images, provides us with a new form of reality, which provokes new experiences and as a consequence new thoughts and emotions. In other words, cinema 'seems to engender a new kind of belief—we recognise its reality as being like ours, but we do not expect its reality to always act like ours (in fact we like it to differ quite a bit)' (Frampton 2006, 155). Here, Frampton is more optimistic about contemporary digital cinema than other writers, such as Shadbolt, who claimed that 'contemporary effects cinema is not interested in alternate aesthetic worlds that might run visually parallel with live action but instead is obsessed with unifying disparate worlds, live action and CGI, into a single seamless reality' (Shadbolt 2013). Her criticism is that unlike stop-motion animation, which creates a distinctly different artistic environment within a film (as outlined in her notion on King Kong quoted above), the blend of digitally animated and real-life action actually denies the potential of alternative creative realities. However, as discussed in the previous paragraphs, the use of digital scenes and shots to create a more contemplative atmosphere may well be able to create an alternative experience that becomes part of the whole rather than a rapture in the viewing process.

Frampton also acknowledges that technical developments may likely proceed to a stage where computer-generated images really become indistinguishable from photographed ones. 'Cinema will then truly become its own new world—able to show anything, be anything, go anywhere, think anything—and animators will be the new gods of this world' (Frampton 2006, 205). This is a bold statement, implying a power to create new worlds and ideas that filmmakers have yet to live up to. Yet according to Frampton, contemporary digital cinema is not primarily about creating entirely new worlds, but altering the image of our own world by adding fresh perspectives and variables. This still provides the audience with familiar elements, so that we engage with the new images and thoughts on a more immediate, intuitive, emotional level and not just on an abstract, aesthetical level, where we appreciate the art and craft without being moved by the story.

Buckland (1999) also discusses the possibilities of 'world creation' in digital cinema. He supports the idea that digital special effects have a function in a film that goes well beyond the creation of spectacle. To analyse CGI and special effects independently from the narrative ignores the films' capability of creating and presenting possible worlds. According to him, a 'possible world is a modal extension of the "actual world"', whereas fiction on the other hand can be described 'as purely imaginary world that runs parallel to, but is autonomous from, the actual world' (Buckland 1999, 177). In this sense, the dinosaurs in Spielberg's *Jurassic Park* were so convincing because they were not entirely fictional, but the product of a—however unlikely—scientific experiment, a 'what if' scenario. Digital cinema has, according to Buckland, a unique capacity to present us with *possible worlds* and not just purely fictional ones, by seamlessly combining actual with virtual images through computer-generated images. This does not only include visible special effects, but more importantly invisible special effects, which are mainly used when a simulation of an event would be too expensive or complicated to produce in reality. Although the films I will discuss later clearly present fictional worlds, we will see that each of the examples discussed makes an attempt at increasing the level of possibility by emphasizing the 'historicity' and humanity within both the story and the presentation. LOTR aims at presenting its universe as preprehistoric, *Troy* has obvious historic links and even *Clash* [*Clash of the Titans*] tries to present its mythical hero in a more 'realistic' world. In that way, the 'digital image can, by means of special effects, make the possible believable' (Buckland 1999, 191). Buckland describes the audience's 'belief' in films, which present possible worlds, as a combination of modal propositions in the philosophical sense.

Pisters (2012) has also pointed out that the notion of belief does not depend on indexical links within an analog image. As Deleuze had already established, links between image and world have been forged, broken and reinstated well before the arrival of digital technologies. Just as Deleuze had argued, Pisters emphasizes that the link between image and world is one of belief, not modes of representation.

Conclusion

As we have seen throughout this chapter, new developments in cinema have always posed a challenge for theorists. When Deleuze classified cinema, he defined two distinct types of images, the movement-image and the time-image. These descriptions did not simply refer to the individual images, but also illustrated how these images relate to each other and create a system of meaning. For Deleuze, the shift from movement-image to the time-image took place after World War II, when the particular circumstances of postwar society inspired new aesthetic approaches towards film. Like Nietzsche and Kracauer before him, Deleuze clearly links aesthetic movements to social and cultural developments and thus emphasizes the reciprocal influence between cinema and society. However, he acknowledges that this shift does not take place in all areas of cinema and that although some new styles of cinema take on new images and structures, the majority of mainstream cinema remains within the concept of the movement-image. Yet, the later discussions on digital cinema have also shown that even mainstream cinema, and particularly digital cinema, has incorporated a number of aspects of the time-image into its more traditional movement-images, which consequently extends the creative possibilities of storytelling in contemporary cinema. The notion of belief here played an important part, as did the idea about a Catholic quality in cinema and the return of grand mise-en-scènes. Scott McQuire (2000, 53) has suggested that rather than complaining about the narrative of contemporary digital cinema (or the lack thereof), a 'more productive framework is to analyse why explicitly "mythological" films … have been able to grip popular imagination at this particular historical conjuncture, marrying the bare bones of fairy-tale narrative structures to the inculcation of a specific type of special effects driven viewing experience'. The second part of this book will aim to find some answers to this question.

From *Philosophy, Myth and Epic Cinema: Beyond Mere Illusions* by Sylvie Magerstädt.
© 2015 by Sylvie Magerstädt. Reproduced with permission of the Licensor through PLSclear.

Note

1. See, for example, Michael Punt, 'Parallel Histories: Early Cinema and Digital Media,' *Convergence* 6, no. 2 (2000): 62–76.

References

Berton, J. A. Jr., 1990. Film Theory for the Digital World: Connecting the Masters to the New Digital Cinema. *LEONARDO Digital Image*–Digital Cinema Supplement Issue, pp. 5–11.

Buckland, W., 1999. Between Science Fact and Science Fiction: Spielberg's Digital Dinosaurs, Possible Worlds, and the New Aesthetic Realism. *Screen* 40 (2): 177–91.

Cubitt, S., 1999. Introduction: Le réel, c'est l'impossible—the Sublime Time of Special Effects. *Screen* 40 (2): 123–30.

Frampton, D., 2006. *Filmosophy*. London and New York: Wallflower Press.

Heim, M., 1993. *Metaphysics of Virtual Realities*. New York and Oxford: Oxford University Press.

Jockenhövel, J., 2011. What Is It If It's Not Real? It's Genre–Early Color Film and Digital 3D. *Cinemascope* 7 (15): 1–14.

King, G., 2000. *Spectacular Narratives: Hollywood in the Age of the Blockbuster*. London: I. B. Tauris.

McQuire, S., 2000. Impact Aesthetics: Back to the Future in Digital Cinema? Millennial Fantasies. *Convergence* 6 (41).

Pierson, M., 1999a. CGI Effects in Hollywood Science-Fiction Cinema 1989–95: The Wonder Years. *Screen* 40 (2): 158–76.

Pierson, M., 1999b. No Longer State of the Art: Crafting a Future for CGI. *Wide Angle* 21 (1): 29–47.

Pisters, P., 2012. *The Neuro-Image. A Deleuzian Film-Philosophy of Digital Screen Culture*. Stanford, CA: Stanford University Press.

Prince, S., 1996. True Lies: Perceptual Realism, Digital Images and Film Theory. *Film Quarterly* 49 (3): 27–37.

Punt, M., 2000. Parallel Histories: Early Cinema and Digital Media. *Convergence* 6 (2): 62–76.

Shadbolt, J., 2013. Parallel Synchronized Randomness: Stop-motion Animation in Live Action Feature Films. *Animation Studies* vol. 8. http://journal.animationstudies.org/jane-shadbolt-parallel-synchronized-randomness-stop-motion-animation-in-live-action-feature-films/.

8 Horrorism; or, On Violence Against the Helpless

ADRIANA CAVARERO

But it touched my heart so forcibly to think of parting entirely with the child, and, for aught I knew, of having it murdered, or starved by neglect and ill-usage (which was much the same), that I could not think of it without horror.

Daniel Defoe, *Moll Flanders*

In the ample repertory of human violence, there is one particularly atrocious kind whose features I propose to subsume in the category of *horrorism*. This coinage, apart from the obvious assonance with the word "terrorism," is meant to emphasize the peculiarly repugnant character of so many scenes of contemporary violence, which locates them in the realm of horror rather than that of terror. Why not simply speak of horror, without going to the trouble of adopting a neologism that may cause some annoyance? A neologism assumes that there exists something new, different, recent. But what is so new about carnage and torture, after all? What is so different about bodies burning under incendiary bombs? What is so recent about the customary, age-old slaughter of the innocents? A simple answer might be that, at first sight and in certain circumstances anyway, what is new is the way in which the massacre is now perpetrated: a body that blows itself up in order to rip other bodies to pieces. And more than that, a female body, as happens ever more frequently; sometimes even the body of a pregnant mother-to-be. Thus the most ancient horror renews itself, reaching the extremity of an axis that originates at its own core. To call it terrorism on the basis that it forms part of a terror strategy of a particularly atrocious kind would be inadequate. Calling it horrorism, on the other hand, helps us see that a certain model of horror is indispensable for understanding our present.

Medusa and Medea are the ancient icons of today's spreading horrorism. Medusa reminds us that the "killing of uniqueness," as Hannah Arendt would say, is an ontological crime that goes well beyond the inflicting of death. Medea confirms that this crime is visited on a body not just vulnerable but reduced to the primary situation of absolute helplessness.

It is worth pointing out that, although the scene of infancy links them and makes them coincide, "vulnerable" and "helpless" are not synonymous terms. The human being is vulnerable as a singular body exposed to wounding. There is not, however, anything necessary about the *vulnus* (wound) embedded in the term "vulnerable," only the potential for a wound to occur at any time, in contingent circumstances. As Saint Augustine said, "the fact that our body in the present moment is not necessarily wounded, does not render it invulnerable."[1] As a body, the vulnerable one remains vulnerable as long as she lives, exposed at any instant to *vulnus*. Yet the same potential also delivers her to healing and the relational ontology that decides its meaning.[2] Irremediably open to wounding and caring, the vulnerable one exists totally in the tension generated by this alternative. As though the null response—neither the wound nor the care—were excluded. Or as though the absence of wound and care were not even thinkable. And yet you might call that indifference, and even bless it, if it were just the absence of wounding, whereas, if it were the absence of caring, we would perhaps have to call it desolation. But exposure to the other that persists over the arc of an entire life renders this absence improbable. In fact, given that every human being who exists has been born and has been an infant, materially impossible.

The infant, the small child—and here lies Hannah Arendt's great intuition concerning the ontological and political centrality of the category of Birth—actually proclaims relationship as a human condition not just fundamental but structurally necessary. This means that, as a creature totally consigned to relationship, a child is the vulnerable being par excellence and constitutes the primary paradigm of any discourse on vulnerability.[3] And at the same time and even more so, the primary paradigm of any discourse on helplessness.

As its etymology suggests, the "helpless one" ("l'inerme," literally "the unarmed one") is he who does not bear arms and thus cannot harm, kill, or wound. But in everyday usage, rather than this incapacity to take the offensive, the term "helpless" tends to designate a person who, attacked by an armed other, has no arms with which to defend himself. Defenseless and in the power of the other, the helpless person finds himself substantially in a condition of passivity, undergoing violence he can neither flee from nor defend against. The scene is entirely tilted toward unilateral violence. There is no symmetry, no parity, no reciprocity. As in the exemplary case of the infant, it is the other who is in a position of omnipotence. But albeit exemplary, the case of the infant has a peculiar characteristic that distinguishes it from all other cases: the defenselessness of a baby does not depend on circumstances. In other words, infancy is not a circumstance but a condition, the essential mode in which the human being comes into the world and, for a certain period, inhabits it. Infancy is precisely the span of time, never exactly calculable and in some cases interminable, in which vulnerability and helplessness are completely conjoined. Only subsequently do they split apart. Though she remains vulnerable as long as she lives, from the first to the last day of her singular existence, an adult falls back into defenselessness only in certain circumstances. She is always vulnerable but only sometimes helpless, as contingency dictates and with a variable degree of intensity. That degree is maximal when, as happens in torture, the circumstances that cause a helpless victim to undergo violence are willed, prepared, and organized by armed tormentors.

Having established that vulnerability is a permanent status of the human being, whereas finding oneself helpless—except for in infancy and, sometimes, extreme old age—depends on circumstances, it should be added that the circumstances may vary widely. Sometimes misfortune of a more or less natural kind, distress, suffering, or illness, can make you feel helpless. In such cases, we sometimes say that an adult is as helpless as a baby. The expression is not without a certain tenderness: it hints at a plea for care and emphasizes that the vulnerable one in this case is unilaterally exposed to wounds against which he cannot defend himself. It would be easy, almost a joke, to batter him—which seems to be the thought in the minds of modern hooligans who, for fun, attack persons already ill or debilitated. Atrocious as it is, and worthy to be classified as an episode of everyday horrorism, violence of this type is nonetheless occasional. The helpless person is helpless already. She is attacked but not produced. The scene of torture is different: the situation centered on the helpless victim, far from being a given or a happenstance, is produced artificially or, as the Italian has it, *con arte* ("artfully"). In this sense, torture belongs to the type of circumstance in which the coincidence between the vulnerable and the helpless is the result of a series of acts, intentional and planned, aimed at bringing it about. Several peculiar aspects of horrorism are thereby fully disclosed. The center of the scene is occupied by a suffering body, a body reduced to a totally available object or, rather, a thing objectified by the reality of pain,[4] on which violence is taking its time about doing its work. Death may come at the end, but it is not the end in view. The dead body, no matter how mutilated, is only a residue of the scene of torture. The special form of horrorism of which the torturer is the featured protagonist actually prefers to consummate itself on the living body, to prolong the suffering inscribed in the *vulnus*, bringing the vulnerable one to the limit of bearability of pain and offense. As every torturer knows, the vulnerable is not the same as the killable. The latter stands poised between death and life, the former between the wound and healing care. That the vulnerable one is also defenseless makes things easier, because, since it is unilateral, the violence can unfold as something irresistible, even unlimitable, except that the death of the vulnerable one (her "*venir meno*," in the untranslatable Italian idiom) always does constitute a limit. And this is precisely the limit against which (and not just in the case of torture) horror measures the peculiarity of its crime and, in competition with terror, founds its dominion.

Although it often has to do with death or, if you like, with the killing of helpless victims, horrorism is characterized by a particular form of violence that exceeds death itself. This is starkly evidenced in the infinite scene of torture, a word whose etymological root lies in the Latin verb "*torquere*" (supplying English with the verbs "to torque" and "to distort" and the nouns "torture," "torment," "torque," "torch," and "tort" but normally translated as "to twist"): to torture is to twist and distort the body, to make it into "a body broken to pieces by *tormentum*."[5] But some cases of violent, or even instant, death yield a superabundance of signifieds, in comparison to the simple crime of homicide. Medea is a good example. After all, the celebrated infanticidal mother confines herself to killing the helpless; she doesn't torture them. Though the myth does relate that she tears the bodies to pieces, she does so only after the victims are already dead. Albeit using other means and with scaled-up effects, our contemporary massacres, including those caused by suicide bombers, evoke a similar image. People unable to defend themselves against an unforeseeable attack and hence, in precisely this circumstance, helpless people are killed by explosive devices that often rip their bodies to shreds. Obviously some are wounded as well, which causes the scene to turn particularly repugnant, but not just because we see the "undoing" effect of *vulnus* on a living and suffering body that arouses compassion rather than on a cadaver. Repugnance wells up not so much because of the homicide in itself as because of the offense against vulnerable people who are also defenseless. On top of that, the body of the suicide bomber explodes and is dismembered in the very act of killing, shattering, and dismembering the bodies of others. And, on top of that, this violent body is also, sometimes, that of a woman. The indices of superabundance with respect to the figure of simple killing accumulate and multiply. It is not death, much less the death of the real or imagined enemy, that looms large. The crime discloses its profundity, going to the very roots of the human condition, which suffers offense at the ontological level.

Notes

1. St. Augustine, *De peccatorum meritis et remissione et de baptismo parvulorum* 1.3.
2. See Luigina Mortari, *La pratica dell'aver cura* (Milan: Mondadori, 2006).
3. This is confirmed, from a specifically Christian point of view, in a work by David Jansen, *Graced Vulnerability: A Theology of Childhood* (Cleveland: Pilgrim, 2005). In a context of theological reflection, it proposes a relational—rather than rationalistic—conception of the human being, taking the vulnerability of the infant as a paradigm.

4. See Elaine Scarry, *The Body in Pain: The Making and Unmaking of the World* (New York: Oxford University Press, 1985).
5. Corrado Bologna, "Tortura," in *Enciclopedia* (Turin: Einaudi, 1981), 14:353. [This multivolume work with a one-word title is informally but universally known to Italian readers as the "Enciclopedia Einaudi." WM]

References

Bologna, Corrado. "Tortura." In *Enciclopedia*, vol. 14. Turin: Einaudi, 1981.

Jansen, David. *Graced Vulnerability: A Theology of Childhood*. Cleveland: Pilgrim, 2005.

Mortari, Luigina. *La pratica dell'aver cura*. Milan: Mondadori, 2006.

Scarry, Elaine. *The Body in Pain: The Making and Unmaking of the World*. New York: Oxford University Press, 1985.

9 Shimmering Phantasmagoria: Trans/Cinema/Aesthetics in an Age of Technological Reproducibility

ELIZA STEINBOCK

Opening a phantasmagoria show in Paris in 1793, Philip Philidor proclaimed to the crowd, "I do not wish to deceive you; but I will astonish you."[1] The Enlightenment's investment in rational, clear thinking achieved by shining a light on the natural world takes a perverse twist in this popular form of entertainment that projects phantoms during an aural and visual dialogue between the living and the dead. The double view of trans bodies as both engineered by medical science and as fundamentally illusory holds the same tension, and protracted appeal, as proto-cinematic phantasmagoria shows. In our twenty-first-century cultural moment when trans characters and talent are inundating televisual series, reality shows, and films, yet still with their transition forming a main attraction and plot device, it seems pertinent to ask, Are trans people the heirs of phantasmagoric visual culture?[2] Taking a historical view, Rita Felski argues that the perceived unde-cidability of gender leads the figure of the transsexual to become a metaphor for cultural crisis. Citing the epigram *fin de siècle, fin de sexe*, Felski notes how the anxieties of suspended sex from the late nineteenth century return before the millennium during the postmodern moment in which "gender emerges as a priv-ileged symbolic field for the articulation of diverse fashionings of history and time," be they apocalyptic or redemptive.[3]

What is missing in trans origin myths and interpretations of their existence—a bellwether—is an appre-ciation for how trans subjects narrate and represent their lives and thereby mold the available conceptual models of gendered embodiment. This chapter submits that diverse conceptualizations for trans embod-iments and identities emerge together with phantasmagorical visual practices that offer them a horizon of intelligibility by interlacing science with entertainment. I foremost explore the continuity of a stuttering, flickering type of transformation as a type of shimmering found in the early cinematographic "fantastic views" of filmmaker George Méliès (1896–1912) and in the (photo) montage of Danish artist Lili Elbe's life writing (1931) about how she became a real girl that was later reprinted (referring to her "sex change"). At the close I consider how shimmering phantasmagoria return in the contemporary trans artworks of Zackary Drucker and A. L. Steiner, who collaborate on a photography series entitled "BEFORE/AFTER" (2009–present), and the flipbook and life-size zoetrope project "Becoming" by Yishay Garbasz (2010), documenting the year before and after her gender clarification surgery. Forgoing the foundational terms of either *trans* or *film* is imperative to tracing the phantasmagoria's lingering hold on how a transformative embodiment is conceptualized within visual culture. Following Elizabeth Freeman's queer historical concept of "temporal drag" to register the pull of the deep past on the present, I focus on how some trans bodies carry forward "the genuine *past*-ness of the past—its opacity and illegibility," that seems intransient and anachronistic, that is, unless viewed from the perspective of the phantasmagoria.[4] To grasp the parallel and overlapping tracks of trans and phantasmagoria's temporal drag, I map the genealogy of an expansive trans concept interacting with invert, hermaphrodite, and deviant sex theories relying on the dichotomy of illusion/real, and I conduct media archaeology to trace phantasmagoric aesthetics of deception/reproduction across divergent cultural series.

A veritable mountain of literature discusses phantasmagoria as the name for the ancient or modern exhibition of optical illusions, or the literary creation of a shifting series of imagined phantasms, or the key term of intellectual and aesthetic discussions during the nineteenth and twentieth centuries. Straddling the era of incipient and full-blown technological reproducibility, Tom Gunning explains, "Phantasmagoria takes on the weight of modern dialectics of truth and illusion, subjectivity and objectivity, deception and liberation, and even life and death."[5] Or, as Terry Castle has shown, in the history of the phantasmagoria we can find the latent irrationalism haunting the rationalist conception of the mind, what she calls the "spectralization" of the world of thought.[6] Its persistence today in the syntax of trans lives and representation points toward the strong undertow of these larger categorical anxieties deflected onto gender then as now, and thus complicates the notions of transsexual and transgender as formatively modern or postmodern.

My argumentation goes against the grain of scholars such as Bernice Hausman or R. Nick Gorton who attribute the emergence of trans identities foremost to the development of surgical technologies by modern science and to the taxonomy of mental and sexual pathologies in sexology.[7] The evolving system of medico-scientific discourses certainly determines the so-called truth about a subject's status vis-à-vis differentiating between pathological and healthy definitions of sexual and gender practices. Trans subjects who articulate the feeling of being in the "wrong body" become a sign of pathology, and therefore a subject to reform back to health. But this view of trans embodiment is limited to explaining discourses of clinical experiences that arose during the modern era, however much of a hold they retain today in spite of competition from juridical definitions of self-determination.[8] In addition, I also contest the conclusion of trans scholars such as Jack Halberstam who claim this modern formation of trans has been superseded by postmodern theories that question any form of universal truth and challenges the fixity of all meaning, including the designations sex and gender.[9] In general, theories of gender performativity in queer and transgender studies embrace the philosophies that gender is more a fiction than a fact, and that identity is a potentiality rather than an achievement. Related to this malleable identity, technology for gender transitioning has accompanied changes in the economic and aesthetic landscape in which neoliberal orders increasingly favor plasticity. Here the prevalence of trans discourses of change are seen to orbit around the economic order, thereby becoming suspect for capitulating to late capitalist choice economies.[10] The growing investment in what Zygmunt Bauman calls "liquid life" and gradually more mainstream calls for fluidity in identity from celebrities like Miley Cyrus and Ruby Rose might well lead to increased possibilities for *some* trans subjectivities to become intelligible, while others become opaque.[11]

However, the modern and the postmodern claims for conceptualizing trans are primarily about epistemological correction, or uncertainty. Running through both claims, and both eras, is the perpetuation of the trans stereotype of *being* illusory or unreal, which places a heavy stigma on those who assert a trans identity. That is, the trans "onto-epistemological" condition, in which being and knowing are always already entangled, appears symbolically as either an aberration or a deconstructive supplement to constructed normal, natural, or healthy binary gender identities that match the sex assigned at birth, often referred to as cisgender.[12] The visual legacies of inscribing gender truths onto the visual body-as-text can be heard in trans vocabularies, such as being read (for trans), passing (for cisgender), female impersonator, or masculine presenting. Trans subjectivity is pulled taut between gestures of concealing and revealing with its literal translation into the violence of the genital reveal I discussed in the introduction. First I address the perilous investment in an one/none visual truth of sex and gender before coming to see how trans subjects engage the phantasmagoria *dispositif* to effectively shift the visual and discursive order toward a model of sensorial reckoning best described as shimmering.

Cultural Series: Machines for Perceiving "Self-Evidences"

The experience of transitioning is often conceptualized as a visual effect of a personal disclosure, a "coming out" of the hidden epistemological closet into the revealing light of truth. Jay Prosser, for example, considers the transsexual to exist only during a medically assisted physical transition to become the desired perceptible gender. "The immediate purpose of transsexuality," he writes, "is to make real the subject's true gender on the body," and in this pursuit he names "the visual media" as being highly valuable for the "promise (like transition itself) to make visible that which begins as imperceptible—there but underexposed."[13] People who "cross over (*trans-*) the boundaries constructed by their culture to define and contain gender" thereby lose access to conventional evidence for making truth claims for their gender identity.[14] This places a tremendous amount of onto-epistemological weight on the indexical, referential, and highly visual dimension of their truth statements. The visual media of photographic images especially "realize the image of the 'true' self that is originally only apparitional" to others and potentially to oneself.[15] The photographic portrait accompanying written testimony functions, for Prosser, as an incarnation of gendered realness, bringing to the apparitional yet truer version of self as described in language a sense of heft paradoxically through its paper or digital materiality. In Prosser's brilliant analysis of how written trans autobiographies often integrate personal and artistic photographs, he is aware of the dangers of awarding visual media with less (perceived) mediation between signifier and soma than writing's rhetorical strategies. Borrowing language from Roland Barthes, the photograph, he notes, appears "co-natural" or fully in alignment with the bodily referent and even confused with it as it begins to function as more referential to the anchored gendered self (I am there, I am that) than the actual body that remains stubbornly in flux. In fact, the photographic portrait that realizes a true gender by index risks over time not offering the indexed subject a sustained form of gendered realness, but rather its illusion. The "now you see it, now you don't" quality of visual trans self-representation can function like a phantasmagoric technique. Like Philidor's disclaimer for his phantasmagoria, the production of visual gendered realness oscillates between deception and astonishment.

The optical device and conceptual vehicle of the phantasmagoria stresses the spectacular and spectral quality of bodies. Not only did the phantasmagoria incorporate the necessary, underlying lens technologies, perspectival physics, and techniques for capturing light for photographic arts, it also readied an audience eager to be astonished by cinematographic views. For a methodological frame to study the continuities between previous popular trick technologies and early film, André Gaudreault suggests the inclusive term of a "cultural series" for moments of transition through "intermedial meshing" between media rather than looking to pinpoint a historical rupture.[16] The process of institutionalization through the normalization of codes later set the animated views of cinema apart from other cultural forms such as magic shows and vaudeville theatre, consolidating it into a relatively autonomous media institution during Hollywood's Golden Age (1917–1960s). Even from a twenty-first-century point of view though, the series element of spectacular and specular bodies continues to play across differing cultural and media forms, linking together phantasmagoric aesthetic impulses with new technical advances. The cultural series approach that tracks intermedial meshing might also be applied to the scientific series of sexual intermediacy in which earlier notions of trans concepts were strongly related to homosexuality and intersexuality as well. Dating from the late nineteenth century, this kaleidoscopic blending and turning of trans-inter-queer inflections has a distinctly visual and psychosexual lineage. Take for example Magnus Hirschfeld's "Yearbooks for Sexual Intermediaries" (1899–1923), which consist of 20,000 pages of images showing the variance of psychic and physical hermaphroditism, transvestism, and homosexuality between the poles of what he called the "full woman" and the "full man."[17] These meshings of sexual intermediacy shifted again when judicial rulings compared intersex and transsexual claims to change gender status (1950s) and when homosexuality was largely replaced by transsexuality in a key reference psychology book on diagnosing mental disorders (1973).[18] My framing of phantasmagoria as a cultural series has the benefit of bringing together, and thinking together, two historical transitional moments: when technological reproducibility first affected visual culture by heightening the volatility of an audiovisual image, and when surgical and sexological science also first acknowledged the mutability of gender.

Michel Foucault's historical method of archeology that accounts for the dimension and direction of power in normalization processes can be usefully combined with studying minute transitions within cultural series.[19] His analysis of different eras focuses on the relation of forces that produce and deploy truth; power produces epistemological formations specific to a period's configuration, enabling something to be said to be, and another thing to be seen as, true. A cultural moment thus consists in the visible and the sayable that enables knowledge to emerge as self-evident. In parsing Foucault's archaeological method, Gilles Deleuze explains that an era consists of a geological threshold that breaks with the previous one through the trans-formation of *statements* (sayable) and *visibilities* (visible)—"an audiovisual archive"—that form bands of discursive knowledge and fields of nondiscursive knowledge.[20]

In the case of the phantasmagoria, I see that it patterns the supposedly self-evident or knowable visi-bilities of both cinema images and trans bodies as astonishing illusions or more generally as a shimmer. Deleuze defines visibilities to be "forms of luminosity which are created by the light [of the era] itself and allow a thing or object to exist only as a flash, sparkle or *shimmer*."[21] The "first light" of an era acts as a virtual visibility producing all perceptible experiences; it "brings forth visibilities as flashes and shimmerings, which are the 'second light.'"[22] Thus, the pervasive lights of an era can be analyzed as a potentate form that is capable of creating other forms and movements.[23] Deleuze proposes that in the same way that state-ments depend on their system for sayability, visibilities are inseparable from the machines that produce their seeability. Such visibility machines do not have to be optical machines like film projectors per se; they are more generally conceived as an assembly of organs and functions that makes something inconspicuously visible: producing a thing as a shimmering. Crucial to entering the visible field as a second light, then, is the proper relation to the machine that acts as a first light. Only then can one (or something) become a shimmer, created as a "light-being" both absolute in one's givenness and yet historical, because a being of light "is inseparable from the way in which it falls into a formation or corpus."[24] The phantasmagoria serves a unify-ing function, acting as a production and distribution center of light and dark, the opaque and transparent, the seen and not-seen—a system of light infused with power relations, as Foucault skillfully analyzes in "Diego Velásquez's" painting *Las Meninas*.[25] As a type of this first light, the cultural series of phantasmagoria not only literally projects a shimmering image, but also is a form of luminosity that allows cinema and trans bodies to exist as self-evident shimmers.

I look methodologically at how the cultural series of the phantasmagoria developed in order to under-stand how the sense of trans right about now is oddly not that anachronistic with trans from back then. Although trans identification and means to attain a gender transition then and now are clearly not the same, the lingering phantasmagoric aesthetic achieves a continued problematic sense of a sex change as self-evidently illusory by wavering on the tip of deception/astonishment. My archaeological method involves "breaking open" the self-evidence of an audiovisual cultural form that is suspended in the "strata" of an age, leading to the question, How did the era of technological reproducibility become filled with this particular cultural series of phantasmagoric shimmerings?[26] Principally, according to a media archeology perspective, as the means of image reproduction became more sophisticated so did the concealment of its production, contributing further to the sense of self-evident realness and the ever-greater popular success of phantasmagoric devices. The original phantasmagoria that used rear projection from behind the screen to keep the audience unaware of the lanterns became improved with new optical technologies of film that further hid the source of production by projecting images from behind audiences' backs. Jonathan Crary's historical study of visual devices and techniques determines that of the many competing optical experiences of the 1830s most disappeared by the 1850s because they were insufficiently "phantasmorgoric" in the sense of creating an illusion of the image's standalone realness.[27] Richard Grusin and Jay David Bolter find that similarly new technologies are taken up only when they come closest to presenting an unmediated reality (i.e., an illusion of the realness of the image because it appears unsupported), concluding that successful "remediation" follows the logic of transparency.[28] The persistent popularity of phantasmagoria since the 1790s is also accounted for by Theodor Adorno's Marxist analysis: "[phantasmagoria indicates] the occultation of production by means of the outward appearance of the product [...] this outer appearance can lay claim to the status of being. Its perfection is at the same time the perfection of the illusion that the work of art is a reality *sui generis* that constitutes itself in the realm of the absolute without having to renounce its claim to image the world."[29] The occultation of production through its concealment makes a commodity a "very queer thing," Marx noted, because it seems to take on an animated life of its own.[30] Hiding the production of gender, sometimes in plain sight with gender-marked clothing, gesture, and so on, enables one's outer appearance to do the work of "claiming the status of being." The very queer shimmer of a thing in the era of technological reproducibility shows up under the aegis of competing phantasmagorical optical novelties that create a world of images so real that they threaten to replace the actual experiences they represent.

The genre of fantastical stories of transformation also trades in the troubling division of illusion from realness. One of the first self-authored memoirs of someone who was relentlessly investigated for their "true" sex and gender identity was written by Herculine (Adélaîde/Abel) Barbin (1838–68), who also referred to herself as Alexina or Camille and was living in France during the phantasmagoria craze. Foucault came across Barbin's story through an entry in a sexological encyclopedia published by Auguste Tardieu that details Barbin's youth spent in an all-girl's convent school and later a women's teaching college. Foucault extracts from the personal narrative and surrounding medical documents an emerging social perception of monstrous and foolish embodiments that deviate from the ideal form of a singular sex—a new shimmer in the audiovisual archive. Changes of sex or claims of multiple sexes increasingly became considered as "insulting to 'the truth,'" or "not adequate to reality," and "soon as belonging more or less to the realm of chimeras."[31] Even if not an outright crime, sexual irregularity is suspected to be fictitious, a mere disguise that should be stripped off through the declaration of one's true sex.

Barbin captured the attention of medical authorities precisely because of her disturbing phantasmagoric appeal to lovers. These lovers were understood to be deceived and perhaps even desired to be astonished by Barbin's shimmering sexes: true and apparent. In Foucault's words: "But if nature, through its fantasies or accidents, might 'deceive' the observer and hide the true sex for a time, individuals might also very well be suspected of dissembling their inmost knowledge of their true sex and of profiting from certain anatomical oddities in order to make use of their bodies as if they belonged to the other sex. In short, the *phantasmagorias of nature* might be of service to licentious behavior, hence the moral interest that inhered in the medical diagnosis of the true sex."[32] Barbin's story does not relish in deceiving the medical or intimate observer, but it certainly savors the delights she experienced in not having a definite, identifiable sex. The world her story relates to readers "was a world in which grins hung about without the cat" in that it imparts how the identity of Barbin and partners had little or no importance next to the feelings that were shared.[33]

This apparently "happy limbo of a non-identity" with its resultant affective intensification became rudely interrupted when she was forced by law to live as a man, and Barbin eventually committed suicide, her memoirs left at her side.[34] Her death portends the many trans and intersex people to come who also cannot find a way to live when forced to have a definite true sex that they either cannot abide or cannot convincingly produce. The phantasmagoria at this time thus dangerously tilts toward the modernist "one true identity" logic of a concealed referent, defining everything else as an illusion. I wager though that the cultural series of phantasmagoria continues in its development to model other visibilities with more accommodating ways of living as a shimmering.

If, as Foucault claims, the specific phantom of the eighteenth century was the transvestite and that of the nineteenth century was the haunting hermaphrodite, it is small wonder that sexological narratives about sexual intermediacy find their outlet as well in the cinematic effects of double exposure, substitution, and transformation.[35] The fantastic view that gender is transformable, and sex changeable, acknowledges an interest in the waning sense of incommensurable difference between the sexes.[36] The cinematographic shimmer of trans, however flickering in and out of focus with hermaphrodites and sexual deviants, indicates that long before Christine Jorgenson attained her international celebrity for having a "sex change" in the early 1950s, the visual field was peppered with sex change–type narratives and morphing imagery. In the scientific series of trans sex transformation, a significant shift occurred when Western scientific traditions of surveillance, measurement, and physical transformation utilized cinema to perform a "fantastic construction of 'human life' as a dynamic entity to be tracked, studied, and transformed in the social 'theatre' of the laboratory."[37] The ontology of cinema, in its special relation to animating life and suspending death in a cinematic theatre, strongly resembles the ontology of the trans body that undergoes surgery, which takes place in an operating theatre. In the phantasmagoria cultural series, cinema, with its system of editing cuts and suturing images, parallels the incisions and sutures that take place in a surgical theatre. Attention to the construction of human life with respect to the ways in which surgical and cinematic cuts refigure bodies may offer insight into the cultural and technical conditions that enabled trans identity to emerge differentiated from an otherwise perplexing limbo identity.

Walter Benjamin's 1936 essay "The Work of Art in the Age of Its Technological Reproducibility" offers such a theory of cinema with respect to its ability to cut into reality in order to reassemble the aesthetic experience of life.[38] In Benjamin's theorization of the cinema–as–surgical theatre, incisions occur on a number of levels: (1) the selection of reality to be captured on celluloid, (2) editing the celluloid, and (3) the viewer's reception of the edited film. First, the cinematographer penetrates deeply into reality's tissue to extract piecemeal parts, slicing into it much like the surgeon "makes an intervention in the patient."[39] Then, during the film's production, the editor assembles the various cuts to create another, transformed perception of reality. Finally, when this artificially "equipment-free" view of reality is foisted on film viewers, the film becomes the surrogate surgeon. Cinema has, based on successive changes of scene and focus made possible through the procedure of cutting celluloid, a "percussive effect" on the spectator: assailing him or her through the tactile quality of the unstoppable and erratic flow of cuts.[40] Film as a whole—not just at either its production or its reception—operates on an ailing relation with reality, in part caused by the phantasmagoric quality of commodities. Benjamin brings the discourse of surgery to bear on cinema in order to underscore the uncertain cultural and political consequences of interacting with reproductive technologies that bring enlivening novelty as well as deadening alienation. In the age of a global movie-going world, cinematic pictures become part of, if not the core of, what Susan Buck-Morss calls the "new urban phantasmagoria" of the commodity-on-display in which purely representational value is paramount.[41]

How reproductive technologies are used and to what ends are critical questions not only for representation politics but also for how gender becomes reproduced in the operating theatre of the social.

Notes

1. Quoted in Laurent Mannoni, *The Great Art of Light and Shadow* (Exeter: University of Exeter Press, 2000), 144.
2. Here I refer to Laverne Cox playing Sophia Burset on *Orange Is the New Black*, Jamie Clayton playing Nomi on *Sense8*, numerous characters on *Transparent*, Scott Turner Schofield on *The Bold and the Beautiful*, *I Am Cait* about Caitlyn Jenner, *I Am Jazz* on the life of a young trans woman, RuPaul's *Drag Race*, and so on. I mention specific films in the introduction and in this chapter refer to Tom Hooper's 2015 dramatization of *The Danish Girl*.
3. Rita Felski, "*Fin de siècle, Fin de sexe*: Transsexuality, Postmodernism, and the Death of History," *New Literary History* 27 (1996): 338.
4. Elizabeth Freeman, *Time Binds: Queer Temporalities, Queer Histories* (Durham, NC: Duke University Press, 2010), 62–64.
5. He further writes, "I know of no word more complex than 'Phantasmagoria,'" in Tom Gunning, "Illusions Past and Future: The Phantasmagoria and Its Specters" (paper presented at the Refresh! First International Conference on the Histories of Art, Science and Technology, 2004). Consulted via Media Art History accessed March 24, 2016, http://plo2.donau-uni.ac.at/jspui/handle/10002/296/.
6. Terry Castle, "Phantasmagoria: Spectral Technology and the Metaphorics of Modern Reverie," *Critical Inquiry* 15, no. 1 (1988): 29.
7. On surgeries see Dwight Billings and Thomas Urban, "The Socio-Medical Construction of Transsexualism: An Interpretation and Critique," *Social Problems* 29, no. 3 (1982): 266–82; and Bernice Hausman, *Changing Sex: Transsexualism, Technology, and the Idea of Gender* (Durham, NC: Duke University Press, 1995).

    On diagnostic categories see Jay Prosser, *Second Skins: The Body Narratives of Transsexuality* (New York: Columbia University Press, 1998); and the provocative R. Nick Gorton, "Transgender as Mental Illness: Nosology, Social Justice, and the Tarnished Golden Mean," in *The Transgender Studies Reader 2*, ed. Susan Stryker and Aren Aizura (New York: Routledge, [2007] 2013), 644–52.
8. Legal and administrative hurdles to gender self-determination in the U.S. context are elaborately discussed in Dean Spade, *Normal Life: Administrative Violence, Critical Trans Politics, and the Limits of Law* (Durham, NC: Duke University Press, 2015).
9. Early examples include Jack (formerly Judith) Halberstam, "F2M: The Making of Female Masculinity," in *The Lesbian Postmodern*, ed. Laura Doan, 210–28 (New York: Columbia University Press, 1994); and Susan Stryker, "My Words to Victor Frankenstein Above the Village of Chamounix: Performing Transgender Rage" [1994], in *The Transgender Studies Reader*, ed. Susan Stryker and Stephen Whittle, 244–56 (New York: Routledge, 2006).
10. On the neoliberal undercurrents to a grossly dividing transnormativity see Jasbir Puar, "Bodies with New Organs: Becoming Trans, Becoming Disabled," *Social Text* 33, no. 3 (2015): 45–75.
11. The first in a series on liquidity is Zygmunt Bauman, *Liquid Life* (London: Polity Press, 2005).
12. Karen Barad, *Meeting the Universe Halfway: Quantum Physics and the Entanglement of Matter and Meaning* (Durham, NC: Duke University Press, 2007).

13. Prosser, *Second Skins*, 211.

14. Susan Stryker, *Transgender History* (Berkeley: Seal Press, 2008), 1.

15. Prosser, *Second Skins*, 211.

16. André Gaudreault, *Film and Attraction: From Kinematography to Cinema*, trans. Timothy Barnard (Chicago: University of Illinois Press, [2008] 2011), 68. Gaudreault acknowledges that Eric de Kuyper articulates ideas similar to his "intermedial meshing" to describe the hodgepodge of technologies among kinematographic phenomena.

17. Vern L. Bullough, "Magnus Hirschfeld, An Often Over-looked Pioneer," *Sexuality and Culture* 7, no. 1 (2003): 62–72. See commentary on the role of Hirschfeld in Merl Storr and Jay Prosser, "Introduction to Part III Transsexuality and Bisexuality," in *Sexology Uncensored: The Documents of Sexual Science*, ed. Lucy Bland and Laura Doan (Chicago: Chicago University Press, 1998), 75–77. Sexology today differentiates cross-gender identification from intersex conditions. Conceptualization of trans identification evolved into a psychic cross-gender desire aligned with requested bodily modifications, whereas intersex was kept from becoming an identity by framing bodies as atypical through diagnosis and (nonconsensual) treatment. Hence, both involve hormonal and surgical practices but deployed in one case to treat the psyche and in the other case, the physical irregularity. Today intersex social movements and trans rights organizations both use the language of self-determination and informed consent models to enable people access to voluntary treatment that is seen from a more holistic perspective.

18. See Stryker, *Transgender History*, 95–98; Ulrike Klöppel, "Who Has the Right to Change Gender Status? Drawing Boundaries between Inter- and Transsexuality," in *Critical Intersex*, ed. M. Morgan Holmes (Farnham, U.K.: Ashgate, 2009), 171.

19. See Michel Foucault, *The Archaeology of Knowledge*, trans. A. M. Sheridan Smith (New York: Taylor & Francis, [1969] 2013).

20. Gilles Deleuze, *Foucault*, trans. Seán Hand (Minneapolis: University of Minnesota Press, [1986] 1990), 50. In his assessment of Foucault's method, Deleuze places emphasis on the covert literary project entitled *Death and The Labyrinth: The World of Raymond Roussel*, trans. Charles Ruas (London: Athlone Press, [1963] 1987), which Foucault conducts under a pseudonym and which outlines his method of production. In his treatment of Roussel's various kinds of writing, Foucault argues that in his extraction of words selected for a poetic line he reveals the secret meanings of phrases and, similarly, he draws images that show the object's shimmering visibility. Deleuze suggests that Foucault's archaeological method of breaking and extracting may be attributed to becoming inspired by Roussel's various methods to scramble and to decode language and everyday imagery. Deleuze also argues that this (borrowed) method is integral to Foucault's development of the notions of relationality, forces, and power. This work on Roussel anticipates Foucault's Nietzsche-influenced reassessment of power in *Discipline and Punish: The Birth of the Prison* (1975) and was written during the period of *The Birth of the Clinic: An Archaeology of Medical Perception* (1963) that studies power's productive capacity. Upon publication of the book about Roussel, Foucault explained that his analysis was highly personal; he tried to bury the manuscript in his pseudonymously written entry on the work of Foucault (himself!) by not mentioning it. Certainly it stands apart in style and argumentation. See the introduction to the text by John Ashbery for more on the reception of Foucault's Roussel book and its place in his oeuvre (xiii-xxviii).

21. Deleuze, *Foucault*, 52, emphasis mine.

22. Deleuze, *Foucault*, 57–58. In Deleuze's reading of Foucault, the method of tracing secret statements and the light that makes a thing shimmer underline all of Foucault's historical works. From *The Archaeology of Knowledge* onward, discourse precedes the visible field he designates as "non-discursive." For Foucault, however, this suggests irreducibility, not a reduction. The nonrelation of words and images implies for Foucault an important cultural process of mutual grappling and capture.

23. Foucault tried to locate visibilities in his study of Roussel and isolate them in Manet, tracing an aesthetics of an era in a manner close to that of the French artist Robert Delaunay (1885–1941), argues Deleuze (*Foucault*, 52).
24. Deleuze, *Foucault*, 58.
25. This analysis composes the first chapter of Michel Foucault, *The Order of Things* (New York: Routledge, [1966] 2006).
26. Deleuze, *Foucault*, 53.
27. Jonathan Crary, *Techniques of the Observer: On Vision and Modernity in the Nineteenth Century* (Cambridge, MA: MIT Press, 1990), 132–36.
28. Richard Grusin and Jay David Bolter, *Remediation: Understanding New Media* (Cambridge, MA: MIT Press, 2000), 20.
29. Theodor Adorno quoted in Crary, *Techniques of the Observer*, 132.
30. Karl Marx, "Section 4 The Fetishism of Commodities and the Secret Thereof," in *A Critique of Political Economy: Vol I Part I—The Process of Capitalist Production*, ed. Friedrich Engels (New York: Cosimo Classics, [1867] 2007), 81.
31. Michel Foucault, "Introduction," in *Being the Recently Discovered Memoirs of a Nineteenth-Century French Hermaprodite (1838) by Herculine Barbin*, trans. Richard McDougall (New York: Pantheon, 1980), x. Foucault's study of Barbin's conjectured hermaphroditism recalls and to an extent reproduces the early entanglements of inversion theory relying on the notion of physical and psychic hermaphroditism that enfolds sexological histories of both transsexuality and homosexuality.
32. Foucault, "Introduction," ix, emphasis mine.
33. Foucault "Introduction," xiii.
34. Foucault, "Introduction," xiii. See also Arnold L. Davidson, "Sex and the Emergence of Sexuality," *Critical Inquiry* 14, no. 1 (1987): 16–48 for an extended treatment of Barbin's memoirs.
35. Foucault, "Introduction," xvii.
36. The shifting notion of sexual difference(s) is documented by Joanne Meyerowitz, *How Sex Changed: A History of Transsexuality in the United States* (Cambridge, MA: Harvard University Press, 2002). From the early twentieth century, she writes, "the concepts of sex change and sex-change surgery existed well before the word transsexual entered the medical parlance" (15).
37. Lisa Cartwright, *Screening the Body: Tracing Medicine's Visual Culture* (Minneapolis: University of Minnesota Press, 1995), 9.
38. Following Miriam Hansen and others, I name the essay more generally for brevity and because there are two English versions I refer to the second version by Walter Benjamin, "The Work of Art in the Age of Its Technological Reproducibility: Second Version (1936)," in *Walter Benjamin: Selected Writings, Vol. 3: 1935–1938*, ed. Howard Eiland and Michael W. Jennings (Cambridge, MA: Belknap Press, 2002), because this was the one Benjamin considered complete. I realize this nomination runs the risk of canonization; I hope the reader can forgive this unintended gesture.
39. W. Benjamin, "Work of Art," 114.
40. W. Benjamin, "Work of Art," 114–19.
41. Susan Buck-Morss, *The Dialectics of Seeing: Walter Benjamin and the Arcades Project* (Cambridge, MA: MIT Press, 1991), 81.

References

Barad, Karen. *Meeting the Universe Halfway: Quantum Physics and the Entanglement of Matter and Meaning*. Durham, NC: Duke University Press, 2007.

Bauman, Zygmunt. *Liquid Life*. London: Polity Press, 2005.

Benjamin, Walter. "The Work of Art in the Age of Its Technological Reproducibility: Second Version (1936)." In *Walter Benjamin: Selected Writings, Vol. 3: 1935–1938*, edited by Howard Eiland and Michael W. Jennings. Cambridge, MA: Belknap Press, 2002.

Billings, Dwight, and Thomas Urban. "The Socio-Medical Construction of Transsexualism: An Interpretation and Critique." *Social Problems* 29, no. 3 (1982): 266–82.

Buck-Morss, Susan. *The Dialectics of Seeing: Walter Benjamin and the Arcades Project*. Cambridge, MA: MIT Press, 1991.

Bullough, Vern L. "Magnus Hirschfeld, An Often Over-looked Pioneer." *Sexuality and Culture* 7, no. 1 (2003): 62–72.

Cartwright, Lisa. *Screening the Body: Tracing Medicine's Visual Culture*. Minneapolis: University of Minnesota Press, 1995.

Castle, Terry. "Phantasmagoria: Spectral Technology and the Metaphorics of Modern Reverie." *Critical Inquiry* 15, no. 1 (1988): 26–61.

Crary, Jonathan. *Techniques of the Observer: On Vision and Modernity in the Nineteenth Century*. Cambridge, MA: MIT Press, 1990.

Davidson, Arnold L. "Sex and the Emergence of Sexuality." *Critical Inquiry* 14, no. 1 (1987): 16–48.

Deleuze, Gilles. *Foucault*. Translated by Seán Hand. Minneapolis: University of Minnesota Press, [1986] 2000.

Drucker, Zackary, and A. L. Steiner. "Before/After 2009–Present." *Art F City* website, Section IMG MGMT, May 16, 2011. Accessed March 24, 2016. http://artfcity.com/2011/05/16/img-mgmt-z-drucker-a-l-steiner-beforeafter-2009-present.

Felski, Rita. "*Fin de Siècle, Fin de Sexe*: Transsexuality, Postmodernism, and the Death of History." *New Literary History* 27 (1996): 337–49.

Foucault, Michel. *The Archaeology of Knowledge*. Translated by A. M. Sheridan Smith. New York: Taylor & Francis, [1969] 2013.

Foucault, Michel. *The Birth of the Clinic: An Archaeology of Medical Perception*. Translated by A. M. Sheridan Smith. New York: Vintage, [1963] 1973.

Foucault, Michel. *Death and The Labyrinth: The World of Raymond Roussel*. Translated by Charles Ruas. London: Athlone Press, [1963] 1987.

Foucault, Michel. *Discipline and Punish: The Birth of the Prison*. Translated by Alan Sheridan. New York: Pantheon, 1977.

Foucault, Michel. "Introduction." In *Being the Recently Discovered Memoirs of a Nineteenth-Century French Hermaprodite (1838)* by Herculine Barbin, translated by Richard McDougall, vi–xvii. New York: Pantheon, 1980.

Foucault, Michel. *The Order of Things*. New York: Routledge, [1966] 2006.

Freeman, Elizabeth. *Time Binds: Queer Temporalities, Queer Histories*. Durham, NC: Duke University Press, 2010.

Garbasz, Yishay. "Installation Process of Becoming at the Busan Biennale 2010." YouTube. Accessed February 20, 2016. https://www.youtube.com/watch?v=F5diBtcul_4.

Gaudreault, André. *Film and Attraction: From Kinematography to Cinema*. Translated by Timothy Barnard. Chicago: University of Illinois Press, [2008] 2011).

Gorton, R. Nick. "Transgender as Mental Illness: Nosology, Social Justice, and the Tarnished Golden Mean." In *The Transgender Studies Reader 2*, edited by Susan Stryker and Aren Aizura, 644–52. New York: Routledge, [2007] 2013.

Grusin Richard, and Jay David Bolter. *Remediation: Understanding New Media*. Cambridge, MA: MIT Press, 2000.

Gunning, Tom. "Illusions Past and Future: The Phantasmagoria and Its Specters". Paper presented at the Refresh! First International Conference on the Histories of Art, Science and Technology, 2004. Consulted via Media Art History. Accessed March 24, 2016. http://pl02.donau-uni.ac.at/jspui/handle/10002/296/.

Halberstam, Judith. "F2M: The Making of Female Masculinity." In *The Lesbian Postmodern*, edited by Laura Doan, 210–28. New York: Columbia University Press, 1994.

Hausman, Bernice. *Changing Sex: Transsexualism, Technology, and the Idea of Gender*. Durham, NC: Duke University Press, 1995.

Klöppel, Ulrike. "Who Has the Right to Change Gender Status? Drawing Boundaries between Inter- and Transsexuality." In *Critical Intersex*, edited by M. Morgan Holmes, 171–90. Farnham, U.K.: Ashgate, 2009.

Mannoni, Laurent. *The Great Art of Light and Shadow*. Exeter, UK: University of Exeter Press, 2000.

Marx, Karl. "Section 4 The Fetishism of Commodities and the Secret Thereof." In *A Critique of Political Economy: Vol. I Part I—The Process of Capitalist Production*, translated by Friedrich Engels. New York: Cosimo Classics, [1867] 2007.

Meyerowitz, Joanne. *How Sex Changed: A History of Transsexuality in the United States*. Cambridge, MA: Harvard University Press, 2002.

Prosser, Jay. *Second Skins: The Body Narratives of Transsexuality*. New York: Columbia University Press, 1998.

Puar, Jasbir K. "Bodies with New Organs: Becoming Trans, Becoming Disabled." *Social Text* 33, no. 3 (2015): 45–75.

Spade, Dean. *Normal Life: Administrative Violence, Critical Trans Politics and the Limits of Law*. Durham, NC: Duke University Press, 2015.

Steiner, A. L., and Zackary Drucker. "Before/After 2009–Present." *Art F City* website, Section IMG MGMT, May 16, 2011. Accessed March 24, 2016. http://artfcity.com/2011/05/16/img-mgmt-z-drucker-a-l-steiner-beforeafter-2009-present.

Storr, Merl, and Jay Prosser. "Introduction to Part III Transsexuality and Bisexuality." In *Sexology Uncensored: The Documents of Sexual Science*, edited by Lucy Bland and Laura Doan, 75–77. Chicago: Chicago University Press, 1998.

Stryker, Susan "My Words to Victor Frankenstein Above the Village of Chamounix: Performing Transgender Rage." In *The Transgender Studies Reader*, edited by Susan Stryker and Stephen Whittle, 244–56. New York: Routledge, [1994] 2006.

Stryker, Susan. *Transgender History*. Berkeley: Seal Press, 2008.

10 Remembering in Art: The Horizontal and the Vertical

SIRI HUSTVEDT

A couple of years ago, I walked into a museum, saw a still life on the wall, and, before I had a single articulate thought, the name "Chardin" jumped to mind. The particular canvas was new to me, but its physiognomy, if you will, was not. I was seeing the face of an old friend who had changed a bit but not beyond recognition. How does memory affect looking at a work of art? Like so many simple questions, this one is difficult to answer. Memory is repetition; a thing from the past recurs in the present. Without repetition, we couldn't recognize anything. "The dialectic of repetition is easy," writes Søren Kierkegaard's pseudonym Constantin Constantius, "for that which is repeated has been—otherwise it could not be repeated—but the very fact that it has been makes the repetition into something new."[1] Kierkegaard's *Repetition* is a bewildering text, but Constantius makes a complex distinction between repetition and recollection, which I will borrow somewhat recklessly for my own purposes. Recollection looks backward; repetition forward.

The "new" Chardin canvas must have unearthed my earlier encounters with the painter's work, but I had no need to think about them before I made the identification. Most of my remembering was unconscious and therefore cannot be broken down into a sequential process I can analyze. My perception of the canvas and the feeling that accompanied it seemed instantly to generate the proper noun. Of course, I have misrecognized art, too. I have seen what I believe is one painter's canvas and discovered it belongs to another or, upon returning to a work, I have realized that I had left out an entire figure or object.

Memory is bound up with time, a concept so ferociously difficult to explicate it remains a torture to philosophers. Conscious memories appear to be a feature of our reflective self-consciousness, knowing that we know, that trick of seeing ourselves through the eyes of someone else. We can consciously remember in images and words what was—we have a mental representation of ourselves in a place and at an event sometime in the past—but we can also imagine what might be in the future. I am not interested here in the time of clocks and calendars or in the time of theoretical physics but rather in the felt rhythms of before and after and the strange reality of a present, which cannot be a vanishing point in time, an impossibly small temporal unit, but a continuum in which the represented past is pulled into the present in anticipation of the future. William James's idea of the stream of consciousness, Henri Bergson's memory as *duration*, and Edmund Husserl's *retention* and *protension* are different versions of this retaining, anticipatory phenomenological present. Memory haunts the present as a ghost of the past, a double of what was, happening again in an extended now, but it is always distinct from immediate perceptual reality. When we look at a work of art we are always remembering, even if we are not at all aware of the shaping memories that make our vision possible, but we are also always projecting from that past into an extended present and future.

The spatial conception of time in Western culture is most often a horizontal line or arrow moving from left to right. We imagine a narrative unfolding in this direction. Events are felt as happening in a left-to-right motion, and research has shown that in artworks figures with greater agency or power usually appear to the left in pictorial space—a phenomenon that was first noticed in a neurological patient who suffered from aphasia. Although he confused subject and object in his speech, he could clarify his meanings by drawing. He consistently placed the narrative agent or subject to the left in pictorial space.[2] It was hypothesized that this placement might have to do with the brain's hemispheres and the specializations of right and left, that perhaps we are anatomically designed to see the world's action in left-to-right terms.

But the fact that in Arabic and Israeli speakers the directional bias is reversed, right to left, and that it appears not to exist in either illiterate speakers or preliterate children has made this theory untenable.[3] The spatial agency bias directly echoes the direction of reading and writing, which suggests that the scanning habits of literacy have fundamentally shaped our perception, a striking example of how linguistic culture shapes the way we see and interpret images, not only time as a horizontal left-to-right movement in space, but its effect on how we configure *power* in space. In Western portraiture it has been noted that faces are more likely to be looking to the left than to the right, and that portraits of men are more likely to be turned to the left than portraits of women, perhaps because the masculine, not the feminine, character is conceived of as "forward looking." Anne Maass and her colleagues looked at 120 Adam and Eve images and found Adam to the left of Eve in 62 percent of the pictures.[4] One could certainly argue that in the Paradise adventure, Eve is more of an agent than Adam, but in these images power trumps story.

Whichever direction your time arrow points, if you try to lift time out of space, you will find yourself confounded. Without the metaphor we lose the concept of personal temporality altogether. Interestingly, it is impossible to have a conscious autobiographical memory without a spatial configuration. The remembered self must be *somewhere*: I remember the picnic by the lake. It must have been 1965. I was ten. In order to remember the events of the picnic, I have to ground it. In harmony with the great traditions of artificial mnemonic systems, those palaces and rooms that root words to a place so they can be remembered, conscious personal memory does not exist without space. Space anchors time in memory.

In the working notes for his unfinished *The Visible and the Invisible*, Maurice Merleau-Ponty proposed an idea of vertical time, a radical break with earlier philosophies, one he related to what he called "wild being," *être sauvage*. What is vertical time? It is surely preliterate time, a time that stays with us even after we are thinking about ourselves thinking and recording those thoughts on paper. Vertical time is not bound purely to self-conscious reflection or to any Cartesian idea of the mental but to a time of embodied animal being, to prepersonal, preconceptual, prereflective time, a time human beings share with mice. "Then past and present," Merleau-Ponty wrote, "are *Ineinander*, each enveloping-enveloped—and that itself is the flesh."[5] Time in this understanding is not something we are "in." It is not a line forward or an ongoing tick of the clock, and it cannot be separated from our perception of the world. The hard lines usually drawn between a body and what is outside it soften in this idea of enveloped and enveloping "flesh."

It is not easy to explicate precisely what Merleau-Ponty meant by this verticality and flesh, nor how he would have developed the idea had he lived, but it is interesting to tip time's direction and keep verticality in mind in relation to the problem of memory and perception in relation to artworks. The philosopher understood that all species are linked. He called these connections *interanimality*. Learning and memory are part of the lives of even simple invertebrate creatures. The sea slug, Aplysia, with only ten thousand neurons, has been the object of many studies, most famously in the memory research of Eric Kandel.[6] The slug will never call up mental images of last week's crawl toward a stone, but sensitization and habituation, primitive forms of learning and remembering, are part of its life.

Human beings are far more complex than sea slugs, but we are their relatives as remembering beings nevertheless. My ability to recognize a Chardin canvas that is new to me through earlier perceptions is not a passive act but a creative one, which relies on memory, most of which is unconscious. Despite increasing knowledge about the brain's visual system, heated debates (both scientific and philosophical) go on about how the human mind perceives and remembers what is out there in the world. There is growing evidence that unconscious inference influences how we see. "Unconscious inference" was a term used by the biophysicist Hermann von Helmholtz, who argued that vision is determined by prior experience.[7] We perceive the world through perceptual repetitions, repetitions that become expectations over time. We fill in what is missing in our perception with inferences from the past. Without such inferences, I could not have recognized that canvas as one by Chardin. There are scientists who argue that the role of our embodied brains in perception is essentially an economic, conservative one and that perceptual inferences help to minimize surprises from the environment.[8] Whether this can stand as a global theory of perception remains open.

What is certain is the past lives on in the bodily present, often without our awareness, and its regular perceptual rhythms and repetitions help shape our organized vision. Research on change blindness demonstrates that many of us fail to notice even dramatic alterations in a visual scene, whether the image is fixed or moving. For example, one actor replaces another in a film, and we haven't a clue that a shift has been made.[9] Similarly, studies on inattentional blindness have shown that if people have a task to perform, counting the number of times a ball changes hands during a game, for example, many of them will miss an unexpected intrusion, such as a woman strolling calmly through the proceedings with an umbrella or a person in a gorilla suit.[10] Even more remarkable is the phenomenon of blindsight, discovered in patients who have lesions in their primary visual cortex and insist they can see nothing. Despite the fact that they have no visual experience, they are able to discriminate objects, colors, and spatial configurations far above chance levels. In other words, blindsight patients can see but they have no conscious awareness of seeing.[11] These forms of blindness are not irrelevant to looking at art. To what degree do we *conventionalize* the images in front of us because we see the patterns we expect to see? How much do we miss? How much of vision is stereotyped? Do we always quash surprise to the degree that it is possible without even knowing we are doing it? And how much visual information do we take in without being at all conscious of it?

Much has been written about the prospective or predictive brain in neuroscience, which may help explain not just gaps in our perception but our notoriously unreliable autobiographical memories. We all know that each person who was present at that family picnic recalls the get-together differently. It is even possible that Uncle Fred, who did not attend the picnic, has vivid memories of that sunny afternoon by the lake and its sensational event: the near drowning of Cousin Thomas and his rescue by the heroic Aunt Angelina. Uncle Fred's certainty that he remembers Thomas in extremis and Angelina's daring dive underscores the contagious nature of stories (he heard all about it), as well as the vivid mental imagery that may accompany them. Imaginary and real events merge in a highly promiscuous manner in the human mind. Nevertheless, Uncle Fred's false memory might make him more alert to struggling swimmers in the future, or at least that is how the evolutionary story about why we have such faulty memories might be told. What matters is not that we see every detail in the visual field but rather that we see what is most salient. Perfect recollections of our pasts may be less important than using its lessons as flexible repetitions in the future.

Merleau-Ponty spoke of the perceiving body as a vehicle for "I can." In 1952, the neuropsychologist Roger Sperry also linked the mental to the motor. "An analysis of our current thinking will show that it tends to suffer generally from a failure to view mental activities in their proper relation, or even in any relation, to motor behavior." He further argues, "Perception is basically an implicit preparation to respond. Its function is to prepare the organism for adaptive action."[12] Perception involves all our senses, but we are so used to thinking of vision as the sense of senses, the supreme form in which the world is made available to us, that the idea that seeing is intimately bound up with bodily motion, that it evolved to help us run or jump or attack, may seem a bit odd. But, as Melvyn Goodale puts it, "Visual systems first evolved not to enable animals to see, but to provide distal sensory control of their movements. Vision as 'sight' is a relative newcomer to the evolutionary landscape."[13] Goodale and his collaborator, David Milner, have hypothesized that there are two distinct visual pathways in the brain—the dorsal and ventral streams. The dorsal stream, which evolved first, informs motor behaviors—vision for bodily action. The ventral stream, which evolved later, informs cognition. This is vision for perception, one that establishes a catalogue of visual representations of the world, which allows us to identify and classify objects and events. What does this have to do with art? Images inspire active responses. The experience of art viewing is not just a visual one; it is muscular and emotional as well.

Perception involves unconscious kinesthetic memories, separable from our vivid or vague mental images of a picnic remembered differently by each member of the family, images that are referred to as declarative, explicit, or conscious memories. Implicit memories include motor-sensory, procedural memories, what Merleau-Ponty, among others, called "habit" learning. Walking, talking, swimming, reading, and writing are skills we once struggled to master but that through repetition have become unreflective. As the spatial agency bias demonstrates, however, such unconscious habits may become essential to our conceptions of time, space, narrative, and social power. The Russian neurologist A. R. Luria coined a beautiful phrase for these learned but automatic motions. He called them "kinetic melodies."[14] A person can lose the ability to retain long-term autobiographical memory without losing the ability to learn new visuomotor skills, as was made clear in the famous case of H.M., whom Brenda Milner studied for years. H.M. suffered from terrible epileptic seizures, submitted to an operation, which stopped the seizures, but he sustained damage to the medial temporal lobe of his brain. His perception, intelligence, and short-term memory (the ability to retain information for seconds) were intact, but he forgot what had happened to him soon after it occurred. He had lost long-term memory. He did, however, learn and retain the ability to perform a complex mirror drawing skill. What he forgot was his experience of learning it.[15]

We see in order to move, but we also vicariously mirror movements we see in others. In *The Expression of the Emotions in Man and Animals* (1872), Charles Darwin notes that some human actions "seem to be due to imitation or some sort of sympathy." He mentions throat clearing among audience members when a singer goes hoarse and the fact that "at leaping matches, as the performer makes his spring, many of the spectators, generally men and boys, move their feet."[16] Darwin was fascinated by imitation and the "social instincts" in both animals and human beings and regarded sympathy as crucial to collective life, a trait he believed was increased through natural selection. Both the artist and the art viewer relate to the work of art with forms of sympathetic connection.

Neuroscience research has demonstrated this human reflectivity in vicarious movement, sensation, and emotion. When we look at another person, see an image of another person, or even read about another person doing or feeling something, we participate in that doing or feeling automatically and subliminally. Neural systems in the premotor and somatosensory cortex are activated in us that allow for an implicit understanding of what is happening to the other person. There continue to be debates about neuronal mirror systems. Much remains to be known, but empirical infant research, along with research on our fellow mammals, confirms that we are social beings oriented toward others from the beginning of our lives and that our development is predicated on that essential bond. My philosophical leanings have caused me to embrace an embodied, motor-sensory-affective relational mammalian reality, of which we human beings are a part.

This virtual connection to the other is embedded in how we see art and to what we understand as the imagination itself. The art historian David Freedberg and the neuroscientist Vittorio Gallese have written about embodied simulation and empathetic experiences in art viewing and argued that this preconceptual, somatic experience plays a vital role in our responses to works of art.[17] A now well-known fMRI—brain scan—study on professional dancers found that this neural participation was stronger when viewers watched movements they had themselves mastered, a finding that suggests learning, which becomes unconscious motor or habit memories, in this case of specific, highly complex gestures, sharpens the self-other link in mirroring others.[18]

I have repeatedly stressed in my writing about visual art that the relation we have to it is a form of inter-subjectivity. It is not a relation between person and thing, between me and a painted silver cup on a canvas. Chardin's silver cup is humanized by the simple fact that he not only produced the work but the gestures of his body remain a part of it. His touch becomes mine in viewing. The artwork is, of course, not fully a "you" but rather a "quasi you," and I engage with it as the other's creation, a thing impregnated with his or her being. It does not matter if the work is figurative or abstract; my relation to it is a sensual, emotional, and intellectual connection between a me and something like a you rather than a utilitarian one—between me and an it. The real cup on my kitchen counter is not a quasi you. It becomes a temporary extension of my hand when I drink from it. The word coined by the psychologist J. J. Gibson is "affordance." The sight of the cup acts as an affordance for my action.[19] Seeing a real cup affords me the chance to drink, and the reach of my arm will secure the sip or gulp.

Chardin's cup, however, is a radiant signifier of cup-ness that will never serve me as a real cup would, but it is also suffused with the emotion of human movement no actual cup in the world has. It beckons to me as an image of a graspable thing that is locked in the imaginary realm created by another person and delineated by its frame. Part of my relation to the unattainable cup is my recognition of cups, my memory of cups and drinks of various potable liquids, as well as the motor memory of the gestures involved in drinking. It is peculiar that a glass, a couple of nuts, three apples, a copper bowl, and a spoon can produce in me a feeling of tenderness for other human beings, persons who do not appear in the canvas at all, but this is the truth. The canvas from 1769 carries within it the ghostly touch of an artist long dead; my perception of it includes his motion and awakens in me my own history of felt touch.

Works of the imagination in all the arts are created from and perceived through unconscious corporeal processes—implicit memory and mirroring—that are never symbolically represented, and in the learned bodily rhythms and repetitions we call skill. Furthermore, a motor skill such as writing from left to right accompanied by the subject-precedes-object convention in English may be used metaphorically to rein-force a cultural stereotype about masculinity as active subject and femininity as passive object. These learned patterns are also made from rhythms of exchange between us that become predictive of feeling. The child who learns that his howling will earn him a slap eventually falls silent. Feelings are conscious, but feeling responses are embedded in an organism's past. They are repetitions of earlier sensations and feelings that have good and bad values, which guide our judgments in life but are not conscious thoughts.

We are not reasoning machines. We reason and judge with emotion. We also know that we remember what we care about. Emotion consolidates and reconsolidates memories in animals and human beings.[20] Emotional events stay alive in us, usually for better, sometimes for worse. They may be conscious or unconscious. We remember what moves us so we may act to protect ourselves or repeat a pleasure in the future. I remember Chardin's pictures because in the past they moved me and, when I saw the new canvas, I recognized the repetition of a particular form of tender melancholy, a feeling I like. When a work of art leaves me cold, I forget it.

Before art became art, before aesthetics was a discipline, before museums and galleries and auction houses, people were making paintings, totems, and myriad other objects that radiated religious or mythical meaning, forms invested with divine or demonic power within a particular culture. It is gener-ally agreed that cave paintings, such as the ones at Lascaux, were made for religious, not aesthetic, purposes. Transubstantiation in the Eucharist is an excellent example of the ordinary miraculously infused with divinity—wafer and wine as body and blood of God ingested by the believer. Images of various kinds continue to be animated by the sacred, the magical, or the merely enchanted in tribal, religious, but also in secular culture. There is surely an argument to be made that the gleaming images of movie stars, athletes, billionaires, and various other beloved (or hated) cultural figures have been invested with something more than human, that the collective imagination has imbued them with an almost supernatural quality not granted the rest of us plebeians. We do not treat blank canvases and tubes of oil paint with reverence, but we do regard certain works of art as sanctified by another kind of memory: collective memory. Some works of art have been invested with a kind of holiness. The names da Vinci, Rembrandt, van Gogh, and Picasso have become signs of artistic grandeur in the West. The artists' names and their works are treated as quasi-deities and, when not priceless, are colossally expensive.

My response to Chardin's silver cup has an animistic quality, one triggered by an embodied simulation of the strokes and touches in the canvas and a corresponding felt empathy, not for the cup, apples, copper bowl, or nuts, but for what I perceive as the delicate, almost unbearably delicate, movements expressed in the canvas itself. But Chardin's cup is not a cup, to rephrase the sentence inscribed in Magritte's famous pipe painting, and the pleasure I derive from the painted cup is at least in part about its *distance* from me, its presence in a parallel world of representation I cannot reach. The mental image of my special coffee mug in my memory is not the cup itself, nor is my fantasy of a cup I hope to receive for my birthday. Art always partakes of symbolic alienation. In her introduction to a book by Ernst Cassirer, whose work influenced her own, the American philosopher Susanne Langer articulates the difference: "In its symbolic image, the experience is conceived, instead of just physiologically remembered."[21] The distinction is crucial. There is a remembered preconceptual past in our moving, perceiving bodies and a remembered subjective conceptual reality that frames our experience symbolically. One might conceive of the preconceptual as vertical animal memory and the symbolic as horizontal, serial memory that is linked to our language and literacy, one that has produced an arrow of time.

In *Feeling and Form*, Langer writes, "Whatever brute fact may be, our experience of it bears the stamp of language."[22] It is hard indeed to return to a time before we could speak, to perceive the world prior to its dissection by words, to enter wild being and vertical time because boundaries, it must be remembered, are often inscribed by the concepts and words we use to erase the ambiguities of overlapping realities. Once we can speak and write, our kinetic music changes. Our spatial views are altered, but we mustn't view concepts and words, spoken or written, as entities suspended over our bodies or lodged exclusively in our heads; they are in us and of us, part of our rhythmical, felt bodily existence and expressive reality. Again and again, I have set my alarm for six o'clock to make sure I will get up in time for the plane I have to take that morning. Again and again, I have slept solidly and woken an instant before the alarm rings. Even my sleeping body can count and somehow remember that artificial interval we call an *hour*. Culture becomes matter—acquired knowledge resides in soma.

In his mostly fragmentary writings in the early twentieth century Aby Warburg tried to make sense of the life and felt movement of static images through a form of cultural memory that made its appearance in what he called *Pathosformel*, recurring emotive images that covered, according to Warburg, everything from "helpless passive absorption to murderous frenzy and all the intervening moments."[23] He was particularly fascinated by how images of the pagan past were revived in Renaissance art that depicted Christian as well as mythological themes. Drawing on Nietzsche's poles of the Dionysian and Apollonian, Jakob Burckhardt's reading of ancient Greek life, Robert Vischer's *Einfühlung* (empathy), Cassirer's idea of myth and symbolic forms, Ewald Hering's biology of ancestral memory, Darwin's theory of the emotions, and the zoologist Richard Semon's theory of the memory engram, Warburg understood the repetition of these forms as a kind of *Nachleben* or afterlife, the survival of primitive, ecstatic, often dangerous impulses into the artistic present.

Following Hering, Warburg believed in a biological transmission of memory, a hereditary unconscious material memory that linked all species and all matter. As Andrea Pinotti points out, Warburg's engram "refer[s] to a moment of accumulation of an energetic charge deriving from a sufficiently intense and often repeated event capable to inscribe itself indelibly in the collective memory as a material track."[24] In other words, the idea of heredity in Warburg's thought is subsumed by the idea of memory. From the point of view of Kierkegaard's Constantin Constantius, Warburg's returns are not recollections but *repetitions*, vivid renewals of forms of wild being that change over time. For Warburg, they were transmitted by the artist and apprehended by the viewer as an electrical emotional charge, and these shock variations are less personal than prepersonal, part of a larger human story rather than a single or particular human story. The notion of collective memory as *biological* is controversial, of course. Lamarck's idea that parental experiences or any acquired characteristics can be passed on to offspring has long been regarded as an embarrassing wrong turn in science. Jung's collective unconscious has suffered a similar fate as a "mystical" notion.

Darwin, who is nothing if not current, proposed another form of hereditary "memory" through natural selection: the ancestral past is alive in our present traits. Semantic issues become pivotal in this context. Some evolutionary psychologists explain just about every human propensity, including popular taste in art, as inherited from our Pleistocene ancestors. These proclivities are present in naturally selected mind modules that are supposed to determine everything from male and female behavior to the kind of landscape paintings most Americans prefer. In *The Blank Slate*, the evolutionary psychologist Steven Pinker argues, "The dominant theories of elite art and art criticism in the twentieth century grew out of a militant denial of human nature. One legacy is ugly, baffling, and insulting art. The other is pretentious and unintelligible scholarship."[25] There is plenty of bad art in every period and plenty of bad writing about art, too, but Pinker approaches aesthetics with a hammer, pounding away at the preening fops and snooty critics who have tromped on the aesthetic preferences of the average guy, which are decided by evolution, not mass marketing.

This is no doubt a popular position to take, but it tells us little about what is nature and what is culture in the experience of looking at art. From Pinker's perspective, those of us who love Henri Matisse or Alberto Giacometti or Joan Mitchell are actively suppressing our true natures, natures that apparently crave soothing calendar landscapes with deer and heroic figures in them. Crude thinking is alive and well, and it is crude from a scientific, philosophical, and aesthetic position to argue that this fixed human "nature" tells us that Modernism is both bad and *unnatural*. It is not crude, however, to ask questions about the human urge to represent and symbolize the world, nor is it crude to ask how this urge is reconfigured over time, from culture to culture, or to ask how prereflective wild mammalian being and reflective symbolic forms are both involved in the experience of art.

There is no question in my mind that we share emotions with other animals, but how would one, for example, parse nature and culture in the pleasure I feel as I look at a painting by Chardin? As an evolved creature with a complex, creative visual system and a literate citizen of the United States, who therefore unconsciously reads time in paintings from left to right, but who also has myriad personal memories of paintings of many kinds, who has read and thought about visual art for years, I am obviously a physiological amalgam of all these factors. Can one actually isolate the natural from the cultural "components" of my pleasure?

Warburg's memory science was of his time, and memory, like many words, has shifting meanings. In the nineteenth century it could encompass broad notions of inherited traits and ideas. It is fascinating to note that in the field of epigenetics there is mounting evidence that environmental stress on an animal creates molecular changes after DNA replication. The nucleotide sequence of the genes is not directly affected but gene expression or suppression is.[26] Such changes, it appears, can be inherited, not forever, but for more than one generation. In science, old ideas have a way of sneaking back in new forms.

Warburg's conception of time and memory was not linear. It might be described as vertical or funnel shaped. The extreme poles of archaic human experience represented in bodily gestures he identified as recurring in artworks and other images, including stamps, postcards, and advertisements, are formulaic expressions of extreme human states of orgiastic mania, traumatic fear, and severe melancholy or depression, states in which there is no room for reflective thought or distance, no distinction between ego and world.

For Warburg, wild being had a terrifying quality. The distance created by symbols was precisely what constituted civilization and culture. "When this interval becomes the basis of artistic production," he wrote, "the conditions have been fulfilled for this consciousness of distance to achieve an enduring social function which, in its rhythmical change between absorption in its object and detached restraint, signifies the oscillation between a cosmology of images and one of signs; its adequacy or failure as an instrument of mental orientation signifies the fate of human culture."[27] In other words, the stakes are high.

In another revealing fragment, Warburg wrote, "The detachment of the subject from the object which establishes the zone for abstract thought originates in the experience of the cutting of the umbilical cord."[28] The dialectic here is between a wild fusion without differentiation between mother and infant during pregnancy and the distance that arrives with separation and eventually self-conscious reflection. Warburg's umbilical cord is at once literal and metaphorical. For the fetus, the umbilical connection is a lifeline that is cut once the newborn is literally separated from its mother's body. A redemptive, metaphorical "space" or "distance" arrives when the child is able to reflect on herself and the world around her. Warburg believed that *Denkraum*, or "thought room" (another spatial metaphor), acted as a vehicle of rescue from drowning in the other. This opening or distance between subject and object created by symbols rescues a person from ecstatic and/or traumatic bodily feeling, in which there is no distinction between me and you or between me and the world, an idea that has strong psychoanalytic resonance. Freud believed the primal sexual drive could be sublimated in cultural and artistic forms.

A pure example of preconceptual memory without *Denkraum* is the traumatic flashback, a particular kind of memory relevant to Warburg's thought. The flashback *feels like* the eruption of a horrific past event in the present—a motor-sensory and sometimes visual "reenactment" of experience. While it is happening, it is as if the horror is *happening again*. It is not a repetition that is renewed or changed; rather, it is an identical experience, which means there is no felt sequential horizontal reality, no forward or backward, no linear quality at all. Unlike an autobiographical memory for which I have mental images and a story, there is no "back then" in the flashback. Time *feels* vertical: a volcanic upward surge, which is wholly unmediated by symbols. After a car accident, I had flashbacks four nights in a row in my sleep. Then, after many years of no recurrence, I had another, a deafening, terrifying explosion that shocked me awake from my sleep. I was certain the house had been bombed or was collapsing on top of me, that a massive attack or wholly unexpected earthquake had struck New York City. It wasn't until I had reassured myself that both I and the house were intact that I realized it must have been another flashback of the now remote accident. The words "car accident" and "flashback" had to be applied to the nameless experience minutes later, however. They were not present during the experience, which did not signify car crash but what can only be described as bodily horror. Whether the flashback is a perfect repetition of an earlier event or not (I don't know how this could be proved), it is a form of memory unlike others and, while it is happening, it has no context, no language, no before or after. It is literally a memory without distance or any time beyond the present. It occurs without reflective symbolic thought room. It is not framed. The flashback is conscious, but it is inscribed in bodily systems outside of consciousness.

Every work of art has an aesthetic frame, which procures a form of *Denkraum* or conscious reflection for the viewer, reader, or listener, no matter how traumatic or frightening the subject. In religion, ritual and taboo provide for an orderly unfolding of events, as well as dissections of space that insulate the practitioner from the power of the sacred. The liturgy is a sequence of precise repetitions that organize the time of the church service according to a prescribed order. The Jewish *mikvah*, the monthly purification ritual for women, turns on a menstruation taboo and is subject to specific laws that define the time of immersion and the structure of the bath in space. For example, the *mikvah* must contain at least two hundred gallons of rainwater and it must not be portable. Representations and symbols alienate and protect us as much as they seduce and lure us into their alternative or parallel space.

A now famous canvas by Artemisia Gentileschi of Judith decapitating Holofernes that was painted sometime between 1614 and 1620, and that hangs in the Uffizi in Florence, presents the viewer with gruesome and arguably traumatic content. Warburg searched figures in art for recurring emotional gestures that leapt across centuries and periods, what Giorgio Agamben called "an indissoluble intertwining of an emotional charge and an iconographic formula" in which form and content are indistinguishable.[29] I am not arguing that Gentileschi's canvas of a beheading represents the return of a pathos formula. I am using it as a test case for memory and perception, a way to demonstrate that memory, expectation, the unconscious and conscious, the biological and the cultural, and vertical and horizontal axes of time collide in us as spectators. (The image can be readily seen online.)

Decapitation is not an archaic form of violence. Those of us who live far from war nevertheless have immediate access to the grisly beheadings of ISIS on the Internet, should we choose to view the documentary footage. As spectators to such horrors, we might be haunted forever, but the films cannot kill us. We see the violence occur in miniature; our vision of it is literally framed by a screen, and yet *knowing that the victims are real people*, not actors, increases our terror. The three people in this Baroque canvas are flat painted figures that do not move. They "live" inside a frame. Still, this image of a woman beheading a man is a terrible one, and embodied mirroring is at work in us, an "as if" kinetic participation in the scene that elicits, at least in me, both fear and fascination. The woman's braced forearms, her strong grip on the sword with one hand, and the fist she makes with the other, which is pressed so hard into the man's forehead that she has pushed the skin of his face into a fold of wrinkles over his eye, and the way she leans back from the blood that spurts from the severed neck of her victim, perhaps to protect her clothing, all create a startling feeling of a fixed, frozen, eternal *now*.

But I am also feeling the painter's kinetic melodies in the paint itself, the gestures of intense or precise movement, an expressive style in a delimited space that pulls me into an I and quasi-you relation, and it is in this encounter that the image's meaning is created, a meaning I may have to struggle to articulate, but if I look long enough and hard enough, the self/other distinction begins to blur. Doesn't the canvas, perceived by my remembering body, virtually enact the represented bodies I see? Doesn't this further summon Merleau-Ponty's evocation of Husserl's *Ineinander*, a back-and-forth or entwining relation, in which the thing outside is also the thing inside me? I ask myself, for example, what the expression on the murderous woman's face means, and, asking it, I am shaken by past feelings of rage and vengeance and seem to recognize in her countenance the cold purpose of hate. The past reappears in me, not as a sequential horizontal march of autobiographical events, but as a nameless vertical eruption of emotional memories I cannot identify, but which nevertheless permits me to step back when needed, to reflect within the safety of the aesthetic frame.

The story of Judith beheading Holofernes was rendered many times at different moments in the narrative. In the deuterocanonical text, Judith seeks out the enemy general, Holofernes. Enchanted by her beauty and with seduction on his mind, he invites her into his tent, drinks too much, and, as he lies in a drunken haze, she cuts off his head and saves the Jewish people from the Assyrian threat. We are therefore looking at a heroine, not a monster, and remembering the story will necessarily affect your reading of the canvas. But stories, too, whether they are true or fictitious, are learned and differently remembered, and their forms inhabit us corporeally as a left-to-right direction, for example, but also as rhythms of tension, crisis, and resolution, evoked by the words we have heard or read. Stories enter and reside in us, bias our expectations, infect our perceptions, and help us decode what we see. The story is the invisible surround for the painting. We know what happened before and we know what comes next.

Compare Gentileschi's canvas to one painted earlier by Caravaggio in 1599. I instantly read this picture from left to right because its long rectangular form is divided exactly in two—with one figure dominating the left side of the canvas and two others dominating the right—so it invites a conventional narrative movement from left to right. In fact, the only thing that brings the two sides of the canvas together is the dark red drapery that hangs in space between the left and right spaces, but there is a bit more fabric on the right. If we consider the spatial agency bias for a moment, it is clear that the person being acted upon (the victim) is on the left and the actor (the murderer) is on the right, a violation of the subject-comes-before-object grammatical structure through which we have come to read space.

Gentileschi's Judith canvas does not conform to the spatial agency bias either. Judith is to the left of Holofernes, but she looms over him. The strength of her sword's motion is evident in her taut arms. I, the spectator, am witness to the fact that the general's head in the immediate foreground will soon fall from his body and drop to the floor if it is not instantly gripped by the heroine. Unlike the Caravaggio painting, the narrative in the Gentileschi painting is one of immediate, terrible violence, produced in part by its spatial configuration of verticality. Judith and her active collaborator, the maidservant, have subdued the man beneath them, which creates not a linear sense of movement from one to the other, as in reading a text, but a disruption of that sequential temporality.

Verticality, unfamiliar as a metaphor for time, is a conventional signifier for rank, power, and worth, so deeply engrained in us that it is inescapable. It finds its way into countless binaries, mind over body, male over female, or the simple fact that feeling high is better than feeling low. I would argue that in the Caravaggio image, the placement of Holofernes to the left, which causes us to read the picture from left to right, undermines the obvious fact that he is the victim in the canvas. He may be a victim, but he's a potent one. What captivates me in this canvas is *solely* the agonized face of Holofernes, which I find extraordinary and awful. It is he who is the painting's emotional "agent," the doer. It is his suffering the viewer feels, not Judith's violence. In stark contrast to her victim, this pretty, benign, delicate Judith appears to have flown in from another world of feminine futility. She does not look as if she could slice a loaf of bread much less a man's neck, and the expression on her face is one of pique and minor discomfort, not rage or determination. Without the presence of Holofernes, one might surmise that she had just spilled wine on someone at a dinner party. The old crone beside her is less an accomplice in assassination than a voyeur.

Artemisia Gentileschi was a renowned and controversial painter in her day, but after she died, her work languished in obscurity until it was rediscovered in the twentieth century. She is now regarded as a brilliant painter of the period, but the fact that she was a woman, that she was the daughter of a prominent painter, Orazio Gentileschi, and that she was raped by another painter, Agostino Tassi, in her father's house, which resulted in a public trial, the records of which are extant, are all part of her complex artistic legacy. Caravaggio was also controversial, rumored to be homosexual, frequently in trouble with the law, and an artist who influenced both Gentileschis, father and daughter.

These biographical facts are part of what some in science call semantic memory. A fact, such as *Helsinki is the capital of Finland*, is not personal to me, and I don't need a spatial mental image of the city to call it up. But semantic memories may become the center of emotionally charged interpretations of all manner of things nevertheless. For years, art historians ascribed paintings, even those *signed by* Artemisia Gentileschi, to her father, especially when they were particularly good. Some scholars have seen Artemisia Gentileschi's *Judith* as the image of revenge for the artist's rape or "defloration," as it was then conceived. Others say no, this is a misinterpretation; we cannot impose our contemporary ideas about rape onto past events. She was a creature of the period and is shaped by its discourses, which do not belong to us.[30] No doubt both stories carry some truth. Gentileschi also defied the conventions of her time by painting subjects usually forbidden to women. Her version of *Judith Beheading Holofernes* shocked her contemporaries and has continued to shock onlookers ever since. The electric charge of the painting has not died.

It seems to me that Gentileschi may have wanted to outdo Caravaggio's canvas, to take on the painter who had influenced her style, and knew she had the stuff to do it. To my mind, anyway, she won this competition hands down. No one can know whether the painting was born of her own traumatic experience, although it is not mad to think this. It is nevertheless true that the tendency to reduce works of art by women to the details of their biographies is nauseatingly familiar. Biography also figures in interpretations of works by men, including Caravaggio, of course, but the male artist is granted a transcendence of his circumstances the female artist is not. Gentileschi has certainly suffered from this diminishment. Then again, every artist carries memories, habit memories, conscious autobiographical memories, and emotional memories, and it is foolish to suppose these do not enter the work along with cultural, collective memories.

Violent acts are read in different ways in different cultures. In the United States, marital rape did not become a crime until the 1970s, and not until 1993 did every state remove the marital exemption from rape law. Laws define and frame actions, but the visceral shock of violent acts, of being beaten, hurt, or forcibly violated is not uniquely human. In response to extreme threats, the parasympathetic nervous system responds with tonic immobility—heart rate and breathing slow, blood pressure drops, muscles relax, and in people, dissociation, a strange feeling of indifference to the life-threatening situation, may take hold. Representations of violence, however, are not violence. It is impossible to pick apart Gentileschi's motives or the feelings she had while she worked on her canvas or the degree to which her thoughts, both conscious and unconscious, were invested with outrage and revenge fantasies. She was an artist, and sublimation in self-reflection is necessarily a part of making art, even when your subject matter is horrific.

Aby Warburg suffered a psychotic break in 1918 and was hospitalized for several years, finally ending up in a clinic in Kreuzlingen, Switzerland, under the care of the psychoanalyst and physician Ludwig Binswanger. Warburg's psychosis was severe. He threatened to murder his family, but he was also under the delusion that his doctor was an anti-Semite advocating the mass liquidation of the Jews. While this fantasy was decidedly false about Binswanger, Warburg's delusions now appear uncannily prescient about Germany's future. And, just as it is tempting to interpret Gentileschi's *Judith* as an image of revenge for her rape or "defloration," it is tempting to attribute aspects of Warburg's thought to his mental state. His brilliance is, at least in part, due to an almost preternatural sensitivity to images, as well as an electric connection to and fear of their bodily meanings. He was a man who had to fight his way back from psychotic confusion to the distance that arrives with symbolic thought, and he did. Although Binswanger diagnosed Warburg with schizophrenia, he was, I think, more accurately diagnosed by Emil Kraepelin, another famous doctor, as suffering from manic depression. One could say Warburg actually *lived* the extreme poles of his *Pathosformel*.

It is crude to reduce art or thought to an artist's or thinker's biography, as it is crude to posit art as either the result of purely cultural constructs or, conversely, of biological "mechanisms." The story is far more complicated. We, all of us, are body subjects, both acted upon by the world and creators of the world in which we live. There is a dynamic reversibility in this that turns us back to remembering. Art historians often march through linear, horizontal time with its periods and changing styles, their language colored by an almost phobic relation to the emotional, pretheoretical, vertical qualities of art viewing, a fear related to biases of agency and power and to the fact that passion and the body have been understood as effeminate and reason and the mental as manly, a dualist tradition that infects our memories, our expectations, and our perceptions. That divide, however, is at once false and dangerous.

"Fixed ideas," Kierkegaard wrote in a journal entry, "are like cramps e.g. in the foot—the best remedy for them is to trample on them."[31] It has been my purpose here to open rather than to close the question of memory in art, to propose plural ambiguities rather than a single "inherited" fixed idea or expectation, borrowed from philosophy, science, or aesthetics. Time is inevitably understood in spatial terms, and it is valuable to upend our fixed metaphor of left-to-right horizontality in the West without abandoning it. It is useful as a concept. But time and memory have verticality, too, if we understand that verticality as part of our mammalian heritage, as part of a prereflective reality that is also embodied experience. Warburg's spatial notion of *Denkraum*, a room for thought or an interval for contemplation of and reflection on the otherness of an artwork, given to us in a protective, aesthetic, symbolic frame, remains fertile. I see. I feel. I remember. The work in front of me is at once of me and not of me. I muse and I wonder. I interrogate my responses. I take time.

From *A Woman Looking at Men Looking at Women: Essays on Art, Sex, and the Mind* by Siri Hustvedt. © Siri Hustvedt, 2016. Reprinted by permission of Siri Hustvedt.

Notes

1. Søren Kierkegaard, *Repetition*, in *Kierkegaard's Writings*, vol. 6, trans. Howard V. Hong and Edna Hong (Princeton, NJ: Princeton University Press, 1983), 149.

2. Catarina Suitner and Chris McManus, "Spatial Agency in Art," in *Spatial Dimensions In Thought*, ed. Thomas W. Schubert and Anne Maass (Berlin: Walter de Gruyter, 2011), 283.

3. Christian Dobel, Gil Diesendruck, and Jens Bölte, "How Writing System and Age Influence Spatial Representations of Actions: A Developmental, Cross-Linguistic Study," *Psychological Science* 18, no. 6 (2007): 487–91.

4. Anne Maass et al., "Groups in Space: Stereotypes and the Spatial Agency Bias," *Journal of Experimental Social Psychology* 45, no. 3 (2009): 495.

5. Maurice Merleau-Ponty, *The Visible and the Invisible Followed by Working Notes* (Evanston, IL: Northwestern University Press, 1968), 268.

6. See Eric Kandel, "The Biology of Memory: A Forty-Year Perspective," *The Journal of Neuroscience* 29, no. 41 (2009): 12748–56.

7. For an account of unconscious perceptual inference in the work of Hermann von Helmholtz, the nineteenth-century biophysicist, see Gary Carl Hatfield, *The Natural and the Normative: Theories of Spatial Perception from Kant to Helmholtz* (Cambridge, MA: MIT Press, 1990), 195–207.

8. Karl Friston, "The Free Energy Principle: A Unified Brain Theory?" *Nature Reviews Neuroscience* (2010), https://doi.org/10.1038/nrn2787.

9. See Daniel J. Simons, "Current Approaches to Change Blindness," *Visual Cognition* 7 (2000): 1–15.

10. Steven B. Most et al., "What You See Is What You Set: Sustained Inattentional Blindness and the Capture of Awareness," *Psychological Review* 112, no. 1 (2005): 217–42.

11. Lawrence Weizkrantz, *Blindsight: A Case Study and Its Implications* (Oxford: Clarendon Press, 1986).

12. Roger Sperry, "Neurology and the Mind-Brain Problem," *American Scientist* 40, no. 2 (1952): 292.

13. Melvin Goodale, "Acting Without Thinking: Separate Cortical Pathways for Visuomotor Control and Visual Perception," www.csulb.edu/-cwallis/cscenter/hvr/abstracts/goodale.html. See also A. Milner and M. A. Goodale, "Two Visual Systems Re-Viewed," *Neuropsychologia* 46, no. 3 (2008): 774–85.

14. A. R. Luria, *Higher Cortical Functions in Man*, 2nd ed., trans. Basil Haigh (New York: Basic Books, 1966), 293.

15. For an overview of the case, see Jenni A. Ogden, *Fractured Minds: A Case Study Approach to Clinical Neuropsychology* (Oxford: Oxford University Press, 2005), 46–63. See also Larry R. Squire, "The Legacy of Patient H.M. for Neuroscience," *Neuron* 61, no. 1 (2009): 6–9.

16. Charles Darwin, *The Expression of the Emotions in Man and Animals* (London: Appleton, 1873), 23.

17. David Freedberg and Vittorio Gallese, "Motion, Emotion and Empathy in Esthetic Experience," *Trends in Cognitive Science* 11, no. 5 (2007): 197–203.

18. D. E. Merino et al., "Action Obervation and Acquired Motor Skills: An fMRI Study with Expert Dancers," *Cerebral Cortex* 15, no. 8 (2009): 1243–49.

19. James J. Gibson, *Ecological Approach to Visual Perception* (New York: Psychology Press, 2015), 119–36.

20. For an accessible overview, see Joseph LeDoux, "Manipulating Memory," *The Scientist Magazine*, March 1, 2009, www.the-scientist.com/?articles.view/articleNo/27171/title/Manipulating-Memory/.

21. Susanne Langer, "On Cassirer's Theory of Language and Myth," in *The Philosophy of Ernst Cassirer*, ed. Paul Arthur Schlipp (New York: Tudor Publishing Company, 1949), 383.

22. Susanne Langer, *Feeling and Form*, 220.

23. Aby Warburg, quoted in Ernst Gombrich, *Aby Warburg: An Intellectual Biography*, 2nd ed. (Chicago: University of Chicago Press, 1986), 246.

24. Andrea Pinotti, "Memory and Image," The Italian Academy for Advanced Studies in America, October 8, 2003, italianacademy.columbia.edu/fellow/andrea-pinotti.

25. Steven Pinker, *The Blank Slate*: The *Modern Denial of Human Nature* (New York: Viking, 2002), 418.

26. For an overview see Tabitha M. Powledge, "Behavioral Epigenetics: How Nurture Shapes Nature," *BioScience* 61, iss. 8 (2011): 588–92.

27. Aby Warburg, quoted in Gombrich, 219.

28. Ibid., 220.

29. Giorgio Agamben, "Aby Warburg and the Nameless Science," in *Potentialities: Collected Essays in Philosophy*, trans. Daniel Heller Roazen (Stanford: Stanford University Press, 1999), 90.

30. For various scholarly views on the question, see the exhibition catalogue *Orazio and Artemisia Gentileschi*, ed. Keith Christiansen and Judith Mann (New York: The Metropolitan Museum of Art, with Yale University Press, 2001).

31. Søren Kierkegaard, *Kierkegaard's Journals and Notebooks*, vol: 1, journals AA–DD, ed. Neils Jørgen Cappelørn, Alastair Hannay, David Kangas, Bruce H. Kirmmse, George Pattison, Vanessa Rumble, and K. Brian Söderquist (Princeton, NJ: Princeton University Press, 2007), 246.

Part 3 Film Phenomenology and Bodies

Introduction

In *Frida*, the 2002 biopic of Frida Kahlo, co-produced by its star Salma Hayek and Sarah Green, and directed by Julie Taymor, we see Frida encased in a plaster cast and bedridden following her involvement in a terrible road traffic accident at the age of eighteen. The film shows the young, energetic and vivacious girl before the accident where she sustained catastrophic injuries, and conveys the pain and restrictions that Frida has to endure afterwards. As time passes, confined to bed, Frida begins to draw colourful butterflies on her cast, and then her parents set up a drawing board for her in bed, and a mirror above her so that she can paint herself (Figure P3.1). The love of her parents and their determination to enable her to express herself, in the face of their heartbreak, is desperately moving. In this mesmerizing image, we can see Frida's confidence in her creativity, but also the film has enabled us to experience the transition from a physically active body to a physically confined and imaginatively creative state of being. As the camera reveals the painting she is working on to be a self portrait, so recognizable from her familiar, distinctive style, the film enlarges our understanding of the circumstances in which Frida began her work, and the intense focus she brought to bear on her art, born out of such physical confinement.

The way in which film can enable us to experience being other bodies, in other situations, is the subject of this Part. The texts here supplement the foundational work in this field by Vivian Sobchack (1992; 2004) and Laura U. Marks (1999; 2002), and bring some diverse and perhaps less familiar perspectives on embodiment. Katharina Lindner's work on queer phenomenology and women's bodies on film that are sporting or dancing, is a major intervention in the field. In *Film Bodies*, Lindner brings together film phenomenology and queer/feminist phenomenology, and asks 'what kind of queer feminist film phenomenology might surface in this encounter?' (Lindner, 2018: 3). In the chapter reproduced in this reader, Lindner's close analysis of *Tomboy* and *Girlhood/Bande de filles* reveals the films' 'sensory, tactile, muscular and kinaesthetic registers' and analyses the tensions between queer film theory, feminist film theory, and cultural constructions of identity and gender. Modes of embodiment in these films have an experimental quality, and their focus on active, youthful bodies enables Lindner to push the boundaries of film phenomenology to consider queer embodiment in a significantly physically and psychologically affective framework.

Elaine Scarry's work holds immense potential for the film philosopher, particularly *Dreaming by the Book* (1999), *On Beauty and Being Just* (1999) and *The Body in Pain: The Making and Unmaking of the World* (1985), from which Chapter 12 is taken. In 'Pain and Imagining', Scarry considers the objects about which it is possible to imagine, and the lack of objects required to experience pain. Moving into a highly pictorial discussion of the relationships between objects, tools, weapons and pain, this piece offers a potentially

Figure P3.1 Frida paints herself from her reflection (*Frida*).

inventive way of considering the affectiveness of images of pain and suffering on screen, and the invasion of our imagination by images of the pain of others.

The pregnant body has received comparatively little attention from film phenomenologists, and Iris Marion Young's essay focuses on 'the experiences of pregnancy from the pregnant subject's viewpoint' in a way that opens up potential encounters with pregnant others on screen. Young's influential 1990 essay 'Throwing Like a Girl' offered a transformative insight into the cultural and societal restrictions on a girl's freedom of movement, and 'Pregnant Embodiment' explains many aspects of pregnancy, perhaps most notably the way it challenges bodily integrity. Young draws attention to many physical and psychical moments that the pregnant subject experiences and which urgently need wider cultural attention. From feeling one's belly upon one's knee when sitting down, to navigating the medicalization of pregnancy and the concurrent alienation, Young's essay offers images and ideas that could inform affective encounters with on-screen pregnant bodies, and attitudes expressed towards them.

In 'The Beasts that Perish', Mary Midgley challenges the misleading divisions between human and non-human animals and calls for consideration of their beings. Considering cross species communication, and relationships of dependence, Midgley's critique of traditional dualism (where animals are seen as a different kind of 'thing' to humans, probably without consciousness) proposes an acknowledged sharing of the world with animals and promotes the urgency of realizing the harm that we do them. This chapter from *Are You an Illusion?* (2014) is but an indication of the clear-sighted philosophy produced by Midgley, consistent with her approach that philosophy is something we are all doing and living every day. Her rejection here of the word 'anthropomorphism' is productively linked to her chapter 'Is a Dolphin a Person?' (1996) and these in turn shed light on the relationships on-screen between humans and non-humans, which are so often accused of sentimentality. Her interest in Gaia, and her lifelong commitment to animal rights, is evident throughout her body of work, and provides a history of such philosophical argument that can usefully be included in contemporary film philosophical work on non-anthropocentric cinema.

References

Lindner, K. (2018), *Film Bodies: Queer Feminist Encounters with Gender and Sexuality in Cinema*, London and New York: I. B. Tauris & Co.

Marks, L. U. (1999), *The Skin of the Film: Intercultural Cinema, Embodiment, and the Senses*, Durham, NC: Duke University Press.

Marks, L. U. (2002), *Touch: Sensuous Theory and Multisensory Media*, Minneapolis: University of Minnesota Press.

Midgley, M. (1996), *Utopias, Dolphins and Computers: Problems of Philosophical Plumbing*, London and New York: Routledge.

Scarry, E. (1985), *The Body in Pain: The Making and Unmaking of the World*, New York and Oxford: Oxford University Press.

Scarry, E. (1999), *On Beauty and Being Just*, London: Duckworth.

Scarry, E. (1999), *Dreaming by the Book*, New York: Farrar, Straus and Giroux.

Sobchack, V. (1992), *The Address of the Eye: a Phenomenology of Film Experience*, Princeton, NJ and Oxford: Princeton University Press.

Sobchack, V. (2004), *Carnal Thoughts: Embodiment and Moving Image Culture*, Berkeley, CA and London: University of California Press.

Young, I. M. ([1990] 2005), 'Throwing Like a Girl: A Phenomenology of Feminine Body Comportment, Motility, and Spatiality', in *On Female Body Experience: 'Throwing Like a Girl' and Other Essays in Feminist Philosophy and Social Theory* by I. M. Young, 27–45, Oxford: Oxford University Press.

11 Céline Sciamma's 'Queer' Cinema: Affirming Gestures of Refusal in *Tomboy* and *Girlhood*

KATHARINA LINDNER

This chapter explores the usefulness of a queer feminist phenomenological approach to 'queer' cinema. With specific reference to Céline Sciamma's body of films, it offers a phenomenologically grounded answer to Davis's Deleuzian-inflected question, as discussed in Chapter 2: 'But what's a queer film?' I read *Tomboy* and *Girlhood* as particularly poignant incarnations of contemporary tensions in queer film (theory), especially around (in)visibility, identity (politics), performativity and representation. Both films engage centrally with questions of gender and sexuality while refraining from inscribing rigid gender and sexual identities onto their characters (and the same goes for *Naissance des pieuvres* (*Water Lilies*, 2007), the first part of Sciamma's female adolescent coming-of-age trilogy, which is not discussed here). The films speak to, and negotiate, the at times conflicting aims and preoccupations of queer film (theory) on the one hand and feminist film (theory) on the other. What the textural encounters in this chapter make graspable, is how those tensions and conflicts are embodied, and 'worked out', via the films' sensory, tactile, muscular and kinaesthetic registers – or what Sophie Mayer might call the films' 'uncommonly sensual figurations.'[1] The films make strange what usually is, and makes, common 'sense' in relation to gender, sexuality, childhood and adolescence in cinema.

While the argument developed here is applicable to questions of queerness and/in cinema more generally, Sciamma's films serve as particularly fruitful case studies as they manage to avoid the drawbacks of a narrowly defined identity politics through a foregrounding of embodiment, corporeality and sensuousness. *Tomboy* and *Girlhood* do feature fairly explicit lesbian/queer/trans content. *Tomboy* is the story of Laure (Zoé Héran) who moves into a new neighbourhood with her family and passes as a boy amongst her new friends, calling herself Mikaël, while *Girlhood* sees its protagonist, Marieme/Vic (Karidja Touré), take on a range of differently gendered appearances and behaviours throughout the film, including specifically male-identified ones in the final segment.[2] However, my concern here (as in the rest of the book) is not with how male, female, trans, straight, bisexual or lesbian identities are represented or given visibility. At the same time, I do not want to lose sight of the situatedness of (gender and sexual) embodiment, which Davis's Deleuzian account risks doing in its attempt to track how 'queerness recedes from lived experience through character and/or narrative politics to an aesthetics and/or affect.'[3] Instead, I propose that a phenomenologically based and queerly orientated textural analysis allows us to make (un/common) sense of the films' queer feminist leanings and attitudes: of how they are orientated, of who or what they are directed towards, and of their resonances with bodily tendencies, gestures and modes of embodiment as they are shaped by and acquired within the textures of the social.[4]

Sciamma's coming-of-age trilogy has emerged within a mainstream media landscape characterised by the proliferation of lesbian, and more recently trans, visibility. As Michele Aaron notes, one of the legacies of the New Queer Cinema has been the more general queering of Western popular culture and the commercialisation and repackaging of queer for mainstream audiences.[5] What is problematic about this co-optation of 'queer' is that it loses its critical, oppositional and transgressive edge. Lesbian sexuality in particular is also often re-appropriated for a heterosexual male gaze in ways that raise important questions about viewing pleasures and about who mainstream films with gay, lesbian or trans content are 'for' and who they appeal to (and why) – *Black Swan* with its (hallucinatory) lesbian sex scene being a notable case in point. It also raises important, and complicated, questions about how queer/gay/lesbian/trans identities, and gender and sexuality more generally, can or should (not) be represented in cinema – and also about whether representations of queer gender and sexual identities are essential, or even necessary, in contemporary queer cinema. It thus links to fundamental questions around where and how we might identify what is, and can be, 'queer' about queer cinema, and about where we might 'locate' its queerness. *Tomboy* and *Girlhood* emerge very specifically from, and arguably in response to, this wider representational and critical landscape: the aftermath of the New Queer Cinema and queer (film) theory, and the resultant tensions around (in)visibility, identity (politics), representability, legibility, recognisability and intelligibility that continue to shape this context.

Both films refrain from representations of specific, stable and narrowly defined gay, lesbian or trans identities. Nonetheless, they are profoundly queer feminist films and the young female protagonists are central to this – but *not* because of the identity categories inscribed on them in conventional cinematic terms. Instead, the films' queer feminist implications and resonances hinge centrally on the modes of movement, comportment and spatiality as well as the sensuous, tactile and kinaesthetic ways of being-in-the-world that take shape around, and in relation to, their troubled and troubling protagonists.

The young female bodies are at the very core of the films – visually, narratively and sensuously – a risky move considering the 'over-determined physicalities' of adolescent girls (in (French) cinema) in particular.[6] Various physical activities are depicted in both films – football, swimming, running, fighting and dancing in *Tomboy*; and American football, dancing and fighting in *Girlhood* – and it is through these performances that the body's more general centrality is made most explicit. However, the female bodies are not 'on display', or staged to-be-looked-at, in conventionally gendered ways. They function as intensely corporeal, tactile and muscular articulations of the phenomenological ways of being-in and becoming familiar with and orientated in the world that take shape in and through the films. They constitute the ground on which gender and sexuality are 'worked out' and 'worked through' *cinematically* in *Tomboy* and *Girlhood*, based on the bodies' textural incorporations. The athletic sequences foreground what is perhaps more subtly woven through the textures of the films as a whole: the making tangible and graspable of queer feminist orientations in tactile and kinaesthetic terms.

As in previous chapters, I am deeply indebted to Ahmed's queer phenomenology, which offers an account of orientation that 'points to how spatial distinctions and awareness are implicated in how bodies get directed in specific ways. In other words, orientation for [Ahmed, as for] me is about how the bodily, the spatial and the social are entangled.'[7] *Tomboy* and *Girlhood* offer sensuous, visceral encounters with the various forms and shapes this entanglement might take – and the young characters' bodies are the very centre, 'the zero point', that the spatial and the social emanate from and that they are 'orientated around' in the filmic worlds they occupy.[8]

While Sciamma's cinema does not subscribe to, or articulate, a particular identity politics, a consideration of the queer feminist embodiments and orientations in and of her films provides the grounds for encountering *Tomboy* and *Girlhood* as sensuous incarnations of an embodied 'politics of refusal', of both gender/sexual and cinematic norms.

Trans, Lesbian or Queer? Passing, (Mis)Recognition and (Dis)Appearance in *Tomboy*

In her second feature, Sciamma moves from the adolescent world of *Water Lilies* into the realm of childhood and pre-pubescent bodies – that is, bodies whose visible markers of sexual difference are not yet developed. Within critical debate, *Tomboy* tends to be situated in relation to the wider cinematic and media contexts of trans representations.[9] With a few exceptions, such as *The Danish Girl* (Tom Hooper, UK/US, 2015), *Dallas Buyers Club* (Jean-Marc Vallée, US, 2013) and *Boys Don't Cry* (Kimberly Pierce, US, 1999),[10] mainstream representations of trans identities are rare, unless we use trans, as Keely Saunders does, as an umbrella term that also includes depictions of drag and cross-dressing, of which there exists a much more visible mainstream cinematic history and an associated set of generic conventions.[11] While the trans trope has tended to serve hetero- and cis-normative narrative purposes in mainstream representation – by functioning as a means of deception, manipulation, comedy or terror – *Tomboy* is an example of more recent representations, which also include *Nånting måste gå sönder* (*Something Must Break*, Ester Martin Bergsmark, Sweden, 2014) and *52 Tuesdays* (Sophie Hyde, Australia, 2013), that are centrally, and largely affirmatively, *about* the trans experience.

Cinematic engagements with female-to-male (FTM) transition in particular are fairly atypical. Keely Saunders notes that, 'along with non-binary, questioning or fluid gender identities,' FTM characters and stories are 'commonly under-represented in the media compared with more familiar male to female translives.'[12] *52 Tuesdays* and *Albert Nobbs*, which variously conjures cross-dressing, trans and lesbian tropes through the mesmerising performances of Glenn Close and Janet McTeer, constitute exceptions, as does *Boys Don't Cry*, which was groundbreaking in its non-rationalising and non-trivialising depiction of the trans experience.[13] It refrains from providing a rationale as to *why* Brandon Teena/Tina Brandon (Hillary Swank) wants to pass as, and *be*, a man, and instead, depicts the process and experience of living a trans life (in not entirely unproblematic terms) and its violent, deathly consequences. *Tomboy* is fairly unusual then in its preoccupation with the FTM trans experience as well as its focus on a pre-pubescent child – if, indeed, how use the trans label to identify what it is the film is 'about' and what it 'does' (*sic*).

Darren Waldron reads *Tomboy* as part of contemporary public discourses in which 'the subject of gender nonconformity in children is a prominent concern.'[14] He also notes a 'preoccupation with boys' within those debates and the narrative and visual conventions through which they are articulated.[15] This preoccupation with boys, and with how they might 'do' femininity, mirrors the more general historical trajectory of trans visibility identified by Saunders as primarily confined to cross-dressing men. This is not too surprising, perhaps, considering the different ways in [which] femininity/femaleness and masculinity/maleness are culturally constructed. Variously, femininity is conceived of as excess, as masquerade, as something to be put on (make-up, jewellery, shoes, clothes, hair, gestures, smiles), whereas masculinity is 'natural', a given. This is reflected in critical discourses more generally that tend to focus on the socio-cultural construction of women and femininity, while 'we hear much less about the "construction of men".'[16]

Waldron also notes that gender fluidity or gender nonconformity is more commonly accepted in girls than in boys, because departures from traditional femininity in girls, exemplified by the figure of the tomboy, are much more pervasive.[17] For Halberstam, this is no great surprise as cross-gender behaviour in girls is 'associated with a "natural" desire for the greater freedoms enjoyed by boys' – as long as sexual difference is not fundamentally challenged.[18] In fact, the tomboy trope – in relation not just to children/adolescents but female character of all ages – is relatively common in mainstream cinema, yet critically neglected. Lynne Stahl provides a rare – to my knowledge, unique – exploration of mainstream cinematic incarnations of the tomboy narrative and suggests that tomboyism functions primarily as a phase to be overcome on the way to acceptable and desirable womanhood. Tomboyism's troubling links with lesbianism (rather than transgenderism!) are thus both gestured towards *and* disavowed through the eventual reaffirmations of heteronormative narrative arcs and conventionality.[19]

While tomboy characters tend to be obsessively domesticated, feminised and/or paired off with male love interests, there are also those characters who emerge from the narrative as tomboys (such as in *Fried Green Tomatoes* (Jon Avnet, US, 1991), for instance). It is in relation to this sustained and uncontained tomboyism that associations with lesbianism are, though not explicitly visible, no longer 'plausibly unnoticeable'.[20] As Stahl points out, however, recalling earlier arguments by White and Whatling, even those films in which tomboyism is heteronormatively contained and tomboy characters end up on the straight and narrow, as it were, 'leave – and sometimes create – room for sustained deviant [spectatorial] possibilities in the same instant that they attempt to smother them.'[21]

What surfaces, perhaps inadvertently, from these discussions is the slippery, messy unruliness of gender and sexual categories (and the political stakes in those categories) that are variously overlapping *and* contradictory. The discourses and debates emerging from and cohering around *Tomboy* thus speak, rather poignantly, to the questions of visibility, representability, legibility, intelligibility and appearance (of sex, gender and sexuality) that the film itself raises and works through. *Tomboy* is variously identified as a trans, lesbian or queer film in popular discourses, while it tends to be read as a trans film within academic debates, with trans inconsistently defined as in-/excluding cross-dressing, drag, passing, gender nonconformity, gender fluidity, tomboyism, non-binarism, transgenderism and transsexuality. Waldron, for instance, situates *Tomboy* within the larger representational and discursive (media, medical and policy) context of 'gender nonconformity' and reads the film as being equally concerned with 'the experiences of a girl who passes as a boy as with those of "boyish" girls.'[22] Stahl, on the other hand, explicitly excludes *Tomboy* from her study of the tomboy narrative in cinema, because she reads it as an example of transgender representation. For Stahl, it thus does not fit a project that is interested 'in a specific narrative and cinematic history that sees tomboyism as inextricably bound up with femaleness and lesbianism, not transsexuality.'[23] Stahl usefully adds that 'the suppression of trans discourses within tomboy narratives could itself make a compelling study'.[24]

There is a slightly problematic slippage here, then, between cinematic representation and critical discourse that hinges on circular relations between meaning, identification and naming. What is tomboyism exactly? If we have identified 'a cinematic history that sees tomboyism as inextricably bound up with femaleness and lesbianism, not transsexuality,' does this not perhaps mean that we have only defined certain gender-nonconforming behaviours and appearances in girls *as* 'tomboyish' *if* they are linked to lesbianism and/or eventually outgrown? And does this mean that the same gender-nonconforming behaviours and appearances, when linked to transgenderism or transsexuality – or even simply *not* linked to a (latent) lesbianism – are then not tomboyish, but … genderqueer?

I am playing devil's advocate here and am certainly not advocating a rigid definition of tomboy-qualifying characteristics. And while it is true that (cinematic) representations play an important part in the discursive construction of networks of meaning that link, for instance, 'tomboyism' with 'lesbianism', we also need to be cognisant of the constitutive, performative implications of naming and of the ways in which critical discourses are implicated in the perpetuation of normative structures of meaning. (We might ask similar questions about the seeming lack of filmic representations of trans men/boys: Does our reading of gender nonconformity in girls and women as tomboyism preclude the transgender trope from 'appearing'?) How the tomboy becomes 'visible' or 'legible', then, and how and under which circumstances the tomboy 'appears' – to adapt Villarejos's argument around 'lesbian appearance' once more – depends on the discursive and interpretive contexts from which we take our clues. Tomboyism has tentative, ambiguous and shifting ties to sex, gender and sexuality, but is crucially implicated in their legibility. It constitutes a kind of gender nonconformity with uneasy links to both lesbianism and transgenderism, via a semiotic chain that is characterised by unpredictable and often contradictory twists and turns.

If considered within the larger context of the tomboy trope, *Tomboy* seems fairly conventional, despite its refusal to reintegrate Laure into hetero-conventionality (Laure emerges from the narrative as a tomboy).[25] If considered within the larger context of trans representation, we might note that the film replays a rather conventional narrative of passing – 'dissimulation, discovery and confrontation'[26] – and a familiar arc of suspense: it is a question of *how*, not *whether*, Laure will be found out. *Tomboy* also breaks the representational, generic mould with its focus on transgenderism in a 'girl' (if what we 'see' is a trans rather than a tomboy narrative), although the film is centrally about, to adapt Tim Palmer's phrase, 'the world of boys,' about ways of being a boy and about boyhood masculinity.[27]

Tomboy posits an understanding of gender as somehow both 'authentic' and 'put on'. Laure unselfconsciously and seemingly 'naturally' engages in the performative reconstitution of masculinity when she is with her family, who equally unselfconsciously and uncritically read and address her as a 'girl' – a girl, it should be noted, who embodies gender very differently than her girly and effeminate younger sister, Jeanne (Malonn Lévana). However, this 'known' disconnect between sex and gender goes unremarked and, importantly, *unfelt* within the confines of the domestic space of the family home. As well as Jeanne, Laure's father (Matthieu Demy) and pregnant mother (Sophie Cattani), who remain nameless, are part of the initially warm and comforting domestic interior where Laure's gender-nonconformity, including her androgynous/boyish appearance, behaviours and tastes, are not only accepted but supported. Heteronormative societal pressures do not seem to encroach upon the familial realm, which constitutes a safe and familiar corporeal and affective space that not only accommodates but embraces Laure's queerly gendered mode of embodiment. It is within this context that Laure is most plausibly read as a 'tomboy', or as a 'boyish girl'. Importantly, however, Laure does not exhibit the kind of unhappiness, anger and rebelliousness (against gender norms) that characterise filmic articulations of the tomboy trope.[28] Laure does not rebel 'against' anything or anyone – she does not seem to *have* to. The domestic space of the home extends the shape of Laure's embodiment unconditionally, at least initially.

The family home is only part of the phenomenal world that Laure inhabits. Waldron notes the 'dialectical configuration of space between the domestic interior,' where Laure is known to be a (tom)boyish girl, and the 'communal exterior', the space outside the home, where Laure interacts with the other children in the neighbourhood her family has just moved into, and where her (tom)boyish demeanour leads her to be (mis)read as a boy.[29] It is when she goes along with the (mis)recognition and begins to pass as a boy that her (entirely unaltered) appearance and behaviours take on transgendered implications. This is crucial, as the variances in what her (tom)boyish demeanour *means* and how it is *read* – by Laure's family ('she is a girl'); by the other children in the film ('this is a boy'); and, in a rather different, shifting manner, by the spectator ('is this a (tom)boyish girl who passes as a boy?'; 'is this "really" a boy?'; 'is this a trans boy?') – is entirely dependent on the knowledge and experience that we bring to the encounter, exposing the conditionality of visibility, legibility and appearance.

Laure's first encounter in the new neighbourhood is with Lisa (Jeanne Disson). It is one of the film's most crucial moments because it constitutes the first instance of (mis)recognition/passing – but also because it leaves a certain ambiguity around agency and intent. We do not quite know whether Lisa assumes Laure is a boy when she says, 'You're shy? […] Won't you tell me your name?', or if she is playing it safe because she is not quite sure – but her cautiously flirtatious manner, which is very plausibly interpreted by Laure as a sign of being (mis)read, as well as the absence of a questioning response to Laure's answer – 'Mikaël, my name is Mikaël' – insinuate as much. The camera lingers on Laure's face after she names herself Mikaël and interpellates herself as a boy, rather than showing us Lisa's reaction directly. Instead, Lisa's acceptance of Laure as Mikaël is confirmed by a cut from the close-up of Laure/Mikaël as s/he holds Lisa's gaze to a scene of both children walking through the woods. Overall, then, this first encounter does not offer a clear sense, due to the ambiguous constellation of dialogue, body language and looks, about whether it is Lisa's (mis)recognition or Laure's 'deceit' that comes first. This ambivalence does not function to encourage the viewer to contemplate the temporality of the encounter, however. It serves instead to downplay the importance of rationality, sequence and cause-and-effect relations and heightens the affective charge of the encounter, which might be best understood as a playful and mutually affirming all-at-once.[30]

In this sense, *Tomboy* diverts from the mainstream conventions of the passing narrative, in that it is 'not preoccupied with "putting on a gender" because Laure's behaviour obtains a permanence and sense of authenticity.'[31] The film is not concerned with questions of intentional deceit, and associated notions of agency, in terms of how gender might be performed. It also, however, and as already gestured towards, stays away from constructing a sense of gender as somehow fixed or innate as it reveals 'the conditionality of all gendering,' both by 'highlighting the performative strategies undertaken by boys to comply with compulsory masculinity' and through Jeanne's overtly feminine appearance and behaviour that are equally depicted as a kind of 'authentic performance', as something she does rather than an innate tendency.[32] *Tomboy* carefully and sensitively negotiates these tensions (between essentialism and a postmodern relativism) without ever fully resolving them – a powerfully affirmative stance.

This is another aspect of the film that sets it apart from conventional, mainstream representational patterns where cross-dressing or passing tend to have specific narrative motivations or aims and tend to be framed as conscious, purposeful deceit. Laure's 'deceit' has no obvious purpose other than passing itself, similar to Brandon Teena's in *Boys Don't Cry*. Laure's 'deceit' is also, at least at first, not a conscious act, *un*like Brandon's mindful attempts to hide the parts of his physical body that might reveal his 'secret', with the process of transformation being explicitly depicted in a lengthy scene early on in *Boys Don't Cry*. When Laure 'appears' as a boy in the initial encounter with Lisa, Laure is not 'putting on an act.' Rather, it is a strictly binary sex/gender system, which is unable to accommodate Laure's mode of being-in-the-world, that leads Lisa to (mis)identify her as a boy in order to enable an interpersonal encounter with an intelligible (i.e., gendered) subject. A similar kind of (mis)identification or (mis)recognition might also be evoked in the viewer's first encounter with Laure in *Tomboy's* opening sequence (discussed in more detail below).

In a gesture of refusal (of cinematic conventions and societal expectations), the film disregards the 'why?' and 'when?' of Laure's gender-nonconformity and focuses instead on the 'how?'. This lack of a rational justification conjures a wonderfully refreshing opening-up of the film's sensuous, embodied and affective resonances. It also has potentially disconcerting or disorientating implications, however, as it prohibits a neat and reassuring categorisation of Laure's gender and sexual identity. Does Laure go along with the initial (mis)recognition because she is attracted to Lisa? Can the gender disguise therefore be read as Laure's attempt to act on her (forbidden) desire for Lisa? Is Laure therefore a 'lesbian'? Or is she really just a (tom)boyish girl, so used to being misrecognised as a boy, that it is just easier, and perhaps more fun, to play along with it? Or does Laure genuinely feel like a boy, and want to be a boy? And are gender nonconformity and passing therefore manifestations of a trans identity? These are just some of the possible ways in which the film might make sense to viewers – and film reviews, online discussion boards and more general public media discourses provide an indication that the film is, indeed, made sense of in all of these ways. Notably, the ascribing of a particular (lesbian or trans) identity to the protagonist can lead to fairly heated debates about why certain identity attributions are/not appropriate and which identity groups might therefore 'claim' the film and its character – an example of (paranoid) identity politics at work in ways that are not entirely productive.

Making 'sense' of (the) *Tomboy*

Halberstam notes that trans narratives tend to be 'dedicated to forcing the transgender subject to *make sense*' – to those who might not, and/or might want to, understand *why* deviance from gender norms takes place, thereby reinforcing the givenness and normativity of binary gender as that which does not need to be explained to make sense.[33] This kind of rationalising is precisely what *Tomboy* refuses to engage in. Rather than making sense of its protagonist by imposing a logical explanation, the film makes sensuous, tactile, muscular and kinaesthetic 'sense' of a particular way of being, and finding one's way, in the world.

The opening sequence introduces us to the protagonist and her world in a specifically tactile, muscular and kinaesthetic manner. It is *Tomboy's* textural, sensory register that shapes our initial contact with the film and thus invites an embodied, haptic mode of spectatorial engagement. Importantly, the film's sensuous qualities are tied closely to its, at this point, unnamed and unidentified protagonist and her sensory engagement with the world. The opening sequence is crucial in its foundational interweaving of the film's textural register with its thematic concerns around sex/gender, visibility and passing, which enables a side-stepping of considerations of trans narratives and the 'transgender gaze'.

We first come into contact with (the) *Tomboy* (the character/figure/film) when the heavy, muffled, enveloping sound of wind, as if reverberating in one's own ears, materialises on the soundtrack, steadily increasing in volume before there is a cut from the black screen with opening credits to a close-up of the back of a child's head. The shot is slightly angled, so we are looking up, and all we see is a slender neck, short, shaggy hair, and the top of skinny, angular shoulders in a blue T-shirt. We are seemingly situated on some kind of vehicle, as we move forward, along with the character, through a tree-covered landscape. The bobbly texture of the washed-out T-shirt, the fine blonde hairs on the delicately textured skin, the wind finding its way through the already ruffled, messy hair and the sun rays gently sliding across the hair, skin and fabric are in focus, while the lush, green surroundings, with the sunlight breaking through the swaying leaves, move past us, envelop us even, in a sensuously blurry play of colour, movement and light. The sounds of the wind, which give the diegetic world a thickly textured feel before we see it, also take shape visually through the swaying movements of the branches and leaves and, perhaps more importantly, through the fluttering strands of hair. The densely reverberating soundscape, together with the finely textured materiality of hair, skin and fabric, provides a tangible sense of the character's sensory world: of whirling air brushing across the skin of the face; of fluttering strands of hair on the scalp; of wind insistently tugging at the fabric of the shirt.

The character we are introduced to here is Laure, the as-yet-unnamed protagonist. It is rather presumptuous to use a gendered pronoun, and to refer to Laure as 'she' at this point, as conventional, legible markers of gender and sexual difference are notably absent. If anything, we might say that what appears in this very first shot is a 'boy', or 'boyishness' – although more knowing audiences, which in this case might include the majority of spectators, given the film's name as well as extra filmic/promotional discourses, are likely to read this first appearance differently, about which further below.

The audiovisual framing of *Tomboy's* opening moments provides a sense of proximity, not necessarily because we are visually close, or because we share the character's visual perspective, but because we are invited to share her phenomenal world in what is an intimately sensory encounter. The soundscape in particular, resembling the wind brushing past and reverberating in one's ears, crucially links sound, touch, proximity and contact. The only sounds we hear are the ones created with, or on, the body as the air makes contact with its surface and even enters its folds, resounding insides the ear cavity and not leaving any space for other, less proximal sounds to intermingle. It is the kind of sound experience that is by necessity tied to the individual and that cannot normally be shared. The wind reverberating in *my* ears can only be heard by *me*. The particular audiovisual framing described here therefore creates an impression of the 'space of the body' as tightly enclosed yet marked by a pleasurable sensory richness.[34] The body is cocooned by the densely textured, cushioned soundscape.

Tomboy's opening provides a graspable sense of how this sensorial envelopment might be experienced and felt. It provokes a spectatorial relation of tactile empathy to a character that does not yet make any 'sense' otherwise: no name, no narrative context, no face. This lengthy opening shot, which lasts for around 15 seconds, gives us time to take in the minute textural details and their sensory resonances, before there is a cut to a point-of-view shot of the trees, branches and leaves moving past and across the screen in a blurry haze of texture and movement, ruptured by the glistening sun rays rhythmically breaking through the leafy layers, blinding us momentarily. The disorientatingly contrasting texture (shadowy leaves – blindingly bright sunlight) is interwoven with the movement of fuzzy shapes and patterns (of leaves and branches) across the screen, which is too fast for our eyes to keep up, serving as an embodied reminder of the intrinsically tactile, kinaesthetic nature of perception. It evokes the kind of haptic gaze that intimately links vision and touch, and thus invites a spectatorial attitude of openness and vulnerability that enables the film to make contact.

When a hand, presumably Laure's, appears on the screen, in front of the blurry background, a sense of three-dimensional (optical) depth returns to the image, while the significance of contact and touch is also reinforced and given a specifically spatial dimension. The small, delicate hand, fingers slightly bent, is in focus in the centre of the screen, as the fine blonde hairs on the wrist and fingers catch the sunlight and become visible on the fair, freckled surface of the skin. The hand and fingers move slightly, responding to the pressure of the wind, engaging in a playful dance with the invisible force of the moving air, crucially linking surface, texture and hapticity with movement, spatiality and orientation. As the hand leaves the frame again, a gradual change in focus increases the blurriness of the leaves and branches in the background, until the screen is filled with a hazy, shifting pattern of fuzzy, overlapping, indistinct circles of green and light. This is followed by a cut to a frontal close-up of the character's face with the textured pattern of the previous shot mirrored by the oscillating movement of sunlight and shade across the skin of her face, the wind tugging at the strands of her short, messy hair. Importantly, her eyes are closed as she moves her head slightly, left and right, up and down, seemingly engrossed in the pleasurable sensation of the wind brushing against her skin, alternately giving in to and pushing against the dense yet malleable pressure of the air, in a playful and sensuously tactile and muscular to-and-fro. The scene conveys an impression of the warm, soothing sensation of sunrays touching the surface of the skin, intermingling with the crisp, clean coolness of the air, and of the muscular effort of resisting, responding to and moving against the pressure of the wind.

The densely textured and richly sensuous register of the film introduced here is intimately tied to Laure and her corporeal presence in the world, which begins to make sensuous, tactile, kinaesthetic, muscular and spatial 'sense' to us. We then see Laure open her eyes and briefly look around, visually taking in her surroundings, before a cut to a shot inside a car provides an initial sense of the spatio-temporal and narrative context: Laure is standing on the passenger seat, her upper body sticking out of the sunroof. This is followed by a cut that returns to a frontal close-up of Laure's face that is held for a few seconds, even when the sound of the wind, deeply entangled as it is with the sensuous texture of the phenomenal world unfolding in the opening sequence, is abruptly replaced by complete silence. The subsequent cut to a black title screen – with '*Tomboy*' first written in blue, then changing to red, before settling on a blue-red-blue-red-blue-red alternation, asserting the incipient blurring of gender boundaries and binaries – marks the end of the opening sequence.

The rich sensory texture of *Tomboy's* opening is intimately tied to Laure's 'unsettlingly androgynous' appearance.[35] Given the film's title, an awareness of the gender nonconformity associated with tomboyism and sensitivity towards a potentially not-quite-straightforward legibility of gender is likely to underpin our initial encounter with the film. Out of context, Laure might conceivably be identified as a boy – a possibility we are invited to contemplate when we first make contact with, and get close to, Laure in the opening scene – prefiguring Lisa's above-mentioned (mis)identification in a later sequence. The interweaving of an intimately sensuous encounter with Laure in/and the film, which makes 'perfect sense', as it were, with the simultaneous foreclosing of a straightforwardly intelligible gender identity evokes a contradictory tension in our spectatorial relation with Laure/the film.

While we get intimately close to the body, giving us (as I have shown) opportunities for identification and empathy with a particular sensory experience and way of being-in-the-world that hinges on Laure's corporeal presence, that body refuses to disclose what it is 'normally' presumed to be ultimately accountable for. The lengthy, lingering shots of the back of Laure's head, and especially of her face, draw us in as they foreground the intricately detailed textures of the body, its surface that makes contact with the world and its sensuous, muscular interiority that negotiates its spatial relations with the world. Yet, gender, that which arguably renders us intelligible as subjects, and which is read off the body *in the last instance*, remains elusive.

Tomboy's opening thus resonates with, and foreshadows, 'the complex relations in time and space between seeing and not seeing, appearing and disappearing, knowing and not knowing' that gather around transgenderism and that, as Halberstam notes, are 'difficult to track.'[36] Halberstam identifies a range of different cinematic treatments of transgenderism 'that resolve these complex problems of temporality and visibility,' most notably the 'rewind'.

> [T]he transgender character is presented at first as 'properly' gendered, as passing in other words, and as properly located with a linear narrative; her exposure as transgender constitutes that film's narrative climax, and spells out both her decline and the unravelling of cinematic time. The viewer literally has to rewind the film after the character's exposure in order to reorganize the narrative logic in terms of the pass.[37]

Whenever a character has been read, and accepted, by the audience as male or female (although how exactly we might determine such a reading/acceptance is not entirely clear) and is subsequently exposed as a trans character, this 'causes the audience to reorient themselves in relation to the film's past in order to read the film's present and prepare themselves for the film's future. When we "see" the transgender character, then, we are actually seeing cinematic time's sleight of hand.'[38]

In *Tomboy*, the androgyny and gender ambiguity that surround Laure from the very beginning mean that cinematic time is unravelling *at the same time* as it is constituted. Laure is never '"properly" gendered' to begin with. There is a certain vagueness about *when* Laure first 'appears' as a boy or as a girl or as trans (to the spectator) – and it is this vagueness that further complicates, and heightens, Halberstam's assertion that:

> the transgender film confronts powerfully the way that transgenderism is constituted as a paradox made up in equal parts of visibility and temporality: whenever the transgender character is seen to be transgendered, then he/she is failing to pass and threatening to expose a rupture between the distinct temporal registers of past, present, and future.[39]

Beyond the 'rewind' (that evokes a reassuring spectatorial reorientation and retrospective sense-making), Halberstam identifies a potentially more useful and affirmative cinematic treatment of transgenderism: the constitution of a transgender gaze that allows us to 'look *with* the transgender character instead of *at* him.'[40] For Halberstam, *Boys Don't Cry* constitutes a 'quantum leap' in trans representations because it articulates 'the specific formal dimensions of a transgender gaze,' rather than locating transgenderism 'in between the male and female gaze and alongside unrelenting tragedy.'[41] However, even as groundbreaking a film as *Boys Don't Cry* does not manage a sustained commitment to a transgender look (Halberstam convincingly argues that the transgender look is replaced by a reassuring lesbian gaze that affirms the binary constitution of sex and gender), in part due to the inherently heteronormative underpinnings of narrative and visual structures, and their associated viewing pleasures, in (mainstream) cinema. *Tomboy's* strength lies in its undercutting of the significance of the gaze, and of the visual more generally, which is no easy feat given that 'gender assignations rely so heavily on the visual,' especially in the context of cinema.[42]

The casting of Héran, with her lanky and troublingly androgynous physique, mesmerisingly enigmatic face, and unselfconsciously tomboyish demeanour, is key to the ways in which *Tomboy's* explorations of gender nonconformity and passing are worked out. Héran's appearance imbues her performance with a sense of corporeal and affective authenticity and makes Laure's diegetic passing unnervingly believable. It underpins the sensuous resonances of the film and our embodied engagement with it, while at the same time conjuring a self-consciousness about the normalised assumptions implicit in our 'reading' of others when we encounter them. Laure's 'appearance' does not change throughout the film and she is not visually transformed in any way – even though she conjures different kinds of gender and sexual identities when she appears to different characters and in different spaces in the film. As spectators, we are unquestionably in on Laure's secret when her body is *visually* exposed in the bathroom scene that takes place relatively early on in the film (immediately following Laure's first encounter with Lisa and the other children in the neighbourhood). However, even given our privileged access to knowledge and the superior spectatorial positioning that arguably comes with it, *Tomboy* evokes a lingering, and periodically resurfacing, impetus for the spectator to engage in a self-reflexive questioning of our perceptual habits. Even towards the end of the film, we are encouraged to ask ourselves: How would we 'read' Laure if we encountered her out of context? This question remains, and remains unanswered, because issues around gender (identity), legibility and passing are worked out of primarily outwith the realm of the visual.

It is a kind of pleasurably puzzling elusiveness that drives our continued spectatorial turning and tending towards Laure: Are there any signs that give her 'real' gender away? Surely we would 'see' them, given how intimately close we are? We might follow Laure's journey in (sheepish) anticipation of a rupture, a glitch in her corporeal performance, that reassures us of our privileged position of spectatorial superiority and omniscience (we 'know' she is 'really' a girl; we have 'seen' evidence of this in the bathroom scene) – but this reassurance never materialises. Yes, *Tomboy* replays an arc of suspense typical of passing narratives, encouraging spectatorial anticipation of the moment in which Laure's secret is discovered – and Laure *is* 'found out' eventually, but not because she somehow fails to appear as a boy; there is no glitch. The children find out that Laure is 'really' a girl when the film's interior/domestic and exterior worlds collide, as Laure's mother becomes aware of and discloses Laure's passing to another parent. It is through the performative speech act of naming, through a *discursive* reshaping of Laure's positionality within the binary sex/gender system, that her appearance becomes troubling, 'disgusting' even, as one of the boys asserts, in the exterior world of the film.

The authenticity and permanency of Laure's queerly gendered mode of embodiment is articulated perhaps most poignantly when her mother forces her to wear a dress, and violently drags her, screaming, out of the apartment to make her apologise for lying to her friends about being a boy. The unshapely dress, which hangs on and clearly does not fit Laure's lanky angular frame, gives her the appearance of a boy in drag. It recalls an earlier, though more humorous, scene in which Lisa wants to play 'girls' with Laure and covers her face in make-up. There is a delightfully potent disconnect between Lisa's assertion that 'It suits you! You look great as a girl,' and the comically grotesque, brightly coloured lipstick, rouge and eye shadow on Laure's face that clash with her short, messy hair and boyish white tank top. During this scene, and while touching Laure's face, Lisa also announces that the group of friends is planning to go swimming the next day, drawing Laure's, and our, attention, to the materiality of her (female) body. This adds yet another layer of complexity to a moment in which a jarring multitude of gendered meanings, resonances, signs, affects and connotations cohere in and around Laure's corporeal presence.

Testing the limits of the body

While *Tomboy* adheres to a range of generic, narrative and visual conventions that guide us on our journey through the film, it is its *physical* dynamic that most powerfully and affectively shapes our spectatorial engagement. Sciamma herself speaks of her film in these (embodied, visceral) terms, noting, for instance, that *Tomboy* is more 'choppy' than *Water Lilies*, because it 'follows the rhythms of childhood' and therefore works with a 'different energy'. More importantly, she sees the 'physical dynamic' of *Tomboy* 'not in the narrative which unfolds, but in the questioning of, "What body do I have?"' For her, 'the body is the limit of the film, and therefore it is also the object of the film.'[43]

The limits of the body, and thus the film, are most vigorously tested in those moments in which it is most explicitly on display. As in *Girlhood* (as we will see) it is in the context of athletic, physical activities that the limits of the body, its shape and its corporeal significance are most tangibly 'worked out'. In *Tomboy*, the muscular and kinaesthetic dimensions of Laure 'finding her feet' as a boy are articulated most graspably in relation to football (a particularly gendered physical activity) and swimming (where the material shape of the body is most visibly exposed).

There are two different football sequences, both relatively early on in the film, when Laure is still 'new' (to the neighbourhood and to her life as a boy) and tries to integrate herself into the existing group, which consist of a handful of boys and Lisa, the only girl. Lisa complains that the boys never let her play because she is 'useless'; football clearly is for boys, not for girls. In the first football scene, everyone is involved in the game, except for Lisa (because she is a girl) and Laure (because she is 'new' and a bit shy). Lisa wonders why Laure is not taking part in the game – because clearly, as a boy, she should be – and notes that Laure is 'not like the others'.

Watching the game from the sideline, Laure is fascinated by the physical performance. It is the excessive display of the boys' performative articulation of normative masculine, which a quintessentially masculine sport such as football enables, encourages and even demands, that appeals to Laure. She smirks, approvingly, as the boys take off their shirts, give each other congratulatory high-fives after scoring and spit on the ground. The sequence ends with a rather comical looking constellation that highlights the chaotic dynamics of sex/gender/desire that emerge from the footballing encounter. The final three shots consist of a medium shot of one of the boys, staring back at Laure in an almost aggressive and confrontational manner, returning a gaze that he might experience as threateningly objectifying; a frontal close-up of Laure who, in turn, holds her gaze (at the boy), unwaveringly; and a close-up that shows Lisa in profile, looking (desiringly?) at Laure. Lisa and the boy direct, albeit very differently charged, gazes at Laure, marked by longing and aggression respectively, granting Laure a 'masculine' position in this network of looks and affirming her ability to pass as a boy.

There is also an important *embodied* dimension to this encounter, however. Despite Lisa's attempts to direct Laure's attention towards her, Laure *faces* the boys and their actions. Facing, for Ahmed, is a '"somatic mode of attention" that allows us to be touched by the proximity of others.'[44] Laure's proximity to the footballing action is articulated through the framing, which approximates her embodied engagement and positioning (rather than point of 'view'). At times, the camera increases our proximity to the muscular

Figure 11.1 Lisa and Laure/Mikaël Watching the Football Game (*Tomboy*).

dynamics of the game, closing in on the boys' performative displays of masculinity (athletic skill, spitting, goal celebrations). The reaction shots of Laure betray her empathetic engagement with the corporeality of the performances (of football and masculinity): her upper body sways when she shifts her weight from one foot to the other; her hands and arms fidget restlessly; she tenses her upper body as she turns to face the action; the twitching muscles around her mouth and pursed lips reveal both an approving smirk and the gathering of saliva in response to the boys' spitting. For Waldron, *Tomboy* shows how 'Laure's embodied consciousness invests in the corporeal strategy of mimesis.'[45] This is *not*, importantly – or certainly not always/necessarily – a conscious or intentional strategy. Instead, what this sequence in particular gestures towards is a sense of muscular, kinaesthetic empathy that is enabled by Laure's corporeal orientations and habits, by who or what she is *facing* – and her bodily tendencies are, in turn, shaped by the encounter. What surfaces here is the mode of spectatorship the film itself makes possible – if we are inclined to *face* it in particular ways.

The muscular and tactile dimensions of Laure's (and the film's) corporeal journey manifest themselves more explicitly in a scene in the bathroom (shortly after the first and before the second football game). Laure is framed from behind, in a mid-shot that shows us both her back (from the waist up) and the front of her body as reflected in the mirror. On the surface, this scene of Laure gazing at her reflection in the mirror might seem to cry out for a psychoanalytic reading. However, the psychic dynamics of looking, recognition, identification and subjectivity, while gestured towards, are not what this moment *centrally* evokes. Laure's relation to her mirror image takes shape as a palpably haptic and muscular encounter. She first pulls up her grey tank top, revealing, and probingly touching, her skinny, flat stomach and chest. She then takes the top off altogether exploring the contours of her lean – emaciated, even – upper body with her hands, squeezing her biceps, tracing the shape of her collarbone, pushing back her shoulder, turning left, then right, so she can see her back, the twisting motion accentuating the outline of her ribs protruding through the skin. The camera moves closer, with a cut to an over-the-shoulder shot/medium close-up about halfway through

Figure 11.2 Touching the Body/Image (*Tomboy*).

the mirror scene, drawing us further into the encounter. We no longer look at Laure looking at herself in the mirror, but we look in the mirror with her.

The scene constitutes a sensuous, tactile remoulding of conventional body-image relations. Laure only looks at her face and meets her own gaze, conjuring the kind of (mis)recognition linked to psychoanalytic conceptions of subject formation, in the very final moments of the scene. Up until then, Laure's eyes follow her hands as they trace the contours of her body, explicitly linking vision, movement and touch. She also takes her eyes off her mirror image at one point and looks directly down at her hands, probing the muscular texture of her arms. Laure's encounter in/with the mirror is not about searching for a coherent sense of self. 'Who am I?' is not the question explored here – Laure knows 'who' she is and the kind of affirmative (self) recognition afforded by the encounter with the mirror image is not what she is 'looking for'.

In the wake of being (mis)recognised as a boy by Lisa and the boys, and after witnessing, and being touched and moved by, the boy's performative display of normative masculinity during the first football scene, the mirror allows Laure to explore and test the limits of her body. Could she pass if she were to take off her shirt and expose her upper body? Laure is comfortable 'in her own skin' – but what are the links between her 'felt' embodiment and the affective resonances this body might evoke? What exactly 'appears' when Laure is present? These are questions we are invited to (at)tend to(wards). Laure's upper body, pre-pubescent as it is, does not yet bear the visible signs of sexual difference. Through the explicit linking of vision, movement, touch and (bodily) texture, the scene foregrounds the corporeal dimensions of appearance, (mis)recognition and identification – as they are explored in and by the film, but also as they shape our encounter with the film. How Laure is read does not depend on what her body looks like, but on how it appears, and on 'what' appears when her body is present – not in terms of fixed or innate biological facts, but with regard to the lived-body's tactile, muscular and kinaesthetic capabilities that shape, and are shaped by, differently gendered modes of embodiment.

It is in the final moments of the scene that Laure lifts her gaze (from the reflection of her body to the refection of her face), looks herself in the eye, as it were, smirks and spits in the sink, mirroring the boys' behaviour during the football game. Her smirking gaze conveys a self-congratulatory confidence in her ability to pass, which she puts to the test when joining in with the boys in the following football scene, which traces, in muscular, kinaesthetic and spatial terms, Laure's entry and subsequent immersion into the world of boys. The game is already in full flow when Laure arrives and she casts an isolated figure in the leafy suburban landscape. She is framed by an extreme long-shot, standing in front of a bluish-grey wall, watching the boys play, before eventually joining in. Her fidgety demeanour (she tenses her shoulders, tucks at her shirt, rubs her hands across the fabric covering her torso and pulls up her shorts) betrays a specifically tactile sense of nervous self-consciousness. Her capabilities for playing football and for 'play[ing] at being a boy' are about to be tested.[46]

Butler asserts the significance of 'the space of concerted collective action and improvisation' that team sports provide with regard to how gender norms and ideals continue to be reconstituted.[47] She proposes a phenomenological understanding of sport that usefully illuminates the embodied implications of the football sequences in *Tomboy*. When collective sporting action takes place, what emerges is:

> a situation in which bodies are being made, in which the tacit sculpting of bodies takes place dramatically and in concert [...] one of the consequences of playing together is that the physiology of the body is transformed through the process of that collective action. The bodies that begin the game are not the same bodies that end the game.[48]

It is by tracing the ways in which Laure is finding her feet and coming to feel 'at home' within the masculine world of boys/football in the remainder of the sequence that *Tomboy* reinforces the already established (tactile, muscular and kinaesthetic) entanglements between visibility, legibility and passing and gendered modes of embodiment. Butler emphasises the significance of bodily action in a *shared* corporeal space and notes the inter-corporeal resonances and mutual shaping of bodies that take place within it. In sport, 'bodies engage in the rituals of self-production *only in relation to other bodies in motion*', and we might claim that:

> bodies are decentered in relation to one another, that they find and pursue their centre outside themselves in a shared corporeal space, what Merleau-Ponty, the phenomenologist, called 'the flesh of the world.' This is a corporeal space that is not simply composed of the various bodies by which it is inhabited; it is rather, a *set of rules, norms, and relations by which a body assumes its bearings and its shape*; in turn, these norms are altered in the course of their inhabitation, those bodily rituals and incarnations by which such ideals and norms are given new life.[49]

It is *Tomboy's* conjuring of precisely these corporeal resonances that grounds its incarnations of gender (ambiguity) more firmly in the realm of lived experience and reasserts the continued privileging of an embodied spectatorial attitude.

When Laure first joins in, she is frequently framed on her own, with the boys appearing in the margins of the frame. The relatively static framing, along with Laure's continued self-conscious touching and tugging at her shirt, gives shape to a hesitant and inhibited intentionality. She is among the boys but has not yet adjusted to the game's rhythms and movements. Encouraged by a few successful footballing moves, which are accompanied by an increasingly mobile camera and more dynamic editing, Laure gradually sheds her inhibiting self-referentiality and her body begins to 'extend the shape' of the game's 'corporeal space' much more comfortably and confidently.[50]

Laure takes off her shirt, again touching her stomach, a specifically tactile affirmation of the self, and then looks around to assess whether her exposed upper body has affected a change in her 'appearance'. The camera follows Laure's initially timid steps – the footballing action taking place, again, outside the frame – and the close framing conveys a sense of the enclosing self-referentiality conjured by the 'pressure' of the binary sex/gender system that underpins the cultural logics of intelligibility However, when Laure's survey of the group confirms a reassuring lack of reaction from the boys, she spits on the ground and engages in the action much more unselfconsciously. What the sequence traces here is what happens when the 'spectatorial point of view' of one's own body, that 'lets the body appear as a bounded kind of thing' is 'relinquished in favour of engaged bodily action.'[51] Laure's initial hesitation is linked to her inability to give up her perspective *on*, and take up a perspective *from*, the body. Crucially, her initial, inhibitingly alienated, perspective *on* the body is articulated as a specifically embodied and tactile perspective: Laure's touching, tracing and probing the surface and contours of her body add a textured, corporeal dimension to Butler's assertion that 'it appears that the spectatorial point of view works to defeat and break apart the sense of kinesthetic continuity that characterizes engaged bodily action, that sense of not knowing where the body ends and its instrument begins,' and that 'too much self-consciousness paralyzes action altogether.'[52]

The gradual shift in Laure's mode of embodiment is made graspable through her increasingly engaged participation in the game: there is no self-referential touching; her gaze and (bodily) attention are directed towards the ball and the footballing action (rather than her own body and others' apprehension of it); and her face betrays concentration and focus. The palpable shift in the modes of directionality, intentionality and spatiality embodied by Laure are emulated by the shift in framing and the more immediate and recipro-cally engaged mode of spectatorship it evokes. The game evolves increasingly around Laure at the centre of the footballing action. While the handheld camera keeps Laure in the centre of the frame it also becomes progressively more mobile, moving among the players, closing in on Laure's grimacing face, flexed muscles and dribbling feet, with quicker cuts between shots and changing angles further adding to the sense of kinaesthetic freedom and energy. Laure's integration into the 'world of boys' and their masculine corporeal

Figure 11.3 Laure/Mikaël in the 'World of Boys' (*Tomboy*).

space is therefore not only shown to us. It is, first and foremost, articulated via a shift in the modes of movement and comportment embodied by Laure *and* the film. The filmic body engages in a mutually empathetic relation with Laure as it simultaneously adjusts to *and* moulds the shape of her embodied consciousness. If, as D'Aloia argues 'watching a film is an experience of a relationship between bodies in space,'[53] then the spectatorial attitude invited by this scene of Laure's emphatic 'occupation' in and of the boys' corporeal world is underpinned by a similarly responsive (tactile, muscular and kinaesthetic) empathy.[54]

Tomboy traces Laure's negotiation of the different ways in which her embodied existence takes shape and makes sense in the interior and exterior worlds of the film. Gradually, these worlds encroach upon each other and ultimately, and not surprisingly, they collide. This collision is instigated by the figure of the mother, who comes to stand, and not entirely unproblematically, for the larger social and institutional contexts in which Laure's queer embodiment is not a viable, and intelligible, option. There is a heart-wrenching moment in the scene cited above, as Laure's mother forces her to wear a dress and drags her into the exterior world of the film, dressed as a girl, in order to 'straighten things out' with her friends and their parents.

The mother explains to a distraught Laure, who does not want to face, and 'come out' to, Lisa in particular, that she does not mind Laure 'playing the boy' and that it 'doesn't even make [her] sad,' but that they 'have no choice' but to come clean because of the impending start of the new school year. It is within the larger social/institutional context that Laure's nonconforming embodiment of gender is unintelligible and thus forecloses subjecthood. As Butler argues, 'the body that one lives is in many ways a body that becomes livable only through first being cast in a culturally intelligible way. In other words, the cultural framing of the body precedes and enables its lived experience.'[55] Laure acquires two different but equally viable kinds of intelligibility throughout the film – she is intelligible as a (tomboyish) 'girl' in the domestic space of the home and intelligible as a 'boy' in the exterior, yet bounded and sheltered, world of childhood. The spectator, however, who, like Laure, moves between these two different corporeal, affective spaces, is confronted with a continued oscillation of sense-making logics, which reinforces a palpably self-reflexive mode of embodied spectatorship.

Figure 11.4 Laure/Mikaël in 'Drag' (*Tomboy*).

It is when these worlds collide *in* the film that Laure's mode of being becomes unintelligible and therefore unlivable. It is at this point in the film – when Laure is 'exposed' by her mother and then confronted by the other children who demand to 'see' evidence of Laure's biological sex in a scene that carries haunting resonances with Brandon's exposure in *Boys Don't Cry* – that a generic ending that somehow falls back on the binary sex/gender system seems inevitable. As the narrative nears its ending, *Tomboy* poses the same questions that Laure, wearing the blue dress, is asked by her mother, just prior to being dragging to Lisa's apartment: 'Got an idea? Cos if you do, please say so, I can't think of any. Have you got a solution?' A solution, that is, other than assuming a clearly defined and legible subject position within the gender binary? Endearingly, the film refuses to provide any kind of clear-cut solution.

In the final scene, we see Laure, by herself, looking out onto the leafy suburban environment from the balcony of the family home. She spots Lisa, standing underneath a tree, gazing up, clearly looking for another encounter. Lisa's turning and tending towards Laure is significant for a number of reasons. The corporeal trajectory of Laure's variously troubling embodiment of gender is interwoven with her increasingly intimate friendship with Lisa. Lisa likes 'Mikaël' and their relationship acquires elements of a romance, including a few timid kisses. Lisa is therefore most directly affected by the revelation of Laure's secret. However, when Laure is cornered and backed up against a tree in the woods by the boys who insist on 'checking' 'if *she* is really a girl', Lisa replies 'Leave *him* alone'. Lisa here engages in the kind of affirmative recognition of Laure's queer identity that Brandon receives from Lana (Chloë Sevigny), his girlfriend, in *Boys Don't Cry*. In a similar, though perhaps more excruciatingly harrowing, scene, in which Lana is forced to check on the physical evidence of Brandon's sex, 'Lana refuses to look when Brandon unbuckles his pants, telling him, "Don't … I know you're a guy."'[56] The boys pressure Lisa to examine Laure, by forcing her to admit that, if Laure is really a girl, their kissing was 'disgusting'. Unlike Lana, Lisa does appear to look, although we cannot be quite sure. Only their upper bodies are in the frame when Laure and Lisa stand facing each other. They continue to look at each other as Lisa seems to unzip and/or pull down Laure's shorts and then briefly glance downwards, at Laure's crotch. We are unable to see what exactly Lisa does, and what exactly she sees.

As Halberstam notes, there are moments, gestures and glances throughout *Boys Don't Cry* that suggest that Lana is somehow aware that Brandon is different – and the same goes for Lisa who realises early on that her new friend is 'not like the others.' This dynamic, in addition to Lisa's return to Laure at the end of the film, imbues her character with queer resonances, which, like Lana's, tend to get lost as they pale in relation to the more explicit queerness of the protagonists. Nonetheless, it is Lisa's instigation of the film's climactic final encounter that enables the refreshingly affirmative opening-up of queer spaces of possibility – rather than the re-establishment of a binary order that narrative closure normally demands. Laure spots Lisa standing outside her apartment. When Laure joins her, they are framed in a two-shot, first coyly staring at the ground, before looking at each other, when Lisa asks 'What's your name?'. The final shot is a close-up of Laure who breathes in heavily before answering 'My name is Laure.' The shot of Laure's serious, thoughtful face is held for various seconds, as Laure's eyes dart around nervously, unsure as to where to look, before fixing her gaze on Lisa. A cut to a black screen signals the end of the film, just as the hint of a smile begins to appear on Laure's face.

Sciamma has commented on the significance of the final scene, noting that the 'end of the film is like the end of a lie – but it doesn't end on "I'm a girl"; it ends with the act of Laure saying her name.' She adds that 'the act of stating who you are asserts the possibility of not having to hide in order to be who you are.'[57] Sciamma considers this to be an act of liberation – and not a return to the norm. The final encounter between Lisa and Laure is one of mutual acknowledgment that queers both characters. It constitutes a subtly emphatic refusal of closure (in all its manifestations) and undercuts the primacy of vision in establishing intelligible and mutually affirmative intersubjective relations. Halberstam notes that *Boys Don't Cry*, creates:

> a position for the transgender subject that is fortified from the traditional operations of the gaze and conventional modes of gendering but also makes the transgender subject dependent on the recognition of a woman. In other words, Brandon can be Brandon because Lana is willing to see him as he sees himself [...] and she is willing to avert her gaze when his manhood is in question.[58]

By anchoring the working out of subjectivity and intelligibility in the realm of embodiment, rather than the disembodied gaze, *Tomboy* manages to sidestep the binary sex/gender system that even a 'transgender subject' like Brandon ultimately reaffirms. Through its making graspable of the phenomenological dimensions of what we might refer to as the non-binary, rather than trans, experience, *Tomboy* gestures towards the possibility of making meaningful contact with ambiguously gendered others. Through its tactile, muscular and kinaesthetic incarnations and negotiations of legibility and appearance, *Tomboy* constitutes a weighty unhinging of the binary sex/gender system that underpins normative configurations of transgenderism, gender nonconformity and passing – in cinema and beyond.

Queer Shape-Shifting: Embodied Trajectories of Transformation and Resistance in *Girlhood*

Girlhood is the final instalment of Sciamma's female coming-of-age trilogy. In many ways, *Girlhood* seems bigger, more serious and more grown-up than its predecessors: it moves from the realms of childhood and early adolescence to late adolescence and the transition to adulthood; it is shot in CinemaScope and is visually grander and more spectacular; and it also opens up the 'world of girls, girls alone' by situating its protagonist(s) in a more specific socio-historical and political context.[59] As Sophie Mayer writes: 'Girlhood goes where the others don't as Marieme/Vic leaves home and enters the adult world on the margins of white French society, full of risks and opportunities.'[60]

Tomboy, like *Water Lilies*, is in some way an 'atemporal' film, in that the young characters' world is fairly self-contained and removed from the wider real-world context, but *Girlhood* is very specifically set in 'the world of today.' Not only does the film feature specific fashion styles, versions of mobile phones and brands of sneakers, soft drinks, alcohol and sweets (entirely absent from *Tomboy*), *Girlhood* also evokes the specific social, cultural and political context of contemporary France through the characters' venturing into various kinds of public, crowded spaces (public transport, the mall, the big open plaza around La Grande Arche) that leads to a range of conflicts and tensions around the intersections of race, gender and class.

Like *Tomboy*, *Girlhood's* appeal hinges, at least in part, on the mesmerising face of its young female protagonist, often framed in close-up, looking on, an indication of her sidelined positioning in the heteropatriarchal, white world of contemporary France. Marieme's face is as mesmerising as it is unrevealing. It is determined yet inaccessible, her often closed, tensed mouth betraying only the lack of 'voice' available to those living at the margins. While the close-up tends to provide access to the inner life and emotions of characters, and thus encourage spectatorial identification, *Girlhood*, like *Tomboy*, privileges a spectatorial encounter with the muscular, kinaesthetic and spatial modes of being-in-the-world embodied by its young female protagonist(s) over more conventional cinematic articulations of subjectivity and agency via the gaze, face and voice and the opportunities for spectatorial identification they provide.

In part, Marieme's face is as spellbinding as it is stoically enigmatic because it is *not* a white face and *Girlhood* certainly plays on, and makes the most of, the 'representational anomaly' of black faces and black

Figure 11.5 Marieme (*Girlhood*).

skin filling the cinema screen, often in close-up.[61] The all-black and predominantly female cast, and a narrative that situates its young black protagonist in the marginalised, violent and (cinematically) overdetermined space of the Parisian banlieue projects, have emerged as some of the key points of discussion around *Girlhood*. The film is often lauded for giving visibility to non-white *female* actors within the larger context of increasing numbers of mostly *male* actors from ethnic-minority backgrounds in France. Ginette Vincendeau ascribes this, in part, to 'the legacy of the *beur* [...] and *banlieue* cinema of the 1980s and 1990s,' which demonstrated 'the viability and relevance of multicultural stories in both mainstream and auteur cinema.'[62]

Within critical debate, *Girlhood* tends to be situated in relation to the broader context of *banlieue* cinema. *Girlhood* is characterised by the generic interweaving of the coming-of-age trope with 'the grammar of the *banlieue* film from which [it] borrows many familiar aspects: concrete buildings, walkways and esplanades frame characters whose clothes and language label them as *banlieue* youth.'[63] Its release also coincided with the 20th anniversary of *La Haine* (1995), Mathieu Kassovitz's quintessential *banlieue* film that sparked an explosion of this type of largely social realist drama in France. *Girlhood* is often considered to be the latest highlight in the cycle of *banlieue* films and comparisons with *La Haine* were rife upon its release.[64]

Girlhood is not characterised by the gritty realism that is linked to the overtly political stance of the *banlieue* social drama, however. Instead, Sciamma adopts what Vincendeau calls 'an intensely aestheticising gaze' in her '"impressionistic" tale of youth.'[65] Sciamma admits that she is interested in 'the choreography of the girls' bodies, the energy of their performances (dancing, fighting), the light on their skin', and fascinated by 'bands of black girls in real life, their "energy and way of speaking."'[66] This aestheticising look at the racial 'other', fuelled by a self-acclaimed fascination with this otherness (which, importantly, has specifically corporeal and visceral undertones), has led to damning critiques of the film as a 'racist, exoticising fantasy of a privileged white filmmaker,' for 'perpetuating the image of black women as victims of oppression' and for 'demonising black men,' countering the praise it received for its making visible of ethnic minority identities and its depiction of 'girls valorising each other.'[67]

A phenomenological approach offers a nuanced alternative to the 'political-aesthetic split' that, as Vincendeau notes, characterises existing debates. In what follows, I trace *Girlhood's* embodied (muscular, kinaesthetic and spatial) trajectory and explore the queer feminist potential of its corporeal and affective resonances. This is, again, an attempt to avoid the drawbacks of a narrowly defined identity politics

– which *Girlhood* itself refuses – while acknowledging the situatedness of experience. *Girlhood* accounts for Marieme's variously marginalised positionality through its unhinging of straightforwardly white and heteropatriarchal modes of embodiment and being-in-the-world, articulated as they are through the muscular, kinaesthetic and spatial dimensions of 'the choreography of the girls' bodies,' 'the energy of their performances' and their appropriation of space 'in a male-dominated [and white] world.'[68]

It is additionally worth noting that Sciamma herself attempts to deflect comparisons with *La Haine* and 'all this cinema about the Urban Western.'[69] Instead, she identifies the 'Janes' as her sources of inspiration – Jane Campion, Jane Austen and Calamity Jane – in order to assert that *Girlhood* is, first and foremost, 'a coming of age story about young women' that happens to be 'set in the suburbs with a black girl.'[70] In doing so, Sciamma attempts to (re)position herself and her film more specifically in relation to a larger trajectory of women's/feminist filmmaking, authorship and criticism – as well as, via the reference to *Calamity Jane* (David Butler, US, 1953), to cinema's variously queer history.[71]

Girlhood is not an obviously queer film – at least in terms of its subject matter. It is only in the final part of the narrative that LGBTI themes are explicitly engaged with. In this sense, it perhaps seems odd to see *Girlhood* featuring so prominently on the queer film festival circuit (despite its out lesbian director). It is *not* so strange, however, if we acknowledge that *Girlhood's* (feminist) queerness lies elsewhere: in its muscular habits and kinaesthetic tendencies; its corporeal resonances and textural entanglements; its embodied twists and turn; and its affective shape-shifting and palpable reorientations. These are woven into the film's textural fabric and shape its sensuous trajectory throughout, before surfacing more explicitly towards the end.

As with her other films, Sciamma refuses to tie her protagonist to a specific and fixed identity (is Marieme straight? bi? trans?), but acknowledges that she is somehow 'queer': 'There are several ways to be queer: [Marieme] is really trying out the different identities that society has set for her. She is not inventing them, she's trying them out.'[72] She goes from being a 'shy, quiet girl' to a 'more iconic, empowered girl, part of a group with this more feminine side,' but she can also be 'one of the boys.'[73] Notably, Marieme's embodiment of these various identities is shaped most significantly through her relations to other *female* characters. If her identity is anchored at all, it is in relation to the variously corporeal and affective resonances that reverberate around the female characters' embodied presence, including in particular her younger sister, the other members of the *bande* and Monica (Dielika Doulibaly), her flatmate, in the final segment of the film. As Sciamma notes, *Girlhood* is 'about how the great love stories and great sentimental journey for girls is among girls.'[74] *Girlhood's* queerness, then, lies in its unhinging of normative modes of gendered embodiment as well as of the normative (lack of affirmative) relations between women that tend to be woven into the fabric of heteronormative patriarchal relations.

In addition to *La Haine*, *Girlhood* also evoked comparisons with Richard Linklater's *Boyhood* (US, 2014), released earlier in the same year, partly because of the coming-of-age subject matter, but mainly due to the films' matching titles. The comparison is in many ways farfetched, however. As Robbie Collins points out, while *Boyhood*, explores 'the passing of time' and 'the making of history,' *Girlhood* is 'set in, and celebrates, the immediate, impulsive here and now.'[75] Sciamma herself variously welcomes and refutes the comparison: the connection of *Bande de filles'* English title to Linklater's film was accidental, she asserts. Although she admits that the films engage in a useful dialogue around growing up and coming-of-age, *Boyhood* and *Girlhood* 'believe very different things in cinema.' While both films 'attempt to encapsulate a universal experience', *Boyhood* offers a conventionally normative account of the coming-of-age trope: 'What's universal in America [and more specifically in US cinema] about teenagehood is a middle-class white boy with average dreams. We pick a character at the margins and say what's universal is a 16-year-old black girl.'[76]

To claim universality for a story with an entirely black cast and a young black female protagonist is problematic, and not only because *Girlhood* was made by a (relatively) privileged white filmmaker. On the one hand, assertions that Marieme is not a *black* heroine, but a 'contemporary heroine', betray a seemingly progressive colour-blindness, and echo non-white filmmakers' and actors' resistance to 'being seen in terms of their ethnic origins for fear of being ghettoised.'[77] This understanding of *Girlhood* as not being *about* race is echoed in various reviews; for example, the claim that '*Girlhood* is not a film about the black experience so much as the trials of youth.'[78] On the other hand, Sciamma's appropriation of the racial 'other', and of the *banlieue*, to her 'auteurist vision' risks discounting the specificity of the experience and situation (in the phenomenological sense) of the racial 'other'.[79]

What *Girlhood* manages to achieve, I want to argue, is a careful negotiation of a range of seemingly binary and mutually exclusive positions: universality vs. specificity; difference vs. otherness; racial stereotypes vs. affirmative/positive images. As with *Tomboy*, Sciamma draws on generic and representational clichés (of *banlieue* cinema; of urban-set films featuring disaffected black youth; of the coming-of-age genre; of the female adolescent in French cinema) while at the same time remoulding these clichés and refusing to follow their straightforwardly white and heteropatriarchal 'lines'. Eric Kohn gestures towards this contradictory ambiguity, noting that '*Girlhood* deals with race by implication,' while 'its main line of inquiry is universal (which, ironically, makes it something of anomaly among movies exclusively focused on minorities).'[80] Similarly, Barbara Speed suggests that while *Girlhood* 'says things about race, class, and French society, […] these are always firmly grounded in Marieme and her story.' This is because we never 'leave Marieme's headspace', which arguably 'stops you drawing out the film to make it answer to a much broader sociopolitical narrative.'[81] In other words, what emerges here, and as I explore further in what follows, is a sense that *Girlhood* engages with questions of race, gender, sexuality and wider socio-political issues not via conventional representational strategies, but through muscular, kinaesthetic and spatial incarnations of the ways in which oppressively racialised and gendered social structures are embodied and felt and, importantly, resisted and refused. It is not necessarily that we never 'leave Marieme's headspace' (although we are firmly positioned 'with' Marieme throughout the film), but that we are offered a visceral encounter with the affectively corporeal trajectory of her shape-shifting journey.

Girlhood conveys this journey in five parts – in addition to the American football opening sequence – that are clearly separated by black screens. The first part introduces us to a shy, quiet and reserved Marieme and her restrictive home life, which consists of taking on a mothering role for her two younger sisters; dealing with a bullying, violent older brother while her mother is mostly absent and at work; her lack of educational prospects (she is told she has to leave school because of her grades); and her first encounter with Lady (Assa Sylla), Fily (Mariétou Touré) and Adiatou (Lindsay Karamoh), the *bande de filles*. Part two shows Marieme growing more confident in the company of the three other girls, as the plain clothes and braids of childhood of the first part are replaced by wavy open hair, tight jeans and a black leather jacket that match the style of the other members of the *bande*. Part two also includes the much-talked-about scene of the four girls dancing to Rihanna's 'Diamonds', as well as the first of two fight sequences, in which Lady, the leader of the *bande*, is defeated by a girl from another gang.

In part three, Marieme asserts herself and her frustrations and desires even more confidently as she dares to pursue a 'forbidden' relationship and sexual intimacy with a boy, Ismaël (Idrissa Diabaté), who is a close friend of Marieme's thuggish brother. She also challenges and defeats the leader of the other gang in a brutal street fight. Part four sees Marieme leave home and her friends; in an attempt to refuse the dead-end life set out for her she agrees to work as a drug dealer for gangster Abou (Djibril Gueye). In the fifth and final part, Marieme undergoes the most dramatic physical transformation, as we see her selling drugs wearing a short blonde wig, heavy make-up, a tight-fitting short red dress and high heels, while she takes on an overtly masculine appearance outside her drug-dealing activities: she wears short braids, plain baggy clothes and even binds her breasts in order to conceal her feminine bodily shape. Marieme also shares an apartment with Monica, a more conventionally feminine character, and the two women 'appear' as a couple at various points, especially in the domestic context of the kitchen and, most poignantly, when they slow dance together at Abou's party towards the very end of the film.

The changes in Marieme's appearance are clearly linked to her transformative journey and are indicative of *Girlhood's* more general non-essentialising stance. As Sciamma notes, her aim was to show how 'identities are worn like costumes' and she likens *Girlhood* to the 'superhero genre' in that Marieme's transformations are tied to the realisation of 'what power the "costume" gives her.'[82] However, *Girlhood* goes beyond the surface layer of the costume that can easily be put on and taken off and locates its protagonist's variously transformative journey in the realm of embodiment, spatiality and sensuousness – and the muscular and kinaesthetic register is asserted from the onset.

Feeling social 'pressures' or: On (not) having a 'voice'

Girlhood opens with a highly aestheticised slow-motion sequence of an American football match. The scene is fairly decontextualised and its ties to the narrative and diegetic world of *Girlhood* are tenuous. It does not really make (rational) sense and echoes, at least in part, the fantastic, ahistorical and utopian register of the musical 'number'.[83] Two teams, fully dressed in American football regalia, emerge from the tunnel as the energetically hypnotic score increases in volume; together with the slow-motion framing of moving bodies, the sonic swell adds to the sense of decontextualised abstraction. Both teams seem to take the game seriously – there are crunching tackles, hostile stares and helmet against helmet standoffs. Yet there is no referee, and there are no coaches or spectators of any kind in the empty stands that are surrounded by the impenetrable black darkness of the night sky. Both teams also wear the same team name on the back of their jerseys and engage in a joint celebration at the end of the game, leaving all sense of rivalry and confrontation behind. There are no references to American football in the remainder of the film and, while the scene is linked to our introduction to *Girlhood's* diegetic world 'proper' (we see the players, including Marieme, returning to the *banlieue* projects following the game), the football sequence itself appears removed in time and space and takes on a utopian register.

Figure 11.6 Celebrating Female Physicality (*Girlhood*).

There is a certain ambiguity around the players' gender as they emerge from the tunnel and run towards and past the camera in the blurry opening shot. Their heads are covered by helmets, their faces obscured by protective grilles and their bodily shapes concealed by thickly padded outfits – but we get occasional glimpses of ponytails sticking out of helmets, and of eye make-up. What is centrally conveyed in this sequence is a sense of uninhibited kinetic energy and corporeal, muscular contact that is shaped by the players' movements and by the energetically rhythmic sync score that gradually intensifies throughout. The sequence is shot entirely in slow motion as the camera puts us in touch with the players' assertively dynamic physicalities and traces the collective contours of taut bodies brimming with energy. Questions of gender, and gendered embodiment, are thus woven into the affective fabric of *Girlhood* from the (utopian) onset. The sequence plays with the masculine associations of American football (including the strong, powerful, energetic and assertive modes of movement and comportment characteristic of those playing the sport) and creates an affectively visceral juxtaposition between the quintessentially masculine modes of embodiment that take shape in the scene and the visible indicators of (and common-sense assumptions about) femininity that are present, albeit ambiguously, throughout.

The opening sequence stands in stark contrast to the general invisibility, in cinema and beyond, of strong, powerful and unrestrained female bodies of various shapes and sizes 'revelling in the joy of their own strength' – especially without being exposed to an intrusive (male) gaze.[84] We are offered an encounter with the collective and exuberant kinetic energy and corporeal dynamism of bodies that extend an ambiguously abstract space which appears unmarked by the restrictive textures of the social. It is a self-enclosed space that is removed from the diegetic world of the film to which we are subsequently introduced. The opening sequence thus not only introduces us to the muscular, kinaesthetic and spatial register, tied as it is to the uninhibited and confident female physicalities. It also provides a contrast to, and thus foregrounds, the imprisoning pressures of the heteropatriarchal white world that the girls normally inhabit and that they return to following the opening sporting action.

Sound, noise and voice also play an important role in *Girlhood's* opening incarnation of the muscular and spatial dimensions of the girls' corporeal presence. When they take off their helmets and begin their post-game celebrations, their voices, initially audible as unintelligible chatter, are the first diegetic sounds that appear on the soundtrack alongside the non-diegetic score. They gradually transform into the rhythmic roars of celebratory chants, almost overpowering the music. The opening sequence ends with a long-shot of the teams in the centre of the floodlit field, with the depthless, impenetrable night sky taking up the majority of the frame, before the floodlights turn off and the entire screen turns to black. The film's title, '*Bande de filles*', appears on the screen and only the girls' echoing chants remain present on the soundtrack. Their voices provide a sound bridge into *Girlhood's* diegetic world as they turn into sonorous yet indecipherable chatter that continues to increase in volume as the silhouettes of the girls walking towards the camera become progressively more distinguishable from the black void from which they emerge. The thickly textured and reverberating entanglement of animated and cheerful voices gives the group a corporeal presence, even when individual bodies and faces cannot be clearly demarcated.

The girls move through the darkness as a lively, hustling and bustling unit, the energy and dynamism of their collective corporeal presence intimately entangled with the enchantingly chaotic vitality of their resounding sonic presence. But as the girls enter the projects, with a low-angle shot emphasising the high-rise apartment blocks towering over the group, the volume (perceived loudness, intensity) of the densely textured, layered sounds enveloping the girls diminishes, along with the volume (size) of the group, as the girls peel off one by one or in small groups to return to their respective homes, as well as the volume (spatiality) of individual bodies, as the girls' assertively confident comportment is replaced by slouched postures, tensed shoulders, hands stuffed in pockets, bowed heads and downcast eyes. The dark shadows of anonymous male figures, cast against the dimly lit walls of the high-rises, line the walkway and assert the sombre and intimidating atmosphere, as their muffled conversations and menacing shouts replace the girls' joyous chatter. Marieme is identified as *Girlhood's* protagonist as we experience the disintegration of the group and the isolating journey through the palpably hostile environment with her. Marieme emerges from the group and there is a gradual shift in spectatorial alignment in our initial encounter, from the corporeal collective to the figure of Marieme.

The opening offers a palpable contrast between an energetic, assertive and expansive physicality on the one hand and an inhibited, self-referential and contained mode of comportment on the other, foregrounding the corporeal resonances of social *pressures*. This juxtaposition resonates with Ahmed's queer phenomenological account, already evoked in relation to *2 Seconds*, where she notes that social 'pressure' to lead a certain kind of life might be experienced as a 'physical "press" on the surface of the body' and that, over time, bodies tend to 'take the shape' of these pressures.[85] What Ahmed articulates here, and what *Girlhood's* opening begins to make graspable, are the ways in which 'persons live out their positioning in social structures along with the opportunities and constraints they produce.'[86] The lived-body and its cinematic incarnations are shaped by, and give shape to, these structures – and *Girlhood's* sensory opening register offers an embodied encounter with their 'pressing' resonances. The film's overall trajectory coheres around the muscular, kinaesthetic and spatial juxtaposition that shapes our entrance into the film and traces Marieme's refusal to give in to the heteronormatively patriarchal norms that 'pressure' her to follow the course of the life set out for her. The gendered (rather than racialised) dimensions of these pressures and of Marieme's 'positioning in social structure' are foregrounded throughout, which is why the film might resonate not so much as being 'about' race and more profoundly as being 'about' gender.

Girlhood's opening also gestures towards the precarious implications of a phenomenological, affective register within larger social and representational contexts in which language and representation are dominant modes of expression and signification. It highlights the juxtaposition not only between different modes of physicality, but also between vocality/noise and voice/speech. The girls' chatter and laughter gives them an aural presence, but also links to their physical, spatial incarnations: these are sounds that are produced by and emanate from, while also gesturing back towards, the body. However, while we can *hear* the girls, and while their voices reverberate beyond the screen, they do not have 'a voice'. Their patter is largely incomprehensible and we are unable to make out exactly *what it is* they say. Overall, their raucous presence in this scene, which also foreshadows the noisy confrontation between the *bande* and another (black) girl gang in a metro station, risks reinforcing stereotypical associations of black femininity with a kind of animalistic, irrational, out-of-control and excessive corporeality. That said, the tone, rhythm and energy of their patter as they walk through the darkness as a group, still resonating with the dynamic energy of the American football sequence, also provide us with a palpable sense of positivity, energy, elation and confidence. Both in the opening sequence and throughout, especially during moments of corporeal collectivity and infectious laughter (about which more later), *Girlhood* opens up different registers of meaning – what Bolton, following Irigaray, calls a 'feminine syntax' or a 'gestural code of women's bodies.'[87]

It is this intertwining of embodiment and spatiality with sound, noise and voice that is key to Marieme's working out of her place in the world *as well as* to the film's working out of a mode of articulation that makes Marieme's corporeally affective transformations graspable. *Girlhood* is a much more 'vocal' film than *Tomboy*. There is more dialogue and there are numerous moments in which Marieme attempts to 'voice' her frustrations with the life set out for her (including her conversation with the guidance councillor who tells her that she cannot stay at school; her confrontation with her mother's boss who offers her a dead-end job as a cleaner; and in the hotel scene in which she says goodbye to the other three members of the *bande* before moving on to become part of Abou's drug cartel). Overall, however, dialogue is of secondary importance with regard to *Girlhood's* articulation of Marieme's working out her options in a world that is not 'for' her and that does not 'extend [her] shape.'[88] As Kohn suggest, 'the themes in play unfold in physical terms.'[89]

Various different kinds of bodily performances take place throughout the film and it is during these moments that the sense of corporeal resistance, refusal and assertion is conveyed most palpably and offers the most profoundly affective resonances. In particular, these moments include the American football match, the *bande's* dancing to Rihanna's 'Diamonds' in a hotel room, another dance sequence in the public space around La Grande Arche and two brutal street fights. Those moments are crucial because they convey a sense of Marieme's and the girls' assertive and unconstrained physicalities, engendering a powerfully visceral contrast with the constrained and pressured modes of embodiment that take shape outside of those moments. As Harris points out, 'to see these same bodies stilled elsewhere in the film by violence and taboo is thus all the more agonising.'[90]

As foreshadowed by the American football scene, affirmative assertions of corporeal collectivity take place when the girls manage to find, and 'occupy' (in Ahmed's sense), spaces that are removed from the otherwise overbearing pressures of the social[91] – spaces, in other words, in which they are amongst themselves and manage to create, at least temporarily, a 'world of girls, girls alone.'[92] Dori Thomas points to *Girlhood's* articulation of a notable difference:

> between who these girls are when they are together and who they are when they are surrounded by those who hold them back or would seek to control them. Throughout the film, the girls are constantly changing their behavior and their appearances to suit their surroundings – they do so, because that's how they survive.[93]

While Marieme's shape-shifting is, in part, about survival, it is also clearly an embodied manifestation of resistance and refusal and an unapologetic assertion of corporeal presence. These assertions are most palpable when the girls are together, when they *do* things together, when they 'connect', when they 'turn towards' each other and when the affective and corporeal resonances between them surface and, at times, erupt in gripping manifestations of profoundly queer phenomenological orientations.

Laughter and 'Diamonds': affecting assertions of collective corporeal presence

These corporeal tropes come together, and are conveyed most affectively, in the first hotel room scene, which also includes the girls' rendition of Rihanna's 'Diamonds'. Sciamma notes that 'there is no safe space for girls' in Marieme's world.[94] Renting a hotel room (with stolen money) is an attempt to create a (temporary) space that allows for abandon and intimacy. The room takes on a utopian quality, evoking the decontextualised feel of the American football match – although the pressures and confines of the outside world are much more proximate and occasionally rupture the confines of the utopian spaces (for instance, through phone calls from Marieme's brother). Hotel rooms are ambiguous sites in that they constitute a complex intersection of the public and the private – they are both and neither. In *Girlhood*, they function as an alternative to the various restrictions, restraints and pressures the girls encounter in the private (their homes) *and* the public realm (school, the metro, the mall, the plaza and the city more generally).

Homes, in particular, are ambivalent spaces in all of Sciamma's films, but *Girlhood* foregrounds the heteropatriarchal pressures of the home most explicitly. To a certain extent, the conventionally gendered implications of the public–private divide are turned on their head. As Sciamma describes, in '[t]he neighborhood outside and even at home, the men make the rules and there is an authority the girls have to live by. But when they go to a public space like in the city, it's kind of a stage where they get to perform.'[95] These public 'performances', in which the girls unapologetically assert their physical, sonic presence include their confident, sassy and loud strutting through the mall; the shouting match with another girl gang on a metro station platform; the dance moves they practice to the music played from their mobile phones on the metro; and the street fights. The girls variously re-appropriate and occupy public spaces that are not 'meant' for them in these moments, through behaviours, appearances and modes of taking up space that disrupt the normatively white, straight, patriarchal expectations and tendencies that normally shape these spaces and the bodies that occupy them. In one particularly touching scene, the girls stage a dance-off in a public plaza in the city, following the stunningly shot set-piece that traces the girls' smiling faces as they stand in front of La Grand Arche at the beginning of the fourth segment of the film. There are [a] number of lengthy closeups that linger on the dancers' gyrating hips and crotches. The framing does not appear intrusive, however, as the joyous and elated performances are contained within the protective bubble of the girls' collective corporeal presence.

The *bande's* get-together in the hotel room earlier (in the second segment of the film) constitutes a key moment in *Girlhood's* gradual incarnation of the powerfully affective resonances of female solidarity, mutuality and intimacy. It is also a corporeal, sensuous manifestation of Marieme's integration *into* the group, as she turns from shy and reserved onlooker to the visceral, muscular, kinaesthetic centre of the group – *and of the film*. In the preceding confrontation with another girl gang in the metro station, for instance, Marieme stays in the background, observing and taking in the aggressive posturing and shouting with a tensely closed mouth and slight frown. As the girls enter the hotel room, Lady, Adiatou and Fily sit down on the bed. Marieme throws herself on top of the entangled bodies with some force; she wants to be 'in the middle'. A less-than-impressed Lady pushes Marieme off her legs and a pillow fight ensues as the girls begin to laugh, at Lady (for being angry) and at Adiatou who gets up to perform a hysterically comical rendition of a pop song before throwing herself back onto the pile of bodies. The girls now laugh uncontrollably, *at* and *with* each other, as high-pitched shrieks alternate with raucous snorts and deep, guttural, resounding howls. They are in stitches, doubled-over, holding their bellies, unable to speak, seemingly taken over by an irresistible force that has their bodies firmly in its grip. Their laughter is overwhelmingly infectious, the kind that is difficult to fake. The scene conveys a palpable sense of corporeal authenticity, as the young actors themselves seem genuinely entangled in the joyous and pleasurable affective resonances that emanate from and reverberate around their bodily intimacy – it is difficult not to laugh along with them, or at least crack the hint of a smile.

Simon Critchley notes that laughter is affective because it is 'a corporal response [...] a muscular phenomenon, consisting of spasmodic contraction and relaxation of the facial muscles with corresponding movements in the diaphragm' – it is precisely the physicality of laughter that is infectious.[06] Bolton very usefully distinguishes between different kinds of women's laughter, not all of which have subversive implications. In cinema, where 'many stories are not about women's lived bodies, [laughter] is usually an indication of their reactivity, rather than activity' and conventionally functions to indicate a type: giggler, hag, bitch, challenge. In films that are also *about* women's lived bodies, such as *Girlhood*, women's *collective* laughter in particular might evoke 'a phenomenological encounter, through which we are able to join them in a place [that is otherwise] inexpressible.'[97] The cinematic incarnation of this kind of hearty, rebellious infectious female laughter:

> reaches out and has an effect on the audience that dialogue does not provide. It is a phenomenological communication of their lived bodies in all their desperation, isolation, alienation, or joyful rejection [...] conveying the lived bodies of women [and] thus enabling viewers to join them in laughter as a *place* where women's voices can be heard.[98]

The moments of laughter in *Girlhood* conjure this kind of affectively embodied engagement and make palpable the confidence, unselfconsciousness and abandon that add a sense of corporeal substance to the girls' collective presence. The moments assert Bolton's suggestion that 'women laughing together can be a form of rebellion – a laugh of solidarity, of denial of patriarchal power.' It can convey a sense of '*refusal* to go along with the societal structures which are being imposed on [women], uniting them in a kind of socio-political sisterliness.'[99] Crucially, women's laughter is often juxtaposed with speech – especially when female characters do not have a 'voice' in the conventional sense. What a broadly phenomenological (Irigarayan) approach enables is a consideration of women's laughter not only as a 'place for women's discourse' but as part of a 'gestural code of women's bodies' that bypasses, as it were, conventionally dominant systems of signification, including language and speech.[100] Laughter, like the various other embodied forms of articulation and assertion that shape *Girlhood's* corporeal trajectory, gains significance when the language that is available is inadequate to the task of conveying experiences, connections, frustrations and desires. The making graspable of the physicality of (collective) laughter in *Girlhood* therefore opens up spaces for spectatorial encounters that make corporeal, sensuous 'sense' of the girls' world and experiences.

The hotel room turns into an even more explicitly abstract and utopian space when a close-up of Lady blowing smoke from a shisha pipe into the camera cuts to a close-up of Lady's downcast face and bare shoulders bathed in shimmering, blue light. Lady lip-syncs to the non-diegetic music, as Rihanna's 'Diamonds' appears on the soundtrack and drowns out any diegetic noise. Lady lifts her head to stare straight into the camera, acknowledging its presence and seemingly performing directly 'for' us. As the camera tracks back, Adiatou joins Lady in the frame and both characters now lip-sync, singing with/at each other, and begin to dance together, hands intertwined. The close, mobile framing conveys a sense of bodily intimacy and mutuality as the girls respond to each others' slow and rhythmic movements, with the blue light giving the scene a dream-like feel. As with the American football match, the performance takes place in an affective sphere that is removed from the reality of the diegesis and any sense of the characters performing *for* an audience, other than each other, disappears. Instead, they clearly revel in the joy of the connections, resonances and kinetic energies generated by their joint presence and their 'tending toward' each other.[101]

Fily then enters the frame and joins the dancers, before we see Marieme still sitting on the bed, watching the dancers, her upper body swaying to the rhythm of the song in almost imperceptibly small movements.

Figure 11.7 Laughter and 'Diamonds' (*Girlhood*).

The camera slowly closes in on Marieme's face, emphasising her gaze that distances her from the performance and the girls' collective elation and energy, while the rhythmic swaying of her body also conveys the emergence of a physical connection. We are drawn towards Marieme as the camera brings us closer and closer, just as Marieme is drawn to the girls' collective corporeal energy. As Sciamma notes, the scene is 'really about how friendship is choreography and the birth of a friendship between the characters but also *between the audience and the character*.'[102] When Marieme joins the others, all four dancers are briefly framed together, in mid-shot, with Marieme dancing in the centre of the frame. The camera then reverts to the closer framing of the characters from the shoulders up, moving amongst the dancers, adding to the sense of kinaesthetic and muscular energy, while also conveying the joyous elation in their faces, always returning to Marieme, who becomes the corporeal and affective centre that the dancers, *and the film*, circulate around.

Towards the end of the song, which is, unusually for the cinematic context, played in its entirety, the girls' voices, singing along, become audible on the soundtrack as the diegetic world begins to encroach upon the utopian space of the performance. The 'number' ends with the girls hugging each other, out of breath and laughing and we then see all four characters sleeping on the hotel bed, before Marieme returns home to her abusive older brother the next morning. Again, the contrast between the affective resonances of the girls' collective laughing/dancing and the isolated figure of Marieme walking timidly through the bleak landscape of tower blocks, quietly entering her home, is palpable. It serves to underscore the significance of embodied experience and the ways in which heteropatriarchal social pressures are lived.

A final (queer) twist

As the narrative progresses, Marieme asserts herself more and more forcefully. This is made viscerally explicitly in the street fight sequence in which a determined and ruthless Marieme defeats her opponent, with the close framing and mobile camera conveying the corporeal intensity and brutality of the fight. It is, however, in the final segment that gender and sexual norms are most profoundly unhinged as Marieme's continually twisting and turning corporeal journey undergoes an unexpected change in direction. Marieme decides to leave behind everything she knows. She refuses to follow the 'line', and the 'life', set out for her.[103] Marieme takes on two contrasting kinds of appearances and identities in this final segment, one of which is explicitly posited as a performance (of gender) with a specific purpose: she dons a short blonde wig, high heels, a tight red dress and make-up when she sells drugs to Abou's clients – and sheds this costume as soon as she has fulfilled her task.

Her new everyday appearance also constitutes a fairly dramatic shift. Marieme takes on a manly appearance and becomes 'one of the guys' of Abou's drug cartel. We might read her adaption of a masculine mode of embodiment as a refusal to be confined by the multiply marginalised social positionality associated with feminine modes of embodiment and womanly appearance, and, in the same vein, as a way of protecting herself from abuse, sexual harassment and other forms of gendered violence – although the exact reasons for the radical change in appearance and mode of embodiment are never clarified. Marieme even binds her breasts, which is revealed when she meets with her boyfriend Ismaël. He is visibly taken aback when he discovers the bandages as he slips his hand underneath her shirt. He wants to know 'why?', but is never given an answer. As in *Tomboy*, Sciamma stays away from *why* in order to focus on *how* her characters live their gender.

This part of the narrative thus combines Marieme's taking on of a male appearance (which is sometimes read as an indication of her trans identity) with her continuing relationship with Ismaël (although this storyline takes up relatively little screen time) as well as with her ambiguous and increasingly intimate relation with the conventionally feminine Monica. It is this twisted and contradictory intermingling of gender and sexuality within the film that evokes a sense of queerness most explicitly. Perhaps surprisingly, it is the final segment that has drawn relatively little attention in critical reviews.

It opens with Marieme walking up the red-carpeted stairs to a stylish apartment to deliver drugs at a party – a white, upper-class space that is otherwise completely invisible in *Girlhood*. She is explicitly, and perhaps excessively, sexualised, for the first time in the film, as her walk up the stairs is aestheticised by the slow-motion framing and the slow and rhythmic sync score that conveys a sense of (sexual) tension, suspense and danger/risk. A low-angle shot closes in on her high heels, ankles and shimmering calves, before moving up her legs, revealing a short, sleeveless red dress and a blonde wig. After delivering the drugs, she returns to the backseat of the car waiting for her in the street and immediately sheds her costume (wig and dress).

We then see her with her new *bande*: two young men, both fellow drug dealers, and Monica. Marieme sits between the men on the couch, wearing short braids and plain, unshapely clothes, her 'manspreading' posture resembling theirs, as they eat pizza and watch a football match on TV. Monica sits curled up at the side of the couch, taking up very little space, and is clearly not interested in the football match. Marieme sports a serious, angry almost, facial expression throughout, as she talks with the guys, one of whom makes unwanted sexual advances towards Monica. Just as Marieme was integrated into the *bande de filles* by adjusting to the rhythm and corporeal dynamic of the group, she is now incorporated into the gang of boys.

We then see Marieme and Monica walking back to their apartment at night. Marieme carries Monica the final part of the way because her feet hurt from walking in high heels. Their laughter and physical proximity recalls the tactile and muscular intimacy amongst the members of the *bande de filles* that Marieme has left behind. This moment also sets up a significant contrast, which structures the final segment, between Marieme's stoic, reserved, cold and aggressive comportment when she is amongst the boys and her relaxed, open and caring tendencies when she is with Monica. As one of the guys, Marieme becomes a part of, and helps perpetuate, the violent pressures exerted on young women (like her) by the heteropatriar-chal world she lives in and that she has previously experienced herself. This shift in behaviour and attitude can certainly be read as a refusal to occupy the position of the female 'victim', but it also adds to the more

Figure 11.8 Twisting Binary Gender (*Girlhood*).

general sense of Marieme as an ambiguous heroine, one who does not invite any kind of straightforwardly comfortable identification. *Girlhood's* foregrounding of an embodied, muscular and kinaesthetic mode of spectatorship mitigates these tensions and posits Marieme's latest and perhaps most extreme shape-shifting as part of *Girlhood's* overall corporeal trajectory.

It is through Marieme's continued, and explicitly sexual, relationship with Ismaël and the simultaneously emerging, far more tactile and embodied, relation to Monica, that *Girlhood* challenges gender and sexual binaries most profoundly. This is encapsulated in the sequence surrounding Ismaël's discovery of Marieme's breast binding. When Ismaël leaves Marieme's room, slamming the door on his way out because he cannot make sense of Marieme's appearance, the camera moves down from her serious, thoughtful face to her bare shoulders, gold necklace and bound torso, with the slight swelling of her breasts bulging over the bandage, and her visibly heavy breathing betraying her inner turmoil. The image encapsulates a multitude of contradictory meanings around gender and sexuality and is then juxtaposed with an equally complex and contradictory scenario: Monica applies makeup to Marieme's eyes and lips, softly smiling as she does so, then tenderly moving blonde strands of hair from the wig out of Marieme's face with her fingers before gazing into Marieme's eyes.

Following the subsequent drug delivery, Marieme joins Monica at one of Abou's rooftop parties. Her appearance is ambiguously gendered as she has taken off the blonde wig, but not the big sparkly earrings, and replaced the short red dress with her baggy clothes, while her face is still covered in make-up. Monica asks Marieme to dance and they engage in an intimate slow dance, arms around each other's shoulders and waist and looking into each other's eyes in an obviously romantic and sexually charged encounter. They are violently interrupted by Abou who pulls Marieme towards him, attempting first to dance with her and then to kiss her. Marieme's physical refusal of Abou's advances (she shoves him away and then slaps him in the face) marks the end of her drug-selling career.

In the end, Marieme turns away from everything: the *bande*, Abou and his gang (including Monica), Ismaël (she tells him she does not want to be 'a good girl' and marry him) and her family. She returns to her family home once more in the final scene of the film and rings the doorbell, but changes her mind at the last minute. The closing shot sees Marieme, with her short braids, make-up, earrings and unshapely, boyish clothes, walk away from the door of the apartment block and the camera, and towards the railing at the edge of the building from where she can oversee the surrounding area. In an interview, Sciamma notes the significance of Marieme's appearance in this scene: 'In the last shot of the film, Marieme wears the braids of childhood, the makeup of a diva, and the clothing of a boy. She's possibly everything or none of those.'[104] We see Marieme, now crying, from behind and then in profile (when she turns around), as the camera begins to track towards and then past her until she disappears from the right side of the frame. The camera stops moving when only the out-of-focus surroundings (leafy trees, other tower blocks in the distance) are visible in the frame as *Girlhood's* signature sync score grows louder on the soundtrack. Marieme then walks back into the frame, her face in profile and close-up, briefly hesitating as she reaches the centre of the screen, breathing in deeply and swallowing, before continuing her move across.

Sciamma says the following about the film's ending and her protagonist's identity:

I don't have this secret story I'm not telling: I'm finishing my movie where I know it should be finished. It's really about leaving her on the side and going to that blurry horizon and you expect the credits to roll because it's like ten seconds. But she's getting back in the frame and you're going to have to put up with her in the frame. It's not that open, it's really saying something. It's the most political shot I ever did in my life.[105]

The final moments of the film are an assertion of Marieme's corporeal presence, of the muscular, breathing physicality, of her kinetic energy and directionality, and her refusal to be stilled and confined, by the heteropatriarchal world she inhabits – and, perhaps most importantly, by the cinematic frame.

Overall, what this queer feminist phenomenological encounter with *Tomboy* and *Girlhood* makes graspable, I hope, is a sense of the films' corporeally affective qualities. It also fleshes out, and gives concrete shape to, the kind of critical tending towards cinema that asserts the centrality of sensuousness and corporeality to the queerness of certain kinds of (queer) films: those that hinge on, and foreground, the materiality of embodiment and performance. The focus on the embodied resonances evoked by the textural entanglement of the bodies in, of and around *Tomboy* and *Girlhood* provides a model for how we might account for cinematic queerness in relation to the spatial and kinaesthetic implications of nonconforming incarnations of gender and sexuality. This project's focus on muscularity, spatiality, movement, temporality and perception has begun to provide a queer feminist phenomenological answer to the questions that Davina Quinlivan raises in her exploration of 'how "queer" cinema might feel': How can we foreground and put to critical use the concordances of embodied film theory and queer spectatorship? And how might we explore the sense of queer cinema as haptic experience *as well as* the queer implications of haptic enquiry.[106] We might say that what has taken shape here, throughout this book, is a reorientation, not just of film criticism (by (at)tending to the sensuous dimensions of cinema) but of *phenomenological* film criticism (by (at)tending to the variously twisted dimensions of embodiment). And this reorientation allows us to grasp the queer feminist cinematic tendencies that variously surface in and through (certain kinds of) queer feminist film.

From *Film Bodies: Queer Feminist Encounters with Gender and Sexuality in Cinema* by Katharina Lindner. © 2018 Katharina Lindner, I. B. Tauris, an imprint of Bloomsbury Publishing Plc.

Notes

1. Mayer, 'Uncommon sensuality', p. 96; referencing Kara Keeling, *The Witch's Flight: The Cinematic, the Black Femme and the Image of Common Sense* (Durham and London: Duke University Press, 2008).
2. 'Marieme' becomes 'Vic' (for *victory/victoire*) when she joins the girl gang/*bande de filles* and is given a gold necklace with her new name on it. She is referred to as Vic by the members of the *bande*, but is known as Marieme in the other contexts and spaces of the film. For reasons of clarity, I refer to the character as Marieme throughout.
3. Ibid., p. 88.
4. Ahmed, *Queer Phenomenology*, pp. 7; 130.
5. Aaron, 'The new queer spectator', in M. Aaron (ed.), *New Queer Cinema: A Critical Reader* (New Brunswick: Rutgers University Press, 2004).
6. Tim Palmer, *Brutal Intimacy: Analyzing Contemporary French Cinema* (Middletown: Wesleyan University Press, 2011), p. 34.
7. Ahmed, *Queer Phenomenology*, p. 181.
8. Ibid., p. 8.
9. See Keeley Saunders, 'Gender-defined spaces, places and tropes: contemporary transgender representation in *Tomboy* and *Romeos*', *Journal of European Popular Culture* 5/2 (2014), pp. 181–93.
10. We might note here the considerable critical acclaim, including Oscar nominations, received by straight and cis actors playing trans characters.
11. Saunders, 'Gender-defined spaces, places and tropes'.

12. Ibid., p. 185.
13. Halberstam, *In a Queer Time and Place*, pp. 54–5.
14. Darren Waldron, 'Embodying gender nonconformity in "girls": Céline Sciamma's *Tomboy*', *L'Esprit Créateur* 53/1 (2013), p. 61.
15. Ibid., p. 62.
16. Marjorie Garber, *Vested Interests: Cross-Dressing and Cultural Anxiety* (London: Penguin, 1993), pp. 101–2; quoted in Saunders, 'Gender-defined spaces, places and tropes', p. 185.
17. Waldron, 'Embodying gender nonconformity in "girls"', p. 62.
18. Halberstam, *Female Masculinity* (London: Durham and London, 1998), p. 185.
19. Stahl, *Unhappy Medium*.
20. Ibid., p. 29.
21. Ibid., p. 10.
22. Ibid., p. 60.
23. Ibid., p. 19.
24. Ibid.
25. Ibid., p. 24.
26. Waldron, 'Embodying gender nonconformity in "girls"', p. 63.
27. Palmer, *Brutal Intimacy*, p. 35.
28. Stahl, *Unhappy Medium*, p. 24.
29. Waldron, 'Embodying gender nonconformity in "girls"', p. 68.
30. I refer to the protagonist as 'Laure' and 'she' (rather than he, s/he, he/she, they), for purposes of avoiding an obscure and confusing writing style – although this might more accurately reflect the lack of clarity around sex/gender, visibility and legibility that continue to surface throughout the film. In using a feminine pronoun I follow Waldron's not entirely unproblematic suggestion that this is a sensible move as it mirrors 'how Sciamma refers to Laure in interviews' and, more importantly, because it avoids 'collapsing transgender subjectivities within an account of gender nonconformity' (Waldron, 'Embodying gender nonconformity in "girls"', p. 72). My referring to Laure as she/her is also a reflection of what 'appears', as it were, in my own encounter with the film.
31. Waldron, 'Embodying gender nonconformity in "girls"', p. 60.
32. Ibid.
33. Halberstam, *In a Queer Time and Place*, p. 54, my emphasis; quoted in Saunders, 'Gender-defined spaces, places and tropes', p. 183.
34. Gil, 'Paradoxical body', p. 97.
35. Céline Sciamma, *Tomboy* DVD interview (2011).
36. Halberstam, *In a Queer Time and Place*, p. 78.
37. Ibid.
38. Ibid.
39. Ibid.
40. Ibid., emphases in original.
41. Ibid., p. 91.
42. Ibid., p. 104.
43. Sciamma, *Tomboy* DVD interview.
44. Ahmed, *Queer Phenomenology*, p. 200; referencing Thomas Csordas, *Body/Meaning/Healing* (New York: Palgrave Macmillan, 2002), pp. 241–6.
45. Waldron, 'Embodying gender nonconformity in "girls"', p. 66.
46. Sciamma, *Tomboy* DVD interview.

47. Butler, 'Athletic genders', para. 6.
48. Ibid.
49. Ibid., my emphases.
50. Ahmed, *Queer Phenomenology*, p. 20.
51. Butler, 'Athletic genders', para. 8.
52. Ibid.
53. D'Aloia, 'Upside-down cinema', p. 155.
54. Ahmed, *Queer Phenomenology*, p. 62.
55. Butler, 'Athletic genders', para. 12.
56. Halberstam, *In a Queer Time and Place*, p. 87.
57. Sciamma, *Tomboy* DVD interview.
58. Ibid., p. 89.
59. Palmer, *Brutal Intimacy*, p. 35.
60. Mayer, '"She's getting back in the frame": interview with Céline Sciamma', *The F Word: Contemporary UK Feminism* (5 May 2015). Available at http://www.thefword.org.uk/2015/05/celine_sciamma_interview/ (accessed 2 April 2017).
61. Dori Thomas, 'A review of Céline Sciamma's *Girlhood*: an honest and emotionally powerful take on the coming-of-age genre', *Side B Magazine* (5 June 2015). Available at http://sidebmagazine.tumblr.com/post/120774164350/a-review-of-c%C3%A9line-sciammas-girlhood-an-honest (accessed 2 April 2017).
62. Ginette Vincendeau, 'Minority report', *Sight & Sound* 25/6 (2015), p. 24.
63. Ibid., p. 27.
64. Sue Harris, 'Film of the week: *Girlhood*' (14 Dec 2015). Available at http://www.bfi.org.uk/news-opinion/sight-sound-magazine/reviews-recommendations/film-week-girlhood (accessed 2 April 2017).
65. Vincendeau, 'Minority report', p. 27.
66. Ibid., quoting Sciamma.
67. Ibid.
68. Ibid.
69. Sciamma, quoted in Mayer, '"She's getting back in the frame"'.
70. Ibid.
71. Barbara Creed, 'Lesbian bodies: tribades, tomboys and tarts', in J. Price and M. Shildrick (eds), *Feminist Theory and the Body: A Reader* (New York: Routledge, 1999).
72. Sciamma, quoted in Mayer, '"She's getting back in the frame"'.
73. Ibid.
74. Ibid.
75. Robbie Collins, '*Girlhood* review: "A coming-of-age classic"', *The Telegraph* (13 May 2015). Available at http://www.telegraph.co.uk/film/girlhood/review/ (accessed 2 April 2017).
76. Sciamma, quoted in James Mottram, 'Céline Sciamma interview: step aside *Boyhood*, it's *Girlhood* time', *Independent* (24 April 2015). Available at http://www.independent.co.uk/arts-entertainment/films/features/cline-sciamma-interview-step-aside-boyhood-its-girlhood-time-10199093.html (accessed 2 April 2017).
77. Vincendeau, 'Minority report', p. 24.
78. Mottram, 'Céline Sciamma interview'.
79. Vincendeau, 'Minority report', p. 27.
80. Eric Kohn, 'Cannes review: Céline Sciamma's *Girlhood* is one of the best coming of age movies in years', *Indiewire* (15 May 2014). Available at http://www.indiewire.com/article/cannes-review-celine-sciammas-girlhood-is-one-of-the-best-coming-of-age-movies-in-years (accessed 2 April 2017).

81. Barbara Speed, '*Girlhood* avoids easy answer in its portrayal of growing up in the Paris suburbs', *New Statesman* (12 May 2015). Available at http://www.newstatesman.com/culture/2015/05/girlhood-avoids-easy-answers-its-portrayal-growing-paris-suburbs (accessed 2 April 2017).

82. Alison Nastasi, '*Girlhood* director Céline Sciamma on reclaiming childhood, casting her girl gang, and how her film mirrors *Boyhood*', *Flavorwire* (30 January 2015). Available at http://flavorwire.com/502100/girlhood-director-celine-sciamma-on-reclaiming-childhood-casting-her-girl-gang-and-how-her-film-mirrors-boyhood (accessed 2 April 2017).

83. Dyer, 'Entertainment and utopia'.

84. Harris, 'Film of the week: *Girlhood*'.

85. Ahmed, *Queer Phenomenology*, pp. 17; 160.

86. Bolton, 'Giggling girls and cackling crones'.

87. Ibid.

88. Ahmed, *Queer Phenomenology*, p. 147.

89. Kohn, 'Cannes review'.

90. Harris, 'Film of the week: *Girlhood*'.

91. Ahmed, *Queer Phenomenology*, p. 62.

92. Palmer, *Brutal Intimacy*, p. 35.

93. Thomas, 'A review of Céline Sciamma's *Girlhood*'.

94. Sciamma, quoted in ReBecca Theodore-Vachon, 'Interview: black women's lives matter in *Girlhood*', *RogerEbert.com* (7 February 2015). Available at http://www.rogerebert.com/interviews/interview-black-womens-lives-matter-in-girlhood (accessed 2 April 2017).

95. Ibid.

96. Simon Critchley, 'Humour as practically enacted theory, or why critics should tell more jokes', in R. Westwood and C. Rhodes (eds), *Humour, Work and Organization* (London and New York: Routledge, 2007), p. 22.

97. Bolton, 'Giggling girls and cackling crones'.

98. Ibid., my emphasis.

99. Ibid., my emphasis.

100. Ibid.

101. Ahmed, *Queer Phenomenology*, p. 129.

102. Sciamma, quoted in Jordan Rossi, 'The interview: Céline Sciamma – *Girlhood*', *Hunger* (8 May 2015), my emphasis. Available at http://www.hungertv.com/feature/the-interview-celine-sciamma-girlhood/ (accessed 2 April 2017).

103. Ahmed, *Queer Phenomenology*; Freeman, *Time Binds*.

104. Sciamma, quoted in Mayer, '"She's getting back in the frame"'.

105. Ibid.

106. Davina Quinlivan, 'On how queer cinema might feel', *Music, Sound, and the Moving Image* 9/1 (2015), pp. 65–6.

References

Aaron, Michele, 'The new queer spectator', in M. Aaron (ed.), *New Queer Cinema: A Critical Reader* (New Brunswick: Rutgers University Press, 2004).

Ahmed, Sara, *Queer Phenomenology: Orientations, Objects, Others* (Durham and London: Duke University Press, 2006).

Bolton, Lucy, 'Giggling girls and cackling crones: the phenomenology of women's laughter', Keynote *Film-Philosophy* Conference, Liverpool John Moores University (6–7 July 2011).

Butler, Judith, 'Athletic genders: hyperbolic instance and/or the overcoming of sexual binarism', *Stanford Humanities Review* 6/2 (1998). Available at: http://web.stanford.edu/group/SHR/6-2/html/butler.html (accessed 28 March 2017).

Collins, Robbie, '*Girlhood* review: "A coming-of-age classic"', *The Telegraph* (13 May 2015). Available at http://www.telegraph.co.uk/film/girlhood/review/ (accessed 2 April 2017).

Creed, Barbara, 'Lesbian bodies: tribades, tomboys and tarts', in J. Price and M. Shildrick (eds), *Feminist Theory and the Body: A Reader* (New York: Routledge, 1999).

Critchley, Simon, 'Humour as practically enacted theory, or why critics should tell more jokes', in R. Westwood and C. Rhodes (eds), *Humour, Work and Organization* (London and New York: Routledge, 2007).

Csordas, Thomas, *Body/Meaning/Healing* (New York: Palgrave Macmillan, 2002).

D'Aloia, Adriano, 'Upside-down cinema', *Cinema: Journal of Philosophy and the Moving Image* 3 (2012), pp. 155–82.

Davis, Nick, *The Desiring-Image: Gilles Deleuze and Contemporary Queer Cinema* (New York: Oxford University Press, 2013).

Dyer, Richard, 'Entertainment and utopia', in R. Dyer (ed.), *Only Entertainment* (London: Routledge, 1992).

Freeman, Elizabeth, *Time Binds: Queer Temporalities, Queer Histories* (London: Duke University Press, 2010).

Garber, Marjorie, *Vested Interests: Cross-Dressing and Cultural Anxiety* (London: Penguin, 1993).

Gil, José, 'Paradoxical body', in A. Lepecki and J. Joy (eds), *Planes of Compositions: Dance, Theory and the Global* (London and New York: Seagull Books, 2009).

Halberstam, Judith/Jack, *Female Masculinity* (Durham and London: Duke University Press, 1998).

Halberstam, Judith/Jack, *In a Queer Time and Place: Transgender Bodies and Subcultural Lives* (New York: New York University Press, 2005).

Harris, Sue, 'Film of the week: *Girlhood*' (14 Dec 2015). Available at http://www.bfi.org.uk/news-opinion/sight-sound-magazine/reviews-recommendations/film-week-girlhood (accessed 2 April 2017).

Keeling, Kara, *The Witch's Flight: The Cinematic, the Black Femme and the Image of Common Sense* (Durham and London: Duke University Press, 2008).

Kohn, Eric, 'Cannes review: Céline Sciamma's *Girlhood* is one of the best coming of age movies in years', *Indiewire* (15 May 2014). Available at http://www.indiewire.com/article/cannes-review-celine-sciammas-girlhood-is-one-of-the-best-coming-of-age-movies-in-years (accessed 2 April 2017).

Mayer, Sophie, '"She's getting back in the frame": interview with Céline Sciamma', *The F Word: Contemporary UK Feminism* (5 May 2015). Available at http://www.thefword.org.uk/2015/05/celine_sciamma_interview/ (accessed 2 April 2017).

Mayer, Sophie, 'Uncommon sensuality: new queer feminist film theory', in L. Mulvey and A. Backman Rogers (eds), *Feminisms: Diversity, Difference and Multiplicity in Contemporary Film Cultures* (Amsterdam: Amsterdam University Press, 2015).

Mottram, James, 'Céline Sciamma interview: step aside *Boyhood*, it's *Girlhood* time', *Independent* (24 April 2015). Available at http://www.independent.co.uk/arts-entertainment/films/features/cline-sciamma-interview-step-aside-boyhood-its-girlhood-time-10199093.html (accessed 2 April 2017).

Nastasi, Alison, '*Girlhood* director Céline Sciamma on reclaiming childhood, casting her girl gang, and how her film mirrors *Boyhood*', *Flavorwire* (30 January 2015). Available at http://flavorwire.com/502100/girlhood-director-celine-sciamma-on-reclaiming-childhood-casting-her-girl-gang-and-how-her-film-mirrors-boyhood (accessed 2 April 2017).

Palmer, Tim, *Brutal Intimacy: Analyzing Contemporary French Cinema* (Middletown: Wesleyan University Press, 2011).

Quinlivan, Davina, 'On how queer cinema might feel', *Music, Sound, and the Moving Image* 9/1 (2015), pp. 63–77.

Rossi, Jordan, 'The interview: Céline Sciamma – *Girlhood*', *Hunger* (8 May 2015). Available at http://www.hungertv.com/feature/the-interview-celine-sciamma-girlhood/ (accessed 2 April 2017).

Saunders, Keeley, 'Gender-defined spaces, places and tropes: contemporary transgender representation in *Tomboy* and *Romeos*', *Journal of European Popular Culture* 5/2 (2014), pp. 181–93.

Sciamma, Céline, *Tomboy* DVD interview (2011).

Speed, Barbara, '*Girlhood* avoids easy answer in its portrayal of growing up in the Paris suburbs', *New Statesman* (12 May 2015). Available at http://www.newstatesman.com/culture/2015/05/girlhood-avoids-easy-answers-its-portrayal-growing-paris-suburbs (accessed 2 April 2017).

Stahl, Lynne, *Unhappy Medium: Filmic Tomboy Narrative and Queer Feminist Spectatorship*, PhD dissertation, Cornell University (2015).

Theodore-Vachon, ReBecca, 'Interview: black women's lives matter in *Girlhood*', *RogerEbert.com* (7 February 2015). Available at http://www.rogerebert.com/interviews/interview-black-womens-lives-matter-in-girlhood (accessed 2 April 2017).

Thomas, Dori, 'A review of Céline Sciamma's *Girlhood*: an honest and emotionally powerful take on the coming-of-age genre', *Side B Magazine* (5 June 2015). Available at http://sidebmagazine.tumblr.com/post/120774164350/a-review-of-c%C3%A9line-sciammas-girlhood-an-honest (accessed 2 April 2017).

Villarejo, Amy, *Lesbian Rule: Cultural Criticism and the Value of Desire* (London: Duke University Press, 2003).

Vincendeau, Ginette, 'Minority report', *Sight & Sound* 25/6 (2015), pp. 22–9.

Waldron, Darren, 'Embodying gender nonconformity in "girls": Céline Sciamma's *Tomboy*', *L'Esprit Créateur* 53/1 (2013), pp. 60–73.

Whatling, Clare, *Screen Dreams: Fantasising Lesbians in Film* (Manchester: Manchester University Press, 1997).

White, Patricia, *unInvited: Classical Hollywood Cinema and Lesbian Representability* (Bloomington: Indiana University Press, 1999).

12 Pain and Imagining

ELAINE SCARRY

The subject in the second half of this study is the opposite of what it was in the first half, for what will be attended to is no longer the deconstruction of the world but that world's construction and reconstruction. Thus, the particular structure of activity that will be isolated here is now not unmaking but making. As will very gradually become apparent over the next few chapters, the activity of creation has an identifiable structure. A recognition of that structure requires as only a first step the recognition of the relation between physical pain and imagining. If that relation, described immediately below, echoes our earlier subject, it is because the uncovering of the structure of torture and the structure of war is the uncovering of the inverted form of that relation. It is impossible to speak of either torture or war without attending to the destruction of the artifacts of civilization in either their interior and mental or exterior and materialized forms; even more significantly, the infliction of pain in torture is inextricably bound up with the generation of a political "fiction" just as the injuries of war are bound up with a process of conferring facticity on unanchored cultural "constructs." Because these events entail the appropriation, aping, and deconstructing of the territory of creating, they entail some of the very elements that will now be looked at in their benign form. When the relation between physical pain and imagining occurs in its forward form, it has the following shape, a shape necessitated by the exceptional place that each has within the psychic arrangements of intentional states and their objects.

It was noticed at an early point in this book that physical pain is exceptional in the whole fabric of psychic, somatic, and perceptual states for being the only one that has no object. Though the capacity to experience physical pain is as primal a fact about the human being as is the capacity to hear, to touch, to desire, to fear, to hunger, it differs from these events, and from every other bodily and psychic event, by not having an object in the external world. Hearing and touch are of objects outside the boundaries of the body, as desire is desire of x, fear is fear of y, hunger is hunger for z; but pain is not "of" or "for" anything—it is itself alone. This objectlessness, the complete absence of referential content, almost prevents it from being rendered in language: objectless, it cannot easily be objectified in any form, material or verbal. But it is also its objectlessness that may give rise to imagining by first occasioning the process that eventually brings forth the dense sea of artifacts and symbols that we make and move about in. All other states, precisely by taking an object, at first invite one only to enter rather than to supplement the natural world. The man "desiring" can see the rain and know it is its cessation that he is longing for, so that he can go out and find the berries he is hungry for, before the night comes that he fears. Because of the inevitable bonding of his own interior states with companion objects in the outside world, he easily locates himself in that external world and has no need to invent a world to extend himself out into. The object is an extension of, an expression of, the state: the rain expresses his longing, the berries his hunger, and the night his fear. But nothing expresses his physical pain. Any state that was permanently objectless would no doubt begin the process of invention. But it is especially appropriate that the very state in which he is utterly objectless is also of all states the one that, by its aversiveness, makes most pressing the urge to move out and away from the body.

The only state that is as anomalous as pain is the imagination. While pain is a state remarkable for being wholly without objects, the imagination is remarkable for being the only state that is wholly its objects. There is in imagining no activity, no "state," no experienceable condition or felt-occurrence separate from the objects: the only evidence that one is "imagining" is that imaginary objects appear in the mind. Thus, while pain is like seeing or desiring but not like seeing *x* or desiring *y*, the opposite but equally extraordinary characteristic belongs to imagining. It is like the *x* or the *y* that are the objects of vision or desire, but not like the felt-occurrences of seeing or desiring. While, then, pain is like other forms of sentience but devoid of the self-extension that is ordinarily the counterpart of sentience, the imagination is like other forms of the capacity for self-extension without the experienceable sentience on which it is ordinarily premised. It may well provide an object for other forms of sentience, an imaginary object of hearing (like Ryle's inwardly hummed tune)[1] or an imaginary object of touch (the way the perfume on Annie's letter conjures up before Sartre's mind for a brief instant the palpable near-proximity of Annie herself)[2] but the object it provides is never provided for any experienceable form of sentience unique to itself.[3]

Although the gerund "imagining" assumes an activity, and although in some philosophic contexts it is described as though it were made up of both an intentional act and an intentional object,[4] in fact (as has long been intuitively recognized in the centuries-old game played by children and philosophers alike) it is impossible to imagine without imagining something. The attributes that the invisible and itself (apart from its objects) inexperienceable activity of imagining is understood to have, tend to be derived from the attributes of whatever "imagined object" happened to have been taken as a representable instance of imagining. If, for example, a discussion of imagining takes either Pegasus or a unicorn as its instance of the imagined object, the imagination is then likely to be itself characterized by the qualities of the specified image. Although the unicorn or Pegasus expresses the imagination's freedom from natural occurrence, its ability to rearrange wings and legs into new combinations, and although it expresses as well the imagination's eventual capacity to create beyond "need," since neither the unicorn nor Pegasus is striking for its usefulness to people in the twentieth century, such an image, by its very frivolity, wrongly suggests that the activity itself is trivial or marginal: that is, discussions conjuring up this type of image tend also to underestimate the centrality and significance of imagining in everyday life. Such an object is especially misleading because it wrongly suggests that the imagination is self-announcing—that it is only at work when its object is immediately recognizable as "made-up."

Very different conclusions about the nature of the imagination will be reached if one takes as an indicative object something more richly implicated in everyday life. If, like Sartre, one contemplates not an imagined Pegasus but an imagined Pierre, not a unicorn but an Annie, then the imagination's relation to daily acts of perception as well as its part in the deepest events of loss, love, and friendship are likely to be more immediately recognizable.[5] Even here, however, inferences about the nature of the activity that produced the objects will follow from and be limited by the attributes of the chosen objects. Sartre, for example, draws conclusions from the fact that his imagined Pierre is so impoverished by comparison with his real friend Pierre, that his imagined Annie has none of the vibrancy, spontaneity, and limitless depth of presence of the real Annie. But, of course, had he compared his imagined friends not to his real-friends-when-present but to his wholly absent friends, his conclusions would have been supplemented by other, very different conclusions. That is, the imagined Pierre is shadowy, dry, and barely present compared to the real Pierre, but is much more vibrantly present than the absent Pierre, and it was that absence that had occasioned the introduction of the image both into Sartre's mental life and into his philosophic account of that life. He only began to imagine Pierre because Pierre was away, lost to him, walking in Berlin down streets far beyond Sartre's sensory and perceptual reach; and thus his choice was not between a two-dimensional Pierre and a real Pierre but between a two-dimensional Pierre and a world utterly devoid of, bereft of, that friend's presence. Further, the same generic embodied imaginer capable of picturing, making present, an absent friend, is also capable of inventing both the idea and the materialized form of the telegraph, as well as devising the specific message, "Come home at once," as he is also capable of inventing many other mechanisms for transforming the condition of absence into presence, the telephone, train, airplane, all of which originate as the imagination's object.

The object that is selected as indicative of the imagination's activity, then, may vary from discussion to discussion; and the attributes that are generalized to the activity tend to be derived from the attributes of the model object. The appropriateness of various kinds of model objects will be returned to at a later moment, but for now the point of central importance is that the imagination is only experienced in the images it produces, and that even discussions of its characteristics as a state tend to be instead discussions of the characteristics of the invoked object. Almost never is the imagination "imagined" without an object, though the Hebraic scriptures come very close to requiring that believers do just that, that they apprehend the capacity for creation devoid of any representable content: attributing to God a representable form is explicitly forbidden, though the objects of mental creation may here be contemplated as the objects that God himself produced, the universe and its inhabitants. The immense problems surrounding that requirement, and the gradual modulation out of that requirement in both the Hebraic and Christian scriptures, will be elaborated in a later chapter. For now, whether the object imagined is God, the imagination itself, Pegasus, Pierre, Annie, a unicorn, a wall, a telegram, or an airplane, the activity producing the object tends to be coterminous with and only knowable through that object.

Physical pain, then, is an intentional state without an intentional object; imagining is an intentional object without an experienceable intentional state. Thus, it may be that in some peculiar way it is appropriate to think of pain as the imagination's intentional state, and to identify the imagination as pain's intentional object. Of course, it is probably inaccurate to identify an essentially objectless state as an "intentional state without an object" since only by having an object does it exist as an intentional state: in isolation, pain "intends" nothing; it is wholly passive; it is "suffered" rather than willed or directed. To be more precise, one can say that pain only becomes an intentional state once it is brought into relation with the objectifying power of the imagination: through that relation, pain will be transformed from a wholly passive and helpless occurrence into a self-modifying and, when most successful, self-eliminating one. But to argue that physical pain and imagining belong to one another as each other's missing intentional counterpart seems only to argue that "hurting and an imagined x" may occur together in a closed loop of interior occurrence that is a structural analogue for other intentional acts like "hearing a voice," "touching a windowpane," whereas it seems possible that something much more important is occurring here. What may instead be the case is that "pain" and "imagining" constitute extreme conditions of, on the one hand, intentionality as a state and, on the other, intentionality as self-objectification; and that between these two boundary conditions all the other more familiar, binary acts-and-objects are located. That is, pain and imagining are the "framing events" within whose boundaries all other perceptual, somatic, and emotional events occur; thus, between the two extremes can be mapped the whole terrain of the human psyche.

That this is an appropriate and useful way of understanding the relation between pain and the imagination is suggested by a number of observable phenomena. The more a habitual form of perception is experienced as itself rather than its external object, the closer it lies to pain; conversely, the more completely a state is experienced as its object, the closer it lies to imaginative self-transformation. So, for example, a woman (perhaps her name is Ruth), working in the fields, touching the wheat, feels not only the wheat but her fingers touching. Touch, as is recognized in traditional descriptions of the senses, lies closer to pain than does vision. Looking across the fields, she is filled with images of grain: though to some degree the perceptual event is feelable as occurring in a horizontal band between her cheekbones and her forehead, she tends "to experience" there the sheaves of wheat and barley rather than any self-conscious state of feeling in her eyes. It is because vision and hearing are, under ordinary conditions, so exclusively bound up with their object rather than their bodily location that they are the senses most frequently invoked by poets as the sensory analogues for the imagination. Through them, one seems to become disembodied, either because one seems to have been transported hundreds of feet beyond the edges of the body out into the external world, or instead because the images of objects from the external world have themselves been carried into the interior of the body as perceptual content, and seem to reside there, displacing the dense matter of the body itself.

But while forms of perception, like touch and vision, can be differentiated from one another by the relative degree of emphasis within them on the feeling state or instead on the object, any one of them in isolation contains the potential for being experienced either as state or as object, and thus has within it the fluidity of moving now toward the vicinity of hurting, now toward the vicinity of imagining. Although vision and hearing ordinarily reside close to objectification, if one experiences one's eyes or ears themselves—if the woman working looks up at the sun too suddenly and her eyes fill with blinding light—then vision falls back to the neighborhood of pain. Or if the objects in the external field—the grain, the figures of other workers, the trees off to the side—begin one year to appear distorted or blurred to her (that is, if the objects begin to become lost to her), she will cease to experience vision only as objectified interior content and will begin to become more self-conscious of the event of "seeing" itself: she no longer experiences the images of grain, persons, and trees without also experiencing her own body in the mode of aversiveness and deprivation (a deprivation that in its most extreme form is physical pain). So, too, though touch always has both somatic and external content, it may be experienced now more as one, now more as the other; and the more it is experienced as the first, the closer it lies to pain; the more it is experienced as the other, the closer it lies to self-displacement and transformation. Thus, if a thorn cuts through the skin of the woman's finger, she feels not the thorn but her body hurting her. If instead she experiences across the skin of her fingers not the awareness of the feel of those fingers but the feel of the fine weave of another woman's work, or if she traces the lettering of an engraved message and becomes mindful not of events in her hands but of the form and motivating force of the signs, or if that night she experiences the intense feelings across the skin of her body not as her own body but as the intensely feelable presence of her beloved, she in each of these moments experiences the sensation of "touch" not as bodily sensations but as self-displacing, self-transforming objectification; and so far are these moments from physical pain, that if they are named as bodily occurrences at all, they will be called "pleasure," a word usually reserved either for moments of overt disembodiment or, as here, moments when acute bodily sensations are experienced as something other than one's own body.[6]

The topography of act and object in sensation and perception is even more immediately recognizable as a description of emotional and somatic states. A state of consciousness other than pain—such as hunger or desire—will, if deprived of its object, begin to approach the neighborhood of pain, as in acute, unsatisfied hunger or prolonged, objectless longing; conversely, when such a state is given an object, it is itself experienced as a pleasurable and self-eliminating (or more precisely, pleasurable because self-eliminating) physical occurrence.[7] The interior states of physical hunger and psychological desire have nothing aversive, fearful, or unpleasant about them if the person experiencing them inhabits a world where food is bountiful and a companion is near.

While it may be immediately apparent in these examples why it is appropriate to identify the objectless state of consciousness as approaching the condition of pain,[8] the appropriateness of identifying the objectified state with the opposite framing boundary of imagining may be less immediately apparent since (in the examples given) the sources of objectification (wheat to eat, another human being to love, golden fields to see) originate in the natural world.[9] The appropriateness of the identification, however, arises from the fact that beyond the expansive ground of ordinary, naturally occurring objects is the narrow extra ground of imagined objects, and beyond this ground, there is no other. Imagining is, in effect, the ground of last resort. That is, should it happen that the world fails to provide an object, the imagination is there, almost on an emergency stand-by basis, as a last resource for the generation of objects. Missing, they will be made-up; and though they may sometimes be inferior to naturally occurring objects, they will always be superior to naturally occurring objectlessness. If no food is present, imagining grain or berries will, at least temporarily, allow the hunger to be experienced as potentially positive rather than as wholly aversive and the imagined image may remind the person to walk over the next hill to find real wheat and berries. The transformation of hunger into eating (a transformation in which there is a literal displacement of the passive, aversive sensation of hunger by the active incorporation of external objects into the body) no longer requires the self-announcing presence of objects, because if they are not themselves sensorially present to vision, they will present themselves to the imagination, and will motivate either a search (an alteration in the ground of the world) or an act of material invention (an introduction of a new object onto the ground of the world). Similarly, imagining a companion if the world provides none, may—at least temporarily—prevent longing from being a wholly self-experiencing set of physical and emotional events that, emptied of any referential content, exist as merely painful inner disturbances. It may be that "dreaming," too, should be understood in this way, as sustaining the objectifying powers of people during the hours when they are cut off from the natural source of objects, so that they do not during sleep drown in their own corporeal engulfment. That is, the particular content of the dream images (now terrifying, now benign; now full of uncanny secret intelligence about the sleeper, now ignorant, arbitrary, and nonsensical) is itself insignificant beside the overall fact of the dreaming itself, the emergency work of the imagination to provide an object—this object, that object, any object—to sustain and to exercise the capacity for self-objectification during the sleep-filled hours of sweet and dangerous bodily absorption.

The appropriateness of identifying imagining as a boundary condition of intentionality may, then, be recognized in the fact that imagining provides an extra and extraordinary ground of objects beyond the naturally occurring ground; it actively "intends," "authors," or "sponsors" objects when they are not *passively* available as an already existing "given." But the appropriateness of the identification may also be understood by phrasing the relation in the opposite direction: rather than apprehending the imagination as an extreme miming of the ordinary given condition in other forms of consciousness, other forms of consciousness can be understood to entail more moderate and modest acts of the authoring, self-alteration, and self-artifice routinely and dramatically at work in imagining. If one takes "hurting and an imagined object" (for example, "acute thirst and an imagined cup of water") as intentional counterparts, and if one sees the two together as one in a series of intentional events—acute thirst and an imagined cup of water, touching a flower, hearing a baby cry, watching a train, fearing a storm—it may at first seem that its essential relation between state and object (where the object comes into existence specifically to *eliminate* the condition) differs fundamentally from the relation between state and object in all the other examples, in each of which state and object co-exist as ongoing counterparts. But even these other ordinary perceptual and emotional acts entail self-alteration and artifice. Although in "seeing a field" the "field" is not "taken" in order to nullify the act of "seeing" (the way water is imagined in order to eliminate the thirst, or a blanket is imagined in order to eliminate the state of being cold), the person may well change the direction of his gaze, and thus "see the city" to his left in order to displace, eliminate, his "seeing the field." Ordinary perception is self-modifying because, at the very least, it alters and nullifies its own content, continually exchanging one object for another, exercising control over the direction and content of touch, hearing, seeing, smell, and taste. Thus the radical alteration that occurs in the landscape of the natural world in pain-and-imagining—"being on a desert and hallucinating a tree-filled oasis," "dying of thirst and 'seeing' water on the next sand dune"—is habitually mimed in daily acts of shifting one's seeing to the east rather than the west, reaching out to touch the objects on the left rather than those on the right, attending to the sounds coming from the room above rather than the room below. Further, it may be that the cancellation not only of the object but of the interior state itself is occurring in ordinary perception since the person tends to alter the object of touch, vision, or taste precisely at the moment when he becomes selfconscious of the bodily state itself—that is, when the already given object fails to permit the ongoing achievement of self-objectification, throwing his attention back onto the body. If the sun is too bright for a woman's eyes, she moves into the shade, and as she does, her eyes again fill with seeable objects rather than aversive sensation; if in turn the shade grows too dark for her to differentiate, without straining, the seeds she is sorting, she moves back out into the light; she may shift her vision to some nearby children to ease her discomfort at remembering her lost child; or if that only "makes" her more acutely selfconscious of her loss, she may watch some birds instead. Through her relation to these objects, she continually modifies the degree to which she displaces selfconsciousness with unselfconscious objectified content. So too in somatic and emotional states like hunger and desire, a person can continually modify the state itself—now minimizing it, now letting it occur, now intensifying and sustaining it, now eliminating it altogether—by continually modifying and adjusting his or her relation to the object.

A third characteristic of the relation between imaginary and real objects that reveals the appropriateness of identifying "imagining" as a framing state of intentionality at the edge of the human world opposite to the boundary formed by physical pain is that the imagination seems to provide a standard for judging the acceptability of objects in the naturally given world. The more exactly the object of desire or hunger or fear fits or expresses the state, the more precise a projection of the state it is, the more will it seem to have been generated by the interior state itself and will it be considered a visionary solution. That is, one of the distinguishing features of the made world, as opposed to the natural world, is that it is brought forth for the precise purpose of being the objects of these states, to be a precise fit; and so when a naturally occurring event seems to have this quality of fit, it seems to belong to the made world. Conversely, the less the object accommodates and expresses the inner requirements of the hunger, desire, or fear, the less there is an object for the state and only the state itself, the more it will approach the condition of pain. The more perfectly Boaz fits the inner shape of Ruth's desire, the more will he seem a kinsman and companion brought forth for her not by a bountiful earth but by a bountiful heaven (by, that is, willed artifice). The less he fits those interior claims, the more will she reside in those interior claims and the more she will suffer. That the imagination is somehow implicated in assessments of objectification does not mean that "made objects" are preferable to natural objects, for one may very much prefer the "given" (raw wheat, raw berries) to the "artificial" (wheat bread, berry jam, berry dumplings, berry pie, whiskey, berry cider, berry wine, and so forth); but it does mean that the very preferability of natural objects at a given moment is itself recognizable because the standard of "perfect fit" has been established by the full array of natural and imagined objects that collectively accommodate hunger in all the varying degrees of its insistence, the nuanced petulance of its claims. This is also true of most other states, and so it is familiar to hear people express their amazement at the natural world by an implicit reference to an imaginary standard: "This stone looks like it was hand-made," "I cannot imagine a more kind person," "The wind in the trees looks like the principle of intelligence itself," "There could not be a planet more physically beautiful than earth."

That pain and the imagination are each other's missing intentional counterpart, and that they together provide a framing identity of man-as-creator within which all other intimate perceptual, psychological, emotional, and somatic events occur, is perhaps most succinctly suggested by the fact that there is one piece of language used—in many different languages—at once as a near synonym for pain, *and* as a near synonym for created object; and that is the word "work." The deep ambivalence of the meaning of "work" in western civilization has often been commented upon, for it has tended to be perceived at once as pain's twin and as its opposite: in its Hebrew and Greek etymological origins, in our spoken myths and unspoken intuitions, and in our tradition of religious and philosophic analysis, it has been repeatedly placed by the side of physical suffering yet has, at the same time and almost as often, been placed in the company of pleasure, art, imagination, civilization—phenomena that in varying degrees express man's expansive possibility, the movement out into the world that is the opposite of pain's contractive potential.[10] Any sense that this duality is arbitrary dissolves when work is seen against the full array of intentional acts and objects; for work (like all the intentional states looked at above but to a much greater degree than was apprehensible there) conforms to this same arrangement. The more it realizes and transforms itself in its object, the closer it is to the imagination, to art, to culture; the more it is unable to bring forth an object or, bringing it forth, is then cut off from its object, the more it approaches the condition of pain. So, as an example of the one extreme, is the fact that the collective artifacts of civilization—its paintings, poems, buildings—are habitually referred to individually as "works." Indicative of the opposite extreme is the fact that historical moments when work has been identified with suffering have been moments in which those persons performing the activity of work have been separated from the benefits of the objects that are the product of that activity. Slavery, whether occurring in ancient Egypt or in the nineteenth-century American South, was an arrangement in which physical work was demanded of a population whose members were themselves cut off from ownership, control, and enjoyment of the products they produced. So, too, the nineteenth-century British factory world is one in which work is described as approaching the condition of pain, not only in the extensive writings of Marx but in the British parliamentary bluebooks on which he relied so heavily. The proximity of work to pain is here specifically attributed to the massive hunger, sores, disease, airlessness, and exhaustion suffered by the industrial population, but all these conditions are in turn attributed to the more fundamental shattering of the essential integrity of act-and-object in the human psyche; for the body at work was separated from the objects of its work; the men, women, and children bringing forth out of their labor a multitude of objects (coal, lace, bricks, shirts, watches, pins, paper, plaited straw), themselves inhabited a space wholly outside the realm on which those objects conferred their benefit, a realm that belonged to a set of people who had not themselves directly participated in the making of the objects.[11]

Far more than any other intentional state, work approximates the framing events of pain and the imagination, for it consists of both an extremely embodied physical act (an act which, even in nonphysical labor, engages the whole psyche) and of an object that was not previously in the world, a fishing net or piece of lace where there had been none, or a mended net or repaired lace curtain where there had been only a torn approximation, or a sentence or a paragraph or a poem where there had been silence. Work and its "work" (or work and its object, its artifact) are the names that are given to the phenomena of pain and the imagination as they begin to move from being a self-contained loop within the body to becoming the equivalent loop now projected into the external world. It is through this movement out into the world that the extreme privacy of the occurrence (both pain and imagining are invisible to anyone outside the boundaries of the person's body) begins to be sharable, that sentience becomes social and thus acquires its distinctly human form.

In this process of externalization, each of the two components is itself diminished, which is in the one case a great benefit and in the other only an apparent loss. Although the activity of work may itself at any given historical moment involve a degree of aversiveness in which it begins to be identical with physical pain,[12] it is by no means an internal requirement of the activity that it have this aversive intensity, and it does not ordinarily do so. It does, however, under all circumstances, and regardless of whether it is primarily physical or mental labor, entail the much more moderate (and now willed, directed, and controlled) embodied aversiveness of exertion, prolonged effort, and exhaustion. It hurts to work. Thus, the wholly passive and acute suffering of physical pain becomes the self-regulated and modest suffering of work. Work is, then, a diminution of pain: the *aversive intensity* of pain becomes in work *controlled discomfort*. So, too, imagining achieves a moderated form in the material and verbal artifacts that are the objects of work. If, for example, a person standing in a field imagines himself to be instead standing by the sea, he has (in imagining) brought about a large alteration in the world, displacing the whole physically "given" context with an invented one. If, in contrast, he fashions out of the clay of the ground a cup and introduces this "new" object into the field, he has again brought about an alteration in the physically "given" world, but a much more modest one than in the first case. While imagining may entail a revolution of the entire order of things, the eclipse of the given by a *total reinvention of the world*, an artifact (a relocated piece of coal, a sentence, a cup, a piece of lace) is *a fragment of world alteration*. Imagining a city, the human being "makes" a house; imagining a political utopia, he or she instead helps to build a country; imagining the elimination of suffering from the world, the person instead nurses a friend back to health. Although, however, artifice is more modest and fragmentary than imagining, its objects have the immense advantage over imagined objects of being real, and because real, sharable; and because the objects are sharable, in the end artifice has a scale as large as that in imagining because its outcome is for the first time collective.

That is, if there were a hundred persons, each of whom imagined himself the inventor of a town, each would find that he could instead in a given week only "make" a few hundred bricks, or construct part of a wagon, or clear a piece of a road. But because each person's made objects now inhabit the sharable external space outside his own body accessible to all, the objects he makes can be coupled with those objects made by the second person, and the third, and so the large imagined town gets made. In imagining the town, each person had to invent and sustain the image individually, and thus the hundred persons continually duplicated each other's efforts. Further, for any one person to make the town continually available to himself, he had to devote each day to sustaining the image, and then the next day (day after day), reinvent it once more. In the collective work of artifice, in contrast, the town becomes a freestanding object; it no longer depends for its existence on the mental labor of daily reinvention. Thus the imaginers may move on to other projects. It may be that in the year the town was being built, more focused and sustained exertion was required than would have been required by a hundred persons daydreaming about a town day after day for three hundred and sixty-five days; but in the long run, the effort required to perpetuate the fantasy city would be much greater, since the act would have to be sustained and renewed over fifty years, while those who built the town will in forty-nine of those years be free of its daily reinvention, except for now and then when it needs to be repaired. The advantage of material culture over a culture of belief is (as will be elaborated in a later chapter) difficult to overstate. In work, then, pain is moderated into sustained discomfort; and the objects of imagining, though individually moderated into fragmentary artifacts, are collectively translated into the structures of civilization that have nothing modest about them.

In the attempt to uncover the structure of creation in later chapters, the assumed starting point will be the framing relation of intentionality, described either as "pain and imagining" or "work and its artifacts." There is one additional word that changes in the movement back and forth between these two sets of companion terms, and that should be briefly clarified before starting. The elementary place occupied by the image of the "weapon" in the first set of terms is the place held by the "tool" in the second set of terms: the projection into intentionality through the mediation of "agency" in the pain-weapon-imagined object arrangement (which is in its deconstructed form, the pain-weapon-power arrangement) becomes now the work-tool-artifact arrangement. The modulation of the weapon into the tool has some of the same characteristics as the modulation of the embodied experience of pain into the embodied activity of work, or as the modulation of an imagined object into a materialized or verbalized artifact, but it also has some additional characteristics.

That the sign of the weapon has an elementary place in the transformation of pain into the projected image was suggested earlier, and was described both in its beneficent and, more elaborately, in its deconstructed form.[13] Although in its benign form the displacement of aversive sentience with the disembodied content of objectified images eventually entails an infinite array of images, and although it is not possible to travel back into the origins of human imagining and chart the chronological sequence in which such images first appeared, there are many outwardly visible indications that the image of the weapon is not just one among thousands of signs but is a sign occupying a primal place in the original moment of transformation. Of such outward indications, perhaps the most important to recall here is the centrality of the image in the language of people in physical pain. Physical pain is not only itself resistant to language but also actively destroys language, deconstructing it into the pre-language of cries and groans. To hear those cries is to witness the shattering of language. Conversely, to be present when the person in pain rediscovers speech and so regains his powers of self-objectification is almost to be present at the birth, or rebirth, of language. That the person in pain very typically moves through a handful of descriptive words to an "as if" construction, and an "as if" construction that has a weapon on the other side, indicates the primacy of the sign in the elementary work of projection into metaphor. To describe one's hurt in an image of agency is to project it into an object which, though at first conceived of as moving toward the body, by its very separability from the body becomes an image that can be lifted away, carrying some of the attributes of pain with it.[14] The primacy of this sign in the projection of human pain into disembodied imagining will, in the next chapter, be more elaborately attended to as it occurs in the Hebraic scriptures, where the relationship between the people and their imagined object (God) is repeatedly represented as a relation between a deeply embodied, suffering human being and a wholly disembodied (i.e., immune from pain) principle of creating, mediated by the recurring image of a colossal weapon that transverses the space between them. The only path connecting the body and the power of creating is apprehended as the vertical line running along the edge of a weapon whose one end is on the ground and whose other end is in heaven; on the other side of the concrete, imaginable image an unimaginable, contentless creator is apprehended to exist. It is also useful to recall that the weapon as a materialized artifact is usually assumed to have been present at the infancy of culture. Long before man extends himself out into the world by making other artifacts, he extends himself out into that world by holding onto a found object (stick, stone) that increases, extends, the length and strength of his arm. This weapon may itself be modified into a tool, or the tool back into a weapon, and it is the identity of the two, as well as the profound mental distance separating them, that must for a moment be held steadily visible.

The weapon and the tool seem at moments indistinguishable, for they may each reside in a single physical object (even the clenched fist of a human hand may be either a weapon or a tool), and may be quickly transformed back and forth, now into the one, now into the other. At the same time, however, a gulf of meaning, intention, connotation, and tone separates them. If one holds the two side by side in front of the mind—a hand (as weapon) and a hand (as tool), a knife (weapon) and a knife (tool), a hammer and a hammer, an ax and an ax—it is then clear that what differentiates them is not the object itself but the surface on which they fall. What we call a "weapon" when it acts on a sentient surface we call a "tool" when it acts on a nonsentient surface. The hand that pounds a human face is a weapon and the hand that pounds the dough for bread or the clay for a bowl is a tool. The knife that enters the cow or the horse is a weapon and the knife that cuts through the no longer alive meat at dinner is a tool. The ax that cuts through the back of a wolf is a weapon and the ax that cuts through a tree is a tool. The hammer that hammers a man to a cross is a weapon and the hammer used to construct the cross itself is a tool.

Although one can conceive of exceptions to this basis of differentiation, the exceptions tend to reaffirm the distinction, as well as to call attention to its complexities. If, for example, someone were to object that the ax that cuts through the tree (in the preceding examples) should be called a weapon rather than a tool, the person making the objection would almost certainly turn out to be one who believes that the vegetable world is sentient and capable of experiencing some form of pain; conversely, if one were to object that the knife that cuts through the cow is a tool, the person would be someone who has retracted the privileges of sentience from the animal world and thinks of cows as already-food and therefore, not-quite-alive (as we more routinely think of trees as not-quite-alive). If an ax strikes the side of a house, that ax may—especially to those whose home it is—be perceived as a weapon even though it acts on a nonsentient surface; but this identification itself exposes the fact that we think of human artifacts as extensions of sentient human beings and as thus themselves protected by the privileges accorded sentience. Again, there are certain instruments (such as those in medicine and dentistry) that we call "tools" even though they enter human tissue; but it should be noticed that this identification is "learned" and that even after it is learned, it requires a conscious mental act to hold steady the perception (which violates all intuition) of the object as a tool. Every child recognizes it as a weapon and responds accordingly. Even adults tend to watch the approach of the knife toward an arm with complete equanimity only if they know that the tissue of the arm has been anesthetized and thus made almost nonsentient. Similarly, contemporary arguments about whether abortion is properly understood as a medical operation (tool) or instead as a murder (weapon) have sometimes turned on the question of whether or not the fetus is capable of experiencing pain.[15]

These and many other concrete instances work to reaffirm the mental and moral distance separating sentient and nonsentient surfaces, a distance so great that the object acting on them is perceived and named as two different objects. If one imagines oneself back at an early moment in culture during which a large knife is suspended above a child (Isaac, Iphigenia, any child), and if before the knife falls, the child is moved out of that space and an animal, goat or lamb, is put in its place, that moment of substitution will be recognizable as one that has always (in the retrospective accounts of the culture which followed) been designated a revolutionary moment in the growth of moral consciousness. But if one now holds steadily visible not two pictures but three pictures—the child and the knife looming above, giving way to the lamb and the knife looming above, and now in turn the lamb is moved out of that location and replaced by a block of wood under the still looming knife—so great in the transition from the second to the third picture is the revolution in consciousness that the object itself is now re-perceived as a wholly different object, a tool rather than a weapon, and the anticipated action of the object is no longer an act of "wounding" but an act of "creating."

This difference will be returned to after looking for a moment at a characteristic that remains common to the two objects. The power of alteration resides equally in weapons and in tools. In each there is a tremendous distance between what is occurring at the two ends, not simply because one end is active and the other passive, but because a fairly inconsequential alteration at one end is magnified into an occurrence full of consequence at the other. A small shift in the body at one end of a gun (so small it is almost imperceptible, only the position of one finger moves) can wholly shatter a body at its other end. The pressure of a hand pushing on the handle of a knife, itself too small to alter (to dent, to scar) even slightly the surface of the handle, will as it begins to be transferred and concentrated across the broad half-inch of the handle to the drastically thin surface edge of the blade, be magnified into a huge power of altering whatever surface it touches at its other end. Thus the object, whether weapon or tool, is a lever across which a comparatively small change in the body at one end is amplified into a very large change in the object, animate or inanimate, at the other end. A person using a weapon or a tool can therefore take credit for, "experience," a large alteration without himself "experiencing" any direct bodily alteration; he experiences alteration without himself risking the aversiveness that ordinarily accompanies self-alteration; he objectifies his presence in the world through the alterability of his world. The difference in the alteration that occurs at each end of the weapon or tool is one not just of scale but of duration. The cut made by a sword or a scythe is not only a much greater change than is that of the motion of the lifted arm that caused it, but it also lasts far longer than that arm motion. In addition to whatever practical benefits are gained by hurting an enemy or harvesting grain, there is a magnification of the actor because he has brought about an alteration not only larger than the one he himself experienced but of much greater duration. Whatever assertion of selfhood might be carried by his performing that lift and swing of his arm over and over again in an unbroken sequence over a week, can instead (if there was a tool or weapon held in his hand) be accomplished by a single movement of the arm, for now the alteration itself, the cut grain or the unhealed wound, is the freestanding sign of that momentary motion that itself endures for a week. The altered object becomes a record that prevents the action from having to be endlessly repeated; presence is registered and need not be continually re-enacted.

Although the primary basis for differentiating a weapon and a tool is that the one acts on a sentient and the other on a nonsentient surface, a more precise account would say that the tool, too, acts on a sentient surface but in a delayed way. The making of an artifact is a social act, for the object (whether an art work or instead an object of everyday use) is intended as something that will both enter into and itself elicit human responsiveness. Though the tool does not, like a weapon, act directly on the human body, it does so at two or three steps removed. Marks on a series of trees register the marker's presence as though he stood in all those places: they allow him to inhabit a space much larger than the small circle of his immediately present body. Those marks are now part of the visual field of anyone else who approaches the grove of trees. Rather than using a weapon on someone's eyes, the world is rebuilt or re-presented (even if only modestly altered) in such a way that it must be reseen. That is, rather than directly altering sentience (as occurs in the use of a weapon on a living body), the tool alters sentience by providing "objects" of sentience. It alters without hurting (often even bringing about the diminution of hurt). Through tools and acts of making, human beings become implicated in each other's sentience. Seeing is seeing of x, and the one who has made the "x" has entered into the interior of the other person's seeing, entered there in the object of perception. The objects of hearing, desire, hunger, touch, are not just passively grasped by the fixed intentional states: the objects themselves act on the state, sometimes initiating the state, sometimes modifying it, increasing, decreasing, or eliminating it. Thus when intentional objects come to include not just the rain, berries, stones, and the night but also bread, bowls, church steeples, and radiators, there comes to be an ongoing interaction at the (once private) center of human sentience; for not only are the interior facts of sentience projected outward into the artifact in the moment of its making, but conversely those artifacts now enter the interior of other persons as the content of perception and emotion. Thus in the transformation of a weapon into a tool, everything is gained and nothing is lost.

One final attribute of the tool in the constellation of "work-tool-artifact" is that it is itself the concrete record of the connection between the worker and the object of his or her work; it is the path from the object back to its sentient source; it is the path that if eclipsed from attention allows the object to be severed from its source. This special position of the tool becomes more apparent when work is seen within the framework of intentionality: work is an intentional act; its object (whether a carved statue or a chunk of coal lifted out of the earth) is an intentional object. The tool, as is visible in its two ends, shares characteristics of each. At once act and object, it can be assimilated in either direction: it belongs to the body and is an extension of the human hand; it is also itself an object (the earliest made object, perhaps preceded only by the weapon) which must itself be made before it can participate in the making of other objects.[16] The tool, then, occupies a remarkable position within the intentional frame. In almost all intentional states other than work, the connection between act and object is invisible and magical, signaled only by a preposition (the "of" and the "for" in fear *of* x, hunger *for* y) that is a "placeholder" and a "zero." In work, the locus of the connection becomes for the first time palpable and concrete in the tool. Across its concrete surface, the interior act and the exterior object become continuous; the "of" and the "for" themselves become subject to direction and control. The benefits to sentience are incalculable.

In the following chapters, there will begin to emerge a more complete account of the interior structure of the act of creating as it is objectified and made knowable in the hidden interior of the created object. As the nature of making becomes visible, the significance of unmaking—looked at in the first half of this book—will itself be more fully apprehended. One of the central problems in exposing the interior of making (which will be called here "imagining" when the activity and its object are interior, and "making" or "creating" when the activity is extended into the external world and has as its outcome a material or verbal artifact) is, as suggested earlier, the selection of an appropriate "model object." Unmaking resides in and can thus be represented by two relatively self-contained events, torture and war, the first of which is its most complete and therefore most perfect representative. But where is the equivalent representative of "making," which manifests itself everywhere, which seems on the one hand fully present in the most fragile and singular of outcomes (a pencil, a white shirt, a clothespin, room, or curtain), yet seems on the other only to be fully present in the overarching structures of civilization whose scale places them beyond the reach of sensory as well as, perhaps, of intellectual apprehension? Any "model object" will be inadequate, either by being too diminutive and fragmentary, or by being too large for description; and the discussion that follows will minimize the problem only by distributing the error in both directions, now erring on the side of the large, now erring on the side of the small, thus moving back and forth between what is fully representative but not representable and what is easily representable but not truly representative. This alternation is itself made easier by the fact that the structure of making appears to remain constant across such changes in scale.

The logic governing the selection of individual material artifacts as model objects will become apparent as those objects are invoked here and there throughout Chapter 4 and centrally in Chapter 5. Such objects (now a blanket, now an altar, now a chair, a coat, or a lightbulb) will be presented in the context of their own self-evident characteristics as well as characteristics consciously or unconsciously attributed to them in, for example, literature and law (a verbal artifact, such as a story or a legal argument, may itself comment on and expose the nature of a material artifact, such as a city or a pennywhistle or an artificial heart). Thus the specific logic of invoking any one of them need not be anticipated here. The logic underlying the selection of fragments from the overarching structure of civilization may not, in contrast, be self-evident when it is encountered in Chapter 4, and so will be very briefly indicated here.

Because the deconstruction of creation takes a specifically political form (torture, war), it might seem most appropriate to trace the outlines of the opposite event again in a specifically political form, such as the moment when a new country is being conceived and constructed (made-up, made-real), or when an already existing country, having been partially destroyed, is being re-imagined and re-constructed (remade-up). As it happens, the human imagination has given a fairly complete account of itself at both such moments. The "creating" of a country, for example the United States, is knowable, *after the fact*, in the freestanding artifact that was its outcome, the United States itself and more particularly, its constitution; but in addition the actual present-tense activity of creating in this instance produced not only an object (a constitution, a country) but also a record of its own present-tense action. In the pages of *The Federalist Papers*, it is possible to see the outline of the act of creation, in part because Madison, Hamilton, and Jay so self-consciously recognize themselves as engaged in an act of "invention," as when Madison stops to differentiate men from angels on the basis that each is self-governing but the first only achieves this through materialized design,[17] or when Hamilton, calling attention to "the interior structure of the edifice we are here invited to erect,"[18] explicitly refers to the nation as a made object. Similarly, the "recreating" or "reconstructing" of partially destroyed nations has a surviving record of both its initial moment of conception and its successive modifications in the written documents and oral history surrounding the Marshall Plan, the Plan for European Economic Recovery, and the European Common Market. If the period between 1939 and 1945 is conventionally identified as one of the darkest in western civilization, then there can also be taken as one of its most luminous the period of years during which Europe was rebuilt, and, in particular, one forty-eight hour period beginning on 5 June 1947 when a quiet speech given before a small audience at an American university set off throughout the night on a faraway continent a series of phone calls between various heads of state who, in a sudden swell of amazement, disbelief, and visionary trust, found themselves (though still standing in the midst of massive rubble, poverty, hunger, and anticipated cold) "imagining" there in the middle of the night a restored Europe, and imagining as well the still only-imaginary path by which they would get there—found themselves also, perhaps, recognizing in some dim corner of their minds that the United States' Secretary of State may have been only speaking hypothetically, may have been only introducing an "as if" clause in the presence of his listeners, but found themselves realizing too (as though participating in a benign conspiracy with some larger, intercontinental imagination) that Europe could invoke its own "as if" clause, and by acting as if the United States quite simply meant what it said, the hypothetical would become real, regardless of original intention.[19] In any event, within one forty-eight hour period, the United States had "supposed," and Europe had begun to act on the supposition.

In both the *Federalist Papers* and the Plan for European Economic Recovery, the work of the human imagination in constructing large units of civilization (for here the unit of shelter is not a room or a house but a country or a continent) is at moments exposed even in the fundamental framing relation between "pain and imagining," for in the first the United States is being described in its conceptual infancy, and thus both the fragility of union and its anticipated strength are co-present on every page; similarly, the success of European recovery was premised on an almost unprecedented willingness on the part of each of the participants to expose its own inner fragility ("For the first time in modern history," Marshall noted, "representatives of sixteen nations collectively disclosed their internal economic conditions and facilities and undertook, subject to stated conditions, to do certain things for the mutual benefit of all").[20] Nevertheless, to step into the intricacies of either the *Federalist Papers* or the Plan for European Economic Recovery is to walk into the middle of the civilizing process when many of its fundamental assumptions are already securely in place, and thus in no need of articulation, and thus not themselves self-announcing. Equally important, though the generic events of torture and war are opposed by the civilizing impulse even when that impulse has a specific and small location, manifesting itself in something as fragmentary as a table, and though, therefore, it is also opposed by the making of something more expansive, like a nation or a group of nations, it is nevertheless misleading to focus on a particular country or continent at a given historical moment, since insofar as they have a true opposite, it is "civilization" itself.

If western civilization is characterized by a long list of attributes, two that must occupy a central position in any list are first, its Judeo-Christian framework of belief, and second, its insistent thrust toward material self-expression. These two attributes have in part guided the selection of the two texts that are invoked in Chapter 4, the Judeo-Christian scriptures and the writings of Marx, in each of which the nature of creating—the relation between body and image, body and belief, body and artifact—is endlessly puzzled over, looked at now from one side and now from another, now from below and now from above, held up before the mind and turned over and around so that all its intricacies and edges become visible. Although the logic of invoking the biblical writings may seem self-evident, the logic of invoking the writings of Marx may seem less so; for Marx is in the United States so often narrowly perceived in his capacity as critic of western economic structures that it is sometimes forgotten that he is our major philosopher on the nature of material objects, that he not only accepts but embraces and applauds the western impulse toward material self-objectification, and that he himself, though an angry opponent of what he perceived to be its injustices, accepted perhaps ninety percent of its materialist premises. Even that part of his work that is revolutionary should probably be seen as what Jacob Talmon has called a "western heresy,"[21] a heresy through which western materialist assumptions have been exported to non-western cultures, a vehicle through which a constellation of premises embedded in materialism has been carried into what were originally less materially centered, or nonmaterial, even in some instances anti-material, societies. If this description is accurate, then his relation to the west is not unlike the relation of Christianity to Judaism; for although there must have been a day long ago when Christianity was perceived as a radical rejection of Jewish belief, at a distance of two thousand years it is self-evident that Christianity accepted ninety percent of Judaic assumptions, and by means of the ten percent by which it strayed, itself became the vehicle through which a stunning artifact invented in a tiny corner of the Mediterranean could be extended out over an entire hemisphere, conferring its benefits not only on the tiny population who were racially related to the original imaginers, but to the populations of several continents, for the relation between the believer and the object of belief no longer depended on the disposition of genetic material residing in the body of the believer.

Although one of these writings appears relatively early in the civilization it helped to sponsor and the other relatively late, in both of them elementary attributes of the nature of creating are made visible because in neither of them is anything silently assumed. In each an extended meditation on the nature of human making is occasioned by the recognition of a problem in the already existing realm of artifice: the largest created object (God in one case; the overarching economic and ideological structures of society in the other) is perceived to be either insufficiently reciprocating or insufficiently self-substantiating, and is thus itself subjected to a process of modification in the course of the meditation. In both works, there is a recognition that the strategies of "wounding" and "creating" have become conflated, and the work of differentiating and holding the two securely separate in the mind comes to depend on a controlling and redirecting of the referential activity of the sign of the weapon or tool, the sign that precisely because of its inherent instability has allowed the partial deconstruction of making into unmaking. Although at the starting point of the analysis that follows, problems analogous to those encountered in earlier chapters will be re-encountered, these texts very quickly carry us to new territory of understanding. The language in which the scriptural and Marxist explorations occur requires no translation into the terms that are of central concern in the present study, for in each of them the overt and undisguised subject matter is that of "creating," "creator," "body," "artifact," "working," "hurting," "making," "maker." The only new term introduced into this otherwise familiar list is the word "believing" which, in its biblical context, is close to being a synonym for what has been called here "imagining": "to believe" is to perpetuate the imagined object across a succession of days, weeks, and years; "belief" is the capacity to sustain the imagined (or apprehended) object in one's own psyche, even when there is no sensorially available confirmation that that object has any existence independent of one's own interior mental activity. Because both of these writings take "making" as their central subject, and because both so regularly traverse the full expanse of ground that separates the extreme framing condition of the body in physical pain from the opposite framing condition of self-objectification as it occurs in its most extended and ample of artifacts, the Judeo-Christian and Marxist narratives themselves become—perhaps to a degree not equalled by any other two texts in the west—epic explorations of the human imagination.

Notes

1. Gilbert Ryle, *The Concept of Mind* (London: Hutchinson, 1949), 267f.

2. Jean-Paul Sartre, *The Psychology of Imagination* (New York: Philosophical Library, 1948; rpt—Secaucus, N.J.: Citadel, 1972), 208.

3. Not only is there no form of sentience specific to "imagining," but it does not, unlike other forms of sensation, even seem to be anchored in a specific part of the body. Though "images" may typically be experienced as appearing in the head, it requires very little effort to "push" the image into some other part of the body: it is almost as easy to make an imagined blue flower arise in the interior of the calf of the leg as it is to make it arise in the head; just as the picture of a foot race can occur along the interior path of the forearm, with its starting point at the elbow and its finishing point at the wrist. The "natural" location within the head (which may occur in part because of the analogue with the objectified content of hearing and seeing) becomes habitual, but is a habit that is subject to alteration.

4. The analysis of it as *both* act and object may be only implicit in a given analysis or may instead be explicit, as in Edward S. Casey, *Imagining: A Phenomenological Study* (Bloomington: Indiana University Press, 1979). Of most importance is the fact that whether or not the language of intentionality is explicitly used, such discussions tend always to include the specification of an object. Casey (49) quotes Ryle (251, 254) as asserting that there is no object in imagining, but in context Ryle seems only to mean there is no perceptual or actually sensed object: Ryle's entire discussion of necessity proceeds through a series of invoked objects.

5. Sartre, 177–212.

6. In some traditions "pleasure" has been understood as the absence of pain rather than as itself an actively experienceable condition, while in others it has been understood as a discrete sensory phenomenon the experience of which does not depend on the prior presence (or even anticipated presence) of pain. Even in the second case, however, it has tended to be understood as a *bodily* state in which something other than *the body* is experienced: see for example, Eugene Minkowski's description of "pleasure" or "contentment" as the feeling that accompanies the expansive, outward movement into the world, as when one completes an act, or makes a decision ("Findings in a Case of Schizophrenic Depression," trans. Barbara Bliss, in *Existence: A New Dimension in Psychiatry and Psychology*, ed. Rollo May, Ernest Angel, Henri F. Ellenberger [New York: Basic, 1958; rpt—New York: Simon-Touchstone, n.d.], 134). Thus the two conceptions of pleasure are not as deeply at odds with one another as they may at first appear, for in each (overtly in the first case, less overtly but recoverably in the second) it is a condition associated with living beyond the physical body, or experiencing bodily sensations in terms of objectified content.

7. It may at first appear that this description would be inapplicable to an intentional state such as fear, since the state itself is elicited by, rather than eliminated by, its object. But, as has often been noted, objectless fear may have a much greater aversiveness than fear-and-object since, in the second case, the existence of the object gives the person a course of action. He may act to eliminate the object, to move away from the object, or to placate the object, all of which are ways of altering the state of fear itself (and are ways not available to him in objectless fear, which thus places him much closer to the aversive passivity of the person in pain).

    This argument would not, however, wholly satisfy the objection, since objectless fear is an unusual condition (except in those descriptions of the ordinary modern state of anxiety as an ongoing state of diffuse, object-less fear). The analysis of the relation between state and object in ordinary intention as occurring within the framing relation of the boundary conditions of pain and objectified self-transformation must be understood as it would apply not only to the alternatives of objectless fear and fear-and-object (where it is clear that the first places the person closer to pain than the second) but to the more ordinary alternatives of no fear and fear-and-object.

To understand this, it is helpful to return for a moment to the relation between pain and its imagined object. The imagined object in pain may be one of two kinds. First, it may be an object (artifact or objectified condition) in which the hurt is eliminated: if one is hungry, imagining food, if one's back aches, imagining and longing for a chair when there is none actually present or perhaps even yet invented. Second, the envisioned object may instead be an imagined cause of the pain, as has been stressed in the many examples given here of the occurrence of agency language: so a person with an acute "stabbing" pain in the leg conceives of it as "stabbing," imagines a causal knife, and may even (as in imagistic therapy) work to diminish the pain by mentally moving the knife away; or, the person may instead conceive of the leg itself as the cause, and imagine himself existing in a world without the offending limb (itself a change in the realm of externalized objects), or a person with pains in his chest and stomach may conceive of God as the cause, and so work for forgiveness and the cessation of pain. Both categories of imagined object are paths toward the elimination of pain (whether effective or ineffective): in the first case, the object (food, chair) directly eliminates the sensation, in the second, the anterior cause of the sensation is imagined, and one then works to alter one's relation to that anterior object (pushing the knife away; having the leg removed, praying to God).

The second category of pain-and-imagined object makes possible an understanding of the nature of fear-and-object that explains how the object, even though responsible for producing the sentient condition of fear that is close to pain, can be itself understood as moving the person away from pain and toward the opposite boundary of objectified self-transformation. Here fear-and-object (or the object and the fear it has evoked) reverse the temporal relation between pain-and-imagined object: seeing a knife in the vicinity of one's leg, one fears it and acts to remove it, push it away, rather than waiting until one's leg is already hurt and trying (much less effectively) to alter the pain by mentally reversing the causal action; or again, fearing God's wrath, one works to heal the relation, preventing the anticipated infliction of hurt. Thus the external object occasions a modified and diminished form of sentient suffering (fear), in order to allow the object to be acted upon, in order to prevent the more extreme form of sentient suffering (physical pain). Fear-and-object can thus itself be understood as a partially objectified, hence halfway eliminated, form of pain.

8. Because ordinary forms of sentience are, when objectless, close to pain, an understanding of pain may eventually make possible a better understanding of the much more inclusive phenomenon of sentience. That is, it would be difficult to approach an understanding of sentience by attending to the sentient experiences of, for example, seeing or hearing or hungering because it is so difficult to hold visible these occurrences separate from their objectified content. Pain, in contrast, makes possible a recognition of the characteristics of sentience (whether that sentience occurs as hurting, seeing, touching, hungering) distinct from the characteristics it (i.e., seeing, touching, hungering) acquires in its habitual interaction with the realm of objects. Thus to some extent, the "language of physical pain" can be understood more broadly as "the language of physical sentience".

9. The class of intentional objects is, in other discursive contexts, commonly understood to include both existing objects and nonexisting ones—hence the widespread use of the term "intentionality" to designate a relation between state and object, one feature of which is that the object "may or may not" exist. The discussion that follows assumes (and takes an interest in) the distinguishability of existing objects and imaginary ones, but does so in order to show the multiple ways by which they become implicated in one another (thus also, in effect, resulting in the "may or may not exist" condition of any one intentional object).

10. The two antithetical conceptions of work are, for example, described by Karl Löwith in his chapter on "The Problem of Work" in *From Hegel to Nietzsche: The Revolution in Nineteenth-Century Thought*, trans. David E. Green (Garden City, N.Y.: Anchor, 1967), 2, ii, 260–283.

11. The centrality of the categories of "act" and "object" in Marx's analyses of work in both *Grundrisse* and *Capital* will be returned to in Chapter 4. Hannah Arendt's important analysis of the distinction between "work" and "labor" as depending on the temporal stability (e.g., table) or instability (e.g., bread) of the object (*The Human*

Condition [Chicago: University of Chicago, 1958; rpt—Garden City, N.Y.: Doubleday-Anchor, 1959], 72–88) may be derived from the much more elaborated account of the distinction between objectless and objectified work in Marx, whose entire political critique depends on it.

12. See, for example, the extensive literature on industrial disease and industrial accidents.

13. Both the benign and the deconstructed form of the relation are summarized in the introductory discussion of "pain and agency"; the deconstructed form is elaborated on in the chapters on torture and war.

14. At many points in the opening chapters of this study, it has been noted that a person attempting to objectify pain will invoke the image of the weapon. It is interesting that philosophic discussions of the imagination also invoke the sign of the weapon (Sartre's nail [84]. Ryle's boxing match [260, 261]), even though the ostensible subject is not pain, thus suggesting the accessibility of this sign, even among the full array of imaginable objects. (That is, the writers are attempting to invoke imaginary objects that the reader will simultaneously be able to imagine, and thus the fact that the image of the weapon is among those invoked suggests that it is presumed to be universally invocable.)

15. L. W. Sumner, *Abortion and Moral Theory* (Princeton: Princeton University Press, 1981).

16. Even if, for example, anthropologists were one day able to show that the "first" artifact had been a bowl rather than a hammer, this would not change the fact that the first artifact was a tool (or weapon) since in order to make the bowl, the hand had to first be "made" a tool—that is, in the making of the bowl, the hand had to be used as a shaping agent.

17. James Madison, "Number 51," *The Federalist Papers*, McLean edition, indexed and introd. Clinton Rossiter (New York: Mentor-New American, 1961), 322.

18. Alexander Hamilton, "Number 27," *The Federalist Papers*, 175.

19. Conversation with Henri Jann, National Humanities Center, Research Triangle Park, North Carolina, September 1979.

20. George C. Marshall, *Assistance to European Economic Recovery: Statement before Senate Committee on Foreign Relations* (8 January 1948), Department of State: Publication 3022, Economic Cooperation Series 2 (Washington, D.C.: GPO, 1948), 2.

21. Jacob Talmon, "Portrait of a Humanist and His Dilemmas: In Memory of Charles Frankel," National Humanities Center, Research Triangle Park, N.C., 25 September 1979.

13 Pregnant Embodiment: Subjectivity and Alienation

IRIS MARION YOUNG

The library card catalog contains dozens of entries under the heading "pregnancy": clinical treatises detailing signs of morbidity; volumes cataloging studies of fetal development, with elaborate drawings; or popular manuals in which physicians and others give advice on diet and exercise for the pregnant woman. Pregnancy does not belong to the woman herself. It is a state of the developing fetus, for which the woman is a container; or it is an objective, observable process coming under scientific scrutiny; or it becomes objectified by the woman herself as a "condition" in which she must "take care of herself." Except, perhaps, for one insignificant diary, no card appears listing a work that, as Kristeva puts it, is "concerned with the subject, the mother as the site of her proceedings."[1]

We should not be surprised to learn that discourse on pregnancy omits subjectivity, for the specific experience of women has been absent from most of our culture's discourse about human experience and history. This essay considers some of the experiences of pregnancy from the pregnant subject's viewpoint. Through reference to diaries and literature, as well as phenomenological reflection on the pregnant experience, I seek to let women speak in their own voices.

Section I describes some aspects of bodily existence unique to pregnancy. The pregnant subject, I suggest, is decentered, split, or doubled in several ways. She experiences her body as herself and not herself. Its inner movements belong to another being, yet they are not other, because her body boundaries shift and because her bodily self-location is focused on her trunk in addition to her head. This split subject appears in the eroticism of pregnancy, in which the woman can experience an innocent narcissism fed by recollection of her repressed experience of her own mother's body. Pregnant existence entails, finally, a unique temporality of process and growth in which the woman can experience herself as split between past and future.

This description of the lived pregnant body both develops and partially criticizes the phenomenology of bodily existence found in the writings of Straus, Merleau-Ponty, and several other existential phenomenologists. It continues the radical undermining of Cartesianism that these thinkers inaugurated, but it also challenges their implicit assumptions of a unified subject and sharp distinction between transcendence and immanence. Pregnancy, I argue, reveals a paradigm of bodily experience in which the transparent unity of self dissolves and the body attends positively to itself at the same time that it enacts its projects.

Section II reflects on the encounter of the pregnant subject with the institutions and practices of medicine. I argue that within the present organization of these institutions and practices, women usually find such an encounter alienating in several respects. Medicine's self-identification as the curing profession encourages others as well as the woman to think of her pregnancy as a condition that deviates from normal health. The control over knowledge about the pregnancy and birth process that the physician has through instruments, moreover, devalues the privileged relation she has to the fetus and her pregnant body. The fact that in the contemporary context the obstetrician is usually a man reduces the likelihood of bodily empathy between physician and patient. Within the context of authority and dependence that currently structures the doctor–patient relation, moreover, coupled with the use of instruments and drugs in the birthing process, the pregnant and birthing woman often lacks autonomy within these experiences.

Before proceeding, it is important to note that this essay restricts its analysis to the specific experience of women in technologically sophisticated Western societies. The analysis presupposes that pregnancy can be experienced for its own sake, noticed, and savored. This entails that the pregnancy be chosen by the woman, either as an explicit decision to become pregnant or at least as choosing to be identified with and positively accepting of it. Most women in human history have not chosen their pregnancies in this sense. For the vast majority of women in the world today, and even for many women in this privileged and liberal society, pregnancy is not an experience they choose. So I speak in large measure for an experience that must be instituted and for those pregnant women who have been able to take up their situation as their own.

I

The unique contribution of Straus, along with Merleau-Ponty and certain other existential phenomenologists, to the Western philosophical tradition has consisted in locating consciousness and subjectivity in the body itself. This move to situate subjectivity in the lived body jeopardizes dualistic metaphysics altogether. There remains no basis for preserving the mutual exclusivity of the categories subject and object, inner and outer, I and world. Straus puts it this way:

> The meaning of "mine" is determined in relation to, in contraposition to, the world, the Allon, to which I am nevertheless a party. The meaning of "mine" is not comprehensible in the unmediated antithesis of I and not-I, own and strange, subject and object, constituting I and constituted world. Everything points to the fact that separateness and union originate in the same ground.[2]

As Sarano has pointed out, however, antidualist philosophers still tend to operate with a dualist language, this time distinguishing two forms of experiencing the body itself, as subject and as object, both transcending freedom and mere facticity.[3] Reflection on the experience of pregnancy, I shall show, provides a radical challenge even to this dualism that is tacitly at work in the philosophers of the body.

To the extent that these existential phenomenologists preserve a distinction between subject and object, they do so at least partly because they assume the subject as a unity. In the *Phenomenology of Perception*, for example, Merleau-Ponty locates the "intentional arc" that unifies experience in the body, rather than in an abstract constituting consciousness. He does not, however, abandon the idea of a unified self as a condition of experience.

> There must be, then, corresponding to this open unity of the world, an open and indefinite unity of subjectivity. Like the world's unity, that of the I is invoked rather than experienced each time I perform an act of perception, each time I reach a self-evident truth, and the universal I is the background against which these effulgent forms stand out: it is through one present thought that I achieve the unity of all my thoughts.[4]

Merleau-Ponty's later work, as well as more recent French philosophy, however, suggests that this transcendental faith in a unified subject as a condition of experience may be little more than ideology.[5] The work of Lacan, Derrida, and Kristeva suggests that the unity of the self is itself a project, a project sometimes successfully enacted by a moving and often contradictory subjectivity. I take Kristeva's remarks about pregnancy as a starting point:

Pregnancy seems to be experienced as the radical ordeal of the splitting of the subject: redoubling up of the body, separation and coexistence of the self and another, of nature and consciousness, of physiology and speech.[6]

We can confirm this notion of pregnancy as split subjectivity even outside the psychoanalytic framework that Kristeva uses. Reflection on the experience of pregnancy reveals a body subjectivity that is decentered, myself in the mode of not being myself.

As my pregnancy begins, I experience it as a change in my body; I become different from what I have been. My nipples become reddened and tender; my belly swells into a pear. I feel this elastic around my waist, itching, this round, hard middle replacing the doughy belly with which I still identify. Then I feel a little tickle, a little gurgle in my belly. It is my feeling, my insides, and it feels somewhat like a gas bubble, but it is not; it is different, in another place, belonging to another, another that is nevertheless my body.

The first movements of the fetus produce this sense of the splitting subject; the fetus's movements are wholly mine, completely within me, conditioning my experience and space. Only I have access to these movements from their origin, as it were. For months only I can witness this life within me, and it is only under my direction of where to put their hands that others can feel these movements. I have a privileged relation to this other life, not unlike that which I have to my dreams and thoughts, which I can tell someone but which cannot be an object for both of us in the same way. Adrienne Rich reports this sense of the movements within me as mine, even though they are another's.

In early pregnancy, the stirring of the fetus felt like ghostly tremors of my own body, later like the movements of a being imprisoned within me; but both sensations were *my* sensations, contributing to my own sense of physical and psychic space.[7]

Pregnancy challenges the integration of my body experience by rendering fluid the boundary between what is within, myself, and what is outside, separate. I experience my insides as the space of another, yet my own body.

Nor in pregnancy did I experience the embryo as decisively internal in Freud's terms, but rather, as something inside and of me, yet becoming hourly and daily more separate, on its way to becoming separate from me and of itself. …

Far from existing in the mode of "inner space," women are powerfully and vulnerably attuned both to "inner" and "outer" because for us the two are continuous, not polar.[8]

The birthing process entails the most extreme suspension of the bodily distinction between inner and outer. As the months and weeks progress, increasingly I feel my insides, strained and pressed, and increasingly feel the movement of a body inside me. Through pain and blood and water this inside thing emerges between my legs, for a short while both inside and outside me. Later I look with wonder at my mushy middle and at my child, amazed that this yowling, flailing thing, so completely different from me, was there inside, part of me.

The integrity of my body is undermined in pregnancy not only by this externality of the inside, but also by the fact that the boundaries of my body are themselves in flux. In pregnancy I literally do not have a firm sense of where my body ends and the world begins. My automatic body habits become dislodged; the continuity between my customary body and my body at this moment is broken.[9] In pregnancy my prepregnant body image does not entirely leave my movements and expectations, yet it is with the pregnant body that I must move. This is another instance of the doubling of the pregnant subject.

I move as if I could squeeze around chairs and through crowds as I could seven months before, only to find my way blocked by my own body sticking out in front of me—but yet not me, since I did not expect it to block my passage. As I lean over in my chair to tie my shoe, I am surprised by the graze of this hard belly on my thigh. I do not anticipate my body touching itself, for my habits retain the old sense of my boundaries. In the ambiguity of bodily touch, I feel myself being touched and touching simultaneously, both on my knee and my belly.[10] The belly is other, since I did not expect it there, but since I feel the touch upon it, it is me.[11]

Existential phenomenologists of the body usually assume a distinction between transcendence and immanence as two modes of bodily being. They assume that insofar as I adopt an active relation to the world, I am not aware of my body for its own sake. In the successful enactment of my aims and projects, my body is a transparent medium.[12] For several of these thinkers, awareness of my body as weighted material, as physical, occurs only or primarily when my instrumental relation to the world breaks down, in fatigue or illness.

> The transformation into the bodily as physical always means discomfort and malaise. The character of husk, which our live bodiness here increasingly assumes, shows itself in its onerousness, bringing heaviness, burden, weight.[13]

Being brought to awareness of my body for its own sake, these thinkers assume, entails estrangement and objectification.

> If, suddenly, I am no longer indifferent to my body, and if I suddenly give my attention to its functions and processes, then my body as a whole is objectified, becomes to me an other, a part of the outside world. And though I may also be able to feel its inner processes, I am myself excluded.[14]

Thus the dichotomy of subject and object appears anew in the conceptualization of the body itself. These thinkers tend to assume that awareness of my body in its weight, massiveness, and balance is always an alienated objectification of my body, in which I am not my body and my body imprisons me. They also tend to assume that such awareness of my body must cut me off from the enactment of my projects; I cannot be attending to the physicality of my body and using it as the means to the accomplishment of my aims.

Certainly there are occasions when I experience my body only as a resistance, only as a painful otherness preventing me from accomplishing my goals. It is inappropriate, however, to tie such a negative meaning to all experience of being brought to awareness of the body in its weight and materiality. Sally Gadow has argued that in addition to experiencing the body as a transparent mediator for our projects or an objectified and alienated resistance or pain, we also at times experience our bodily being in an aesthetic mode. That is, we can become aware of ourselves as body and take an interest in its sensations and limitations for their own sake, experiencing them as a fullness rather than as a lack.[15] While Gadow suggests that both illness and aging can be experiences of the body in such an aesthetic mode, pregnancy is most paradigmatic of such experience of being thrown into awareness of one's body. Contrary to the mutually exclusive categorization between transcendence and immanence that underlies some theories, the awareness of my body in its bulk and weight does not impede the accomplishing of my aims.

This belly touching my knee, this extra part of me that gives me a joyful surprise when I move through a tight place, calls me back to the matter of my body even as I move about accomplishing my aims. Pregnant consciousness is animated by a double intentionality: my subjectivity splits between awareness of myself as body and awareness of my aims and projects. To be sure, even in pregnancy there are times when I am so absorbed in my activity that I do not feel myself as body, but when I move or feel the look of another I am likely to be recalled to the thickness of my body.

I walk through the library stacks searching for the *Critique of Dialectical Reason*; I feel the painless pull of false contractions in my back. I put my hand on my belly to notice its hardening, while my eyes continue their scanning. As I sit with friends listening to jazz in a darkened bar, I feel within me the kicking of the fetus, as if it follows the rhythm of the music. In attending to my pregnant body in such circumstances, I do not feel myself alienated from it, as in illness. I merely notice its borders and rumblings with interest, sometimes with pleasure, and this aesthetic interest does not divert me from my business.

This splitting focus both on my body and my projects has its counterpart in the dual location I give to myself on my body. Straus suggests that in everyday instrumental actions of getting about our business, comprehending, observing, willing, and acting, the "I" is located phenomenologically in our head. There are certain activities, however, of which dancing is paradigmatic, where the "I" shifts from the eyes to the region of the trunk. In this orientation that Straus calls "pathic" we experience ourselves in greater sensory continuity with the surroundings.[16]

The pregnant subject experiences herself as located in the eyes and trunk simultaneously, I suggest. She often experiences her ordinary walking, turning, sitting as a kind of dance, movement that not only gets her where she is going, but also in which she glides through space in an immediate openness. She is surprised sometimes that this weighted solidity that she feels herself becoming can still move with ease.

Pregnancy roots me to the earth, makes me conscious of the physicality of my body not as an object, but as the material weight that I am in movement. The notion of the body as a pure medium of my projects is the illusion of a philosophy that has not quite shed the Western philosophical legacy of humanity as spirit.[17] Movement always entails awareness of effort and the feeling of resistance. In pregnancy this fact of existence never leaves me. I am an actor transcending through each moment to further projects, but the solid inertia and demands of my body call me to my limits not as an obstacle to action, but only as a fleshy relation to the earth.[18] As the months proceed, the most ordinary efforts of human existence, such as sitting, bending, and walking, which I formerly took for granted, become apparent as the projects they themselves are. Getting up, for example, increasingly becomes a task that requires my attention.[19]

In the experience of the pregnant woman, this weight and materiality often produce a sense of power, solidity, and validity. Thus, whereas our society often devalues and trivializes women, regards women as weak and dainty, the pregnant woman can gain a certain sense of self-respect.

This bulk slows my walking and makes my gestures and my mind more stately. I suppose if I schooled myself to walk massively the rest of my life, I might always have massive thoughts.[20]

There was a time when the pregnant woman stood as a symbol of stately and sexual beauty.[21] While pregnancy remains an object of fascination, our own culture harshly separates pregnancy from sexuality. The dominant culture defines feminine beauty as slim and shapely. The pregnant woman is often not looked upon as sexually active or desirable, even though her own desires and sensitivity may have increased. Her male partner, if she has one, may decline to share in her sexuality, and her physician may advise her to restrict her sexual activity. To the degree that a woman derives a sense of self-worth from looking "sexy" in the manner promoted by dominant cultural images, she may experience her pregnant body as being ugly and alien.

Though the pregnant woman may find herself desexualized by others, at the same time she may find herself with a heightened sense of her own sexuality. Kristeva suggests that the pregnant and birthing woman renews connection to the repressed, preconscious, presymbolic aspect of existence. Instead of being a unified ego, the subject of the paternal symbolic order, the pregnant subject straddles the spheres of language and instinct. In this splitting of the subject, the pregnant woman recollects a primordial sexual continuity with the maternal body, which Kristeva calls "juissance."[22]

The pregnant woman's relation to her body can be an innocent narcissism. As I undress in the morning and evening, I gaze in the mirror for long minutes, without stealth or vanity. I do not appraise myself, ask whether I look good enough for others, but like a child take pleasure in discovering new things in my body. I turn to the side and stroke the taut flesh that protrudes under my breasts.

Perhaps the dominant culture's desexualization of the pregnant body helps make possible such self-love when it happens. The culture's separation of pregnancy and sexuality can liberate her from the sexually objectifying gaze that alienates and instrumentalizes her when in her nonpregnant state. The leer of sexual objectification regards the woman in pieces, as the possible object of a man's desire and touch.[23] In pregnancy the woman may experience some release from this alienating gaze. The look focusing on her belly is one not of desire, but of recognition. Some may be repelled by her, find her body ridiculous, but the look that follows her in pregnancy does not alienate her, does not instrumentalize her with respect to another's desire. Indeed, in this society, which still often narrows women's possibilities to motherhood, the pregnant woman often finds herself looked at with approval.

> As soon as I was visibly and clearly pregnant, I felt, for the first time in my adolescent and adult life, not-guilty. The atmosphere of approval in which I was bathed—even by strangers in the street, it seemed—was like an aura I carried with me, in which doubts, fears, misgivings, met with absolute denial. This is what women have always done.[24]

In classical art this "aura" surrounding motherhood depicts repose. The dominant culture projects pregnancy as a time of quiet waiting. We refer to the woman as "expecting," as though this new life were flying in from another planet and she sat in her rocking chair by the window, occasionally moving the curtain aside to see whether the ship is coming. The image of uneventful waiting associated with pregnancy reveals clearly how much the discourse of pregnancy leaves out the subjectivity of the woman. From the point of view of others pregnancy is primarily a time of waiting and watching, when nothing happens.

For the pregnant subject, on the other hand, pregnancy has a temporality of movement, growth, and change. The pregnant subject is not simply a splitting in which the two halves lie open and still, but a dialectic. The pregnant woman experiences herself as a source and participant in a creative process. Though she does not plan and direct it, neither does it merely wash over her; rather, she *is* this process, this change. Time stretches out, moments and days take on a depth because she experiences more changes in herself, her body. Each day, each week, she looks at herself for signs of transformation.

> Were I to lose consciousness for a month, I could still tell that an appreciable time had passed by the increased size of the fetus within me. There is a constant sense of growth, of progress, of time, which, while it may be wasted for you personally, is still being used, so that even if you were to do nothing at all during those nine months, something would nevertheless be accomplished and a climax reached.[25]

For others the birth of an infant may be only a beginning, but for the birthing woman it is a conclusion as well. It signals the close of a process she has been undergoing for nine months, the leaving of this unique body she has moved through, always surprising her a bit in its boundary changes and inner kicks. Especially if this is her first child she experiences the birth as a transition to a new self that she may both desire and fear. She fears a loss of identity, as though on the other side of the birth she herself became a transformed person, such that she would "never be the same again."

Finally her "time" comes, as is commonly said. During labor, however, there is no sense of growth and change, but the cessation of time. There is no intention, no activity, only a will to endure. I only know that I have been lying in this pain, concentrating on staying above it, for a long time because the hands of the clock say so or the sun on the wall has moved to the other side of the room.

Time is absolutely still. I have been here forever. Time no longer exists. Always, Time holds steady for birth. There is only this rocketing, this labor.[26]

II

Feminist writers often use the concept of alienation to describe female existence in a male-dominated society and culture.[27] In this section I argue that the pregnant subject's encounter with obstetrical medicine in the United States often alienates her from her pregnant and birthing experience. Alienation here means the objectification or appropriation by one subject of another subject's body, action, or product of action, such that she or he does not recognize that objectification as having its origins in her or his experience. A subject's experience or action is alienated when it is defined or controlled by a subject who does not share one's assumptions or goals. I will argue that a woman's experience in pregnancy and birthing is often alienated because her condition tends to be defined as a disorder, because medical instruments objectify internal processes in such a way that they devalue a woman's experience of those processes, and because the social relations and instrumentation of the medical setting reduce her control over her experience.

Through most of the history of medicine its theoreticians and practitioners did not include the reproductive processes of women within its domain. Once women's reproductive processes came within the domain of medicine, they were defined as diseases. Indeed, by the mid–nineteenth century, at least in Victorian England and America, being female itself was symptomatic of disease. Medical writers considered women to be inherently weak and psychologically unstable, and the ovaries and uterus to be the cause of a great number of diseases and disorders, both physical and psychological.[28]

Contemporary obstetricians and gynecologists usually take pains to assert that menstruation, pregnancy, childbirth, and menopause are normal body functions that occasionally have a disorder. The legacy that defined pregnancy and other reproductive functions as conditions requiring medical therapy, however, has not been entirely abandoned.

Rothman points out that even medical writers who explicitly deny that pregnancy is a disease view normal changes associated with pregnancy, such as lowered hemoglobin, water retention, and weight gain, as "symptoms" requiring "treatment" as part of the normal process of prenatal care.[29] Though 75 percent to 88 percent of pregnant women experience some nausea in the early months, some obstetrical textbooks refer to this physiological process as a neurosis that "may indicate resentment, ambivalence and inadequacy in women ill-prepared for motherhood."[30] Obstetrical teaching films entitled *Normal Delivery* depict the use of various drugs and instruments, as well as the use of paracervical block and the performance of episiotomy.[31]

A continued tendency on the part of medicine to treat pregnancy and childbirth as dysfunctional conditions derives first from the way medicine defines its purpose. Though medicine has extended its domain to include many bodily and psychological processes that ought not to be conceptualized as illness or disease—such as child development, sexuality, and aging, as well as women's reproductive functions—medicine continues to define itself as the practice that seeks cure for disease. E. D. Pellegrino and D. C. Thomasma, for example, define the goal of medicine as "the relief of perceived lived body disruption" and "organic restoration to a former or better state of perceived health or well-being."

> When a patient consults a physician, he or she does so with one specific purpose in mind: to be healed, to be restored and made whole, i.e., to be relieved of some noxious element in physical or emotional life which the patient defines as disease—a distortion of the accustomed perception of what is a satisfactory life.[32]

These are often not the motives that prompt pregnant women to seek the office of the obstetrician. Yet because medicine continues to define itself as the curing profession, it can tend implicitly to conceptualize women's reproductive processes as disease or infirmity.

A second conceptual ground for the tendency within gynecological and obstetrical practice to approach menstruation, pregnancy, and menopause as "conditions" with "symptoms" that require "treatment" lies in the implicit male bias in medicine's conception of health. The dominant model of health assumes that the normal, healthy body is unchanging. Health is associated with stability, equilibrium, a steady state. Only a minority of persons, however, namely adult men who are not yet old, experience their health as a state in which there is no regular or noticeable change in body condition. For them a noticeable change in their bodily state usually does signal a disruption or dysfunction. Regular, noticeable, sometimes extreme change in bodily condition, on the other hand, is an aspect of the normal bodily functioning of adult women. Change is also a central aspect of the bodily existence of healthy children and healthy old people, as well as some of the so-called disabled. Yet medical conceptualization implicitly uses this unchanging adult male body as the standard of all health.

This tendency of medical conceptualization to treat pregnancy as disease can produce alienation for the pregnant woman. She often has a sense of bodily well-being during her pregnancy and often has increased immunity to common diseases such as colds and flu. As we saw in the previous section, more-over, she often has a bodily self-image of strength and solidity. Thus, while her body may signal one set of impressions, her entrance into the definitions of medicine may lead her to the opposite understanding. Even though certain discomforts associated with pregnancy, such as nausea, flatulence, and shortness of breath, can happen in the healthiest of woman, her internalization of various discussions of the fragility of pregnancy may lead her to define such experience as signs of weakness.

Numerous criticisms of the use of instruments, drugs, surgery, and other methods of intervention in obstetrical practice have been voiced in recent years.[33] I do not wish to reiterate them here, nor do I wish to argue that the use of instruments and drugs in pregnancy and childbirth is usually inappropriate or danger-ous. The instrumental and intervention orientation that predominates in contemporary obstetrics, however, can contribute to a woman's sense of alienation in at least two ways.

First, the normal procedures of the American hospital birthing setting render the woman considerably more passive than she need be. Most hospitals, for example, do not allow the woman to walk around even during early stages of labor, despite the fact that there is evidence that moving around can lessen pain and speed the birthing process. Routine breaking of the amniotic sac enforces this bed confinement. Women usually labor and deliver in a horizontal or near-horizontal position, reducing the influence of gravity and reducing the woman's ability to push. The use of intravenous equipment, monitors, and pain-relieving drugs all inhibit a woman's capacity to move during labor.

Second, the use of instruments provides a means of objectifying the pregnancy and birth that alien-ates a woman because it negates or devalues her own experience of those processes. As the previous section described, at a phenomenological level the pregnant woman has a unique knowledge of her body processes and the life of the fetus. She feels the movements of the fetus, the contractions of her uterus, with an immediacy and certainty that no one can share. Recently invented machines tend to devalue this knowledge. The fetal-heart sensor projects the heartbeat of the six-week-old fetus into the room so that all can hear it in the same way. The sonogram is receiving increasing use to follow the course of fetal devel-opment. The fetal monitor attached during labor records the intensity and duration of each contraction on white paper; the woman's reports are no longer necessary for charting the progress of her labor. Such instruments transfer some control over the means of observing the pregnancy and birth process from the woman to the medical personnel. The woman's experience of these processes is reduced in value, replaced by more objective means of observation.

Alienation within the context of contemporary obstetrics can be further produced for the pregnant woman by the fact that the physician attending her is usually a man. Humanistic writers about medicine often suggest that a basic condition of good medical practice is that the physician and patient share the lived-body experience.[34] If the description of the lived-body experience of pregnancy in the previous section is valid, however, pregnancy and childbirth entail a unique body subjectivity that is difficult to empathize with unless one is or has been pregnant. Since the vast majority of obstetricians are men, then, this basic condition of therapeutic practice usually cannot be met in obstetrics. Physicians and pregnant women are thereby distanced in their relationship, perhaps more than others in the doctor-patient relation. The sexual asymmetry between physician and patient also produces a distance because it must be desexualized. Prenatal checkups follow the same procedure as gynecological examinations, requiring an aloof matter-of-factness in order to preclude attaching sexual meaning to them.[35]

There is a final alienation the woman experiences in the medical setting, which drives from the relations of authority and subordination that usually structure the doctor-patient relation in contemporary medical practice. Many writers have noted that medicine has increasingly become an institution with broad social authority on a par with the legal system or even organized religion.[36] The relationship between doctor and patient is usually structured as superior to subordinate. Physicians often project an air of fatherly infallibility and resist having their opinions challenged; the authoritarianism of the doctor-patient relations increases as the social distance between them increases.[37]

This authority that the physician has over any patient is amplified in gynecology and obstetrics by the dynamic of gender hierarchy. In a culture that still generally regards men as being more important than women and gives men authority and power over women in many institutions, the power the doctor has over the knowledge and objectification of her body processes, as well as his power to direct the performance of her office visits and her birthing, are often experienced by her as another form of male power over women.[38]

Philosophers of medicine have pointed out that the concept of health is much less a scientific concept than a normative concept referring to human well-being and the good life.[39] I have argued that there exists a male bias in medicine's concept of health insofar as the healthy body is understood to be the body in a steady state. This argument suggests that medical culture requires a more self-consciously differentiated understanding of health and disease.[40] Contemporary culture has gone to a certain extent in the direction of developing distinct norms of health and disease for the aged, the physically impaired, children, and hormonally active women. Such developments should be encouraged, and medical theorists and practitioners should be vigilant about tendencies to judge physical difference as deviance.

Moreover, to overcome the potentialities for alienation that I have argued exist in obstetrical practices, as well as other medical practices, medicine must shed its self-definition as primarily concerned with curing. Given that nearly all aspects of human bodily life and change have come within the domain of medical institutions and practices, such a definition is no longer appropriate. There are numerous life states and physical conditions in which a person needs help or care, rather than medical or surgical efforts to alter, repress, or speed a body process. The birthing woman certainly needs help in her own actions, being held, talked to, coached, dabbed with water, and having someone manipulate the emergence of the infant. Children, old people, and the physically impaired often need help and care though they are not diseased. Within current medical and related institutions there exist professionals who perform these caring functions. They are usually women, usually poorly paid, and their activities are usually seen as complementing and subordinate to the direction of activities such as diagnostic tests, drug therapies, and surgical therapies performed by the physicians, usually men. The alienation experienced by the pregnant and birthing woman would probably be lessened if caring were distinguished from curing and took on a practical value that did not subordinate it to curing.

Postscript, November 2003

"Pregnant Embodiment" was first published in 1983. Despite the enormous technological changes that have taken place in the United States and elsewhere that affect the experience of pregnancy and childbirth, I have left the text in its original form. The basic description of pregnant embodiment remains valid, I believe, as does the analysis of alienation of this subjectivity under the gaze of medicine. At least one technologically induced change in the experience of pregnancy, however, deserves an afterword comment. Description of the experience of pregnancy in this essay does not take into account the influence of sonogram technology, which arguably has altered the experience of pregnant women and their partners in significant ways. It is now routine for obstetricians to order one or more sonogram images after the fetus is large enough to distinguish features through its use. The sonogram projects an image of the developing fetus. Pregnant women, their partners and others who view the image often speak of the thrill of first seeing it. I have met more than one proud father who carries around a print of the image of a two-month-old fetus to show to his friends and colleagues.

The frequency of the routine use of sonogram in American obstetrical practice does not change the basic analysis of this paper. Indeed, it reinforces that analysis. This essay has two parts that describe a tension in the experience of pregnancy and childbirth for the woman who lives them. On the one hand, she *is* a pregnant person; it is she and only she who lives this growing body and moves within it. She and only she has a privileged relation of *feeling* with the developing fetus. The pregnant woman feels the weight, position, and motion of the fetus as part of herself yet not herself. Others have access to feeling this developing life only by contact with and through her.

On the other hand, however, the second section of the essay describes the conversion of this subjective experience into objective entities that can be observed by anyone with the proper instruments. These objectified observables come to be defined as the authoritative knowledge of the process of gestation and the state of the fetus, and thereby the pregnant woman's privileged insider knowledge comes to be devalued. In the last twenty years in the United States, as well as many other advanced industrial societies, this objectifying process has accelerated, I suggest. Sonogram technology makes it possible for anyone to experience fetal movement by looking at the same projected image. The pregnant woman's experience of that image is just the same as anyone else's who views it. This shared and shareable experience of the fetus tends to have more status as "reality" than the feelings only she can report. It is no accident, it seems to me, that this authoritative reality comes to those who witness it by way of *vision*. Sonogram technology has revolutionized the experience of pregnancy and expectant parenting by putting a visual representation of the fetus at the center, in the context of a modern epistemological system that has always given priority to the visual over the tactile or even the oral.

Originally published in *The Journal of Medicine and Philosophy*, 1984, 9, 45–62, https://doi.org/10.1093/0195161920.003.0004. Reprinted by permission of Oxford University Press on behalf of *The Journal of Medicine and Philosophy*; permission conveyed through Copyright Clearance Center, Inc.

Notes

1. Julia Kristeva, "Motherhood According to Giovanni Bellini," in *Desire in Language* (New York: Columbia University Press, 1980), 237.

2. Erwin Straus, *Psychiatry and Philosophy* (New York: Springer-Verlag, 1969), 29.

3. J. Sarano, *The Meaning of the Body*, trans. James H. Farley (Philadelphia: Westminster Press, 1966), 62–63.

4. Maurice Merleau-Ponty, *Phenomenology of Perception*, trans. Colin Smith (New York: Humanities Press, 1962), 406.

5. See Rosalind Coward and John Ellis, *Language and Materialism* (London: Routledge and Kegan Paul, 1977).

6. Julia Kristeva, "Women's Time," trans. Alice Jardine and Harry Blake, *Signs: Journal of Women in Culture and Society* 7 (1981): 31; cf. Kristeva, "Motherhood According to Giovanni Bellini," 238.

7. Adrienne Rich, *Of Woman Born* (New York: W. W. Norton, 1976), 47.

8. Rich, *Of Woman Born,* 47–48.

9. See Merleau-Ponty, *Phenomenology of Perception,* 82.

10. On the ambiguity of touch, see Merleau-Ponty, 93; see also Straus, *Psychiatry and Philosophy,* 46.

11. Straus discusses an intentional shift between the body as "other" and as self; see *The Primary World of the Senses* (London: Free Press, 1963), 370.

12. Merleau-Ponty, *Phenomenology of Perception,* 138–39.

13. Hans Plugge, "Man and His Body," in *The Philosophy of the Body*, ed. Stuart Spicker (Chicago: Quadrangle Books, 1970), 298.

14. Straus, *Primary World of the Senses,* 245.

15. Sally Gadow, "Body and Self: A Dialectic," *Journal of Medicine and Philosophy* 5 (1980): 172–85 https://doi.org/10.1093/jmp/5.3.172.

16. See Erwin Straus, "Forms of Spatiality," in *Phenomenological Psychology* (New York: Basic Books), especially 11–12.

17. See Elizabeth V. Spelman, "Woman as Body: Ancient and Contemporary Views," *Feminist Studies* 8 (1982): 109–23 https://doi.org/10.2307/3177582.

18. On the relation of body to ground, see R. M. Griffith, "Anthropology: Man-a-foot," in *Philosophy of the Body,* 273–92; see also Stuart Spicker, "Terra Firma and Infirma Species: From Medical Philosophical Anthropology to Philosophy of Medicine," *Journal of Medicine and Philosophy* 1 (1976): 104–35 https://doi.org/10.1093/jmp/1.2.104.

19. Straus's essay "The Upright Posture" well expresses the centrality of getting up and standing up to being a person; see *Phenomenological Psychology,* 137–65.

20. Ann Lewis, *An Interesting Condition* (Garden City, N.Y.: Doubleday, 1950), 83. When I began reading for this essay I was shocked at how few texts I found of women speaking about their pregnancies; this book is a rare gem in that regard.

21. Rich discusses some of the history of views of pregnancy and motherhood; see *Of Woman Born,* chapter 4.

22. Kristeva, "Motherhood According to Giovanni Bellini," 242. Marianne Hirsch makes a useful commentary in "Mothers and Daughters," *Signs* 7 (1981): 200–222 https://doi.org/10.1086/493870.

23. See Sandra Bartky, "On Psychological Oppression," in *Philosophy and Women*, ed. Bishop and Weinzweig (Belmont, Calif.: Wadsworth Publishing Co., 1979), 330–41.

24. Rich, *Of Woman Born,* 6.

25. Lewis, *An Interesting Condition,* 78.

26. Phyllis Chesler, *With Child: A Diary of Motherhood* (New York: Thomas Y. Crowell, 1979).

27. Ann Foreman, *Femininity as Alienation* (London: Pluto Press, 1977); Sandra Bartky, "Narcissism, Femininity, and Alienation," *Social Theory and Practice* 8 (1982): 127–43.

28. Barbara Ehrenreich and Deirdre English, *For Her Own Good* (Garden City, N.Y.: Doubleday, 1978), chapters 2 and 3.

29. Barbara Katz Rothman, "Women, Health, and Medicine," in *Women: A Feminist Perspective*, ed. Jo Freeman (Palo Alto, Calif.: Mayfield Publishing Co., 1979), 27–40.

30. Quoted in Gena Corea, *The Hidden Malpractice: How American Medicine Treats Women as Patients and Professionals* (New York: William Morrow, 1977), 76.

31. Rothman, "Women, Health, and Medicine," 36.

32. E. D. Pellegrino and D. C. Thomasma, *A Philosophical Basis of Medical Practice* (New York: Oxford University Press, 1981), 122; earlier quotes from 76 and 72, respectively.

33. Suzanne Arms, *Immaculate Deception: A New Look at Women and Childbirth in America* (Boston: Houghton Mifflin, 1975); D. Haire, "The Cultural Warping of Childbirth," *Environmental Child Health*, 19 (1973): 171–91; and Adele Laslie, "Ethical Issues in Childbirth," *Journal of Medicine and Philosophy* 7 (1982): 179–96 https://doi.org/10.1093/jmp/7.2.179.

34. Pellegrino and Thomasma, *A Philosophical Basis of Medical Practice,* 114.

35. J. Emerson, "Behavior in Private Places: Sustaining Definitions of Reality in Gynecological Examinations," in *Recent Sociology*, ed. H. Dreitzen, no. 2 (London: Macmillan, 1970), 74–97.

36. See E. Friedson, *The Profession of Medicine* (New York: Dodd and Mead Co., 1970); Irving K. Zola, "Medicine as an Institution of Social Control," *Sociological Review* 2 (1972): 487–504; and Janice Raymond, "Medicine as Patriarchal Religion," *Journal of Medicine and Philosophy* 7 (1982): 197–216 https://doi.org/10.1093/jmp/7.2.197.

37. See G. Ehrenreich and J. Ehrenreich, "Medicine and Social Control," in *The Cultural Crisis of Modern Medicine*, ed. John Erenreich (New York: Monthly Review Press, 1979), 1–28.

38. See B. Kaiser and K. Kaiser, "The Challenge of the Women's Movement to American Gynecology," *American Journal of Obstetrics and Gynecology* 120 (1974): 652–61.

39. Pellegrino and Thomasma, *A Philosophical Basis of Medical Practice,* 74–76; see also Tristram Engelhardt, "Human Well-Being and Medicine: Some Basic Value Judgments in the Biomedical Sciences," in *Science, Ethics and Medicine*, ed. Engelhardt and Daniel Callahan (Hastings-on-Hudson, N.Y.: Ethics and the Life Sciences, 1976), 120–39; and Caroline Whitbeck, "A Theory of Health" in *Concepts of Health and Disease: Interdisciplinary Perspectives*, ed. Arthur L. Caplan, Tristram Engelhardt, and James J. McCartney (Reading, Mass.: Addison-Wesley, 1981), 611–26.

40. Arlene Dallery, "Illness and Health: Alternatives to Medicine," in *Phenomenology in a Pluralistic Context: Selected Studies in Phenomenology and Existentialism*, ed. E. Schrag and W. L. McBride (Albany: State University of New York Press, 1983), 167–76.

14 The Beasts that Perish

MARY MIDGLEY

Machines on legs

We need here to consider another bad consequence of our traditional dualism – a quite misleading conception of the nature of non-human animals. This confusion still haunts us, though it is now under attack. Descartes notoriously ruled that animals could not be conscious because they were simply automata. Like his contemporaries he was fascinated by the ingenious clockwork models that were beginning to be produced in his day. And, since many of them were actually images of animals, he readily supposed that real animals could be worked in the same way. This idea fitted well with the physicists' current view that all motion was produced by impact, something that cogs and sprockets could easily produce. It made mechanism seem a plausible explanation for movement throughout the realm of nature.

Its drawback was, of course, that it didn't fit the actual behaviour of animals at all. For a clockwork duck to perform the exact movements that have been programmed into it is not at all the same thing as for a real duck to respond flexibly to the unexpected things that happen around her all the time, including, of course, the social signals of her ducklings. Descartes and his contemporaries entirely ignored this business of social signals, even though in practice their whole lives depended on the social signals they constantly exchanged with their horses, and indeed those they exchanged with other humans. It should have struck them that when a sheepdog responds to his master's command, taking the sheep through complicated manoeuvres far off from the signaller, it is hard to see how anybody could explain the process in terms of a clockwork mechanism.

The trouble was that the dualist background only allowed for two alternatives. Animals must either have souls, which would have awkward consequences such as sending them to heaven and entitling them to considerate treatment, or they must simply be material machines. These machines could conveniently be provided in some form like clockwork. No doubt the solution chosen to this dilemma was somewhat influenced by our culture's bias towards meat-eating, and also towards performing scientific experiments. The suggestion (made by a disciple of Descartes) that the screams coming from experimental subjects were merely the insignificant creaking of their rusty mechanism does not sound entirely disinterested. But the materialist view that animals were not conscious still seemed to scientifically minded people for a long time an objective and convincing story.

Voltaire, however, promptly attacked it:

Barbarians seize this dog, which in friendship surpasses man so prodigiously; they nail it on a table, and they dissect it alive in order to show the mesenteric veins. You discover in it all the same organs of feeling that are in yourself. Answer me, machinist, *has nature arranged all the means of feeling in this animal, so that it may not feel?* Has it nerves in order to be impassible? Do not suppose this impertinent contradiction in nature.

(Regan & Singer 1976: 67, quoting Voltaire, *Philosophical Dictionary*, "Animals", emphasis added)

Plenty of people agreed with him and more do today, but the researchers' impression that science demanded belief in the unconsciousness of animals persisted and became increasingly fixed in the tradition.

From a real scientific point of view, however, this belief is surely a mysterious one. What, if anything, is the basis for assuming that *Homo sapiens* is unique in this respect? The argument about the nerves is surely conclusive. As time went on and evolutionary explanations began to be more widely accepted, the suggestion of an unbridgeable gap in perception between us and all the other animals looked more and more mysterious. Yet animal behaviour has continued for a long time to be studied in these reductive, physicalist terms, as far as possible without any reference to the animals' possible consciousness or their views on what it all meant. The aim has always been to design and report these experiments in a way that would have been appropriate if the subjects had indeed been clockwork automata. Animals, it seemed, did not howl or moan, they "vociferated". They did not "respond" they "reacted". And they never behaved in any way that was not required by the purpose of the experiment.

How persistent this approach has been can be seen from an impressive proclamation called the "Cambridge Declaration on Consciousness", presented as recently as 2012 by a number of authoritative scientists at (pleasingly enough) the Francis Crick Memorial Conference on Consciousness in Human and Non-Human Animals. It testified that they *do* now think that actually animals may well be conscious. But how do you set about proving something as obvious as that, something that every baby knows and which adult experience has never thrown any doubt on? The compilers face this problem with heroic determination and a load of neurological statistics. At length they conclude that:

> While comparative research on this topic is naturally hampered by the inability of non-human animals, and often humans, to clearly and readily communicate about their internal states, the following observations can be stated unequivocally …

> The weight of evidence indicates that humans are not unique in possessing the neurological substrates that generate consciousness. Non-human animals, including all mammals and birds, and many other creatures, including octopuses, also possess these neurological substrates. (Low *et al.* 2012: 2)

So they *can* be conscious (even the octopuses) and when they act in an intelligent manner, it is reasonable to conclude that they are.

How can it possibly be necessary to say this today? The admission certainly comes better late than never, but why has it taken scientists three hundred years to get rid of an error that a little attention to their own domestic animals could quickly have cured? As we are beginning to realize, the explanation of this slowness does not lie in any scientific counter-evidence but in a background myth, a set of assumptions that is essentially religious.

That myth shows humans as exalted above the rest of creation, not now by the will of God but because their intellectual faculties allow them to perceive a supersensible semi-divine world – essentially the world of numbers – which forms the explanation of everything. We saw in Chapter 3 where this idea came from and in Chapter 12 we shall encounter some more of its consequences. It teaches us that human uniqueness is not just a matter of being rather different from other species, as elephants or giraffes are. Nor is it only a difference in the mental faculties. It is a metaphysical privilege that sets us altogether apart. That is why doing justice to it has gone on requiring radical dualism just as much as the book of Genesis used to. To prove our distinctness we still need our peculiar ontological status, even though we have lost the worldview that used to support it.

What about evolution?

The trouble is, of course, that this sense of separateness is quite incompatible with an evolutionary approach, with a real conviction that all earthly development is gradual and continuous. But it still shouts down that conviction in the souls of the scientistic. This is why accounts of animal behaviour were long required to show it as completely unlike human behaviour and as like as possible to the behaviour of gases. To ensure this, two particularly misleading words have been constantly employed in describing this behaviour: *anecdotal* and *anthropomorphic*.

"Anecdotal" is used to discredit any account of particular concrete events, no matter how well attested it may be. This rule is just an exaggeration of the quite proper requirement that we should support particular accounts by suitable evidence, but, as such single occurrences can at times be really relevant, it is sometimes a serious nuisance. "Anthropomorphic" on the other hand, is a really bad word, one that has long ago escaped from its proper usage into suggesting errors. It originally referred to ideas of God that credited him with having a human shape. When it was transferred to talk about animals, it made sense at first in a particular kind of situation: one where the animals were actually being credited with behaviour that could only be human, as in "a parliament of rooks". But it very quickly came to be used whenever an animal was described in words that would be appropriate for describing a human at all, especially emotion words.

Thus phrases such as "the cat was upset – surprised – terrified or affectionate" had to be translated into strictly behavioural terms, however probable, and indeed however important, it might be that the cat actually did have those feelings. The idea was that, even if the feelings existed, which was still thought to be unlikely, we could not possibly identify them. Claiming to detect them would therefore be anthropomorphism.

This usage simply neglects the fact that *we too are animals* – social animals endowed with good powers of expression – so that both our feelings and the ways in which we express them come directly from our nature and are designed to fit with those of our relatives. All kinds of animals need to be able to read the mood of others around them, not only because those others may pose a threat, or may be food, but also because they may be acquaintances with whom we shall want to socialize, even when they are not of our own species. Racehorses, for instance, often become friendly with a cat or a goat who shares their lodging and they may pine if it is taken away.

The extent to which social signals revealing these moods can be understood across species is indeed somewhat surprising. It shows how deeply we all depend on each other. Warning cries, for instance, are understood everywhere, even across the very deep canyon of evolutionary time that divides mammals from birds. The rich development of these signalling powers on both sides is one of those fascinating convergences that show the shared directions that underlie all of evolution.

All this has, however, been thoroughly neglected until very lately. Darwin, who fully understood its importance, wrote an excellent book about it that he called *The Expression of the Emotions in Man and Animals* (1872). In that book he very properly combined and compared human examples directly with those from other species. For this he used the everyday human language to describe all cases equally, and that language proved perfectly adequate to its task: not surprisingly, since it has been honed for centuries in all kinds of situations, including ones for interspecies communication. (People have always known whether their horses were frightened or angry.) He often pointed out differences between the responses of different species, but he also noted the many close parallels. He drew many of his examples from domestic animals because these were the ones that could be most fully studied in detail. These examples were often "anecdotal" – that is, not repeated – and were used because they were needed to fill in significant details that cast light on a general tendency.

The result of this common-sense approach was that his official followers dismissed the book as the embarrassing lapse of an ageing investigator – an amateur clearly tainted by folk psychology – and said as little as possible about it during his centenary celebrations. They thought it unscientific. How wrong this was is surely now clear. That stress on our natural powers of communication was just what was needed in order to shake up the absurd isolation in which the human race was still supposed to be existing. It cuts through some of the partitions that have been erected to divide us from the rest of nature. It shows that, peculiar and sublime though we may be in some ways, we can still feel at home on the earth alongside its other inhabitants, instead of having no company except numbers.

Plenty of people can appreciate that approach. And it ought at once to have been followed up after Darwin's book came out. But it wasn't, and it was some time before his example was really followed. At the beginning of the twentieth century the behaviourists, then ruling psychology, brushed it aside and constantly supported their doctrines by research on animals that was conducted entirely on artificial mechanistic principles. They silenced any other suggestions.

Realism about animals

The scientist who eventually broke this monopoly and produced a more realistic approach was Konrad Lorenz, an Austrian ethologist who understood animals deeply and did not care in the least what his colleagues thought of him. Writing in the 1930s, he described the life of geese, jackdaws and other creatures clearly and directly, using everyday psychological language as Darwin had done, and using it – just as Darwin did – so intelligently that anybody could see it was appropriate to the animals. His friend Niko Tinbergen did the same good service for gulls and other birds. Their example launched a whole new tradition of vigorous animal studies in which people like Jane Goodall responded directly to the thoughts and wishes of the animals while still supplying plenty of scientific detail.

This was a drastic change. When Goodall first started to write about chimpanzee behaviour, her supervisor told her at once to stop referring to her animals by names. Scientific procedure required her to use only numbers. She replied that names made it much easier to remember the events – something that had indeed already been established by other psychologists – and eventually he reluctantly allowed her to go on doing so. Now, of course, investigators do it all the time.

This episode shows the extraordinary power of dualist habits. In theory, dualism was already becoming discredited at this time; the movement was already towards materialism. But the dualist myth was still strong, presenting its imaginative picture of a divided world, a world in which animals loomed on the non-human side of a stark division as menacing extras, needing to be controlled. To suit this picture, many people still thought it was a basic scientific truth that animals were, in a peculiar sense, *things*: things in a way that people were not.

The behaviourists, when they were feeling strong, dealt with this awkward situation drastically by saying that, of course, humans were only things too. As Skinner put it, "We should not be anthropomorphic about man". Most of the time, however, they had to allow some space to the mental story in studying people. Why didn't they do so about other species? The reason for this was extremely simple; they were too ignorant about them to see the point at all.

Lorenz's contribution was crucial here. By filling in some of the real details about animals he cleared away the symbolic fantasies that had gathered around them, fantasies expressed by the associations attached to words such as rat, snake, wolf, cow, bitch, ape, raven, crocodile, shark and so forth. He showed that these fancies bore no relation to the actual behaviour of the creatures. Wolves, for instance, display all the domestic virtues and do not go ravening out of savagery but simply for survival. The beasts were being used as figures onto which all sorts of fears and fantasies could be projected.

By describing their actual lives more fully, Lorenz showed not just that they were less dangerous than we thought but that they were not the frighteningly alien beings that people imagined. They were normal fellow inhabitants of the earth. They are, he said, much more like us emotionally than we have supposed, although they are often less like us intellectually. This new understanding made it possible for people to share their world with animals imaginatively rather than trying to get rid of them. It showed nature itself as a system that we could well be part of, rather than as an alien force against which we had to fight. (The need to wage a "war against nature" had been a favourite theme of thinkers in the early twentieth century, notably Freud and William James.)

This change was crucial, not just because it improved our relations with the animals but because it made us more aware of our own vulnerability, of the pace at which we were damaging our planet. Throughout the nineteenth century and much of the twentieth, most influential people in the West simply did not consider this at all. The environmental costs of the Industrial Revolution scarcely crossed their minds. When their attention was drawn to particular kinds of damage, their reassuring answer was always that science and technology would be able to find cures for any harm they might happen to do. They thought that civilization was self-perpetuating. The dualist world picture that showed us as observers and engineers, organizing from a distance a scene over which we had total authority, left no room for the thought that we ourselves could be in real danger.

If we had not been ruled by that picture – if we had had a more realistic vision of our relation to the earth – we would surely have understood much more quickly the harm that we were doing. Here again it is striking to notice how myths – imaginative visions – can stop people from seeing plainly visible facts. And the interesting point about this particular case is that it was the myth – not the facts – that was deemed to be scientific. For a long time, talk about planetary damage was dismissed as fanciful – sentimental, frilly, feminine – "new age", even though it often came from well-qualified scientists.

The trouble is that what people were used to thinking of as scientific was the mechanistic vision in which nothing could really go wrong. That vision is still powerful today, notably in the USA where it does most damage, but also in countries like the UK where, although we may believe the news about the danger, droughts and floods have not yet brought that message home.

What all this means is that our belief in our detachment from the other animals, and from the earth that has produced them, is surely one more example of what may well be called scientistic superstition: an opinion maintained by convention contrary to well-known evidence in order to suit an imaginative habit. As far as animals are concerned, this notion differs from some others in that, at least in certain situations, it does seem to be seriously believed. Meat-eating and uncontrolled animal experimentation are indeed activities consistent with the idea that animals are unconscious, although they may well not be consistent with people's attitudes towards their cats and horses. Similarly, the belief that earth cannot be hurt by our abuse is consistent with our policy of doing hardly anything to protect it, although not, of course, with the news about it that we are getting every day. But there are other parts of these strange pseudoscientific conventions that quite plainly are not seriously believed since they do not produce appropriate behaviour. The most striking of these is the denial of free will.

From *Are You an Illusion?* by Mary Midgley. © Mary Midgley 2014.
Reproduced with permission of Taylor & Francis Group through PLSclear.

References

Darwin, C. 1872. *The Expression of the Emotions in Man and Animals*. London: John Murray.

Low, P., D. Edelman & C. Koch 2012. "The Cambridge Declaration on Consciousness". Proclaimed at the Francis Crick Memorial Conference on Consciousness in Human and Non-Human Animals at Churchill College, Cambridge. http://fcmconference.org/img/CambridgeDeclarationOnConsciousness.pdf (accessed December 2013).

Regan, T. & P. Singer 1976. *Animal Rights and Human Obligations*. Englewood Cliffs, NJ: Prentice Hall.

Part 4 Film and the Time Machine

Introduction

In the striking image from *The Edge of Heaven/Auf der anderen Seite* (Fatih Akın, 2007), a grief-stricken mother awakes in the last bed that her dead daughter had slept in. Susanne (Hanna Schygulla) has travelled to Istanbul in an attempt to find some connection to her daughter before she died, and after they had fallen out over the telephone. She goes to the apartment where her daughter was staying, lies on her bed, and reads her diary, before falling asleep. When she awakes, in the morning light, she lifts herself up with a smile on her face. She looks towards the camera, and a reverse shot shows her daughter, Lotte's (Patrycia Ziolkowska) face smiling broadly at her. The precise moment in Figure P4.1 is when Susanne's consciousness is hovering between sleep and wakefulness; a pause, but also a moment of stillness filled with the most metaphysical and spiritual import. Here is one of the infinite ways in which film can manipulate time in order to create meaning and profound metaphysical affect.

In a field of film philosophy that has been dominated by the name of Gilles Deleuze, this Part places Maya Deren at the forefront of re-thinking the dimension of film time. In her 1946 essay, reproduced here, Deren begins by stating that 'motion pictures are concerned with time and with movement'. Forty years before Deleuze's *Cinema 1* (1989a) and *Cinema 2* (1989b) meditated on the movement-image and time-image respectively, Deren spoke about the 'time potentialities of film' and that it 'rests upon the rhythm of movement'. Deren's analysis of her knowing manipulation of space and time in her films is directed at potential filmmakers, as she calls for them to produce work that is unique to the medium of film rather than forms from other mediums. This is a pleasing progression from Woolf's warning to filmmakers, twenty years before, that they did not yet realize what their medium could do: here Deren develops the specificity of film's capabilities and implores future filmmakers to be inventive with the form.

Brydie Kosmina's 2020 essay is a beautiful reflection on the possibilities that the concept of hauntology offers for past, present and future feminist temporalities. Kosmina's corpus is a literary one, but not only have several of her exemplar novels been adapted into films, but also the pertinence to film thinking of the ghosts and memories she describes is clear. Drawing on many sources from Virginia Woolf to Jacques Derrida, and Sara Ahmed to José Esteban Muñoz, Kosmina succeeds in her aim of 'bringing together [...] different ideas in a new pattern to craft a new material on which to embroider'. This reference to fabric recalls Woolf's comparison, in *Orlando* (1928), of memory with woven fabric. In this way, Woolf is a spectre haunting Kosmina's essay, and we are all reminded of her ingenious and intricate metaphor for memory.

Gail Weiss is concerned with the multiplicities of our identities, and the identities of others whom we encounter, and the role that temporality plays in their formation. Identifying the tensions around visible and non-visible characteristics, and the variable status accorded to them, Weiss turns to Linda Alcoff's concept of identities as interpretive horizons and develops the idea that there is transformative potential through encounters with others which are based on mutual respect and sharing of a common present. This offers

Figure P4.1 Susanne wakes to a vision of Lotte (*The Edge of Heaven/Auf der anderen Seite*).

insight into meetings and encounters that do not fit a conventional narrative pattern and closed-down ending, but rather occur as time periods of interest and transformation, and the basis of that shared time, and indeed how those partaking in the meeting may have been transformed.

The final piece in this Part is the influential writing of Elizabeth Freeman on temporal drag and erotohistoriography. Through close engagement with Mary Shelley's *Frankenstein, or, The Modern Prometheus* (1818), and Woolf's *Orlando* (Woolf clearly haunts this anthology), Freeman demonstrates the ways in which erotohistoriography works in these novels that play with bodies and queer time. Moving on to analyse features of the novels that appear in the lesbian time-travel movie *The Sticky Fingers of Time*, Freeman sees the film as showing historical and temporal disjunction being experienced as illicit pleasure, and lesbian sex forging an encounter across time. Freeman's argument takes in the formal and the metaphorical elements of the film that construct the erotohistoriography and presents a compelling analysis of this little-seen gem as a figuration of her temporal reading methods.

References

Deleuze, G. (1989a), *Cinema 1: The Movement Image*, trans. H. Tomlinson and B. Habberjam, London and New York: The Athlone Press.
Deleuze, G. (1989b), *Cinema 2: The Time Image*, trans. H. Tomlinson and R. Galeta, London and New York: The Athlone Press.

15 Creating Movies with a New Dimension: Time

MAYA DEREN

The biggest kick we film-makers get out of life is in showing an audience something new, in watching the reactions of our neighbors, friends, and strangers, to the end result of the hours of work which we have put into our films. Sometimes the audience is pleased, sometimes not. But whatever the emotion, as soon as the showing is over, there are questions. And the favorite question from my audience is: "Where do you get the ideas for your pictures? How can I get originality like that into my films?"

My answer is: Do not approach motion-picture photography in the conventional manner. Do not look upon movies as a mere extension of the still photograph. And pay *no* attention to those who tell you that the best approach to film-making is a sure grounding in photographic techniques through still photography. All this may sound revolutionary, and I mean for it to. For, apart from the problem of proper exposure and other basic technical routines (and these can be learned directly in connection with movies), the imaginative method of motion picture photography is very different from that of still photography. The superficial similarity of the fact that both techniques employ a lens and sensitive film usually serves to start the film-maker off on the wrong foot—full of habits of vision highly valuable to the still photograph, but actually harmful to the motion picture. Thus, I would say that the best study for the embryonic film-maker is one of the time arts—i.e., the dance or music—since, after all, motion pictures are concerned with time and with movement.

The basic difference between still and motion pictures can be simply explained. A still photograph is concerned with the isolation of a moment or a second of time. The wealth of detail which usually escapes our attention as each moment passes is here arrested for our leisurely scrutiny and examination. The moment is stayed, is composed *within* a stable frame. But in films the problem is directly opposite, for films are concerned with the way in which the moment passes and becomes the next one. This metamorphosis cannot be composed within a frame, but only *through* frames, from one frame to the next. Such movement concerns itself not with details of space, but with details of movement in time.

Such a consideration may seem abstract, academic, or esoteric; yet it comes into play immediately in the selection of a lens for a specific shot. The sense of pace in a film is given by the time it takes for an object to travel from one side of the frame to another. Obviously if the area of the lens covers the length of two strides, the person will seem to be going faster than if it takes him many strides to go from edge to edge of the frame.

A movement which takes place at right angles to a long focal length lens (more than one inch) will seem to pass much more rapidly than if it takes place at right angles to a short focal length, wide angle lens. This is true either in the case of a person running across the field of vision of the camera frame or in the case of the camera's making a panoramic move across a landscape. This is the kind of timing concept which has no function at all in still photography but is of primary importance in motion pictures.

But, such specialized techniques should never be used as ends in themselves. Always, technique must be subordinate to idea. For example, my film, *A Study in Choreography for Camera*, is a demonstration of the idea that in dancing one achieves a more magic relationship to space than one does in the course of ordinary walking. After all, dancing is not only a way of moving one's limbs—it also brings the dancer into a different relationship with his surroundings (both objects and space as a whole). It is, in short, qualitatively different from normal, naturalistic movement. And I wanted to show this not in terms of theater space but, by using techniques peculiar to the motion-picture camera, I wanted to put the entire world at the feet of the dancer.

In one shot for this film, I used a certain lens because of its effect on a time-space relationship. The location of this particular shot is the Egyptian Hall of the Metropolitan Museum of Art. The Hall (which has natural illumination through a glass roof) is square, and small enough to permit a dancer to travel its length and back in a short period of time. If I had used the regular one inch lens, the shot might have been pleasing but hardly startling. However, I used a wide angle lens—my main purpose in doing this was not so much to solve the follow-focus problem, as it was to use the exaggerated perspective of a wide angle lens to achieve a startling relationship between time and space.

Through the lens, the dancer—moving towards the back of the hall—seemed to become distant in terms of size without taking a normally long time to do so. In terms of normal vision, the dancer would have had to run much longer and farther. But in a matter of seconds, with the aid of the wide angle lens, through which the hall appeared much deeper, the dancer, starting in close-up, danced into the depth of the hall where he looked tiny and distant, and, returning rapidly became large and close again. A still photographer, photographing a dancer in the Egyptian Hall, would have had entirely different considerations in mind.

Concern with the time elements of film is important, also, in the handling of the camera frame. For a motion picture camera presents one with all the potentialities of a moving frame. For example, in *Meshes of the Afternoon* a camera tilting from side to side was used to give the impression of a rocking stairway. This scene comes at a moment in the film in which it was necessary to convey an impression that even an ostensibly inanimate staircase conspired (as do other objects in the film) to frustrate a girl in her effort to arrive somewhere. The figure which had preceded the girl climbed the stairs with ordinary ease. But those same stairs became active and seemed to throw the girl back when she tried to follow.

To shoot the scene, Alexander Hammid photographed with the camera hand-held, standing at the top of the stairs, and I, who happened to act in this sequence, started up the bottom of the stairs, towards the camera, simulating a heavy, uneven fall first to the right and then to the left. We so synchronized our movements that when I fell to my right, he tilted the camera to his left and vice versa. Thus, my falls seemed to be induced by a pitching of the stairs.

Here again, no special attention was paid to the spatial composition within an individual frame, but the movement over a series of frames was composed for a period of time. And note that the tilting was not merely a display of the technical virtuosity of which the motion picture camera is capable, but that it was used as the best method through which a particular emotion could be described.

The moving frame of a motion picture camera also makes it possible to determine not only *what* the audience sees (which is the completed intention of a still photograph) but also *when* they see it. This function can be used to portray not only the emotion of surprise and discovery—as when a room is revealed bit by bit during a panoramic shot—but it can also be used to conceal a manipulation of the camera. In one sequence of my film *At Land* I wished to establish the continuity of a girl walking down a road, and at the same time her relationship to a person walking with her, to her right, while the identity of that person remained fluid and uncertain. It is really a "change of identity" scene similar to the common dream in which one person's identity changes to another's before our eyes.

The scene begins with a long-shot of a deserted country road. A girl walks towards the camera, and when she has advanced into a closeup, the camera begins traveling with her, keeping her in a front view at a constant distance. When the camera shifts the view to the girl's side, it reveals a boy walking with her, also in medium closeup (although when we saw the girl at a distance, he was not there). He starts talking to her, and the camera shifts back to her as she answers him, and then back to him—except that now it is another boy. He picks up the conversation, the camera pans to her as she answers, then back to the right, but it is now still another boy. This same thing happens a number of times.

The effect was achieved very simply. The first boy fell in step with the girl while the camera held her in closeup. The other, alternating men, waited behind the camera, on the right side of the road. As the girl and first boy advanced towards them, the camera panned to the girl. Meanwhile, on the right side of the road, which was now out of frame, the first boy ducked behind the camera while the second boy took his place, so that when the camera returned to the right side of the road, it found another person there. Thus, the almost unreal effect, the almost dreamlike quality, was easily achieved.

The fact that a camera can be moved from one location to another, and that the various shots can follow each other immediately, in the process of editing, is also a capacity unique to motion pictures. In the dance film, *A Study in Choreography for Camera*, I took a shot of the dancer Talley Beatty as he began to lower his leg in a birch tree forest. Then I took a shot, in closeup, of the leg being lowered into an apartment. When these two shots are cut together so as to keep the leg movement continuous, it seems as if he steps, without pause, from a forest exterior to an apartment interior, and conveys a sense of movement through space. In other words, I have used the integrity of a human movement—its continuity of rhythm and pacing—to bind together locations which are otherwise unrelated. This is obviously a use of the time potentialities of film, in that it rests upon the rhythm of movement and upon the fact that two separate locations can be cut together on the strength of that rhythm.

The same technique was employed in *Meshes of the Afternoon*, where the girl rises from a chair and begins a walking movement forward. This is followed immediately by a series of closeups of the feet as the first stride lands on sand, the second on grass, the third on pavement, and the fourth on a rug. In walking across the room, the girl has covered the immense distance from ocean, through all the other elements, to another chair.

Still another manipulation of the time element in film—and its relationship to space—is made possible by the fact that the motion picture camera records as it runs, that the running can be interrupted at any moment, and resumed on the same frame. This is a camera function that can be used to express a quality best described as follows: All of us are given to day dreaming as we walk down streets or roads, across fields and beaches. We may walk several blocks without noticing how much space we have covered, how many stores we have passed by, how many buildings—which have not become a part of our conscious thought. That is the emotional reaction I wanted to reproduce in a part of my film *At Land*.

The sequence takes place on a series of sand dunes. It begins with a long shot of the dunes as a girl enters from the left edge of the frame, climbs a dune in the foreground, and disappears behind a dune on the right of the frame. At this point the camera stops, and great care is taken that it does not jar while it is not running.

Meanwhile, the girl walks on a considerable distance, and then disappears behind a dune much further along. At this point the camera motor is again started, but since it starts on the spatially identical frame as it stopped on there is nothing to indicate that the running was interrupted. As soon as it starts, it begins panning towards the right, as if it had followed her while she was hidden behind the dune. However, instead of seeing her emerge from that dune, it discovers her emerging from a dune much further away. When it discovers her, the camera stops panning while she again climbs one dune and disappears behind another.

Again the camera is stopped, again the girl walks ahead to a further dune. Then the camera starts again, pans, and discovers her—this time a mere speck, very far away.

Since the spatial location is not interrupted but is kept in continuity—that is, since the starting frame of the second part is identical with the stopping frame of the first shot—the action seems continuous. But it is not continuous in time, for it is actually interrupted to permit a certain activity—the long walking—to take place unregistered. And so the girl, who started out so near us, has, in a magic way, become rapidly distant. The alienation is out of proportion to the actual movement, just as in the course of personal relationships there grows, between two persons, a coolness which cannot be traced to any action on the part of either of them.

By these few examples, taken from my own work, I have attempted to explore new creative fields within the scope of the motion picture camera for the beginning film-maker. True, it is fun to picture the baby's third birthday party exactly as it occurs; but it is stimulating and exciting to translate the magic of thoughts and dreams to film. My purpose is to call the attention of all potential film-makers to those creative elements which are unique to the motion-picture camera, so that their efforts may result in new discoveries and new forms, rather than in imitations of the forms created by other mediums.

It is possible that people may take exception to the basic premise of my work. They may feel that it is the function of the photographer, or of any artist, to reproduce life as we see it. My opinion is that there is no particular value in duplicating something which already exists—except, of course, for purposes of personal or historical record (as birthday parties or news events), or of greater circulation (as travelogues of countries which few people have had an opportunity to see at first hand). I am bored, frankly, and I believe most persons are, with repetitions and reiterations. And I am immensely grateful when someone creates, out of his talent and effort, something which I never could have experienced except through his creation of it.

The desire to discover and to experience something new is responsible for growth and development in the individual, progress in civilization. And so it seems to me that a labor which results in something created, to add to the sum total of the world, is infinitely more valuable than a labor devoted to the reproduction of something already familiar. Thus, the fact that the motion picture camera is capable of creating new relationships between time and space, different from those of any other medium, is what has led me to this emphasis upon the temporal considerations of filmmaking. But remember—whatever the technique, it must serve the form as a whole, it must be appropriate to the theme and to the logic of its development, rather than a display of method designed to impress other movie makers.

First published in *Popular Photography*, 1946. Reprinted from *Essential Deren: Collected Writings on Film*, edited by Bruce R. McPherson, copyright © 2005 by The Estate of Maya Deren, by permission of McPherson & Company, Publishers, Kingston, New York.

16 Feminist Temporalities: Memory, Ghosts, and the Collapse of Time

BRYDIE KOSMINA

In *Orlando: A Biography*, Woolf ((1928a) 1998, 75–76) writes that '[m]emory is the seamstress, and a capricious one at that. Memory runs her needle in and out, up and down, hither and thither. We know not what comes next, or what follows after'. Memory, in Woolf's formulation, holds a certain material status, as the fabric of disparate ideas and temporalities are threaded together: the warp and the weft woven together just as past and future are woven together. The fabric of memory can be embroidered as necessary, or as desired, and thus presents a peculiar temporal collapse and revisionist attitude to time that can prove useful for feminists seeking to imagine a more equitable future. Critiquing linear temporalities and teleological narratives of progress has long been a concern of feminist philosophers, particularly new materialist feminist philosophers, according to Sellberg (2019). After all, as Ian Baucom has written (2001, 80), '[t]ime does not pass, it accumulates'. In this paper, I build on Sellberg's exploration of the connection between feminist philosophies, non-linear temporalities and materiality. The recurrent use of memory and ghosts in feminist literary, historical, and philosophical writing represents an inherent challenge to linear temporalities and conceptions of materiality. Memory and ghosts have long existed in women's writing as spectres of the past drawn into the present, functioning as *present absences*, underlining their apparent immateriality. I posit that a feminist ghost analytic underpinned by Jacques Derrida's hauntology and future-oriented understandings of memory enables *re-materializing* these revenants of the past, making their absence an inescapable presence, their transparency an undeniable solidity, and reconfiguring their status as fragments of the past into harbingers of an utopian future. In this sense, I mirror Woolf's mnemonic weaving in threading together multiple means of grappling with and blurring the temporalities of feminist politics, memory, and ghosts. This paper is thus both synthesis and synthetic: the bringing together of different ideas in a new pattern to craft a new material on which to embroider.

Past

In an era defined by what Lyotard (1984, xxiv, 37) labels an 'incredulity' towards metanarratives, postmodern theorists have characterized the past as inaccessible, sublimated to the dominance of the present. For instance, Jameson (1991, 18) argues that in post-modernity, 'the past is thereby itself modified' as the historical record has become a multitudinous *simulacrum* of narrative cohesion, existing instead as a 'vast collection of images'. Consequently, Newman, Clayton, and Hirsch (2002) see the postmodern rejection of the past as an accessible or coherent time and/or space as a consequence of the suspicion of metanarratives; the past and the future as organizing categories are viewed with ambivalence, condensing time into the pure present. Jacques Derrida proposes the term 'hauntology' in *Spectres of Marx* (1994) to describe the multiple, destabilized temporalities of postmodernity, embodied in the figure of the spectre. Writing specifically about the ghosts of Marxism and Soviet Communism following the Fall of the Berlin Wall, Derrida argues that the arrival of the spectre heralds the collapse of modal notions of time, as it is a figure of the past (something from the past which has died) and the present (the moment of the haunting) simultaneously. The postmodern condition, then, is a process of 'learning to live [with the spectre] [...] And this being-with specters would also be, not only but also, a *politics* of memory, of inheritance, and of generations' (Derrida 1994, xviii-xix, emphasis original). This resonates with Jameson's claim (1991, ix) that postmodernism is best defined as 'an attempt to think the present historically in an age that has forgotten how to think historically in the first place'. If the past is difficult (if not impossible) to access in the postmodern present, then the spectre functions as a mechanic to draw the past *into* the present, creating fissures or fractures in the present through which the haunting ghosts of the past can slip. A 'spectral moment', therefore, is 'a moment that no longer belongs to time' (Derrida 1994, xix). As Shaw (2018, 2) writes, the spectre, in Derrida's formulation, 'dissolv[es] the separation between now and then', and therefore represents a 'compulsion to repeat the past, and an anticipation of the future'. The ghost denotes time in multiple ways: 'it is *le temps*, but also *l'histoire*, and it is *le monde*, time, history, world' (Derrida 1994, 21, emphasis original), and is thus a useful figure through which to consider a feminist temporality as it pertains to the current moment (*le monde*) as much as it does to the past (*l'histoire*).

The (in)accessibility and (in)coherence of the past as an organizing category and the consequent spectralization of narratives of the past is of particular urgency for feminist activists and scholars, for whom history and the past must be rewritten, revised, and recuperated. Perhaps this tension between the availability and the accessibility of the past for marginalized groups is why there is such a strong thread in feminist historical and literary scholarship of recovery and recuperation of past figures, events, narratives, or motifs. Woolf, for instance, writes of the need for women's history in *A Room of One's Own* ((1928b) 2009), a call taken up by women's historians, and later feminist historians, in the late 1960s and early 1970s. History is not the past itself, but rather is a narrative of that time, and feminist revisionist and recuperative scholarship reflects an explicitly political feminist intervention in these narratives of the past. Feminist historical work is underpinned by a recognition that prior narratives of the past have excluded marginalized identities, stories, and agency, and must therefore be embellished, or even rewritten entirely, for those groups to access the past at all. Lerner (1993, 4), for instance, a feminist theologian and historian, distinguishes between the events of the past (things that happened) and history (historians' interpretation of the past that is influenced by and influences patriarchal hegemony in the present). Lerner argues that women consequently have 'a relationship to History and to historical process different from that of men', as women have been 'obliterated or marginalized' from the record (1993, 4). This strand of feminist historical work is inextricably tied to contemporary feminist politics, and often focuses on making invisible or hidden figures and narratives material and visible once more (Cowman and Jackson 2003). Invisibility is in fact a recurring metaphor in this early period of second-wave feminist historical scholarship, as evidenced by texts like Sheila Rowbotham's *Hidden from History* (1973) and Renate Bridenthal and Claudia Koonz's *Becoming Visible* (1977). This feminist revisionist historiography represents an intervention in narratives of past temporalities according to the necessities of feminist activism in the present, which, unconsciously or not, reproduce long-standing metaphors of women's status as hidden or invisible figures, and reinforce the connection between spectral metaphors and the feminine.

Similarly, literary scholars have sought to re-discover and recuperate forgotten women's voices and texts, critiquing patriarchal literary canons, and often positioning the authors of these recuperated or newly-rejuvenated texts as foremothers to twentieth-century feminist movements (Marsden 2002). In creating a matrilineal heritage of authors and historical figures, feminists can, in Marsden's words (2002, 659), 'envision a new literary history, one distinct from the traditional masculine canon'. The work of feminist recovery in history and literary studies is not without problems: as Marsden points out, it can encourage value judgements based on how these historical figures and texts align with contemporary feminism, and ignores those women who may be objectionable or not useful for present-day feminist work. It also can create a situation where women scholars are *expected* to study women, and lose their feminist credentials if they fail to. Nevertheless, as with feminist historical work, the recovery and recuperation of women's writing from the forgotten (or deliberately erased) canons of the past serves an explicit contemporary political purpose. Not only does it bring these writers and texts once more into the light, but it also creates a canon of one's own for feminists looking to the past for templates of action in the present.

Feminism itself is spectralized and 'haunted by its past', argues Hesford (2005, 227, 228), and is figured as 'a kind of remembering – a collective cultural remembering of the second wave movement – that is also a haunting'. Hesford (2005, 230) goes on to write that '[f]or feminists in particular, to have a haunted relationship with the feminist past is to be able to bear witness to the possibilities, often unrealized, of that past'. Consequently, despite the problems that an exclusive focus on recovery work can have for feminist scholars, scholarship of recovery and recuperation remains, and will remain, a mainstay of feminist scholarship and activism. As Rowbotham (1989, 261) writes, feminist activism has always had 'a respect for memory and a desire to reinterpret history'. Further, as Sandra Gilbert and Susan Gubar write in their seminal *The Madwoman in the Attic* (1979, 98–99), 'the woman poet [...] reconstruct[s] the shattered tradition that is her matrilineal heritage' and thus 'the female artist makes her journey into what Adrienne Rich has called "the cratered night of female memory" to revitalize the darkness, to retrieve what has been lost, to regenerate, reconceive, and give birth'. As Cowman and Jackson (2003) have argued, feminist scholarship concerned with the past, history, and women's heritage implicitly underlines feminist understandings of temporality as non-linear, as it presents a challenge to patriarchal narratives of human experience. The long traditions of feminist rhetoric concerned with writing a new narrative of the past for, of, and by women reveal the necessity of a means to access past temporalities for political ends.

These understandings of feminist history and literary studies presuppose a situation in which women's pasts are always invisible and that feminist scholarship renders them visible again. This renders the past transparent: the time and space between *then* and *now* becomes a barely-opaque veil or shroud that hides these figures from view in the present, who exist as absent presences (or present absences, depending on perspective). This use of invisibility or transparency extends to women's writing, which for centuries has been dominated by recurring metaphors of perhaps the most obvious motif of an invisible presence: the ghost. Charlotte Brontë's *Jane Eyre* (1847) and Emily Brontë's *Wuthering Heights* (1847), for example, abound with ghosts and spirits, both literal and metaphorical. Du Maurier's ((1938) 2015) eponymous *Rebecca* haunts the narrative and the characters without ever becoming wholly visible. Toni Morrison's *Beloved* ((1987) 2010) is both haunted and haunting on multiple levels: haunted by the 'Sixty Million or more' victims of the African slave trade, by Sethe's dead baby, and by the eternal presence of past trauma. These seminal texts in the canon of women's writing demonstrate a recurring concern with ghosts and spirits as metaphors for both the haunting of past trauma, and for the subject haunted by that trauma.

En-*vision*-ing women's pasts is thus an exercise (or exorcise) in grappling with the invisibility of the ghost, an exercise that entails balancing the recurring haunting presence of the past in the pure present of postmodernity. Derrida's conception of the ghost as heralding temporal collapse is consequently useful: past and present, immaterial and material can exist simultaneously. The ghost and spectrality represent the beginnings of a non-linear feminist temporality that repurposes narratives of the past for and in the present, while also functioning as a means of lifting the veil and making these ghosts of the past visible. A feminist ghost mechanic for re-writing the past represents a means through which hidden pasts can be brought into the light of the present, and alternate times may be envisioned and created.

Present

While ghosts and memories are living fragments of the past, or reanimated revenants of past events, figures, and symbols, these spectral figures exist within the pure present. Further, these spectres of the past are a *requirement* for conceptualizing the present. As Paul Connerton writes (1989, 2):

> our experience of the present very largely depends upon our knowledge of the past. We experience our present world in a context which is causally connected with past events and objects, and hence with reference to events and objects which we are not experiencing when we are experiencing the present. And we will experience our present differently in accordance with the different pasts to which we are able to connect that present. Hence the difficulty of extracting our past from our present: not simply because present factors tend to influence – some might want to say distort – our recollections of the past, but also because past factors tend to influence, or distort, our experience of the present.

The cyclical loop of past and present feeds evolving discourses of each, blurring temporalities into a Möbius strip that draws the past into the present, and projects the present back into the past. This cycle of past and present represents a more equal relationship between temporalities than has been conceived of in postmodern treatises on temporalities, which tend to privilege the present moment over all other times. The emphasis on the present is, in part, a consequence of postmodern categories of time and space: Harvey (1989, 240), for instance, argues that postmodern thinking is characterized by an emphasis on the pure present, as 'time horizons shorten to the point where the present is all there is'. Heise (1997, 64, 67) similarly argues that the 'focus on the present' is a central narrative feature of postmodern literature, and that this is 'a way of dealing aesthetically with an altered culture of time in which access to the past and especially the future appears more limited than before in cultural self-awareness'. Despite these rather pessimistic pronouncements on the status of alternate temporalities to the present under postmodernity, access to the past is not shut off, but is fundamentally altered. The affective structures of the 'stretched-out present' that Lauren Berlant writes about in *Cruel Optimism* (2011, 5) demonstrate the present's status as 'a thing that is sensed and under constant revision' (4). Alternate pasts are drawn into the present, making it thick or stretched with potential: the constant re-interpretation and re-evaluation of the past in line with renewed necessities and anxieties of the present.

Consequently, interventions in the past do not exist independently of politics in the present: the recovery or revision of the past is determined by the necessities and anxieties of the present, as these temporalities are mutually dependent. While historical writing has been a dominant means of writing the past, memory is an equally useful mode of accessing the past from inside the present. Karlsson (2010) writes that 'memory can provide the individual with a comforting notion of a connection or a continuity in relationship to history, a kind of "presence of the past", which itself may bring about an understanding of being part of something larger than a single, isolated human life'. Memory studies have become an increasingly urgent field of study, particularly since the 1990s, perhaps in response to the postmodern instability of history and the past. Memory, a fragment of the past, is simultaneously always a 'phenomenon of the present', to quote Nora (1992, 3). Hite and Jara (2020, 247, 250) characterize this mnemonic persistence of the past in the present as 'fissures' that can 'tear open a new form of imagining emancipative possibilities [...] interrupt[ing] the present radically, persistently, sometimes in democratizing ways'. Grosz (2004, 251) similarly describes the persistence of memory as a mechanism that 'fracture[s]' and 're-fract[s]' the present with 'the murmurs of the past and the potential of the future. Every present is riven by memory'. The potential of memory to disrupt the 'stretched-out present' (Berlant 2011, 5) to contain past and future can be turned to any number of political avenues[1] but is particularly compelling when viewed in relation to remembering oppressed or marginalized pasts.

Just as with the recurring metaphor of the ghost, there is a clear trend for women using memory as a literary motif to explore their connection to the past from within the present, particularly given the patriarchal status of history and the exclusion of women from recorded pasts. Thinking of women's pasts as spectral and veiled or shrouded is particularly compelling (and potentially paradoxical) when viewed with Woolf's description of memory as a woven fabric: remembering becomes a means of lifting the veil. Memory, as Woolf writes, weaves together time: it makes time a material thread to be braided and entwined into the fabric of the present as needed. Woolf had earlier played with the fluid stream of memory and its status as both past and present in *Mrs Dalloway* ((1925) 2004, 6): Clarissa Dalloway thinks to herself as she walks towards Bond Street, '[s]he remembered once throwing a shilling into the Serpentine. But every one remembered; what she loved was this, here, now, in front of her'. Daphne du Maurier writes in *Rebecca* ((1938) 2015, 40) of the desire to bottle memory: '[i]f only there could be an invention […] that bottled up a memory, like scent. And it never faded, and it never got stale. And then, when one wanted it, the bottle could be uncorked, and it would be like living the moment all over again'. Perhaps the most famous discussion of the function of memory in revising past and present in women's writing is Morrison's notion of rememory in *Beloved* ((1987) 2010). Rememory, in Morrison's formulation, is both a noun and a verb: it is both the material presence of the past in the present, and the action of drawing that ghostly past into the present through re-remembering it. *Beloved* is a story haunted by ghosts of the past made material flesh through memory, as Sethe's dead child returns as Beloved. These texts, and others, reflect a recurring motif in women's writing of the twentieth century in which past trauma is re-examined, revised, and turned to some future purpose through the mechanisms of memory and ghosts. As Dilek Direnç writes, 'in female memory women's wisdom, knowledge, and strength are preserved and can be transmitted' (2002, n.p.).

The loop of past and present in memory and history works in both directions: feminist work is influenced and shaped by memories of the past, just as memories of the past are influenced and shaped by feminist activism in the present. By using memory as a device for constructing women's shared pasts, these feminist historians, literary scholars, and writers are writing a 'history of the present', to use Foucault's description of genealogy ((1975) 1977, 31). Memory serves not just a literary purpose in feminist temporal work, but a sociological one too: Cowman and Jackson (2003, 45–47) point to the 'interest in life stories and personal narratives' in feminist historical projects. In using memory as a central and enduring mechanic through which to access the past, these feminist writers can draw the past into the present, expanding narrow time horizons, and thus creating scope for the irruption of femininity into past temporalities. Memory provides an alternative to history as a means of passing down narratives, ideas, and lineages for present day purposes.

The imbrication of past and present temporalities that memory entails mirrors the collapse of past and present that the arrival of the ghost heralds. These revenants of the past cannot be exorcized, though, and forever return and are re-remembered. Memory and the ghost are linked in their collapse of past and present, their simultaneous and paradoxical immateriality and the nevertheless material repercussions of its arrival in the present moment, and their recurrent use as a motif of the transparency or absence of women's pasts in both scholarly and fictional work. To speak *to* and *with* the ghosts of the patriarchal past is simultaneously to bear witness to the haunting of the present and to imagine a more just future. Given the recurring motifs of memory and ghosts in women's writing, and the non-linear turns of feminist temporalities, hauntology is a useful mechanic through which to understand these blurred temporal and spatial lines.

Future

The ghost functions as a mechanic through which the past can be made present in the present, just as memory functions as a means of fracturing that present for the past to interrupt. What these mnemonic and spectral revenants of the past that haunt the present have in common is their *future* orientation. The ghost is not only a figure of the past and present, but of the future too: the spectre is '[t]urned toward the future', according to Derrida (1994, xix). 'Spectres', Shaw (2018, 7) similarly argues, 'disturb the present with the possibility of alternative pasts and futures. In doing so they also defy time and space'. Hauntology, therefore, 'is the idea that there is something from the past which is always present in the present; and, also that this something is waiting for its return to a future to come [...] The spectre is thus both past and future' (Hughes 2012, 15). As Fisher (2012, 16) argues, '[t]he future is always experienced as a haunting: as a virtuality that already impinges on the present, conditioning expectations and motivating cultural production'. The ghost represents a 'compulsion to repeat the past, and an anticipation of the future', and living with the spectre requires 'recognition of the future inside the past, [and] the possibilities opened up by new knowledge of that which went before' (Shaw 2018, 2, 107). Similarly, memory presumes and constructs a future in the recollection of the past. As Grosz (2004, 117) argues, '[t]he past is what gives us that difference, that tension with the present which can move us to a future in which the present can no longer recognize itself'. To remember the past in a certain way or with a certain intention presupposes an implicit assumption of what the future is, or could be. The spectre and its ghostly companion memory represent a means of grappling with non-linear understandings of past, present, and future meanings, and thus demonstrate a mechanic for handling past and future temporalities in the pure present of postmodernity.

This recurrent rhetoric of the past in the present has implications for feminist futures: as Ahmed (2003, 236) writes, '[t]he question of "feminist futures" cannot be asked without reference to the pasts and presents of different feminisms'. As Ahmed goes on to argue, feminism itself exists as a critique of past conditions specifically to ensure that the future does not repeat those conditions. Similarly, Grosz (2004, 253–255) writes,

[w]hat is this persistence of the past in the present? And how does it help us rethink questions of politics, which are ultimately questions of change, of desirable futures? [...] [the question of history] is about the production of *conceivable futures*, the future understood not as that which is similarly contained in the present, but rather, as what diverges from the present, what produces a new future, one uncontained by and unpredicted from within the present. This is indeed what I understand feminist politics – at least at its best – to be about: the production of futures for women that are uncontained by any of the models provided in the present.

Feminists have always *implicitly* grappled with multiple temporalities at once, due to the very nature of activist work. *Explicitly* addressing the collapsed temporalities of feminist work enables *changing* the past and present as needed for the future. Derrida's hauntological figure of the ghost thus holds political potential for feminists seeking to imagine a future free of patriarchy. Not only is spectralisation a useful mechanism for feminists seeking to play with temporal lines, but the ghost is always turned towards future justice, resonating with feminist futurity. The arrival of the spectre requires the haunted subject to address the unfinished business of the past that the ghost represents and remedy the problems that cause the ghost to be unable to move on. As Derrida (1994, xviii, emphasis original) argues, '[i]t is necessary to speak *of the* ghost, indeed *to the* ghost and *with* it [...] no justice [...] seems possible or thinkable without the principal of some *responsibility*.' Shaw (2018, 107) similarly points out that the arrival of the ghost 'demands justice or, at the very least, a response from the haunted subject'. The spectre demands justice from those it haunts, and consequently represents the potential to revise the past in line with feminist needs in the present and utopian visions of the future. Similarly, remembering the past according to the necessities of the present also presupposes a desired future. Feminist memory serves the broader purpose of imagining a future different to, or aligned with, that past.

Derrida proposes the spectre as a wholly temporal phenomenon, rendering it a mechanic without material affect. However, re-materializing the ghost, and making it a spatial as well as temporal phenomenon, renders it not a present *absence*, but an absent *presence*. A haunting happens 'in specific moments, and specific locations' (Blanco and Peeren 2010, xi): the irruption of the ghost into the present moment is consequently not just a temporal phenomenon but a material one too. The figure of the ghost as a *material* mechanic through which to grapple with non-linear feminist temporalities is particularly compelling in light of Elizabeth Freeman's discussion in *Time Binds: Queer Temporalities, Queer Histories* (2010, 3) of queer time and the temporal negotiation of the body, writing that 'naked flesh is bound into socially meaningful embodiment through temporal regulation'. Re-materializing the ghost entails acknowledging that its temporal rupture has material effects on the body (individual, social, politic), and, further, that its temporal rupture is made possible only by its transparent materiality. The ghost represents both the material and the immaterial, the visible and the invisible, and the spectre consequently represents the potential to disturb temporality as both an experiential and conceptual phenomenon. The ghost appears when and where it is required in the present to demand justice in the future for the past. A feminist ghost analytic does not empty out the political undercurrent of feminist histories, but draws these into the present, and into the future. Memory, similarly, is made material in feminist writing, as seen in the earlier quotes from Woolf, du Maurier and Morrison. Memory becomes a fabric to be woven; a coin to be tossed in the river; a scent to be bottled; or a child to be loved.

Inscribing the spectre as the harbinger of a non-linear approach to temporality is not unique to the feminist hauntological use of memory proposed in this paper. Freeman (2010, 10) argues that queer hauntological formulations of temporality demonstrate how '[queer] time can produce new social relations and even new forms of justice that counter the chrononormative and chronobiopolitical'. Framing the haunting presence of the past in the present for the future as 'temporal drag', Freeman posits that this backward-directed temporal pull simultaneously creates forward movement by 'connecting queer performativity to disavowed political histories' (2010, 65). Feminist hauntological utopianism which is predicated on the irruption of memory and the spectre into the present demonstrates the materiality of this temporal drag, and resonates with a feminist hauntological temporality that utilizes the figures of the spectre and of memory. The spectre irrupts into the present, bringing with it the haunting past and future hopes, and thus creates present-day action or response. The present becomes stretched or thick as it contains past and future times, and this in turn creates material affect in the haunted subject who, in turn, reconsiders present-day conditions.

The spectre is not only future-oriented, but directed towards a *utopian* future. Anti-utopian trends in scholarship in the latter twentieth century and twenty-first century have made hope seem trite: Jacoby (2005, 6) writes that '[t]he movement from utopia to dystopia ratifies history'. Nevertheless, as we live through a time characterized by the 'in these troubling times' email, utopian thought is not just a mode of critical enquiry but a requirement of surviving. Future temporalities opened up through a feminist ghost analytic are utopian by necessity: the arrival of the ghost demands action, and the haunted subject must act for justice. In using the spectre to understand the collapsing of temporalities, feminists thus imagine a more open future free from patriarchy. Similarly, while memory may seem to be oriented wholly towards the past, as Gutman, Sodaro, and Brown argue (2010), memory studies has always challenged linear temporalities. Memory studies, Gutman, Brown, and Sodaro (2) write, holds as a central assumption the insistence 'that temporality is not unidirectional; we do not carry the past with us into the present unchanged, but rather it is recreated in and by the present' and, further, that this increasingly is being turned to the future. A feminist use of memory consequently reflects what Huyssen (2003, 29) calls 'productive remembering': it is remembering *for* a cause and *for* a future.

Utopias have had a long history from Thomas More's 1516 original treatise. Wilde (1891, 303–4) famously wrote of the crucial place Utopia has in the human imagination: '[a] map of the world that does not include Utopia is not worth even glancing at, for it leaves out the one country at which Humanity is always landing. And when Humanity lands there, it looks out, and, seeing a better country, sets sail. Progress is the realization of Utopias'. Utopia holds a crucial space in the cultural imaginary, although utopians come in many varieties. Jacoby (2005, xiv, xv) distinguishes between blueprint utopians, who 'map out the future in inches and minutes' and iconoclastic utopians, who 'dreamt of a superior society but who declined to give its precise measurements'. While blueprint utopians are criticized for the precision of their utopian societies which can become oppressive in their limitations, iconoclastic utopians suffer from the opposite problem: the utopian society they aim towards is unspecified. Nevertheless, iconoclastic utopianism has a strong philosophical tradition: philosophers such as Walter Benjamin, Herbert Marcuse, and Ernst Bloch all demonstrate the open future of this utopian tradition. Utopianism may seem trite in the current, unstable global climate but it is essential to survival. Further, a utopian sensibility underpins feminist activism: fighting for a world free of patriarchy requires utopian thinking.

Of more pressing concern than the naivety of utopian thinking is the inaccessibility of the future in postmodern thinking, and thus the potential exclusion of utopian thought from postmodern conceptions of time. Postmodern utopianism is consequently predicated on simultaneous acceptance of the pure present of postmodernity, and the haunting presence of the past and the future. Michael J. Griffin and Tom Moylan thus define the postmodern utopian impulse as the simultaneous

> negation of the present moment and a figuration of a better reality that can be articulated through a variety of texts and social practices [...] Utopianism, consequently, is best understood as a process of social dreaming that unleashes and informs efforts to make the world a better place, not to the letter of a plan but to the spirit of an open-ended process (2007,11).

Utopian thought requires consideration of the present and the past, as the world is imagined as a better place in contrast to the status quo. Utopia has long been written about as a spectre, a ghost, a spirit, or a haunting (Beaumont 2011), but the connection between utopia and the spectre is not just a metaphorical one, but also a temporal one. The emphasis on future justice in contrast to the present moment and past conditions makes the spectre's collapse of temporalities a useful mechanic through which to reach utopia. McManus (2007) argues that utopian thought is 'nonlinear' and that it maps 'time's layered excess as the overlap of the future into both present and past, and of past into present and future', and O'Brien (2007) similarly sees utopianism as hauntological in its emphasis on future justice in relation to the present. Further, Bartkowski (1989, 12) argues that the utopian thought, by necessity, 'decenters questions of time and history'. The spectre thus reflects a 'revolutionary temporality' (McManus 2007, 72), which links hope and history in the present moment.

Again, the utopian inflection of the spectre and of memory in feminist temporalities is compelling to view in light of queer futurity and utopianism, particularly José Esteban Muñoz's notion of queer utopian futurity, outlined in *Cruising Utopia: The Then and There of Queer Futurity* (2009). 'Queerness', Muñoz writes, 'exists for us an as ideality that can be distilled from the past and used to imagine a future [...] We must strive, in the face of the here and now's totalizing rendering of reality, to think and feel a *then and there*' and 'the *then* that disrupts the tyranny of the *now* is both past and future' (2009, 1, 29, emphasis original). What these feminist and queer interventions in past, present, and future temporalities represent is the re-orientation of time into a spatial and material phenomenon. What understandings of queer time and feminist hauntological time share is a recognition of the utopian potential of the affective structures of past, present, and future. Time, in these formulations, is material, affective, and holds the potential for revolution. The spectre of a feminist utopia haunts feminist work just as the spectre of the patriarchal past does. Feminist utopianism is not new, but has a long tradition in feminist activism, philosophy, and literature, which mirrors the eternally hopeful project of feminist activism. Ahmed writes that 'hope is also implicit in the very attachment to protest: it suggests that what angers us is not inevitable, even if transformation can sometimes feel impossible' (2003, 251). Considering feminist utopianism in conjunction with the recurring concern with memory in feminist work introduces a complex temporal loop. The constant turn to memory draws the past into the present, while using that memory for the future.

Utopia

Envisioning the future is always a difficult project, particularly in the unstable times we now live in. As the emails piling up in my inbox all say, these are unprecedented times, and new modes of thought that provide a means of thinking a better future that simultaneously uphold the status of past and present are consequently required. This is particularly important for feminist scholars, for whom the unfinished business of the past and the open horizon of the future exist in tension. Given the long recurrence of motifs of memory and ghosts in feminist writing and scholarship, reanimating these revenants of the past, and exercising them (rather than exorcising them) in the imagining of a better future uses their immateriality to serve a feminist purpose. It turns the long philosophical tradition of casting women and the feminine as absence, as the ghostly shadows in the background, into a means of imagining a more just future, as the haunted subject in the present must respond to the injustices that the ghost represents. Using a feminist ghost analytic derived from hauntological notions of collapsing temporalities enables the consolidation of a utopian future-oriented feminist practice that builds long traditions that centre the motifs of the spectre and of memory in women's and feminist writing. Weaving together the threads of memory, ghosts, history, and utopia creates the rich tapestry of an open, non-linear feminist temporality.

Originally published in *Continuum*, 34(6) (2020), 901–13. https://doi.org/10.1080/10304312.2020.184 2126. Reprinted by permission of Taylor & Francis Ltd, https://www.tandfonline.com.

Note

1. Although this paper has focused on examining the gendered and feminist dimensions of hauntology and memory, there is an equally urgent argument to be made for investigating the spectral and mnemonic legacies of colonialism and white supremacy, and anti-racist and postcolonial activism. Ian Baucom, for instance, touches on the hauntological memories of the slave trade in *Spectres of the Atlantic: Finance Capital, Slavery, and the Philosophy of History* (2001), and María del Pilar Blanco and Esther Peeren discuss unexamined people, including undocumented migrants, in *Popular Ghosts: The Haunted Spaces of Everyday Culture* (2010). How does the spectre of memory function in re-remembering the pasts and presents of colonization and race-based oppression, and, equally, of Civil Rights movements, for the future, and what are the implications of using a figure like the spectre or like memory in accessing and utilizing these temporalities?

References

Ahmed, S. 2003. 'Feminist Futures.' In *A Concise Companion to Feminist Theory*, edited by M. Eagleton, 236–254. Maiden, MA and Oxford: Blackwell Publishing.

Bartkowski, F. 1989. *Feminist Utopias*. Lincoln and London: University of Nebraska Press.

Baucom, I. 2001. 'Specters of the Atlantic.' *The South Atlantic Quarterly* 100 (1): 61–82. https://doi.org/10.1215/00382876-100-1-61.

Beaumont, M. 2011. *The Spectre of Utopia: Utopian and Science Fictions at the Fin de Siècle*. Oxford: Peter Lang.

Berlant, L. 2011. *Cruel Optimism*. Durham: Duke University Press.

Blanco, M. D. P., and E. Peeren. 2010. *Popular Ghosts: The Haunted Spaces of Everyday Culture*. New York and London: Continuum.

Bridenthal, R. and Koonz C. (eds.) 1977. *Becoming Visible: Women in European History*. Boston: Houghton Mifflin.

Brontë, C. (1847) 2016. *Jane Eyre*. Collins Classics edition. London: HarperCollins.

Brontë, E. (1847) 2003. *Wuthering Heights*. Penguin Classics edition. London: Penguin Books.

Connerton, P. 1989. *How Societies Remember*. Cambridge: Cambridge University Press.

Cowman, K., and L. A. Jackson. 2003. 'Time.' In *A Concise Companion to Feminist Theory*, edited by M. Eagleton, 32–52. Malden, MA and Oxford: Blackwell Publishing.

Derrida, J. 1994. *Specters of Marx: The State of the Debt, the Work of Mourning and the New International*. Translated by Peggy Kamuf. New York and London: Routledge.

Direnç, D. 2002. 'Between Generations across Cultures: Exploring Female Memory in Women's Fiction.' *International Fiction Review* 29 (1 and 2). https://journals.lib.unb.ca/index.php/IFR/article/view/7717

Du Maurier, D. (1938) 2015. *Rebecca*. Reprint. London: Virago Press.

Fisher, M. 2012. 'What Is Hauntology.' *Film Quarterly* 66 (1): 16–25. https://doi.org/10.1525/fq.2012.66.1.16.

Foucault, M. (1975) 1977. *Discipline and Punish: The Birth of the Prison*. Middlesex, England: Penguin Books.

Freeman, E. 2010. *Time Binds: Queer Temporalities, Queer Histories*. Durham: Duke University Press.

Gilbert, S. M., and S. Gubar. 1979. *The Madwoman in the Attic: The Woman Writer and the Nineteenth-Century Literary Imagination*. New Haven and London: Yale University Press.

Griffin, M., and T. Moylan. 2007. 'Introduction: Exploring Utopia.' In *Exploring the Utopian Impulse: Essays on Utopian Thought and Practice*, edited by M. J. Griffin and T. Moylan, 11–18. Oxford: Peter Lang.

Grosz, E. 2004. *The Nick of Time: Politics, Evolution, and the Untimely*. Durham: Duke University Press.

Gutman, Y., A. Sodaro, and A. D. Brown. 2010. 'Introduction: Memory and the Future: Why a Change of Focus is Necessary.' In *Memory and the Future: Transnational Politics, Ethics and Society*, edited by Y. Gutman, A. D. Brown, and A. Sodaro, 1–11. Basingstoke, UK: Palgrave Macmillan.

Harvey, D. 1989. *The Condition of Postmodernity: An Enquiry into the Origins of Cultural Change*. Cambridge, Massachusetts and Oxford: Blackwell Publishing.

Heise, U. K. 1997. *Chronoschisms: Time, Narrative, and Postmodernism*. Cambridge: Cambridge University Press.

Hesford, V. 2005. 'Feminism and Its Ghosts: The Spectre of the Feminist-as-lesbian.' *Feminist Theory* 6 (3): 227–250. https://doi.org/10.1177/1464700105057361

Hite, K., and D. Jara. 2020. 'Presenting Unwieldy Pasts.' *Memory Studies* 13 (3): 245–252.

Hughes, C. 2012. 'Dialogue between Fukuyama's Account of the End of History and Derrida's Hauntology.' *Journal of Philosophy: A Cross-Disciplinary Inquiry* 7 (8): 13–26. https://doi.org/10.5840/jphilnepal201271813

Huyssen, A. 2003. *Present Pasts: Urban Palimpsests and the Politics of Memory*. Stanford: Stanford University Press.

Jacoby, R. 2005. *Picture Imperfect: Utopian Thought for an Anti-Utopian Age*. New York: Columbia University Press.

Jameson, F. 1991. *Postmodernism, Or, the Cultural Logic of Late Capitalism*. Durham: Duke University Press.

Karlsson, K.-G. 2010. 'The Uses of History and the Third Wave of Europeanisation.' In *A European Memory?: Contested Histories and Politics of Remembrance*, edited by M. Pakier and B. Stråth, 38–55. New York and Oxford: Berghahn Books.

Lerner, G. 1993. *The Creation of Feminist Consciousness: From the Middle Ages to Eighteen-Seventy*. New York and Oxford: Oxford University Press.

Lyotard, J.-F. 1984. *The Postmodern Condition*: A *Report on Knowledge*. Translated by Geoff Bennington and Brian Massumi. Manchester: Manchester University Press.

Marsden, J. I. 2002. 'Beyond Recovery: Feminism and the Future of Eighteenth-Century Literary Studies.' *Feminist Studies* 28 (3): 657–662. https://doi.org/10.2307/3178795.

McManus, S. 2007. 'Truth, Temporality, and Theorizing Resistance.' In *Exploring the Utopian Impulse: Essays on Utopian Thought and Practice*, edited by M. J. Griffin and T. Moylan, 57–82. Oxford: Peter Lang.

Morrison, T. (1987) 2010. *Beloved*. Reading guide edition. London: Vintage Books.

Muñoz, J. E. 2009. *Cruising Utopia: The Then and There of Queer Futurity*. New York: New York University Press.

Newman, K., J. Clayton, and M. Hirsch. 2002. 'Re-Reading the Present.' In *Time and the Literary*, edited by K. Newman, J. Clayton, and M. Hirsch, 1–10. New York and London: Routledge.

Nora, P. 1992. *Realms of Memory, Vol. 1 Conflicts and Divisions*. Translated by Arthur Goldhammer, and edited by Lawrence D. Kritzman. New York: Columbia University Press.

O'Brien, E. 2007. '"Towards Justice to Come": Derrida and Utopian Justice.' In *Exploring the Utopian Impulse: Essays on Utopian Thought and Practice*, edited by M. J. Griffin and T. Moylan, 43–56. Oxford: Peter Lang.

Rowbotham, S. 1973. *Hidden From History: 300 Years of Women's Oppression and the Fight Against It*. London: Pluto Press.

Rowbotham, S. 1989. *The Past Is Before Us: Feminism in Action since the 1960s*. London, Boston, Sydney, Wellington: Pandora.

Sellberg, K. 2019. 'The "Turns" of Feminist Time: Evolutionary Logic, Life and Renewal in "New Materialist" Feminist Philosophy.' *Australian Feminist Studies* 34 (99): 93–106. https://doi.org/10.1080/08164649.2019.1605488.

Shaw, K. 2018. *Hauntology: The Presence of the past in Twenty-First Century English Literature*. Cham, Switzerland: Palgrave Macmillan, https://doi.org/10.1007/978-3-319-74968-6

Wilde, O. 1891. 'The Soul of Man under Socialism.' *Fortnightly Review* 291: 212–319.

Woolf, V. (1925) 2004. *Mrs Dalloway*. Reprint. London: Vintage.

Woolf, V. (1928a) 1998. *Orlando: A Biography*. Reprint. Oxford: Oxford University Press.

Woolf, V. (1928b) 2009. *A Room of One's Own*. Reprint. London: Penguin Books.

17 Sharing Time Across Unshared Horizons

GAIL WEISS

The focus of this essay arises out of a political issue with which I have been concerned for some time, namely, the very real social barriers that divide individuals and groups of people with very different histories and experiences from one another when there are no corresponding temporal or spatial barriers preventing their communication. Both phenomenology and hermeneutics, I would argue, provide us with extremely useful ways of grappling with this problem. In phenomenological terms, we might understand it as a question of how it is possible to "share time" across unshared horizons, that is, how it is possible for people to, in Alfred Schutz's language, "grow old together" with all the intimacy that this implies, even when they lack a shared "stock of knowledge" that constitutes the typical parameters of daily life. From a hermeneutical perspective, this lack of shared understanding is clearly tied to significant interpretive differences that can stem from conflicting or even incompatible horizons of significance. The challenge of communicating with others with whom we share space and time across varying cultural horizons clearly has direct implications, both positive and negative, both for how one is identified by others as well as how one comes to identify oneself. In particular, I would like to explore how "sharing time across unshared horizons" can promote new understandings of personal as well as group identity that are grounded in a recognition of and respect for difference.

Using the Bergsonian distinction between time and temporality, or between "outer time" and "inner time," the problem I am interested in examining is how people can share what Schutz calls "civic" or "standard time," that is, quantitative time, and attribute completely different (sometimes even incompatible) meanings to their experiences. Of course, from a Bergsonian perspective, no two people will "live" time in the same way; there will always be differences between the durée of one person and that of another even when they are engaged in the same activity. Each individual's distinctive corporeal relationship with the world of her concern is sufficient to guarantee the idiosyncratic nature of her respective temporal experience, and thus, the unique significance of specific events in her life.[1] Nonetheless, Schutz claims that "because it is common to each of us, standard time makes an intersubjective coordination of the different individual plan systems possible."[2] He appeals to the universality of what he calls the "world of working," or the concrete, ongoing engagement of our bodies in specific motor tasks, as a ground for a common intersubjective experience. In a passage that echoes Husserl's famous description of the natural attitude in *Ideas I*, Schutz asserts:

> The wide-awake man within the natural attitude is primarily interested in that sector of the world of his everyday life which is within his scope and which is centered in space and time around himself. The place which my body occupies in the world, my actual Here, is the starting point from which I take my bearing in space. It is, so to speak, the center 0 of my system of coordinates. Relatively to my body I

group the elements of my surroundings under the categories of right and left, before and behind, above and below, near and far, and so on. And in a similar way my actual Now is the origin of all the time perspectives under which I organize the events within the world such as the categories of fore and aft, past and future, simultaneity and succession, etc.[3]

Although Schutz doesn't say this explicitly, his implication is that because human bodies share basic physiological similarities despite their manifest differences of age, sex, skin, hair, eye color, height, weight, and so on, there will be corresponding structural similarities in our temporal experiences. However, recent work by disability theorists has challenged even this rudimentary assumption. For someone who is incapable of assuming the vertical posture typical for children and adult human beings, for instance a quadriplegic, the body *might* still serve as the "center *0* of her system of coordinates" and her "actual Now" may still serve as "the origin of all the time perspectives under which" she "organizes the events within the world," but this world itself will not have the same spatiality, nor I would argue, the same temporality as it would for someone who is able-bodied. Moreover, the inhospitability of our built environment for quadriplegics, paraplegics, and other people with serious motor disabilities virtually guarantees that they cannot be full participants in the "world of working" that, according to Schutz, forms the basis of the natural attitude. This does not mean that the disabled, too, don't have their own "world of working," just that the presuppositions that govern the world of working for the able-bodied individual (presuppositions regarding their basic manner and mode of engaging the world) are often inoperative or just simply inapplicable in the former's world. Not being able to draw upon the same basic motor capacities as "normates" (a term used by leading disability theorist Rosemarie Garland Thomson) and being socially stigmatized for this "failure" certainly lead to different ways of experiencing the world for disabled and non-disabled individuals. Because our bodies comprise an ongoing horizon of significance in all aspects of our lives, it is inevitable that disabled individuals and able-bodied individuals face significant challenges in bridging the physical barriers that spatially, temporally, socially, and politically divide them.

While it is perhaps easier to see how someone who is physically impaired, who continually experiences what Thomson calls a "mis-fit" between her body and her environment, may bring different horizons to bear upon her experience than an able-bodied person, disabled people are certainly not the only ones who may experience themselves as "misfits" in relation to the "world of working" that, as previously mentioned, comprises the basis for a shared, intersubjective existence for Schutz. People who are socially and politically disenfranchised, physically and/or psychically oppressed, because they are deemed to be the "wrong" race, the "wrong" ethnicity, or the "wrong" gender, or to possess the "wrong" sexuality also, I would argue, may find that the horizons of significance that structure the meaning of daily life for their oppressors are not salient for them. This experience of "unshared horizons," in turn, is often concretely manifested through what Ruth Frankenberg calls "racial social geographies," the powerful, yet often invisible, barriers that physically, socially, and psychically segregate groups of people who are perceived (and/or perceive themselves) to be essentially different from one another, even when they inhabit a single, shared space and time such as daily lunch period in a high school cafeteria.[4]

Linda Alcoff's discussion of both the positive and the negative ways in which identities are visibly marked, in *Visible Identities: Race, Gender, and the Self*, has a direct bearing on the question of incommensurable durées, for she is concerned with how identities that have been sedimented through oppressive experiences can nonetheless serve as positive "interpretive horizons" for those who live them. More specifically, Alcoff defends many people's strong sense of pride in their distinct racialized, ethnic, and gendered identities, even when these latter have resulted from long histories of oppression. Her rich and provocative descriptions of how race and gender actually function as social identities in the United States today accords well with Husserl's emphasis on providing as comprehensive a description as possible of the phenomenon one is investigating, and she well recognizes that to achieve this latter goal philosophy needs to move beyond rigid methodological and disciplinary boundaries. Philosophy, in other words, to echo Judith Butler's concerns articulated in the final chapter of her book, *Undoing Gender*, needs to confront its own othering practices, and needs to let that which has been designated other speak, in its own words, on its own terms, and I might add, in a manner that expresses the other's own sense of time.[5]

In its Cartesian zeal for "clear and distinct knowledge," the legacy of the modern philosophical tradition (and the Socratic and Aristotelian traditions as well) has been an intolerance for ambiguity, and, as Alcoff persuasively shows throughout her work, this poses huge problems for understanding the evolving meanings of racialized and gendered identities since these latter are paradigmatic sites of ambiguity, confusion, and discomfort. Turning now to Alcoff's work, I hope to open up a more general discussion of how we can best continue the dialogue to which she has so richly contributed, a dialogue concerned with identifying the concrete strategies that can best serve to alleviate the deleterious effects of oppressive identities as they unfold over time without devaluing the personal, political, theoretical, and practical significance of identity and the durées that constitute them.

At the very outset of *Visible Identities*, Alcoff makes it clear that she is offering "a sustained defense of identity as an epistemically salient and ontologically real entity."[6] "The reality of identities," she tells us, "often comes from the fact that they are visibly marked on the body itself, guiding if not determining the way we perceive and judge others and are perceived and judged by them."[7] Although she explicitly links the "realness" of identities to their "visibility," Alcoff also repeatedly acknowledges that visibility is woefully inadequate as a criterion for assessing a given individual's identity. Indeed, in her discussion of mixed-race individuals, including her own experience, Alcoff stresses that it is frequently the case that one's skin color, hair texture, and other physiognomic features may reflect only one identity rather than two or more, leading others to falsely identify the individual exclusively with one race alone. As Alcoff affirms, the rule of hypodescent described by Gloria Marshall and many other critical race theorists is alive and well, revealing the strong historico-political motivation for identifying a mixed-race individual, even with racially ambiguous features, with the racial group that is most oppressed.[8]

Hybrid identities, especially identities that are usually thought to be oppositional to one another, can produce confusion and anxiety not only for those who embody them but also for those who recognize their coexistence in another person's life. Not only do they reveal the limits of the clear-cut categorical distinctions that philosophers hold dear, but they also pose challenges to our most basic ontological, epistemological, and temporal presuppositions.[9] In *The Republic*, Plato attempts to justify the purity of identity categories through the "Myth of the Metals," famously proclaiming that each person is formed out of one metal alone, gold, silver, or bronze.[10] The metal we are made of, he argues, determines our aptitudes in life and, in his view, should therefore dictate the individual's goals and aspirations. Although the concept of racial identity did not exist as such in Plato's time, the legacy of this seemingly harmless myth that defines an individual in terms of his possession of a specific "natural" aptitude and holds him accountable for how well or poorly he develops it is readily found in racist ideologies that either implicitly or explicitly argue that a given individual's race can or should determine the type of person they are, the occupations for which they are most suited, the accomplishments of which they are capable, and the social class with which they should be associated.

Despite the dangers of viewing an individual's identity as if it were a simple, singular, or "pure" entity, Alcoff nonetheless affirms that identities help to make sense of and unify our lived experience. "Identities," she tells us, "must resonate with and unify lived experience, and they must provide a meaning that has some purchase, however partial, on the subject's own daily reality."[11] On the surface, it might seem that the best way to accomplish this would be if our identities themselves were unified. Indeed, our proper names serve symbolically as unifiers of our identity, and, as Louis Althusser and Judith Butler respectively maintain, they facilitate our interpellation as singular individuals.[12] Both Althusser and Butler emphasize, however, that while it is through interpellation that we become subjects in our own right, at the same time, it is also through being interpellated by others that we are subjected to those others. While neither Althusser nor Butler specifically focuses on the temporality of the interpellative process, it is evident that a great deal of the power of the act of interpellation arises out of its repetition over time; the sedimentation of both individual and group identities that results is thus an intersubjective temporal phenomenon. Moreover, the process of subjectivation that occurs through the act of interpellation is depicted by Butler in particular as both enabling and disabling: enabling insofar as it grants us social recognition, disabling because we ultimately lack control over the forms that recognition will take since it issues from others and not from ourselves.[13]

To the extent that our identities are constituted out of multiple facets of our own experience, including multiple encounters with (the experiences of) others, it is inevitable that our identities themselves will express that very multiplicity, even when they appear to be unified and coherent. Indeed, the different temporal and spatial contexts within which these identities are performed contribute to this sense of multiplicity even as these identities themselves become consolidated in and through their repetition in varying situations. Appealing to Teresa de Lauretis's work, Alcoff reinforces these points when she claims that "the fluid historical context in which we negotiate our identities is a context in which we are both subjects of and subjected to social construction."[14] If we view our identities as involving a constant negotiation between our own view of ourselves and the perspectives others have of us, or between what Alcoff refers to as our subjective lived experience on the one hand and our social identities on the other, it is evident that even the most rigidly defined identity is never fixed in stone but can always be transformed.[15]

There are countless historical examples of such transformations in both individual and group identities. For instance, as Michel Foucault emphasizes in *Discipline and Punish*, a single illicit action may forever after brand an individual with the identity of criminal, an all-encompassing identity that has the power to fundamentally alter how that individual views himself and how he is viewed by others. And, as Lewis Gordon, Frantz Fanon, and many other critical race theorists have argued, the very appearance of a black man in an antiblack world is capable of generating a phobic response that becomes part and parcel of his identity in a racist state, placing "ontological limits" on his own subjectivation.[16] Accordingly, Alcoff argues, "identities are constituted by social contextual conditions of interaction in specific cultures at particular historical periods, and thus their nature, effects, and the problems that need to be addressed in regard to them will be largely local."[17]

Since it is clear that there may be contexts in which I ascribe a particular identity to myself that others do not ascribe to me (or vice versa), we must reckon in any discussion of identity with a traditional philosophical concern, namely, with how to resolve the self/other binary according to which there is a fundamental separation between my view of myself and the view the other has of me.[18] Within this dualistic framework, identity is seen as encompassing both a "subjective" perspective that reflects and expresses my own view of myself and, at the same time, the perspective of the other (or others), which is distinct from my own. Working within such a binary model, the central issue then becomes, how are these dual (and often competing) perspectives reconcilable into a coherent identity that is lived by and associated with a concrete individual?

As Alcoff discusses, Merleau-Ponty raises this type of concern in relation to Sartre's ontological distinction between the experience of being-for-itself (*être pour-soi*) and the experience of being-for-others (*être pour-les-autres*). Merleau-Ponty attempts to move beyond this oppositional framework by positing a chiasmatic relationship between the perspective we have of ourselves and the perspective the other has of us. To call the relationship between my own perspective and the perspective of the other chiasmatic means that it is a reversible relationship that allows us to experience the perspective of the other toward ourselves (even without having full access to it) even as the other can do the same for us, all the while preserving the differences between the two perspectives. In the essay *Eye and Mind*, he suggests that we chiasmatically encounter inanimate as well as animate others. On his account, we are reckoning with the perspective of others all the time, even if we can never *know* them with Cartesian clarity and distinctness. Insofar as we can enter into chiasmatic relationships with nonconscious entities, it should be evident that a chiasmatic relationship does not, for Merleau-Ponty, presuppose that one or both of us must be aware of that relationship in order for it to exist. In his most famous example of a mundane chiasmatic encounter, namely, one hand touching the other, one doesn't have to be *aware* that one hand is touching the other in order to have the experience. Awareness does, undeniably, affect and transform the experience (of touching and being touched) and therefore alters its meaning, but it does not create the experience in the first place *nor* is it required to make the special temporal reflexivity that is operative within the experience significant in our lives.

Merleau-Ponty opposes the self/other binary because he maintains that even *before* the recognition of the unique perspective of the other occurs, we are always already acting within an intersubjective context and so are already affected by the perspective of the other, whether or not we are aware that this is occurring. This is why he proclaims that

> what is given … is the taking up of each subjectivity by itself, and of subjectivities by each other *in the generality of a single nature, the cohesion of an intersubjective life and a world*. … True reflection presents me to myself not as idle and inaccessible subjectivity, but as identical with my presence in the world and to others, as I am now realizing it: I am all that I see, I am an intersubjective field, not despite my body and historical situation, but, on the contrary, by being this body and this situation, and through them, all the rest.[19]

Irigaray, though accusing Merleau-Ponty of ultimately privileging subjectivity (and male subjectivity at that) over intersubjectivity, agrees with his claim that subjectivity is grounded within a fundamentally intersubjective experience. The experience of the look, as Sartre describes it in *Being and Nothingness*, or of the master's need and demand for recognition by the slave, as depicted by Hegel, both of which Alcoff discusses at some length, highlights the moments we are forced to *acknowledge* the radical alterity of the other; but they fail, Irigaray argues, to acknowledge properly the significance of more primordial contacts with the other, most particularly, the encounters that begin even before we are born, as our bodies grow over time within the bodies of our mothers.[20]

Through a compelling historical analysis of the rationalist philosophical tradition, Alcoff reinforces Irigaray's critique, demonstrating that the inherently intersubjective features of identity have most often been seen as a threat to our status as autonomous moral agents. Within this tradition, with relatively few exceptions, the roles played by others, society, history, politics, and even, I would argue, temporality itself in the formation of our identities have often been downplayed. To the extent that these influences are acknowledged, they have frequently been seen as collectively determining the "accidental" features of our identities, not the essential ones. And, Alcoff contends, within these accounts the most essential aspect of identity turns out to be general and universal (and, I might add, it is also depicted as atemporal), namely the capacity for rationality itself.

A major problem with such an ahistorical approach to identity is that there are countless individuals (all of whom possess their own distinctive identities) whose disabilities, sex, and/or race have precluded them from being seen as having the capacity for rationality in the first place.[21] Not surprisingly, with regard to the self/other binary that frames these discussions, the emphasis is overwhelmingly placed on the autonomous self's ability to express its own identity through its willed choices. And, as feminists, critical race theorists, and disability theorists have all emphasized, those individuals who are viewed as unable to do this often have their very humanity placed in question.

On this Cartesian view, then, the perspective of the other is not granted the same legitimacy as one's own perspective, and, as Heidegger illustrates in his condemnation of the perspective of the "they" in *Being and Time*, the choice to give weight to the view of the other regarding oneself can even be regarded as potentially inauthentic.[22] Existentialists, then, as well as rationalists have placed the primary weight upon the self in determining its own identity even while recognizing that to be human means, to use Sartre's language, to be not only a being-for-itself but also a being-for-others.[23]

In his essay "Identity: Cultural, Transcultural, and Multicultural," Peter Caws reinforces this position, maintaining that "there is a sense—the existentialists were good at dramatizing it, but I think they were also right—in which I am alone in the world and have to forge my identity in isolation."[24] From this perspective, identity is an individual project, and Caws distinguishes it from an identification, which can be imposed on one by others. This occurs, for instance, when one is identified as a citizen of a particular country (e.g., a Spaniard or a Turk). Caws observes that children are born into a "first" or "native" culture that is "imposed from without." It is a culture, he claims, that they belong to but that they have not "made their own."[25] For Caws and other existentialist thinkers, identity is something we fashion ourselves, working from the "raw" (and not-so-raw) materials provided by the world around us, including all the people, places, and things we come in contact with on a daily basis. In Caws's words, "Identity, psychologically as well as logically, is a *reflexive* relation, a relation of myself to myself, but it can be a mediated relation: I relate to myself through my interaction with others *and with the world*."[26] Ultimately, for him as well as for Sartre, identity is something we individually *choose*; however, it also must be distinguished from the mundane choices we make from moment to moment throughout our lives. For Sartre, the choice of an identity should be understood as an *existential* choice that unifies my less momentous choices such as which outfit to wear in the morning, what to eat for lunch, and with whom to spend time.[27]

In contrast to the strong individualist emphasis in the existentialist tradition, Marxists maintain that others play the crucial role in determining an individual's identity (including how it is temporally constructed and experienced), and they understand this identity to be primarily a function of one's social class. Even when one emerges from the "false consciousness" of believing one's class status to be natural and inevitable, one does so not by affirming one's individuality but by recognizing that one is a member of a socially constructed, subjugated (or dominating) economic group. In short, one attains *class consciousness*.

While the recognition that others play a central role in the formation of one's identity is a compelling feature of a Marxist position, on the other hand, this view also runs the danger of making it seem as if the individual has virtually no agency in determining her identity. Moreover, it is not only Marxists who are subject to this critique. In her book *Volatile Bodies*, Elizabeth Grosz calls positions that emphasize the role of society in determining the identity of the individual "outside in" perspectives, and she argues that Friedrich Nietzsche, Michel Foucault, Gilles Deleuze, and Félix Guattari all ascribe to this model, in which the individual's identity is primarily constructed not by herself but by the society in which she lives.[28] Pierre Bourdieu's discussions of the power of the habitus to shape an individual's desires, hopes, fears, and beliefs in accordance with the standards of taste operative for their social class are a perfect example of this view. It should not be surprising that, just as the Cartesian emphasis on the autonomous self has been critiqued for its "subjectivism," so too have serious objections been made concerning Bourdieu's reduction of an individual's aesthetic predilections to the taste that has been indexed for that individual's social class.

Rather than embracing one side of the self/other binary or the other, Alcoff attributes equally primary roles both to the self and to the other in the constitution of identity. Like Merleau-Ponty, she views subjectivity and intersubjectivity as inseparable from one another; both philosophers maintain that we always emerge as subjects in and through our interactions with others. Insofar as these interactions are multiple, it follows that our identities themselves are multiple. This helps us to understand why even if an individual has a dominant identity, the meaning of that identity is never fixed in her life but changes over time and in different situations in accordance with her own experiences as well as with the way society as a whole and other individuals respond to (or fail to respond to) her. While society may promulgate specific standards for particular identities, it is clear that even the person most devoted to these standards will inevitably end up embodying them in her own way. This is why Alcoff declares that "social identities are relational, contextual, *and* fundamental to the self."[29]

Up to now, I have focused more generally on the complexity of the issues that must be addressed when one seeks to make claims about the meaning of particular identities. As we have seen, there are a variety of conflicting perspectives regarding how much weight to give to the self and how much weight to attribute to the other (including society at large) in the construction of an individual's identity. Since I cannot do justice to all of the possible issues that can be raised with regard to the changing meanings of an individual's multiple identities over time, I would like to turn instead to a particular set of concerns, namely, how multiple identities seem to be very inclusive insofar as they can provide access to different horizons simultaneously, and yet, how the often competing demands placed upon one by dual identities are frequently so all-encompassing that it is virtually impossible to live these identities in a unified, coherent manner throughout one's life. Rather than abandoning the notion of multiple identities or even a hybrid identity as an impossible project, I would argue, both with and against Alcoff, that we need to recognize the limits of privileging a unified identity as a goal we should be striving for to live meaningful lives. Moreover, I would also argue that we need to stop privileging *visible* identities over invisible identities, since the latter can be just as salient for a given individual and her community even if there are no visual markers present to indicate that that identity is present and operative in her life.

In an all-too-brief section of *Visible Identities*, Alcoff argues for what she calls a "pluritopic hermeneutics," though, unfortunately, she doesn't develop what this involves in much depth. She explains this notion by observing that "one's very own horizon, constitutive of one's identity, is itself pluritopic and multicultural, constituted by sometimes contradictory background meanings or value assumptions."[30] She goes on to claim that "we cannot assume that any hermeneutic horizon or background of understanding is in fact coherent or closed to other horizons."[31] This leads her to conclude: "Thus, it is not simply that the other makes up the self, but that multiple others are constitutive aspects of our interpretive horizon, offering alternative and in some cases competing background assumptions and perceptual practices, fracturing the meanings of visible appearance and complicating embodied knowledge."[32]

If we accept, as I think we should, Alcoff's view of identity as an interpretive horizon, and acknowledge that this latter is intersubjectively constituted out of "competing background assumptions and perceptual practices" that fracture "the meanings of visible appearance" and complicate "embodied knowledge," then why privilege visible appearance at all? Although I agree with much of what Alcoff says about identity, the places I find myself least persuaded with her account are precisely those places where she is at pains to distinguish racialized and gendered identities from other types of identity, such as religious or ethnic identity, on the basis of the visibility of the former as compared to the latter. Even though Alcoff acknowledges that other types of identity can certainly be visible, she nonetheless doesn't acknowledge sufficiently that many individuals' ethnic or religious identities may be even more visible (to themselves as well as to others) than their racial identity, if not their gender identity, and that, as Robert Murphy and other disability scholars have argued, the visibility of a wheelchair can render *invisible* its user's race or gender altogether.[33] Alcoff does *not* argue that race and gender are more important or more meaningful aspects of our identity because they are allegedly the most visible aspects of one's identity, but her emphasis on the salience of visibility for identity opens up her account to this type of misreading. Moreover, as she herself acknowledges in the case of mixed-race individuals, racial identity is not always visible, and as transsexuals' experiences frequently attest, neither is gender identity. So, the questions I am posing for Alcoff are: (1) Why do we need to distinguish between visible and non-visible identities, especially if this isn't a salient distinction in an individual's own life? (2) Are race and gender really more visible than other kinds of identities? I realize that one of the reasons why Alcoff emphasizes visibility so much is because it so readily reveals the materiality of identity to the "eye of the beholder," and yet the materiality and even temporality of our non-visible identities can be revealed through other sensory avenues as well.

By calling identities interpretive horizons, Alcoff is suggesting that our identities serve as indispensable frameworks that structure the meaning we give to our everyday experiences. At the same time, our identities, as we have seen, are not fixed but fluid, continually being reshaped over time and across space by the events and relationships through which they are constructed in the first place. In his chapter "On Multiple Realities" in *The Problem of Social Reality*, Schutz argues, following William James, not only that different people can construct different "realities" but also that each of us inhabits more than one reality. These latter include not only the "world of working" that undergirds the natural attitude but also the "world of phantasms," the world of memories, the world of anticipations, and so on. Rather than seeing the distinctiveness of these multiple realities as separating one person from another, Schutz also reminds us that "the world of daily life into which we are born is from the outset an intersubjective world. This implies on the one hand that this world is not my private one but common to all of us; on the other hand that within this world there are fellow-men with whom I am connected by manifold social relationships."[34]

When the other communicates with me, when I listen to the other and try to figure out what he is saying, Schutz maintains, I am engaged in interpretive activity. Through this inter subjective engagement, he argues, "a new dimension of time" is established.[35] In his words: "He and I, *we* share, while the process lasts, a common vivid present, *our* vivid present, which enables him and me to say: '*We* experienced this occurrence together.' By the We-relation, thus established, we both—he, addressing himself to me, and I, listening to him—are living in our mutual vivid present, directed toward the thought to be realized in and by the communicating process. *We grow older together*."[36] Unlike Alcoff, however, Schutz does not focus intently on the personal, social, and political obstacles that often keep individuals from entering into "we-relationships" with one another, that is, on the self-imposed and socially imposed "limits" of interpretation.

If we view identities as interpretive horizons, as Alcoff suggests, this can, I would argue, help us to understand how and why temporal experiences can be so radically different even when the individuals in question are "spending time together." If an individual refuses the possibility of establishing a "we-relationship" with another person because the horizons that constitute the basis for the latter's own interpretive activity are seen to be too different from her own, this means, on Schutz's account, not only that she is foreclosing the possibility of expanding her own interpretive horizons but also that she is depriving herself of the potential to establish new ways of experiencing time. Schutz's emphasis on the temporal implications of forming or even refusing to form "we-relationships" thus has the potential to deepen Alcoff's account of how identities are formed by attuning us to one of the most important yet less visible aspects of identity construction, namely, that identities are themselves products of time and can in turn transform how time is embodied and expressed.

While Bergson, Schutz, Merleau-Ponty, Alcoff, and I would all agree that the uniqueness of our respective durées is a source of experiential richness that contributes inexhaustible depth and meaning to our collective being-in-the-world, nonetheless, it is also crucial to acknowledge, as Alcoff does, the very real individual and cultural prejudices, as well as the political and physical barriers, that form part of the fabric of the "natural attitude" and that must be denaturalized in order to be overcome. Anticipating Levinas, Schutz stresses the importance of the face-to-face relationship in this process. The face-to-face relation, he tells us, is "a basic structure of the world of daily life."[37] The importance of this direct encounter with the other cannot be underestimated, because, Schutz argues, "all the other manifold social relationships are derived from the originary experiencing of the totality of the other's self in the community of time and space."[38] As Schutz himself would acknowledge, however, "the community of time and space" is not homogeneous, nor can it be taken for granted insofar as it is possible for "multiple realities" to be experienced in and through this primary intersubjective encounter. Or, as Bergson might argue, several different durées can and do unfold within what Schutz is calling a community of time and space. While Levinas would disagree that we ever do experience the "totality of the other's self" in the face-to-face relation, both he and Schutz emphasize the transformative potential this relationship has precisely because it is an encounter with the alterity of the other, an encounter that enables us to transcend the limits of our own "stock of knowledge."

To take seriously Alcoff's view of identity as an interpretive horizon enables us to explore the possibilities available to us to transform our own identities, our own horizons, and thereby the very meaning of our experiences, through our interactions with others. Taken together with Schutz's analysis of the temporal possibilities opened up by the we-relationship, we can see the cost not only to the marginalized other but also to the dominant individual who refuses to engage in this process. For, as the numerous anti-immigrant protests that ushered in the new millennium in France, the United States, and elsewhere in the world poignantly reveal, the refusal to enter into we-relationships with those who are deemed to be too different from oneself inevitably not only harms these others (both visibly and invisibly) by attacking, diminishing, and literally delegitimizing key features of their identity, but also impoverishes one's own lived possibilities insofar as one closes oneself off from alternative ways of living space and time.

Does this mean that oppressed individuals should feel compelled to enter into we-relationships with their oppressors?[39] Aren't some ways of living space and time more desirable and enriching to experience than others? These are important questions raised by my analysis, and though they deserve more attention than I can give to them here, let me conclude by observing that since a we-relationship requires a willingness of both parties to "share a common present," this relationship is impossible to enact when the horizons of significance that each party brings to bear on the situation are viewed (by either or both parties) to be incommensurable. Thus, while no two individuals can or should share the same horizons (indeed if they did, they would have nothing of interest to *share* with one another), there must nonetheless be a ground of *mutual* respect for the differences between our identities and experiences in order for we-relationships to be established and maintained. We-relationships, then, presuppose not sameness of experiences, but a genuine openness to and appreciation for difference. This means that respect for the alterity of the other must always be present in order for time to be shared across unshared horizons. The mutuality of this respect is impossible when one party dominates another. Nor is it something that can be achieved once and for all, since it is an ongoing, intersubjective project that both unfolds within and also makes possible a shared experience of time.

From *Time in Feminist Phenomenology* edited by Christina Schües, Dorothea E. Olkowski, and Helen A. Fielding, pp. 171–88. © 2011 Indiana University Press. Reprinted with the permission of Indiana University Press.

Notes

1. Bergson, *An Introduction to Metaphysics*.
2. Schutz, *The Problem of Social Reality*, 222.
3. Ibid., 222–23.
4. Frankenberg, *White Women, Race Matters*.
5. Butler, *Undoing Gender*.
6. Alcoff, *Visible Identities*, 5.
7. Ibid.
8. Marshall, "Racial Classifications."
9. One temporal presupposition disrupted by mixed-race individuals includes the common belief that an individual can have only one identity at a time rather than two identities (or some sort of amalgamation of two identities) at the same time.
10. It is important to note, however, that the myth didn't even apply to all people, just to recognized citizens or potential citizens of the Republic. This eliminated slaves from consideration altogether, and, given Plato's own ambivalent views about women's capacity for rationality, it renders the applicability of the account to freeborn women very problematic as well.
11. Alcoff, *Visible Identities*, 42.
12. See Althusser, "Ideology and Ideological State Apparatuses" and Butler's chapter "Arguing with the Real" in *Bodies That Matter*, as well as her subsequent book, *Excitable Speech: A Politics of the Performative,* for in-depth accounts of the power of interpellation.
13. Althusser emphasizes the role of the state even more than the role of other individuals in this process. Subjectivation, he argues, is ideological through and through. In his words, *"the category of the subject is only constitutive of all ideology insofar as all ideology has the function (which defines it) of 'constituting' concrete individuals as subjects"* (Althusser, "Ideology and Ideological State Apparatus," 116). For Althusser (following Marx), the state ideology that "constitutes concrete individuals as subjects" is always the dominant ideology of the ruling class. In *Bodies That Matter,* Butler further develops Althusser's insight that the disabling aspects of subjectivation produce enabling effects by granting the subject recognition as a subject, albeit a subordinated subject. In her words, "This 'subjection,' or *assujettissement,* is not only a subordination but a securing and maintaining, a putting into place of a subject, a subjectivation" (Butler, *Bodies That Matter,* 34). Butler traces this enabling/disabling view of subjectivation back to Hegel's famous discussion in the lordship and bondsman chapter in *Phenomenology of Mind* of the subordination of the master to the slave insofar as the master requires the slave's recognition of his status as master (and therefore a confirmation by the slave of the slave's own subordinated status) in order to secure his own subjectivation as master.
14. Alcoff, *Visible Identities*, 146.
15. This goes against William James's strong claim in the "Habits" chapter of *The Principles of Psychology* that a person's character is "fixed like plaster by the time we are thirty" and is more in keeping with the existentialist emphasis upon the ongoing re-creation of the self espoused by both Jean-Paul Sartre and Simone de Beauvoir.
16. I am using Lewis Gordon's expression "antiblack world" to capture the all-pervasive presence of antiblack racism in social life, that is, the ways in which antiblack racism operates as an "ontological limitation of human reality" for blacks (as well as for non-blacks) (Gordon, *Bad Faith and Antiblack Racism,* 1).
17. Alcoff, *Visible Identities,* 266, 9.
18. Alcoff provides an excellent historical survey of both political and philosophical approaches to identity in chapters 2 and 3 of *Visible Identities*.

19. Merleau-Ponty, *Phenomenology of Perception,* 452.

20. Irigaray, *Speculum of the Other Woman.*

21. Eva Kittay offers one of the most moving accounts of just such a person in chapter 6 of *Love's Labor,* namely her oldest child, Sesha, who has had no trouble expressing her identity with caretakers, family, and friends, despite severe mental and physical disabilities that render her incapable of using language or of getting about in the world independently.

22. The same point holds for Sartre as well, and it is illustrated in depth both in the "Bad Faith" section of *Being and Nothingness* and in his play *No Exit.*

23. Kierkegaard's, Heidegger's, and Sartre's respective understandings of the authentic individual as someone who is at least conceptually able to separate herself from others have been integral to both the phenomenological and the existential traditions. It is a major reason for the ongoing critique of these traditions as being too "subjectivist." Alcoff provides an excellent explanation of this critique and a response to it in chapter 4 of *Visible Identities.* Sara Heinämaa also tackles this critique head-on in chapter 1 of *Toward a Phenomenology of Sexual Difference,* with reference to both Kierkegaard and Beauvoir, arguing that it is possible to affirm the "Kierkegaardian notion of the separation of the self" without this affirmation leading to "solipsism or subjectivism" (Heinämaa, *Toward a Phenomenology of Sexual Difference,* 10).

24. Caws, "Identity: Cultural, Transcultural, and Multicultural," 379.

25. Ibid., 371.

26. Ibid., 379. It is striking that Caws claims that identity, as reflexive, "can" be mediated rather than that it is mediated. This suggests that it might be possible for the self to relate to itself without mediation by others and/or by the world of her concern. In fact, Caws supports this interpretation when he maintains that one can and should transcend one's culture of origin, though he is quick to clarify that this "does not mean turning one's back on it" (385). To make one's identity one's own, as we have just seen, involves stepping away from identifications that have been imposed on one by one's society. In his words, "the mature person is likely to leave his or her culture of origin behind as limiting to the development of personal identity" (372). While he acknowledges the positive role that an ethnic identification can play in an individual's life, he views it as exceedingly problematic for the individual to merely accept this identification as her identity. Instead, appealing to Sartre, Caws maintains that she needs to actively commit to this particular identity as a self-conscious choice in order to avoid the charge of bad faith. In what follows, I will argue that though this may seem like a very appealing view of identity, especially to individuals who were oppressed growing up within their native cultures, it presupposes that we can, indeed, transcend the influence of our culture of origin through our rational choices. Moreover, it is exceedingly problematic to imply, as Caws does, that the "mature" person leaves her native culture behind. This makes it seem as if one's native culture resembles the immature Freudian id that must be repudiated. However, even Freud recognized that the desires of the id can never be transcended or vanquished altogether. Instead we must reckon with them on an ongoing basis, just as, I would argue, we continue to reckon with the influence of our native culture, which we have a tendency to regard as immature when we are most in tension with it!

27. See the "Existential Psychoanalysis" chapter of *Being and Nothingness* for a good description of what it means to make an existential choice.

28. See part 3 of *Volatile Bodies* for an in-depth description of these types of theories. Grosz herself seems more sympathetic to "outside in" perspectives, despite her recognition of their shortcomings, than to the "inside out" perspectives she associates with the phenomenological and psychoanalytic traditions.

29. Alcoff, *Visible Identities,* 90.

30. Ibid., 125.

31. Ibid.

32. Ibid.

33. Murphy, *The Body Silent*.

34. Schutz, *The Problem of Social Reality,* 218.

35. Ibid., 219.

36. Ibid., 219–20.

37. Ibid., 221.

38. Ibid.

39. I am indebted to an anonymous reviewer for drawing my attention to the danger of ignoring the power differentials that make it not only unfeasible but also undesirable for oppressed individuals to seek to engage in "we-relationships" with their oppressors.

References

Alcoff, Linda. *Visible Identities: Race, Gender, and the Self*. Oxford: Oxford University Press, 2006.

Althusser, Louis. "Ideology and Ideological State Apparatus (Notes towards an Investigation)." In *Lenin and Philosophy and Other Essays*, trans. Ben Brewster, 85–126. New York: Monthly Review Press, 2001.

Bergson, Henri. *An Introduction to Metaphysics*. Trans. Thomas E. Hulme. New York: Macmillan, 1955.

Bourdieu, Pierre. *The Logic of Practice*. Trans. Richard Nice. Stanford, Calif.: Stanford University Press, 1990.

Butler, Judith. *Bodies That Matter: On the Discursive Limits of "Sex."* New York: Routledge, 1993.

Butler, Judith. *Excitable Speech: A Politics of the Performative*. New York: Routledge, 1997.

Butler, Judith. *Undoing Gender*. New York: Routledge Press, 2004.

Caws, Peter. "Identity: Cultural, Transcultural, and Multicultural." In *Multiculturalism: A Critical Reader*, ed. David Theo Goldberg, 371–87. Oxford: Blackwell, 1994.

Fanon, Frantz. *Black Skin White Masks*. Trans. Charles Lam Markmann. New York: Grove Press, 1967.

Foucault, Michel. *Discipline and Punish: The Birth of the Prison*. Trans. Alan Sheridan. New York: Vintage Books, 1977.

Frankenberg, Ruth. *White Women, Race Matters: The Social Construction of Whiteness*. Minneapolis: University of Minnesota Press, 1993.

Gordon, Lewis R. *Bad Faith and Antiblack Racism*. Atlantic Highlands, N.J.: Humanities Press, 1995.

Gordon, Lewis R. *Existentia Africana: Understanding Africana Existential Thought*. New York: Routledge, 2000.

Grosz, Elizabeth. *Volatile Bodies: Toward a Corporeal Feminism*. Bloomington: Indiana University Press, 1994.

Hegel, Georg W. F. *The Phenomenology of Mind*. Intro. George Lichtheim. Trans. James B. Baillie. New York: Harper and Row, 1967.

Heidegger, Martin. *Being and Time*. Trans. Joan Stambaugh. Albany: SUNY Press, 1996.

Heinämaa, Sara. *Toward a Phenomenology of Sexual Difference: Husserl, Merleau-Ponty, and Beauvoir*. Lanham, Md.: Rowman and Littlefield, 2003.

Husserl, Edmund. *Ideas Pertaining to a Pure Phenomenology and to a Phenomenological Philosophy*. First Book. Trans. Fred Kersten. Dordrecht: Kluwer Academic Publishers, 1982.

Irigaray, Luce. *An Ethics of Sexual Difference*. Trans. Carolyn Burke and Gillian C. Gill. Ithaca, N.Y.: Cornell University Press, 1993.

Irigaray, Luce. *Speculum of the Other Woman*. Trans. Gillian C. Gill. Ithaca, N.Y.: Cornell University Press, 1985.

James, William. *The Principles of Psychology*. Vol. 1. New York: Dover Publications, 1950.

Kierkegaard, Søren. *Fear and Trembling/Repetition*. Ed. and trans. Howard Hong and Edna Hong. Princeton, N.J.: Princeton University Press, 1983.

Kittay, Eva. *Love's Labor: Essays on Women, Equality, and Dependency*. New York: Routledge, 1999.

Marshall, Gloria. "Racial Classifications: Popular and Scientific." In *The Racial Economy of Science: Toward a Democratic Future*, ed. Sandra Harding, 116–27. Bloomington: Indiana University Press, 1993.

Merleau-Ponty, Maurice. "Eye and Mind." In *The Merleau-Ponty Aesthetics Reader*, ed. Galen A. Johnson. Translation ed. Michael Smith. Evanston, Ill.: Northwestern University Press, 1993.

Merleau-Ponty, Maurice. *Phenomenology of Perception*. Trans. Colin Smith. London: Routledge and Kegan Paul, 1962.

Murphy, Robert F. *The Body Silent*. New York: W. W. Norton, 1990.

Plato. *The Republic*. Trans. Francis MacDonald Cornford. Oxford: Oxford University Press, 1978.

Sartre, Jean-Paul. *Being and Nothingness*. Trans. Hazel E. Barnes. New York: Washington Square Press, 1956.

Sartre, Jean-Paul. "No Exit." In *No Exit and Three Other Plays*. Trans. S. Gilbert, 1–47. New York: Vintage Books, 1976.

Schutz, Alfred. *The Phenomenology of the Social World*. Trans. George Walsh and Frederick Lehnert. Evanston, Ill.: Northwestern University Press, 1967.

Schutz, Alfred. *The Problem of Social Reality: Collected Papers I*. Ed. Maurice Natanson. The Hague: Martinus Nijhoff, 1982.

Thomson, Rosemarie Garland. *Extraordinary Bodies: Figuring Physical Disability in American Culture and Literature*. New York: Columbia University Press, 1997.

18 Time Binds, or, Erotohistoriography

ELIZABETH FREEMAN

From the vantage point of temporal drag, what would a genealogy of history itself look like? Any search for the origins of queer historiographical pleasure, it seems, would resurrect the very impulses that the texts that I have explored thus far resist. But in the texts that follow, pleasure — instead of appearing as foundational to a discipline or identity — flashes up from the past as the loser in bygone battles over what the discipline of history itself should become. As the winners of a battle between sensory and cognitive modes of apprehending history declared it, history should be understood rather than felt, and written in a genre as clearly separable from fiction (if not from narrative) as possible.[1] Yet from at least the 1800s, fiction has offered traces not only of unrealized pasts but also of the unrealized past of history itself.

The conflict between rational and emotional understanding, reportage and fiction, is visible in a rather old chestnut of both literary and queer theory, Mary Shelley's *Frankenstein, or, The Modern Prometheus*. Shelley's novel is in many ways critical of both the genealogical logic and domestic-sentimental chrononormativities that Dougherty, Bonder, and Harris would undermine over a century and a half later, as I detailed in chapter 1. And *Frankenstein*, as I will show, is also committed to the performance of anachrony I called "temporal drag" in chapter 2. But most important, *Frankenstein* allows us access to a counterhistory of history itself — an antisystematic method that informs other, much later artistic productions traveling more explicitly under the sign of queer.

I call this method *erotohistoriography*. Erotohistoriography is distinct from the desire for a fully present past, a restoration of bygone times. Erotohistoriography does not write the lost object into the present so much as encounter it already in the present, by treating the present itself as hybrid. And it uses the body as a tool to effect, figure, or perform that encounter. Erotohistoriography admits that contact with historical materials can be precipitated by particular bodily dispositions, and that these connections may elicit bodily responses, even pleasurable ones, that are themselves a form of understanding. It sees the body as a method, and historical consciousness as something intimately involved with corporeal sensations. And If erotohistoriography does not begin with *Frankenstein*, that novel at least offers us figures for witnessing the history of a discredited form of knowledge and for tracking its afterlife.

Frankenstein: Bodying Forth History

As many critics have recognized, *Frankenstein* is fiercely antigenealogical. Judith Halberstam writes that in the novel, the family is "as fragmented and incoherent as the monster himself" and seems most authentic and normative when its members are apart.[2] Certainly the novel's kin groups — the fictionalized Byrons and Shelleys who meet near Lac Leman, Switzerland, to tell ghost stories in Mary Shelley's 1831

"Author's Introduction"; Robert Walton and his sister Mrs. Saville, whose letters frame the novel; its main narrator Victor Frankenstein; and the De Laceys, who are at the center of the tale the monster tells — are marked by the same "unnatural" suture and disaggregation that mark the monster's body. For instance, the historical Byrons and Shelleys were entangled in all kinds of adulterous liaisons, out-of-wedlock children, bisexual affairs, and custody disputes, which histories are at least partially visible in the rivalry of their fictionalized counterparts as they compete to tell the best horror tale. Then, too, the ostensibly devoted Walton never appears in the same diegetic space as his supposedly beloved sister. The Frankenstein family of whom Victor Frankenstein speaks to Walton is a mix of adopted and biological kin eventually torn asunder by murders and accusations of betrayal. And the De Laceys, whom the monster describes to Victor Frankenstein, shelter their son's Turkish/Arabian fiancée from her vengeful father, in a hut that the monster eventually destroys.

But at least two of these families are also *temporally* out of joint in ways that parallel the monster's composition out of bits and pieces of dead flesh. For the Waltons' and Frankensteins' attempts and failures to achieve domestic synchronicity occur in the process of sending one another letters. Walton's narration is entirely epistolary; within the tale Victor Frankenstein tells him, letters between family members and friends constantly circulate. On the one hand, these letters forge a sense of immediacy and intimacy: these families know their members and recognize their status as kin through being addressed and represented in letter form. The letters also construct and perform familial status to an extra-domestic audience: as Jürgen Habermas reminds us, eighteenth- and early-nineteenth-century letters were often written not only to their addressees but also implicitly to larger publics within and beyond the extended family.[3] The structure of *Frankenstein* captures this process of "publishing the family," for the monster's self-narrated autobiography and tale of the De Laceys appear within a story that Victor Frankenstein, his creator, tells to the sympathetic stranger Robert Walton, whose record of it in letters to his sister Margaret Saville constitutes the novel as a whole, whose audience is both the group at Lac Leman and Shelley's eventual readers.[4] The result is a kind of closed circuit of writing and telling in which the monster is simultaneously the center (for he is the innermost narrator, framed first by Victor's narrative which in turn is framed by Walton's letters) and the margin (for though he speaks, he never writes, and this, I would argue, symptomizes his lack of familial connection).

Even as letter writing for a familial audience produces a kind of virtual coherence, though, it also opens up temporal fissures that undermine that very coherence. Most works of epistolary fiction play on the gap between the moment of writing a letter and the moment of receiving and reading one: among other things, this conceit allows the reader of an epistolary novel to know things before characters do, and for a plot element to be obsolete (that is, already undone by another event) even as it is revealed. Like the monster's body, then, many letters are dead on arrival. If the family form gains coherence through the virtual *space* or "worlding" enacted by writing letters, it is made dangerously incoherent by the *time* lags that this spacing depends on: this is most evident in the juxtaposition between Elizabeth's cheery and incongruous letter to Victor, relating the history of Justine Moritz's arrival into the family (which Victor presumably already knows), and the subsequent letter from Victor's father telling of young William Frankenstein's murder, eventually blamed on that same Justine. And of course, Victor's own role in the novel is also to arrive too late to prevent the deaths of his family members by the monster's hands. *Frankenstein* is nothing if not a novel of the *après-coup*.

Just as the Frankenstein family (and to a lesser extent the Walton family) is temporally dispersed by the very letters that spatially bind them, the body parts that supposedly make the monster a synchronized whole are ineluctably unjoined, insofar as they belong to different moments in history. Thus while Halberstam and others have read the monster as gothically and queerly hybrid because he collapses and interchanges any number of social structures (class, race, gender), I'd like to consider him queerly hybrid in a temporal sense. First, the monster embodies the wrinkled time that marks both the gothic and, as I have argued up to this point, the queer. As a genre, the gothic traffics in alternate temporalities or a-rhythms that present themselves in concretely historical terms, as dead bodies coming back to life in the form of vampires, ghosts, and monsters. These undead bodies, in turn, catalyze bodily sensations such as skipped heartbeats, screams, shudders, tears, and swoons in gothic characters, and presumably in some readers (who may also laugh, admittedly, but this is simply another physiological effect). Just as the monster's body is composed of dead flesh touching more dead flesh, the gothic character often experiences both a fleshly touch from the dead and an unpredictable fleshly response to it: the monster is, in many ways, a double for both the genre he inhabits and for the disaggregated sensorium of the gothic character and reader. Indeed, the literary critic Mike Goode speculates that gothic novels themselves enacted a kind of "ecstatic history."[5] That is, the genre transduced religious experiences — which always appeared at the boundaries of what could be encompassed by earthly knowledge — into terror, hallucinations, or sexual transport, themselves alternative or subjugated knowledge practices. In this sense, the gothic was a kind of historical novel *in extremis*, a register for encountering the past felt precisely at the boundaries of what could be encompassed by secular, disciplinary, and even "scientific" notions of history. And as the sociologist Avery Gordon argues, ghosts are the paradigmatic figure for these historical limit-cases, often appearing in gothic novels as tactile experiences not only of dead people but also of repressed events and social formations.[6] While Frankenstein's monster is not a ghost, precisely, his striated and heterogeneous anatomy can certainly be read similarly, as a figure for both the social conflicts of which history consists and the genre in which history announced itself in other terms. The monster, like Goode's and Gordon's undead, figures the outside of not only the human but also — crucially — of what can count as history and as its proper mode of apprehension.

On the face of it, this reading of *Frankenstein* as a novel about the writing and experiencing of history seems implausible. The knowledge that Victor seeks is not historical knowledge per se but scientific knowledge — specifically, the secret of life, and the ability to create new life, which he wishes to wrest from God and/or women. But interestingly, before he ever touches a cadaver, Victor begins his quest for knowledge through contact with the dead, for his early studies consist of reading obsolete, outmoded scientific works. Even once he discovers the fundamental error of this approach in college and joins the world of modern science, he eventually turns back to past ideas and methods for imparting life to dead matter. As he begins to raid charnel-houses in order to create his monster, he transfers his allegiance from dead authors to dead bodies. It might be argued that Victor cannot be characterized as a historian precisely insofar as he reads primary documents as if they inform him about the present, as if they were "live." But he is certainly what some Romantic-era historians condemned as an "antiquarian," someone whose obsession with the past threatened to become an end in itself.[7] In fact, Victor has not only the wrong method but also the wrong relationship to knowledge. His learning distracts him from attending to his family, as critics generally agree, but this is not benign neglect; indeed, his love for old texts takes a perverse turn. His passion for ancient science slides into literal contact with the dead when he begins robbing graves, and his obsession with his project of bringing this dead flesh to life substitutes for his romance with Elizabeth and his manly friendship with Henry Clerval. Eventually Victor's own body dessicates because of both his misguided intellectual program and his ghastly creation: Victor's studies and the monster's body are allegories for one another insofar as the monster is not only flesh but text, a body condensing Victor's, Shelley's, and a generation of critics' *knowledge*.

Indeed, *Frankenstein* is preoccupied with the relationship between cognition and the body, and specifically, as I will demonstrate, between historical understanding and the male body. In this sense, the novel reflects discussion among historians in the long nineteenth century, who were keenly interested in the question of how feelings and sensations in the present could illuminate past events.[8] The idea of apprehending and representing collective experiences from the past in avowedly embodied, not always painful ways might seem repugnant both to traditionalist historicist methods that rely on the principle of objective and disinterested analysis, and to Marxist understandings that genuine historical consciousness is precipitated by oppression. But this idea was absolutely viable in the Anglo-American eighteenth and nineteenth centuries. Goode writes that Enlightenment and Romantic-era discussions about historical method — specifically, a debate in 1790–91 between Edmund Burke and Thomas Paine — centered on how the male capacity for sensibility, figured in terms of bodily constitution, was crucial to historical understanding.[9] In Burke's account, manly somatic responses were considered a legitimate relay to historical knowledge. The era's "man of feeling" properly encountered history through sympathetic identifications with its personae and modes of living. This transferential relationship took place not only in the mind but also through more visceral attachments, identifications, and attempts to reinhabit past worldviews, all of which in turn reconstituted the historian's body as a finer instrument of sensibility. In other words, history was a use of physical sensation that, in a dialectical turn, *made* the very bodies capable of properly receiving those sensations. This process, as Goode describes it, was a sort of Foucauldian *ars erotica* of historical inquiry.[10]

But this relationship between the historian and his object always threatened to become carnal, a mismanaged encounter that could variously dehumanize, dry up, or even kill off the properly masculine body. Thus, argues Goode, the discipline of history arose in conjunction with, and partook in, a crisis about masculinity. Pamphlets and published cartoons from the 1790s figure antiquarians' obsessive interest in the archives as a sort of sexual perversion. The era's term "bibliomania" did not correlate directly with modern homosexuality, but it certainly included a morbid disinterest in women and, at times, a homoerotic interest in the lives of great men. Goode provides the hilarious example of a satirical cartoon from 1811, Thomas Rowlandson's *Modern Antiques*, in which a wizened and lecherous old man fondles the genitals of an ancient Greek statue in a museum storehouse, while a robust young heterosexual couple have sex in an empty Egyptian sarcophagus.[11] In this light, we can see Victor's obsession with building his monster from dead bodies as a turn from a vaguely perverse and homoerotic bibliomania to a deeply perverse necrophilia, in which physical contact with the dead substitutes for healthy sex between the living. Victor's morbid disinterest in women, or at least in Elizabeth, is part and parcel of his obsession with the dead. And his encounter with the past in the form of corpses, rather than textbooks or even marble statues, becomes more horrifyingly carnal than the old man's fondlings in the cartoon.

But beyond this analogy between dead bodies and the archive, it is also possible to read *Frankenstein*'s much-discussed emphasis on sympathy as a plea for a particular relationship to historical knowledge. In the moment Shelley wrote, "sympathy" was the key term for a liberal notion that justice, polity, and freedom rest on the capacity of human beings first to respond to the plight of others, and then to abstract and redistribute this capacity into a general, reciprocal political obligation among members of a group.[12] This response to others extended to the dead. For Edmund Burke, writing *Reflections on the Revolution in France* (1790), both jurisprudence and historical method involved a certain amount of sympathy, manifest in the ability to imaginatively inhabit and reenact the behavior codes of prior times, even if those codes were, in Goode's words, "malformed" and potentially unsuitable for the present.[13] Crucially, though, the Burkean historian must use this identificatory process to apprehend *differences* between his feelings and those of the past, in order to grasp the larger historical differences that would make precedent more or less applicable.[14] In other words, the man of feeling must first feel the feelings of the past and then feel their disruptive contact with the present. Seen in Burkean terms, then, Frankenstein's monster, deformed though he may be, is a much better historian than his creator. Victor applies his passion for knowledge to the wrong textual corpus, learning codes of scientific conduct from Paracelsus and Agrippa that are absolutely inappropriate for the present. He does not compare them with modern-day methods and interests until he is forced to do so at college, at which point he turns to dead bodies.

By contrast, the monster may wear and perform anachronistic behaviors in the literal form of mismatched body parts, but he actually learns virtue from precedent. He also "civilizes" himself by choosing rationally among thoughts and behaviors of long-past eras and fitting them to his present situation. For crucially, the monster learns about human culture and sympathy through books, including history books. Overhearing the cottagers reading Volney's *Ruins of Empires* to one another gives him "a cursory knowledge of history," but he also imitates their weeping "over the hapless fate of [America's] original inhabitants."[15] Here, historical events engender the proper feeling of compassion for others. Having learned to read, the monster also finds a copy of *Plutarch's Lives*, from which he learns "to admire peaceable lawgivers, Numa, Solon, and Lycurgus, in preference to Romulus and Theseus" (170). He remarks that "if my first introduction to humanity had been made by a young soldier, burning for glory and slaughter, I should have been imbued with different sensations" (170), suggesting that his character and sensory apparatus are malleable in exact proportion to the kind of history he reads. Through imaginatively projecting himself into the lives of history's oppressed and into the mindsets of the right heroes from the past, the monster develops virtue, much as Burke advocated the mimetic transmission of established manners and ethics.

Shelley clearly elevates the monster's sympathetic relationship to the past (including the life-histories of the cottagers) over Victor Frankenstein's combination of perverse antiquarianism, obsessive fixation, and eventually, cold, hard science. Indeed, what critics have generally seen as Shelley's commitment to the *feminine* sphere of the domestic affections may equally well represent her commitment to properly *manly* Romantic-era historical sensibilities. For she figures Victor Frankenstein in much the same terms as Thomas Paine figured Burke's affective historicism. As Goode explains, Paine reviled Burkean historicism because it animated and depended on feelings that were historically derived rather than spontaneous, on codes of conduct that were appropriated from the past rather than inborn. Paine accused Burke's approach to history of bringing the living too close to the dead, and so ruining the living body's constitution.[16] As if to embody Paine's fears, in *Frankenstein* the scientist himself becomes at least as hideous as the monster, degenerating into the withered, dried-up, sickly scholar caricatured in the popular presses of the 1790s. Indeed, popular rhetoric of the era cast those with an unnatural interest in the past as enslaved, their devotion to precedent diminishing their capacity for self-government in the present. We see a hint of this in a scene in which Victor tours an aspect of British history:

> We passed a considerable period at Oxford, rambling among its environs, and endeavouring to identify every spot which might relate to the most animating epoch of English history. Our little voyages of discovery were often prolonged by the successive objects that presented themselves. We visited the tomb of the illustrious Hampden, and the field on which that patriot fell. For a moment my soul was elevated from its debasing and miserable fears, to contemplate the divine ideas of liberty and self-sacrifice, of which these sights were the monuments and the remembrancers. For an instant I dared to shake off my chains, and look around me with a free and lofty spirit; but the iron had eaten into my flesh, and I sank again, trembling and hopeless, into my miserable self. (215)[17]

Here, "animating" recalls Victor's project of bringing the dead to life, yet it refers to history's proper effect on bodily constitution: Hampden's grave "elevates" its viewers from what is "debasing and miserable" and inculcates a revivifying notion of liberal freedom. Official national history seems to free Victor of his body and his particular past, to offer him a truly republican release from both. But Victor is, at the end of their outing, bound like a slave by chains of obligation to another past, fetters that have scourged his very body. The monster, too, refers to Victor as "Slave" in his long soliloquy at the novel's center. And the figure of the living body shackled to dead matter also appears more pointedly near the end of the novel, when Victor chases the monster over the Arctic ice in a dogsled: "Once, after the poor animals that conveyed me had with incredible toil gained the summit of a sloping ice-mountain, … one, sinking under his fatigue, died … I disencumbered the dogs of their dead companion" (281–82). The dogs, at least momentarily harnessed to a corpse, double Victor's enslavement not only to the monster but also to the dead.

For Paine, then, the Burkean body was just that — an artificial lump of matter tantamount to a corpse, composed as it was of other people's values and ideas, rather than a natural body whose sense of liberty and self-governance was innate. In this sense, Paine championed an ahistorical relationship to knowledge, and by extension the ahistorical body constituted by such a relation: the Paineite subject would just "feel right," as Harriet Beecher Stowe would later put it in *Uncle Tom's Cabin* (1852), knowing how to act and what to do rather than being constituted by forces that preceded him. As Goode's work clarifies, in the Paineite formulation bodily feeling, including feeling historical, doesn't *have* a cultural history, and any inherited codes, including those for gendered or sexual behavior, repress the body's natural inclinations. Frankenstein's monster, by contrast, is a body that contains a history of bodies and of bodiliness and thus figures a gender and a sexuality that themselves write a history of genders and sexualities. After Foucault, the monster suggests, we are all Frankensteinian monsters: or, after *Frankenstein*, the Foucauldian body emerges.

At the end of *Frankenstein*, the Victorian era of "hard" historical science that would succeed Romantic historiography glimmers out proleptically for a moment. Victor corrects Walton's transcription of his narrative in the Arctic: "Frankenstein discovered that I [Walton] made notes concerning his history: he asked to see them, and then himself corrected and augmented them in many places; but principally *in giving life and spirit* to the conversations he held with his enemy. 'Since you have preserved my narration,' said he, '*I would not that a mutilated one should go down to posterity*'" (285, both emphases mine). It is as if, here, Victor aims to bring the dead to life but is afraid of yet another monstrous creation, this time in the form of a historical narrative. Putting together a proper history in the frigid Arctic, he literalizes the Victorian turn to a colder, more objective, scientific relationship to the past. He intends that this history, unlike the one he constructed from dead bodies, will not engender such a frenzy, instead seeking one that, unlike his creature, will persevere as the unified corpus of knowledge sought by academic historians. The later Romantic era had already subordinated the monster's stigmatized passionate attachments to the past to a larger, decorporealizing project: while privileging a Burkean sensitivity to the past, the Romantics demanded that the archivist connect or coordinate small details to what they called "the spirit of the age" in which those details dwelt.[18] And the Victorians, in the name of science, would altogether distance themselves from Romantic historiography. Victor the mad chemist, then, is out of time in more than one direction. Not only does he revivify the stereotype of the scholar as pervert but he also prefigures the Victorian movement toward a disinterested, unsentimental, avowedly scientific approach to history. That the monster finally arranges and lights his own funeral pyre suggests how unbearable the weight of a more self-reflexively historical being, and the burden of visceral apprehension, must be in a culture that will increasingly demote these ways of knowing.

In sum, Frankenstein's monster is monstrous because he lets history too far in, going so far as to embody it instead of merely feeling it, even to embody the historicity of the body revealed when erotic contact with the past produces sensations that are unintelligible by present sexual and gender codes. He certainly emblematizes the passionate attachments to archival materials that were increasingly barred from historicist methodology as the nineteenth century progressed. But he also figures history's ability to effect shifts in bodily constitution in ways that were increasingly demonized, problematized, or disavowed.

In *Frankenstein*, we can also see the erotic relation to history that would suture contemporary affective historiography, which in its attachment to melancholia seems so pleasure-shy, to the model of *jouissance*, from whose ahistoricism queer theory has turned away. By locating the scene of gothic encounter in the hymeneal bed itself where Elizabeth sees the monster for the first time, *Frankenstein* suggests that Elizabeth's response to the dead, to Victor's secret history as the monster's creator, and to the presence of another historical moment in embodied form is directly sexual. In the famous wedding night scene, the return of history (in the form of the monster's retribution for Victor's murder of his beloved) ravishes Elizabeth far more completely than anything her new husband could offer. Or perhaps it ravishes Victor, who declares, "As I heard [Elizabeth's scream] … my arms dropped, the motion of every muscle and fibre was suspended; I could feel the blood trickling in my veins and tingling in the extremities of my limbs" (264). In light of the way this scene hints at a literally, even genitally ecstatic relation to the past, I would argue that *Frankenstein* is a novel explicitly concerned with the erotics of historical consciousness. Over and over, the novel codes contact with the past as a meeting of sensate body, historical understanding, and representation. In the erotohistoriographic mode, *Frankenstein* stages the very queer possibility that encounters with history are bodily encounters, and even that they have a revivifying and pleasurable effect.

In figuring both a threatening nearness to the materials of the past and the effect of that nearness on the body, the monster is a precursor to Virginia Woolf's famous Orlando, who chases his lovers across the time-line even as he is chased by his biographer, and, in a hilarious parody of the Romantic "spirit of the age," whose body morphs from male to female under the pressures of historical change. What distinguishes *Orlando* from *Frankenstein*, though, is the lesbian possibility that historical knowledge might depend not only on sympathetic feelings but also on sexual pleasure directly administered, and that the body might pleasure itself with the past. In the history of erotohistoriography that I am sketching out here, *Orlando* may stand as the first lesbian work in the genre.

Orlando: Fingering History

In the early 1800s, the London *Morning Chronicle* published a daily fashion column that was always prefaced by the epitaph "To shew / The very age and body of the time, / Its form and pressure."[19] In *Orlando*, Woolf seems intent on literalizing that body of "the time." Like Victor Frankenstein, Orlando is the historian as pervert figured by Burke's detractors. He/she also loses a self and what would otherwise be a normal and natural body by too much contact with the dead — yet he/she claims this loss exuberantly. Unlike Victor Frankenstein, Orlando's body does not wither, nor does he/she lose interest in women; Orlando simply changes genders. And if anything, contact with the past and the forces of historical change make him/her more robust, for he/she ages only about fifteen years in three hundred.

Woolf figures this departure from what by the Edwardian era were the norms of historical inquiry not as a contest between forms of masculinity but as a struggle among masculinity, femininity, and queerness. She rejects both a masculine national progress narrative and the dilettantish and anhedonic hobbies left to female antiquarians, embracing a juicily queer mode of seeing and writing the past. Woolf is merciless in her skewering of disciplinary history: her acknowledgments facetiously thank her husband, Leonard Woolf, "for the profound historical knowledge to which these pages owe whatever degree of accuracy they may attain" and laud "Miss M. K. Snowdon's indefatigable researches in the archives of Harrogate and Cheltenham [which] were none the less arduous for being vain."[20] Later in the novel, the narrator counter-poses two fictional diary accounts of Orlando's coronation as Duke, in Constantinople: a bombastic and self-congratulatory report from one naval officer John Fenner Brigge on how the ceremony impresses the natives, and a gushing letter from one General Hartoppe's daughter Penelope, full of exclamation points and comments about fashion and good-looking men. But Woolf's predominant figure for the academic historian is the unnamed, ostensibly gender-neutral narrator, a professional biographer. The narrator claims to "enjoy the immunity of all biographers and historians from any sex whatever" (220) and declares that "the biographer who records the life of such a one [need never] … invoke the help of novelist or poet. From deed to deed, from glory to glory, from office to office he must go, his scribe following after, till they reach what ever seat it may be that is the height of their desire" (14–15). Here, even as Woolf satirizes supposedly objective and passionless history, she deconstructs its disavowed sexual basis, jokingly implying a sodomitical relationship between biographer and subject with her reference to their shared "seat" of desire.

In Woolf's own biography, this relationship was not sodomitical but Sapphic. As critics from Nigel Nicolson onward have recognized, the eroticized chase between Orlando and his/her biographer mirrors Woolf's attempt to textually seduce Vita Sackville-West.[21] If we read *Orlando*'s biographer as historiographer, and his object Orlando as a figure for the past itself, then the writing of history is also figured as a seduction of the past and, correspondingly, as the past's erotic impact on the body itself. Historiography even has the ability (if the narrator's obsession with Orlando's legs is any example) to seduce the seducer. Woolf's methodology, then, centers on an avowedly erotic pleasure: an *ars erotica* of historical inquiry that takes place not between the hearts of emoting men, as in Burke, but between and across the bodies of lusting women.

Woolf's novel tells the story of young Orlando's excursion through English literary and cultural history, an experience of history not only *on* but *as* a body. Our hero(ine) lives three hundred years, waking up one morning to find her sex changed from male to female midway through his/her journey. Of course, this is in part a story about the constructedness of gender: for instance, prose styles and costumes that are resoundingly masculine in Elizabethan England become foppishly feminine by the Restoration. But *Orlando*'s more interesting conceit, for my purposes, is that the protagonist him/herself experiences historical change as a set of directly corporeal and often sexual sensations. In a parody of the kind of historiography that speaks knowingly of a given era's zeitgeist, Woolf literalizes political or cultural climate as weather. The end of the Elizabethan period announces itself by thawing the frozen River Thames; the nineteenth century is ushered in with a damp that increases the birthrate and the vegetation; the twentieth century dries everything up. Orlando feels these various centuries not only as fluctuations in weather but also as reorganizations of his/her body, succinctly captured by the narrator's observation that "one might see the spirit of the age blowing, now hot, now cold, upon [Orlando's] cheeks" (236).

Not surprisingly for a feminist who had read Freud, Woolf also plays hard and fast with the motif of castration, describing three muses who, on encountering Orlando's change from man to woman during the Restoration era, "peeped in at the door and threw a garment like a towel at the naked form which, unfortunately, fell short by several inches" (138), the ambiguous "which" here referring not only to the towel but to the "naked form" and its suddenly missing inches. But Woolf also *historicizes* castration, figuring Orlando's morphing body in terms of the parts that become salient at different historical moments: the castration complex becomes a more generally somatic trauma in which the relation of particular body parts to the whole body shifts from era to era. In Orlando's Elizabethan incarnation as a man, for instance, his legs take center stage. As the scene with the three muses suggests, the Restoration era has a rather dramatic effect on his penis. By the nineteenth century, the now-female Orlando feels historical change as finger trouble:

> The nerve which controls the pen winds itself about every fibre of our being, threads the heart, pierces the liver. Though the seat of her trouble seemed to be the left finger, she could feel herself poisoned through and through, and was forced at length to consider the most desperate of remedies, which was to yield completely and submissively to the spirit of the age, and take a husband. (243)

Here, Woolf hints that not only gender but also the anatomical basis for "sex" itself may be historically contingent. The two-sex system in which Orlando finds herself trapped, Woolf seems to argue, is a product of rather than the precursor to the heterosexual-marital imperative. Castration, then, centers not only on the penis but also on the left ring finger: here, we might say, the Oedipal narrative meets the annular one.

Orlando is possessed of a radically metahistoricized body, a body like that of Shelley's monster insofar as it incarnates the history of sexuality. But during the male period of his life, he is also an antiquarian of sorts, obsessed with artifacts of the past in ways that echo Victor Frankenstein. Indeed, *Orlando* opens with a living person disturbing a fragment of dead flesh: we first see our hero/ine slicing at the rafters, trying to strike the head of an African "pagan" killed by one of his ancestors. In this contretemps, "Africa" represents both Orlando's place in an imperial venture and a racialized, racist trope for the past itself. Yet it also immediately establishes that Orlando is, temporally speaking, as out of joint as the desiccated head with which he parries. And as the novel progresses, Orlando becomes increasingly compelled by dead body parts and then relics in general. Several times, he visits the tomb of his noble ancestors, fondling their possessions and skeletal remains:

> [Orlando] would take a skeleton hand in his and bend the joints this way and that. "Whose hand was it?" he went on to ask. "The right or the left? The hand of man or woman, of age or youth? Had it urged the war horse, or plied the needle? Had it plucked the rose, or grasped cold steel? Had it ——" but here either his invention failed him or, what is more likely, provided him with so many instances of what a hand can do that he shrank, as his wont was, from the cardinal labour of composition, which is excision. (71)

The passage stages a conflict between a labile historiography and the selective principles of "disinterested" academic writing evidenced by Victor Frankenstein's editorial work on Walton's manuscript: in *Orlando*, proper scholarship appears as "excision" or castration of the hand. Orlando's problem as a historian, foreshadowed by his antics with the "pagan" head and appearing more overtly in his struggles to end his long poem "The Oak Tree," is that he can't cut anything out. Or off. Here, his surfeit of responses to the dead part-object in the tomb suggest what Carla Freccero refers to as "an alternate path to the Western melancholic's incorporation of the lost other and its permanent, if uneasy, entombment within the crypt of history." Freccero suggests that this alternate relationship to the past might take the form of "a penetrative reciprocity, a becoming-object for an other subject and a resultant joy or ecstasy."[22] This suggests a kind of bottomy historiography: the potential for collective queer time — even queer history — to be structured as an uneven transmission of receptivity rather than authority or custom, of a certain enjoyably porous relation to unpredictable futures or to new configurations of the past.[23] Woolf's inside reference to "what a hand can do" alludes to this sort of flexible erotics between women as, also, a historiographic method.

Later, Orlando begins to practice erotohistoriography more methodically than his tomb fondlings suggest, for he becomes obsessed with official history's cast-offs. Lovingly fondling Queen Mary's prayer book, Orlando adds a flake of tobacco to the hair, bloodstain, and crumb of pastry already stuck to its pages. These marks of use are all connected to the body, which seems to variously shed, bleed, eat, and smoke a sedimented history that interests Orlando far more than the textual materials enclosing it. Woolf here seems to gesture toward the late-eighteenth-century Burkean ideal of the historian as a man of feeling. But she also releases the erotic energies that this ideal, in its appeal to virtuous manhood, ultimately disavows.

Her trope for such a method is the hand, which redeems that aforementioned aching left-hand finger. Early in the novel, Orlando is presented to Queen Elizabeth, whom he encounters by way of her royal hand; from this appendage he infers her ancient, decayed body buried underneath its brocade and jewels. That night, the queen seduces him, insisting that he bury his head in her skirts. "'This,' she breathed, 'is my victory!' — even as a rocket roared up and dyed her cheeks scarlet" (25). This militarized orgasm, following from what looks like oral sex with a person so old she might as well be dead, prefigures what will later develop into an explicitly desirous relationship between the individual historian and the materials of a collective past. For at another point the narrator, struggling to piece together the facts of Orlando's life, apotheosizes the joking possibility of a lesbian historiography: "Just when we thought to elucidate a secret that has puzzled historians for a hundred years, there was a hole in the manuscript big enough to put your finger through" (119). Here again, history is a hole to penetrate, but not with the usual instruments.

That Sapphic finger, in turn, has already appeared in veiled form, in the question Orlando puts to the skeletal hand of his ancestors, of whether it belonged to a man or a woman, "urged the war horse, or plied the needle" (71). Woolf's narrator later muses upon the needle in another figure for lesbian erotohistoriography:

> Nature, who has played so many queer tricks upon us … [has] added to our confusion by providing a perfect rag-bag of odds and ends within us — a piece of a policeman's trousers lying cheek by jowl with Queen Alexandra's wedding veil — but has contrived that the whole assortment shall be lightly stitched together by a single thread. Memory is the seamstress, and a capricious one at that. Memory runs her needle in and out, up and down, hither and thither. (77–78)

Taken together, these passages suggest that the hand that plies the needle, the needle that is itself a kind of finger penetrating the holes in memory and manuscript, the nerve system that controls the pen and yet is wrapped around the fibers of our whole being, are figures for a more affective and embodied form of historical inquiry. Orlando neither celebrates a merely cognitive or imagistic memory nor subordinates any response to material detail toward an apprehension of "the spirit of the age." Instead, the novel pursues a kind of visceral encounter between past and present figured as a tactile meeting, as a finger that in stitching, both touches and is touched, and that in reading, pokes and caresses the holes in the archival text even as it sutures them.

Orlando's aesthetic of lesbian fingerplay, as I have described it, offers up erotohistoriography as the model for a truly digital history. But insofar as it tantalizes us with the possibility of manually encountering the past, it also takes pleasure in the analog. For in analog technology, information is borne along in continuous, linear sequences of physical matter such as light waves or sound waves. Analog technology tends also to be indexical, incorporating a trace of that which is represented into the representation, as with light in a photograph, or sound waves in a recording. Digital technologies, which convert this material to binary code, create infinitesimal gaps in this continuum and enable endless shuffling. But because of its high speed and the homogeneity of its materials (numbers), digital also seems "smoother" than analog. Digital code effaces the visible seams, audible noise, palpable textures that accompany analog transitions from one material or state to another: in an analog experience of the real, the gears jam momentarily when things change, as in the small skip in spliced film or audiotape, the pops and hisses between tracks on LP records, the layers of paint overlapping or bleeding slightly as they meet in a painting, the finger interrupting a stream of text as it flips the pages of a codex. With her digits that penetrate, sew, and dangle, then, Woolf proleptically figures an analog version of the digital, even as Orlando retrospectively looks back toward to discredited historiographic methods and restores an eroticized materiality to the gaps and imperfect sutures between past and present.

The Sticky Fingers of Time: Analog and Digital Pleasure

Though *Orlando* precedes the digital era by quite a few decades, the independent filmmaker Hilary Brougher's feature-length film *The Sticky Fingers of Time* (1997) owes something to that novel's way of bodying as opposed to minding the gap between then and now. Significantly, Brougher made *Sticky Fingers* on a very low budget, using no special effects: if its conceit of shuffled times is digital, its technology is entirely analog.[24] Like *Orlando*, the film explores lesbian sex and time travel as figures for one another and for the erotics of apprehending history. In this small masterpiece, the slightly butch Drew (Nicole Zaray) eventually travels from her own 1990s to the 1950s and falls in love with a midcentury high femme, Tucker (Terumi Matthews). Tucker, in turn, is involved with both Isaac (James Urbaniak), an androgynous male from her own era, and Ofelia (Belinda Becker), a very feminine female from an unspecified future. The time-traveling journey begins with Drew attempting to rescue Tucker from her impending death by murder but, in the spirit of *Orlando*, becomes a romantic chase as well.

Here is a brief summary of this incredibly complicated plot. Sometime in the 1950s, as Tucker sits down to begin writing her novel *The Sticky Fingers of Time*, her live-in lover Ofelia kisses her and asks her to buy coffee. Stepping out, Tucker suddenly finds herself on her own street, but in the 1990s. Meanwhile in the 1990s, inside Tucker's former apartment, Drew has deleted the novel she had nearly finished and goes to meet her friend Gorge (Samantha Buck), so Gorge can borrow Drew's dental insurance card. After this meeting, Drew and Tucker bump into one another outside a bookstore, where Drew has just bought a vintage copy of Tucker's now-completed novel. As the two women separate, a clipping flutters out of the novel; Tucker picks it up, puts it in her purse, and follows Drew into a bar. There, they introduce themselves to one another and examine the clipping, which reveals that Tucker died of a gunshot wound in 1953. Isaac appears in the bar and surreptitiously asks Drew to help him rescue Tucker, which he cannot do himself since he has already lived through that moment in time once. He also explains that Tucker can time travel because of radiation sickness, and that Ofelia murdered her in 1953, splattering Tucker's irradiated DNA, called Code, into other, future souls — of whom Drew is now one. Drew, somewhat infatuated, follows Tucker in and out of the 1990s, with Ofelia fast behind her. Returning home, Drew finds her friend Gorge inexplicably absent. Ofelia appears and takes Drew back in time to the dentist's office, where Drew relives another murder: Ofelia's henchmen, posting as assistants, have mistakenly killed Gorge thinking she was Drew. Ofelia then takes Drew further back in time to the scene of Drew's parents' divorce, mocking Drew and then channeling her soul into a cactus. From within her cactus consciousness, Drew realizes that she has traveled to the scene of Tucker's murder once already, in a "blackout" caused by her parents' final argument, and this realization allows her soul to burst through the plant. Drew then travels to the 1950s, before Ofelia has broken up Isaac and Tucker, and steals Tucker's plane tickets to Nevada, where she had planned to see the H bomb test that   had she arrived to see it — would have resulted in her time-traveling abilities, and hence both Drew's and Ofelia's as well. Once Drew has stopped Tucker's trip, she has effectively prevented anyone, including herself, from being able to time-travel. With Ofelia now presumably stuck in the future, Drew and Tucker settle together in the apartment, and, we can assume, live happily ever after in the 1950s.

"Fingers, why fingers?" muses Tucker at the beginning of *The Sticky Fingers of Time*. Filled with images of hands on the keys of a manual typewriter, a mouse, and a keyboard, the film seems obsessed with the act of writing, particularly the writing of lesbian pulp novels and science fiction. As with *Orlando*, its scenes of writing are obviously conventional postmodern devices to call attention to the constructedness of gender, sexuality, and time. But the film's title suggests that a certain literality, even *materiality*, gloms onto even the most rigorous deconstruction — that historical details may obstinately stick to or gum up the gears of queer theory. For *Sticky Fingers'* sticky fingers, digital clocks of a sort, are explicitly connected to time-travel. In the film's opening scene, Tucker is at the typewriter starting to write her own 1950s pulp novel, presumably the historical parallel to Drew's unfinished one. Tucker murmurs to herself, "Time has five fingers: one is for the present, two is for the past, three is for the future." Ofelia, who is her lover at this point, completes her sentence: "And four is for what could have been, and five is for what yet could be." In other words, in this film, two fingers are subjunctive. If Tucker's and Ofelia's description of the "fingers of time" were correlated with ordinary hand gestures, the index finger, one, would point to the present; the middle finger, two, would indicate the past; the heterosexual-marital ring finger would correspond to the future, as it does for Woolf's Orlando. The pinkie and the thumb, the outer limits of the hand, would signal "what could have been" and "what yet could be," respectively. But Ofelia has already scrambled the sequence, for though the audience does not know of these events yet, within the chronological order of the film she has already kidnapped Isaac from 1953, reengineered him into a time traveler by chopping off his index and middle finger and stapling prosthetic ones to the stumps, and usurped his place as Tucker's lover. Ofelia's surgery, then, has already disordered the logic of counting by hand that Tucker depends on for her novel, making Isaac's index and middle fingers into the agents of change: "what could have been" and "what yet could be" are precisely the interventions into past and future that Isaac's two primary digits allow.

One could certainly read Ofelia's act as an act of castration (and given Brougher's casting of an African American woman in the role of Ofelia, as castration of white manhood by black womanhood, a particularly pernicious cliché — about which more below). But insofar as the prosthetic fingers allow Isaac to hop the timeline, they are actually quite a bit better than the originals. Then, too, Isaac's name recalls the biblical character whose birth to an elderly and therefore presumably infertile couple already marks a certain queer fold in time, and whose status as a potential victim of infanticide reverses the Oedipal narrative. Here, though, the binding of Isaac is not a covenant between God the Father and Man his son. Instead, *time* binds Isaac to Drew: he has already returned once to the "slice of time" in which the murder has taken place and failed to rescue Tucker, and so he finds Drew and tells her that she must do so. Thus Ofelia's act seems less to castrate a masculine subject than to found a queer alternative to the sequential logic of generations, a bond between subjects who neither descend from one another nor coexist at the same moment.

The index and middle fingers may be the ones most often used for typing (if my own is any example), enhancing the film's play with the idea that writing itself is an act of intervention into time. But they are also the ones most often used in the initial stages of lesbian sex. Thus Isaac's stapled digits, the most literal reference to the film's eponymous "sticky fingers," function as a sort of temporal dildo. Or perhaps this is reductive, insofar as fingers are capable of but not limited to phallic activity, and in Isaac their sexual flexibility is matched by a certain temporal flexibility. As time-travel devices, Isaac's fingers don't seem to register the Oedipal drama of penis envy. For they "think" sexuality entirely outside the two-sex sequencing of conventional psychoanalysis, in which the mother is the past and the father is the future, and history outside the two-sex sequencing of orthodox Marxism, in which the mother is Nature on which "man" works to produce himself and his future. Exploring and reorganizing relations between now, then, and hereafter, these digits are a *tactile* unconscious, or as Walter Benjamin describes the cinema's function as optical unconscious, a surgeon's hand palpitating the organs in a patient's body.[25] In *Sticky Fingers* and the cinema alike, the patient is the present tense.

Of course, if manual sex often starts with the first two fingers, the others frequently follow, and very often the fingers eventually double back upon themselves. Likewise, Isaac's subjunctive fingers are intended to bring the past, present, and future into new conjunctions, to double time back upon itself as they insert new possibilities into the course of human events. Thus Brougher's unspoken figure for historical rupture is what may be the only sex practice invented in the twentieth century — namely, fisting. The fist is a feminized, reverse image of the Freudian toothache I described in my introduction, the pain around which an always melancholic subjectivity organizes itself: while the tooth, an instrument of penetration, turns into an orifice by way of the cavity and the dentist's drill, the hand, an instrument of receptivity in its capacity to hold things, becomes as fist an instrument of penetration. But hands, even fists, also receive touch even as they give it. Thus the film's queer "touch across time," as Carolyn Dinshaw has called it, is troped as a reciprocal tactility between disjunctive moments.[26]

Along the way, this film also pays explicit homage to *Frankenstein*. Though Drew has deleted the only copy of her novel-in-progress from her computer, Gorge remains enthusiastic about it when they meet to exchange the dental insurance card: "I love that part," Gorge says, "when Frankenstein splits his stitches and he dies, fertilizing the earth where that little girl grows tomatoes." This little snippet of dialogue, the film's slightly befuddled nod to Mary Shelley — for Gorge, like many readers, confuses the monster and his creator — seems at first glance to revise *Frankenstein* in exactly the communitarian terms that critics who see that novel as a plea for family values might have prescribed for the original monster and his creator. Rather than escaping society on an ice floe, in Gorge's account Drew's revised monster joins the human scheme of obligations and dependencies, preparing the earth for regrowth and for the next generation. The scene Gorge describes also initially seems to follow the heterosexual, masculine logic that both Shelley and Woolf would eschew. Neither Drew's novel nor this part of it ever appears directly in the film itself, so it is unclear whether the monster fertilizes the earth with his blood, his rotting corpse, or both. But given that the remainder of the film deals with disseminative modes of transmission such as radiation, it is fair to imagine that the monster sheds blood when he bursts his stitches. Here, then, in a heteronormative reading, we can see the monster figuratively inseminating the little girl. But in *choosing* to die for the next generation, the monster also accrues a particular form of Christian masculinity. He transcends the "natural" pain of childbirth, and hence the cyclical time of reproduction, and in doing so enters into a sequential temporal scheme that is the precondition for modern, Western disciplinary history. In a secular version of the Christ story that organizes the meaning of empires and nations, wounds catalyze or serve as metonyms for battle narrative, becoming the signs and guarantees of history proper. When retold across time, wounds facilitate social continuity between male generations in homosocial ways that merely biological fatherhood cannot.[27]

In this light, the monster merely serves dominant historiographical modes. His body, composed as it is of cadavers, may well contain a wounded soldier or two — but in his own death scene as Drew apparently rewrites it, historical continuity seems at first to supersede textuality, taking the more corporeal form of a delayed communion at which the little girl will presumably eat the tomatoes nourished by the monster's blood and body. Within this revised Frankenstein story, the singular and irreplaceable event of a wound on a male body does indeed install the "deep time" of at least a *generational* "before" and "after." And the possibility that this temporal schema might become *historical* appears in the scene's frame, in the form of Gorge telling this sacrifice story so that it might be handed over, handed down: this scene is all that is left of Drew's novel, and Gorge dutifully preserves it. She sublimates and displaces Frankenstein's act into a narrative fragment that might eventually count as part of official, if not precisely national, history — that is, that might be exchanged between men, across time. Indeed, this exchange is already partially underway, for the androgynously named Gorge is speaking to Drew, who bears a similarly gender-undifferentiated name. In short, the monster's masculine self-wounding has literally "engendered" a potential historicity, also structurally masculine, that the rest of the film plays out — and plays with — in terms of time travel.

Within *Sticky Fingers*' complicated intertextual moment we can certainly see a version of the dictum that "history is what hurts": Shelley's monster is stuck within a visual cultural regime that reads his soul from his deformed body and thus denies him an object for his desires, and perhaps Brougher's queer character Drew identifies with this. But we might also return to the Frankenstein scene to witness a different story

— one in which bodies are the relentlessly plural sign of being *in* time rather than escaping from it, wounds a sign of being open to the possibility of change. For as the figure of the little girl suggests, these very same injuries are portals into futurity itself. And in opening himself up to a future he cannot see, the monster enacts a certain historical agency irreducible to biological reproduction between man and woman, or narrative transmission of events between men. Instead, this scene captures a tremendously polymorphous fantasy about how the queer corpus might encounter temporality and historicity. First, there is no actual event here: Gorge, a fictional character in a film, speaks of another fictional character from a nineteenth-century novel reappearing in Drew's twentieth-century novel, which Drew herself has already destroyed in despair. In fact, because Brougher (or Gorge, or Drew) has conflated the scientist and the monster, not even the "original" Frankenstein appears. Within the scene, this Frankenstein, himself assembled of cadavers with all the historical seams showing, bursts the boundaries of his own physique. A queer reader might understand this as a form of male lactation or as an ejaculation that crosses the divide between adults and children. But perhaps most importantly, we will remember that even in Shelley, the monster's body is not at all a sign of full presence outside of history, nor is it simply a sign of the wounding necessary to enter history, nor even a sign of the discontinuous body of gender nonnormativity. It is an index of temporal heterogeneity — specifically, of dead bodies persisting in the present and the future, of nonreproductive yet still insistently corporeal kinship with the departed. This revised monster's act suggests a historiographic practice wherein the past takes form of something already fragmented, "split," and decaying, to which the present and future are somehow porous in an analog way, and for which bodies are both metaphor and medium. In this sense,

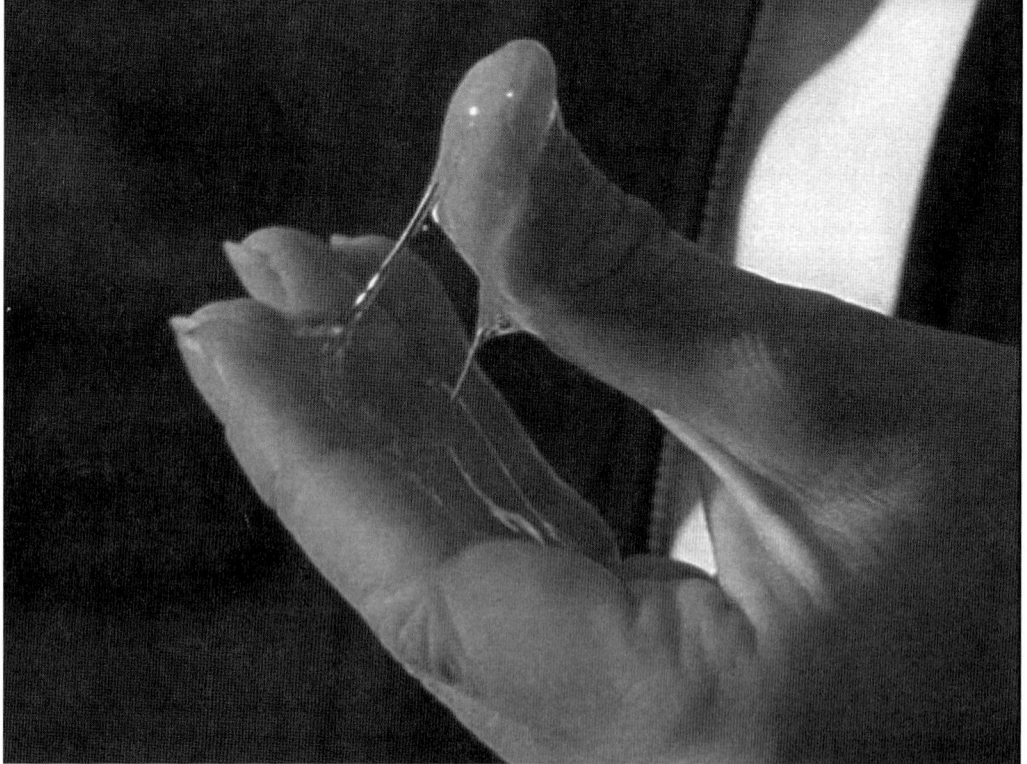

Figure 18.1 The sticky substance (*The Sticky Fingers of Time*).

his body is not a "body" at all but a figure for relations between bodies past and present. It marks the return from the late eighteenth century of a *corporealized* historiography, and, extending *Orlando*'s project, it suggests a future-making project of the sort that contemporary queers might embrace.

Like *Frankenstein* and *Orlando*, Brougher's film desublimates the eroticism of affective historiography, allowing us to think that history is not only what hurts but what arouses, kindles, whets, or itches. In theorizing the relations among the senses, subjectivity, and the social that make historical consciousness possible, *Sticky Fingers* argues, perhaps it is time to return to the orifice, to holes, as Woolf has put it, "big enough to put your finger through." For when Drew and Tucker time travel, they black out and wake up in another era, rubbing their eyes only to find them filled with a clear, viscous liquid, the bodily register of contact with other moments (see Figure 18.1). It's possible that the clear substance that floods their eyes is intended to invoke tears, the bodily response most obviously correlated with the sympathetic histories practiced by the Burkean man of feeling. But the stretchy, slippery properties of this liquid make it look much more like personal lubricant of the sort with which many lesbians of the 1990s became familiar through the grass-roots sex-positive lesbian presses. Taking this substance as a figure for a different kind of encounter with history, we might say that history is what pleasures. In other words, the boundaries of the properly historical, the retreating edge of a legibly historical formation, may appear in or through a directly sexual version of the gothic ecstasy that I referred to at the beginning of this chapter.

If we read Drew's Frankensteinian scene in terms of queer bodily pleasures, then, the little girl matters very much: she is, we can assume, going to eat those lovely tomatoes. In this sense, she is both a feminine subject and, shall we say, a sexual bottom. But in contrast to Freud's and Butler's formulations, Frankenstein's wound passes over from his pain to her pleasure, his openings to hers, without necessarily having to become a phallus at all. Flowing from multiple openings, his fluids fertilize tomatoes to nourish her through the mouth. In short, as with *Orlando*, holes beget holes. Here, Frankenstein's transfer of energies across time appears not as sacrifice but rather as a gender-undifferentiated discharge to be received pleasurably in the future, in a future imagined *as* pleasure. The great surprise of the scene, then, lies in the missing feast it suggests: the hint that erotic bliss may be as potentially "historical" as trauma.

Giorgio Agamben suggests that pleasure could found the new concept of time presently missing from historical materialism: "For everyone there is an immediate and available experience on which a new concept of time could be founded. This is an experience so essential to human beings that an ancient Western myth makes it humankind's original home: it is pleasure."[28] More problematically, he locates that pleasure in man's "originary home," which sounds a great deal like the Kristevian maternal body I critiqued in chapter 1. In contrast, the scene from *Sticky Fingers* offers neither mother nor father in its imagining of relations between time and history, no original, maternal body of plentitude but only a scarred and striated body on the one side, an absent prepubescent one on the other, a dumb vegetable in between, and crucially, the mouth as a tactile rather than a verbal instrument for historical transactions, for scenes of historicist binding. I have argued for the body and the hand as historiographical instruments; let us now turn to the mouth.

In work that has been crucial for queer theory, Nicholas Abraham and Maria Torok describe melancholia in corporeal terms, as the "crypting" of a lost object, an attempt to embed the object into or make it part of the body itself in a process they call "incorporation."[29] Incorporation is the pathological form of introjection, where the lost loved object serves as the means through which the subject reworks its originary erotic autonomy. In introjection, the object is a placeholder for the self whom the subject must return to loving as in primary narcissism, and this process also creates a permeable self capable of integrating the new. In the theory of introjection, time synchs up again, the uninterrupted present corresponds to an integrated self. Incorporation, on the other hand, is out of synch; it produces an unintegrated, Frankensteinian body and psyche. Interestingly, incorporation reveals itself through an oral symptom — a set of behaviors that includes binging on food, or a fetish-word, even a way of speaking, that simultaneously preserves and obscures the loss. Incorporation, then, is another kind of "fat" writing and performance, overloading both the body and the sign in ways reminiscent of Hayes's, Subrin's, and Mitchell's temporal drag.

As with melancholia compared to mourning, the "pathological" form of incorporation seems eminently queerer; it preserves the past *as past*, in a crypt imperfectly sealed off from the present, in a psyche with unpredictable leakages, in a body semiotically and sensually at productive odds with itself. But what are these odds? Despite Abraham and Torok's temporally normalizing logic, what is most crucial about the work on introjection that Torok did by herself is the fact that the past is not wholly defined in terms of trauma. Instead, it consists of latent excitations not yet traversed by the binary between pain and pleasure, preserved and suspended in this very ambivalence and capable of being released *as pleasure* rather than simply being repeated as incomplete mastery over pain. Venturing where Sigmund Freud would not, Torok has theorized a version of the possibility of a fully sensual rather than merely verbal or narrative relationship to the past. In "The Illness of Mourning and the Fantasy of the Exquisite Corpse," she works her way into the most opaque part of Freud's essay on melancholia — the section on mania where Freud notes but fails to theorize the eruptions of frenzied joy that often follow the loss of a loved one. Torok considers a series of unanswered letters in which Freud's contemporary Karl Abraham (no relation to Nicholas) pressed him to consider mania. Apparently, Abraham suggested several times that in the wake of what is supposed to be a terrible event, "mania" very often consists of a sudden influx of erotic feelings, but Freud seems not to have answered this call to examine the phenomenon. Torok suggests that the melancholic's entombed secret is not a loss at all; rather, it is "an erotic effusion" repressed and mnemonically preserved: "*The illness of mourning* [i.e., melancholia] *does not result, as might appear, from the affliction caused by the objectal loss itself, but rather from the feeling of an irreparable crime: of having been overcome with desire, of having been surprised by an overflow of libido at the least appropriate moment, when it would behoove us to be grieved in despair.*"[30]

In their later essay, Abraham and Torok claim that melancholic incorporation itself "perpetuate[s] a clandestine pleasure," a long-ago interrupted idyll of erotic contact with the lost object.[31] For Torok, then, the melancholic psyche is a doubled effect of pleasures past: first, pleasure is severed and remade as unpleasure or trauma; then, the object that gave pleasure itself disappears. Affect, scene, and object reemerge in the crypt, to be released in the grieving subject's sudden lust. In short, as a component of melancholia, mania revisits an inappropriate sexual response from the past.

With Torok's sense of melancholia as a lost idyll preserved, we reach the contemporary form of what I have been calling erotohistoriography: a combination of femme historiography and bottom historiography, a way of imagining the "inappropriate" response of eros in the face of sorrow as a trace of past forms of pleasure. As a mode of reparative criticism, erotohistoriography honors the way queer relations complexly exceed the present, insisting that various queer social practices, especially those involving enjoyable bodily sensations, produce forms of time consciousness — even historical consciousness — that can intervene into the material damage done in the name of development, civilization, and so on. Within these terms, we might imagine ourselves haunted by bliss and not just by trauma; residues of positive affect (idylls, utopias, memories of touch) might be available for queer counter- (or para-) historiographies. Camp performance, as I have described in the previous chapter, might be seen as a kind of historicist *jouissance*, a *frisson* of dead bodies on live ones, fading constructs on emergent ones. Or, what Annamarie Jagose has called "the figure of 'history' — its energizing of the very tropes of before and after" — might be seen in queer patterns of courtship and cruising, in sexual and more broadly tactile encounters, even in identity formations such as butch/femme or FTM, all of which suggestions *Sticky Fingers* makes.[32] Or — and — historicity itself might appear as a structure of *tactile* feeling, a mode of touch, even an erotic practice.

In *The Sticky Fingers of Time*, Drew's unfinished novel seems to have imagined this queer version of continuity, conjuring up a way for the dead to enter our bodies neither through the solely psychoanalytic means of introjection nor through the mass-popular means of psychic channeling. Instead, the lost passage on *Frankenstein* evokes Torok's notion of incorporation, of literally consuming an object that partakes of the lost body and thereby preserving it. If Frankenstein's monster enacts what seems to be a particularly melancholic futurity, the little girl's future will also emerge within the supposedly pathological delights of incorporation as she eats the ripened tomatoes. The name of the woman who narrates this scene, "Gorge," only makes explicit the incorporative logic of Drew's fantasy, for as a noun it means a narrow passage, while as a verb it means to eat to the bursting point.[33] Following the same oral logic of historical transmission, a third character hailing from the future, Ofelia, has the ability to transport others involuntarily across the time-line by kissing them. And most crucially, the film's very first intervention into linear time comes in the form of a murder that takes place in a site dedicated to the oral, if not to the erotic — a dentist's office.

In the scene where Gorge uses Drew's insurance card to have a tooth abscess examined, the Freudian "jaw tooth's aching hole" is an opening into the future for Gorge, insofar as she meets it in the form of a zombie nurse who kills her, and/or an opening into the past for the nurse, insofar as she meets it in the form of Gorge. It's also an opening into the past for Drew, insofar as Ofelia, by kissing Drew, yanks her first back to this scene and then into the cactus and her repressed past. Here teeth seem to signify two ways. In classical psychoanalytic terms, they operate as symbol for the reorganization of Drew's libido in genital terms: kissed back to the scene of a toothache, Drew emerges as all the more lesbian. In terms of temporality, Derrida has described the interval between temporal instances as a diastema, literally a break between different kinds of teeth.[34] In the dentist's office scene, then, teeth are a symbol for the collision of historical moments at the mouth, itself an intersection between the exterior and the interior of the body.

But unlike the Freudian toothache, Gorge's abscess never does get reworked into the phallus. Instead, it replicates itself in any number of references to the mouth as a temporal device. After sleeping with her ex-boyfriend one last time, for instance, Drew remarks that "relapse sucks," condensing temporal regression and the oral in a single phrase. Later, Isaac claims that "time is a pie. You can eat the slices in any order, but you can't eat the same slice twice." We might thus read the film as productively, radically melancholic in some ways, insofar as melancholia is classically regarded as a form of "relapse" to the oral phase in which teeth are absent, neither temporal spacing nor physiological boundaries are stable, and interior and exterior are thoroughly confused. Then, too, these figures make literal Torok's model of incorporating or eating the past. They invoke and dare to affirm the hunger for historical referentiality itself, that pull toward the disappearing moment, however present we know that moment never was.

In this film, orality and digitality also meet one another in a specific trope for history, one that makes good on Orlando's dreamy insertion of a tobacco flake into an ancient prayer book. *Sticky Fingers* plays several times on the film noir and pulp novel cigarette — phallic emblem, instrument of seduction, relay to *après-sex* bliss, and dykedom's most compressed display of manual and labial dexterity. But it transforms that classic cigarette scene into mutual marijuana toking. Sue-Ellen Case argued quite some time ago that we must attend to specific historical formations of erotic coupledom in order to expose poststructuralism's focus on the individual subject — or, as she puts it, we must use butch-femme to turn the Lacanian slash of self-alienation into a lesbian bar.[35] These pot-smoking scenes suggest that now it's time to turn that couple-centered lesbian bar into an even more affiliative historical joint of the sort that *Coal Miner's Granddaughter* and *The Physics of Love* also suggest. For recalling the onetime definition of a joint as "a connecting point of time," the film portrays Tucker and Drew getting wasted in bed twice, once in the 1990s and once in the final sequence.[36] These scenes redescribe the famous Shakespearean joints of time in corporeal terms not limited to the skeletal or to a single body: locations and dislocations occur through membranes and orifices; as with *The Physics of Love*'s intraveneous merging of mother and daughter, here inhalations and exhalations are the very media of temporal contact. In short, *Sticky Fingers* moves from lips and teeth to lungs, correlating Drew's entry into lesbianism with a mild hallucinogenic drug, followed up by an increasing number of shocks to her sense of chronology and temporal location. Each smoking scene hastens the attraction between these denizens of different eras, gesturing toward social possibilities exceeding but not canceling out the sexual: indeed, the toking scenes rework the visual metaphor of Walter Benjamin's "profane illumination" into something like an apostatic high.[37] Drifting the smokers across time, the joint disarticulates bodies and reorganizes subjectivities. Or as Benjamin himself might put it, as if to rework Freud's narcissistic toothache, the dream-state of being stoned "loosens individuality like a hollow tooth."[38]

In short, here historical and temporal disjunction, experienced as illicit pleasure, define and enable queer sociability. Against a developmental and specular logic of "coming out," Brougher's film suggests lesbianism as an oscillation between dreaming and waking states, and a movement among various microtemporalities that do not add up. And smoke is not the only way that history seeps in. The sticky substance that Tucker and Drew find in their eyes after time traveling literalizes the transition from an ocular logic to a tactile one; it exchanges a gay and lesbian history in which lesbians become progressively more visible, for a textural logic suggested by the film's title, in which queer history both announces itself as a suggestively lubricated touch and clings stubbornly to the (proto-?)lesbian body. Tucker also gets continual nosebleeds, a result of the radiation sickness she acquired while watching H-bomb tests in the 1950s before Drew intervened and stopped her from going. As well as needing to be lubricated, then, time travel produces a different set of bodily fluids from those considered vital to biological reproduction, itself the supposed precondition for an enduring humanity and thus for history. Yet in the face of historical rupture, these women's bodies also do not dissolve into sentimental tears. Instead, they discharge something else, some new form of subjectivity neither imprisoned within nor fully free from past forms. The oozy eyeballs and bloody noses turn the certainty of chronology and continuity into unpredictable temporal flows, and they move the biological location of futurity away from the uterus, vaginal canal, or tear ducts, and onto new bodily sites.

These effluvia and their sites of emergence, in turn, evoke a loss of control reducible neither to genitalized orgasm nor to sentimentalism's hydraulic release of desexualized emotions. In *Sticky Fingers* time, and eventually history, are gathered and redispersed through the edges and breaks of the body itself. The film's various seepages suggest corporeal connections across bodies but beyond sex, across historical moments but beyond generationality, across social movements but beyond concepts of activism that relegate sex practice and erotic style to the margins of what can count as political. They are examples of what, following the film critic Laura Marks, might be called *haptic* historiography, ways of negotiating with the past and producing historical knowledge through visceral sensations.[39]

The Dialectics of Feeling

If Woolf emphasizes hands to invoke the pleasures of both reading and writing history, Brougher's use of them also calls forth a historical-material development in which the index finger is key: the invention of the camera. As Walter Benjamin puts it in his essay on Baudelaire, "A touch of the finger now sufficed to fix an event for an unlimited period of time."[40] While previously I discussed the role of the camera in turning reproductive sequence into historical consequence, here I would like to discuss its uses for alternative modes of affiliation across time. For the camera also unfixed the event of representation itself, reducing a series of laborious steps into one push of a button that would then trigger a hidden sequence of automated motions. Indeed, Benjamin traces the temporal work of the camera back to the invention of the match, suggesting that the profane illumination or historiographic flash he describes in his *Theses on the Philosophy of History* does indeed have its literal referent in the act of lighting up: "The invention of the match around the middle of the nineteenth century brought forth a number of innovations which have one thing in common: one abrupt movement of the hand triggers a process of many steps."[41] By the time of the movie camera, the role of the index finger was paradoxical: pushing a button both stopped time, staying the process of change and decay as it captured images one by one, and initiated the inexorably forward movement of frames as the film stock scrolled through. Benjamin also argued, famously, that in stopping time film and photography possessed the power to reveal previously invisible structural elements of a given moment in history, even as their very apparatus effaced material process, labor, and duration. But in his analysis these haptic experiences of "switching, inserting, pressing, and the like" were eventually supplanted by the optic experiences engendered by a city filled with images.[42] By the time Benjamin wrote "The Work of Art in the Era of Mechanical Reproduction," he had relegated the hand to a mere metaphor, speaking of the audience's ability to "grasp" formerly inaccessible artworks and bring them closer.

In contrast, *The Sticky Fingers of Time*, like *Orlando*, both literalizes and lesbianizes the hand that can freeze and reorder time, yet it refuses to develop the results of this act into a properly image-bound dialectic. To put it more simply, Brougher's film retains its medium's commitment to the indexical — not only to the history of the index finger, but to the indexical as the very quality linking film to historiography. For film contains a trace of the light hitting an object. The film's moments of bodily encounters with temporal alterity recall Benjamin's concept of the mimetic faculty, perhaps the most directly corporeal of the several revolutionary cognitive practices he advocates. For Benjamin, mimesis combines similarity on the visual plane and sensuality on the tactile plane. In his essay "On the Mimetic Faculty," he traces the human gift of analogy — another aspect of the aforementioned analog — which relies on the meanings produced by physical contiguity. Analogy, far from being a merely linguistic trope, consists of making and understanding likenesses, from the one-to-one correspondences of children's gestural imitations, through the more abstract signs of dance, through representation via runes and hieroglyphs, to the "nonsensuous similarity" of language itself, a binding element between perceiver and perceived that retains a trace of indexicality.[43] Countering the Saussurian model in which sound-patterns have an arbitrary relation to what they call forth in the mind, Benjamin suggests the possibility of a motivated or material (yet also nonrepresentational) bond between signifier and signified: the semiotic, a lost or decayed imitative element. In short, he grants even speech and writing an indexical trace, a time-binding of past and present.

While Benjamin's theory of mimesis in language has not inspired a school of thought, several media critics in his tradition — most notably Andre Bazin and Roland Barthes — have recognized that cinematography itself is mimetic in the sense Benjamin describes. The camera cannot represent or mime its object without direct contact with the light rays that have touched that object, yet it immediately ceases to be dependent on that object and preserves the trace of a past moment only as light. Crucial to the semiotic, then, is a repressed link to the body (here, the eyes), a buried moment of physical contiguity not unlike Torok's aforementioned erotic idyll. Psychoanalysis tends to locate this moment out of history, in a universalized primal relation to the mother. But Benjamin's essay on Surrealism, which can be read as a companion to the one on mimesis, suggests that the semiotic can be both historicized and brought into view, developed like invisible ink (or like Braille) through a tactile version of thinking.

For as extensions of the mimetic faculty, Benjamin's more fully elaborated concepts of the optical unconscious and the dialectical image paradoxically demand a heightened sense of attention to the body. In his view, the Surrealist project was to think as if intoxicated or dreaming, to master the world of commodities by seizing the revolutionary energies of outmoded objects, juxtaposing them with natural, mythic, or futuristic signs, making them touch one another, sensing the ways in which objects from different times or domains inadvertently repeat one another or exist in a metonymic relationship.[44] Mimesis, that is, is the Surrealistic "grab," the prehensile "seize" of appropriation. It seems more like incorporation, which Torok describes as "instantaneous and magical," than like introjection, with the latter's steady accretion of new capacities and meanings.[45] In these terms, mimesis might be thought of both as the invisible adhesive that binds of otherwise incongruous elements (and thus as the mortar of the dialectical image) and as the physical means of dissolving frozen images back into mobile practices, dead identities into live social acts (and thus as an acid bath for congealed meanings). Broadly thought, Benjaminian mimesis denotes a kinesthetic apprehension of the object-world, albeit one subject to changes in technology that variously demand, repress, or transform the kinetic element of perception, and in doing so historicize this object-world. This tactile register lends itself to the kind of antinarrative leaps across time, the achronic "correspondences" that Benjamin so valued: these are felt as well as seen. Whatever "appears" as a formless brush of one thing against another, a sensual meeting irreducible to resemblance, is a sign of something that the discursive regimes and narrative genres of official history cannot contain — even as they depend on it.

Following Benjamin (as well as Sir James Fraser), Michael Taussig reminds us that mimesis itself has two elements — copying, which depends on the visual apprehension of sameness, and contagious magic, which is more like infiltration and depends on contact. *Sticky Fingers* plays with this double sense of mimesis, with the way that lesbian bodies only seem to copy one another visually, while actually oozing into one another and in doing so mutually reconstellating one another and themselves. As if to follow the logic of the copy, Brougher gave the parts of Drew and Tucker to two actresses who look quite a bit alike. These characters also live in the same apartment at two different moments, and one name actually suggests artistic replication ("Drew" as the past tense of "draw"). But Drew is actually *made of* Tucker, rather than just resembling her, as is Ofelia. Recall that in the film's 1953 plot, the H-bomb test scrambles Tucker's "Code," the DNA-like semiotic substance that makes up the human soul, and this reorganization allows her to travel across the timeline. Knowing this, Ofelia has murdered Tucker, splattering her Code so that it recombines with the Code of people in the future, including herself and Drew. In contrast to the replicative function signaled by Drew's name, then, Tucker's suggests a more active relation between bodies ("Tuck her," "Fuck her," or even "Touch her"), and indeed her body, in the form of its Code, has "touched" Drew's long before they meet. Tucker has likewise touched Ofelia, whose name itself lingers on the sound "feel" (and also brings us back to *Hamlet*'s temporal juggernauts). Finally, it is by tactile appropriation, that is, by the lure of lesbian sex, that Tucker eventually draws Drew into the 1950s to fuck her forever. The film thus moves from copy to contact, turning this latter form of contagious magic into an encounter across time rather than just space.

In this case of tactile appropriation, history — the political unconscious consisting not only of repressed social conflict but also and crucially in this film of effaced or foreclosed social bonds of which lesbianism is only one — opens up to a lesbian hand. Or, following Taussig again, "the history of mimesis flows into the mimesis of history."[46] In other words, we might think of mimetic historiography as a nonrepresentational encounter with traces of the past or future. The very inaccessibility of other times to touch guarantees a binding that cannot be reduced to the literal, the physical — yet cannot be thought elsewise than with the erotic at the center. Mimetic historiography does not privilege the steady cumulation of meaning over time but works in fits and starts, torques and seizures. And mimesis itself is historically contingent: as Benjamin recognized in his description of the role of cinema as a mimetic technology and as Taussig echoes in his phrase "the history of mimesis," the sensorium itself is temporally heterogeneous. Indeed, we might think of Raymond Williams's "structures of feeling" not only as traces of residual, dominant, and emerging modes of production but also as more literal assemblages of older and newer sensations dependent on modes of *re*production — that is, enabled or disabled by mediating technologies and social forms as they come and go, in what I'd like to call a *dialectics* of feeling. To put it simply, we feel through and with representational, technological, and social forms whose histories are uneven and overlapping. This, too, involves the power of the analog, where edges show and make themselves felt.

Sticky Fingers hints at the historical specificity of mimesis and at the erotic power of scrambling mimetic modes when Tucker, hiding in Drew's apartment, attempts to put a compact disc onto a turntable and then to listen to the entertainment center as if it were a radio — here, there are no means of digital conversion that could seamlessly blend one medium and another. Immediately thereafter, Tucker surprises any understanding of her as a diehard lesbian by having sex with her now ex-boyfriend Isaac (doubling Drew's "relapse" with her own ex-boyfriend). Tucker's screwball mixup in Drew's bedroom, prefigured by electronic components and their sensory regimes, moves eroticism beyond the play between male and female, or even the presence and absence of components like the penis, and toward the play between sensations available then and not now, or vice versa.

More broadly, the film's very cinematography mimics the dialectic between seepage and rupture, older and newer modes of sensory engagement, that I have described. Rather than splicing together black-and-white and color film stock to move between the 1950s and the 1990s, for instance, Brougher's cinematographer shot the 1950s sequences in the same color film as the 1990s ones, after which her editor took the color out from the 1950s scenes. As the film's opening scene shifts into the 1990s, the colors and the era literally bleed into Tucker's face, and just as she has found herself with a nosebleed in the black-and-white 1950s, her gummy eyes greet the colorful 1990s. The 1990s scenes and those set in Ofelia's historically indeterminate milieu are not differentiated by color or stock at all, so they too simply fold "naturally" into one another. But the 1970s scenes that Ofelia forces Drew to witness look different, for they were shot on a different color film stock, Fuji color-negative, which Brougher saw as a useful way to duplicate the red-yellow tones and flatness of filmic images from that era. Here, the analog technique of splicing suggests in formal terms that the 1970s are the only era truly out of time or sequence, the one least accessible to the travelers.

And this turns out to be the case: just as Sharon Hayes offers up a dead slogan from the feminist movement, just as Subrin's *Shulie* seems to stall out before "women's lib," *Sticky Fingers* theorizes the limits of erotohistoriography by way of that era. In a scene near the end of the film, Ofelia kisses Drew, thrusting her backward in time to a hotel room in the Poconos, where Drew's family once spent a summer vacation that ended in her parents' divorce. At the time, Drew had passed out during her parents' final argument. But in this revisit, Ofelia and her assistants bind Drew's arms and legs tightly, forcing her to stand in the hotel doorway and watch what she missed when she blacked out as a child: her mother, dressed in a crochet vest and turtleneck, storms out of the hotel shouting, jumps in the family station wagon, and drives off by herself. Drew's mother's actions suggest that like many heterosexual white women of her time, she has come to realize that her marriage is a trap — as she leaves, she shouts that it's not the kids, it's that her husband simply doesn't listen to her. In other words, in this return to the past, what had been a *personal* loss for Drew is here subtly reframed as a political moment, a moment in social time.

Yet unlike other slices of the historical pie in this film, this one is indigestible; unlike other historical portals, this one is impenetrable. For after Drew turns away from the scene, Ofelia transmits Drew's Code into a cactus — an unusable instrument of penetration if ever there was one, whose spiny "fingers" may stick but cannot hold anything. From inside the cactus, Drew relives the blackout that had allowed her to escape from her parents' final argument as a child and learns that during that blackout she had time traveled to discover Tucker's murdered body on the street in 1953. Thus the 1970s were inaccessible to Drew even in their own present tense: having blacked out and gone elsewhere in time, Drew neither remembers nor even

Figure 18.2 Drew watches her mother's departure (*The Sticky Fingers of Time*).

initially experiences her mother's primal feminist scene yet remains, like Elisabeth Subrin, Sharon Hayes, and other artists I have discussed, haunted by it.

As Drew watches her mother's departure from the doorway of the hotel room, Ofelia stands behind her (see Figure 18.2). On the face of it, this staging seems to put past (the mother), present (Drew), and future (Ofelia) in their proper relation. But we can also read this sequence as a rupture of the pattern in which a butch-femme or straight feminist past, a queer 1990s present, and a multiracial cybernetic future mutually illuminate one another. For insofar as Ofelia is played by an African American actress, she — like *Shulie*'s "Negroes" — links the problem of the timeline with the problem of the color line. As Frances Negrón-Muntaner has explored in detail, Brougher's decision to cast an African American woman in the role of Ofelia has implications of which the film is not fully in control.[47] I cannot do justice to Negrón-Muntaner's intricate, psychoanalytically informed argument, which pivots on an understanding of Ofelia as the black phallus who guarantees the time-hopping that engenders a white lesbian relationship. Nor do I wish to perform a racial/racist "rescue" of the film. Rather, I'd like to use Negrón-Muntaner's critique to question the terms of this chapter thus far. Is claiming pleasure for historiography a queer act that nevertheless recapitulates the film's erasure of a specifically black social time, or repeats its disavowal of the founding violence so often enacted upon people of color in the name of white pleasures?

It's fair to say that the color-blindness that Brougher claims animated her choice of actors is also a form of historical blindness: intentionally or not, she cast Ofelia as the "time freak" (the film's words) from a de-historicized future, while casting the two white women and the white man as representatives of particular decades. Ofelia seems to have control over the timeline, but she has no access to the markers of historicity; her red satin kimono and straightened updo could come from almost any twentieth-century moment. This may be an attempt to avoid the cheesiness of futuristic costuming, but it does contrast with the loving attention to period detail lavished on the other characters, the props, and the setting. Just as Subrin's "Negroes" are trapped in the post office, Ofelia's own era, whenever it is, is limited to interior domestic scenes in a suburb. For instance, a long scene takes place in Ofelia's home on Staten Island, with no evidence of the public street life that marks the film's 1950s and 1990s alike, or of the protofeminist anti-domesticity that marks Drew's mother's 1970s in this film. Neither does Ofelia have an interior life: despite her suggestively Shakespearean moniker, she is the least melancholic character. While the others brood their way across the timeline, she continually and enigmatically smiles. Nor does she black out like Drew, or bleed like Tucker, or leak around the eyes like both white women. Ofelia, then, can exist in the past and the future and perhaps in the subjunctive tense, but she neither fully resides in her own historical moment nor has a body that opens out into historical time. In fact, the whole thrust of the film is to get Drew back to the moment before Tucker sees the H-bomb, thereby preventing Ofelia from ever breaking the timeframe of her nonhistory to murder Tucker in 1953. And Drew is successful; she steals Isaac's and Tucker's plane tickets to Nevada, leaving Isaac out of the love triangle, herself and Tucker happily stuck in the 1950s in sanitary white coupledom, and Ofelia out of both time and love. African American female interventions — especially if we read Ofelia as, allegorically, the force of black feminism and/or lesbianism in and before the 1970s — are effaced in both the film's present and its past and relegated to an unspecified future that may not even happen. Ofelia has "no future" in a way that belies the power of queerness alone, as Lee Edelman has described it, to signal destruction of linear political imaginings.[48] Or, as the film puts it, Ofelia now has "nothing to kill but time itself."

Ofelia's character asks us to consider: is queer "time binding" — even, specifically, the elliptical time-hopping that seems to animate the white butch-femme styles that Drew and Tucker play with — a way to willfully forget interventions into lesbian history by people of color? Is it a way of claiming correspondences across time that represses what to a white body might not even be tangible? Perhaps we might even pause to ask whether some white butch-femme practices of the 1990s and beyond, grounded as they have been in a certain kind of time-play with the 1950s rather than in any genuine engagement with the coeval gender systems of other contemporary ethnic groups, may also engage Jim Crow as well as Joan Crawford or Johnny Cash. Or perhaps we might ask, *whose* 1950s are available for this kind of play? In other words, if the film is read as an excursus on lesbian history that transforms the latter into a genuine erotohistoriography, Ofelia's sudden blockage in the 1970s of the very time-binding she has seemed to catalyze throughout the film may tell a different story. For even when the butch-femme renaissance of the 1980s and 1990s questioned gender separatism, its theorists and practitioners did not always engage with racial segregation, with the history or present tense of lesbians of color.[49] Furthermore, though I would like to be able to imagine a broadly applicable historiographic practice grounded in bodily pleasures reclaimed, the specifics of particular racialized histories include bodily experiences that do not necessarily center on the sexual in the way I have described and may thus demand more careful working out.

Erotohistoriography *Noir*

Here is one such example of what such working out might look like (the other will follow in the next chapter). In the 1970s scene I have described, Drew stands at the doorway of the hotel room, unable to enter the past, with Ofelia standing behind her as an augur of things to come. Ofelia's own body thereby registers the very future to which Drew's back is turned like the Benjaminian angel of history. Looking backward in time, Drew witnesses the personal catastrophes of a divorce and the social irruption of the women's movement. But she cannot see the H-bomb, the global catastrophe that has made all the film's characters possible. As a woman of color Ofelia has the only body that even remotely registers what the film elides — the decimation of and damage to Asian populations in Japanese and Hawaiian nuclear test sites, of Native American populations in Nevada sites, of poor and brown bodies compromised by nuclear and other toxic waste dumped into regions whose populations are politically marginalized. Though Tucker's typewriter, Drew's computer, and even Isaac's time-traveling fingers could represent technological developments that have led to greater expressive freedom for women and queers, the nuclear holocaust that haunts the film is, as Benjamin puts it, "proof that society has not been mature enough to incorporate technology as its organ."[50] The only significant piece of vintage stock footage in the entire film is a short filmstrip of an atomic bomb test, which is spliced into a montage at the beginning and therefore never appears diegetically within the film. The H-bomb, then, is even less accessible in the formal terms of editing than the scenes shot on the Fuji stock make the 1970s. As Ofelia looks out the doorway into the past, perhaps only she can see beyond the deracinated 1970s that Drew witnesses, and even beyond Tucker's sanitized 1950s, into the technological development that has caused one of the United States' most potent historical blackouts and, arguably, a continuation of its genocidal policies toward people of color.

How does Ofelia feel historical or historically, if she is blocked from both triumphalist linear narrative and from erotohistoriography, white-lesbian-style? In cinema, Gilles Deleuze suggests, tactility can figure a release from the visual and its enchainment with cause-effect relations, only if the hand can "relinquish its prehensile and motor functions to content itself with a pure touching."[51] Shelley, and to a greater extent Woolf, offer up literary versions of this relinquishment: the monster's body figures a "pure touching" of past and present, and Orlando's hand pokes, prods, caresses, penetrates as opposed to grasping. But Ofelia rejects this pastoral vision of what an appendage might do. For her body alone incorporates an organ that registers the greatest number of temporalities at once and can both penetrate and encircle. In addition to engineering Isaac's interestingly les-bionic fingers, Ofelia has designed a prehensile tail for her own body. Perhaps this detail unwittingly invokes racist equations of African Americans and animals. But juxtaposed with Ofelia's status as symbol of the future, the self-manufactured tail hints at what Mark Dery and others, following Sun-Ra, have called "Afro-futurism" — a critical dialogue between technoculture and racial justice crucial for populations consistently troped as primitives.[52] Ofelia teasingly remarks that her tail "even has extra chakras," which at least locates the tail in *some* culture or other. Given the number of inside jokes in the film, this culture is very likely that of the 1990s yoga craze, with all its appropriations of non-Western practices and icons. But Ofelia's teasing suggestion also tells of other possibilities. Iconographically serving as a weapon, an emblem of godlike or human powers, an element of the Indian flag, the chakra encompasses the differential times of body, religion, and nation; that is, it condenses linear time without losing history.

While Ofelia's tail is not a time-travel machine per se, it does constitute the film's stickiest "finger of time"; it is the digit that most effectively stalls the machinery of escape from the past and future into the present. Midway through the film, when Isaac takes Drew to Ofelia's Staten Island home of the future, Drew tries to sneak back into her own timeframe. As she touches a doorknob, Ofelia's tail suddenly strikes out like a whip and encircles Drew's leg and then folds back to drag her away from the door (see Figure 18.3). Following Taussig, we can see Ofelia's tail as a historiographic whip, quite literally "dislocating the chains of [historical] concordance with one hand, reconstellating them in accord with a mimetic snap, with the other," as she consistently refuses to grant Drew access to and ownership over a continuous past and forces her to understand relations between events Drew cannot remember.[53] Ofelia has already remarked to Drew in the

Figure 18.3 Ofelia's tail encircles Drew's leg (*The Sticky Fingers of Time*).

1970s scene, "You can't travel. You're not strong enough." Only Ofelia herself, she seems to suggest, has the capacity to sustain competing marks of historicity on her own body, to have a physiology, sartorial style, and gestural repertoire that do not unfold inevitably out of one another — even by way of the discontinuous resemblances of Surrealism, the dialectical image, or camp. Ofelia's tail is at once the sign of an invented past and a self-generated future, of atavism and prolepsis, of the natural and the constructed, of phallicism and invagination, of remainders and ruptures. Far from *being* an anachronism, like Tucker and Drew in their temporal switchings, Ofelia fits into neither and both of their historical moments and *wears* an anachronism on her body, as if to materialize the meeting of history with bodies, desire, and even — insofar as the tail is prosthetic — commodities. Yet the vestigial/futuristic tail is also the paradoxical sign of society's longed-for maturity, what Benjamin calls its ability to incorporate technology into its organ, except that here society, technology, and the social organ include the sexual body.

Like the body of Frankenstein's monster, like *Orlando*'s many fingers, Ofelia's tail is a crucial binding device that leashes bodies to one another even across time. With her ability to literally take hold, to seize, to grasp the past and bring it into conjunction with the present, to rub the two violently together, Ofelia is the sign of an embodied, frictive historical method that cannot be contained even by the film's oral and manual logics. Hers is a truly *epidermal* temporality, one that substitutes black skin's tangibility for its visibility and the historical burden the latter has borne. Furthermore, unlike Drew or the United States, Ofelia does not "black out." Though this may suggest that she does not have an unconscious, as Negrón-Muntaner argues, I think it also indicates her status as the film's best historiographer, the one who doesn't black out blackness. Ofelia neither forgets nor repudiates the past, but she also refuses to dissolve it into something with which she unproblematically identifies. Through the looking-glass of Frankenstein's tale is Ofelia's tail, which refuses the (often racialized) sacrificial logic of even queer becoming. As an erotohistoriographic tool, Ofelia's tail counts more than any other digit and points to the way that the movement of history on and between particular bodies can encode and incite collective desires.

As it turns out, Ofelia has the most promisingly Frankensteinian body of all the ones I have described in this chapter. First, she resembles Victor Frankenstein in her capacity to engineer the human and her occasional appearance in a white lab coat. Second, born like the monster of a scientific experiment (here, in the form of the H-bomb), Ofelia turns against her progenitor Tucker, whose Code has created her. Possessed of a physique that amalgamates flesh and technology, past and future, and seemingly chained to the past as she vengefully chases Tucker and Drew across the timeline, Ofelia, like the monster and his creator, turns her white masters into slaves. Her zombie nurses, her technological subordination of Isaac, her lashing tail suggest that if the encounter with history has erotic dimensions, these must be also squared with the use of particular bodies — black bodies, slave bodies — to motor modernity's "progress." Reading backward through Ofelia, it is possible to see Shelley's Frankenstein not only as a novel about relations between men across space and time but as a novel about relations between black people and white people. Indeed, as the literary critic Elizabeth Young has persuasively demonstrated, Frankenstein's monster was a powerful metaphor in both abolitionist and anti-abolitionist discourse, where it figured the construction of a black underclass with the potential to turn against its "masters."[54] Frankenstein's questions about absolute power and enslavement, though, interlace not only with its subtle intimations of racial difference (figured most powerfully, perhaps, by the image of a monster with "yellow skin and black hair" bounding across a relentlessly white Arctic snowscape) but also with its famous homoeroticism. If Victor and the monster are master and slave, they are also mutually desirous, albeit in terms of the paranoia, projection, and identification that often accompany disavowed lust.[55] Ofelia's tail, then, also shadows forth the specter of interracial sadomasochism that at least retrospectively haunts Frankenstein. Sadomasochism, or leathersex, is all about wearing the skins of the dead: as "skin drag," leathersex invokes the "stitching" of skin onto body, and its traffic in skins can be read as a discourse on blackness even when it does not involve people of African descent. Conversely, Ofelia's tail reminds us that Frankenstein haunts sadomasochism, for if S/M's skins are not precisely those of the human dead, they do come to life, warming up and moving with the body they clothe.

What happens, then, when sex mimics the postures and costuming of chattel slavery? Would that be temporal drag's most embarrassing performance, erotohistoriography's inverse nightmare? Or with S/M, might we risk claiming the most monstrous — some would say — mode of bodying forth a past we can barely look in the face?

Notes

1.   On the gendering of "sensory" history, see Smith, The Gender of History.
2.   Halberstam, Skin Shows, 30.
3.   Habermas, The Structural Transformation of the Public Sphere, 43–50.

4. The phrase "publishing the family" is from Howard, *Publishing the Family*.

5. Goode, *Sentimental Masculinity and the Rise of History, 1790–1890*, 161.

6. Gordon, *Ghostly Matters*.

7. Goode, "Dryasdust Antiquarianism," 63 and *Sentimental Masculinity*, 71.

8. In fact, Goode notes that Mary Wollstonecraft's *Vindication of the Rights of Men* condemned sentimental history. *Sentimental Masculinity*, 13 and 30.

9. Ibid., 79–86.

10. Ibid., 45–46. In *The Gender of History* Smith attributes some of these modes of doing history to amateur female historiographers.

11. Goode, *Sentimental Masculinity*, 105.

12. Bentley, "Family, Humanity, Polity," 327–28.

13. Goode, *Sentimental Masculinity*, 39.

14. Ibid., 34.

15. Shelley, *Frankenstein*, 155. Hereafter cited in text by page number.

16. Goode, *Sentimental Masculinity*, 84–85.

17. My thanks to Timothy Morton for pointing out the relevance of this passage to my larger discussion.

18. For a history of "the spirit of the age," see Chandler, *England in 1819*, 105–8 and 125.

19. Ibid., 274.

20. Woolf, *Orlando*, ix, vii. Hereafter cited in text by page number.

21. Vita Sackville-West's son Nigel Nicolson called *Orlando* "the longest and most charming love letter in literature" in his *Portrait of a Marriage*, 202.

22. Both quotes are from Carla Freccero, *Queer/Early/Modern*, 102.

23. I follow Ann Cvetkovich's call for thinking an expansive receptivity in terms of actual lesbian sex acts in "Recasting Receptivity."

24. Material about the production of *The Sticky Fingers of Time* is taken from the commentary of the director, Hilary Brougher, and the cinematographer, Ethan Mass, on the DVD of the film distributed by Strand Releasing.

25. Benjamin, "The Work of Art in the Age of Mechanical Reproduction," 233.

26. Dinshaw, *Getting Medieval*, 21. See also Pellegrini, "Touching the Past."

27. Fradenburg and Freccero, "The Pleasures of History," 373.

28. Agamben, "Time and History," 104. Thanks to Gregory Dobbins for bringing this essay to my attention.

29. Abraham and Torok, "Mourning or Melancholia." Following Torok via Butler, we might think of drag, tattooing, piercing, hormones, and other body modifications up to and including phalloplasties as ways of incorporating lost attachments.

30. "Erotic effusion," Torok, "The Illness of Mourning," 103; long quote, 110, her emphasis.

31. Abraham and Torok, "Mourning or Melancholia," 131.

32. Jagose, *Inconsequence*, xi.

33. Thanks to Brad Epps for pushing me to think about these names.

34. Derrida, *Specters of Marx*, 64.

35. Case, "Toward a Butch-Femme Aesthetic," 295.

36. *Oxford English Dictionary* online, 2nd ed. (1989), "joint," n. 6 (*Obs. rare*).

37. Chisholm, "The City of Collective Memory," 124. I take my analysis of smoke in part from the Harlem Renaissance writer Bruce Nugent's short story "Smoke, Lillies [*sic*] and Jade," first published in 1926 in the journal *Fire!*, and Faulkner's use of breath and dust in *Absalom, Absalom!* (1937).

38. Benjamin, "Surrealism" (1929). The translation "hollow tooth" is Richter's, in his *Walter Benjamin and the Corpus of Autobiography*, 35.

39. Marks writes that "haptic *perception* is usually defined by psychologists as the combination of tactile, kinesthetic, and proprioceptive functions, the way we experience touch both on the surface of and inside our bodies ... In haptic *visuality*, the eyes themselves function like organs of touch." Marks, *The Skin of the Film*, 162.
40. Benjamin, "On Some Motifs in Baudelaire," 175.
41. Ibid., 174.
42. Ibid.
43. Benjamin, "On the Mimetic Faculty," 334.
44. Benjamin, "Surrealism."
45. Torok, "The Illness of Mourning," 113.
46. Taussig, *Mimesis and Alterity*, xviii.
47. Negrón-Muntaner, "Ofelia's Kiss."
48. Edelman, *No Future*.
49. Some foundational thinking about butch-femme in the 1980s came from women of color: see Moraga and Hollibaugh, "What We're Rollin' Around in Bed With"; Moraga's *Loving in the War Years*; and the oral histories in Kennedy and Davis, *Boots of Leather, Slippers of Gold*. Yet the racial axis of butch-femme gender practices disappeared from view in slightly later classic works such as Case, "Toward a Butch-Femme Aesthetic"; Faderman, *Odd Girls and Twilight Lovers*; and Rubin, "Of Catamites and Kings."
50. Benjamin, "The Work of Art in the Age of Mechanical Reproduction," 242.
51. Deleuze, *Cinema 2*, 12.
52. See Dery, "Black to the Future," 180.
53. Taussig, *Mimesis and Alterity*, 19.
54. Young, *Black Frankenstein*.
55. See Sedgwick, *Between Men*.

References

Abraham, Nicholas and Maria Torok. "Mourning *or* Melancholia: Introjection *versus* Incorporation." *The Shell and the Kernel: Renewals of Psychoanalysis*, vol. 1, ed. Nicholas T. Rand, 125–38. Chicago: University of Chicago Press, 1994.

Agamben, Georgio. "Time and History: Critique of the Instant and the Continuum." *Infancy and History: The Destruction of Experience*, 91–105. New York: Verso, 1993.

Benjamin, Walter. "On Some Motifs in Baudelaire." (1939). *Illuminations*, ed. Hannah Arendt, 155–200. New York: Schocken Books, 1968.

Benjamin, Walter. "On the Mimetic Faculty." (1933). *Reflections: Essays, Aporisms, Autobiographical Writings*, ed. Peter Demetz, 333–36. New York: Schocken Books, 1978.

Benjamin, Walter. "Surrealism: The Last Snapshot of the European Intelligentsia." (1929). *Reflections: Essays, Aporisms, Autobiographical Writings*, ed. Peter Demetz, 177–92. New York: Schocken Books, 1978.

Benjamin, Walter. "The Work of Art in the Age of Mechanical Reproduction." (1935). *Illuminations*, ed. Hannah Arendt, 217–51. New York: Schocken Books, 1968.

Bentley, Colene. "Family, Humanity, Polity: Theorizing the Basis and Boundaries of Political Community in Frankenstein." *Criticism* 47, no. 3 (summer 2005): 325–51.

Case, Sue-Ellen. "Toward a Butch-Femme Aesthetic." *The Lesbian and Gay Studies Reader*, ed. Henry Abelove, Michèle Aina Barale, and David Halperin, 294–306. New York: Routledge, 1994.

Chandler, James. *England in 1819: The Politics of Literary Culture and the Case of Romantic Historicism*. Chicago: University of Chicago Press, 1999.

Chisholm, Dianne. "The City of Collective Memory." *GLQ* 7, no. 2 (2001): 195–203.

Cvetkovich, Ann. "Recasting Receptivity: Femme Sexualities." *Lesbian Erotics*, ed. Karla Jay, 125–46. New York: New York University Press, 1995.

Deleuze, Gilles. *Cinema 2: The Time-Image*. Trans. Hugh Tomlinson and Robert Galeta. Minneapolis: University of Minnesota Press, 1989.

Derrida, Jaques. *Specters of Marx: The State of the Debt, the Work of Mourning, and the New International*. Trans. Peggy Kamuf. New York: Routledge Classic Editions, 2006

Dery, Mark. "Black to the Future: Interviews with Samuel R. Delany, Greg Tate, and Tricia Rose." *Flame Wars: The Discourse of Cyberculture*, ed. Mark Dery, 179–222. Durham, N.C.: Duke University Press, 1995.

Dinshaw, Carolyn. *Getting Medieval: Sexualities and Communities, Pre- and Post-Modern*. Durham, N.C.: Duke University Press, 1999.

Edelman, Lee. *No Future: Queer Theory and the Death Drive*. Durham, N.C.: Duke University Press, 2004.

Faderman, Lillian. *Odd Girls and Twilight Lovers: A History of Lesbian Life in Twentieth Century America*. New York: Columbia University Press, 1991.

Faulkner, William. *Absalom, Absalom!* (1936). New York: Modern Library, 1993.

Fradenburg, Louise (now L. O. Aranye), and Carla Freccero. "The Pleasures of History." *GLQ* 1, no. 4 (1995): 371–84.

Freccero, Carla. *Queer/Early/Modern*. Durham, N.C.: Duke University Press, 2006.

Goode, Mike. "Dryasdust Antiquarianism and Soppy Masculinity: The Waverley Novels and the Gender of History." *Representations* 82 (spring 2003): 52–86.

Goode, Mike. *Sentimental Masculinity and the Rise of History, 1790–1890*. Cambridge: Cambridge University Press, 2009.

Gordon, Avery. *Ghostly Matters: Haunting and the Sociological Imagination*. Minneapolis: University of Minnesota Press, 2007.

Habermas, Jürgen. *The Structural Transformation of the Public Sphere*. Trans. Thomas Burger. Cambridge, Mass.: MIT Press, 1991.

Halberstam, Judith. *Skin Shows: Gothic Horror and the Technology of Monsters*. Durham, N.C.: Duke University Press, 1995.

Howard, June. *Publishing the Family*. Durham, N.C.: Duke University Press, 2001.

Jagose, Annamarie. *Inconsequence: Lesbian Representation and the Logic of Sequence*. Ithaca, N.Y.: Cornell University Press, 2002.

Kennedy, Elizabeth, and Madeline Davis. *Boots of Leather, Slippers of Gold: The History of a Lesbian Community*. New York: Routledge, 1993.

Marks, Laura. *The Skin of the Film: Intercultural Cinema, Embodiment, and the Senses*. Durham, N.C.: Duke University Press, 2000.

Moraga, Cherríe. *Loving in the War Years: Lo Que Nunca Pasó Sus Labios*. Boston: South End Press, 1983.

Moraga, Cherríe, and Amber Hollibaugh. "What We're Rollin' Around in Bed With: Sexual Silences in Feminism." *Powers of Desire: The Politics of Sexuality*, ed. Ann Snitow, Christine Stansell, and Sharon Thompson, 440–59. New York: Monthly Review Press, 1983.

Negrón-Muntaner, Frances. "Racing *The Sticky Fingers of Time*." *GLQ* 5, no. 3 (1999): 425–35.

Nicolson, Nigel. *Portrait of a Marriage: Vita Sackville-West and Harold Nicolson*. New York: Atheneum, 1973.

Nugent, Richard Bruce. "Smoke, Lillies and Jade." (1926). *Gay Rebel of the Harlem Renaissance: Selections from the Work of Richard Nugent*, ed. Thomas Wirth, 75–87. Durham, N.C.: Duke University Press, 2002.

Pellegrini, Ann. "Touching the Past; or, Hanging Chad." *Journal of the History of Sexuality* 10, no. 2 (2001): 185–94.

Richter, Gerhardt. *Walter Benjamin and the Corpus of Autobiography*. Detroit: Wayne State University Press, 2000.

Rubin, Gayle. "Of Catamites and Kings: Reflections on Butch, Gender, and Boundaries." *The Persistent Desire: A Femme-Butch Reader*, ed. Joan Nestle, 466–82. Boston: Alyson Publications, 1992.

Sedgwick, Eve Kosofsky. *Between Men: English Literature and Male Homosocial Desire*. New York: Columbia University Press, 1985.

Shelley, Mary. *Frankenstein, or, The Modern Prometheus*. (1831). New York: Modern Library, 1999.

Smith, Bonnie. *The Gender of History: Men, Women, and Historical Practice*. Cambridge, Mass.: Harvard University Press, 1998.

Taussig, Michael. *Mimesis and Alterity: A Particular History of the Senses*. New York: Routledge, 1993.

Torok, Maria, "The Illness of Mourning and the Fantasy of the Exquisite Corpse." *The Shell and the Kernel: Renewals of Psychoanalysis*, vol. 1, ed. Nocholas T. Rand, 107–24. Chicago: University of Chicago Press, 1994.

Woolf, Virginia. *Orlando: A Biography*. (1928). New York: Harcourt Brace Jovanovich, 1973.

Young, Elizabeth. *Black Frankenstein: The Making of an American Metaphor*. New York: New York University Press, 2008.

Part 5 Film's Political Power

Introduction

The image of a young girl who is being paraded on a television chat show as a witch is both ridiculous and horrific (Figure P5.1). The child is dressed in robes and headwear that swamp her, and her steady, composed gaze belies her vulnerability. *I Am Not a Witch* (2017), directed by Rungano Nyoni, tells the story of a girl named Shula (Maggie Mulubwa) who lives in a Zambian village and is accused of being a witch. Shula is sent to live in a community with older women who have also been deemed witches, and whose freedom is curtailed by white ribbons to stop them from flying away. These images contain beauty and horror, and the film sits uneasily on a breathtaking seesaw between comedy and tragedy. Inspired by real-life accusations of witchcraft in Zambia, Rungano Nyoni's debut feature film highlights misogyny and superstition, but also financial extortion and cynical exploitation.

I Am Not a Witch is a powerful and unforgettable film that uses stunning cinematography, uncomfortable comedy and social satire to create a feminist critique of the abuse and imprisonment of women who are deemed to be witches. This calls attention to the complex ways in which a film can be crafted to both increase knowledge, unsettle, and draw attention to oppressive and exploitative practices. The bold and revolutionary pieces in this Part challenge us to rethink and reconceive fundamental ideas about the raced and gendered and disabled body, in our work and in our viewing, demonstrating film's feminist political power and bringing it into the purview of feminist film philosophy.

The collection of essays and speeches by Audre Lorde in *Sister Outsider* is a wealth of inspirational, challenging and provocative material which can support and inspire philosophical thinking about film. In 'Uses of the Erotic: the Erotic as Power' she sets out her arguments for women to be in touch with our erotic feelings and to recognize our power which has been repressed and devalued within western society. Lorde says that empowering ourselves through embracing the erotic will change our ways of being in society, releasing creativity and joy. This is so relevant to thinking through innumerable women characters in film, who are objectified and victimized, with no outlet for their eroticism in stories that close them down and punish them for sexuality and independence. As a means of analysing women in film, and identifying the conditions that crush them in racist, patriarchal and anti-erotic narratives (and societies), this generative concept unlocks possibilities for both understanding those that exist and creating powerfully erotic and unleashed women characters in future.

'Whose pussy is this?' asks bell hooks in her reflection upon Spike Lee's *She's Gotta Have It*. Having been told she shouldn't miss it because it is about a liberated black woman, bell hooks and her friends go along to the cinema. It is a generous and authentic model of recording her and her friends' response to the film which opens out the essay in a mode of inclusive activity and contemporaneity. hooks likens the film to *The Color Purple* in terms of its power to generate discussions of black feminism and to reveal ignorance of feminist politics. This essay alongside Lorde's inevitably begs the question as to whether Nola Darling (Tracy

Figure P5.1 Shula on the Chat Show (*I am Not a Witch*).

Camilla Johns), the protagonist of the Spike Lee film, is a woman in touch with erotic power, or whether she is a perfect example of a woman character who needs to be. One scene, hooks argues, exemplifies 'how cinema can be effectively used to raise consciousness about political concerns'. This film overall, however, needs to be aware of the 'same old sexist content in a new and more interesting form'.

Rosi Braidotti calls for an overhaul of the Humanities away from the human as its subject, and most especially the man. In the 'posthuman era of the anthropocene', universities, Braidotti argues, need to move the activity of thinking into the real world: 'The epistemic and the ethical walk hand in hand in the complicated landscapes of the third millennium.' The university needs to become a 'multi-versity', focusing on community and independent research, forging new disciplinary relationships and influencing the present and the future. I include this piece because it suggests the need for scholars to embrace new disciplines and subjects on a newly configured playing field, where there is more than enough room for feminist film philosophers and our critical, theoretical and collaborative skills.

In her essay 'Notes on an Alternative Model – Neither/Nor', Hortense Spillers tackles a difficult concept with a long history and which remains a site of contestation and controversy. The figure of the 'tragic mulatto/a' is familiar from literature and cinema, and indeed Hollywood in the 1950s seems to have been obsessed with casting the top female stars of the time to play women who were wrestling with a secret about their racial background: Elizabeth Taylor in *Raintree County* (1957), Ava Gardner in *Showboat* (1951), Audrey Hepburn in *The Unforgiven* (1960). Spillers unpacks the raced and gendered mythologies that surround the character of the 'mulatta', and the mysterious notions about blood and sex – and judgement – which persist.

Jane Stadler's work engages with the intention and attention involved in our ethical understanding of film. Using two films about women who live with horrific domestic abuse, *Once Were Warriors* (1994) and *Nil By Mouth* (1997), Stadler demonstrates how 'moral vision' (the term used by Iris Murdoch in her essay in this volume) at the cinema requires sensitive attunement to particular situations of characters. Through close formal analysis, calling on the work of Martha Nussbaum, Vivian Sobchack, Simone Weil and others, Stadler meticulously sets out the complexity of perception cultivated by film goers, and the rewards that ensue. Both films situate domestic violence as a matter of moral and political concern, precisely through the sensitivity and detail of the depiction of the characters. Stadler stresses the intersubjective involvement in difficult scenes of violence, and the complex family situations that surround the women, and how the very fact that the films are on screens that are within our visual field, rather than immersing us, enables contemplative reflection in conceptual terms. For Stadler, this type of attentive engagement has a vital political potential, and needs to call our attention to those whose stories are not told and who are underrepresented.

19 Uses of the Erotic: the Erotic as Power

AUDRE LORDE

There are many kinds of power, used and unused, acknowledged or otherwise. The erotic is a resource within each of us that lies in a deeply female and spiritual plane, firmly rooted in the power of our unexpressed or unrecognized feeling. In order to perpetuate itself, every oppression must corrupt or distort those various sources of power within the culture of the oppressed that can provide energy for change. For women, this has meant a suppression of the erotic as a considered source of power and information within our lives.

We have been taught to suspect this resource, vilified, abused, and devalued within western society. On the one hand, the superficially erotic has been encouraged as a sign of female inferiority; on the other hand, women have been made to suffer and to feel both contemptible and suspect by virtue of its existence.

It is a short step from there to the false belief that only by the suppression of the erotic within our lives and consciousness can women be truly strong. But that strength is illusory, for it is fashioned within the context of male models of power.

As women, we have come to distrust that power which rises from our deepest and nonrational knowledge. We have been warned against it all our lives by the male world, which values this depth of feeling enough to keep women around in order to exercise it in the service of men, but which fears this same depth too much to examine the possibilities of it within themselves. So women are maintained at a distant/inferior position to be psychically milked, much the same way ants maintain colonies of aphids to provide a life-giving substance for their masters.

But the erotic offers a well of replenishing and provocative force to the woman who does not fear its revelation, nor succumb to the belief that sensation is enough.

The erotic has often been misnamed by men and used against women. It has been made into the confused, the trivial, the psychotic, the plasticized sensation. For this reason, we have often turned away from the exploration and consideration of the erotic as a source of power and information, confusing it with its opposite, the pornographic. But pornography is a direct denial of the power of the erotic, for it represents the suppression of true feeling. Pornography emphasizes sensation without feeling.

The erotic is a measure between the beginnings of our sense of self and the chaos of our strongest feelings. It is an internal sense of satisfaction to which, once we have experienced it, we know we can aspire. For having experienced the fullness of this depth of feeling and recognizing its power, in honor and self-respect we can require no less of ourselves.

Paper delivered at the Fourth Berkshire Conference on the History of Women, Mount Holyoke College, 25 August 1978. First published as a pamphlet by Out & Out Books. Now published as a pamphlet by Kore Press.

It is never easy to demand the most from ourselves, from our lives, from our work. To encourage excellence is to go beyond the encouraged mediocrity of our society is to encourage excellence. But giving in to the fear of feeling and working to capacity is a luxury only the unintentional can afford, and the unintentional are those who do not wish to guide their own destinies.

This internal requirement toward excellence which we learn from the erotic must not be misconstrued as demanding the impossible from ourselves nor from others. Such a demand incapacitates everyone in the process. For the erotic is not a question only of what we do; it is a question of how acutely and fully we can feel in the doing. Once we know the extent to which we are capable of feeling that sense of satisfaction and completion, we can then observe which of our various life endeavors bring us closest to that fullness.

The aim of each thing which we do is to make our lives and the lives of our children richer and more possible. Within the celebration of the erotic in all our endeavors, my work becomes a conscious decision – a longed-for bed which I enter gratefully and from which I rise up empowered.

Of course, women so empowered are dangerous. So we are taught to separate the erotic demand from most vital areas of our lives other than sex. And the lack of concern for the erotic root and satisfactions of our work is felt in our disaffection from so much of what we do. For instance, how often do we truly love our work even at its most difficult?

The principal horror of any system which defines the good in terms of profit rather than in terms of human need, or which defines human need to the exclusion of the psychic and emotional components of that need – the principal horror of such a system is that it robs our work of its erotic value, its erotic power and life appeal and fulfillment. Such a system reduces work to a travesty of necessities, a duty by which we earn bread or oblivion for ourselves and those we love. But this is tantamount to blinding a painter and then telling her to improve her work, and to enjoy the act of painting. It is not only next to impossible, it is also profoundly cruel.

As women, we need to examine the ways in which our world can be truly different. I am speaking here of the necessity for reassessing the quality of all the aspects of our lives and of our work, and of how we move toward and through them.

The very word *erotic* comes from the Greek word *eros*, the personification of love in all its aspects – born of Chaos, and personifying creative power and harmony. When I speak of the erotic, then, I speak of it as an assertion of the lifeforce of women; of that creative energy empowered, the knowledge and use of which we are now reclaiming in our language, our history, our dancing, our loving, our work, our lives.

There are frequent attempts to equate pornography and eroticism, two diametrically opposed uses of the sexual. Because of these attempts, it has become fashionable to separate the spiritual (psychic and emotional) from the political, to see them as contradictory or antithetical. "What do you mean, a poetic revolutionary, a meditating gunrunner?" In the same way, we have attempted to separate the spiritual and the erotic, thereby reducing the spiritual to a world of flattened affect, a world of the ascetic who aspires to feel nothing. But nothing is farther from the truth. For the ascetic position is one of the highest fear, the gravest immobility. The severe abstinence of the ascetic becomes the ruling obsession. And it is one not of self-discipline but of self-abnegation.

The dichotomy between the spiritual and the political is also false, resulting from an incomplete attention to our erotic knowledge. For the bridge which connects them is formed by the erotic – the sensual – those physical, emotional, and psychic expressions of what is deepest and strongest and richest within each of us, being shared: the passions of love, in its deepest meanings.

Beyond the superficial, the considered phrase, "It feels right to me," acknowledges the strength of the erotic into a true knowledge, for what that means is the first and most powerful guiding light toward any understanding. And understanding is a handmaiden which can only wait upon, or clarify, that knowledge, deeply born. The erotic is the nurturer or nursemaid of all our deepest knowledge.

The erotic functions for me in several ways, and the first is in providing the power which comes from sharing deeply any pursuit with another person. The sharing of joy, whether physical, emotional, psychic, or intellectual, forms a bridge between the sharers which can be the basis for understanding much of what is not shared between them, and lessens the threat of their difference.

Another important way in which the erotic connection functions is the open and fearless underlining of my capacity for joy. In the way my body stretches to music and opens into response, hearkening to its deepest rhythms, so every level upon which I sense also opens to the erotically satisfying experience, whether it is dancing, building a bookcase, writing a poem, examining an idea.

That self-connection shared is a measure of the joy which I know myself to be capable of feeling, a reminder of my capacity for feeling. And that deep and irreplaceable knowledge of my capacity for joy comes to demand from all of my life that it be lived within the knowledge that such satisfaction is possible, and does not have to be called *marriage*, nor *god*, nor *an afterlife*.

This is one reason why the erotic is so feared, and so often relegated to the bedroom alone, when it is recognized at all. For once we begin to feel deeply all the aspects of our lives, we begin to demand from ourselves and from our life-pursuits that they feel in accordance with that joy which we know ourselves to be capable of. Our erotic knowledge empowers us, becomes a lens through which we scrutinize all aspects of our existence, forcing us to evaluate those aspects honestly in terms of their relative meaning within our lives. And this is a grave responsibility, projected from within each of us, not to settle for the convenient, the shoddy, the conventionally expected, nor the merely safe.

During World War II, we bought sealed plastic packets of white, uncolored margarine, with a tiny, intense pellet of yellow coloring perched like a topaz just inside the clear skin of the bag. We would leave the margarine out for a while to soften, and then we would pinch the little pellet to break it inside the bag, releasing the rich yellowness into the soft pale mass of margarine. Then taking it carefully between our fingers, we would knead it gently back and forth, over and over, until the color had spread throughout the whole pound bag of margarine, thoroughly coloring it.

I find the erotic such a kernel within myself. When released from its intense and constrained pellet, it flows through and colors my life with a kind of energy that heightens and sensitizes and strengthens all my experience.

We have been raised to fear the *yes* within ourselves, our deepest cravings. But, once recognized, those which do not enhance our future lose their power and can be altered. The fear of our desires keeps them suspect and indiscriminately powerful, for to suppress any truth is to give it strength beyond endurance. The fear that we cannot grow beyond whatever distortions we may find within ourselves keeps us docile and loyal and obedient, externally defined, and leads us to accept many facets of our oppression as women.

When we live outside ourselves, and by that I mean on external directives only rather than from our internal knowledge and needs, when we live away from those erotic guides from within ourselves, then our lives are limited by external and alien forms, and we conform to the needs of a structure that is not based on human need, let alone an individual's. But when we begin to live from within outward, in touch with the power of the erotic within ourselves, and allowing that power to inform and illuminate our actions upon the world around us, then we begin to be responsible to ourselves in the deepest sense. For as we begin to recognize our deepest feelings, we begin to give up, of necessity, being satisfied with suffering and self-negation, and with the numbness which so often seems like their only alternative in our society. Our acts against oppression become integral with self, motivated and empowered from within.

In touch with the erotic, I become less willing to accept powerlessness, or those other supplied states of being which are not native to me, such as resignation, despair, self-effacement, depression, self-denial.

And yes, there is a hierarchy. There is a difference between painting a back fence and writing a poem, but only one of quantity. And there is, for me, no difference between writing a good poem and moving into sunlight against the body of a woman I love.

This brings me to the last consideration of the erotic. To share the power of each other's feelings is different from using another's feelings as we would use a kleenex. When we look the other way from our experience, erotic or otherwise, we use rather than share the feelings of those others who participate in the experience with us. And use without consent of the used is abuse.

In order to be utilized, our erotic feelings must be recognized. The need for sharing deep feeling is a human need. But within the european-american tradition, this need is satisfied by certain proscribed erotic comings-together. These occasions are almost always characterized by a simultaneous looking away, a pretense of calling them something else, whether a religion, a fit, mob violence, or even playing doctor. And this misnaming of the need and the deed give rise to that distortion which results in pornography and obscenity – the abuse of feeling.

When we look away from the importance of the erotic in the development and sustenance of our power, or when we look away from ourselves as we satisfy our erotic needs in concert with others, we use each other as objects of satisfaction rather than share our joy in the satisfying, rather than make connection with our similarities and our differences. To refuse to be conscious of what we are feeling at any time, however comfortable that might seem, is to deny a large part of the experience, and to allow ourselves to be reduced to the pornographic, the abused, and the absurd.

The erotic cannot be felt secondhand. As a Black lesbian feminist, I have a particular feeling, knowledge, and understanding for those sisters with whom I have danced hard, played, or even fought. This deep participation has often been the forerunner for joint concerted actions not possible before.

But this erotic charge is not easily shared by women who continue to operate under an exclusively european-american male tradition. I know it was not available to me when I was trying to adapt my consciousness to this mode of living and sensation.

Only now, I find more and more women-identified women brave enough to risk sharing the erotic's electrical charge without having to look away, and without distorting the enormously powerful and creative nature of that exchange. Recognizing the power of the erotic within our lives can give us the energy to pursue genuine change within our world, rather than merely settling for a shift of characters in the same weary drama.

For not only do we touch our most profoundly creative source, but we do that which is female and self-affirming in the face of a racist, patriarchal, and anti-erotic society.

From *Sister Outsider* by Audre Lorde. © 1984, 2007 Audre Lorde.
Reproduced by permission of Abner Stein.

20 "Whose Pussy is this?" A Feminist Comment

bell hooks

Before I see Spike Lee's film *She's Gotta Have It*, I hear about it. Folks tell me, "It's black, it's funny, it's something you don't want to miss." With all this talk, especially coming from black folks who don't usually go to the movies, I become reluctant, even suspicious. If everybody is liking it, even white folks, something has got to be wrong somewhere! Initially, these are the thoughts that keep me from seeing the film but I don't stay away long. When I receive letters and phone calls from black women scholars and friends telling me about the film and wanting to talk about whether it portrays a liberated black woman, I make my way to the movies. I don't go alone. I go with my black women friends Beverly, Yvette, and Maria, so we can talk about it together. Some of what was said that evening in the heat of our discussion informs my comments.

A passionate viewer of films, especially the work of independent filmmakers, I found much to appreciate in the technique, style, and overall production of *She's Gotta Have It*. It was especially refreshing to see images of black people on-screen that were not grotesque caricatures, images that were familiar, images that imaginatively captured the essence, dignity, and spirit of that elusive quality known as "soul." It was a very soulful film.

Thinking about the film from a feminist perspective, considering its political implications, I find it much more problematic. In the article "Art vs. Ideology: The Debate Over Positive Images," Salim Muwakkil raises the question of whether a "mature African-American community" can allow "aesthetic judgments to rest on ideological or political criteria," commenting:

> The black cultural nationalists of the 60s and 70s demonstrated anew the deadening effect such ideological requirements have on creative expression. Their various proscriptions and prescriptions aborted a historical moment pregnant with promise. It seems clear that efforts to subordinate the profound and penetrating creative process of black people to an ideological moment suffocates the community's creative vitality.

While I would emphatically assert that aesthetic judgments should not rest *solely* on ideological or political criteria, this does not mean that such criteria cannot be used in conjunction with other critical strategies to assess the overall value of a given work. It does not imply a devaluation to engage in critical discussion of those criteria. To deny the validity of an aesthetic critique that encompasses the ideological or political is to mask the truth that every aesthetic work embodies the political, the ideological as part of its fundamental structure. No aesthetic work transcends politics or ideology.

Significantly, the film *She's Gotta Have It* was advertised, marketed, and talked about in reviews and conversations in a manner that raised political and ideological questions about both the film and the public responses to it. Was the film "a woman's story"? Did the film depict a radically new image of black female sexuality? Can a man really tell a woman's story? One viewer posed the question to me as "Is Nola Darling a liberated woman or just a WHORE?" (This is the way this sentence was written in a letter to me by a black woman professor who teaches film, who wrote that she was "waiting for the feminist response.") There has been no widespread feminist response to the film, precisely because of the overwhelming public celebration of that which is new, different, and exciting in this work. Given the pervasive antifeminism in popular culture, in black subculture, a feminist critique might simply be aggressively dismissed. Yet for feminist thinkers to avoid public critique is to diminish the power of the film. It is a testimony to that power that it compels us to think, to reflect, to engage the work fully.

Recently, the film version of Alice Walker's *The Color Purple* evoked more discussion among black folks of feminist issues (sexism, freedom of sexual expression, male violence against women, etc.) than any theoretical and/or polemical work by feminist scholars. *She's Gotta Have It* generated a similar response. Often these discussions exposed grave ignorance about feminist political movement, revealing the extent to which shallow notions of feminist struggle disseminated by nonfeminists in popular culture shape and influence the way many black people perceive feminism. That all feminists are man-hating sexually depraved, castrating, power-hungry, and so forth, are prevailing stereotypes. The tendency to see liberated women as sexually loose informed the way many people viewed the portrayal of black female sexuality in *She's Gotta Have It*. To some extent, this perception is based on a narrowly defined notion of liberation that was acceptable in some feminist circles at one time.

During the early stage of contemporary women's movement, feminist liberation was often equated with sexual liberation by both feminist activists and nonfeminists. At that time, the conceptualization of female sexual liberation was informed by a fierce heterosexist bias that saw sexual liberation primarily in terms of women asserting the right to be sexually desiring, to initiate sexual relationships, and to participate in casual sexual encounters with varied male partners. Women dared to assert that female sexuality was not passive, that women were desiring subjects who both longed for and enjoyed sex as much if not more than men. These assertions could have easily provided the ideological framework for the construction of a character like Nola Darling, the main female character in *She's Gotta Have It*. Nola expresses again and again her eagerness and willingness to be sexual with men as well as her right to have numerous partners.

Superficially, Nola Darling is the perfect embodiment of woman as desiring subject—a representation that does challenge sexist notions of female sexual passivity. (It is important to remember that from slavery on, black women have been portrayed in white racist thought as sexually assertive, although this view contrasts sharply with the emphasis on chastity, monogamy, and the male right to initiate sexual contact in black culture, a view held especially among the middle classes.) Ironically and unfortunately, Nola Darling's sexual desire is not depicted as an autonomous gesture, as an independent longing for sexual expression, satisfaction, and fulfillment. Instead her assertive sexuality is most often portrayed as though her body, her sexually aroused being, is a reward or gift she bestows on the deserving male. When bodybuilder Greer Childs tells Nola that his photo will appear on the cover of a popular men's magazine, she responds by removing her clothes, by offering her body as a token of her esteem. This and other incidents suggest that Nola, though a desiring subject, acts on the assumption that heterosexual female sexual assertion has legitimacy primarily as a gesture of reward or as a means by which men can be manipulated and controlled by women (what is vulgarly called "pussy power"). Men do not have to objectify Nola's sexuality, because she objectifies it. In so doing, her character becomes the projection of a stereotypical sexist notion of a sexually assertive woman—she is not in fact liberated.

While Nola is not passive sexually, her primary concern is pleasing each partner. Though we are led to believe she enjoys sex, her sexual fulfillment is never the central concern. She is pleasured only to the extent that she is able to please. While her partners enjoy being sexual with her, they are disturbed by her desire to have frequent sex with several partners. They see her sexual longing as abnormal. One male partner,

Mars, says, "All men want freaks (in bed), we just don't want 'em for a wife." This comment illustrates the sexist stereotypes about female sexuality that inform Mars's perceptions of Nola. When Jaime, another partner, suggests that Nola is sick, evoking sexist stereotypes to label her insane, depraved, abnormal, Nola does not respond by asserting that she is sexually liberated. Instead she internalizes the critique and seeks psychiatric help. Throughout the film, she is extremely dependent on male perceptions of her reality. Lacking self-awareness and the capacity to be self-critical, she explores her sexuality only when compelled to do so by a man. If Nola were sexually liberated, there would be no need for her to justify or defend herself against male accusations. It is only after the men have passed judgment that she begins the process of coming to consciousness. Until that point, we know more about how the men in the film see her than about how she sees herself.

To a very grave extent the focus of the film is not Nola but her male partners. Just as they are the center of attention sexually, they are also central personalities in the film. In telling us what they think about Nola, they tell us more about themselves, their values, their desires. She is the object that stimulates the discourse, they are its subjects. The narrators are male and the story is a male-centered, male-biased patriarchal tale. As such, it is not progressive nor does it break away from the traditional portrayal of female sexuality in film. *She's Gotta Have It* can take its place alongside a growing body of contemporary films that claim to tell women's stories while privileging male narratives, films that stimulate audiences with versions of female sexuality that are not really new or different (*Paris, Texas*, for example). Another recently acclaimed film, *Mona Lisa*, objectifies black womanhood and black female sexuality in a similar way.

Overall, it is the men who speak in *She's Gotta Have It*. While Nola appears one-dimensional in perspective and focus, seemingly more concerned about her sexual relationships than about any other aspect of her life, the male characters are multidimensional. They have personalities. Nola has no personality. She is shallow, vacuous, empty. Her one claim to fame is that she likes to fuck. In the male pornographic imagination she could be described as "pure pussy," that is to say that her ability to perform sexually is the central, defining aspect of her identity.

These sexually active, sexually hungry men are not "pure penis," because there is no such category. They are each defined by unique characteristics and attributes—Mars by his humor, Greer by his obsession with bodybuilding, Jaime by his concern with romance and committed relationships. Unlike Nola, they are not always thinking about sex, do not suffer from penis on the brain. They have opinions on a variety of topics: politics, sports, lifestyles, gender, and so on. Filmmaker Spike Lee challenges and critiques notions of black male sexuality while presenting a very typical perspective on black female sexuality. His imaginative exploration of the black male psyche is far more probing, far more expansive, and finally much more interesting than his exploration of black femaleness.

When Nola testifies that there have been "dogs" in her life—men who were only concerned with getting into bed—a group of black men appear on the screen in single file delivering the lines they use to seduce women, to "get it." In this brief segment, sexist male objectification of females is exposed along with the falseness and superficiality of the men. This particular scene more than any other in the film, is an excellent example of how cinema can be effectively used to raise consciousness about political concerns—in this case sexist male objectification of females. Without any particular character making a heavy-handed statement about how shallowly these black men think about women and sexuality, this point is powerfully conveyed. Filmmaker Spike Lee acknowledges that he intended to focus critically on black male behavior in the film, stating, "I know that black men do a lot of things that are fucked up and I've tried to show some of the things that we do."

While his innovative portrayal of black men in this scene (which is shot in such a way as to assume a documentary stance—the men appearing in single file before a camera as though they were being individually interviewed—acts to expose and, by implication, critique black male sexism, other scenes reinforce and perpetuate it. The deconstructive power of this scene is undermined most glaringly by the rape scene that occurs later.

Often talking with folks about the movie, I found my people did not notice that there was a rape scene, while others questioned whether what happened could be accurately described as a rape. Those of us who understand rape to be an act of coercive sexual contact, wherein one person is forced by another to participate without consent, watched a rape scene in *She's Gotta Have It*. When I first saw the film with the black women friends mentioned earlier, we were surprised and disturbed by the rape scene, yet we did not yell out in protest or leave the theater. As a group, we collectively sunk in our seats as though hiding. It was not the imaginative portrayal of rape that was shocking and disturbing but the manner and style of this depiction. In this instance, rape as an act of black male violence against a black woman was portrayed as though it was just another enjoyable sexual encounter, just another fuck. Rape, the film implies, is a difficult term to use when describing forced sexual intercourse with a sexually active female (in this case it is called a "near rape"). After all, as many black folks—women and men—stressed in conversation with me, she called him—she wanted to be sexual—she wanted it. Embedded in such thinking is the sexist assumption that woman as desiring subject, as active initiator, as sexual seducer is responsible for the quality, nature, and content of male response.

Not surprisingly, Nola sees herself as accountable, yet her ability to judge situations clearly has been questioned throughout the film. While she is completely in character when she labels the rape a "near rape," the fact remains that she is raped. Though she is depicted as deriving pleasure from the act, this does not alter the fact that she is forced to act sexually without her consent. It is perfectly compatible with sexist pornographic fantasies about rape to show a woman enjoying violation. Since the sexist mindset places responsibility on the female, claiming that she is really in control, such a fantasy allows that she (who is in actuality a victim) has the power to change this violent act into a pleasurable experience.

Hence the look on Darling's face during the rape, which begins as a grimace, reflecting pain, ends as a game of pleasure, satisfaction. This is most assuredly a sexist imaginative fantasy of rape—one that we as passive, silent viewers condone by our complicity. Protests from the audience would have at last altered passive acceptance of this depiction of rape. In keeping with the reality of patriarchy, with sexism in our culture, viewers who were pleased with the rape cheered and expressed their approval of Jaime's action when I saw the film.

As Jaime rapes Nola and aggressively demands that she answer the question "Whose pussy is this?" we arrive at the moment of truth—the moment when she can declare herself independent, sexually liberated, the moment when she can proudly assert through resistance her sexual autonomy (for many partners, to belong to no one). Ironically, she does not resist the physical violence. She does not assert the primacy of her body rights. She is passive. It is ironic because until this moment we have been seduced by the image of her as a forceful woman, a woman who dares to be sexually assertive, demanding, active. We are seduced and betrayed. When Nola responds to the question "Whose pussy is this?" by saying, "Yours," it is difficult for anyone who has fallen for the image of her as sexually liberated not to feel let down, disappointed both in her character and in the film. Suddenly we are not witnessing a radical questioning of female sexual passivity or a celebration of female sexual self-assertion but a reconstruction of the same old sexist content in a new and more interesting form. While some of us were passively disgusted, disturbed, sexist male viewers feeling vilified cheered, expressing their satisfaction that the uppity black woman had been put in her place—that male domination and patriarchal order were restored.

After the rape, Nola ceases to be sexually active, chooses to be in a monogamous relationship with Jaime, the partner who has coerced her. Ideologically, such a scenario impresses on the consciousness of black males, and all males, the sexist assumption that rape is an effective means of patriarchal social control that it restores and maintains male power over women. It simultaneously suggests to black females, and all females, that being sexually assertive will lead to rejection and punishment. In a culture where a woman is raped every eighteen seconds, where there is still enormous ignorance about rape, where patriarchy and sexist practices promote and condone the rape of women by men as a way to maintain male domination, it is disturbing to witness this scene, not only because it reinforces dangerous stereotypes (a central one being that women enjoy rape), but because it suggests that rape does not have severe and grave consequences for victims. Without counselling, without support, Nola is restored to her cool, confident self by the end of the movie. Silent about her sexuality throughout much of the film, she suddenly speaks. It is she who will call the rape a "near rape," as though it was really no big deal.

Yet it is the rape that shifts the direction of the film, of Nola Darling's fictional self-exploration. As an expression of her newly acquired self-assertion, she calmly denounces the "near rape," explains that the relationship with Jaime has not worked, and stresses her right to be autonomously self-defining. Expressed without the bravado and zest that has characterized that we have witnessed a woman being disempowered and not a woman coming to power. This perception seems to be reconfirmed when Nola's choice to be truly self-defining means that she will be alone, with no sexual partner.

In perfect contrast to *The Color Purple*, wherein same-sex relationships between women are depicted as a source of mutual, nonexploitive erotic affirmation and serve as catalysts for self-development, the lesbian sexuality in *She's Gotta Have It* is negatively portrayed. It does not represent an alternative to destructive heterosexual practice. The lesbian character is predatory, as much a "dog" as any of the men. Significantly, Nola does not find it difficult to reject unwanted sexual advances from another woman, to assert her body rights, her preferences. Utterly male-identified, she does not value her women friends. Though they are underdeveloped characters in the film, her two female friends are compelling and interesting. The apparent dedication and discipline the bass player shows in relationship to her music stand in sharp contrast to Nola's lackadaisical approach to her art, whereas the bass player appears comfortable with her autonomy in a way that Nola is not.

Autonomy is not depicted as a life-enhancing, empowering choice for Nola. Her decision to be self-defining leaves her as vacuous and as empty as she has previously appeared without the savvy she had in her role as vamp. Finally we see her at the end of the film alone, wrapped in her sheets, a familiar image that does not suggest transformation. Are we to imagine that she has ceased to long for the "it" she's gotta have? Are we to think that the "it" is multiple in implication after all, that it may not be sex but a sense of self she is longing for? She has had sex throughout the film; what she has not had is a sense of self that would enable her to be fully autonomous and sexually assertive, independent, and liberated. Without a firm sense of self her attempts at becoming a desiring subject rather than an object are doomed to fail. Nola cannot enter the sexual power struggle between women and men as object and become subject. Desire alone is not enough to make her a subject, to liberate (the film does make this point, but this is no new revelation). A new image, the one we have yet to see in film, is the desiring black woman who prevails, who triumphs, not desexualized, not alone, who is "together" in every sense of the word. Joan Mellen in her introduction to *Women and Their Sexuality in the New Film* emphasizes that the recent attempt to portray radical and transformative images of female sexuality has proven to be a disappointment, in most instances a failure:

The language of independent women may be reluctantly allowed, but the substance goes unaltered. If lip service provides a pseudo-anticipation of challenge to old values and images, the real business at hand is to refurbish the established view, now strengthened by nominal reference to "awareness." This sleight of hand is the method of co-option. Cinema is an arena in which the process had been refined.

Thus the very image of liberated or self-sufficient women, when it is risked on the screen, is presented unpalatably and deployed to reinforce the old ways.

Even though filmmaker Spike Lee may have intended to portray a radical new image of black female sexuality, *She's Gotta Have It* reinforces and perpetuates old norms overall. Positively the film does show us the nature of black male-female power struggles, the contradictions, the craziness, and that is an important new direction. Yet it is the absence of compelling liberatory reconciliation that undermines the progressive radical potential of this film. Even though nude scenes, scenes of sexual play constitute an important imaging of black sexuality on-screen since they are not grotesque or pornographic, we still do not see an imaging of mutual, sexually satisfying relationships between black women and men in a context of nondomination. It does not really matter if the woman is dominating and a male submitting—it is the same old oppressive scenario. Ultimately, it is a patriarchal tale—one in which woman does not emerge triumphant, fulfilled. While we can applaud Nola's feeble attempt to tell a new story at the end of the film, it is not compelling, not enough—it is not satisfying.

21 Posthuman Humanities: Life beyond Theory

ROSI BRAIDOTTI

The 'Proper' Subject of the Humanities is not 'Man'

I have argued throughout this book that posthuman theory rests on a process ontology that challenges the traditional equation of subjectivity with rational consciousness, resisting the reduction of both to objectivity and linearity.[1] The nomadic vision of the posthuman knowing subject as a time continuum and a collective assemblage implies a double commitment, on the one hand to processes of change and on the other to a strong ethics of eco-sophical sense of community. Co-presence, that is to say the simultaneity of being in the world together, defines the ethics of interaction with both human and non-human others. A collectively distributed consciousness emerges from this, a transversal form of non-synthetic understanding of the relational bond that connects us. This places the relation and the notion of complexity at the centre of both the ethics and the epistemic structures and strategies of the posthuman subject (Braidotti, 2006).

This view has important implications for the production of scientific knowledge. The dominant vision of the scientific enterprise is based on the institutional implementation of a number of Laws that discipline the practice of scientific research and police the thematic and methodological borders of what counts as respectable, acceptable, and fundable science. In so doing, the laws of scientific practice regulate what a mind is allowed to do, and thus they control the structures of our thinking. Posthuman thought proposes an alternative vision of both the thinking subject, of his or her evolution on the planetary stage, and the actual structure of thinking.

Deleuze and Guattari's idea that the task of thinking is to create new concepts is a great source of inspiration for the Humanities because it rests on the parallelism between philosophy, science and the arts. This is not to be mistaken for a flattening out of the differences between these intellectual pursuits, but rather a way of stressing the unity of purpose among the three branches of knowledge. Deleuze and Guattari take care to stress the differences between the distinctive styles of intelligence that philosophy, science and the arts respectively embody. They also argue that they remain indexed on a common plane of intensive self-transforming Life energy. This continuum sustains the ontology of becoming that is the conceptual motor of posthuman nomadic thought. In so far as science has to come to terms with the real physical processes of an actualized and defined world, it is less open to the processes of becoming or differentiation that characterize Deleuze's monistic ontology. Philosophy is at an advantage, being a subtler tool for the probing intellect, one that is more attuned to the virtual plane of immanence, to the generative force of a generative universe, or 'chaosmosis', which is nonhuman and in constant flux. Thinking is the conceptual counterpart of the ability to enter modes of relation, to affect and be affected, sustaining qualitative shifts and creative tensions accordingly, which is also the prerogative of art. Critical theory therefore has a major role to play.

Manuel De Landa (2002) analyses brilliantly the intensive mode of Deleuzian science and stresses the crucial importance of processes of actualization of virtual possibilities, over and above universal essence and linear realizations. De Landa points out that, apart from the anti-essentialism, intensive nomad science also aims to avoid typological thinking. The ruling principle of resemblance, identity, analogy and opposition has to be avoided in thinking about the virtual and intensive becoming. Deleuze demands 'that we give an account of that which allows making such judgements or establishing those relations' (De Landa, 2002: 42).

The important aspect of nomadic vitalism is that it is neither organicist nor essentialist, but pragmatic and immanent. In other words, vital materialism does not assume an over-arching concept of life, just practices and flows of becoming, complex assemblages and heterogeneous relations. As I argued in chapter 2, there is no idealized transcendental, but virtual multiplicity. The monistic ontology that sustains this vision of life as vitalist, self-organizing matter also allows the critical thinker to re-unite the different branches of philosophy, the sciences and the arts in a new alliance. I see this as a dynamic contemporary formula to redefine the relationship between the two cultures of the 'subtle' (Humanities) and 'hard' (Natural) sciences. They are different lines of approaching the vital matter that constitutes the core of both subjectivity and its planetary and cosmic relations.

Bonta and Protevi (2004) stress that Deleuze's 'geo-philosophy' encourages the Humanities to engage with contemporary biology and physics in very creative ways. The emphasis falls on complexity in distinguishing between actualized states and virtual becoming – on the basis of a vision of matter as auto-poietic. The former constitute the object of 'Royal Science', the latter the frame for 'minor science'; both are necessary at different points in time, but only 'minor science' is ethically transformative and not bound to the economic imperatives of advanced capitalism and its cognitive excursions into living matter. As a consequence, one can venture the preliminary conclusion that the main implication of posthuman critical theory for the practice of science is that the scientific Laws need to be retuned according to a view of the subject of knowledge as a complex singularity, an affective assemblage and a relational vitalist entity.

It follows from all this that the Humanities in the posthuman era of anthropocene should not stick to the Human – let alone 'Man' – as its proper object of study. On the contrary, the field would benefit by being free from the empire of humanist Man, so as to be able to access in a post-anthropocentric manner issues of external and even planetary importance, such as scientific and technological advances, ecological and social sustainability and the multiple challenges of globalization. Such a change of focus requires assistance from other social and scientific actors as well.

The question is whether the Humanities are allowed to set their own agenda in relation to contemporary science and technology, or whether they are confined to places they did not choose to be in the first place. There is in fact a distinct tendency, for instance in the public debates about climate change or biotechnologies, to assign to the institutionally under-funded field of the Humanities all subjects related to the human component of these complex debates. This tendency has made the institutional fortunes of ethics, which is expected – and often claims itself the prerogative – to issue new meta-discourses and normative injunctions suited to the dilemmas of our age. This meta-discursive claim, however, is unsubstantiated. Moreover, it perpetuates the institutionalized habit of thought – reactive and sedentary – of erecting philosophy to the role of a master theory. The image of the philosopher as the legislator of knowledge and the judge of truth – a model rooted in the Kantian school – is the exact opposite of what posthuman critical theory is arguing for: post-identitarian, non-unitary and transversal subjectivity based on relations with human and non-human others.

Another discursive field that gets regularly evoked as the single responsibility of the Humanities is the controversial issue of the 'social and cultural aspects' of complex issues such as climate change or the impact of bio-technologies. In other words, the Humanities are actively confined to the anthropocentric corner, while being simultaneously blamed for this limitation, which is the perfect illustration of the paradox noted by Whimster (2006: 174): 'a science of the human would seem either to have the capacity to be inhuman or, alternatively, to be humanistic but hardly scientific'. Damned if you do, damned if you don't.

My point is that the Humanities need to embrace the multiple opportunities offered by the posthuman condition. The Humanities can set their own objects of enquiry, free from the traditional or institutional assignment to the human and its humanistic derivatives. We know by now that the field is richly endowed with an archive of multiple possibilities which equip it with the methodological and theoretical resources to set up original and necessary debates with the sciences and technologies and other grand challenges of today. The question is what the Humanities can become in the posthuman era and after the decline of the primacy of 'Man' and of *anthropos*.

The Global 'Multi'-versity

The question now is what is the institutional practice best suited to posthuman critical theory and to the twenty-first-century Humanities. The discussions about the Humanities' ability to cope with the challenges of the third millennium beg the question of the crisis of the university as idea and as representation.

A brief historical survey of the debate about the idea of the university can give an idea of the extent of this crisis. The Renaissance model of the Humanist academy defined by the scholar as an artist or artisan handcrafting his or her research patiently and without constraints, over a long period of time, is simply over. It has been replaced by a modern 'Fordist' model of the university as a chain-production unit mass-producing academic good. Nussbaum's claim (1999) that [the Renaissance] model is still carried on today by the American Liberal Arts college is both elitist and nostalgic, as I mentioned in chapter 2. Immanuel Kant's classical text on 'The conflicts of the faculties', first published in 1789 (Kant, 1992) presents the blueprint for the modern university, based on the model of industrial production. Kant divided the university into 'higher' faculties – Law, Medicine and Theology – which are practically oriented and 'lower' faculties – the Arts, Humanities and Sciences – which are responsible for criticism and hence are withdrawn from markets and practical concerns.[2] This blueprint is still quite valid, in spite of several historical modifications. Probably the most significant is the nineteenth century von Humboldt model of the university as the place for training the highly selected, and until recently exclusively male, elites for leadership and intelligent citizenship. That model is still prevalent in Europe.

In his stimulating and at times devastating anatomy of the contemporary university, Bill Readings (1996) argues, however, that the institution has become 'post-historical', in that it has 'outlived itself, is now a survivor of the era in which it defined itself in terms of the project of the historical development, affirmation and inculcation of national culture' (1996: 6). All the previous models of the university I mentioned above: the Kantian, the von Humboldt and even the British colonial defended by Cardinal Newman (1907), have been destabilized by the global economy. In this respect, the decline of the nation-state has negative consequences for the university as a whole and especially for the Humanities. The central figure in academic life today is not the professor, argues Readings, but the administrator and the university is no longer a pillar of national identity, or an ideological arm of the nation-state and the state apparatus:

> The university is now no more of a parasitical drain, on resources, than the stock exchange or the insurance company are a drain on industrial production. Like the stock exchange, the university is a point of capital's self-knowledge, of capital's ability not just to manage risk or diversity, but to extract a surplus

value from that management. In the case of the university, this extraction occurs as a result of speculation on differentials in information. (1996: 40)

In this context, the much-flaunted notion of 'excellence' means nothing substantial, but is a crucial factor in the trans-national exchange of academic capital. A mere 'techno-bureaucratic ideal' (Readings, 1996: 14), it has no content reference. This 'de-referentialization' of academic standards has both negative and positive consequences.

On the negative front, the lack of specific referents means that 'excellence' is indexed on money, markets' demands and consumers' satisfaction. On a more positive note, 'de-referentialization' opens up the possibility for new spaces 'in which we can think the notions of country and community differently' (1996: 124). What can we do with these models of university today?

Let us start by looking at the classical conservative model, exemplified by John Searle in his defence of the key ideas in the Western rationalist tradition (1995), as the core values of Humanities research. Firmly grounded in a realist practice of truth, the rationalist tradition is text-based and deploys theory in a self-critical manner. It rests on linear thinking because it assumes that the function of language is to communicate effectively. Consequently, truth is a matter of the accuracy of representation – according to a correspondence theory of truth which grounds statements in observable factual realities. It follows that knowledge is expected to be objective – because it relies on representations of an independently existing reality and not on subjectivist interpretations. Rationality rules supreme and formal reason – as opposed to practical reason – has its own inner logic which provides standards of proof and validity. As a result, intellectual standards are non-negotiable and grounded in objective criteria of excellence.

The traditional idea of the university is supposed to embody and uphold these criteria. Searle opposes to this the 'post-modernist' university, influenced by imported anti-realist theories of truth which weaken the scientificity of the academic practice. The representativeness of the curriculum in terms of gender, race, and ethnicity – regrettably for Searle – becomes more important than its truth value, introducing a shallow intellectual egalitarianism under the guise of multiculturalism. This causes confusion between a domain to be studied and a cause to be defended, which disrupts the deployment of traditional Humanities methods and practices and erodes its self-confidence.

In an eloquent response to Searle, Richard Rorty (1996) criticizes the over-emphasis on rationalism as 'a secularized version of the Western monotheistic tradition' (1996: 33). Realism and the correspondence to reality are rather meaningless concepts, or rather 'a term without content' (1996: 26). The much-praised 'objectivity of science', argues Rorty, rests on active inter-subjectivity and social interaction. Emphasizing the importance of socio-political factors in shaping meanings and truths, Rorty strikes a more pragmatic note:

A healthy and free university accommodates generational change, radical religious and political disagreement and new social responsibilities as best it can. It muddles through. (1996: 28)

The question of theory and the aftermath of the 'theory wars' comes back to haunt this discussion. Searle's conservative remarks are accurate as the expression of his emotional involvement in the Humanities' self-defence. He is nonetheless ruthless in blaming the postmodern theorists for the situation. Contrary to the facile anti-postmodernism of his approach, I would stress the serious methodological challenges that this approach has thrown to the Humanities. Indeed, blaming the postmodern messengers for bringing the sobering message that the humanistic master narratives are in trouble is a sleight of hand that does not help further the cause of the Humanities today. It is a great pity that the serious debate about the future of humanistic higher education is caught up in the legacy of the 1990s 'theory wars' and the polemical in-fighting about feminism, postmodernism, multiculturalism and French philosophy. Joan Scott puts it brilliantly:

> As if postmodernists were the cause of all the problems of disciplinary uncertainty scholars are now facing; as if their banishment would end the questions about difference posed by demographic changes in university populations, by the emergence of postcolonial critiques of colonial assumptions, by developments in the history of philosophy that reach back to at least the nineteenth century, by the more recent end of the Cold War and by the extraordinary economic constraints of the last years. (Scott, 1996: 171)

Referring back to John Dewey's[3] notion of the university as a disciplinary community, Scott deplores the politicized contests about postmodernism and knowledge, which over-emphasize 'the presumed political implications of one's scholarly ideas, not the ideas themselves'. Louis Menand (1996) goes further and suggests that conservative political forces are manipulating 'theory wars' as a pretext to interfere in the internal academic affairs of the university, as evidence by the particularly targeted attacks against feminism, multi-culturalism and post-colonialism. This critical insight is picked up by Edward Said, who connects the identity crisis of the Humanities to the displacement of Eurocentric curricula in US universities and adds, quite ironically:

> Some critics have reacted as if the very nature of the University and academic freedom had been threatened because unduly politicized. Others have gone further: for them the critique of the Western canon, with its panoply of what its opponent have called Dead White European Males [...] has rather improbably signalled the outset of a new fascism, the demise of Western civilization itself, and the overturn of slavery, child marriage, bigamy and the harem. (Said, 1996: 214–15)

Irony left aside, it is quite clear that the real target of the conservatives' wrath is the threat that these new areas of studies pose to the power of corporate disciplines in two major ways: through their radical epistemologies and their methodological interdisciplinarity. The meltdown of disciplinary boundaries and the subsequent loss of corporate power by the old disciplines is less of a theoretical than an administrative crisis. As Menand astutely observes, given that the disciplines are not timeless entities, but historically contingent discursive formations, their de-segregation is not itself a source of anxiety for the scholars, some of whom are even driving the process. It is, however, a major headache for the administrators in charge of the machinery of self-governance of Humanities faculties, who tend to 'take advantage of the state of flux to reduce spending and increase forceful retrenchments' (1996: 19). But what does the posthuman have to do with any of this?

Instead of pursuing this polemic, I would rather start from the empirical imperative to think global, but act local, to develop an institutional frame that actualized a posthuman practice that is 'worthy of our times' (Braidotti, 2011) while resisting the violence, the injustice and the vulgarity of the times. Confronting the historicity of our condition means moving the activity of thinking outwards, into the real world, so as to assume accountability for the conditions that define our location. The epistemic and the ethical walk hand in hand into the complicated landscapes of the third millennium. We need conceptual creativity and intellectual courage to rise to the occasion, as there is no going back.

Although the issues of pastoral care and intergenerational justice are more topical than ever in the academic classroom, it is also the case that, since the Cold War era, the function of the university has been mostly research and development for the sake of social development and industrial growth and technological advances, including but not only the military, as we saw in the previous chapter. This is especially true of the USA, but Europe and vast parts of Asia are also part of this model. According to Wernick, since the 1960s the university has mutated into a 'multi-versity', fulfilling a variety of social and economic functions, often linked to the Cold War militarization of the social space and geo-political conflicts. The term 'multi-versity' was coined in 1963 by the then Chancellor of the University of California system Clark Kerr (2001) to refer to the explosion of tasks and demands imposed on major universities. The university continued to mutate so that, over the next twenty years, 'universities have become corporate, oriented to performance and de-traditionalized. Under the aegis of professional managers they have become post-historical institutions without a memory' (Wernick, 2006: 561). As the professoriate and students' representative bodies lost their powers of governance to neo-liberal economic logic, the Humanities dispersed their foundational value to become a sort of luxury intellectual consumer good.

Can this trend be reversed? What is the most adequate model of the university for the globalized era? I want to argue that the posthuman predicament affects also an issue as crucial as the civic responsibility of the university today. How can the academic and civic space interact in our globalized, technologically mediated world? The digital revolution paves the way for at least a partial answer: the new campuses will be virtual and hence global by definition. This means that the universal ideal of transcendent values defended by Searle is over. It is being rapidly replaced by the infrastructural vision of the university as a hub of both localized knowledge production and global transmission of cognitive data. This need not necessarily result in either de-humanizing or dis-embedding the university, but in new forms of re-grounding and of accountability. Thus, in an article pointedly called 'The twenty kilometer university', an interdisciplinary team (Phillips et al., 2011) analyses the changing relationship between the university and the contemporary global city in China and draws some inspiring consequences for the mission of the academic institution today.

The global city space requires and depends upon intelligent spaces of high-technological interactivity and can thus be defined as a 'smart' city space with dense technological infrastructure. Ambient technology rests on infrastructural networks which, being non-hierarchical and user-friendly, defeat the traditional organization of both knowledge production and knowledge transfer. In some ways, the technologically smart urban space displaces and replaces the university, by inscribing knowledge and its circulation at the heart of the social order. What happens then to the formerly segregated and, at least in Europe, highly sacralized academic space? The authors argue that the academic needs to unfold onto the civic and become embedded in the urban environment in a radical new manner. The city as a whole is the science park of the future. The university consequently needs to transform itself into a 'multi-versity' (Wernick 2006: 561), capable of interacting with the city space so as to create 'a collective ethos of communal intelligence with a common goal of economic progress through the means that sustain and streamline city life' (Phillips et al., 2011: 299). The branding of cities and their universities – which was initiated in the Cold War era – enters a new phase of intensifying marketing practices, promotional efforts and a financial culture of private and public investments that are often unrelated to the actual content matter.

The global multi-versity is the place where technology and metaphysics meet, with explosive but also exhilarating consequences. This globalized, technologically mediated 'multi-versity' is a new entity: 'with its role in relation to citizen-formation and *bildung* fading into the background if not outright obscurity' (Phillips et al., 2011: 300). Stefan Collini (2012: 13) stresses the same point by arguing that we must stop thinking in terms of nineteenth-century European ideals and 'focus instead on how it is the Asian incarnation of the Americanized version of the European model, with schools of technology, medicine and management to the fore, which most powerfully instantiates the ideal of the university in the twenty-first century'.

In other words, the contemporary university needs to redefine its posthuman planetary mission in terms of a renewed relationship to the global city where it is situated. This implies both a revision of the urban space and a redefinition of civic responsibility. All the more so as, according to the United Nations, there will be 22 mega-cities in the world by 2015 and that by 2050 two-thirds of the world population will dwell in urban centres. In 2012 we officially registered the fact that 50 per cent of the world population now lives in cities. More Internet-backed interactivity will allow citizens to participate in all forms of planning, managing and assessing their urban environment. The key words are: open source, open governance, open data and open science, granting free access by the public to all scientific and administrative data. Contemporary twenty-first-century cities, as in the case of the Chinese study quoted above, are not only sprawled out or 'exploded' urban spaces. They are also – in the best of cases – technologically mediated, 'smart' urban surfaces. Just as in the past, in Europe, universities and their cities grew together, weaving a complex web of urban, social, economic, political and civic ties, so today a new network of relations is being set up. Because of the high degree of technological intervention involved in contemporary network societies, this new urban space can be considered as post-anthropocentric and well beyond the Vitruvian frame of reference of a humanist scale. Responding to local concerns and global challenges, the contemporary 'multi-versity' faces up to both the demands of a competitive labour market, global culture and the corporate world, while pursuing its century-old missions of scientific excellence and enlightened citizenship. The cities of tomorrow will be living centres of learning, information brokering and shared cognitive practice, based on intense social networking. After naval ports and airports, Internet ports will be the gateways to navigating the cities of the third millennium.

This takes me to the second aspect of the new covenant between the university and the city in the third millennium: the civic dimension. More than ever, the university needs to pursue its aim of ensuring independent research, constructive pedagogical practice and critical thinking. Compounded by the role that contemporary universities can play as major technological hubs and global centres of knowledge transfer, the mix of innovation and tradition can sustain the continuing relevance of the institution of the university in the contemporary world. The combination of technical skills and civic responsibility, a concern for social and environmental sustainability, and a discerning relationship to consumerism, are the core values of the contemporary multi-versity. Bill Readings (1996) was hinting at this when he referred to the possibility that the contemporary university may help redefine community and belonging away from classical nationalism on the one hand, and crass consumerism on the other. Referring to Blanchot's work, Readings calls for a new model of the university as a community of post-identitarian, posthuman subjects. The model will be a community without steady identity or fixed unity, for a people and a multi-versity to come.

This has deep implications for the role and place of theory. I remember the day when this specific penny dropped inside my head. I was at a Laurie Anderson concert in Paris in the late 1980s. She is one of those conceptual artists who seamlessly unfold into a public intellectual, creating acoustic and aesthetic expressions for the transformations of our times. 'O Superman' was the first cyber song to become a global hit – a premonition of posthuman things to come – whereas 'Strange Angels' is a critical re-appraisal of Walter Benjamin's theses on the philosophy of History, hinting at a new continuum between the remembrance of things past and the sustainability of the future. At this particular concert, Anderson, who would soon embark on her artist residency with NASA, defined the work of people who used to call themselves 'intellectuals' as having become 'content-providers'. That was the late 1980s. Last week I received the announcement of a major conference on the future of European education in which an entire panel was devoted to papers by and about 'ideas brokers'. That entails marketing and advertising ideas, rather than fundamental research and experimentation; it does not even particularly require imaginative creativity. Academics are left to brokering ideas, while information networks do the content provision and are increasingly autonomous in decision making. All around, an exploded and expanded 'smart' city space distributes the knowledge products to students-users who are literate in infrastructural knowledge production. Welcome to the future!

That future has already started in the endless re-organizations and financial restrictions that plague the contemporary academic world and are particularly acute in the Humanities. Louis Menand argues that the modern research university is neither the embodiment of eternal truths and universal ideas, nor the paragon of truth, beauty and virtue. It is actually a rather cumbersome and expensive bureaucracy:

> [I]t is philosophically weak and it encourages intellectual predictability, professional insularity and social irrelevance. It deserves to be replaced. But if it is replaced, it is in the interests of everyone who values the continued integrity of teaching and inquiry to devise a new institutional structure that will perform the same function. Otherwise academic freedom will be killed by the thing that, in America, kills most swiftly and surely: not bad ideas, but lack of money. (Menand, 1996: 19)

This negative social and economic context of financial scarcity has caused a distinct deterioration of the working conditions of all staff in the average neo-liberal university worldwide. Stefan Collini comments on this issue with customary wit: 'The distracted, numbers-swamped, audit-crazed, grant-chasing life of most contemporary academics departments is far removed from classical ideals of the contemplative life' (Collini, 2012: 19). As a matter of fact, academics function more like mid-ranking executives in a business organization run by accountants and financial advisors than as independent scholars in a self-organized community. The more successful ones have become very skilful in obtaining external grants and funding. They are also known as the 'tender'-preneurs. Rosalind Gill (2010), on the other hand, not only deplores the working conditions in the academic world, but also attempts to assess the damage they cause to both individuals and the institutions where stress and competitiveness rule. The precariousness of younger staff members is a source of special concern. Collini concurs: 'the conditions of work of junior and temporary staff in some unfavoured institutions may, in limiting cases, suggest comparisons with those of staff in a call center' (2012: 19).

Yet, it does feel slightly incongruous to think about all this from my specific location, in the ancient city of Utrecht, in the heart of the old world. City and university here have become so interwoven over the span of centuries that it is difficult to tell the urban, civic structure apart from the academic one. *Civitas* and *Universitas* are two sides of the same coin and it may not be simple to shift the grounds of their inter-action in the name of the posthuman predicament. What might the blueprint for the future look like? I want to resist the apocalyptic visions of the last professors as a dying species (Donoghue, 2008). Posthuman Humanities, marked by a new alliance between the arts and the sciences, and enriched by the ancient European academic and civic tradition, can sponsor multiple allegiances and new ecologies of belonging. They can redefine cosmopolitanism, fulfilling the posthuman definition of Europe as the place that is histor-ically and morally bound to the critical re-elaboration of its own history.

By extension, we need a university that looks like the society it both reflects and serves, that is to say a globalized, technologically mediated, ethnically and linguistically diverse society that is still in tune with basic principles of social justice, the respect for diversity, the principles of hospitality and convivi-ality. I am aware but do not mind the residual Humanism of such aspirations, which I take at best as a productive contradiction. Against the social construction of wilful forgetfulness and of crass ignorance, I defend a fundamental aspiration to over-arching principles of posthuman bonding. A university that is seri-ously committed to representing today's world needs to tackle these issues by instituting trans-disciplinary areas which explore the production of knowledge in a technologically mediated world; the new relationship between arts and sciences; and the poly-lingual realities engendered by globalization. In a new outpour of intellectual creativity, posthuman Humanities in the global multi-versity will include: Humanistic Informatics, or digital Humanities; Cognitive or neural humanities; Environmental or sustainable Humanities; Bio-genetic and Global Humanities. They will also pursue the project of investigating what kind of research methods and insights are developed by literary and art practices. They will continue to support 'the human mind's restless pursuit of fuller understanding' (Collini, 2012: 27) which is the essential mission of the Humanities.

In other words, I think the Humanities can and will survive and prosper to the extent that they will show the ability and willingness to undergo a major process of transformation in the direction of the posthuman. To be worthy of our times, we need to be pragmatic: we need schemes of thought and figurations that enable us to account in empowering terms for the changes and transformations currently on the way. We already live in permanent states of transition, hybridization and nomadic mobility, in emancipated (post-feminist), multi-ethnic societies with high degrees of technological intervention. These are neither simple, nor linear events, but rather multi-layered and internally contradictory phenomena. They combine elements of ultra-modernity with splinters of neo-archaism: high-tech advances and neo-primitivism, which defy the logic of the excluded middle.

Contemporary culture and institutional education are often unable to represent these realities adequately. They favour instead the predictably plaintive refrains about the end of ideologies, run concurrently with the apology of the 'new'. Nostalgia and hyper-consumerism join hands, under the hold of neo-liberal restoration of possessive individualism. This unitary vision of the humanist subject, however, cannot provide an effective antidote to the processes of fragmentation, flows and mutations that mark our era. We need to start from non-unitary, relational subject positions so as to learn to think differently about ourselves and our systems of values, starting with adequate cartographies of our embedded and embodied posthuman locations.

A university that looks like the world of today can only be a 'multi-versity', is an exploded and expanded institution that will affirm a constructive post-humanity. As such it cannot support education for the sole purpose of integration into the labour market, but also for its own sake. We do need to embrace non-profit as a key value in contemporary knowledge production, but this gratuitousness is linked to the construction of social horizons of hope and therefore it is a vote of confidence in the sheer sustainability of the future (Braidotti, 2006). The future is nothing more or less than inter-generational solidarity, responsibility for posterity, but it is also our shared dream, or a consensual hallucination.[4] Collini puts it beautifully (2012: 199): 'we are merely custodians for the present generation of a complex intellectual inheritance which we did not create, and which is not ours to destroy'. Posthuman Humanities are already at work in the global multi-versity, not only to fend off extinction, but also to actualize sustainable posthuman futures.

From *The Posthuman* by Rosi Braidotti, Polity 2013. © Rosi Braidotti 2013.

Notes

1. For an excellent critical account of the notion of objectivity, see Daston and Galison (2007).
2. For a contemporary critical update on Kant's vision of the university, see Lambert (2001).
3. Dewey played an important role in launching the American Association of University Professors in 1915.
4. This is William Gibson's definition of cyberspace.

References

Bonta, Mark and John Protevi. 2004. *Deleuze and Geophilosophy. A Guide and Glossary*. Edinburgh: Edinburgh University Press.
Braidotti, Rosi. 2006. *Transpositions: On Nomadic Ethics*. Cambridge: Polity Press.

Braidotti, Rosi. 2011. *Nomadic Theory. The Portable Rosi Braidotti*. New York: Columbia University Press.

Collini, Stefan. 2012. *What Are Universities For?* London: Penguin Books.

Daston, Lorraine and Peter Galison. 2007. *Objectivity*. New York: Zone Books.

De Landa, Manuel. 2002. *Intensive Science and Virtual Philosophy*. London: Continuum.

Donoghue, Frank. 2008. *The Last Professors: The Corporate University and the Fate of the Humanities*. New York: Fordham University Press.

Gill, Rosalind. 2010. Breaking the silence: the hidden injuries of the neoliberal universities. In: Rosalind Gill and Roisin Ryan Flood (eds.) *Secrecy and Silence in the Research Process: Feminist Reflections*. London and New York: Routledge.

Kant, Immanuel. 1992. *The Conflict of the Faculties*. Lincoln, NE: University of Nebraska Press.

Kerr, Clark. 2001. *The Uses of the University*. Cambridge, MA: Harvard University Press.

Lambert, Gregg. 2001. *Report to the Academy*. Aurora, CO: The Davis Group Publisher.

Menand, Louis (ed.) 1996. *The Future of Academic Freedom*. Chicago, IL: University of Chicago Press.

Newman, John. 1907. *The Idea of a University*. London: Longmans, Green & Co.

Nussbaum, Martha C. 1999. *Cultivating Humanity: a Classical Defense of Reform in Liberal Education*. Cambridge, MA: Harvard University Press.

Phillips, John, Andrew Benjamin, Ryan Bishop, Li Shiqiao, Esther Lorenz, Lui Xiaodu and Meng Yan. 2011. The twenty-kilometer university. Knowledge as infrastructure. *Theory, Culture & Society*, 28 (7–8), 287–320.

Readings, Bill. 1996. *The University in Ruins*. Cambridge, MA: Harvard University Press.

Rorty, Richard. 1996. Does academic freedom have philosophical presuppositions? In: Louis Menand (ed.) *The Future of Academic Freedom*. Chicago, IL: University of Chicago Press.

Said, Edward. 1996. Identity, authority and freedom: The potentate and the traveller. In: Louis Menand (ed.) *The Future of Academic Freedom*. Chicago, IL: University of Chicago Press.

Scott, Joan. 1996. Academic freedom as an ethical practice. In: Louis Menand (ed.) *The Future of Academic Freedom*. Chicago, IL: University of Chicago Press.

Searle, John R. 1995. Postmodernism and the Western rationalist tradition. In: John Arthur and Amy Shapiro (eds.) *Campus Wars*. Boulder, CO: Westview Press.

Wernick, Andrew. 2006. University. *Theory, Culture & Society*, 23 (2–3), 557–79.

Whimster, Sam. 2006. The human sciences. *Theory, Culture & Society*, 23 (2–3), 174–6.

22 Notes on an Alternative Model—Neither/Nor

HORTENSE J. SPILLERS

Language has always been the companion of empire.

Antonio de Nebrija, 1492—"The Year of the Other"

In an inventory of American ideas, the thematic of the "tragic mulatto/a" seems to disappear at the end of the nineteenth century.[1] Even though certain writers in the United States have pursued this configuration of character well into the twentieth, with varying and divergent purposes in mind,[2] it is as though both the dominant and dominated national interests eventually abandoned the vocation of naming, perceiving, and explaining to themselves the identity of this peculiar New World invention. A retrieval of this topic will, therefore, appear anachronistic and irrelevant to African-American critical projects at the moment. Furthermore, the term itself and the issues that it raises are so thoroughly circumscribed by historical closure and apparently bankrupt in the situation of their origin that my attempt to revivify them is burdened, already, in the beginning, with doubt, with the necessity to prove their revised critical point. But it seems to me that the mulatto figure, stranded in cultural ambiguity, conceals the very strategies of feministic violence and displacement that have enabled a problematics of alterity regarding the African-American community in the United States. Created to provide a middle ground of latitude between "black" and "white," the customary and permissible binary agencies of the national adventure, mulatto being, as a neither/nor proposition, inscribed no historic locus, or materiality, that was other than evasive and shadowy on the national landscape. To that extent, the mulatto/a embodied an alibi, an excuse for "other/otherness" that the dominant culture could not (cannot now either) appropriate, or wish away. An accretion of signs that embody the "unspeakable," of the very thing that the dominant culture would forget, the mulatto/a, as term, designates a disguise, a cover up, in the century of Emancipation and beyond, of the social and political reality of the dreaded African presence. Behind the African-become-American stands the shadow, the unsubstantial "double" that the culture dreamed *in the place of* that humanity transformed into its profoundest challenge and by the impositions of policy, its deepest "un-American" activity.

To understand, then, the American invention of the mulatto, a term imported from the European lexis,[3] is to understand more completely, I feel, the false opposition of cultural traits that converge on the binary distribution of "black" and "white." My further aim in exploring this topic, however, is to try to discover how "mulatto-ness," the covering term, explains the workings of gender as a category of social production that has not yet assimilated to women of color. Rather than proof of the point, I see these notes as a trial of it.

Before pursuing these observations further, I should point out certain difficulties of this analysis. Those historical subjects subsumed under "mulatto/a" cannot be so easily banished to the realm of the mythical, nor is it my wish to do so. I should make it clear that I am drawing a distinction throughout between historical figures like Frederick Douglass, or Lemuel Haynes, Vermont preacher of the early nineteenth century, and the *appropriation* of the interracial child by the genocidal forces of dominance. The latter concerns a violence, or fatal ignorance, of naming and placing that is itself paradigmatic of the model of alterity, and to discover its ways and means is our persistent and urgent aim.

To compare, then, historical subjects with idea-forms, or iconographic content, or characters from novels might suggest an incommensurability, or even inaptitude of critical method, but the comparison could be instructive, since it alerts us to the subtleties that threaten to transform the living subject into an inert mass and suggests the reincarnations of human violence in their intellectual and symbolic array. The "mulatto/a," just as the "nigger," tells us little or nothing about the subject buried beneath the epithets, but quite a great deal more concerning the psychic and cultural reflexes that invent and invoke them. I am suggesting that in the *stillness* of time and space eventuated by the "mulatto/a"—its apparent sameness of fictional, historical, and auto/biographical content—we gain insight into the *theft of* the dynamic principle of the living that distinguishes the subject from his/her objectification. Such difference remains evident in the institution of New World enslavement and the captivity and production of, for example, William Faulkner's narrator's "wise supine" female of *Absalom, Absalom!*

The questionable paternity of the mulatto character in fiction, just as its parallel in the historical sequence, marks the beginning and end of cultural and symbolic illegitimacy. We shall try to see more fully how and why that is the case. In a very real sense, America's historic mulatto subject plays out his/her character on the ground of a fiction made public and decisive by dimensions of the spectacular and the specular. In his/her face, the deceits of a culture are mirrored; the deeds of a secret and unnamed fatherhood made known: "My father was a white man. He was admitted to be such by all I ever heard speak of my parentage. The opinion was also whispered that my master was my father, but of the correctness of this opinion, I know nothing."[4]

Frederick Douglass by any other name would tell the same tale over and over again with frightening consistency. But mulatto-ness is not, fortunately, a figure of self-referentiality.[5] Neither the enslaved man/woman, nor the fugitive-in-freedom would call *himself/herself* "mulatto/a," a special category of thingness that isolates and overdetermines the human character to which it points. A semantic marker, already fully inhabited by a content and an expectation, America's "tragic mulatto" exists for others—and a particular male other—in an attribution of the illicit that designates the violent mingling and commingling of bloodlines that a simplified cultural patrimony wishes to deny. But in that very denial, the most dramatic and visible of admissions is evident.

The site of a contamination, this marked figure has no name that is not parodic. In Faulkner's *Light in August*, Joe Christmas, for example, connected with the realm of pure nature makes no claim to rational force in the eyes of his maker. Standing outside the ruined house of Joanna Burden, at the broken gate, in thigh tall weeds, Christmas, in an erection scene, engages gestures of alienation that overlap the erotic: "watching his body, seeming to watch it turning slow and lascivious in a whispering of gutter filth like a drowned corpse in a thick still black pool of more than water."[6] Shortly following this bizarre moment, a car emerges in Christmas's hearing, as he observes his body "grow white out of the darkness like a kodak print emerging from the liquid." Just as the photograph releases an inherent biochemical response, Christmas materializes the unarticulated, unaccommodated American identity—raw and fundamental in a portrayal of basic, unmitigated urge. We cannot even call Christmas's compulsion desire yet, since it is untouched by the mediations and remediations of culture. Transformed into naked, grotesque, hungry man at the world's margin, Christmas speaks the radical disjuncture of human experience as his own private chaos. Christmas's narrative takes hold of a conscious infinity of pain as we see him refracted through an endless regression of events in the re-encounter of former selves. We observe a figure drowning in a sea of phenomena, enacting and re-enacting a purposeful purposelessness of movement that is bizarre, madly pointed.

Animated by forces beyond his knowing, Christmas provides an analogy on the deracinated person, fixed in cultural vestibularity. Time passes for him, over and around him, but it has no subjective properties that he might call his own.

A "unanimity-minus-one,"[7] who assumes the terror and crucifixion of his natal community's "expendable figure," Christmas is Faulkner's powerful effort to give a grammar to American race magic. But "race" itself is already a mystification by 1929, which year witnesses the publication of Nella Larsen's *Passing*, another sortie into the intrigues of genetic determinism. "Race" becomes for Faulkner, as for Larsen and Jessie Fauset, a metaphor through which the chaotic and primitive urges of human community find systematic expression. In that sense, "community" comes weighted with the burden of history, since, in Faulkner's case, its ultimate embodiment is one Percy Grimm, one's perfect kamikazi. It is, therefore, both stunning and to be expected that, for Grimm and his kind, Christmas's jugular relocates in his genitals: the flight of Joe Christmas, arrested in the kitchen of the outraged Reverend Gail Hightower, ends in a bloodbath. Grimm pursues him through the mob that wants his flesh for the death of Joanna Burden, but more precisely, his killing is a castration, as Grimm hacks away at the forbidden "cargo" in the name of white women's honor.

It would seem, then, that the mulatto *in the text of fiction* provides a strategy for naming and celebrating the phallus. In other words, the play and interplay of an open and undisguised sexuality are mapped on the body of the mulatto character, who allows the dominant culture to say without parting its lips that "we have willed to sin," the puritan recoil at the sight and the site of the genitals. In that regard, Percy Grimm is his culture's good little factotum, who understands on some dark level of unknowing that the culture, more pointedly, the culture of the fathers, can never admit, as Joe Christmas's wildness reminds them, that the law is based on phallic violence in an array of other names and symbols. The term "mulatto/a," then, becomes a displacement for a proper name, an instance of the "paradox of the negative" that signifies what it does not mean. In Faulkner's work, at least, sexuality is literally monumental, with none of the antiseptic saving grace that psychoanalysis lends it. The unavoidable bedrock of human and fictional complication, sexuality is here restored to nearness to the terrible.

If, as old mad Doc Hines, in enraged and consistent babble contends, Joe Christmas—his probable grandson—describes "the mark and the knowledge," then Christmas is the first and last victim on his way out, given the peculiar occasion to understand history and culture, or those economies of violence that carefully differentiate "inner" and "outer," "order" and "degree."

In his *Conquest of America*,[8] Tzvetan Todorov distinguishes three dimensions of the problematics of alterity: (1) the *axiological* level—"the other is good or bad, I love or do not love him, or … he is my equal or my inferior (for there is usually no question that I am good and that I esteem myself)"; (2) the *praxeological* level—the placing of distance or proximity between oneself and an imagined other—"I embrace the other's values, I identify myself with him; or else I identify the other with myself, I impose my own image upon him; between submission to the other and the other's submission, there is also a third term, which is neutrality, or indifference"; (3) the *epistemic* level—"I know or am ignorant of the other's identity … of course, there is no absolute here, but an endless gradation between the lower or higher states of knowledge."

As an instance of the exterior other in *negative* identity, Christmas, on Todorov's levels of analysis, is made the absolute equivalent of anomie. At no time in his fictional development do we not see him in clear association with wild, untamed plenitude, from Faulkner's version of terrifying female sexuality in the figures of Joanna Burden and Burden's good double in the pregnant Lena Grove, to the unspeaking, unspeakable neologism of filth—the "womanshenegro" of a particular Christmas nightmare—to the moonscape of urns, associated with the menses and Christmas's initiation into the rites of the sexual and sacrificial, to the cosmic infinity of days and space that swallow him up in a hideous repetition crisis that precedes his end.

But if it is possible to say so, we observe in Faulkner instances of the exterior other in positive identity whose laws of behavior are much harder and more challenging to detect.

The exterior other in positive identity is, for Faulkner, a female, and in the Faulknerian situation of the female, we gain good insight into the processes of gender-making as a special outcome of modes of dominance. But even more importantly, we observe gender as a special feature of a racialistic ideology. In other words, the African-American female, in her historic identity, robbed of the benefits of the "reproduction of mothering," is, consequently, the very negation of femaleness that accrues as the peculiar cultural property of Anglo-American women, in the national instance, and more generally, of the female of not-color: Faulkner's *Absalom, Absalom!* might be considered a case in point.[9]

This novel renders a fiction of misplaced incestuous longings and the play of homoerotic motives by way of a Freudian family drama.[10] It is key that the children of unreconstructed Thomas Sutpen, the great obsession of Rosa Coldfield's furious speaking, are actually and symbolically "white" and "colored." In effect, this character out of the Virginia wilds, with a crucial *stop* in Haiti (or a Francophone location in the Caribbean), lends an analogy on a fatherhood that founds a "civilization" and a continuity that terminates in a version of return of the repressed—French *Bon*-become-black *Bond*, that Faulkner's Luster says the law puts on you when it catches up with you. The route from Haiti, say, to New Orleans, to Sutpen's Hundred, Yoknapatawpha County, is purposefully and gravidly suggestive, as it involves the worlds of sub-Saharan Africa, the Caribbean, and the United States in the replay of an economic triangulation whose wealth is built solidly on the backs and with the blood of captive human cargo. It is, then, not at all accidental, or academic, to the scheme of history implied by Faulkner's fiction that the savage and dangerous denial of Charles Bon's paternity has precedent in the cultural institution of New World enslavement, as attested by Frederick Douglass, and that this enslavement has a special place, meaning, and economics for the female, as witnessed in the narrative of Linda Brent.[11]

Vagaries of Faulkner's trammeled semantics aside for the moment, this novel quite simply concerns a man who had two sons, one of them the would-be morganatic byblow of an obscure white male on the run, except that Sutpen did marry the mother of Charles Bon to discover, after the fact, that he had been betrayed by the makers of this contrived connubial arrangement. The overseer of a sugar plantation on an island like Santo Domingo—scored into historical memory by the successful revolt of Touissant L'Ouverture—Sutpen tells his version of his story to his contemporary, the grandfather of Quentin, and that, heroically, singlehandedly, he quelled a siege of insurgent African captives on the island. The reward for his bravery, the dowry of the marriage bed, so to speak, is the hand of the master's daughter, whose mother, in turn, is Spanish, the dark suggestion, not French. When Sutpen discovers that the woman to whom he is married has "Negro blood" in her veins, that single most powerful drop of deoxyribose nucleic acid, he decides simultaneously that she cannot, for that reason, contribute to the increment of his "design." He then abandons her and her son, or repudiates them in the name of a higher social and moral purity, but compensates, he imagines, by relinquishing his legal right to various island properties accruing to him as marital lagniappe. Said properties revert back to the plantation owner's daughter.

Leaving the West Indies for other New World territory, Sutpen arrives in Mississippi to take up land and build his "empire." With white Ellen Coldfield, of the indubitable blood, Sutpen has a daughter and son, Henry and Judith. But in the Caribbean a full decade before, Charles, the Good—forced into the estate of the prodigal—has been denied the name, if not the connubial inheritance, of the father. At "Ole Miss" on the eve of civil war, brother and brother meet—the marked and the untainted—their consanguinity not known to either. This disastrous encounter that possibly ends in fratricide bears the earmarks of sexual attraction, incestuously linked. But parallel to it is the complementing sybaritic tale, staked out in massive erotic display, of Charles Bon, installed with his mother in New Orleans under conditions of a severe and privileged privacy. In the narrative of Quentin Compson's father, not definitively informed by the apposite "facts" of the case, a probable fiction is hatched—or a fiction true enough—concerning Bon's octoroon mistress and the intricately manufactured arts of pleasure that distinguish the fictive New Orleans whorehouse.

Compson's social and political sense makes a few things evident at once: he imagines himself the embodiment of that "heritage peculiarly Anglo-Saxon—of fierce proud mysticism" (108). The world that he narrates through his son Quentin is permeated by notions of caste and hierarchy. This order of things, eminently linear, is identified by its interdictive coloring, whose primary object of desire and placement is the female. But in this instance, femaleness is abstracted by legal practice and social custom into an idea that may be sealed off at any concrete point as forbidden territory. In other words, female, in the brain of the creating male narrator, allows access only insofar as she approximates physical/sexual function. A curious split of motives takes place here so that on the one hand the last woman in this hierarchical scale of values—the "slave girls," for instance—are both more and less female, while, on the other, the same may be said for the first "lady," albeit for radically different reasons. Compson's "ladies, women, females" specify an increasingly visual and dramatic enactment of male heterosexuality along three dimensions of female being—"the virgins whom gentlemen someday married, the courtesans to whom they went while on sabbaticals to the cities, the slave girls and women upon whom the first caste rested and to whom in certain cases it doubtless owed the very fact of its virginity" (109).

In this economy of delegated sexual efficacies, the castes of women enter into a drama of exchange value, predicated on the dominant male's self-deceit. The third caste robs the first of a putative clitoral and vaginal pleasure, as the first purloins from the third a uterine functionality.[12] Only the first caste gains here the right to the rites and claims of motherhood, blind to its potential female pleasure and reduced, paradoxically, in the scale of things to a transcendent and opaque Womanhood. In fact, we could say that whatever "essence," or "stuff" of the female genitalia that is lost in Compson's first estate of females is more than compensated by the third estate, inexorably fixed in the condition of a mindless fertility, just as bereft as the first of the possibilities of its own potential female pleasure.[13] But quite obviously the ways and means of domination are not adopted with cultural/historical subjects-become-objects in mind, nor is "gender" here any more than, or other than, an apt articulation of a divided male heteroticism.

Inside the split ego of the dominant male falls the "mulatta," or the "octoroon," or the "quadroon"—those disturbing vectors of social and political identity—who heals the rupture at points of wounding. Allowing the male to have his cake and eat it too, or to rejoin the "female" with the "woman," the mulatta has no name because there is not a locus, or a strategy, for this unitarian principle of the erotic in the nineteenth-century mentality of Faulkner's male character. Bon's female forebear and his octoroon mistress, the unvoiced shadowy creatures who inhabit the content of the narratives of three male figures in the novel, suggest both the vaginal and the prohibitive pleasure.

The patriarchal prerogatives outlined by Compson are centered in notions that concern the domestication of female sexuality—how it is thwarted, contained, circumscribed, and above all, *narrated*, and not a single female character here escapes the outcome, from the infantilized, doll-like figures of the master class, to the brutalized who serve them. Under these conditions, sexuality is permissible, but silenced, only within the precincts of the father's house. We should say in the place of the *permissible* that sexuality is *clean* only in the father's house. Beyond the sphere of domesticity, the sexual—tenaciously named—effects synonymity with the illicit, the wild, the mysterious; without permutation.[14] And one of its signs is the "mulatta," who has no personhood, but locates in the flesh a site of cultural and political maneuver. Unlike African female personality, implied in her presence, the "mulatta" designates those notions of femaleness that would re-enforce the latter as an object of gazing—the dimensions of the spectacular that we addressed before as the virtually unique social property of the "mulatto/a."

Noted for his/her "beauty," the "mulatta/o" in fiction bears a secret, the taint of evil in the blood, but paradoxically, the secret is vividly worn, made clear. Unlike Joe Christmas, whom we pointed as an example of the exterior other in negative identity, the mulatta, in positive identity, has value for the dominant other only insofar as she becomes the inaccessible female property that can be rendered, at his behest, instantly accessible. Teasing himself with her presence, the dominant other re-intersects the lines of sexuality and "civilization" forced to diverge by the requirements of the family, the private property, and the state. "Virility" reveals itself in the whorehouse as the scandal that is not only *sufferable*, but also primarily *applauded* as the singular fact and privilege of the phallus.

It doesn't matter if the principle of virility is, among living historic male subjects, an engagement fraught with *chance*, or the erection that occasionally fails, or the sporadic impotence about which living historic female subjects remain loyally silent. We are talking about myth here, or those boundaries of discourse that fix and determine belief, practice, and desire. To that extent, all "gendering" activity—"male," "female," and its manifold ramifications—constitutes the Grand Lie about which novels are written and for which cause history hurts.[15]

Even though Compson the narrator does not entirely grasp the political and ironic trenchancies of his own conjecture (as *reported* to Shreve by Quentin at Harvard), nor know in those recalled narrative moments that Charles Bon is not an Anglo-Saxon male, he adequately identifies the complementary strands of relationship between chattel slavery and a eugenics of pleasure. Imagining what young Henry Sutpen, the Mississippi provincial, might have observed in his exposure to certain peculiarities of New Orleans life, Compson draws out the hidden exchange value of female use here as a commodification of the flesh that takes place according to intricate rules of gallantry. The caste/cast of octoroon females (in which Bon's mistress with child is installed) literally belongs to a class of masters, who protect their property by way of various devices that cluster in notions of "honor." It would not do, for instance, for Henry Sutpen to call Bon's mistress a "whore," since he, or any other male committing the *faux pas*, would be "forced to purchase that privilege with some of [his] blood from probably a thousand men" (115). The protection of chattel property in this instance occasions the ethics of the duel as the vertical version of the tumescent male. In other words, maleness is centered here almost entirely in sexual activity covered over by acts of courtesy and carefully choreographed through an entire field of manners from a certain architectural structure and accoutrements of the interior, to modes of dress and address.

This relocated mimesis of European courtly love traditions places "gender" squarely within the perspective of cultural invention whose primary aim is the gratifying appetites of the flesh. This materialist philosophy, modulated through various points of human valuation, would suggest that culture itself elaborates a structure of production and reproduction that posits, quite arbitrarily, "higher" and "lower" reaches of human society, immersed in the principle of desire in the Dominant Other. But it seems that powers of domination succeed only to the extent that their permeation remains silent and concealed to those very historical subjects—"higher" and "lower"—upon whom the entire structure rests, upon whom it depends. In other words, the fictions and realities of domination are not only opaque (not everywhere and at once visible) to the subject (and *narrated*) community, but also remain evasive, in their authentic character as raw and violent assertion, to the dominant (and *narrating*) community. Compson, for example, as a materialized fictive presence, assumes a piacular, or religious, function of female use. His hyperbolic sense of "Anglo Saxon" male mission is grammatically similar to Perry Miller's classic analysis of the puritan colonial's "errand in the wilderness."[16] That Compson's grammar crosses its wires with the "religious impulse" suggests not only the vanities of self-deceit, but also the implicit obscenities of an unironized view of any human and social scheme. Further, his shortsightedness problematizes the religious itself as a special means of domination; as a dominant discourse hiding its hand, veiling its baser motivations.

But Compson initiates the first half of his analysis in correct assessment: the invention of the octoroon mistress rests on the "supreme apotheosis of chattelry … human flesh bred of the two races for that sale" (112). That the sentence does not finish itself, overwhelmed by intervening and obstructing periods, ambiguates meaning: "that sale" *of*? "*that* sale," period? And no presumption of ignorance on the hearer's part—we all know, I think, *which sale that is*. "Apotheosis" proximate to "chattelry," however, gives rise to an untenable—one might even say godless—oxymoron. It is also a filthy joke. But none need call it "sacrilege," though, since, in Compson's view at least, this very discourse of contiguity has been ordained by God Himself.

A divine prosthesis, the narrator's "thousand, the white men—made [the octoroon mistress], created and produced them; we even made the laws which declare that one eighth of a specified kind of blood shall outweigh seven eighths of another kind" (115). This refined prattle of a pseudo human science is not entirely misleading since it designates the bestial character of human breeding. If "mulatto" originates etymologically in notions of "sterile mule," then mulatto-ness is not a genetically transferable trait. It must be calculated and preserved as a particularistic project in "race." The southern personality's historic fear that the binary "races" might come together in the spawn of the "miscegenous" is absolutely assured and pursued in the presence of the "mulatto." In fact, it would seem that this presence describes that point of intersection between the *fulfillment* of the prohibitive wish and the *prohibition* itself,[17] so that the narrative energies of the narrator's recalled text are part and parcel of an enormous struggle to ward off a successfully *willed* and *willful* compulsion:

> the white blood to give the shape and pigment of what the white man calls female beauty, to a female principle which existed, queenly and complete, in the hot equatorial groin of the world long before that white one of ours came down from trees and lost its hair and bleached out—a principle apt docile and instinct with strange and curious pleasures of the flesh (which is all: there is nothing else) which her white sisters of a mushroom yesterday fled from in moral and outraged horror—a principle which, where her white sister must needs try to make an economic matter of it like someone who insists upon installing a counter or a scales or a safe in a store or business for a certain percentage of the profits, reigns, wise supine and all-powerful, from the sunless and silken bed which is her throne. (116–17)

What Compson imagines concerning "the hot equatorial groin of the world" can be guessed only too well and has, embarrassingly, no historic basis and needn't, for the narrator, since the subject, one narrator remove, is addressing its own overdetermined sexuality. In the process, "black" remains unnamed except by implication in an imagined metonymic substitution. To return a moment to Todorov's dynamics of alterity, we observe that the narrator has (1) *epistemically* no valuable, or enviable knowledge of the female subjects in question; (2) distances himself *praxeologically* from the subjects so that they reveal to him no dynamic historical movement, remaining for the reader the fictional counters that they are; (3) accommodates *axiologically* those subjects in a stunning act of obverted condescension that objectifies the other at the same time that the other is isolated as a potentially sacred feature.

What has been created here is not so much a fiction of the octoroon heroine as a text of an evoked "Anglo-Saxon" male presence *having*, essentially, a creation myth, not unlike one's giving birth or begetting. But this behaving as *though* the fictive text were "real," that it ought to give the reader valuable information about the historical sequence, contravenes the assumptions of our present critical practices, but the misstep is useful, nevertheless, in what might be abstracted from it. "White" women and those historical subjects trapped in the figuration of "hot equatorial groin of the world" modulate into the very same economic, if not cultural, principle by sheer semantic proximity. The distinction that I wish to make here between "economic" and "cultural" is meant to identify in the economic instance those social and political uses to which the subject is put, while the cultural is intended to define the translation of such uses—in actual cash value, but more ordinarily, in the symbolic and figurative currencies entailed by such translation. The processes that I would keep discrete here so overlap in actual social practice that a distinction seems wrong. But the narrator's insistence on the "economic matter" of, by implication, a hired vaginal substance makes clear that dollars and ledgers are what *he* means as the materialized figurative value of the "white sister." It is less clear, from his point of view, though doubtless true, that the reign of the "wise supine" is just as costly and dear for the very same commodity, even if a "sunless and silken bed" carries a richer poetic and visual echo than counters and scales and stores and business.

Thrown down into the narrator's sentences as extended parentheses, these abrupt elaborations yoke "white" and "not-white" female in figurative alliance and likely, historic alignment that only the ahistoricity of "color," or the "proud fierce mysticism" of "Anglo-Saxon" race ideology, has excised. If the Compsons of the world enforce order and degree in their "casting" of women, then at least they suspect that fundamentally, the female substance—everywhere the same—acquires *different* value according to the very same standard of measure—its *imagined* and *posited* worth to a client, made supreme by his ability to command desire.

The missing *persona* from Compson's scheme is already there in what the metonymic figure keeps concealed. But "equator," in its cotermity with portions of the sub-Saharan African continent, proclaims the narrator's suggested meaning. But indirection in this case, which is itself a mode of figurative elaboration, brings us to a crucial point. In attempting to articulate a theory of difference regarding African-American women, we have begun the effort by looking at semantic processes of appeal that occur in certain textual evidence, including fiction. The Faulknerian excerpt, though isolatable in its persistent, stylistic mannerisms, provides, in that regard, points of concentration in what we might call the historical narratives that refer to this community of women. I have in mind here not primarily, if at all, those written texts of history, or those texts based in self-conscious historiographical pursuit. I mean, rather, those configurations of discursive experience *about* … that appear dispersed across a range of public address and that may or may not find their way to topics of the historical discipline. These configurations, embedded in public consciousness, enact a symbolic behavior that is actually metatextual in its political efficacy, in its impact on the individual life-narratives of historical subjects.

Though "African-American women's community" and "mulatto/a" may appear to be widely divergent structures of appeal, the one claimed by the historical dimension, the other stalled on the terrain of the reified object, they share common ground in two crucial ways: (1) The proximity effected between *real* and *imagined* properties. The "mulatto/a" appears, historically, when African female and male personality become hyphenated American political entities, at that moment when they enter public and political discourse in the codes of slavery, the rise of the fugitive, the advertisement of the run-away man/woman.[18] (2) Both effecting a radical alterity with the dominant one, they demonstrate the extent to which modes of substitution can be adopted as strategies of containment. In other words, if African-American women's community can be silenced in its historic movement, then it will happen because the narratives concerning them have managed successfully to capture the subject in time's vacuum. By denying the presence of the black female, or assimilating her historic identity, more precisely, to a false body, ventriloquized through a factitious public discourse concerning the "blood" and "breeding," the dominant mode succeeds in transposing the real into the mythical/magical.

The situation of the "mulatta" in the same field of signification with the black female juxtaposes contrastive social and political uses, but their simultaneous appearance at the time of the national consolidation of slave-holding power is, on the one hand, no longer a secret—if it ever were—and a problem of meaning on the other. That class of historical subjects fathered by captive owners and following the condition of the mother were never, color of skin aside, surrogate Anglo-American, though they did stand in for black, for African. I am less interested in the class implications of this cultural phenomenon than its symbolic processes and their outcome. Subsequent to the intrusion of a middle term, or middle ground—figuratively—between the subjugated and dominant interests, public discourse gains, essentially, the advantages of a lie by orchestrating otherness through degrees of difference. The philosopher's "great chain of being" ramifies now to disclose within American Africanity itself literal shades of human value so that the subject community refracts the oppressive mechanism just as certainly as the authoring forms put them in place. This fatalistic motion that turns the potentially insurgent community furiously back on itself proceeds by way of processes we might call "archaizing." Faulkner's narrative voices provide examples of this trait when Quentin as Compson posits in the "hot equatorial groin of the world" and "those white ones of ours [come] down from trees and … bleached out" aspects of the magical, or the ahistorical, not at all responsive to context, or contingency. The "mulatta," in prominent isolation from the living subject, just as, by suggestion, "black" and "white" women are, shows this process in concision. "Power" in this instance consists in the prerogative to name human value, to distribute and arrogate it.

The world according to captives and their captors strikes the imagination as a grid of identities running at perpendicular angles to each other: *things* in serial and lateral array; beings in hierarchical and vertical array. On the serial grid, the captive—the chattel property—is the equivalent of inanimate and other living things (see Figure 22.1).

This itemized excerpt from the accounts from an African Trade-Book for the colony of Rhode Island vividly illustrates the dehumanization of African personality.[19] Frederick Douglass, however, provides a narrative a full century later for such a scenario, remembering the division of property upon the death of one of his former masters. Having to return from Baltimore to the site of Captain Anthony's estate, he writes of the occasion: "We were all ranked together at the valuation. Men and women, old and young, married and

	ANAMABOE 1736			Oz.	Acky
		oz.	A.	20	8
Nov. 24th	Sold Capt. Hammond 4 Women for				
	Recd. the following goods				
	Viz. 16 perpets	5			
	7 half Says	3	8		
	3 half Ells	1	8		
	1 ps Niconee		5		
	4 qr bb powder	2			
	14 Sheets		14		
	2 paper Sleties		5		
	112 galls rum	7			
		oz. 20	8		

Figure 22.1 Excerpt from an African Trade-Book.

single, were ranked with horses, sheep, and swine. There were horses and men, cattle and women, pigs and children, all holding the same rank in the scale of being, and were all subjected to the same narrow examination."[20]

From Donnan's accounts of the slave galley's logs and bills of lading and of sales, to Douglass's *Narrative*, we discover time and again the collapse of human identity adopted to the needs of commerce and economic profit. But even more startling than this nominal "crisis of degree" (which renders an equality of substances not unlike the figurative collapse of disparities in metaphorical display) is the *recovery* of difference in a hierarchical and vertical distribution of being, as though this cultural disarray stood corrected, or compensated. In the intersection of these axes, at the point of "mules and men"—the human ownership and possession of other human beings—the notion of property so penetrates the order of things that the entire structure is undermined by a simple change and overwhelming paradox: those subjects located at this juncture of saturated elements are both more and less human, the former because they enter into a wider ecumenicalism with named and claimed things, or vocabularies of experience; the latter because it is their destiny by virtue of Christ's church, by whom the country swears, and the spirit of national insurgence and constitutionality to be human first and only. That we find no comparable "list" of being, as we do the carefully accounted for commercial item, simply suggests to me that "laterality" had done its job, and no more needed to be said, if it were possible to rank human with animal. In effect, the humanity of African personality is placed in quotation marks under these signs and problematized as a leading question for public policy and a philosophical inquiry of the nicest sort.

Alterity, therefore, describes not only an inauthentic human status, but also the locus of a relationship between non-historical elements that come to rest beyond the pale of human and its discourses; this lack of movement in the field of signification seems to me the origin of "mulatto/a-ness"—the *inherent* name and naming—the *wedge* between the world of light and the step beyond—into the undifferentiated, unarticu-lated mass of moving and movable *things*.

Between these dualities, the "shadow" of the "mulatto/a" is interposed. It is a matter of surprise to me that there is in William Faulkner, writing in the twentieth century, and Frances E. W. Harper, writing in the nineteenth, a certain lexical recurrence that initiated my observations in the opening pages of this essay: Quentin/Compson the narrator describes Charles Bon in terms of an appropriation that are just as apposite to his octoroon invention. In fact, Charles Bon is thrice made—once by the attenuated concepts of history that haunt the characterization; once by the structure of mimesis that the character is purported to display; and yet again by the appropriating speaker as a "shadowy" presence: "A myth, a phantom: something which [Ellen and Judith Sutpen] engendered and created whole themselves; some effluvium of Sutpen blood and character, as though as a man he did not exist at all" (104). Frances Harper entitled her 1893 novel *Iola Leroy, or Shadows Uplifted*. Though it is appropriately not clear what dramatic and rhetorical function the topos of "shadow" serves in the novel, it is at least probable that its ambiguity complements its topic—the fate of Iola Leroy, mulatta girl remanded back into slavery and overcoming, at last, the pain and confusion of her biography. But the novel just as certainly concerns the reunion of mothers and children—the blood line of slavery—divided across the cleavage of "race."

In each instance of re-encounter, the pilgrimage that precedes it seems compelled by the mulatto status of the character, as though, as in comic resolution, the peace and order of the world were restored in *their* happiness. For Harper's narrator, at least, only the mulatto characters enter an ascension, as Iola Leroy, in the closure of the novel, is not only a character, but also Character Extraordinaire. These agents "too white to be black, too black to be white" share with Bon and Christmas the magical status of liminality (as it is not clear, recent criticism argues, just what "color" Joe Christmas is),[21] but in the case of Harper's eponymous heroine, the piously sacred overtakes her. Just so, she assumes the equally ambiguous estate of the blessed: "The shadows have been lifted from all their lives; and peace, like bright dew, has descended upon their paths. Blessed themselves, their lives are a blessing to others."[22]

In effect, the law and the order of this world have not simply been fully regained. This world has ended as the character slips away from earth into the non-historical eternity of the unchanging. This false movement takes us back to the notion of the intruded wedge between opposed dualities. In this instance, the mulatta mediates between dualities, which would suggest that at least mimetic movement, imitating *successful* historical movement, is *upward*, along the vertical scale of being. The only "black" in this case who can move is not quite "black" enough, or certainly not enough that the people who need to know can tell. We observe in the female a similar complex of assumptions at work in the Faulknerian case.

The "shadow" as a center of ambiguity in Faulkner's and Harper's work might disclose the dramatic surprise that lends these divergent writings a stunning mutuality. As a way of concluding these notes, I want to point out three moments of crux: the lifting of the shadows from the one-dimensionality of Harper's characters' lives; the phantom-like, shadowy aspects that cluster in Compson's version of Charles Bon; the terrible, ascensive epiphany of Joe Christmas's slaughter: "Then his face, body, all seemed to collapse, to fall in upon itself, and from out the slashed garments about his hips and loins the pent black blood seemed to rush like a released breath. It seemed to rush out of his pale body like a rush of sparks from a rising rocket; upon the black blast the man seemed to rise soaring into their memories forever and ever."[23]

In all three moments, the character achieves, at last, the superior talismanic force, a preponderance, or a preponderant lack, of humanity. This attribution of extraordinary humanity obviously works in contrastive ways: as we have seen in the case of *Iola Leroy*, the closural device points toward a divine and beneficent ground of potentialities; in the case of *Light in August*, toward a sacrificial torture. In *Absalom, Absalom!* Charles Bon, immersed in the secrecies of origin, is invested by effects of adoration, as he becomes the veritable love object of brother and sister Sutpen. But these opposing indices—pointing upward and downward—mobilize character toward the very same region of finality. "Hell" is "heaven" turned upside down, as "heaven" comprehends "hell" in the classic scheme of cosmogony.

That the semantic field here clings tenaciously to notions of the transcendent without openly declaring them as such provides what seems an apt demonstration of Foucault's "enunciative field" by way of concomitance.[24] In this instance of discursive relations between what I would call a founding concept and "forms of succession," "quite different domains of objects" are involved that "belong to quite different types of discourse." Concomitance is generated "either because they serve as analogical confirmation [of the founding concept] or because they serve as a general principle and as premises accepted by a reasoning, or because they serve as models that can be transferred to other contents." The founding concept here may be generally regarded as a religiously discursive pointer, as we observed in Compson's blank parody of the creation process. But the analogues on a religious discursivity in these works fracture in contradiction: the "sacred" mulatto figure simultaneously repels and attracts because of his/her blood-crossed career. Faulkner's narrators attribute to Joe Christmas the "pent black blood" and to the octoroon female "seven-eighths" of the *right* blood type. It is not until Bon's blood connection is revealed that Henry Sutpen most probably commits fratricide of the "blood" brother whom he has loved.

Throughout Harper's work the narrator refers to blood along various lines of stress: the "tainted blood" of "white Negroes"; the "trick of the blood"; "outcast blood in the veins"; "traditions of blood" and the human estate; "the imperceptible infusion of Negro blood," etc. As the life essence, the human blood, for all that scientific knowledge teaches concerning it, persists in notions of the mysterious. At least one tends to regard it mysteriously, as if the scientific topicality of it were insufficient to exhaust its range of figurative notions.

The blood to which these fictive narrators speak has little to do with the scientific, even when they suggest, and perhaps all the more so, mensural dimensions of the substance, as in one-half, one-fourth, one-eighth "black." It appears that medical and scientific knowledges are not, after all, the arbiters of the blood *where we live*, nor yet the origin of recourse when genealogies, or the "transfer" of time through children and properties, are concerned. The blood remains impervious, at the level of folklore and myth, to incursions of the "reasonable" and inscribes the unique barrier beyond which human community has not yet passed into the "brotherhood of man" and the "Fatherhood of God." But this very difficulty of the blood is the hinge upon which the concept of community, as we now understand it, appears to turn; extends itself.

Like the *pharmikon*, the blood is both the antidote and the poison,[25] as the intrusion of mystery in its place segregated the menstruating female, banished the "ugly and deformed" infants of the unhusbanded woman,[26] and rendered "femaleness" itself the site of absence. On its basis, American Africanity was assigned to the axis of "thingness" in a vision of human community that replicates time and again notions of hierarchical order. If there is mystery or spirit drooping down in the midst of things, then someone must safeguard its secrets; traditionally, the offices of the priestly function (and here I mean any structure of the esoteric), of the recondite in general, of the Dominant One, of a hyperbolean phallic status have fallen to the lot of the male. It is this inner and licit circle of a coveted and mystified knower and knowledge that determines the configurations of the law and the order. But the mystery apparently yields its secret, despite the covering names, as the glorification of a male heteronormativity, which designates the only "maleness" that can lay claim to the phallic principle. Under these conditions of culture and acculturation, we regard the "mulatta" as the recovery of female gender beyond the father's house, beyond the lights of the female who falls *legitimately* within its precincts. The borders of the endogamous arrangement are extended without guilt. But the "master," not always sufficiently protected against the burden of incest, might well have discovered his daughter (by African female personality) in the bed of his wife. The invention of the American "mulatta" virtually assured his success.

Originally published in *The Year of the New Left*, Spring 1987. Rev. and rpt. in *The Difference Within: Feminism and Critical Theory*, ed. Elizabeth Meese and Alice Parker (Amsterdam: John Benjamins, 1989). https://doi.org/10.1075/ct.8. Reprinted with permission.

Notes

1. Winthrop Jordan, *White Over Black: American Attitudes Toward the Negro 1550–1812* (Baltimore: Penguin Books, 1969), remains one of the most thoroughgoing analyses of this subject from the point of view of the United States and its colonial antecedents. Part IV, "Fruits of Passion: The Dynamics of Interracial Sex" concerns specifically the historical context against which sexual mores, or an American behavior of sexuality, were played out. In this "cultural matrix of purpose, accomplishment, self-conception, and social circumstances of settlement in the New World, the mulatto child violated the strictest intentions of a binary racial function" (167). For Jordan, the situation of the mulatto reflects a persistent historicity: the configurations assumed by a cultural phenomenon, or structure of attention, against the perspective of time.

   Barbara Christian, *Black Women Novelists: The Development of a Tradition, 1892–1976* (Westport, Conn.: Greenwood Press, 1980), looks closely at the theme of the mulatta in certain nineteenth and twentieth century fiction, including that of Frances E. W. Harper, William Wells Brown, Jessie Fauset, and Nella Larsen. See especially, "From Stereotype to Character," 3–61.

Mary V. Dearborn, *Pocahontas's Daughters: Gender and Ethnicity in American Culture* (New York: Oxford University Press, 1986), 158, explores the specific connection between the thematics of the mulatta heroine in fiction and the act of incest: the denial of paternity and of blood rite to the interracial child creates an ignorance of identity that can redound to the distinct disadvantage of certain lateral kin relations. Even though Dearborn does not employ Judith and Henry Sutpen as an instance of the fatal unknowing, I think that a case can be made for it. Because they are ignorant of the existence of Charles Bon—their "black" brother—incest becomes a distinct possibility for all of Sutpen's children. Drawing out the symbolic and rhetorical resonances of the mulatto theme, Dearborn defines both the fictive character and the historical subject, we infer, as "a living embodiment of the paradox of the individual within society." She suggestively describes the "fictional mulatto" as the "imaginative conjunction of a cultural disjunction."

Henry Louis Gates's guest-edited volume of *Critical Inquiry* 12 (Autumn 1985) does not propose to look specifically at the mulatto/a as an aspect of the problematics of alterity. But the various other issues of alterity explored in the volume are suggestive in a number of ways, specifically, Israel Burshatin's "The Moor in the Text: Metaphor, Emblem, and Silence," 98–119. Burshatin's "moor," like the "mulatto/a," might be viewed as an already inspissated identity before the particulars of context have had an opportunity to do their work.

2.   The following listing of fictional texts on the mulatto/a is not offered as an exhaustive survey. We regard them as impression points that the reader achieves in tracing the career of the subject from Harper's era through the 1930s:

James Weldon Johnson, *The Autobiography of an Ex-Colored Man*, intro. Arna Bontemps (New York: Hill and Wang, 1960). Jean Toomer, *Cane*, intro. Darwin Turner (1923; New York: Liveright, 1975). The reader should see specifically the closing section of this powerful work for the tale of Kabnis. Here, the exteriority of the mulatto figure has been revised and corrected into a structure of internal, or psychic, complication.

Nella Larsen, *Quicksand* (New York: Alfred A. Knopf, 1928); rpt. New York: Negro Universities Press, 1969); idem, *Passing* (New York: Alfred A. Knopf, 1929), rpt. *Afro-American Cultural Series: The American Negro, His History and Literature*, ed. Arthur P. Davis and Darwin Turner (New York: Arno Press, 1969). It would be fair to say that Larsen criticism comes into its own with the explosive critical work of Deborah McDowell, whose introductory essay to the reprinted edition of *Quicksand* and *Passing* (New Brunswick, N.J.: Rutgers University Press, 1986) brought out features of these novels that prior readings had simply missed. For other biographical and critical work on Larsen, see: Thadeous Davis, *Nella Larsen: Novelist of the Harlem Renaissance* (Baton Rouge: Louisiana State University Press, 1994); Jacquelyn McClendon, *The Politics of Color in the Fiction of Jessie Fauset and Nella Larsen* (Charlottesville: University Press of Virginia, 1995); and Charles R. Larson, *Invisible Darkness: Jean Toomer and Nella Larsen* (Iowa City: University of Iowa Press, 1993).

Jessie Redmon Fauset, *The Chinaberry Tree: A Novel of American Life* (1933; College Park, Md.: McGrath Publishing Company, 1969); idem, *Comedy: American Style* (1931; College Park, Md.: McGrath Publishing Company, 1969).

The reader might consult the opening section of Barbara Christian's work for a more comprehensive account of the fiction of the mulatto/a. A fine study of Pauline Hopkins, contemporaneous with Frances Harper and in pursuance of the mulatto thematic, is provided by Claudia Tate, "Pauline Hopkins: Our Literary Foremother," in *Conjuring: Black Women, Fiction, and Literary Tradition*, ed. Marjorie Pryse and Hortense Spillers (Bloomington: Indiana University Press, 1985).

3.   The Oxford English Dictionary on "mulatta" situates the term in Spanish. Born of a "Negra and a fayre man," "mulatta" in the English lexis appears c. 1622. Among its permutations in Portuguese is "mullato," young mule, or one of a mixed race.

4. Frederick Douglass, *Narrative of the Life of Frederick Douglass, An American Slave, Written by Himself* (1845; rpt. New York: Signet Books, 1968), 21–22.

5. Werner Sollors points out that "mulatto/a," as a term of self-reference, was recurrent in the work of certain black writers and intellectuals in the 1980s and 1990s. I am hardly aware, however, of any widespread currency of the term, now or then, either as a mode of self-reference, or a way to describe someone else. The two examples that he evinces in support of his claims are simply the exception that proves the rule; Trey Eilis's "cultural mulatto," one of the examples pressed into service by Sollors, is a different order of cases altogether from "mulatto/a" as a phenotypic designation. My whole point in the essay was to suggest that, *historically*, black people in the U.S. context—whatever their skin tone might have been—did not refer to themselves as "mulatto/a," and that the "mulatto/a" should be distinguished, *as a literary device*, from *interracial* progenies *and* cultural commingling. See Werner Sollors, *Neither Black Nor White Yet Both: Thematic Explorations of Interracial Literature* (Cambridge, Mass.: Harvard University Press, 1997), 128ff.

6. William Faulkner, *Light in August* (1932; New York: Random House Modern Library, 1959), 100.

7. Girard's explosive work offers a background against which we might view the fundamental structuration of human community as the deployment of the dynamics of violence and the fear of violent reprisal. By isolating an "expendable figure," the "unanimity-minus one," community purges itself of various impurities, including guilt. Community also discovers the One Man or Woman (or the substitute) whose elimination would not generate the operations of revenge. Faulkner's Joe Christmas is perfectly placed to carry out all the requirements of Girard's sacrificial program. Essentially unfathered, Christmas is Every man/woman *before* the name of the Father "cleanses" him/her, or releases from the terrors of "unculture."

8. Tzvetan Todorov, "Typology of Relations to the Other," *The Conquest of America*, trans. Richard Howard (New York: Colophon Books, 1984), 185–201, at 185. Todorov's interesting conceptual narrative concentrates in the career of the Native American at the hands of the European explorer, but its application lays hold of a broader frame of reference.

9. William Faulkner, *Absalom, Absalom!* (1936; New York: Random House Modern Library, 1951).

10. John Irwin's brilliant structuralist reading of incest in Faulkner traces its manifestations in the agency of Quentin Compson (*Doubling and Incest/Repetition and Revenge* [Baltimore: Johns Hopkins University Press, 1975]). Overlapping *The Sound and the Fury* and *Absalom, Absalom!*, Quentin reflects his own incestuous urges toward his sister Caddy (*Sound and Fury*) in the narrative that he "repeats" concerning Charles Bon.

    A critical reevaluation of Marxist theory in perspective with the contemporary scene of criticism occasions Fredric Jameson's *Political Unconscious: Narrative as a Socially Symbolic Act* (Ithaca: Cornell University Press, 1981). The opening chapter of the work questions the adequacy of a Freudian "Family Drama" as a comprehensive paradigm and theory of processes of social production. (See "Faulkner Adds Up" in this volume.)

11. The economic uses of African female personality under the onus of captivity are alluded to in Linda Bront's chapter, "Sketches of Neighboring Slaveholders," *Incidents in the Life of a Slave Girl*, ed. I . Maria Child, intro. Walter Teller (New York: Harcourt Brace Jovanovich, Harvest Books, 1973), 45–53. Not commenting specifically on the mulatta's value, the writer sounds, nonetheless, the profit connections between the female body/sexuality and the oppressive conditions of enslavement.

12. The informing conceptualization of the relevant paragraph here is suggested by the brilliantly speculative work of Gayatri Chakravorty Spivak in "French Feminism in an International Frame," *Yale French Studies*, no. 62, Feminist Readings: French Texts/American Contexts, 154–84.

13. Various aspects of female sexuality in conjunction with history and politics are examined in *Pleasure and Danger: Exploring Female Sexuality*, ed. Carole Vance (Boston: Routledge and Kegan Paul, 1984). My own essay here, "Interstices: A Small Drama of Words," looks specifically at the grammar of sexuality in relationship to African-American Women's community (in this volume.) The essays in *Pleasure and Danger* are based on papers

delivered by the participants at the controversial "Feminist and Scholar Conference, IX," at Barnard College, Spring 1982.

14. Foucault, re-opening the problem of Victorian sexuality, considers the discursivity of his subject. Victorian Europe was not, in his view, a sexually muted culture, but seized instead every occasion to induce and excite discourse about it. Illegitimate sexuality in the historic context he examines becomes one of the "forms of reality" subjected to a discourse that is "clandestine, circumscribed, and coded" in reference to the brothel, the mental institution, and other spaces of marginality (*The History of Sexuality: Volume 1–An Introduction*, trans. Robert Hurley [New York: Pantheon Books, 1978], 4ff.). We would regard the site of the mulatta mistress as a marginalized class of objects erotically configured.

15. "History is what hurts" profoundly informs Jameson's sense that "History" is the "ground and untranscendable horizon [that] needs no theoretical justification." He offers its inexorability as the fundamental scene against which the critical praxis unfolds; against which we gauge the efficacy and completeness of any critical system (102).

16. Perry Miller, *The New England Mind*, vol. 1, *The Seventeenth Century*; vol. 2, *From Colony to Province* (Boston: Beacon Press, 1961).

17. The classic reading of the tensions engendered between the wish-fulfillment and its prohibitive mechanism is given in Freud's *Totem and Taboo*, vol. 13 of *The Standard Edition of the Complete Psychological Works of Sigmund Freud*, trans. James Strachey (London: Hogarth Press, 1955).

18. The codification of law that underscores the institution of slavery in the United States is sporadically examined in numerous texts of history. But a work contemporaneous with the final days of the "Peculiar Institution" provides not only a detailed reading of the code, but also an instance of a parallel and *counter* sensitivity that takes on historic appeal in its own right: William Goodell, *The American Slave Code in Theory and Practice: Its Distinctive Features Shown by its Statutes, Judicial Decisions, and Illustrative Texts* (New York: American and Foreign Anti-Slavery Society, 1853). Apparently the "runaway slave" was neither rare nor forgotten. The plentifulness of advertisements describing the *person* of the fugitive—the model, we might suppose, for the contemporary "All Points Bulletin" of the Federal Bureau of Investigation and those mug shots that grace the otherwise uniform local post office—argue the absolute solidification of captivity—the major American social landscape, in my view, for two and a half centuries of human hurt on the scene of "man's last best hope": *Runaway Slave Advertisements: A Documentary History from the 1730s to 1790*, comp. Lathan A. Windley, vol. 1, *Virginia and North Carolina*; vol. 2, *Maryland* (Westport, Conn.: Greenwood Press, 1983); on the "mulatto," see Joel Williamson, *New People: Miscegenation and Mulattoes in the United States* (New York: The Free Press, 1980).

19. Elizabeth Donnan, ed. and comp, 1932. "Accounts from an African Trade Book, 1733–1736," from the Archives of the Newport Historical Society, *Documents Illustrative of the History of the Slave Trade to America*, vol. 3, *New England and the Middle Colonies* (Washington, D.C.: The Carnegie Institute, 1932), 130.

20. Frederick Douglass, *Narrative of the Life of Frederick Douglass*, 59–60.

21. Michael Cobb, "Racial Blasphemies" (Ph.D. diss., Cornell University, 2001).

22. Frances Harper, *Iola Leroy, or Shadows Uplifted* (1893; rpt. New York: AMS Press, 1971), 281.

23. Faulkner, *Light in August*, 440.

24. Michel Foucault, *The Archaeology of Knowledge and the Discourse on Language*, trans. A. M. Sheridan Smith (New York: Harper Colophon Books, 1972), 56–64, at 58.

25. A description of the paradoxical nature of the *pharmikon* is provided by René Girard, *Violence and the Sacred*, trans. Patrick Gregory (Baltimore: Johns Hopkins University Press, 1977).

26. The dispatch, in Roman society, of the illegitimate children of unwed mothers becomes a striking item of anthropological interest. See chap. 8, n. 2.

23 Seeing in the Dark: Attentive Engagement

JANE STADLER

This chapter proposes a way of approaching ethical understanding through sensitive, intentionally directed perception. In order to establish the value of attentive engagement in the cinema, the discussion moves from arguing for the ethical importance of attention, through examining how it is inscribed in film texts, to exploring how it is practiced by film spectators. The perceptual capacity referred to as ethical attention, or (in a sense that suggests more intense personal involvement) as attentive engagement, is characterized by concern for the specific needs and vulnerabilities of a unique individual or situation, within a concrete and particular ethical context. Ethical attention is a practice that involves the resources, faculties, and forms of responsiveness, resistance, and perceptiveness explored in the preceding chapters. It requires emotional, imaginative, and perceptual engagement, as well as acts of narration and narrative interpretation.

The objective of ethical attention is to progressively build up layers of understanding[1] comprised of different perspectives, situational detail, and an awareness of the interwoven influences of personal history, significant relationships, and other cultural and contextual factors that have bearing on questions of ethical choice. Ideally, such a perceptive practice produces a detailed, just, and caring awareness that enables an ethical agent to respond more appropriately to the unique requirements of a situation than the application of general ethical rules, guidelines, values, or principles would, on their own, allow.

Attentive engagement is an ethical process that contrasts with and can be seen as complementary to deductive or inductive reasoning based on the application of moral principles. Since the very concept of ethical attention diverts emphasis from such moral standards (though it might be balanced or guided by them), it is open to criticisms about the lack of criteria for moral deliberation, evaluation, and response and, consequently, to charges of moral relativism. Because attention is both contextually specific and a skill or disposition attributable to an individual, it is often thought to be as weak and indefensible a justification for an ethical action or judgment as intuition or "gut feelings." The responses arising from a practice of ethical attention are difficult to generalize or extend to other situations. Because of this it is hard to see how the moral insights and values which come to light through attention and which govern the ensuing ethical response might be based on understandings shared amongst a community in the manner that makes ethical life coherent.

More specifically, without reliance on principles or rules of conduct prescribing moral duties and obligations, clarity of ethical insight could be in danger of being clouded by ego, or personal and cultural bias. In practice, in each conception of ethical attention taken up in this chapter, the direction of attention extends outward from the self toward others rather than being primarily an act of introspection or reflection, though at the same time ethical attention may include and often necessitate self-scrutiny. Though these altruistic and self-reflexive characteristics of attention ameliorate concerns about self-centered perception, they raise equally disturbing questions about practitioners of ethical attention becoming self-sacrificing. If the ego does not assert itself and the act of attending is directed toward the needs of others then, in extreme cases, an unhealthy form of selfless servitude to others[2] may be enacted.

In this chapter, three different theoretical approaches to attention are considered, addressing the ways in which this central complex of difficulties surrounding relativism, moral criteria, and the ego's attachments is negotiated in each. The descriptive frameworks of these approaches center on philosophical accounts by Simone Weil and Martha Nussbaum of "moral vision" in narrative fiction and within lived ethical situations; on Maurice Merleau-Ponty's theory of attention in *Phenomenology of Perception* and Vivian Sobchack's phenomenological discussion of "the inscription of vision as movement" in film texts; and on attentive engagement as a cinema spectator. In film spectatorship, perception in the cinema is necessarily related to and partially directed by the expression and inscription of the film's own visible, visual activity. Consideration of the forms in which attention is enacted helps to illustrate and extend philosophical accounts of what ethical attention is and ought to be.

Examples from the films *Once Were Warriors* (directed by Lee Tamahori in 1994), and *Nil by Mouth* (Gary Oldman, 1997) are used throughout the chapter to illuminate how acts of attention are instantiated in film texts and in our engagement with them. In addition to treating filmic style as the expression or practice of a form of ethical attention (which in turn engages the attention of spectators), I contrast the styles of these two films, using them as metaphors for the different forms of ethical attention theorized by Weil and by Nussbaum.

After detailing the ethical significance of different modes of perception and ethical attention, the chapter explores the inscription of attention in film texts. Once again Sobchack's work provides a theoretical perspective and an analytical vocabulary to describe movements of attention in screen texts as films give visible expression to acts of perception. Here the possibilities for entwining an awareness of the ethics of attention with Sobchack's phenomenological film analysis are elaborated. As well as gaining opportunities to access and reflect upon examples of various modes of perception made visible in the visual style of the films we watch, as spectators we also participate in and practice the form of perception expressed by the film and by its characters. In the final section of the chapter the conjunction of the film's visual activity and the attentive engagement of spectators with film texts is explored, concluding by suggesting that film spectatorship itself is an attentive practice that provides a model for ethical attention.

Perception and Attention

In a metaphor reminiscent of the spotlight that focuses on the emotional core of memories in *Eternal Sunshine of the Spotless Mind*, Merleau-Ponty compares acts of attention to a searchlight's beam that illuminates hidden aspects of a dark landscape, exploring the possibility that "perception awakens attention" and attention subsequently "develops and enriches" the life of consciousness (Merleau-Ponty 2002, 31). As any cinematographer knows, intensity of illumination or clarity of focus affects the ability of viewers to perceive detail and to understand what we see. By acting as a filter or a focus puller for the chaos of sensory impressions and by delineating a perceptual or mental field of clarity and concentration, attention "presupposes a transformation of the mental field, a new way for consciousness to be present to its objects" (Merleau-Ponty 2002, 33). Thus, Merleau-Ponty concludes, "To pay attention is not merely further to elucidate pre-existing data, it is to bring about a new articulation of them" through "the active constitution of a new object which makes explicit and articulate what was until then presented as no more than an indeterminate horizon" (2002, 35).

According to Sobchack, perception itself is an evaluative, intentional act, not simply a passive, receptive, and uninterpretive physiological process. Perception makes intentionality manifest, that is: intention points or extends toward significant things in the visual field, picking them out from their surroundings. Sobchack claims that perception is a fundamental mode of engagement with the world, and a structuring activity of consciousness (1992, 72). In order for sense perceptions to have meaning or conscious significance, perception must involve the exercise of something like categorization and evaluation: perception, then, can be thought of as the reception and identification of something through sensory engagement with it. The process of evaluative perception, however, often occurs on what might be called an automatic or subconscious level (hence the value of phenomenological analysis, which brings to light such "naturalized" aspects of experience by delving into the processes of recognition and categorization). Perception, though we may rarely notice this, is inseparable from recognition and understanding: "It works on us without us; it hides itself in making the object visible" (Merleau-Ponty 1964, 167).

With Merleau-Ponty, Sobchack links perception with judgment, deliberation, and evaluation: "Perception is the diacritical emergence of judgment in existence … the empirically formal link between embodied consciousness and any significance the world might have for it" (Sobchack 1992, 71–72). This suggests that the perception of phenomena is inherently qualitative and selective, and that it entails value judgments (often of a covert nature). Noticing, overlooking, and ignoring, like more discerning and deliberative evaluations that recognize something as important or as devoid of interest and value, are acts that can have ethical ramifications. For instance, it is often easier to allow people like the Sprague brothers, or Nola, in *The Boys*, or Matthew Poncelet in *Dead Man Walking* to remain outside the zone of our attention, than to focus on them and their difficulties. Once an injustice has been acknowledged, it can exert an ethical claim.

As a precursor to a more systematic working through of modes of attending, an example from Gary Oldman's film *Nil by Mouth* details how perception can have ethical consequences if we shift the context of our perception slightly to include particular and relevant details. *Nil by Mouth* takes a close look at abuse and dependence in the lives of Val (Kathy Burke) and Ray (Ray Winstone), a dysfunctional couple living in council flats in South London.[3] Val's appearance throughout the film is unattractive: she looks dowdy and never fixes her hair or wears anything remotely presentable. In perceiving Val's image on the screen, we not only see her physical appearance, but we also unavoidably see her appearance *as* something good or bad, important or insignificant. We evaluate her appearance, perhaps without consciously realizing it, by comparing her with others and by interpreting our perceptions within the context of her life and our own range of experiences. "Dowdy" is not a term of appreciation. Such an observation and the accompanying evaluation merely seem derogatory if we stop at the level of sense-perception or aesthetic judgment. To stop there would constitute a failure of ethical attention, a failure to discern the relevant details and to deepen understanding of another person's situation. As ethical attention, the act of perception must reach further, moving through successive levels of insight and accumulating layers of narrative detail and context.

As distinct from ordinary perception, ethical attention may extend to the recognition that Val's unkempt state is indicative of her inability to adequately care for herself or receive care from others. This point might remain unnoticed if the attender does not care about Val, or if her image is frozen and abstracted from its context (as in still photography, a description in a news article, or a note in a case record), but it reveals itself when her appearance is set against the circumstances of her life and read as symptomatic of depression, poverty, a lack of support and care through pregnancy, and debased self-esteem.

For a different individual, or even for the same individual in a situation that differed in some significant way, the same "symptom" (a dowdy appearance) might stem from completely different causes. Val's appearance could be a matter of practicality and economy, or a positive choice expressing her personal

Figure 23.1 *Nil by Mouth*: Val's dowdy appearance.

preferences or political convictions; equally, it could indicate a lack of time or inclination to focus on something considered trivial, or a means of resisting dominant ideological positions relating physical appearance to personal-worth. While our attention to Val is, in this instance, reliant on vision, it is also inseparable from evaluations related to an imaginative and conceptual grasp of her situation. This example brings to light the link between ethical attention and contextually specific details, as well as demonstrating how the qualitative dimension of embodied, sensory perception constitutes a fundamental practice of engaging with the world on an ethical level.

Although the terms perception and attention are often used interchangeably, or in senses that overlap with one another, a variety of philosophical distinctions have been drawn between the two, and different philosophers often use the same term in disparate ways. For instance, Martha Nussbaum counts perception[4] as central to the nature of practical reason. Following Aristotle, she claims that discerning the correct decision in an ethical situation rests on perception, understood as "complex responsiveness to the salient features of one's concrete situation" (1990, 55). Nussbaum's conception of the nature of perception is not incompatible with Sobchack's; however, the two theorists emphasize differing objectives in their descriptions of the same capacity. Nussbaum investigates the ethical implications of the involvement of attender and attendee; she considers the significance of responsibility and responsiveness, and attitudes of care and concern. In *Address of the Eye*, Sobchack's concern lies principally with the embodied, hermeneutic, and mediated nature of perception in film. However, she has taken up the ethical implications of cinematic vision in relation to documentary film in "Inscribing Ethical Space" (1984), an article which I draw upon below because it details a number of different ways of encoding an ethical gaze on film.

In Simone Weil's moral philosophy a very different distinction is drawn between the terms perception and attention. Weil classes attention as an active form of looking, yet she believes its ethical value lies in the activity remaining rigorously noninterpretive. Since, for Weil, just and truthful vision incorporates the revelation of reality,[5] subjective acts of evaluation are unnecessary and the attender must actively abstain from interpretation and from engaging in the kinds of implicit evaluations with which personal involvements, attachments, and experiences may be laden.

Nussbaum, in contrast, understands moral attention as necessitating deep involvement: intensity of emotion, reflection, and responsiveness of the physical senses (1990, 207) and a caring engagement with actual individuals (1990, 189). The form of attentive engagement that Nussbaum advocates is very like that of a reader engrossed in a literary work, feeling themselves drawn deeply into the lives of the characters therein. This is an analogy she develops in various ways throughout many of the essays in *Love's Knowledge: Essays on Philosophy and Literature* (1990) an analogy that Wayne Booth also takes up in *The Company We Keep: An Ethics of Fiction* (1988).

In the following analysis, the term attention will be used to describe a deliberately directed, differential awareness or perception, which delineates one element or figure from another and places it in a meaningful relation to background and circumstance. Thus attention is understood as an active, purposeful form of perceiving that entails evaluation on a more conscious level than the naturalized process of identification and categorization that is involved in the phenomenological understanding of ordinary perception discussed above, or in the truthful revelations resulting from Weil's ideal of attention.

Moral Vision

One important sense in which ethical attention has been taken up within philosophy is that of moral vision. As derived from the work of Nussbaum and Weil, moral vision[6] requires a sensitive attunement to the particular situation that allows points of ethical salience to come to light. This ability to see what counts and what is at stake entails an open and receptive disposition. Later, I will examine how this disposition may be cultivated by the process or practice of film spectatorship.

As with a phenomenological approach, Simone Weil's attitude to understanding experience requires a certain "bracketing away" or dislocation of those aspects of the self that generate assumptions, preconceptions, personal involvement, and other complications that might interfere with pure, impartial, objective knowledge. Weil's conception of ethical attention (which differs from the notion of attentive engagement I will develop in this chapter, but balances and informs it in significant ways) implicitly situates the attender outside the space in which the moral action unfurls, rather than as an integral part of it. In a sense the structural features of cinematic spectatorship (as distinct from the practices and processes of spectatorship) provide the ultimate manifestation of Weil's ideal of ethical attention. Not only are the will and the ego, and all personal relationships de-emphasized in the context of cinematic spectatorship, but the physical body is also excluded from the arena in which attention is focused. Though this may be appropriate for a spectator, it is not necessarily appropriate for an agent participating in ethical life.

Once Were Warriors, a film which deals with domestic violence in a contemporary Maori family, is interesting because the way in which it is filmed has remarkable parallels with the form of attention that Weil describes as being fully and appropriately ethical. With the exception of the opening sequence, the film is shot almost entirely from middle distance, rather than using close-ups or long-shots, and the camera is usually static with few zooms, pans, or tracking shots (and when these are utilized, the motion is slow and smooth). Editing also moves at a measured pace and each shot tends to be held for some time, rather than being cut rapidly. This film utilizes the transparent, naturalized editing conventions of "seamless suture" rather than using arty, obvious, or jarring techniques that draw attention away from the narrative to the means, mode, and medium of production and elicit a more self-conscious form of engagement. Similarly, the soundtrack and lighting are unobtrusive. Apart from half a dozen instances where conventional techniques (such as the extradiegetic siren of an ambulance that segues into a human scream, the halo effect of backlighting, or extreme high and low angle shots) are used to highlight a significant element of the narrative, the contrivances of the film recede into the background. In consequence, the film is like a hidden observer, allowing the story and the characters to reveal themselves to its patient eyes, and thus also to the spectators. While these well established realist conventions certainly don't preclude emotive engagement with characters in the narrative, I will argue that they implicitly position the spectator in a particular ethical relation to the story world.

The judicious use of medium-close-ups and forward zooms, and the complete absence of extreme close-ups in *Once Were Warriors* maintains a distance between the viewing subject and the characters which might be associated with a desire to be unobtrusive or to maintain a degree of detachment.[7] In many cases, close-ups invite a certain intensity of engagement with the viewed subject, perhaps because the perceptual proximity afforded by close-ups position the viewer inside the personal space boundary that is usual in Western culture; such framing is often associated with an intimate gaze. Of course, intimacy is not the only function that close shot-scale can fulfill. Like any other cinematic technique, the effects of perceptual proximity are largely contextual. Tight framing that brings us right up against Ray, or Val's bruises, or Brett Sprague in *The Boys* can be confronting, disturbing, or oppressive rather than intimate, and wide shots can also evoke empathy with characters, by conveying feelings of insignificance or alienation as the view of ugly, impersonal council flats in *Nil by Mouth* does. Furthermore, in *Lost Highway*, the opening close-ups of Fred Madison are enigmatic rather than empathic whereas the extreme close-ups of Alice's scarlet lips whispering into the phone have an undeniably fetishistic quality to them. In the latter context, fragmentation of the body transforms Alice into a viewed object, rather than a subject, and objectification sits uneasily alongside intimacy.

Although it is clear that cinematographic devices need to be interpreted in relation to the narrative they feature in, consistent avoidance of close-ups does work to maintain a perceptual distance between the film and the characters and, in doing so, between the audience and the characters. *Once Were Warriors* seems to do this, to an extent.[8] However, this too needs qualification in relation to the phenomenological description of cinematic vision. As we have already established, while the audience's gaze is mediated by the gaze of the filmic body, spectators can also look away, we can use our imaginations to explore beyond the fringes of screen space, or we can focus in and look more closely and attentively at details that are embedded in the context of the frame. This means that the viewing distance determined by shot-scale can be described as a mode of perception that keeps us at arm's length from the characters, but it doesn't necessarily follow that the audience will maintain an emotional distance. As much as *Once Were Warriors* holds the ethical situation it perceives and narrates in perspective for us, it also offers an invitation to wonder, to wander further into the story world and to think beyond its boundaries to its implications for social reality. Thus this "detached" form of moral vision is not practiced at the expense of attending to details or engaging with character and context.

Once Were Warriors' filmic style enunciates a mode of attending to the story that seems to allow information to be disclosed, rather than using attention as a tool to extract or define meaning, or to share knowledge as part of a close relationship with the subjects of attention.[9] This attitude of detachment and "bearing witness" parallels the attitude that Weil advocates as appropriate for an ethical agent when attending to another, for Weil believes "attention should be a looking and not an attachment" (Weil 1978, 174). The driving force behind this idea is that the distance that detachment offers allows the observer to keep the ethical situation in perspective, and thus to remain "objective" about it. The mode of attention inscribed in the visual style of *Once Were Warriors* is not coded as a subjective gaze, but rather as a universal perspective and thus as a more just viewpoint. In a discussion of the ethical implications of different ways of looking at death (or at moral atrocities) via film, Sobchack characterizes the "humane stare" as one in which:

> [T]he image is inscribed by the mark of a steady camera, placed in a generally measured distance from its visual object, and by smooth technical and physical activity. When zooms occur, they are controlled and steady. Vision is purposefully framed and clearly focused. (Sobchack 1984, 297)

Although it is not the only possible form of ethical vision, the nonjudgmental, nonintrusive, objective "humane stare" about which Sobchack writes perfectly describes the mode of vision enacted by *Once Were Warriors'* filmic body. Such a gaze can be a way of attending to the ethical agents whose lives are being documented by the film with respect, depending on the nature of the scene we view. Attending in a detached manner allows disclosure and opens up a valuable space for the unexpected to reveal itself in the absence of the personal projections and expectations that can arise if one is too deeply immersed.

My main concerns with the description of moral vision Weil has developed are that the ideal of detachment implies that ethical truths are revealed to the mind at the cost of emotional intimacy and embodied involvement, and that perception itself can be innocent or devoid of evaluation. Like filmic perception and attention, human vision is an act of composition, of framing what we see within a context in order to narrate its place in life and understand it. While I believe that Weil's notion of attention is an unattainable ideal due to the intersubjective, embodied, and evaluative nature of perception, her insight into the importance of a form of moral vision that is neither invasive, nor judgmental is valuable. It changes the character of ethical insight from something that can be extracted from or applied to a situation, to a valuable gift of understanding that arises from the experience of attending and that is offered freely to the attentive observer.

The primary objectives of ethical attention are similar for Nussbaum and Weil, but the strategies each theorist offers are very different. In direct contrast with Weil, Nussbaum defends the view that ethical perception ought to involve active engagement of the whole person, without restricting the ethical resources and faculties that one might otherwise productively draw upon. Again, supporting an Aristotelian approach to ethics, Nussbaum says that:

> With respect to any complex matter of deep human importance there is no "innocent eye," no way of seeing the world that is entirely neutral and free of cultural shaping … Even where sense perception is concerned, the human mind is an active and interpretative instrument, and that its interpretations are a function of its history and its concepts as well as of its innate structure. [Furthermore] the nature of human world interpretations is holistic. (Nussbaum 1993, 260)

For Nussbaum, Weil's ideals of perception and attention are impossible, in that it is never possible to fully rise above or stand outside of one's own point of view. A practice of attending and engaging at close range, being involved in emotional and empathic contact can lead to perception of the extent and depth and impact of the relevant details of a situation, and may even prevent unethical actions:

> If you really vividly experience a concrete human life, imagine what it's like to live that life, and at the same time permit yourself the full range of emotional responses to that concrete life, you will (if you have at all a good moral start) be unable to do certain things to that person. Vividness leads to tenderness, imagination to compassion. (Nussbaum 1990, 209)

Such vivid insights into other lives may be blurred by a quest for ethical understanding that was practiced in more general or more abstract ways. Nussbaum makes this point when she suggests that sometimes maintaining a calculated, impartial distance and refraining from feeling a sense of attachment and emotional responsiveness constitutes an ethical oversight or failure. Indeed, voyeurism and objectification, two problematic forms of cinematic vision, are reliant on distanciation, which suggests a requirement for another way of seeing.[10] In "Perceptive Equilibrium" Nussbaum critiques perception devoid of strong, affective, emotional involvement, suggesting that in a "perceiver's impartiality, the equipoise of the body drawn strongly to no extreme—there is an almost voyeuristic 'curiosity,' the curiosity of the uninvolved gaze" (1990, 187). According to Nussbaum's argument, which I took up earlier when discussing Stevie's insensitivity in *The Boys*, such a form of perception can lead to becoming distanced from others, seeing them in an abstract way, and consequently it can prevent us from perceiving crucial facts about the ethical situation.

Nil by Mouth can be seen to exemplify a practice of attending that differs substantially from Weil's ideal of ethical attention as detached, receptive observation. *Nil by Mouth* is shot almost entirely in close-up: it infiltrates the lives of the characters in a very intimate way, zooming in close in its efforts to focus on subtle shifts of expression.[11] This close, confronting view of human beings is in no way a fetishistic fascination. Cinematic vision in *Nil by Mouth* eludes ready classification as either voyeurism or fetishistic scopophilia. On the contrary, it is more aptly likened to an ethical mode of cinematic vision that Sobchack describes as an "endangered gaze," which is encoded with markers of subjective proximity of the viewer to the violent events being viewed. In this form of attention, "The representation is marked by the relative instability of its framing … vision is frequently obstructed, inscribing its fragile yet concerned relation to the horrors of mortality it grasps" (Sobchack 1984, 295). Often the film will pull focus to follow a change in the balance of power, or shift in the locus of interest when several characters are engaged in conversation. The presence of the film's body is tangible throughout *Nil by Mouth*, not least because the camera is almost always hand-held. This gives the impression that the film is, indeed, a living body, in a way that is not as apparent in *Once Were Warriors*, where the camera is stable and often motionless, seemingly calm and certainly uninvolved in the action. Even in the midst of the most tumultuous and chaotic fight scenes in *Once Were Warriors*, the tempo of the editing alters minimally and the camera remains like a dispassionate observer, resting safely in the middle distance.

The spectator gets a very different sense of perceptual participation when the film's body occupies the narrative space like a participant, closely aligned with the experiential, intentional, and attentional movements of the characters. In *Nil by Mouth*, the picture we see is constantly reframed or visibly and visually readjusted in response to new information. The use of whip pans makes it seem as though the film turns its head, darting glances toward the action as it moves in close proximity with those it attends to. In this style of filmmaking the film attends to its subject matter in a way that emphasizes the value of getting close, engaging with the characters on an intimate, emotional level, empathizing and feeling involved in their lives.[12] This is not to say that *Once Were Warriors* lacks a sensitive engagement with its subject matter, or fails to induce an empathic reaction in its spectators. On the contrary, it succeeds in engaging its audience on many different levels. Different ways of seeing are instantiated in the two films, which parallel two different approaches to attention. Since we can never fully set aside our own embodied viewing position or transcend our personal histories and commitments, Weil's account of attention seems to be more useful as a theoretical ideal[13] than it is in practice. However, both forms of attention have ethical possibilities. It is a movement between these two extremes that best represents the form of attentive engagement for which I will argue.

In *Once Were Warriors* the filmic body stands back and bears witness to the unfolding story, allowing the elements of ethical salience to reveal themselves and be received by a patiently waiting, attentive entity.[14] *Nil by Mouth*, on the other hand, establishes a more dynamic relationship between the film's body and the characters; it engages in active participation with the story in order to be better placed to see a change of mood. An early scene from *Nil by Mouth* illustrates this active movement of attention when Ray and his mates are sitting around the lounge room chatting, telling stories about their sexual conquests and drug experiences. The flat is tiny and the camera is very close to the characters in the confined space, watching as they smoke cigarettes and talk and laugh. The camera moves from one face to another as the conversation flows, transferring attention by pulling focus if two characters are in the same frame and interest shifts from one to the other. For instance, when Ray's friend Mark is telling a story in this scene, his face takes up over half the screen. Ray is just visible, out of focus beside and behind Mark until he interrupts his friend, at which point the film racks focus, clarifying its vision of Ray and blurring the image of Mark. Unlike *Once Were Warriors*, *Nil by Mouth* has a characteristically shallow depth of field, instead of maintaining an equitable clarity of focus across everything in the visual frame. This film often looks closely at one thing at a time, rather than holding everything in focus.

Another thing that is significant about this scene is its length. The conversation dribbles on incessantly, without driving the plot. Ordinarily for a scene in which the temporal span of the film's attention is so extended, the content of the conversation upon which we dwell would contribute crucial information to the story-line. In *Nil by Mouth* the longest scenes are the ones that must seem interminable in the life of the protagonist, Val, and that are a repetitive and integral part of her everyday existence. The length of these scenes helps spectators to feel what her life must be like. They are not there to make a point; they *are* the point, and the film attends to them at length for this reason. Close aural attention to the content of the dialogue divulges little of significance. Any "point" contained by verbal content of the long scenes could have been made in less than a minute of screen time, but we can observe where the power rests among the speakers, and such interactions illustrate Val's disempowerment.

Another very long scene in the film shows Ray in a drunken rage after Val leaves him. We watch as he becomes progressively incoherent, alternately repentant and violent over what must be a period of about six or eight hours of his life. We see him on the phone to Val several times, slurring and sobbing out his confusion, pleading his love and need. The length of this scene is a torment. Like Ray, it just goes on and on and on, stumbling over the same ground until it is almost as familiar to us as it must be to his wife.

This aspect of *Nil by Mouth*, where the camera stays with a particular scene or shot for reasons that are not immediately apparent or that do not serve the narrative in an obvious way, tends to involve the spectator in the process of attention and interpretation on a different level than the tactics used in *Once Were Warriors*. *Once Were Warriors* articulates ethically salient details primarily by including them in the narrative content, focusing only on significant moments. As I suggested earlier, because the process of deciding which events and conversations are significant is not itself foregrounded, it implies that those particular scenes *revealed themselves* to the patient gaze of the film, and that attentive observation is best practiced discretely, with minimal active engagement in the unfolding picture of an ethical situation. While the selective, evaluative process of narrative composition also occurs in Val and Ray's story, the style and structure of *Nil by Mouth* complements and underwrites the narrative content, directing attention to *the way* of experiencing, seeing, sensing, and framing a situation, as well as to *what* is seen, sensed, or experienced in the frame.

The gritty detail and narrow focus allows us to see a fuller picture in a different way. Here the claim that the form in which the story is told is inseparable from its content is once again substantiated. To see or show the content of an ethical situation from a distance, or to capture it calmly with the sense of being uninvolved is to know a different world and tell a different story. There is a sense in which the inclusion of more detail in *Nil by Mouth* makes the spectator attend more carefully because we know that we must piece it together ourselves and search for or construct its relevance. Furthermore, and importantly, the mode of attention each film practices is appropriately responsive to the particularity of the situation into which it endeavors to gain insight and which, as a screen text expressing the process of its own perception, it illuminates for us. From a more detached or distant vantage point it may not be apparent why Val is unable to see beyond and escape her abusive relationship. Conversely, the attentive practices of the filmic body in *Once Were Warriors* express, and allow spectators to experience the sense of perspective Beth has on her own life and possibilities, and thus to better understand how she, but not Val, is capable of changing her situation.

One of the most striking aspects revealed by the style of cinematography employed in *Nil by Mouth* (as well as by the film's content) was just how painful it was for the characters to even attempt to look at their own lives outside the present moment. They looked back on a history of disadvantage and abuse and looked forward to much of the same, or to loneliness and half-way houses, prison, poverty, and unemployment. They were so enmeshed that they could not face the bigger picture; they could only struggle on from day to day. Coming to terms with the past and looking into the future or attempting to envision change was too frighteningly difficult. Val's past and her heritage are as miserable as her present: she continues a long line of suffering. When Val's Nan asks her mum, Janet, "Why doesn't she leave him?" Janet replies, "Where's she gonna go? To a half-way house with a five year old and another one on the way? Leave off Mum!"

The film offers only brief, stark glimpses of the "bigger picture" within which the lives explored in *Nil by Mouth* are situated, showing a depressing view of massive blocks of concrete council flats set against the dismal backdrop of a desolate section of London. This is significant precisely because a fundamental part of their lives, and one that determines their actions and attitudes to a large extent, is that the characters cannot see outside their own lives. They are not able to see a way out; they don't have access to a bigger picture including better possibilities, a picture that might place things in context and identify avenues of escape. What they can see, beyond their immediate problems, is an unbearable view of more of the same. In attention to gritty detail and the restricted glimpses of unpromising surroundings, we sense the presence of a bigger social picture, an ethical problem extending beyond the borders of the frame.

Once Were Warriors is startlingly different in this respect, in terms of its visual style and its narrative. In it we are shown the broader perspective because the film practices a nonintrusive form of attention that values cultivating an awareness of the wider cultural contexts influencing a particular situation. Regarding the film's content, Beth is able to invoke a positive sense of strength and stability from her past, and reach out to access social support; she is intelligent and confident enough to see a way forward and to see herself as something other than a victim. Beth's pride as a member of a long line of brave people who fought with honor for their land, livelihood, and culture is what gives the film its title and the narrative of Maori heritage gives the film social significance by problematizing the present and future of indigenous communities in New Zealand. Everything in *Once Were Warriors* locates the individual within a larger discourse, framing their particularity in a sociocultural narrative, rather than zeroing in on its detail. Even as the detail is disclosed it is given importance as part of a broader picture. The detail attracts the film's attention, but never fills it—even the closest shots in this film are medium-close-ups, characterized by their brevity and rarity.

A mode of ethical attention in which the balance between detail and context is woven together into an intelligible whole so that detail finds its place within a broader context often entails a narrative form of understanding. If perception or attention is a fundamental organizing structure of intentional consciousness, then narrative form is fundamental to the placement of phenomena that we attend to within meaningful contexts. Tracing the pathways of attention through a film in the above examples reveals how narration and interpretation can structure the practice of ethical attention.

Filmic Attention

In Sobchack's understanding, attention in film texts has to do with things being "noticed" (by both the film and the spectators who are a constituent part of it) to a greater or lesser extent: "That is, in their relative importance as the destination of our attention, certain figures dominate other figures. Less dominant figures are still figures and visible as such, but they are less present in their visible presence in our vision" (Sobchack 1992, 240). Here the word "dominant" (and other terms such as "submissive" or "subordinate" with which it is implicitly associated) foregrounds one way in which the practice of attending can be taken up as an ethical concern, enmeshed with the power relations or hierarchies of significance that permeate the perceptual field.

In a discussion of the extensions and contractions of attention made possible by the "phenomenological frame" the cinema screen offers to the viewer, Stanley Cavell claims that "the altering frame is the image of perfect attention" (1996, 163). Cavell distinguishes between the attentive possibilities offered by different cinematographic techniques. There are, he suggests, cinematic means of expressing perception that actively direct attention (such as racking focus), and there are those (such as deep focus) that give the viewer's vision more freedom to wander within the frame and to respond to the objects in our field of vision:

> Early in its history the cinema discovered the possibility of calling attention to persons and parts of persons and objects; but it is equally a possibility of the medium not to call attention to them but, rather, to let the world happen, to let its parts draw attention to themselves according to their natural weight. (Cavell 1996, 163)

Certainly, the later form of attention is still inescapably selective, evaluative, and focused, but it is a qualitatively different form of cinematic vision, and of ethical attention. Having already drawn the distinction between the ways of seeing enacted in *Nil by Mouth* and *Once Were Warriors*, I would like to explore this qualitative difference further and apply it to cinema and ethical life in a broader sense.

Although literature allows us to explore other perspectives imaginatively, emotively, and conceptually, it cannot *physically* make the actual movement of other eyes and bodies, and thus the passage of their attention, visible to its readers. There is something practically useful in such a physical demonstration of attention in action. In a unique manner, the cinema grants us access to a space of shared vision, allowing us inside the world of someone else's outlook. The intersubjective quality of film, in which spectators are offered insight into other perspectives, is one of the medium's great strengths. We see so much more on the cinema screen than the images of characters looking at one another: we see the representation of an aspect or interpretation of their perceptual experience. As Sobchack remarks, "What is so unique about the cinema's 'viewing view' … is that it presents and represents the activity of vision not merely as it is objectively seen by us, but also as it is introceptively lived by another" (1990, 25).

Since the mode in which one views the world frames it in a certain way, capturing some aspects in the centre, marginalizing, excluding or obscuring others, the way in which each individual sees, views, or attends to a situation is qualitative. The quality of attention affects interpretations and responses to a given situation, hence tracing the process and passage of attention and investigating the qualitative dimensions of perception through focusing on our own and others' perspectives can be a valuable part of developing ethical understanding.

Differentiating between various forms of perception is important within film theory because, though film expresses and describes perception, filmic perception also differs from ordinary perception due to the fact that it is a technologically mediated representation. As Singer observes, the value of cinema "rests precisely in its distance and difference from natural vision. [...] as a supplementary discourse which amplifies and enhances the breadth, range and depth of our perception" (Singer 1990, 65). The film renders the structured, selective aspects of perception evident, providing a visible record of the latent bias that may distort the process of ethical attention. As spectators, we are able to see who the film (and its characters) overlooks, who is listened to and concentrated on, whether the focus is clear, whether the whole person is seen or certain parts of them are objectified, and so on. Although we may not always fulfill the potential, the medium of film gives spectators the opportunity to see and analyze how ways of looking reveal evaluations that are usually concealed in the subjective nature of vision.

The distinctive opening shot in *Once Were Warriors* illustrates the material differences between human and filmic perception, and demonstrates the ethical and communicative value of these differences from ordinary perception. In this shot, which is complemented by soft, melodious extradiegetic music, we see nothing but a tranquil, pastoral scene in the New Zealand countryside for the first moments of the film. Slowly the camera begins to move backward including more and more of the picture, and finally, with the intrusive blare of diegetic sound, moving to the left and revealing that we were looking at an advertising billboard for ENZ Power in the middle of a dirty, depressing industrial area.

This wider view still stops short of adequately grasping the scene, but then we perceive further layers of information: as the camera moves back and cranes down to take in the streetscape, the sound of cars speeding by overwhelms us[15] and involves us even more intensely in the scene. The billboard represents a prevalent, if superficial impression publicized in the postcard image of itself that New Zealand expresses and exports, but the film exercises what can be interpreted as a form of ethical attention committed to filling out the picture and allowing more details to reveal themselves. With camera movement, the film gives a sense of coming down to earth, descending from illusion into reality.

Figure 23.2 *Once Were Warriors*: An idyllic, pastoral opening shot.

Figure 23.3 *Once Were Warriors*: The camera pulls back to reveal urban reality.

The human eye doesn't have access to exclusive framing or zoom lenses: though we can notice one detail to the exclusion of its surroundings, we cannot see *only* that upon which we focus our attention. Nor can we actually turn the volume of the traffic down momentarily (we can only tune it out, withdrawing attention from it). However, conceptually, we can achieve precisely the same effect that the camera and microphone express perceptually: we view something one way and then, with a shift in perception (like changing the framing or the volume) we realize it to have been illusory or incomplete. By changing perspective, we perceive that something was missing or excluded from the position we had previously occupied. Techniques like altering camera position, pulling focus, and reframing function metaphorically to represent the subtle shifts in perspective and attention, and to cue a particular way of viewing and interpreting the subject matter. The opening shot in *Once Were Warriors* suggests that film's intent is to inform the audience (utilizing the visual metaphor) that it will divulge to us a sense of "the bigger picture," placing the issue of domestic violence into a cultural context.

Sobchack explores the experiential differences between zooming in and forward tracking shots, speaking in terms of the film's body inhabiting space and directing (its own and our) attention. Cutting between close-ups and long-shots, or the use of Steadicam, dollies and tracking shots in which the camera actually moves around, toward or away from its subject are experienced, in Sobchack's terms, as movements of the film's body. Such bodily movement is similar to the movement of subjects in the frame, in that it increases or decreases proximity to the viewing subject. Either of these forms of physical movement alters the nature of the material depicted within the frame—they represent a shift in the proximal relationship of the viewed subject to both the camera and the spectators. In cinematographic techniques such as shifting focus, zooming in or out, or changing the lens (to a wide angle, for instance), the picture also "moves," but different changes in the nature of perception are traced on the screen. Spectators notice this visual movement, but it is experienced only as a movement of attention, rather than physical movement of the film's body:

> Attention, then, is a lived-body movement which does not involve movement of the material body through space … Attention is a creative act, an alteration of the subject's relation with the world … Always contingent and motivated, always situated as the concrete relation of the body-subject living its changing projects (its autobiographical narrative) in the world. (Sobchack 1990, 27)

There are important distinctions between and within pictures of motion (*Once Were Warriors* classical tripod-mounted cinematography) and moving pictures (exemplified by *Nil by Mouth*'s inquisitive and restless hand-held camera). As Sobchack suggests, if the picture or frame itself moves, rather than the subjects within it, this represents a change of the frame of reference of the attender, the viewer. This is ethically significant because it represents a change in understanding and value, an active, actual shift in perspective and, especially in the case of pulling focus, a qualitative difference in the way the subject of perception is interpreted.

In similar ways to the optical movement of the film camera, the movement of ethical attention of human beings is also a "lived-body movement" which, though it can be expressed by actually moving closer to someone, can also be unrelated to physical movement toward or away from the attendee. Moving closer to an object (either with our actual bodies, or by increasing the intimacy and intensity of our attention) alters our awareness of it, effecting a change in the way the object appears and is meaningful for us in terms of its contextual location, framing, or focus. With such a perceptual movement, the object swells or diminishes in importance in relation to the viewing subject and we access more or less of the fine detail or the surrounding context.

The understanding of perception as active and mobile in ways that are not limited to, or by, physical movement indicates that although perception (and with it, ethical attention) is embodied, and clearly bound in important ways to particular contexts, situations, and unique individuals, it is not necessarily tied to relations of physical proximity. This point adds strength to Nussbaum's argument that ethical attention is not only instructively exemplified in certain works of art, but can also be cultivated and practiced by those who engage with such art.

Cultivating an awareness of what is included in our visual field is far from being the only way in which we are able to attune our attention to a situation. Movements of attention can also be experienced as imaginative leaps, as the tightening or loosening of emotional ties, and as varying intensities of reflection and self-reflection. (Consider, for instance, the scene from *Dead Man Walking* depicting the intersubjective nature of understanding with the metaphoric use of actual reflections in the glass.) Nondiegetic material and gaps in the narrative can also be of considerable significance, just as the things that are not said sometimes lie at the heart of a story. This brings to mind the point in *Nil by Mouth* when Val was severely beaten by her husband because of his unfounded jealousy, and deep-seated rage and insecurity. In the treatment of Val and her daughter Michelle, this scene highlights two of the ways in which off-screen space can be used as part of the sphere of attention addressed by the film.

In this scene attention was concentrated outside the frame as Val was beaten—her body is not present in the frame itself. The camera certainly does not ignore Val (though its eye, and ours, are averted); it is more as though it cannot bear to look or is unable to do so. The inability to see Val's body also links the spectator across off-screen space to the couple's small daughter Michelle who we later see cringing out of Ray's sight on the stairwell. Like us, she is also following the action but unable to see all that is going on.

Throughout the film Michelle is mostly out of frame and silent to the extent that it might appear that the film overlooks her, as the characters within it often do. However, on closer inspection it is evident that the film's perception of Michelle is keen and sympathetic. The single most beautiful shot in the film shows Michelle's delicate, serious little face in profile as she spells her own name to her Nan, who carefully writes it on a bright red helium balloon, which seems to represent all the freedom, vibrancy, and buoyancy lacking in her life. In other scenes we see that Michelle is too good and too quiet and obedient for a five year old child, suggesting that her unobtrusive demeanor articulates her fear as well as her desire to do anything required to be loved and accepted. She is not rendered invisible by the film so much as perceived by the film as attempting to avoid drawing attention to herself. The film *does* notice Michelle as it repeatedly shows how she makes herself invisible. Like her mother, she desperately wants Ray's attention, but knows she is often safer without attracting it.

As with the treatment of Michelle, the fact that the film refrains from looking directly at Val's beating does not constitute a failure to attend to her. Despite the lack of graphic detail the beating is felt acutely, imagined vividly and heard with clarity. In the closing shots of this scene we are separated from Val by a partition in the kitchen that prevents us from seeing her body and we are only able to see Ray's absorption in his own irrational rage, however, our attention is engaged below the screen and to the right, where Val lies bleeding at Ray's feet.

As the scene concludes we encounter a moment of ellipsis in the narrative, unlike *Once Were Warriors*, where we see Jake, the male protagonist's callous response to his wife's wounds, and we see Beth's reaction and her attempts to clean herself up and deal with the situation, listening as she is sick in the toilet, watching as she confronts her own reflection and winces in the mirror.

Figure 23.4 *Once Were Warriors*: Beth faces her injuries in the bathroom mirror.

In *Nil by Mouth*, our concern stays with Val, focused on her injuries and her pain for some time before the camera finally visibly discloses the detail of her wounds. We never see her look at herself, and we never see Ray look directly at what he has done to her. When eventually the camera moves in close, we see Val show her lacerations and bruises to her mother while she describes being hit by a car in the parking lot at the local shopping center (the make-up artist worked her over with convincing skill, so when we finally do see, we perceive the full extent of her injuries).

We feel Val's inability to face the reality of her own situation in this scene as we hear her tell a desperately reassuring lie about the doctors at the hospital informing her that her unborn baby is mercifully unharmed. Because of the blank interval of time between the beating and this next scene, the viewer is at first uncertain whether Val has indeed sought medical attention. Then, as we listen to the lie unfold it becomes evident that this woman is unable to face up to her situation, even to the extent of confronting her image in the mirror, looking after herself and seeking the most basic level of help: physical care.

Both *Nil by Mouth* and *Once Were Warriors* address the subject of domestic violence directly as a matter of moral and political concern. In a sense the creation of a film narrative (and other forms of art), can be understood as a "project of envisioning" (Singer 1990, 65) which is projected toward an audience who will participate in that vision. Some films create and project a "moral vision" involving the depiction of ethical practices and role models. However, as Nussbaum rightly points out, even if the subject matter is not specifically of an ethical nature, both the form and the content of a text express a "view of life" and convey a sense of what information is important to know, and what faculties are important for knowing (1990, 7).

Figure 23.5 *Nil by Mouth*: Val is unable to face up to the gravity of her situation.

Not only do the films *Once Were Warriors* and *Nil by Mouth* attend to similar subject matter of an explicitly ethical nature and make a social comment on the actions of their characters and the cultural contexts in which they are implicated, but they share a sensitive approach which aims to enrich understanding of the characters without vilification or polarization of their positions. In addition, they share claims about "what matters" intrinsic to the form of film production and reception that are dealt with in the concluding section of this chapter. However, in demonstrating through visual movement their individual "views of life" the two films exhibit stylistic differences expressing variations in ethical values and practices. These stylistic differences articulate differing practices of ethical attention and disparate attitudes regarding the degree and type of involvement an ethical agent ought to experience in relation to the subject of his or her attention.

Spectatorship

When viewing a film we are often "present" in a way that we might not be when watching television, reading, or even listening to a friend relate a personal story because of the specific ways in which we are drawn, bodily, into the narrative space. Our attentive, perceptual presence is incorporated into the story as an active part of the technologically mediated filmic perception, and many of the distractions of the external world are removed in the dimly lit, quiet cinema. While we do come to the cinema with our personal history, beliefs, values, and relationships intact, at the same time we step away from the claims that these elements exert upon us in everyday life.

Often, life's competing demands distract and disperse attention, but in the cinema attention can be more sustained and focused for the duration of the film. Though the process of interpretation is ongoing, our responses, along with the possibility for interruptions and interjections, are suspended until the entire story has been told. As Singer so aptly puts it, "The situation exacts an investment of attention" (1990, 55). Singer suggests that the "zone of inattention" that is created by the dark space surrounding the bright screen and the silence of the audience facilitates fascination and engagement by clearly delineating the parameters of attention (1990, 57). There is a significant difference between the investment of attention described here and the idea of a sponge-like spectator who passively absorbs the contents of the cinema screen. As Sobchack points out in a discussion of the dialogic experience of cinematic spectatorship:

> Certainly, a form of absorption can and does occur in the film experience. But it is not a concrete absorption into the *body* of the other or the *consciousness* of the other. Rather, it is a mutual absorption in the world, a mutually directed interest that converges in the visible and its significance. (Sobchack 1992, 273, original emphasis)

The cinema gives us the luxury of a more contemplative space, and in doing so it actually diverts the focus from the ego's interests, channeling it toward the narrative. Thus, in the model of cinematic spectatorship the problem of "unselfing"[16] (or, alternatively, the tension between evading the distractions of the ego and its desires, and recognizing the significance of partiality, emotion, and one's personal investment in the process of interpreting and responding) is resolved, at least in part, by the contextual conditions in which the narrative is received. We do, and we don't, "lose ourselves" in the practice of attentive engagement. We are present in the act of attending in an unsteady oscillation between personal involvement and immersion in someone else's story. The self, in this understanding, does not distract us from the story, rather, it is through the self (and its intersubjective incorporation into the larger body of the film) that we are able to engage with and understand the story and form connections with the characters within it. The importance of the sense of connection to others that the cinema can offer need not exist at the expense of, or diminish the value of more detached forms of discernment and the role they play in ethical deliberation.

Just as physical distance is essential if the picture is to be comprehensible (if one is too close to the action, perspective is lost and one only sees blotches of color moving on the screen) a kind of distance is also essential to obtain "breadth and clarity" of understanding.

In order to illustrate further the ethical implications of film spectatorship, consider one final sequence from *Nil by Mouth*: a scene in which Billy has appropriated some drugs belonging to Ray, his brother in law. Ray discovers the theft and assaults Billy, despite Val's attempts to intervene. As the scene begins, Billy passes in front of the camera and sits down on the couch in such close proximity to the "film's body" that our vision is disturbed. Short panning movements, as though the film is turning its head to follow Billy's motions, trace the passage of Billy's attention to the illicit "gear" in his hands, and to the threat of being approached from behind and caught in the act. The film uses the evocative *mise-en-scene* and the nondiegetic sound track to describe its perception of Billy's experience. The dull, melancholic blue light and the blues guitar work in conjunction with the unsettled camera movement to articulate a sense of despair and distress surrounding the subject we (film and spectators) are viewing.

In two of only five extreme long shots in a film dominated by close-ups of the human figure, the film moves its attention briefly to the context in which Billy is surreptitiously indulging in an interlude of drug-assisted escapism. We see for a moment the bleak bulk of endless blocks of council flats in the chilly, grey light of a windy dawn. With this interstitial image the film reflects on the alienating social conditions of the urban environment that contains, and to a certain extent gives rise to the problems of the dysfunctional family whose story we are involved in. It is important to note that this shot, and the other extreme long shots are not taken from the visual perspective of any of the screen characters. The oppressively close visual style of the film is, as I have already suggested, indicative of the inability of the characters themselves to step back and look beyond their immediate problems to other possibilities. When we do see a glimpse of what lies beyond the immediate scenario, it seems that there is no escape in sight.

In the remainder of the scene whip pans, short, fast zooms, and unsteady hand-held shots locate us inside the confined space in which the conflict erupts and focus our attention on Ray's aggression and those to whom it is directed in a confronting dialectic of repulsion and fascination. As much as spectators might get the sense of being so close to the action that they may well need to duck or dodge the next assault, there are also times when, with the film's body, spectators experience the scene from behind a barrier that obstructs vision and effects a partial separation from the characters. The lounge room in which the conflict takes place is separated from the kitchen by low wainscoting and a glass partition. At times (particularly when there is no "innocent" perspective to occupy and one is most reluctant to be implicated in the action) the film's body moves behind this, and we see a confused view of the action through reflections on the glass. Filmic techniques such as these, which leave spectators with a sense that the action is difficult to follow, are appropriate to convey a sense of the complex nature of the ethical situation the film is describing. Thus the film engages spectators in the ethical practices involved in the different levels of narrative configuration: composition, attention, and interpretation.

As a pregnant woman with an abusive and drug-dependent spouse Val may attract sympathy; however, the film does not allow a straightforward identification with her as an innocent victim. One of the most uncomfortable moments in the film occurs when we witness Val lash out at her brother for causing trouble, after he has just been beaten by Ray.[17] At this point we are confronted with the pervasive impact violence has on the lives of those involved. The complexity inherent in the situation thus portrayed highlights the inadequacy of reductive moral principles which, by labeling actions as right or wrong in isolation from the surrounding causal influences, often fail to further ethical understanding.

As spectators we experience an intersubjective involvement in this scene: we engage with the film's subjective perception of the situation as it articulates its own point of view, and we literally have our sensory experience aligned with that of Ray, Val, and Billy momentarily. The transition between shots exclusive to the film's subjective vantage point, and those also associated with the viewing positions of the characters makes us, as spectators, feel their sense of entrapment in circumstance, and sense the way in which this perpetuates the victim–victimizer dynamic.

In order to trace or tune into shifts in perspective and disentangle from one another the levels of vision that are experienced in film spectatorship, I am going to return to and enlarge upon the understanding of technologically mediated vision proposed by Sobchack. As Sobchack states, the film's vision is experienced "as our own vision, in our own vision, and in addition to our own vision" (1992, 271). While the film's optical movement explores the horizons of its world, our own vision merges with the film's, overlapping with what the film sees: the image framed by the screen. Thus, as spectators, we actively participate in the film's vision and practice seeing *as* another, and from another's perspective inside the screen space. Our attention traverses the gap between our bodies and the screen, entering into the story world and exploring it in fusion with the film, practicing the very movements of attention that the film is expressing through its own bodily engagement with the narrative. (There may also be another layer of vision hidden here: when the film "borrows" a character's point of view, spectators also adopt that perspective.) Since our sensory experience of the narrative is enabled by our own bodily perceptual capacities and mediated by the filmic technology (to which we are joined as active, integral parts of the film's body), cinematic spectatorship is a practical exercise in the cultivation of the modes of embodied, attentive engagement demonstrated and enacted on the screen.

At the same time, the cinema screen itself is an object situated *in* the spectator's visual field. We are not actually situated inside the screen space; we are seated in the dark cinema looking at a screen text. The spectator is not totally subject to or immersed in another's vision (we also see the cinema, the edges of the screen etc.), additionally, the filmmaker or camera's viewing position often really does change, whereas ours is actually static (however mobile our attention may be). Superimposed on the film's vision of its subject is the spectator's vision of it and, as Sobchack states: "In so far as the visual space I see before me is not completely isomorphic with the bodily space from which I see, there will be a pressure from, an echo of, the machine that mediates my perception" (1992, 172).

Here Sobchack is suggesting that, as a result of the differences between human perception alone and the humanlike, instrument mediated perception visibly expressed on the cinema screen, the audience is constantly reminded of the mediated and intersubjective nature of the visual experience. On this level we can see the film in more conceptual terms as the inscription and description of attention: the articulation of attentive-perceptive practices (its own and those of the characters). This awareness may not always be at the forefront of our consciousness (centered in our attention), however, it indicates that although spectators are drawn into the screen space and the subjective outlooks rendered visible there, we are not seduced into collapsing their own perspectives into the perspectives represented on the screen.

Finally, film spectatorship is an attentive practice in its own right, a practice that involves the vision of the spectator *in addition to* the vision of the film. As attentive spectators we experience moments of resistance and rapport as we draw from off-screen perspectives informed by our own lived experience and mediated by our own abilities. As such, spectatorship is an intersubjective dialogue of vision and interpretation that transcends the individual (but indivisible) units of text and viewer, and incorporates the external world of the spectators' lived experience, to which narrative films refer.

When Sobchack describes these three levels on which the film's vision is experienced, she does not explicitly address a fourth dimension of visual experience associated with film, but elsewhere in her work she refers to ways in which film sometimes offers us what might be understood as a view *of* our own vision, referring to "those moments in which we grasp ourselves in the recognition that our vision differs from that of the other" (Sobchack 1992, 276). In such moments the focus shifts back to the self, to the attender and her or his personal responses to the text.

Occasionally our own view becomes clearer when we recognize how it differs from the vision expressed on the screen. For example, the striptease sequence in *Nil by Mouth* might reinforce spectators' perspectives on the objectification of women by differentiating their views from those of Ray and his friend Mark. Occasionally we also recognize our own biases for what they are when we see them represented in some way on the screen. For instance, perhaps our concern for Michelle's well-being in *Nil by Mouth* might cause us to admit to the limitations of a previously unexamined perspective or opinion, if we recognize ourselves in the view that associates quiet children with good children.

Teasing out the various layers of attention in the cinema generates a better sense of how and why we can come away from a film that moves us with a more developed sense of understanding our own and other's stories, perspectives, and values. This is partly because the film engineers in us or elicits from us a process of discernment and interpretation as it structures information, puts things in perspective, changes frame and focus, shifts, and borrows viewpoints. As attentive spectators we find engaging with and exploring other people's narratives a pleasure or a fascinating challenge, rather than a grueling discipline as Weil believes ethical attention must be. In part this is due to the fact that the physical viewing context provided by the cinema does for us the work of focusing attention on the narrative rather than on the extraneous distractions of the ego and its attachments. Ironically, though the practice of attention Weil describes has much in common with the methods of transcendental phenomenology, and though phenomenology itself aims to describe experience or consciousness, it is Nussbaum's account that more accurately describes the embodied, self-conscious experience of attending on an interpersonal level. In any actual or cinematic context we can no more divorce ourselves from our ego, will, and emotional attachments or relationships than we can amputate our physical body from the process of perception.

Conclusion

I have demonstrated how films (in Sobchack's understanding of the filmic body as a viewing subject) can at once practice modes of ethical attention, provide visible examples of attentive practices for critical reflection, and evoke ethical responses from the spectators who participate in the modes of attention exemplified in the filmic style and structure. The filmic expression of perception is simultaneously an act of representation and a redescription of the object of vision, in which changes (in perspective and value) can be brought about by swelling or diminishing the importance of the viewed object in relation to the attender. Since the spectators' attention is closely linked to the film's, the attentive practices of both film and spectators contribute to the production of a "new" object (an object that is experienced and understood in a different way, a way that can enhance possibilities for ethical insight). The act of viewing a film also produces "new subjects" to the extent that the instrumental mediation of perception and participation in the technologically mediated filmic body effects a transformation of the spectator's subjectivity, rendering it an intersubjective state. Viewed in this way, the cinema might be seen as a richly attentive way of engaging with others and with the world in search of narratively understood ethical insight, through all the confusion of detail and the multiplicity of perspectives that complicate moral vision. Though the vision of a "new object" offered to us in the cinema is ethically limited in that it lacks the possibilities for responsiveness that are present in life, practicing attentive engagement in the cinema can still advance our self-understanding and alter the way in which we relate to others, making the dimensions of our care and understanding keener and more inclusive.

As Laura Marks writes, "Attentive recognition is a participatory notion of spectatorship, whose political potential shouldn't be ignored" (2000, 48). This political potential necessarily broadens the scope of attentive engagement, opening it out beyond interpersonal ethics, or individual responses to particular films. It highlights the necessity of buttressing the ideal of attentive engagement and the particularist responses of care, with compensating ethical structures that balance the partiality of emotion, failures of imagination, the arbitrariness of attention, or the limitations of compassion with some reference to general principles of justice. We need, on principle, and not on the chance that the story of an individual moves us, to counteract the economic imperatives of media production by paying attention to those whose stories are not told, who are underrepresented and who cannot manage to call attention to themselves as individuals or as social groups. Attentive engagement with film can do no more than identify structuring absences and systematic misrepresentation—spectatorship alone cannot redress such injustices. The conclusion of this book considers some of the possibilities and limitations surrounding the transfiguration of ethical experience and understanding resulting from practices of attentive engagement with film narratives, practices that draw deeply on a broad range of ethical resources.

From *Pulling Focus: Intersubjective Experience, Narrative Film, and Ethics* by Jane Stadler.
© 2008 by Jane Stadler, Continuum US, an imprint of Bloomsbury Publishing Inc.

Notes

1. Peta Bowden describes this clarification of moral situations and values through ethical attention as a process of "accumulating understandings" (1998, 60).
2. Bowden addresses the problems that can arise when the flow of care and attention is continuously unidirectional, arguing that the character of moral attention must "focus explicitly on the shared and communal aspects of attenders and the potential for collaboration and mutual support that such connections hold" (1998, 71) in order to avoid falling prey to imbalances in relationships.
3. Samantha Lay's book *British Social Realism: From Documentary to Brit-Grit* (2002) contextualizes Brit-Grit within contemporary developments in the media industry and notes current trends in style, characterization, theme, and reception, including a good case study of *Nil by Mouth* in final chapter "1990s and Beyond: Contemporary Social Realism." She writes:

    All the features and conventions of British social realism can be found in *Nil by Mouth:* "loose" episodic narrative structure with a cyclical resolution and ambiguity defying the closure demanded by mainstream cinema; the use of location shooting; the use of non-professional actors and well-respected "small picture" actors like Ray Winstone and Kathy Burke (surely the Albert Finney and Carol White of our times), in an ensemble cast; the use of naturalistic light, sound and dialogue; high angled shots of depressed urban environments, along with the "gritty" sights and sounds of a certain way of London life. (Lay 2002, 111)

    These features of the British social realist style have clearly influenced the work of Australian director Rowan Woods, and have themselves been influenced by earlier film movements like Italian Neo-Realism and *Cinéma Vérité*, and by parallel developments like the Danish Dogme95 movement. In each instance, there is an important relationship between style, story, politics, and a particular vision of what is ethically important in life that is distinct from much mainstream cinema.

4. Nussbaum uses the terms perception, discernment, moral vision, and moral attention in closely related ways throughout her work on moral insight. Of these terms, discernment is the most actively deliberative. See

especially two essays in *Love's Knowledge*: "Finely Aware and Richly Responsible" (Nussbaum 1990, 148–149) and "The Discernment of Perception" (Nussbaum 1990, 54–55).

5. Weil says that while practicing ethical attention, "what is real becomes evident … in the end illusions are scattered and the real becomes visible" (1952, 174). This has similarities with the phenomenological project of bracketing away preconceptions to perceive the "essence" of a thing.

6. "Moral vision" is also discussed by Iris Murdoch (1970, 35–43) in relation to the moral imagination.

7. In "Inscribing Ethical Space," Sobchack suggests that a distanced mode of vision can connote the helplessness of the viewer in relation to the moral atrocity that is being viewed. From a distance, one cannot be expected to intervene (1984, 295).

8. Alan Duff's book (1990), on which the film *Once Were Warriors* is based, was considered radical at the time of its publication and it raised strong sentiments in New Zealand. Perhaps to avoid alienating the prospective audience, in the adaptation to film some of the more disturbing and confrontational elements were omitted, such as the intimation that Jake Heke, Grace's father, may have been her rapist. A more subjective, confronting form of visual storytelling in the film may have been considered inflammatory, implying value judgments that the filmmakers wished to avoid.

9. A willingness to see and an ability to wait for revelation are two attributes that Cavell places great emphasis upon in documentary filmmaking because, he says, "the only thing that really matters [is] that the subject be allowed to reveal itself" (1979, 127).

10. Within the framework of feminist psychoanalytic film theory, Mary-Ann Doane (1992) and Gaylyn Studlar (1990) suggest the immersive, masochistic gaze of fetishistic scopophilia as one such alternative to the sadistic aspects of voyeurism described by Laura Mulvey (1992).

11. Samantha Lay argues that the Griersonian legacy of naturalism and social realism that informs *Nil by Mouth* is best suited to small screen, which helps to explain the predominance of close-ups in the film as tight framings work better on television (2002, 101–102).

12. As Samantha Lay writes in her analysis of *Nil by Mouth*, "The criticism of this focus on the personal and the private argues that the concentration on the family's problems undermines any sense of the social and economic reasons that might lie behind alcoholism and domestic violence" (2002, 111–112). However, I would counter that understanding Ray and Val's family helps us to understand the broader social problems in which their story is enmeshed.

13. By this I do not mean that the way of seeing Weil advocates *is ideal*, but rather that as a theoretical ideal it shows that we tend to see what we look for, and therefore we must guard against interpreting everything we see in ways that merely reinforce our existing presuppositions. In practice, I think that the greatest lesson that might be derived from Weil's account of attention would involve acknowledging the necessity of examining what we see in terms of what we look for, and thereby developing self-understanding and critically evaluating our own viewing positions.

14. The emotional response of spectators to a film that maintains reflective distance on a stylistic or formal level will not necessarily mirror the film's own attitude of detached observation, nor will we necessarily engage more thoroughly with a film that is shot in close-up. The film's attitude to the subject of its attention and the spectators' responses to the expression or articulation of that attitude are not the same issue, and this is further complicated by the spectators' own attitudes to the narrative content.

15. In some films, such as those directed by David Lynch, the film's body expresses itself and demonstrates its attention with heightened aural/oral sensitivity. For example, the musical lyrics and the nondiegetic sound in Lynch's work often articulate the attitude the film takes to its subject and at the same time suggest a position or attitude that spectators might adopt. Consider, for instance, how the "various ominous drones" in *Lost Highway*

both *express* and *instill* a sense of uneasiness, which is compounded by the vocal cues of the opening track, "I'm Deranged" (by David Bowie).

16. "Unselfing" involves directing one's attention and moral imagination away from one's own interests, toward the needs of others (Murdoch 1970, 84).

17. In a striking parallel, *Once Were Warriors* unsettles viewers with a similar realization when a drunken Beth slaps her son Nig across the face, immediately before she herself is beaten by Jake.

References

Booth, Wayne. 1988. *The Company We Keep: An Ethics of Fiction*. Berkeley, CA: University of California Press.

Bowden, Peta. 1998. "Ethical Attention: Accumulating Understandings." *European Journal of Philosophy*, 6.1: 59–77.

Cavell, Stanley. 1979. *The World Viewed: Reflections on the Ontology of Film*, enlarged edition. Cambridge, MA: Harvard University Press.

Cavell, Stanley. 1996. "The Same and Different: The Awful Truth." In *The Cavell Reader*, ed. S. Mulhall, 167–196. Cambridge, MA: Blackwell Publishers.

Doane, Mary-Ann. 1992. "Film and the Masquerade: Theorizing the Female Spectator." In *Film Theory and Criticism: Introductory Readings* (Fourth Edition), ed. Gerald Mast, Marshall Cohen, and Leo Braudy, 248–256. New York: Oxford University Press.

Duff, Alan. 1990. *Once Were Warriors*. Auckland, New Zealand: Tandem Press.

Lay, Samantha. 2002. *British Social Realism: From Documentary to Brit-Grit*. London: Wallflower Press.

Marks, Laura U. 2000. *The Skin of the Film: Intercultural Cinema, Embodiment and the Senses*. Durham and London: Duke University Press.

Merleau-Ponty, Maurice. 1964. *The Primacy of Perception and Other Essays on Phenomenological Psychology, the Philosophy of Act, History and Politics*, ed. James M. Edie, trans. C. Dallery. Evanston, IL: Northwestern University Press.

Merleau-Ponty, Maurice. 2002. *Phenomenology of Perception*. London: Routledge.

Mulvey, Laura. 1992. "Visual Pleasure and Narrative Cinema." In *Film Theory and Criticism: Introductory Readings* (Fourth Edition), ed. Gerald Mast, Marshall Cohen, and Leo Braudy, 746–757. New York: Oxford University Press.

Murdoch, Iris. 1970. *The Sovereignty of the Good*. London: Routledge and Kegan Paul.

Nussbaum, Martha. 1990. *Love's Knowledge: Essays on Philosophy and Literature*. New York: Oxford University Press.

Nussbaum, Martha. 1993. "Non-Relative Virtues: An Aristotelian Approach." In *The Quality of Life*, ed. Martha Nussbaum and Amartya Sen, 242–269. New York: Oxford University Press.

Singer, Linda. 1990. "Eye / Mind / Screen: Toward a Phenomenology of Cinematic Scopophilia." *Quarterly Review of Film and Video* 12.3: 51–67.

Sobchack, Vivian. 1984. "Inscribing Ethical Space: Ten Propositions on Death, Representation and Documentary." *Quarterly Review of Film Studies* 9.4: 283–300.

Sobchack, Vivian. 1990. "Active Eye: Optical Movement: Transformations of Attention." *Quarterly Review of Film and Video* 12.3: 21–36.

Sobchack, Vivian. 1992. *Address of the Eye*. Princeton, NJ: Princeton University Press.

Studlar, Gaylyn. 1990. "Masochism, Masquerade and the Erotic Metamorphosis of Marlene Dietrich." In *Fabrications: Costume and the Female Body*, ed. Jane Gaines and Charlotte Herzog, 229–249. New York: Routledge.

Weil, Simone. 1952. *Gravity and Grace*, trans. E. Craufurd. London: Routledge and Kegan Paul.

Weil, Simone. 1978. *Lectures on Philosophy*, trans. H. Price. Cambridge: Cambridge University Press.

Part 6 Changing the Dominant Imaginary

Introduction

This is perhaps one of the most exciting and important Parts of the book. Taking on board the brilliant work set out in this collection overall, the calls for change and the suggestions of what needs to happen, here are four essays that strike right at that target. What do we need to see in today's films?

One of the most innovative British horror films of the twenty-first century so far is *Saint Maud*, directed by Rose Glass (2019). In this terrifying tale, an ex-nurse who has become a devout Christian following the death of one of her patients now works as a palliative care nurse for hire who takes care of patients in their final days. Maud's religious convictions, and her intense personality, lead to her becoming obsessed with saving the soul of her latest charge, a dying former dancer without any religious beliefs. In a film that references some familiar images from the horror genre, such as a levitation and demonic visual effects, Glass's film also features striking images of disturbance and delusion. In one scene, Maud sees a typhoon in her beer glass, and in another she puts drawing pins in her shoes to pierce her feet as she walks. The final shot, as Maud believes she is ascending to heaven, shows Maud with angel wings amid celestial lights (Figure P6.1), before cutting for a split second to the reality of her agonizing self-immolation as the very final frame of the film. This image – and many others throughout the film – challenge the image of the female subject of horror as a pursued and punished victim, and create a truly original character who is a passionate and disassociated loner, and who constitutes a real danger. The film is focused on nursing and care, hedonism and sex, populated mainly by women and with a story that unfolds through women's conversations. These characters, and these images, indicate the contemporary reinvention of horror films by a generation of women filmmakers (Peirse 2020).

There can be no argument that breasts are a significant and ubiquitous cultural image and that cinema has always fetishized and spectacularized this physical feature. Howard Hughes designed a bra for Jane Russell in *The Outlaw* (1943), in order to show her breasts at what he perceived as their best, resulting in numerous clashes with the Breen Office. Alfred Hitchcock paid a great deal of attention to Janet Leigh's bra in *Psycho*, including making it the focus of the film's poster. Hitchcock changed Marion Crane's bra from a white bra in the opening hotel scene to a black bra after she has decided to steal the money from her estate agent boss: a surefire indication of her turn to the wrong side of the law. The nudity of women on screen, especially stars, has always attracted attention and featured in marketing campaigns as well as reviews and critiques of the films themselves (Bolton 2009). Rosemarie Garland-Thomson cites many other examples of breasts as ubiquitous cultural icons, observing that 'As both symbol and flesh, no other bodily mark of sexual identity is so routinely or ritualistically offered up to the public eye.' Describing the

Figure P6.1 Maud's fantasy of ascension during self-immolation (*Saint Maud*).

'visual magnetism' of breasts, Garland-Thomson analyses the circumstances of staring at breasts in public, and sets out various categories of breasts that we encounter. Featuring photographs of cancer survivors with surgical scars, and a discussion of images of breasts and breastlessness, this chapter challenges the 'ceaselessly circulated erotic breast' and examines what happens to looking, and staring, when the image of the nude is not what we are used to seeing. This exposé demands analysis in the context of cinema and its perennial obsession with peddling the perfection of the female form.

Alison Kafer's work on the visibility of disability similarly draws our attention to the bodies whose experiences and desires are absent from spaces we might be in, including ostensibly feminist spaces. Kafer considers access to bathrooms and the relationship between arguments based on gender and disability regarding who has access to which type of toilet. Considering also the realms of environmental and reproductive justice, Kafer's arguments insert questions around disability into ableist culture in spaces where they are often unanswered or ignored. Questions about the visibility of disability on screen and in film analysis need to progress, as does the analysis of its scarcity and the reasons and ramifications. I include this piece because Kafer argues that the work of various coalitional movements is happening – it is not absent – and 'alternative political imaginaries are being debated and discussed in and through these various political practices'. In the epigraph to Kafer's chapter in the original publication of her book, she quotes Catriona Sandilands who stresses the significance of constructing 'connections among struggles that may be not only diverse, but opposed to one another in many respects' (1999: 100). Sandilands is working in the fields of ecofeminism and democratic politics, and this conversation and coalition is a model for disability theory and politics as part of feminist film philosophy.

Patricia Hill Collins begins her essay on 'Mammies, Matriarchs, and Other Controlling Images' with a epigraph from Trudier Harris about how 'the Black American Woman has had to admit that while nobody knew the troubles she saw, everybody, his brother and his dog, felt qualified to explain her, even to herself' (1982: 4). This resonates profoundly with Angela Davis's article on 'Afro Images: Politics, Fashion, and Nostalgia' (1994), where she writes how she is persistently recognized by and remembered for her 'Afro' haircut. Finding this reduction of her historical politics to hair fashion understandably infuriates and disturbs Davis, not least because it was the circulation of various photographic images of her at the time that played a major role in creating her notoriety and featured on the FBI poster citing her as one of America's ten most wanted criminals.[1] It is the sight of this poster image, emptied of its content in relation to her legal case and her politics, that so unsettles Davis. It has become a 'controlling image', such as those described by Patricia Hill Collins. Collins writes about 'other controlling images' of Black women as 'mammies, matriarchs, welfare recipients, and hot mommas', and how challenging these images has been a core theme in Black feminist thought. Collins argues that these stereotypical images manipulate ideas about Black womanhood, othering Black women and keeping them othered in order to define the field of who belongs. This brings to mind the work of Kathleen Collins, director of *Losing Ground* (1982), who stated that in American society, and in Christian metaphysics, Black women are projected as sinners as opposed to saints. In a Masterclass that Collins delivered to students at Howard University in 1984, Collins declares that she will not let anybody 'mythologize [her] life'.[2] In *Losing Ground*, Collins explores the lives of a middle class Black couple where the wife is an academic and the husband is an artist: she escapes stereotypes and clichés of Black lives in America in the 1980s and tells the tale of a couple who are mismatched due to their intellectual and creative preferences: she insists that they are 'neither insiders or outsiders'. Patricia Hill Collins's analysis of 'controlling images' demonstrates how the stereotypes support racial oppression through their persistent circulation in contemporary media. Echoing the work of Kafer and Garland-Thomson, Collins looks at the relation of reductive and stereotypical images to concepts of beauty, highlighting both the standards and exceptions that societal and cultural images enforce. She identifies 'the value Black women filmmakers place on Black women's emerging self-definitions', and the work of Patricia Hill Collins, and Kathleen Collins, engenders understanding of the dangerous and oppressive 'controlling images' in cinema history as well as in contemporary society.

The final essay in *The Feminist Film Philosophy Reader* is the enticingly – and succinctly – titled 'Women and Bugs'. Cynthia Freeland's analysis of some inventive images in a selection of horror films mainly from the 1980s and 1990s argues that their relationships with bugs affords women new examples of agency in horror. There are roots of this dynamic in classic Hollywood horror, but Freeland sees women from 1930s and 1940s mainly as victims requiring help. Carol Clover's influential invention of 'the Final Girl' named a role that women played in many horror films of the 1970s, but did not make a claim for their agency or feminist credentials (Clover 1992). Freeland proposes the 'women and bugs' scenario enables women both to be monsters and to defeat them, and she argues against some established character types such as Barbara Creed's 'monstrous mother' (Creed 1993). There is a different dynamic, Freeland argues, if the female monster is defeated by the female hero, which may in fact raise the possibility of reactionary body politics focusing women's bodies on child bearing and nurturing. Freeland's chapter was published in her book, *The Naked and the Undead: Evil and the Appeal of Horror*, in 2000 and in many ways prefigures the above-mentioned reinvigoration and reclamation of the horror genre by women which has taken place in the twenty-first century.

Notes

1.   I am grateful to Vincent Brown who brought Angela Davis's article to my attention in response to my observation that the FBI poster was on display as part of the DIVA exhibition at the V&A, London, June 2023 to April 2024.
2.   Kathleen Collins can be seen delivering a Masterclass at Howard University in 1984, made available by Milestone Films and the estate of Kathleen Collins, to be found here: https://vimeo.com/203379245 (accessed 3 May 2025).

References

Bolton, L. (2009), '"Meg Gets Naked!" Exposing the Female Star in Jane Campion's *In the Cut*', in C. Kevin (ed.) *Feminism and the Body: Interdisciplinary Perspectives*, 153–64, Newcastle upon Tyne: Cambridge Scholars Publishing.

Clover, C. (1992), *Men, Women and Chainsaws: Gender in the Modern Horror Film*, London: BFI.

Creed, B. (1993), *The Monstrous Feminine: Film, Feminism, Psychoanalysis*, London: Routledge.

Davis, A. Y. (1994), 'Afro Images: Politics, Fashion, and Nostalgia', *Critical Inquiry*, 21 (1): 37–45.

Harris, T. (1982), *From Mammies to Militants: Domestics in Black American Literature*, Philadelphia: Temple University Press.

Peirse, A. (2020), *Women Make Horror: Filmmaking, Feminism, Genre*, New Brunswick: Rutgers University Press.

Sandilands, C. (1999), *The Good-Natured Feminist: Ecofeminism and the Quest for Democracy*, Minneapolis, MN: University of Minnesota Press.

24 Breasts

ROSEMARIE GARLAND-THOMSON

Iconic Breasts

Breasts are ubiquitous cultural icons.[1] From the sacred fount of the Maria Lactans, the titillating cleavage of Miss America, the ample bosom of Mammy, to the erotic blast of the Playboy centerfold, the sight of breasts signifies woman. As both symbol and flesh, no other bodily mark of sexual identity is so routinely or ritualistically offered up to the public eye. Even though the penis and vagina carry perhaps equal cultural significance, representations tend to finesse the way we see these parts of our bodies. The penis stands in for phallic power but seldom shows itself in public.[2] Michelangelo's famous statue, for example, expresses David's masculinity through his commanding demeanor and musculature, not the incidental bit of flesh between his potent thighs. Phallic forums, such as the Washington Monument, are stylized rather than mimetic representations of penises. Vaginas appear even less often in respectable representations. Artists such as Georgia O'Keeffe, Judy Chicago, or Eve Ensler rework the vagina's image as a dark, secret snare into flamboyant flowers, dinner plates, or storytellers.[3] Symbolic hotspots as they are, penises and vaginas for the most part demurely decline stares. Breasts, by contrast, are in your face.

Maternal breasts have been on view from prehistory through the beginning of the modern era. The Venuses of the prehistoric fertility cults are enormous bosoms with vestigial limbs attached. Over twenty globular imbricated breasts adorn the elegant torso of the pre-classical Artemis of Ephesus. The bountiful, fertile breast takes on the human scale with the ever-lactating madonnas, reaching an apotheosis in the Madonna-del-latte of the Italian Renaissance. The Dutch Golden Age domesticated the lactating breast as a symbol of secular comfort. The new French Republic of the late eighteenth century offered images of maternal breasts to its new citizenry. People even see breasts where they are not. A long tradition of projecting the maternal breast onto the landscape exists as well, from the Virgin Land to the Grand Tetons, named by a trapper after the French slang for *breasts*.[4] In 1498, Christopher Columbus likened the newly sighted South America to an Edenic nipple projecting out from a mammary globe (Yalom 1997). In our contemporary era, the maternal breast has vanished, however, and the erotic breast has proliferated (87), responding in part to consumerism's more-and-bigger ethic. The comely pinup with her 36-24-36 measurements and the plastic, perky, rocket-titted Barbie figure have obliterated the sturdy fertility goddesses as the breasts we see.[5]

Hidden Breasts

The maternal breast has almost entirely receded from view in our day. Museums or a few churches are the only remaining public spaces where maternal breasts can be seen, safely contained there as aesthetic or sacred relics. The sight of an actual fleshly maternal breast in modern America raises controversy and even legal clashes. A particular flashpoint is breastfeeding in public. In 2004, for example, thirty mothers with infants held a "nurse-in" at a local Starbucks in a Washington, D.C., suburb to protest after a nursing mother was asked to cover up or move to the restroom. Amid the gush of rancorous public responses, one editorial called this sight of breastfeeding, "the latest assault on the right to a peaceful cup of [coffee]" (Roberts 2004, C01). The *Washington Post* writer, herself a former nursing mother, explained her complaint as being "about the slippery and ever-changing slope of social standards" (Roberts 2004, C01). Such skirmishes about which breasts we ought and ought not to stare at ended up in local courts, where breast feeding advocates argued, in short, that nursing women should be accorded civil inattention in public.

Confrontations about public breastfeeding are less about the merits of bottles versus breasts and more about monitoring staring. For the miffed editorial writer who wanted to drink her latte in peace, the issue apparently was not protecting the rights of breastfeeding mothers but rather protecting starers from the lure of starees. Her complaint was that the nursing mother "expects me to avert my eyes" (Roberts 2004, C01). In other words, she wanted to be shielded from her own impulse to stare. Perhaps more, she wanted to spare her fellow patrons from staring. Her plea to the nursing mother, "Please, please, please. Just don't," suggests moreover that she sought to protect her fellow mother from being a staree. The latte lament tells us something about social anxieties over what and how we see in public spaces. We expect maternal breasts to be sequestered in private spaces whereas erotic breasts are unremarkable staples of public visual culture. This moves the nursing breast from a space of simple looking into the territory of staring. Seeing maternal breasts where erotic breasts are expected makes people starers and nursing mothers starees. The social violation that provokes most anxiety, then, may not be breastfeeding in public but rather staring at it.

Exposed Breasts

The naked breast before the naked eye holds a potential charge, both in the past and today. Exposed breasts bespeak varying ideas of womanhood. Deep, inviting cleavage modestly promises sexual thrills. The bountiful maternal breast, whether Mommy or Mammy, whispers comfort to the child. The pierced breast of a rock star shouts down feminine modesty. The Madonna's breast intercedes for souls. The bikinied breast teases and withholds. The pert, pushed-up breast sells everything from lettuce, cars, drinks, dolls, to wars. The pastied breast of the go-go dancer goes almost all the way.[6] The appearance of breasts makes women legible as women; but—perhaps more important—staring at breasts supposedly tells us who a woman *really* is. The choreography and comportment of women's breasts, more than any other part of her body, are an index of her person. Although a woman's understanding of herself may differ wildly from the message that her breasts convey to the eyes of the world, her breasts nevertheless announce the essence of her womanliness.

The visual magnetism of breasts can make both starers and starees anxious. Women often feel self-conscious about their breasted appearance. Too much breast means too much femininity; too little breast means not enough. Flat-chested women may hide behind bulky sweaters or compensate with padded bras. Buxom women may defend against ogling with baggy clothes. One big-breasted woman says, "If a man stares at my breasts, I just don't give him a chance. I wish just once a man would look into my eyes with the same interest that he looks at my breasts" (Latteier 1998, 21). Men too can be wary of visually crossing into forbidden territory if they stare at women's breasts. Breast starers can be thought rude, insensitive, or lascivious. The staring scene at Starbucks worried people, in part, because staring—or not—at nursing breasts is unfamiliar visual territory.

Even though breasts entice stares, the border between what can and cannot be seen gets cautiously negotiated. The tensions between hiding and exposing breasts, between who should look when, fuel fierce debates. Moralists rage against immodest breast display while breasts doing sex work shout out from street corners. Big breasts sell products while breastless cancer survivors display their scars in protests. Mothers get arrested for nursing babies in public while public health advocates promote extended breastfeeding. Mothers and adolescent daughters struggle over necklines while commercialism makes children into sex pots. The surgical shaping of breasts escalates while implants are deemed dangerous. This deep cultural ambivalence turns the female breast into a perpetual peep show (Figure 24.1).

Proper looking gets complicated, then, when breasts are the object of stares. One perspective on anxiety about who should and should not stare at breasts comes from a person who was born intersexed. After living for twenty-four years as a woman, this person transitioned to being a man, an identity with which he felt more comfortable. In addition to comportment and costuming adjustments, testosterone treatments accomplished his transition into manhood.[7] Testosterone provided some of the visible marks of manhood such as facial hair, a more manly body, and a lower voice. Hormonally becoming a male, much to his surprise, affected his staring behavior. He reports that after taking testosterone for several weeks, he began noticing women's bodies differently from before, when he had mostly only looked at people's bodies

Figure 24.1 Marc Tyler Nobleman, "Does my résumé mention my breasts somewhere? I can't think of any other reason you'd continue to stare at them." November 8, 2001. Copyright © Marc Tyler Nobleman. https://linktr.ee/marctylernobleman/.

to simply note differences. Now that he is hormonally a man, he says when he first sees women in public he finds that he rarely looks at their faces anymore but begins his visual acquaintance with them by staring at their breasts. Having lived as a woman, he finds it mortifying to have developed what he calls "guy's eyes" and become a "breast man." Nonetheless, even when his brain tells him not to stare at breasts, he has difficulty not doing so. Despite his initial resistance, he now says that he accepts and even relishes this stereotypical looking practice as part of everyday life as a man (anonymous, 2006 interview). His new social position as a male, in other words, grants him permission to stare at breasts. Here then, the privileges of proper masculinity override the social proscription against staring.

When the expected meanings of a woman's breasts are not clearly decipherable, the sight of them can escalate to visual frenzy. Add to the controversy over public breastfeeding the fury over pop superstar Janet Jackson's fleetingly exposed nipple that 140,000,000 Americans gaped at during the halftime entertainment at the 2004 Super Bowl. The so-called Nipplegate controversy swirled around whether people were supposed to see Jackson's breast. It was an American spectacle: the public was outraged; the FCC launched an investigation; Jackson publicly asked for forgiveness for her inadvertent wardrobe malfunction; Viacom stock went way up. People debated the meaning, not so much of Jackson's nipple, but of our collective, momentary, astonished peek. Moreover, that startled stare defined the mythic cultural spectacle that is the Super Bowl. Those who argued that the Super Bowl is a wholesome American ritual that families share together were irate about Jackson's nipple while complacent about her edgy bump-and-grind performance. Jackson's apology reassured the public that nipples should remain a private resource in the patriarchal family, not a titillating girlie show.

By slipping into view, Jackson's nipple startled her viewers because it went too far beyond the expected visual tease of cleavage. Nipples are the ground zero of a breast's meaning, the sign that animates the breast's contradictions. Both child and lover lay claim to the nipple as a site of pleasure. But Jackson's nipple introduced a third claim. What people ogled was not a nipple presenting itself simply as maternal or erotic, but rather one marked as autoerotic. In full view was the nipple accoutrement that, Jackson had explained earlier on the Oprah Winfrey Show, provided her many pleasures as she moved through her day. The explicitly self-pleasing nipple scandalized by announcing that the pleasures of Jackson's nipple were hers alone. The significance of Jackson's stareable nipple intensifies further when layered with the racist and sexist history of black women's bodies. African-American women have been exploited for their sexual, reproductive, and domestic labor and stigmatized as sexual predators or docile servants. The sign of a black woman owning her own sexual pleasure was an unexpected sight at the All-American Super Bowl.[8] Jackson's nipple became a cultural touchstone—so to speak—for contradictory meanings of breasts.

For women, the visual significance of breasts is their magnetism. The female breast is for the male eye. Breasts are women's erotic capital. Dolly Parton, Jayne Mansfield, Jane Russell, and Carol Doda found wealth and fame by inviting men to stare at their breasts. Throngs of nameless belly dancers, strip teasers, beauty queens, porn stars, and fashion models strut their breasts for a living. What propels this visual avalanche of breasts is an assumed gendered division of looking, as we saw in chapter 6.[9] In short, the social role of men is to be starers, and the social role of women is to be starees. The breast acts as the cultural icon for this visual relation. The social ritual of breast staring reiterates two fundamental lessons for man. First, looking at breasts reminds man of what he is not. Second, looking at breasts reminds man that he can and must get what he desires. Starers see the iconic breast as abundant and available, but always only for others, not the woman herself. The erotic breast provides sexual pleasure for male starers. The maternal breast provides nourishment for the child. Breasts almost never belong to the woman to whom they are attached, but are either ornaments or implements for male viewing comfort, excitement, or mastery.

As a result, women often dissociate from their breasts or worse yet are alienated from them. They are not-me but for-another. And yet, the breast is a source of profound sensual pleasure for everyone. Nipples are made for mouths, and all of nature urges their coupling. For women, however, the pleasure of the breast is in the touching, the feeling—whether that touch comes from the body of the lover, the mouth of the baby, her own hand, or Janet Jackson's self-pleasing sex toy. For women to take pleasure in their own breasts, they must move breasts from sight to touch.[10] The public sighting of a celebrity breast hinting at its own tactile pleasures is not what American viewers expected to see on Super Bowl Sunday. Whether startled, stimulated, or outraged, Americans stared.

Unexpected Breasts

If we are indeed a nation of gawkers, as Neil Postman (1985) and others have argued, unexpected breasts are stareable sights that rouse satisfactions, discomforts, and ambivalences.[11] The endlessly presented image of breasts is at once titillating—so to speak—and monotonous. Even though breasts can invoke visual boredom or excitement, almost all public breasts look remarkably uniform. One day at the beach or a short visit to the women's locker room, however, will reveal the truth that women's breasts are as distinct as the features on their faces. This difference between public breasts and real women's breasts is where commercialism does its most profitable work. Women labor to create and maintain media breasts, using normalization aids that range from shaping garments such as brassieres, to exercise machines, implants, and surgical modification. They learn early on that having proper breasts is the ticket to the good life, and in some way they are right.

Not only do we expect breasts to appear in certain places and shapes, we expect breasts to come in matched pairs. Symmetrical, bilateral conjoinment is the signature of proper feminine personhood and breastedness. A lone breast seldom appears outside of the maternal context. A third breast, which is not uncommon and which may have been part of Anne Boleyn's undoing, was called a "witch's teat" and thought to be a sign of having consorted with the devil. The twoness of breasts contributes to its visual fetish as well. Cleavage announces the breasts, promises their charms, and invites starers to nestle. Alluring necklines catch eyes; the luscious notch draws the tongue—and it all promises thrills. Cleavage depends upon the mates on either side for its definition. When that landscape is disrupted, when the elements of the scene do not match expectations, we are visually aghast.[12] An unpredictable, unrecognizable breasted landscape shocks the eye because it is something we do not know how to see.

The divergence between the breasts we see and the breasts we have provided the breast cancer advocacy movement with an effective visual tool beginning in the 1970s.[13] The national breast-cancer movement has developed widely to include a political advocacy agenda of aggressive lobbying, rallying public support, creating awareness and early detection campaigns, demanding action and funds, speaking out, and founding organizations such as the National Breast Cancer Coalition and events such as Race for the Cure. The first visual element was to put influential breast cancer survivors such as Shirley Temple Black, First Lady Betty Ford, and Happy Rockefeller, wife of the vice president, on view to speak out. Before these women went public, breast cancer was unmentionable and certainly unviewable in public. Later, however, protest and aggressive public engagement edged out the ladylike approach to presenting breasts in public.

Women who had cancer began to bare their breasts by the late 1970s when the women's movement was most strongly pushing against institutionalized sexism. Breastlessness on view sharply violated what people had learned to expect of breasts. These women mobilized American staring behavior to demand that people pay attention to breasts in new ways. Staring forces people to reorganize their understandings, which was exactly what the breast cancer movement sought to do. The shocking sight of amputated breasts pulled the public eye toward political awareness. This use of visual novelty to focus public attention on a political goal was a forerunner to the displays of Sierra Leonians' amputated hands we saw in the last chapter.

The first stareable sight was the now familiar photograph by Hella Hammid called "The Warrior" which shows writer Deena Metzger with outstretched arms, baring her naked chest toward the sky in a triumphant gesture of exuberance (Figure 24.2). She intended the picture to accompany her 1978 publication of *Tree*, the book based on the journal she kept of her breast cancer experience, but the publishers were reluctant. The poster, however, slowly gained circulation and recognition in women's circles after she published it herself. "Warrior" is now a classic image of the women's positive identity politics initiative that honors differences among women. Metzger's triumphant pose celebrates survival, but more, it celebrates breastlessness. In the 1997 edition of her book, the picture is on the cover.

A grimmer look at breast cancer attends to the medical experience of breast cancer treatment rather than survival. The self-portraits of English photographer Jo Spence, for example, call up stares to reveal the realities of breast cancer treatment. Many of Spence's photographic series blend documentary and portraiture to put the middle-age breast at the center.[14] The most arresting of these pictures document her ten-year experience of breast cancer, starting in 1982. Spence's huge, saggy, scarred, and asymmetrical breasts are the central focus of "The Cancer Project," "The Picture of Health," and "The Final Project" (Figure

Figure 24.2 Hella Hammid, "The Warrior." Copyright © 1988 by Deena Metzger. Distributed as an 18" x 24" print by Donnelly/Colt (email: info@donnellycolt.com).

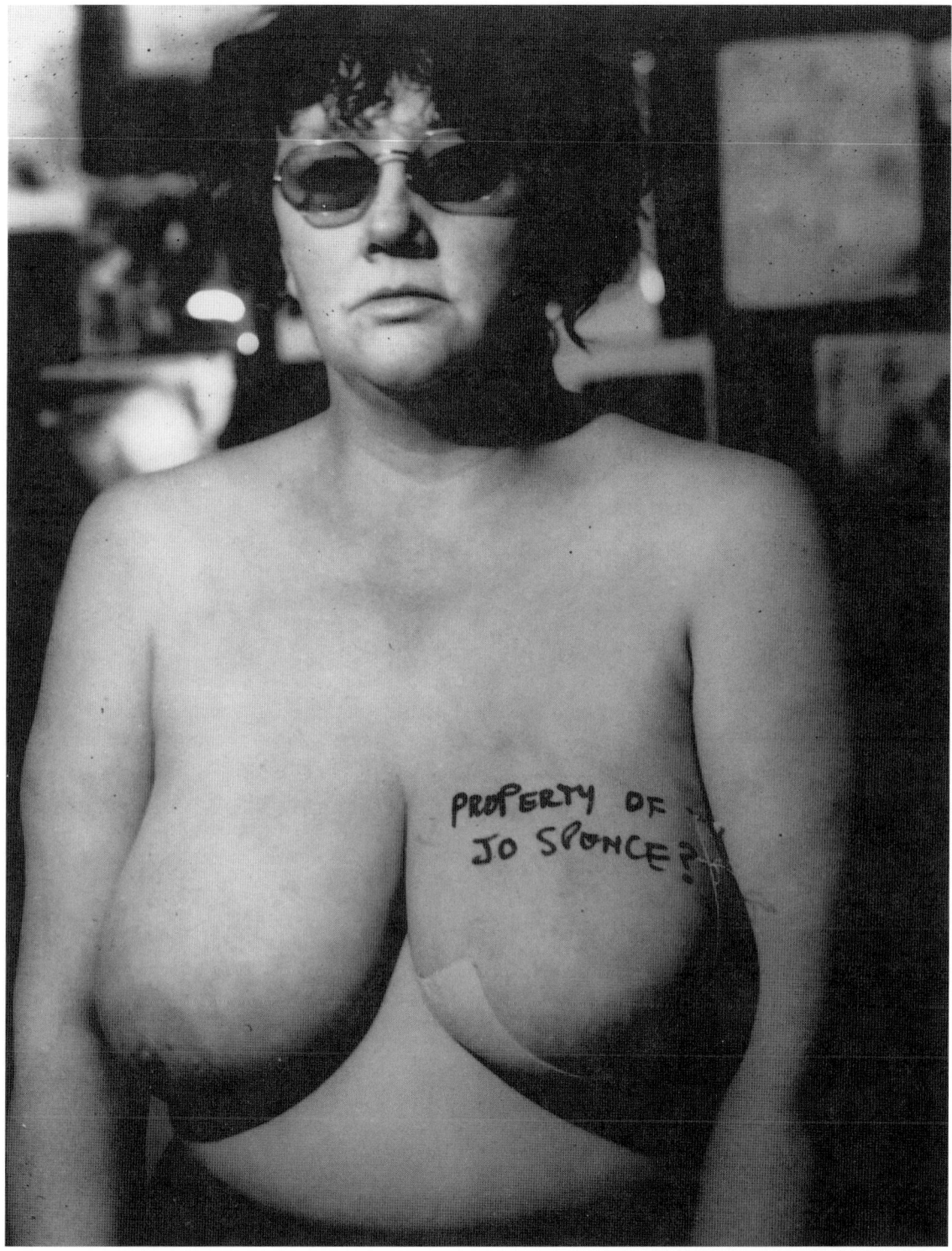

Figure 24.3 Jo Spence, Cancer Shock series (1982). Copyright © Jo Spence Memorial Archive, The Image Centre, Toronto. https://theimagecentre.ca/.

24.3). Spence's pictures resemble bad family snapshots or even mug shots. So far are hers from the usual pert and sculpted breasts that they unsettle. There is not a hint of the cover girl or centerfold. Instead of the generic erotic breast we are used to seeing, Spence is all particularity in these pictures. One image shows Spence's surgically targeted breast with a huge X, scrawled with labels such as "property of Jo Spence?" while another mimics a mug shot, with Spence holding a sign with the date printed on it just under her stark breasts. One portrait juxtaposes a scarred and shrunken breast with a face concealed behind a motorcycle helmet. In another, called "Marked up for Amputation," a huge white X-ed breast emerges from her robe as a grim-faced Spence, with tinted granny glasses, coldly stares back at her gawkers. The last of these sensational and ironic self-portraits is set in a hospice just before she died in 1992. In the tradition of edgy, radical art, Spence's photographs have an enthusiastic but self-selected audience. People have to come to see Spence's pictures, rather than the pictures coming to them.

In 1993, breastlessness showed up where no one expected to see it. That year, a flamboyant, fabulous-looking artist and model who calls herself Matuschka changed the way we stare at breasts. Matuschka has made a career of showing her body; she was a go-go dancer, lingerie model, and photographer who began by making pictures of herself nude among abandoned buildings. She is obsessed with documenting her own figure, particularly her torso. One might say that Matuschka is a professional staree. In 1991, a cancer diagnosis and mastectomy forced her to reconsider her body, work, life, and mortality. With characteristic audacity, she continued making photo-biographic portraits, taking up the challenge of continuing to use her body to make beautiful pictures. Instead of luring eyes with a perfectly matched proper pair of breasts, however, these disquieting portraits compel astonished attention with a spectacular, jagged scar running half way across her chest where her right breast had been. In her post-mastectomy portraits, the stark center of interest gathers around a shocking scar that leaps out of the picture in loud contrast to the familiar stuff of the fashion shot or the smartly posed beautiful woman of art photography. Of the photographs, Matuschka says triumphantly, "now I can make art out of anything" (1993, 162).

Matuschka did not simply now have a body that looked different from before, but people looked at her differently from before. Her striking looks had always attracted stares, and her breasts had often been a destination for eager eyes. Her new body startled her spectators, and their responses startled her. She began to understand her photographs as "a new vocabulary of images" that gave breast cancer activism more than a face (Peterson 2003, 1). At that time, silence and invisibility shrouded breast cancer. There were no pink ribbons, walk-a-thons, talk shows, awareness campaigns, or Dr. Susan Love books—and almost no pictures of breastlessness. So she put together a series of self-portraits called "Beauty Out of Damage" (Figures 24.4 and 24.5). These photos flung into the public's face an image that had only appeared in women's centers and activist offices. At first it seemed no one wanted to buy Matuschka's "honest photographs" (Matuschka 1993, 162). But then a writer for the New York Times saw the artist walking around a rally with her photographs hanging on her body like a sandwich sign and called her for an interview. In August 1993, one of the self-portraits from "Beauty Out of Damage" appeared on the cover of the Sunday New York Times Magazine, and Matuschka became what she calls "the first topless cover girl" in the emerging breast cancer movement (Matuschka 2005, 8; Figure 24.6).[15] What distinguished Matuschka's single-breasted "Beauty" picture from Deena Metzger's earlier "Warrior" poster and Jo Spence's sensational photographs was simple: Matuschka was a fashion model on the cover of a slick, high-end news magazine. Whereas Jo Spence occupied the alternative realm of radical art photography, Matuschka beckoned stares from within a mainstream visual arena. With her high fashion portraits, Matuschka takes up the visual aesthetic tradition of the nude, whereas Spence captures nakedness with a hint of the tabloid. Matuschka made breastlessness a public spectacle that almost no one expected to see.

Figure 24.4 Matuschka, "The New Deal" (1993). Copyright © Matuschka. http://matuschka.net/.

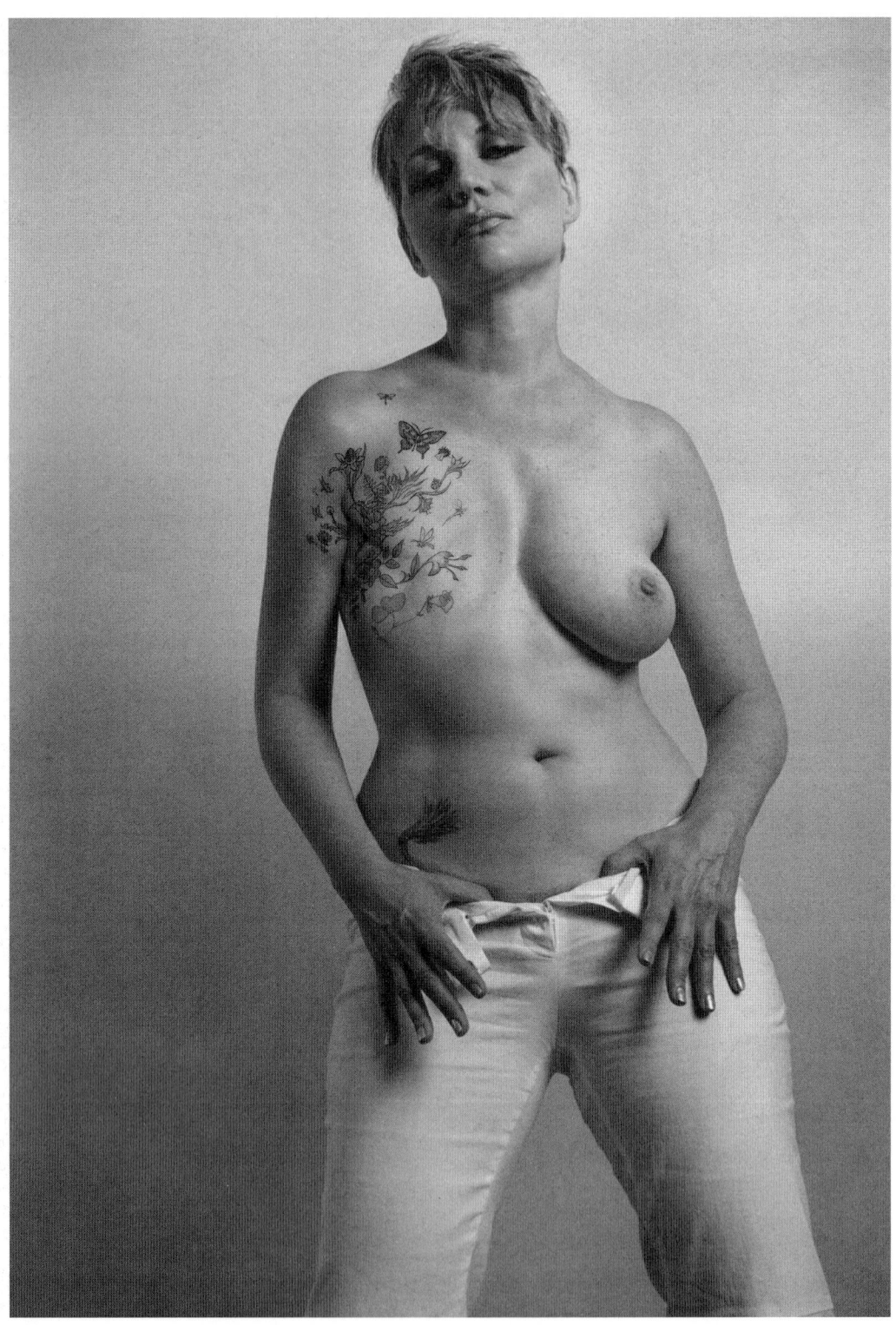

Figure 24.5 Matuschka, "Tattooectomy" (2003). Copyright © Matuschka. http://matuschka.net/.

Figure 24.6 Matuschka, "Beauty Out of Damage" (1993). Copyright © Matuschka. http://matuschka.net/.

People stared. They had seen lots of lovely breasted women in the *New York Times*, but they had never seen breastlessness on such a woman. What we first see seems an unremarkable picture that follows the conventions of high fashion photography. A slender elegant model strikes a chic pose, face in a sophisticated profile, head stylishly turbaned, full front torso with a plunging, off-the-shoulder white gown. The image gains some drama from a not-so-subtle allusion to the goddess Diana. But there, at the literal heart of the picture, is a purplish scar snaking across the place where we expect to see the soft globe of a breast. The picture is stunning, in both senses of the word. It arrests by fusing expected with unexpected, familiar with strange. The unholy visual union of a very sightly figure and a very unsightly scar invites us to look.

Matuschka's at once gorgeous and shocking image drew more than stares; it also pulled in hundreds of letters to the editor at the *New York Times*, as well as a rush of television, radio, newspaper, and magazine interviews, personal phone calls, hate mail, and love letters to Matuschka herself. Some called it "embarrassing," "disgraceful," or thought it exploited suffering for "shock value" (Matuschka 1993, 162). Breast cancer survivors, whose response Matuschka most wanted, generally praised the photograph for making their reality visible, putting forward here to be seen the body that matched their own. Many women responded negatively, however, feeling that the picture violated their privacy, that "what they really looked like" was now exposed to the stares of everyone. Others worried that the shocking revelation of Matuschka's appearance would turn women away from mammograms and treatment. The photograph stirred a conversation about the scandal of ignoring breast cancer by insisting that breast cancer happened and that people should do something about that.

Matuschka's picture stokes anxieties about cancer—but also about staring. The headline printed over the photograph on the *New York Times Magazine* taunts: "You Can't Look Away Any More." That exposed wound and the unexpected difference of her body make people awkward starers in spite of their mothers' injunctions. She forces everyone to look hard, not so much at what we do not want to see, but that at which we are not supposed to stare. To see a wound where we expect a breast demands not just attention, but an explanation, a new reality. That we cannot look away anymore occasions a moment of political ripeness that breast cancer advocates have harvested particularly effectively. Unwavering stares at Matuschka's scar are a kind of upscale rubbernecking. The gut response may be horror, fascination, or stimulation, but the eye response is baroque staring. That stuck look is the raw material of political activism.

Matuschka's portrait on the cover of the *New York Times Magazine* was in a way a turning point for breast cancer advocacy, which has evolved an entire culture of visual symbolism, ranging from ubiquitous pink ribbons to intricate tattoos adorning mastectomy scars. In 2000, for instance, The Breast Cancer Fund, a San Francisco-based nonprofit organization dedicated to research and education, mounted a public awareness campaign called "Obsessed with Breasts" (Figure 24.7).[16] The campaign put up three different posters in public bus shelters and on building walls. One poster looked like the cover of Cosmopolitan magazine; another simulated an ad for a Calvin Klein perfume line called Obsession; the other replicated a Victoria Secret catalog cover. Instead of the expected visual offering of usual breasts, however, these models boldly flaunted scars. This campaign pushed Matuschka's cover girl image toward politicized parody. Not unlike Janet Jackson's autoerotic breast, these images provoked controversy and roused political protests over what constitutes acceptable and unacceptable looking at women's breasts.[17]

Switching out the ceaselessly circulated erotic breast for startling scars snags eyes by fusing two opposing visual genres: the pinup girl and the medical photograph. The medical subject would have been posed with slumping and resigned posture and a black rectangle covering the eyes; the pinup would have been properly cleavaged. The cognitive confusion intensifies our impulse to resolve the contradiction between these divergent expected sights. By mocking the sensationalism of both kinds of images, these pictures protest against the refusal of contemporary America to literally and figuratively look at breast cancer.

IT'S NO SECRET

SOCIETY IS OBSESSED WITH BREASTS

BUT WHAT ARE
WE DOING ABOUT
BREAST CANCER?

Figure 24.7 *Obsessed with Breasts*, ad campaign by Breast Cancer Prevention Partners (formerly Breast Cancer Fund). Copyright © Breast Cancer Prevention Partners. https://www.bcpp.org/.

Figure 24.8 People watch as British artist Marc Quinn's white, thirteen-ton statue inspired by artist Alison Lapper, who was born with no arms and shortened legs, is unveiled in central London's Trafalgar Square, Thursday, September 15, 2005. Lapper posed naked for Quinn when she was eight months pregnant, in what the artist says was a tribute to motherhood and people with disabilities. The sculpture remained in place for two years. Copyright © Lefteris Pitarakis/Associated Press/Alamy Stock Photo.

A perhaps even more novel sight than breastlessness appeared in London's Trafalgar Square in September 2005. A statue called "Alison Lapper Pregnant" was unveiled to the curious eyes of the public gathered for the momentous occasion (Figure 24.8). This much-anticipated and controversial statue by the British sensationalist artist Marc Quinn was selected to occupy the Fourth Plinth, a public spot of honor that had been vacant for 150 years in a public space dominated by the towering memorial to Lord Nelson, Britain's one-armed famed war hero. Quinn's realistic portrayal of a nude, pregnant woman—which won over proposed statues of both Nelson Mandela and the Queen Mother—stirred up disagreements about what ought to be seen in public.

Viewers' responses to "Alison Lapper Pregnant" ranged widely, judging it as "indecent," "confrontational," "repellent," "ugly," and "beautiful" (Jury 2005; Leitch 2005; Reynolds 2005). One observer wrote in a letter to a newspaper that there was "discomfort with the subject matter" (Olsen 2004). The statue's sculptor, Marc Quinn, offers an insight as to why people stare at his statue. Quinn asserts that most public sculpture is "invisible" to most people because it is such an unremarkable sight. "Alison Lapper Pregnant," however, is "vexingly visible." Quinn says that his statue makes people "see things that are there." In other words, it invites them to stare because it is something novel they do not expect to see. "That's why people are outraged by it," Quinn concludes (Darwent 2005).

A fifteen-foot high white marble nude woman on a pedestal is not uncommon among works of art. But to publicly memorialize a pregnant belly flanked with its heavy breasts presents a radical view of womanhood.

Pregnancy, like mastectomy scars, is a usually hidden aspect of women's bodies. A look at "Alison Lapper Pregnant" jolts you with this visual juxtaposition between the familiar female nude and the rarely displayed pregnant woman. "Alison Lapper Pregnant" gets people staring, however, for more than just the unexpected trio of the heavily fecund belly and breasts naked in Trafalgar Square.[18] Surrounding the realistic representation of Alison Lapper's seldom-exposed but still ordinary torso is that of her actual, very unusual set of limbs. Lapper is armless and has shortened legs ending with singularly shaped feet.[19]

Lapper's marble portrait does similar cultural work to the picture of Matuschka on the cover of the *New York Times Magazine*. The venue, pose, medium, and context of both representations are familiar and legible to viewers: one is a white marble nude statue in a public square; the other a high fashion magazine cover shot. Embedded in these ordinary sights, however, are forbidden sights, the sort that would elicit a mother's "don't stare!" These hybrids of the to-be-looked-at and not to-be-looked-at create a stareable scene. They demand baroque staring, that intensely interrogative looking in response to startling visual novelty.

New sights ask new questions that can lead to new understandings. What Matuschka's picture asks is how what we have learned to think of as beauty—the ideal woman—might be crosshatched by what we think of as ugly—a scar replacing the breast. What "Alison Lapper Pregnant" asks is how a woman with significant disabilities merits being seen in Trafalgar Square with national heroes such as Nelson, how she might be sexual, and how she might be fit to parent a child. Viewers may come to these public sights with often unacknowledged ideas that the kinds of bodies such as Matuschka and Lapper have are somehow disqualified from womanhood. The cultural work of these images is to make us look at them long enough to change our minds. We may be discomforted, moved, outraged, enlightened, or offended. But we cannot look away any more.

Recognition

If staring has done its work, the next time people see such bodies, they will be familiar, if only vaguely. When the visual novelty that sparks stares subsides, the bodies that life has given Matuschka and Lapper can be recognizable as belonging to the human spectrum. In other words, these representations put the distinctive details of these women's bodies in people's faces until they get used to them. The individual shapes and marks of these bodies bear witness to human variation, to the way our particular life etches itself onto our bodies. This work is the potentially mutually revivifying aspect of staring encounters.

Recognition, according to the political philosopher Nancy Fraser (2003), is essential not simply for individual self-realization but, more important, is the cornerstone of an ethical political society. Recognition is "an ideal reciprocal relation between subjects in which each sees the other as its equal and also as separate. … [O]ne becomes an individual subject only in virtue of recognizing, and being recognized by, another subject" (2003, 10). Implicit in Fraser's concept of political recognition is that persons be seen as they are, as particular individuals embedded in their own lives. To be recognizable a person must appear as distinct from a generic, generalized figure. To be recognized is to become familiar, no longer strange, to be seen and accorded the status of fellow human. Recognition, then, relies on a combination of identification and differentiation. The trajectory of recognition is this: I recognize you by seeing your similarity and your difference to me, and then I make your strangeness familiar. In other words, I see you as you are.

But all too often we see each other not as we are, but as we are expected to be. This misrecognition disparages or ignores a person's "distinctive characteristics," according to Fraser, which "prevent[s] one from participating as a peer in social life" (2003, 29). What's wrong about misrecognition is that it is unjust.[20] Misrecognition is a form of discrimination that Kenji Yoshino (2006) terms "covering." People of racial, ethnic, and sexual minorities, as well as people with disabilities, often try, according to Yoshino, to meet dominant group expectations by either minimizing or hiding the visible markers of their subordinated status. In other words, they mute their "distinctive characteristics," the ones Fraser calls to be recognized in an ethical society. This is why, according to Yoshino, blacks might straighten hair, the blind wear sunglasses to hide their eyes, or the unusually shaped get reconstructive surgery. This is also, to return to an earlier example, why Sergeant Doyne sometimes wears a "normal" hand. These appearance adjustments help quiet stigmatization and provide civil inattention, but they also invite misrecognition.[21]

Covering, in Yoshino's sense of the term, is an escape from stares. The problem with covering our distinctiveness is that it forfeits recognition. By literally refusing to cover themselves, Metzger, Matuschka, Spence, and Lapper provoke recognition by making themselves stareable sights. They initiate a feminist activist tradition that performance poets Cheryl Marie Wade and Lezlie Frye follow in baring their unusual hands. Moreover, these visual revelations rebuke the cover-ups of padded bras, falsies, implants, cosmetic prostheses, or baggy clothes. One particular cover-up they challenge are breast prostheses, which are an expected response to mastectomy. The self-proclaimed "warrior poet" Audre Lorde writes in *The Cancer Journals* of being urged toward a prosthetic breast so that "nobody'll ever know the difference" (1997, 42). Lorde rejects the prosthesis, not for its look, but for its feel. She elects sensation over appearance, concluding that the prosthesis is "awkwardly inert and lifeless, and having nothing to do with me …" (44). Facing herself in the mirror after her surgery, her new body makes her stare at herself: "I look strange and uneven and peculiar to myself, but somehow, ever so much more myself, and therefore so much more acceptable than I looked with that thing stuck inside my clothes. For not even the most skillful prosthesis in the world could undo that reality, or feel the way my breast had felt, and either I would love my body one breasted now, or remain forever alien to myself" (44). Lorde expresses in words here what Metzger and Matuschka convey in pictures.[22] These women exchange the visual anonymity that an artificial breast affords for the same opportunity Lorde seeks in refusing to cover: to "come to terms with their own pain and loss, and thereby, with their own strength" (49). The exposed bodies of the women who bare their breasts cover the reality of all our distinctive bodies. What breast cancer advocates and the larger disability rights movement wants is not simply stares but recognition, not separated but engaged stares. To look hard is potentially to recognize that devalued human variations do not diminish but testify to our humanness.

From *Staring: How We Look* by Rosemarie Garland-Thomson. ©2009 Oxford University Press. Reproduced with permission of the Licensor through PLSclear.

Notes

1. In this chapter, I am indebted to Iris Marion Young's seminal essay on breastedness, "Breasted Experience," in *On Female Body Experience* (2005).
2. See Susan Bordo (1994).
3. The floral paintings of American artist Georgia O'Keeffe suggest vaginas, even though the artist has insisted they are simply pictures of flowers; American artist Judy Chicago's 1979 feminist celebration of women's culture, "The Dinner Party," explicitly uses stylized vaginal imagery in its series of dining plates; and Eve Ensler's 1996 blockbuster play, "The Vagina Monologues," which is a meditation on the significance and semantics of vaginas, is filled with narrative accounts of looking at vaginas.
4. See Annette Kolodny (1975).
5. See Urla and Swedlund (1995).

6. See Yalom (1997) as well as Latteier (1998).

7. For a provocative, subjective account of testosterone's effects, see Sullivan (2000).

8. Kimberly Wallace-Sanders (2008) discusses this question in her essay "Nipplegate: Black Feminism, Corporeal Fragmentation and the Politics of Public Consumption."

9. This gender dynamic of seeing describes normative cultural scripts, not necessarily the behavior or motivations of actual individuals. How people place themselves along the continuum of sexual identity structures the way actual people look at men and women, of course (Berger 1972).

10. See Young (2005).

11. See Postman (1985) and Debord (1994).

12. About one out of two hundred women have a supernumerary nipple (Yalom 1997, 61).

13. The breast cancer movement was a political recognition initiative that was part of not only the women's movement but the larger cluster of civil rights movements that characterized and transformed the political and social landscape of mid-twentieth-century America.

14. See works by Jo Spence (1988, 1995, 2006).

15. See Ferraro (1993).

16. In 1998, the Breast Cancer Fund published a book called *Art.Rage.Us: Art and Writing by Women with Breast Cancer*. Composed of writing and art by women with breast cancer, this beautiful coffee-table book with an epilogue by breast cancer survivor and environmentalist novelist Terry Tempest Williams is representative of the activist art produced by a breast cancer advocacy movement.

17. At present, the user-populated Internet image archive Flickr hosts a number of self-portraits of breast cancer survivors presented in the mode of these public displays of breastlessness.

18. See, for example, Annie Liebovitz's controversial *Vanity Fair* magazine cover photo of pregnant Demi Moore published in August 1991.

19. Alison Lapper is herself an artist and a single mother. Abandoned to a foundling home for disabled children at birth, she eventually earned a First in Fine Art at Brighton University and became a successful artist. In her youth, she discovered increased freedom and flexibility by discarding the prosthetic limbs she was encouraged to wear. She works for the Mouth and Foot Painting Artists Association designing greeting cards that are sold in seventy-three countries. She also has made a series of photographic self-portraits and in 2006 published an autobiography with Guy Feldman called *My Life in My Hands*.

20. The philosopher Charles Taylor also explored political recognition, using the example of how Canadian Francophone culture gets recognition through legislated bilingualism; see Taylor (1994).

21. See Goffman (1986).

22. For a dissenting argument on breast prostheses, see Herndl (2002).

References

Art.Rage.Us: Art and Writing by Women with Breast Cancer. San Francisco: Chronicle Books, 1998.

Berger, John. *Ways of Seeing*. London: BBC and Penguin, 1972.

Bordo, Susan. "Reading the Male Body." In *The Male Body*, edited by Laurence Goldstein, 265–306. Ann Arbor: University of Michigan Press, 1994.

Darwent, Charles. "A Marble Sculpture of a Pregnant Woman with Shortened Legs and Arms" *The Daily Telegraph* (London), 16 September 2005: 6.

Debord, Guy. *The Society of the Spectacle*. New York: Zone Books, 1994.

Ferraro, Susan. "The Anguished Politics of Breast Cancer." *New York Times Magazine*. 15 August 1993: 24–27.

Fraser, Nancy, and Axel Honneth. *Redistribution or Recognition? A Political Philosophical Exchange*. London: Verso, 2003.

Goffman, Erving. *Stigma: Notes on the Management of Spoiled Identity*. New York: Simon & Schuster, 1986.

Herndl, Diane Price. "Reconstructing the Posthuman Feminist Body: Twenty Years after Audre Lorde's *Cancer Journals*." In *Disability Studies: Enabling the Humanities*, edited by Sharon L. Snyder, et al., 144–55. New York: Modern Language Association of America, 2002.

Jury, Louise. "New hero takes seat in Trafalgar Square… but what do artists and the public think?" *The Independent* (London). 16 September 2005. https://www.independent.co.uk/news/uk/this-britain/new-hero-takes-seat-in-trafalgar-square-but-what-do-artists-and-the-public-think-313003.html.

Kolodny, Annette. *The Lay of the Land: Metaphor as Experience and History in American Life and Letters*. Chapel Hill: University of North Carolina Press, 1975.

Lapper, Alison, and Guy Feldman. *My Life in My Hands*. London: Simon & Schuster, 2006.

Latteier, Carolyn. *Breasts: The Women's Perspective on an American Obsession*. Haworth Innovations in Feminist Studies. New York: Haworth Press, 1998.

Leitch, Luke. "Repellent Lapper Statue Looks Like Soap, Says Critic," *The Independent* (London), 16 September 2005, 11.

Lorde, Audre. *The Cancer Journals: Special Edition*. San Francisco: Aunt Lute Books, 1997.

Matuschka. "Why I Did It." *Glamour Magazine* 91 (November 1993): 162.

Matuschka. "Balancing a Lopsided Act" (By Crinkle Tit). Unpublished essay, 2005.

Olsen, Hanne. "More than a message." *The Guardian*, 20 March 2004. https://www.theguardian.com/theguardian/2004/mar/20/guardianletters.

Peterson, Jennifer. "Case Re-Examined," 2003. http://www.matuschka.net/interviews/interview2003a.html (accessed 24 August 2006).

Postman, Neil. *Amusing Ourselves to Death: Public Discourse in the Age of Show Business*. New York: Viking, 1985.

Reynolds, Nigel. "Whatever Would Nelson Think?" *The Telegraph*, 16 September 2005. https://www.telegraph.co.uk/news/uknews/4197485/Whatever-would-Nelson-think.html.

Roberts, Roxanne. "Do Me a Favor, Keep a Lid on Your Double Latte." *Washington Post*, 15 August 2004, C01.

Spence, Jo. *Beyond the Perfect Image: Photography, Subjectivity, and Antagonism*. Barcelona: Museu d'Art Contemporani de Barcelona, 2006.

Spence, Jo. *Cultural Sniping: The Art of Transgression*. London: Routledge, 1995.

Spence, Jo. *Putting Myself in the Picture: A Political, Personal and Photographic Autobiography*. Seattle: Real Comet Press, 1988.

Sullivan, Andrew. "The He Hormone." *New York Times Magazine*, 2 April 2000, Health, SM 46–57.

Taylor, Charles. "The Politics of Recognition." In *Multiculturalism: Examining the Politics of Recognition*, edited by Amy Gutmann, 25–74. Princeton, N.J.: Princeton University Press, 1994.

Urla, Jacqueline, and Alan Swedlund. "The Anthropometry of Barbie." In *Deviant Bodies: Cultural Perspectives in Science and Popular Culture*, edited by Jennifer Terry et al., 277–313. Bloomington: Indiana University Press, 1995.

Wallace-Sanders, Kimberly. "Nipplegate: Black Feminism, Corporeal Fragmentation and the Politics of Public Consumption." In *Women in Popular Culture: Representation and Meaning*, edited by Marian Meyers. Cresskill, N.J.: Hampton Press, 2008.

Yalom, Marilyn. *A History of the Breast*. New York: Alfred A. Knopf, 1997.

Yoshino, Kenji. *Covering: The Hidden Assault on Our Civil Rights*. New York: Random House, 2006.

Young, Iris Marion. *On Female Body Experience: "Throwing Like a Girl" and Other Essays*. Studies in Feminist Philosophy. New York: Oxford University Press, 2005.

25 Accessible Futures, Future Coalitions

ALISON KAFER

When describing disability studies to my students, I often draw on Douglas Baynton's insight that "disability is everywhere in history once you begin looking for it."[1] For Baynton, "looking for it" entails not only recovering the stories of disabled people or tracing histories of disability discrimination but also exploring how notions of disability and able-mindedness/able-bodiedness have functioned in different contexts. Baynton issues his provocation to historians, but disability studies scholars in other fields have extended its reach, pushing their own colleagues to recognize disability as a category of analysis. Deeply influenced by and indebted to this work, I use this final chapter to read Baynton's assertion differently. Rather than direct his insight outward, to those not currently working in disability studies, I turn inward, directing it to the field itself. If "disability is everywhere … once you begin looking for it," where do we, as disability studies scholars and activists, continue *not* to look? Where do we find disability and where do we miss it? In which theories and in which movements do we recognize ourselves, or recognize disability, and which theories and movements do we continue to see as separate from or tangential to disability studies?

These questions, and potential answers to them, have surfaced in previous chapters, but in this final chapter I address them more directly. In imagining what accessible futures might look like or might include, I find myself thinking about the possibilities of cross-movement work, both intellectually and politically. If disability is everywhere once we start looking for it, then why not look for it in the other social justice movements at work in contemporary culture? My understanding of disability rights, justice, politics, culture, and scholarship has always been informed by my investments in feminist and queer theories and practices. Reading disability into and alongside those investments is one way to imagine disability differently. In other words, looking within disability studies for the traces of other movements while simultaneously looking for disability in places it has gone unmarked is one way of moving us toward accessible futures.

I begin "looking for disability" in a canonical feminist studies text—Bernice Johnson Reagon's influential essay on coalition politics—that is not widely recognized as being "about" disability. Reading disability into it not only allows for an expansion of feminist and disability studies genealogies but also offers a framework for imagining future work. I then move outward from Reagon's text to explore three potential areas of growth for feminist, queer, crip theory and activism: bathroom politics and contestations over public space; environmental justice; and reproductive justice. Zeroing in on each of these sites allows us to think through how different formulations of disability encourage (and discourage) unexpected but generative alliances. I close by invoking still more connections and coalitions, making clear the multiple and overlapping possibilities for feminist, queer, crip futures.

Reagon's text serves as an apt introduction to this chapter because of her frank acknowledgment of and engagement with practices of dissent and strife. Throughout the essay, she encourages us to recognize that the *benefits* of coalition politics are bound up in the *difficulties* of such politics. Disagreement pushes us to recognize and acknowledge our own assumptions and the boundaries we draw around our own work; without such disagreement, and the ways it compels us to reexamine our positions, we can too easily skim over our own exclusions and their effects. I have chosen each of the sites I highlight here—trans/disability bathroom politics, environmental justice movements, and reproductive justice movements—in large part because they, too, are contentious. They force our attention to the formation of the identities, positions, and practices we name as feminist and/or as queer and/or as crip. They also offer contradictions that are not easily resolvable, contradictions that make difficult any facile claims to "unity" or sameness.

I am influenced here by the work of feminist theorists such as Audre Lorde, Chantal Mouffe, and Ranu Samantrai, each of whom argues for the value, and necessity, of dissent. Samantrai explains that "dissenters draw attention to the border zones where … norms are negotiated," subjecting "the terms of membership" in a political community to "continual revision."[2] Indeed, rather than "expelling conflicts and suppressing their annoying reminders," a coalition politics that embraces dissent can begin to ask "how we can take advantage" of such conflicts.[3] Thus, in using the language of "coalition," I am less interested in imagining coalition politics "as a process of dealing with already-constituted interests and identities"—women as discrete group working with disabled people as discrete group—than in thinking through coalitions as a process in which the interests and identities themselves are always open to contestation and debate.[4] How does "disabled" shift, expand, or contract in these various movements and theories? In other words, part of what excites me about the coalitions I examine here is that they often trouble the boundaries of the constituencies involved. Thinking through trans/disability bathroom politics, then, means not only accounting for "disabled people" working alongside "trans- people," or even people who are both trans and disabled, but also questioning the very categories of "disabled people" and "trans- people."

Finding Disability: Feminist Texts, Disability Theory

I teach in a feminist studies program at a small liberal arts college, and my courses are marked "feminist studies" far more often than "disability studies." The productive overlaps between the two fields, however, allow me to insert disability studies insights and analyses into conversations that are not marked as such; disability often surfaces in our conversations even though we were not explicitly looking for it. In that spirit, I want to offer here a rereading of a text familiar, even canonical, to feminist studies audiences, but one that is not widely recognized as a "disability studies text." Reading it again, through the lens of disability, opens up additional possibilities for overlap and critique between disability and feminist studies. As my understandings of crip futurity and feminist cross-movement work have been deeply influenced by this essay, it feels fitting to explore it in this final chapter.

"Coalition Politics: Turning the Century," by Bernice Johnson Reagon, was published in Barbara Smith's *Home Girls: A Black Feminist Anthology* in 1983.[5] Reagon reflects on the process of coalition building, asserting that forming coalitions across difference is both necessary and terrifying: necessary, in that in order to create political change we need to recognize the interrelations among different issues and identities; terrifying, in that we often are working with people unlike us, people who might frame the issues in different ways or to different effects, people who come from different perspectives or with different histories, people who might challenge our founding assumptions.

Reagon's essay is based on a presentation she gave at the 1981 West Coast Women's Music Festival in California's Yosemite National Forest. As many scholars have noted, her piece bears the traces of this location; her focus on coalitions, and on the limitations of monolithic constructions of "woman," was clearly based on contemporary conversations about racism and classism within the women's movement and the role (and composition) of women-only spaces.[6] I want to highlight, however, the ways in which her essay bears the traces not only of the women's music festival but also of the Yosemite National Forest.

Reagon begins the essay with this paragraph:

> I've never been this high before. I'm talking about the altitude. There is a lesson in bringing people together where they can't get enough oxygen, then having them try to figure out what they're going to do when they can't think properly. I'm serious about that. There probably are some people here who can breathe, because you were born in high altitudes and you have big lung cavities. But when you bring people in who have not had the environmental conditioning, you got one group of people who are in a strain—and the group of people who are feeling fine are trying to figure out why you're staggering around, and that's what this workshop is about this morning.[7]

Reagon is undoubtedly speaking metaphorically here. She uses this story of being out of breath as a way of talking about how coalitions are hard, uncomfortable, stressful places where we can never fully let go and relax; in coalition, as on the mountain, we can never fully catch our breath. As she explains in the next paragraph, "I feel as if I'm gonna keel over any minute and die. That is often what it feels like if you're *really* doing coalition work. Most of the time you feel threatened to the core and if you don't, you're not really doing no coalescing."[8] Coalition politics, for Reagon, entails working beyond the limits of one's comfort zone, being pushed into dangerous territory, engaging with people or practices or principles that frighten because of their difference.

But to read this anecdote solely as metaphor is to erase the specificities of Reagon's experience.[9] Immediately before stating that she feels like keeling over, Reagon explains that she "belong[s] to the group of people who are having a very difficult time being here" because of the high altitude; she is *literally* having a difficult time catching her breath.[10] Thus, for Reagon, "coalition politics," both the eponymous essay and the practice, begin with a focus on the body. And not just any body, but a limited body, an impaired body. Reagon is theorizing from the disabled body, using her embodied experience of disability—having a physical limitation in a sociopolitical setting that acts as if that limitation were nonexistent, or at least irrelevant—as a springboard for thinking about difference, relation, and politics. She illustrates the ways in which experiences of disability can be useful not only in informing our understandings about bodies but also our understandings of ethical relations and political practice.

Part of this analysis, on both the literal and metaphorical level, means reckoning with the bodies that cannot survive, let alone thrive, in particular settings. Reagon's breathing difficulties at this altitude, combined with her reflections on whose bodies are absent from this "women's" space, raises questions about the assumptions that undergird feminist practice. Whose bodies, whose experiences, whose desires, and whose identities shape the issues that get framed as feminist, and who does the framing? How accessible—financially, culturally, intellectually, physically—are feminist spaces, spaces in and through which feminist futures are imagined? In other words, Reagon calls feminism to task for creating spaces, both literally and metaphorically, in which certain bodies/minds play no role, or can participate only at great personal risk. She offers a powerful illustration of how the kinds of spaces we imagine often determine the kinds of bodies/minds that can inhabit those spaces. As a result, the conversations that occur in those spaces are dramatically—and all too often invisibly—diminished by the absence of those folks who, for reasons of inaccessibility or exclusion or ignorance, cannot participate.

Reagon explicitly directs her critique to feminism and the women's movement, but we can read her text as offering a challenge to disability studies and disability movements as well. Although the word "disability" appears only in passing in Reagon's text, and she does not identify herself as disabled or describe her breathing difficulties in those terms, we can easily read her essay as a narrative of inaccessibility or as an illustration of the insights to be gained from disability.[11] Recognizing this text as a crip text then allows for a whole set of necessary questions: In focusing so intently on disability identity, how have disability studies and disability rights movements overlooked the crip insights of people like Reagon? How might her formulation of coalition politics, of the need for feminism to acknowledge and grapple with racialized differences, inform a disability studies marked by whiteness, or disability rights movements slow to deal with issues of race and ethnicity? Or how might her focus on breathing difficulties inspire disability analyses of asthma, perhaps even prompting the field to recognize itself in or ally with environmental studies and environmental justice movements? In other words, what can disability studies and disability movements learn from our own exclusions?

Reading Reagon as a crip theorist is one way to begin answering these questions. Such a reading, and the expansive approach to disability politics it entails, means locating the subject of disability studies not just in bodies identified as disabled but in minds and bodies surviving inaccessible spaces, with both "access" and "spaces" defined broadly. It means recognizing contestations over whiteness, or economic disparity, or heteronormativity as part of disability studies and disability activism, not merely side projects or subdisciplines. It means challenging the homophobia and transphobia that lurk within the disability rights movement, marginalizing the experiences of queer- and trans-identified people with disabilities. It requires a continued examination of the whiteness and ethnocentrism of disability studies and disability activism in the United States, as well as committed engagement with the work of disability rights, antiglobalization, and antipoverty activists around the globe.

Like Reagon, however, we can pair our internal criticisms of our own positions and movements with engaged critiques of our partners and allies. Thinking through accessible spaces and accessible futures means addressing the exclusions of feminist and queer political visions of the future, highlighting these theories' reliance on ideologies of wholeness, complicity in compulsory able-bodiedness/able-mindedness, and marginalization of disabled people. What is needed, then, is not only a trenchant critique of ableism but also a desire to think disability otherwise.

This kind of robust combination of future dreams and present critique is essential to politics, and it requires leaving open the parameters of our political visions. Our animating questions could then include the following: Who is included or excluded in our political imaginaries? How are "disability" and "disabled person" (or "woman" or "queer" or "race" or …) being defined in these dreams of the future? Who has access to these imaginaries, and how is access being described? Which issues are being marked as feminist or queer or crip? And, to return to my earlier questions, where are disability studies or disability movements going to look for disability? Where does disability studies see or recognize itself?

The rest of this chapter profiles sites where answers to these kinds of questions are happening. Each of the following sections offers a snapshot of coalitions in progress, and I include them here as stories of disability told, or being told, otherwise. These stories are necessarily incomplete, but in their incompleteness they provide examples of how to imagine disability differently: finding it in unexpected places, using it to make connections to other social justice movements, and recognizing in it the possibilities of desire. These are, potentially, more accessible futures.

"Calling All Restroom Revolutionaries!" Coalescing around Bodies in Space

Reagon's text bridges feminist and disability concerns by drawing our attention to the political implications of space, and questions of access and inaccessibility continue to be productive points of overlap across multiple movements for social justice.[12] Public toilets, in particular, have long been sites of exclusion and activism; as Judith Plaskow explains, because "access to toilets is a prerequisite for full public partici-pation and citizenship … almost all the social justice movements of the last century in the United States have included struggles for adequate toilet facilities."[13] Women moving into traditionally male spaces often discover the bathroom, or lack thereof, to be a key site of sexual harassment and discrimination; the toilet serves as an indicator of the kinds of gendered bodies expected in particular spaces.[14] In response, women have turned public restrooms into sites of political agitation and activism, challenging the architectural and political assumption of the male body as the ideal citizen.[15] Of course, this ideal citizen is not only male but white, and bathrooms have created not only gender dyads but racial ones: for much of the twentieth century, "urinary segregation" taught users powerful lessons about the intertwining of gender and race in public spaces, particularly in the south. There, too, public restrooms were made into contentious sites of struggle and citizenship, and Elizabeth Abel notes that African American men living under Jim Crow were violently punished for refusing to use restrooms marked "colored."[16] Public toilets continue to be heavily policed for inappropriate behavior or inappropriate users. Homeless people are frequent targets of attempts to "clean up" public restrooms, as are those practicing public sex, with cities doing everything from locking "public" facilities to refusing to build or install new public restrooms. Private businesses and restaurants typically designate their restrooms as "for customers only," a restriction that affects not only the homeless but also people who enter public spaces for reasons other than shopping or consumption.[17]

Given these practices of exclusion and resistance, it is not surprising that the toilet has also been a site of intellectual exploration and scholarly engagement, and there has been a vast expansion of toilet talk in the past few years.[18] This work clearly supports Plaskow's observation that toilets are sites of intersectional study and activism, but gender is heavily foregrounded here; histories of gender segregation, policy analy-ses of "potty parity," and speculations about nonsexist bathrooms dominate these discussions. This focus on gender, especially on gender presentation and identity, often feels absolutely necessary given that using the "wrong" bathroom for one's perceived gender can lead to harassment, arrest, and violence; moves to create unisex or gender-neutral restrooms continue to meet ridicule and hostility, even as more and more groups lobby for their creation.[19]

Two clear exceptions to the strict gender segregation of toilets (and to the hostility greeting attempts to desegregate such toilets) are the "family" restrooms increasingly popular in airports and the single-stall restrooms marked with a wheelchair.[20] The notion that people of one gender might need to assist a child or elder of another gender is much more readily accepted and accommodated than the notion that people with different gender presentations or identities might use the same restroom (even if, as in the case of single-stall toilets, at different times).[21] Similarly, we are more willing to accept people of all gender identities and sexes using the same space if those people are already seen as separate from the body politic because of their disabilities.[22] Simply put, unisex/gender-neutral bathrooms are neither threatening nor ridiculous as long as gender nonconformity is not the main reason for their use or creation.

Once they are created, however, such bathrooms are easily taken up for other purposes. In a queer expansion of the meanings of both "family" and "accessible," these spaces are increasingly recognized as options for genderqueer and trans users. Women's rooms, Sally Munt explains, are sites of uncomfortable and often threatening exchanges with those who cast her butch body as dangerously out of place. In this context, the third space of the accessible stall offers a much-needed "stress-free location, a queer space in which I can momentarily procure an interval from the gendered public environment, and psychically replen-ish."[23] Munt's pleasure is tempered, however, by her feelings of trespass; she sees herself as "treading on another borderline, not worthily disabled."[24] Yet cripping her account—not to mention cripping the disabled stall itself—leads to the recognition that gender-segregated spaces are not any more accessible to her than narrow doorways are to me, although the forms such inaccessibility takes are different.[25] The solution to this issue is not to assign more "worthiness" to my use than Munt's (or vice versa) but rather to recognize the possibility for queercrip alliances in the space of the toilet. If, as Munt suggests, the disabled toilet is a "room set aside for the disjunctive, ungendered and strange," then we can use the potential openness of those terms as grounds for coalition.[26]

PISSAR (People in Search of Safe and Accessible Restrooms) offers one example of this kind of collaboration. Founded at the University of California–Santa Barbara in 2003, PISSAR explicitly linked disability access with gender access, creating a bathroom checklist that assessed a restroom's disability-accessibility (e.g., door width, dispenser heights, Braille signage) right alongside its genderqueer-accessibility (e.g., functioning door locks, gender-specific signage, location) (see Appendix A).[27] "PISSAR Patrols," which featured activists carrying clipboards and wearing "free 2 pee" shirts, used the checklist to rate and map campus restrooms. In so doing, they brought people together around the issue of access, regardless of whether or how they identified in terms of disability and gender. More recently, TransBrandeis, part of the GLBT/Queer Alliance at Brandeis University, expanded their mapping and survey project to include attention to disability access, and disability activists at the University of Washington have included attention to trans and gender-queer needs in their own access activism.[28]

It remains rare, however, for issues of disability access and trans access to be raised concurrently on GLBTQ organizational websites or in the (often sensationalized) news coverage about trans campus activism.[29] The frequency with which activists, administrations, and reporters use the language of "gender-blind," as opposed to "gender-neutral," "unisex," or "nongendered," suggests that critical disability perspectives are not at play here.[30] By the same token, my own experiences with PISSAR suggest reluctance on the part of some disability activists to engage with trans and genderqueer issues: one of the disabled students initially opposed forming PISSAR for fear that addressing trans access would dilute the struggle for disability access. The annual conference of the Society for Disability Studies has yet to consistently include gender-neutral restrooms as a required component of access, and too few disability studies scholars include attention to the relationship between trans and disability in our work on access, sexuality, stigma, or medicalization, only a few potential areas of overlap.[31] Trans essayist and activist Eli Clare is widely cited in disability studies, but scholars usually treat his writings on transphobia or on transgender experiences in general as an aside to his work on disability (as if the two were not intimately, and often explicitly, intertwined).

In his introduction to *Toilet: Public Restrooms and the Politics of Sharing*, Harvey Molotch points to the political dilemma facing disability communities as we look to the loo: "Should disabled people demand to be part of the convention [of gender segregated bathrooms]? Or should they be the leaders of a movement to combat it?"[32] One could certainly make the argument that, given the link between access to public spaces and access to the body politic, not to mention the link between hegemonic gender identities and cultural intelligibility, we should lean toward the former. Disabled people should have access to gendered restrooms just as nondisabled people do. The problem with that answer, though, is that it fixes—in both senses of the word—the problem of access too narrowly; rather than transform existing structures, both physical and political, it merely argues for including more people within them (by excluding others). Not only does it overlook the reality that some disabled people are also, simultaneously, trans and genderqueer people (a possibility similarly erased in Molotch's framing of the question), it also forecloses on the possibility that disability studies and activism could ally with other movements.

Thus, I argue for the latter response, with disabled people and disability movements working to undo the gendered conventions of the toilet as part of our larger struggles for access to public space. Such a move feels all the more necessary given that transgender and transsexual people were explicitly excluded from coverage under the ADA.[33] We can treat the public toilet as a site for undoing this exclusion, recognizing public inaccessibility as a problem that connects both those authorized to claim disability and those who are not. Thinking through access can then become a way of thinking through questions of disability identity, analyzing when it is deployed, and by whom, and to what effects. As Tanya Titchkosky argues, "[A]ccess [is] not … a synonym for justice but a beginning place for critical questioning."[34]

Recognizing bathroom access as a site for coalition building can potentially move us beyond the physical space of bathrooms, turning our critical attention to the acts of elimination that occur *beyond* the socially sanctioned space of the toilet, public or private. As Carrie Sandahl explains, "Our society cannot tolerate incontinence; once beyond infancy, incontinence divides the human from the non-human."[35] Not only is there profound shame and disgust directed toward those who "cannot control themselves," as the common colloquialism puts it, but the inability to control oneself is often what drives elderly or disabled people into nursing homes and other institutions. Indeed, this link between continence and full citizenship is too often written into policy and practice: Sandahl condemns the fact that often "Medicare and Medicaid will pay for these products [adult diapers and other incontinence products] if you're in a nursing home, but not if you're living at home."[36] Coalitions of feminists, queers, and crips lobbying not only for broadly accessible toilets but also affordable and accessible diapers may not yet be familiar, but I hope it is starting to sound necessary. We should not limit the "restroom revolution" to the four walls of the restroom.

Indeed, part of the pleasure and possibility of restroom revolutions is that they offer the opportunity to expand the terms of our movements and our theories. As Lisa Duggan notes in her praise of *Toilet*, "Peeing is political"—and so are the places where peeing happens (or doesn't) and the bodies doing the peeing. Attending to the space of the toilet not only makes room for coalitions between trans and disability concerns, it continues the crip theory move of keeping the meanings and parameters of disability, access, and disability studies open for debate and dissent.

Finding Disability in Environmental Justice

Typing "environmentalism" or "environmental justice" into databases alongside "illness" or "disability" brings up hundreds of hits, but the majority of them are public health articles describing conditions linked to environmental exposure (e.g., asthma, cancers, and skin rashes). These pieces map disease clusters, detail specific exposures, record pollutant levels, and/or track chemicals and other pollutants suspected of being carcinogenic or teratogenic ("teratogenic" is from *terata*, or monster, and refers to birth "defects" or "malformations").[37] Finding illness or disability in these texts means finding stories of error and aberration; illness and disability appear almost exclusively as tragic mistakes caused by unnatural incursions into or disruptions of the natural body and the natural environment. These were not the kind of pieces I had in mind when I began researching links between disability and environmentalism.

Those were not the kind of pieces I had in mind, but that is not to say that they play no role in this book or in disability studies more broadly. On the contrary, such questions of body/environment interaction belong squarely within the purview of disability studies, as do public health analyses of toxic neighborhoods and sick buildings. We need a disability studies and disability activism that can challenge the siting of power plants or waste dumps in neighborhoods already overburdened by toxic industries; we need disability analyses that condemn the poisoning of bodies (human and otherwise) by both catastrophic spills and explosions as well as the "everyday" pollution of dry cleaners, contaminated water, and landfills. Disability and environmental movements can find common cause in their concern with the built environment; lead paint and cracked or missing sidewalks create disabling environments for everyone living around them.[38]

The essays I tracked down, then, are essential *to* disability studies, but most of them have yet to be influenced *by* disability studies (much as disability studies has yet to engage fully with this literature). What is needed, then, are analyses that recognize and refuse the intertwined exploitation of bodies and environments without demonizing the illnesses and disabilities, and especially the ill and disabled bodies, that result from such exploitation. As Valerie Ann Johnson argues in "Bringing Together Feminist Disability Studies and Environmental Justice," one of the few essays explicitly doing this kind of bridge work, "We [in the environmental justice movement] tend to conflate disability, disease and environmental injustice. What is needed is to disaggregate the possible results of environmental injustice (i.e., exposure to toxic substances emanating from landfills or hog operations that injure the body) from the *person*, however they are embodied."[39]

This kind of disaggregation requires a more complex and interconnected understanding of disability than is currently circulating in both disability studies and environmental studies. In terms of disability studies, the continued reliance on the social model (and its corollary assumption that there can be no room for medical approaches) makes it difficult to engage with antitoxics movements that work to eliminate or at least decrease disability. My own reluctance to recognize articles warning of birth defects and deformities as part of my project is an example of this difficulty. Yet, as Stacy Alaimo argues, disability studies and activism would "be enriched by attending not only to the ways in which built environments constitute or exacerbate 'disability,' but to how materiality, at a less perceptible level—that of pharmaceuticals, xenobiotic chemicals, air pollution, etc.—affects human health and ability."[40] Similarly, environmental studies and activism could benefit from a more critical approach to disability, one that recognizes disability as a cultural, historical, and political category, rather than simply a medical one. We need environmental analyses that do more than cast disability and disabled bodies/minds as tragedies or aberrations, in part because focusing exclusively on disabled people as the signs of environmental injustice effaces the ways in which we are all affected by toxic pollution and contamination, not just those of us with visible or diagnosed "abnormalities."

Moreover, by relying on the specter of disability to motivate public response, environmental movements rely on what Giovanna Di Chiro calls "eco(hetero)normativity."[41] Making connections across disability, environmental, and queer studies, Di Chiro offers a model for the kind of coalitional thinking that can lead to more accessible futures. She documents how environmentalists "mobilize socially sanctioned heterosexism and queer-fear" by creating and circulating sensationalized accounts of "sexual abnormalities" in fish, animals, and humans. In so doing, mainstream environmentalists reify hegemonic ideals of gender and sexuality, thereby foreclosing on the possibility of cross-movement work. Rather than relying on uncritical concepts of "normal" bodies and orientations, Di Chiro argues that antitoxics activists should focus on more "serious health problems associated with POPs [persistent organic pollutants]," such as "breast, ovarian, prostate, and testicular cancers, neurological and neurobehavioral problems, immune system breakdown, heart disease, diabetes, and obesity."[42]

We can extend Di Chiro's concern about the normalizing strains of antitoxic environmentalism by questioning not only the queer fear embedded within these discourses but also the disability fear.[43] How can we continue the absolutely necessary task of challenging toxic pollution and its effects without perpetuating cultural assumptions about the unmitigated tragedy of disability? How can we attend to "serious health problems" while also deconstructing the stigma attached to those problems or even historicizing the very construction of such conditions as problems? One way is to challenge environmental representations of disability that are completely removed from the experiences of people living with those very disabilities. Or, to put it differently, disability scholars and activists can work to ensure that descriptions of the possible impairments linked to toxic exposures do not replicate ableist language and assumptions. Surely we can find ways to protest lead and mercury poisoning without resorting to warnings about how "developmental delays, learning disabilities, ADHD, and behavioral disorders extract a terrible toll from children, families, and society. … The costs associated with caring for these children can be high for families and society. Special education programs and psychological and medical services drain resources."[44] These statements, posted on the website of the Collaborative on Health and the Environment, not only perpetuate long-standing fears about the economic burden of disabled people but, more disturbingly, imply that disabled people—*rather than polluting industries*—are the ones responsible for draining resources. Disability studies and activism can be a resource here, helping environmental movements avoid this kind of misdirection and create broader coalitions against pollution.

Breast cancer lends itself to these kinds of complex, tangled, and ambiguous reckonings, and feminist theorists and activists continue to produce rich work analyzing its connections. Audre Lorde's *The Cancer Journals* has found a home in disability studies, with scholars pointing to Lorde's searing indictment of prosthetics and passing; Lorde's refusals to become a compliant patient and, relatedly, to hide her mastectomy behind puffs of wool have been a welcome resource for disability movements searching for models of how to refuse medicalized silence. Environmental studies has found the book useful as well for "its insistence on the interconnections between body and environment, which poses cancer as a feminist, antiracist, and environmental justice issue."[45] As Alaimo's reading of the text makes clear, the book serves as a bridge between these various movements. Lorde refuses breast prosthetics in order to transform silence not only about illness and the body but also about the environmental causes of illness. "Lorde displays her scars against the cancer establishment," explains Alaimo, challenging its denial of "the environmental causes of cancer."[46]

Environmental and disability studies and activisms can find common cause in critically examining the medical industrial complex and its current approach to cancer. Organizations such as Breast Cancer Action (BCA) can be understood as simultaneously deploying disability and environmental analyses. Breast Cancer Action offers a strong challenge to cancer rhetorics that present breast cancer as primarily a problem of individual bodies, a challenge that echoes critiques of the medical model of disability. In insisting that we attend to both voluntary and involuntary exposures to carcinogens, BCA moves away from individualized models of cancer to more structural ones; similarly, in arguing that it is "not just genes, but social injustices—political, economic, and racial inequities—that lead to disparities in breast cancer outcomes," BCA argues for a more political/relational model of illness and, by extension, disability.[47]

The Disability Rights Education and Defense Fund (DREDF) is one of the pioneers in this work, laying the groundwork for environmental justice projects informed by disability rights. Silvia Yee, one of the staff attorneys at DREDF, is positioning the organization as a resource for people living in communities overburdened by toxic industries and emissions. The Disability Rights Education and Defense Fund understands that those living in such communities may not have accurate information about the availability of disability protection laws and social services; even though many of the people living in overburdened communities are already ill or disabled, or may become so because of their exposure to toxins, they may not identify themselves as disabled or recognize themselves within disability rights movements. Yet, as Yee explains, federal and state disability laws could potentially be used to

> reduce environmental hazards for the entire community. For instance, children with respiratory disabilities in a public school using chemical pesticides could potentially bring a cause of action that will reduce pesticide exposure for all their classmates as well as the surrounding community. These litigation ideas have been largely unexplored, both theoretically and in practice.[48]

Recognizing the links between disability and environmental justice opens the door to such explorations. Yee and DREDF position disability laws as a way to protect entire communities; "disability rights" thus becomes a tool used not only on behalf of disabled people, and affecting not only disabled people, but for all people.

Activism by and on behalf of people with multiple chemical sensitivities (MCS) provides another example of deploying categories of disability to do environmental justice work. As with trans and genderqueer folks using the language of access to disrupt gender segregation, MCS activists discuss their need for scent- and chemical-free spaces as a component of accessibility. "How and Why to Be Scent-Free," a flyer distributed to attendees of the Queer Disability Conference (held in San Francisco in 2002), offers one such example (see Appendix C); the flyer first details the physical and cognitive effects of toxic exposure in order to testify to the necessity of safer spaces:

> Symptoms of chemical exposure include dizziness, nausea, slurred speech, drowsiness, irritation to mouth, throat, skin, eyes, and lungs, headache, convulsions, fatigue, confusion, and liver and kidney damage. As you can imagine, these symptoms constitute serious barriers for people with chemical sensitivities in work, life, and of course, conference attendance. Promoting scent-free environments is very much like adding ramps and curb-cuts in terms of the profound difference in accessibility it can produce.[49]

Reading the work of scholars and activists with MCS makes this point abundantly clear, as they describe feeling trapped in their homes, or forced out of their homes, or made ill by their encounters with other bodies and environments.[50] Disability studies scholars and activists, with their experience linking *access to spaces* with *access to the body politic*, can serve as useful allies here; these stories of chemically disabling environments are also stories of inaccessibility. Both disability studies and environmental justice disrupt what Mel Chen calls "the fiction of independence and of uninterruptability"; we can see in this shared disruption the possibility for coalition.[51]

Meet Reproductive Justice

Women of color have been at the forefront of struggles to shift the focus of reproductive rights movements and public discourses about reproduction away from a single-issue focus on abortion.[52] Without denying the importance of legal abortion (and especially *access* to legal abortion), activists have long argued for a much broader approach, one that takes into account the widespread social and economic disparities among women. Andrea Smith explains that "the pro-life versus pro-choice paradigm reifies and masks the structures of white supremacy and capitalism that undergird the reproductive choices that women make."[53] As Smith and other activists and scholars detail, the language of choice presents women more as consumers than citizens, opening the door for some women to be cast as bad decision makers and for some choices to be deemed bad or inappropriate. Moreover, the language of choice fails to take into account how different women have different access to different choices; it removes from analysis the conditions under which women and families make decisions about reproduction. Indeed, choice rhetoric can easily be deployed to cover over sterilization abuses: informed consent policies, which would seem to support women's "choices," have often been compromised by racism, classism, ableism, and xenophobia.[54] As a result of these histories and practices, many activists within these movements use the language of "reproductive justice" to "emphasize the relationship of reproductive rights to human rights and economic justice."[55]

I offer this brief overview of reproductive justice for three reasons. First, I want to highlight that both reproductive justice activists and disability activists interrogate the rhetoric of choice found in reproductive rights movements. Much as the experiences of women of color, immigrant women, poor women, and indigenous women exceed the notion of "free choice," the language of choice fails to account for the ableist context in which women make decisions about pregnancy, abortion, and reproduction in general. As Marsha Saxton notes, only certain choices are recognized as valid choices, and only certain choices are socially supported; "Our society profoundly limits the 'choice' to love and care for a baby with a disability."[56] Shelley Tremain echoes Saxton, warning that ableist notions of "prenatal impairment" "increasingly limit the field of possible conduct in response to pregnancy."[57] Disability studies scholars and activists also argue that the continued commodification of pregnancy, a process enabled and perpetuated by the framework of choice, facilitates ableist rhetoric of fetuses, babies, and children as "defective"; positioning women as consumers and babies as products makes possible conversations about and practices toward "selecting" the baby one wants (and deselecting or terminating the babies one doesn't want). A critique of choice, then, bridges both movements.

Second, I want to encourage a greater familiarity with, and support of, reproductive justice movements and frameworks on the part of disability studies and activism. As the definitions above suggest, reproductive justice insists upon a cross-movement approach to reproductive issues, recognizing that questions of reproduction cannot be disentangled from those of race, class, and sexuality, not to mention poverty, welfare, health care, social services, environmental justice, and so on. Disability is an essential piece of this assemblage, and reproductive concerns about disability cannot be untangled from these other factors. Thinking about disability and reproduction requires the kind of cross-movement analysis promised by reproductive justice. Even if reproductive justice movements do not always live up to this promise in terms of disability (as when a major reproductive justice text relegates disability to a single footnote), the possibilities remain.[58] In fact, I think reproductive justice frameworks offer the possibility not only of cross-movement analyses that fully integrate disability but also of fuller *cross-disability* analyses. Physical disabilities and intellectual disabilities are often construed differently in debates about prenatal testing and selective abortion, and disability movements need to acknowledge (even as we interrogate) those distinctions.

Third, thinking about reproductive politics only in terms of abortion and the pro-choice/pro-life binary makes coalition building among disability and reproductive rights and justice activists more difficult. As Smith argues, the pro/anti binary fosters "simplistic analyses of who our political friends and enemies are," which can lead us to "lose opportunities to work with people with whom we … have sharp disagreements, but who may, with different political framings and organizing strategies, shift their positions."[59] Smith's warning strikes me as especially salient for the disability and reproductive rights relationship. Within the logic of the pro/anti abortion binary, anyone who expresses concern about particular abortion practices or rhetorics can too easily appear as an enemy of feminism and an opponent of reproductive rights. Reproductive rights activists are then wary of engaging with disability critiques of prenatal testing and selective abortion; within this context, to take up these critiques, seriously wrestling with the ableist implications of prenatal testing, feels dangerously close to dismantling abortion rights. Similarly, disability rights activists are wary of engaging with reproductive rights groups who continue to use disability as a justification for abortion; it can be hard to find common ground with organizations that take for granted the undesirability of disability. Reproductive justice approaches, which insist as much on the right to continue a pregnancy (and be supported in doing so) as the right to terminate one, offer one possible means of connection.[60]

This kind of connective work is necessary as antireproductive rights activists increasingly use progressive rhetoric for their own purposes.[61] Capitalizing on the eugenic and ableist histories of the reproductive rights movement, opponents of abortion are moving steadily to present themselves as the better ally to disability movements. Feminists for Life (FFL), for example, explicitly defines abortion as a form of discrimination against disabled people, appropriating the rhetoric of disability movements in their campaign against abortion.[62] This deployment of disability rights is evident in their poster series, "It's time to *question abortion*," which includes a poster equating abortion to eugenics. The black-and-white poster features a photograph of an unsmiling dark-skinned man sitting in his manual wheelchair; he has his arms crossed and a defiant expression. "Would you say that to my face?" appears in handwritten script across the photograph, while the following text appears below the picture: "Would you tell me that I never should have been born? That is the message sent when people talk about aborting 'gross fetal anomalies.' People who overcome adversity inspire, challenge and enrich our world." I have often heard disability activists respond to ableist abortion rhetoric with that very question: "Would you tell me that I never should have been born?" Debates about the proliferation of prenatal testing often draw similar responses, with disabled people wondering aloud whether they would have been aborted if their mothers had had the chance.[63] In making space for this line of thinking, the FFL presents itself as more aligned with the interests of disability communities than the pro-choice movement is; according to this logic, advocates for abortion and other reproductive rights are too closely tied to eugenic practices and histories to support disabled people.

Yet working with reproductive rights and justice organizations can be a way for disability movements to make progress on long-held goals, as seen with the Prenatally and Postnatally Diagnosed Conditions Awareness Act of 2008 (also known as the Kennedy Brownback Act). The legislation requires doctors, genetic counselors, and other medical professionals to provide current, accurate, and comprehensive information about disability when they consult with women about their pregnancies. Its purpose is to ensure that women are adequately informed before they make any decisions about continuing or terminating their pregnancies; covered information includes available social services, support groups, and the experiences of disabled people and families with similarly-disabled children. Although it is still too early to evaluate the law's efficacy in terms of the quality of information parents receive, the very passage of the law is significant. By stressing parents' need for information prior to decision making, the Kennedy Brownback Act underscores the fact that there is a decision to be made; it begins to unravel the assumption that abortion is the only viable, rational response to a positive test. Indeed, by focusing on the right to true informed consent, the act acknowledges that women have typically been given inaccurate or incomplete information about disability, information that both reflected and perpetuated cultural fears and stereotypes about disability.[64]

The law is also significant in that it was supported by both disability and reproductive rights and justice organizations. Generations Ahead, recognizing in the bill the potential for cross-movement collaboration, fostered a partnership among the World Institute on Disability, the Disability Rights Education and Defense Fund, the National Women's Health Network, and the Reproductive Health Technologies Project. Together the five organizations disseminated an information sheet about the bill, urging their allies to support the legislation.[65] It was, admittedly, an easier sell for disability rights groups. Reproductive rights organizations were wary of the bill, worried that it was another sideways attempt to restrict women's access to abortion; then Senator Sam Brownback's cosponsorship of the bill fueled these fears because of his longstanding and vocal opposition to reproductive rights. The coalition of disability and reproductive rights groups eventually convinced their allies not to oppose the bill, making the argument that everyone would benefit from more and improved information about disability. They posed the problem not in terms of abortion per se, thereby sidestepping the entrenched pro-choice/pro-life binary, but rather in terms of eliminating the ableist bias in genetic counseling and improving the information and supports given to women expecting a disabled baby.

Two seemingly disparate events in early October 2010 set the stage for another moment of coalition building between disability and reproductive rights and justice movements: Robert Edwards was awarded the Nobel Prize in medicine for his work developing in vitro fertilization; and Virginia Ironside, a British advice columnist, generated controversy over her comments about the alleged suffering of disabled children. Both figures publicly promoted the use of reproductive technologies to select against disability. Edwards argued that it would be a "sin of parents to have a child that carries the heavy burden of genetic disease. We are entering a world where we have to consider the quality of our children."[66] Several pro-life and antiabortion groups seized upon this quote in their condemnation of Edwards's award, but his position on disability was otherwise ignored in the media coverage; it was unremarkable.[67] Ironside's position on disability, on the other hand, is precisely what generated media coverage, but there, too, the assumption that disability is best met with abortion went largely unchallenged. In a televised debate about abortion, Ironside described the abortion of "a baby [that] is going to be born severely disabled" as the "act of a loving mother"; she then offered that, faced with such "a deeply suffering child," she would not hesitate to "put a pillow over its face," as would "any good mother."[68] Although Ironside's comments about infanticide were quickly condemned, her assumption that abortion was the best response to disability generated little discussion.[69] More to the point, her decision to use the specter of disability as a justification for abortion continued a long pattern of pitting disability rights against reproductive rights.

In response to these events, which happened within a couple of days of each other, a group of six scholars and activists (including myself) drafted a statement articulating a disability and reproductive rights and justice position; it currently has over 150 signatories, both organizations and individuals (see Appendix D).[70] Titled "Robert Edwards, Virginia Ironside, and the Unnecessary Opposition of Rights," the statement presents reproductive rights and justice as fully intertwined with the rights of and justice for people with disabilities:

> As people committed to both disability rights and reproductive rights, we believe that respecting women and families in their reproductive decisions requires simultaneously challenging discriminatory attitudes toward people with disabilities. We refuse to accept the bifurcation of women's rights from disability rights, or the belief that protecting reproductive rights requires accepting ableist assumptions about the supposed tragedy of disability. On the contrary, we assert that reproductive rights includes attention to disability rights, and that disability rights requires attention to human rights, including reproductive rights.

In drafting the statement, we rehearsed familiar debates over terminology and affiliation: Were we discussing human rights or women's rights? Did we want to refer to ourselves as feminists or leave such identifications more open? Should we use the language of disability rights or disability justice? Would it be accurate to describe current practices as eugenic or would that be too inflammatory? On each count, we opted to use the broadest and most familiar terms and frames possible; although some of us might individually make different decisions, we wanted a critical mass of "people committed to both disability rights and reproductive rights" to recognize themselves in our call. Indeed, it is these kinds of questions that can, we hope, lead to further articulations, coalitions, and conversations.

What seemed key to any document was a refusal of the bifurcation of disability rights and justice from reproductive rights and justice. We knew that disability activists, particularly those less directly engaged with reproductive justice movements and frameworks, desperately needed a clear statement from reproductive rights activists and organizations that they would not accept "the rhetorical use of disability as an argument for abortion rights."[71] Similarly, reproductive rights groups needed a signal that a significant number of disability activists and scholars were willing to articulate their support for women's reproductive rights. As with the Prenatally and Postnatally Diagnosed Conditions Awareness Act, the statement in no way condemns or limits individual women's choices but rather speaks to the widespread cultural disparagement of disability and disabled people. In identifying shared values between disability and reproductive movements, the statement explicitly calls for continued collaboration:

> We hope, with this statement, to support other activists and scholars who are equally committed to both reproductive rights and disability rights. We hope that as advocates in movements that share similar

values around civil and human rights we can continue to speak out against the use of reproductive rights to undermine disability rights and the use of disability rights to undermine reproductive rights.

This statement was made possible by the work of feminist and disability studies scholars who have been steadfastly refusing the bifurcation of reproductive rights and disability rights for decades.[72] Adrienne Asch, Anne Finger, Rayna Rapp, Dorothy Roberts, Marsha Saxton: all demonstrate that challenging ableism, even within the context of reproductive politics, is not necessarily the same as challenging or limiting women's access to abortion.[73] Perhaps to make that point clear, especially in a context in which disability is being deployed to undermine abortion rights, those trying to bridge the two movements have often been very explicit about their allegiances. In "Abortion and Disability: Who Should and Who Should Not Inhabit the World?" Ruth Hubbard states four separate times that she supports a woman's right to abortion, whatever her reasons.[74] The fact that she felt compelled to repeat this belief over and over again testifies to the difficulty facing those who want to question the ableist underpinnings of the system of prenatal testing without questioning access to abortion. Yet these very scholars, as well as those involved in the actions I describe here, argue that having to make decisions about reproduction in the face of ableist representations of disability and in a culture "that promises much grief to parents of children it deems unfit" harms everyone.[75] To put it plainly: critically examining the reasons why women choose to terminate pregnancies based on disability, challenging reproductive rights movements for using disability as a justification for legal abortion, and deconstructing the assumptions about disability built into prenatal testing policies and practices—none of these necessarily translate into denying women's access to abortion.

In fact, failing to do these things may in fact undermine women's access; at the very least, it makes it more difficult for reproductive rights and justice movements to support and be supported by disability rights and justice movements. I close this section with a provocation, one that also appears in one of the founding texts of feminist disability studies. In their contribution to their anthology *Women with Disabilities: Essays in Psychology, Culture, and Politics*, Adrienne Asch and Michelle Fine argue for the right to abortion "for any reason [women] deem appropriate."[76] Following Asch and Fine, rather than "presume or prescribe any reason (for example, 'the tragedy of the defective fetus')," we should defend women's right to make their own decisions about reproduction, fully supporting them in having or not having a child.[77] Abortion for any reason and under any circumstance must then be accompanied by accessible and affordable prenatal care for all women, as well as reliable and affordable child care, access to social services, and the kind of information about and supports for disability mandated in the Kennedy Brownback Act.

I know that I am arguing for an impossibility, at least in the current political climate. We are moving farther and father away from the radical feminist call of "abortion on demand," seeing more and more burdens on abortion as acceptable rather than unduly prohibitive. Yet when we force women (and reproductive rights, health, and justice movements) living in an ableist culture to prove that their abortions are "justifiable," disability remains a convenient and effective justification for preserving at least a minimal right to abortion. Even those who are uncomfortable with seeing disability as the grounds for abortion may find themselves in the untenable situation of deciding which conditions are grounds for abortion and which are not. When the legality of abortion hinges on some pregnancies being seen as "abortable," drawing lines between impairments becomes inevitable: it is acceptable to abort for blindness but not deafness; it is permissible to abort for Down syndrome but not for an atypically-formed hand; this condition is too severe but that one is not. Disability movements cannot win in these conversations; I agree with Adrienne Asch and others who argue that casting some impairments as justification for abortion harms those currently living with those impairments.[78] Making disability do the work of defending abortion may be effective in securing abortion rights in the short term, but it does so by trafficking in discriminatory stereotypes about disability. Moreover, its long-term effectiveness is doubtful, as it opens the door to a continued interrogation of individual women's reasons and decisions.

It is still true that "neither the pro-choice nor the disability rights movement has consolidated around a position on 'choice' and disability," and neither have reproductive rights and justice movements more broadly.[79] Even in arguing for unrestricted access to abortion, I am not calling for such consolidation, at least not consolidation around a single position. I offer this provocation, one that has been offered many times before by others, in order to continue the process of articulating feminist disability positions on reproduction. We need to expand the terrain of dialogue, moving away from such a limited focus on suffering, quality of life, and unlivable disabilities—notions that often perpetuate ableist assumptions—and toward creating opportunities to support reproductive justice for all, including for and by disabled people. Continuing to accept disability as the reason to keep abortion legal, and casting abortion as the only reasonable choice when dealing with disability, is a narrowing of both abortion rights and the terms of debate. So, too, is the assumption that the meaning of "suffering" or "quality of life" is self-evident and monolithic; rather than using these concepts as if they "obviously" led us to only one conclusion, we could attend instead to their shifts in meanings across different registers, contexts, or bodies/minds. As Sujatha Jesudason argues in her description of Generations Ahead's methodology, coalitions around genetic and reproductive technologies require a willingness to take risks and have frank dialogue about the issues that divide us. Having these kinds of difficult conversations can help different movements discover and articulate their shared values while also laying the groundwork for future conversations as values, identifications, and goals change.[80]

Accessible Futures

In presenting these three possibilities of crip coalition as accessible futures, or as feminist/queer/crip futures, I have focused on only a few possibilities out of many. I could have discussed antiwar protests, for example, and the need to speak out against the disabling effects of the US war on terror. The military-industrial complex causes illness, disability, and death on a global scale, and there is much work to be done in theorizing how to oppose war violence and its effects without denigrating disability and disabled people in the process. (We can see still further links here with environmental justice movements, as the US military is one of the world's worst polluters.)

Or what of potential links between the prison abolition movement and deinstitutionalization movements? There certainly is much to be gained in critically examining the prisons, nursing homes, and asylums of the past and present. The prison industrial complex serves as the primary source of (inadequate) health care for increasing numbers of poor people and people of color, notes Dorothy Roberts, who offers as an example the fact that the psychiatric wing of the Los Angeles County Jail "is the largest mental health facility in the country."[81] Prisons, moreover, not only house disabled people but *produce* them: violence, isolation, and inadequate and inconsistent access to medicine and health care have a disabling effect on the bodies and minds of inmates and prisoners.[82] How might probing these links allow us to recognize the problem Liat Ben-Moshe describes as "trans-incarceration" or "the move from one carceral edifice such as a psychiatric hospital to another such as a jail"?[83]

Or I could have explored connections between disability movements and movements for the rights of domestic workers. At a 2009 protest in Oakland challenging state budget cuts to health care, I watched a group of disabled people and union workers not trade but share chants: "We are the union, the mighty, mighty union!" they all shouted, followed by "We're out, we're loud, we're disabled, and we're proud!" As I watched these interactions, and participated in both sets of chants, I kept thinking about Robert McRuer's concept of "the nondisabled claim to be crip" and his reminder that it is often useful, "for the purposes of solidarity, to come out as something you are—at least in some ways—not."[84] Yet we can also see these union workers' claiming of disability not only as an act of solidarity or affiliation but also as a recognition of what McRuer calls "the disability to come." Some of these women (and they were mostly women) are themselves sick or disabled, and many more will become so through this hard work.[85] In other words, not only are there overlaps between those communities (many care workers are disabled or will become so), there are also overlaps between their needs: both groups will benefit in a system that values attendant care and the workers who provide it.[86]

Or, to turn a critical eye on my own coalitional imaginings, we can trace how each of the issues and movements I have discussed separately in this chapter are themselves intertwined. These imaginings are, in Donna Haraway's framing, "partial": I have selected moments that I myself am involved in and partial to, and they are necessarily incomplete. Not only could we add still other coalitions to this list, we could also complicate, extend, critique, refute, and enrich the cases I have included here.

Indeed, these coalitional moments will be known to many of you; my provocations may feel more familiar than provocative. Yet that possibility is part of my motivation for including them here. Not only am I interested in pushing the parameters of disability studies to include these not-really-so-disparate sites, I am also invested in making clear that this work is happening. In other words, I mention these various coalitional moments not because they currently are absent but because they are present, vibrant, and ongoing. There is rich disability (and feminist, and queer, and environmental, and racial justice, and reproductive, and …) work happening in each of these locations; alternative political imaginaries are being debated and discussed in and through these various political practices. Disabled people have more than a dream of accessible futures: we continue to define and demand our place in political discourses, political visions, and political practice, even as we challenge those very questions and demands. More accessible futures depend on it.

From *Feminist, Queer, Crip* by Alison Kafer, © 2013 by Alison Kafer.
Reprinted with permission of Indiana University Press.

Notes

1. Douglas C. Baynton, "Disability and the Justification of Inequality in American History," in *The New Disability History: American Perspectives*, ed. Paul K. Longmore and Lauri Umansky (New York: New York University Press, 2001), 52.

2. Ranu Samantrai, *AlterNatives: Black Feminism in the Postimperial Nation* (Stanford, CA: Stanford University Press, 2002), 1, 25.

3. Ibid., 132. Audre Lorde makes a similar point, urging, "Do not let the differences pull you apart. Use them, examine them, go through them, grow from them." Jennifer Abod, *The Edge of Each Other's Battles: The Vision of Audre Lorde* (Long Beach, CA: Profile Productions, 2002), VHS.

4. Chantal Mouffe, "Feminism, Citizenship, and Radical Democratic Politics," in *Feminists Theorize the Political*, ed. Judith Butler and Joan W. Scott (New York: Routledge, 1992), 380; Samantrai, *AlterNatives*, 132.

5. Bernice Johnson Reagon, "Coalition Politics: Turning the Century," in *Home Girls: A Black Feminist Anthology*, ed. Barbara Smith (New York: Kitchen Table, 1983): 356–68. I thank Sue Schweik for encouraging me to focus on this text.

6. These struggles were part of the 1981 festival itself. For brief descriptions of what transpired, see Barbara Gagliardi, "West Coast Women's Music Festival," *Big Mama Rag* 9, no. 10 (1981): 3, 22; and Loraine Hutchins, "Trouble and Mediation at Yosemite," *off our backs* 11, no. 10 (1981): 12–13, 25. For an analysis of Reagon's

presentation in the context of the festival and the women's movement more broadly, see Becky Thompson, *A Promise and a Way of Life: White Antiracist Activism* (Minneapolis: University of Minnesota, 2001), 201–04.

7. Reagon, "Coalition Politics," 356.

8. Ibid., 356.

9. Stacy Alaimo makes a similar move in her reading of Audre Lorde's *Cancer Journals*. She argues against reading the memoir "as an abstraction disentangled from the context of Lorde's breast cancer," seeing it only "as a generalized call to refuse to be silenced." Divorcing the text from Lorde's physical, embodied experience dilutes the political thrust of the text, suggests Alaimo. Stacy Alaimo, *Bodily Natures: Science, Environment, and the Material Self* (Bloomington: Indiana University Press, 2010), 85–86.

10. Reagon, "Coalition Politics," 356.

11. Reagon mentions disability in her discussion of how women find themselves identified with, or identify themselves with, other groups; gender is not always primary: "You are Black or you are Chicana or you are Disabled or you are Racist or you are White." Ibid., 349.

12. I take the first part of my title from the title of an article I cowrote with fellow members of PISSAR (People In Search of Safe and Accessible Restrooms). This section, as well as my understandings of coalition politics and queer activism, has benefited tremendously from my time with them; I remain grateful for our intellectual and political work together. Simone Chess, Alison Kafer, Jessi Quizar, and Mattie Udora Richardson, "Calling All Restroom Revolutionaries," in *That's Revolting: Queer Strategies for Resisting Assimilation*, ed., Mattilda (aka Matt Bernstein Sycamore) (Brooklyn: Soft Skull Press, 2004), 189–206.

13. Plaskow lists "the civil rights movement, feminism, disability rights, and rights for transgendered persons." Judith Plaskow, "Embodiment, Elimination, and the Role of Toilets in Struggles for Social Justice," *Cross Currents* (Spring 2008): 52.

14. For an early articulation of the argument that public toilets are a necessary site for feminist theorizing and activism, see Taunya Lovell Banks, "Toilets as a Feminist Issue: A True Story," *Berkeley Women's Law Journal* (1990): 263–89. See also Mary Anne Case, "Changing Room? A Quick Tour of Men's and Women's Rooms in U.S. Law over the Last Decade, from the U.S. Constitution to Local Ordinances," *Public Culture* 13, no. 2 (2001): 333–36; and Patricia Cooper and Ruth Oldenziel, "Cherished Classifications: Bathrooms and the Construction of Gender/Race on the Pennsylvania Railroad during World War II," *Feminist Studies* 25, no. 1 (1999): 7–41.

15. Judith Plaskow offers one example from her personal history, describing a feminist takeover of a campus bathroom during her career as a graduate student. The library at Yale's divinity school had no toilet for women, so she and her comrades put flowers in the men's room urinal and declared the space unisex. Plaskow, "Embodiment, Elimination, and the Role of Toilets," 55.

16. Elizabeth Abel, "Bathroom Doors and Drinking Fountains: Jim Crow's Racial Symbolic," *Critical Inquiry* 25 (Spring 1999): 439. See also Cooper and Oldenziel, "Cherished Classifications."

17. Laura Norén reveals the difficulty that New York cabdrivers and other officeless workers (e.g., bike messengers and street vendors) have in finding a toilet that they can safely and reliably use. Restaurant and other business owners often refuse to let them use their facilities ("for customers and employees only"), and the city has closed a significant number of its public toilets. Laura Norén, "Only Dogs Are Free to Pee: New York Cabbies' Search for Civility," in *Toilet: Public Restrooms and the Politics of Sharing*, ed. Harvey Molotch and Laura Norén (New York: New York University Press, 2010): 93–114.

18. See, for example, Sheila L. Cavanagh, *Queering Bathrooms: Gender, Sexuality, and the Hygienic Imagination* (Toronto: University of Toronto Press, 2010); Olga Gershenson and Barbara Penner, eds., *Ladies and Gents: Public Toilets and Gender* (Philadelphia: Temple University Press, 2009); Molotch and Norén, *Toilet: Public Restrooms and the Politics of Sharing*; and Christine Overall, "Public Toilets: Sex Segregation Revisited," *Ethics and the Environment* 12, no. 2 (2007): 71–91.

19. In the past decade or so, activists have become increasingly vocal about the importance of accessible restrooms for genderqueer and trans-identified people. San Francisco–based PISSR (People In Search of Safe Restrooms); *Toilet Training*, Dean Spade's documentary film and teaching kit; and student groups on college campuses across the country, from Harvard to the University of Washington—all make the case for expanding access to include the needs of genderqueer people, casting the presence of gender-neutral restrooms as necessary for a space to be considered accessible. A number of activist and academic conferences have re-signed the doors on (at least some of) the public toilets in their meeting places, rendering them temporarily unisex; my first exposure to such activism was at the 2002 Queer Disability Conference in San Francisco. For an overview of an early site of toilet activism, the University of Massachusetts, see Olga Gershenson, "The Restroom Revolution: Unisex Toilets and Campus Politics," in Molotch and Norén, *Toilet*, 191–207. For a comprehensive overview of toilet activism in general, see Dean Spade, *Toilet Training: Companion Guide for Activists and Educators*, Sylvia Rivera Law Project (New York: Urban Justice Center, 2004).

   This kind of activism is necessary, explains Leslie Feinberg, because having to decide over and over again which bathroom to use takes a toll on one's humanity. Yet the decision keeps repeating because gender-segregated public toilets place genderqueer people at risk: "If I go into the women's bathroom, am I prepared for the shouting and shaming? Will someone call security or the cops? If I use the men's room, am I willing to fight my way out? Am I really ready for the violence that could ensue?" Leslie Feinberg, *Trans Liberation: Beyond Pink or Blue* (Boston: Beacon, 1998), 68–69.

20. History provides other examples of moments when gender was not the primary organizing principle at work in public toilets, or, rather, when the toilet served as a way to un-gender some bodies but not others. During the era of Jim Crow, "white" bathrooms were strictly segregated by gender, while many "colored" restrooms were not. The imperative to protect women's purity and safety, or to preserve strict distinctions between male and female, applied only to whites; black women were not seen as needing such protections, and unisex bathrooms served as yet another way to deny the manhood of black men. See Abel, "Bathroom Doors and Drinking Fountains," 440–41n5. As Cooper and Oldenzeil note, both race and gender were "cherished classifications" when it came to public spaces. Cooper and Oldenzeil, "Cherished Classifications."

21. While large, single-stall restrooms with diaper-changing tables and room for small children are necessary, labeling them "family," with a male icon and a female icon surrounding an icon of an infant, simply creates a different kind of (hetero)sex-segregation.

22. Sally Munt notes that "the disabled toilet provides isolated privacy and secrecy for the marked body," but we can also see it as offering privacy *from* the marked body. Cultural fears of disability intertwine with shame about elimination and taboos of contamination; although Sheila Cavanagh's interviewees document intense curiosity about what disabled people do in the bathroom, it is a curiosity that prefers a "safe" distance from the disabled body. Sally R. Munt, "The Butch Body," in *Contested Bodies*, ed. Ruth Holliday and John Hassard (London: Routledge, 2001), 102; Cavanagh, *Queering Bathrooms*, 101–03.

23. Munt, "The Butch Body," 102.

24. Ibid., 103.

25. Reading disability narratives alongside trans or genderqueer narratives makes this shared inaccessibility readily apparent. For example, Connie Panzarino, a wheelchair user unable to transfer independently in and out of her chair, explains that as a child she was allowed to attend public schools only if she could refrain from using the restroom while on campus. For years, she restricted her fluid intake and controlled her bladder in order to get an education. Respondents to a survey about gender-segregated toilets describe disciplining their bodies much like Panzarino, restricting their liquid intake or altering their plans in order to avoid having to use gender-specific restrooms. Banks traces a historical parallel in the experiences of African Americans living under Jim Crow who tried to anticipate their toilet needs before leaving home. Banks, "Toilets as a Feminist Issue," 287;

Connie Panzarino, *The Me in the Mirror* (Seattle: Seal Press, 1994); and the Transgender Law Center, accessed May 4, 2007, http://www.transgenderlawcenter.org/. See also Kath Browne, "Genderism and the Bathroom Problem: (Re)Materialising Sexed Sites, (Re)Creating Sexed Bodies," *Gender, Place, and Culture* 11, no. 3 (2004): 331–46.

26. Munt, "The Butch Body," 102.

27. PISSAR was inspired in part by materials created for the 2002 Queer Disability Conference. Participants at the conference were given a "Statement on Bathrooms and Gender" that was also posted on bathroom doors throughout the conference center (see Appendix B). The "Statement" explicitly framed the issue of gender-neutral restrooms as an access issue: "Part of making this conference accessible is recognizing that sex segregated bathrooms are limiting for people who do not fit easily into Men's or Women's Rooms." Queer Disability Conference Organizers, "Statement on Bathrooms and Gender," Queer Disability Conference, San Francisco, California, June 2002. For more on PISSAR, see Chess et al., "Calling All Restroom Revolutionaries!"

28. TransBrandeis, "Mapping Brandeis Bathrooms," accessed July 24, 2011, http://people.brandeis.edu/~trisk/brms/concept.html.

29. Contrast TransBrandeis, for example, with the Harvard Trans Task Force, accessed July 24, 2011, http://www.hcs.harvard.edu/queer/ttf/activism.html.

30. Tobin Seibers makes a similar point about "color-blind" and "race-blind," arguing that they need "to be interrogated from a disability perspective alert to the metaphor of blindness." Tobin Siebers, *Disability Theory* (Ann Arbor: University of Michigan, 2008), 206n4.

31. See, for example, two studies about the inaccessibility of public toilets that make no mention of gender segregation or trans and genderqueer exclusion: Rob Kitchin and Robin Law, "The Socio-spatial Construction of (In)accessible Public Toilets," *Urban Studies* 38, no. 2 (2001): 287–98; and Tanya Titchkosky, "'To Pee or Not to Pee?': Ordinary Talk about Extraordinary Exclusions in a University Environment," *Canadian Journal of Sociology/Cahiers Canadiens de Sociologie* 33, no. 1 (2008): 37–60. For an overview of potential connections between the two fields, see Ashley Mog and Amanda Lock Swarr, "Threads of Commonality in Transgender and Disability Studies," *Disability Studies Quarterly* 28, no. 4 (2008), http://www.dsq-sds.org.

32. Harvey Molotch, "Learning from the Loo," introduction to *Toilet: Public Restrooms and the Politics of Sharing*, ed. Harvey Molotch and Laura Norén (New York: New York University Press, 2010), 17.

33. Jennifer Levi and Bennett Klein, "Pursuing Protection for Transgender People through Disability Laws," in *Transgender Rights*, ed. Paisley Currah, Richard M. Juang, and Shannon Price Minter (Minneapolis: University of Minnesota, 2006), 77. For more on the relationship between trans and disability in terms of legal protections, see Anna Kirkland, "When Transgendered People Sue and Win: Feminist Reflections on Strategy, Activism, and the Legal Process," in *The Fire This Time: Young Activists and the New Feminism*, ed. Vivien Labaton and Dawn Lundy Martin (New York: Anchor, 2004): 181–219; and Dean Spade, "Resisting Medicine, Re/modeling Gender," *Berkeley Women's Law Journal* 18 (2003): 15–37.

34. Titchkosky, "'To Pee or Not to Pee?'" 39.

35. Carrie Sandahl, "Anarcha Anti-Archive: Depends®," *Liminalities: A Journal of Performance Studies* 4, no. 2 (2008), accessed July 24, 2011, http://liminalities.net/4-2/anarcha. John B. Kelly notes how often discussion of assisted suicide and euthanasia turns to, and turns on, discussion of incontinence. Reading through news coverage of Dr. Jack Kevorkian, he explains, makes clear how profoundly afraid our culture is of those who cannot toilet themselves, so much so that death begins to look better than diapers. John B. Kelly, "Incontinence," *Ragged Edge*, no. 1 (2002), accessed July 24, 2011, http://www.ragged-edge-mag.com/0102/0102ft3.htm.

36. Sandahl, "Depends®."

37. For more on teratology, see Rosemarie Garland-Thomson, ed., *Freakery: Cultural Spectacles of the Extraordinary Body* (New York: New York University Press, 1996).

38. As a wheelchair user, I can easily tell when I have rolled into a poor, undervalued neighborhood: The sidewalk becomes cracked and curb cuts get increasingly precarious or disappear altogether. In his poem "Two Cities Separated Identities," Leroy Moore contrasts Berkeley with Oakland by making reference to the cities' sidewalks: "The most accessible city shares roads/leading to potholes, crack sidewalks and mountain curbs of Oaktown." Anne Finger makes a similar observation about race, class, and infrastructure in her rumination on disability and Hurricane Katrina, noting that the sidewalks of New Orleans were in trouble long before the storm hit. Anne Finger, "Hurricane Katrina, Race, Class, Tragedy, and Charity," *DSQ: Disability Studies Quarterly* 25, no. 4 (2005), accessed May 9, 2011, http://www.dsq-sds.org/article/view/630/807.

39. Johnson focuses on the persistence of "food deserts," or areas without affordable and reliable access to safe, fresh, and healthy foods, as an issue linking both disability and environmental justice. Andrew Charles and Huw Thomas similarly call environmental justice movements to task, but their focus is more on encouraging those movements to support local improvements to disability access; they urge greater recognition that the built environment of cities is part of the environment. I share their concerns, but my interest is more with encouraging disability studies scholars and activists to engage more fully with environmental justice movements. Valerie Ann Johnson, "Bringing Together Feminist Disability Studies and Environmental Justice," Barbara Faye Waxman Fiduccia Papers on Women and Girls with Disabilities, Center for Women Policy Studies, February 2011, 3, http://www.centerwomenpolicy.org/programs/waxmanfiduccia/BFWFP_ BringingTogetherFeministDisabilityStudiesandEnvironmentalJustice_ValerieAnnJohnso.pdf; and Andrew Charles and Huw Thomas, "Deafness and Disability—Forgotten Components of Environmental Justice: Illustrated by the Case of Local Agenda 21 in South Wales," *Local Environment* 12, no. 3 (June 2007): 209–21.

40. Alaimo, *Bodily Natures*, 12.

41. Giovanna Di Chiro, "Polluted Politics? Confronting Toxic Discourse, Sex Panic, and Eco-Normativity," in *Queer Ecologies: Sex, Nature, Politics, Desire*, ed. Catriona Mortimer-Sandilands and Bruce Erickson (Bloomington: Indiana University Press, 2010), 202.

42. Ibid., 202; see also 218–19.

43. And, as Di Chiro's analysis suggests, queer fear and disability fear are hard to untangle. LGBT people and intersexed people appear as "disabled" within this literature, their bodies and orientations "unjustly harmed" by their environments. Acknowledging that link, I still think it is useful to focus on the disability fear in addition to, and separately from, fears about sexual abnormalities. The imperative to eliminate disability—"defects" in environmental discourses—is firmly entrenched in environmental movements and discourses.

44. Ted Schettler, "Developmental Disabilities—Impairment of Children's Brain Development and Function: The Role of Environmental Factors," The Collaborative on Health and the Environment, February 8, 2003, http://healthandenvironment.org/learning_behavior/peer_reviewed.

45. Alaimo, *Bodily Natures*, 86.

46. Ibid., 86–87.

47. Breast Cancer Action, "Our Priorities," accessed July 24, 2011, http://bcaction.org/about/priorities/. Stacy Alaimo and Giovanna Di Chiro extend this critique, arguing that attending exclusively to genetic factors opens the door to conceptualizing individual people or "genomic subsets of the population" as particularly susceptible to toxic exposures; the problem to "solve" then becomes those people's susceptibility rather than the release or use of those toxins. Di Chiro refers to this scenario as creating "Roundup Ready®" or "Beryllium Ready" communities. See Alaimo, *Bodily Natures*, 127–28; and Giovanna Di Chiro, "Producing 'Roundup Ready®' Communities? Human Genome Research and Environmental Justice Policy," in *New Perspectives on Environmental Justice: Gender, Sexuality, and Activism*, ed. Rachel Stein (New Brunswick, NJ: Rutgers University Press, 2004), 146, 149.

48. Disability Rights Education and Defense Fund, "Environmental Justice," accessed July 15, 2011, http://www.dredf.org/envirojustice/index.shtml.

49. Queer Disability Conference Organizers, "How and Why to Be Scent-Free," Queer Disability Conference, San Francisco, California, June 2002. For a more recent example of a conference responding to, and struggling with, scent-free/low-scent spaces, see nolose (a conference for folks "dedicated to ending the oppression of fat people and creating vibrant fat queer culture"), accessed May 9, 2011, http://www.nolose.org/10/access.php.

50. See, for example, Mel Y. Chen, "Toxic Animacies, Inanimate Affections," *GLQ: A Journal of Lesbian and Gay Studies* 17, nos. 2–3 (2011): 265–86; Anna Mollow, "No Safe Place," *WSQ: Women's Studies Quarterly* 39, nos. 1–2 (2011): 188–99; Peggy Munson, "Fringe Dweller: Toward an Ecofeminist Politic of Femme," in *Visible: A Femmethology*, vol. 2., ed. Jennifer Clarke Burke (Ypsilanti, MI: Homofactus Press, 2009), 28–36; and Rhonda Zwillinger, *The Dispossessed: Living with Multiple Chemical Sensitivities* (Paulden, AZ: The Dispossessed Outreach Project, 1999).

51. Chen, "Toxic Animacies, Inanimate Affections," 274.

52. Although their influence on this project is not limited to this section, I am deeply grateful to my colleagues in Generations Ahead (GA) for the ideas and actions discussed here, as well as to the disability and reproductive rights and justice activists who participated in the GA roundtables and convenings on disability. Thanks especially to Patty Berne, Julia Epstein, Anne Finger, Emily Galpern, Sujatha Jesudason, Jessica Lehman, Mia Mingus, Dorothy Roberts, Marsha Saxton, Tracy Weitz, and Silvia Yee.

53. Andrea Smith, "Beyond Pro-Choice versus Pro-Life: Women of Color and Reproductive Justice," *NWSA Journal* 17, no. 1 (2005): 120.

54. See, among others, Jennifer Nelson, *Women of Color and the Reproductive Rights Movement* (New York: New York University Press, 2003); Dorothy Roberts, *Killing the Black Body: Race, Reproduction, and the Meaning of Liberty* (New York: Vintage, 1999); Jael Silliman, Marlene Gerber Fried, Loretta Ross, and Elena R. Gutiérrez, *Undivided Rights: Women of Color Organize for Reproductive Justice* (Boston: South End Press, 2004); Rickie Solinger, *Beggars and Choosers: How the Politics of Choice Shapes Adoption, Abortion, and Welfare in the United States* (New York: Hill and Wang, 2001); and Rickie Solinger, *Pregnancy and Power: A Short History of Reproductive Politics in America* (New York: New York University Press, 2005).

55. Silliman et al., *Undivided Rights*, 4.

56. We saw how this limitation played out in the case of a Deaf lesbian couple in chapter 3. Marsha Saxton, "Disability Rights and Selective Abortion," in *Abortion Wars: A Half-Century of Struggle: 1950–2000*, ed. Rickie Solinger (Berkeley: University of California Press, 1998), 375. See also Laura Hershey, "Choosing Disability," *Ms.* (July/August 1994): 26–32; and Ruth Hubbard, "Abortion and Disability: Who Should and Who Should Not Inhabit the World?" in *The Disability Studies Reader*, ed. Lennard J. Davis (New York: Routledge, 2006): 93–103.

57. Shelley Tremain, "Reproductive Freedom, Self-Regulation, and the Government of Impairment in Utero," *Hypatia* 21, no. 1 (2006): 37.

58. Silliman et al., *Undivided Rights*, 22n36.

59. Smith makes this argument from the position of indigenous feminism and the need to challenge those pro-choice activists who have allied with population control groups; she singles out Planned Parenthood. Smith, "Beyond Pro-Choice versus Pro-Life," 132–33.

60. The organization Asian Communities for Reproductive Justice offers a particularly compelling definition of reproductive justice, one that easily encompasses attention to disability: "We believe Reproductive Justice exists when all people have the social, political and economic power and resources to make healthy decisions about our gender, bodies, sexuality and families for our selves and our communities. Reproductive Justice aims to transform power inequities and create long-term systemic change, and therefore relies on the leadership of

communities most impacted by reproductive oppression. The reproductive justice framework recognizes that all individuals are part of families and communities and that our strategies must lift up entire communities in order to support individuals." Asian Communities for Reproductive Justice, accessed December 14, 2010, http://reproductivejustice.org/what-is-reproductive-justice.

61. Examples would include attempts to ban race- and sex-selective abortions and billboards describing black children as "endangered species." Organizations such as SisterSong and Generations Ahead have posted responses to these kinds of campaigns on their websites.

62. For a feminist analysis of FFL and pro-life feminism, see Laury Oaks, "What Are Pro-Life Feminists Doing on Campus?" *NWSA Journal* 21, no. 1 (2009): 178–203.

63. See, for example, Generations Ahead, "Bridging the Divide: Disability Rights and Reproductive Rights and Justice Advocates Discussing Genetic Technologies," (2009), accessed March 8, 2010, http://www.generations-ahead.org/resources; and Saxton, "Disability Rights and Selective Abortion." Of course, even as they agreed with the poster's critical stance toward selective abortion, many disability activists and scholars would challenge the poster's positioning of disability as an adversity to be overcome.

64. Brian Skotko has conducted several studies asking women about the kind of information they received about disability, particularly Down syndrome, in conjunction with prenatal testing and genetic counseling. They report widespread dissatisfaction with both the content and the tone of the information they were given by their doctors. Brian Skotko, "Prenatally Diagnosed Down Syndrome: Mothers Who Continued Their Pregnancies Evaluate Their Health Care Providers," *American Journal of Obstetrics and Gynecology* 192 (2005): 670–77.

65. For a description of Generation Ahead's work on the bill, see "Dodging Old Traps: Aligning, Affirming, and Addressing Disability Rights and Reproductive Autonomy," accessed August 19, 2011, http://www.generations-ahead.org/files-for-download/success-stories/K_Brownback_2011.pdf.

66. Edwards made this statement during his comments to the 1999 meetings of the European Society of Reproduction and Embryology. Lois Rogers, "Having Disabled Babies Will Be Sin, Says Scientist," *Sunday Times* (London), July 4, 1999.

67. For examples of pro-life/antiabortion criticisms that condemn Edwards's statements on disability, see Jenna Lyle, "Vatican Official Objects to IVF Scientist's Nobel Prize Win," *Christian Post*, October 5, 2010, http://www.christianpost.com/news/vatican-official-objects-to-ivfscientists-nobel-prize-win-47083/; and "Pro-Life Group Objects to Nobel Honors for IVF Co-inventor," *Catholic News Agency*, October 5, 2010, http://www.catholicnewsagency.com/news/pro-life-group-objects-to-nobel-honors-for-ivf-co-inventor/.

68. Vanessa Allen, "Outrage as Agony Aunt Tells TV Audience 'I Would Suffocate a Child to End Its Suffering,'" *Daily Mail*, October 5, 2010, http://www.dailymail.co.uk/news/article-1317400/Virginia-Ironside-sparks-BBC-outrage-Id-suffocate-child-end-suffering.html.

69. During the television program, disability activist Clair Lewis called in to the show to challenge Ironside's comments, and she describes the encounter and her position in a blog post. See Clair Lewis, "Why I Called Virginia Ironside a Eugenicist on Live TV," *Heresy Corner*, October 5, 2010, http://heresycorner.blogspot.com/2010/10/why-i-called-virginia-ironside.html. In her column in the *Guardian*, Zoe Williams agreed with those condemning Ironside for her comments on euthanasia, but she defended Ironside's position on abortion and disability. See Zoe Williams, "Abortion and Euthanasia: Was Virginia Ironside Right?" *Guardian*, October 5, 2010, http://www.guardian.co.uk/world/2010/oct/04/virginia-ironside-tv-euthanasia-abortion.

70. Julia Epstein, Laura Hershey, Sujatha Jesudason, Dorothy Roberts, Silvia Yee, and I wrote the text collaboratively over email and the telephone. The statement remains active, and new signatories are still being added. "Robert Edwards, Virginia Ironside, and the Unnecessary Opposition of Rights," accessed October 15, 2010, http://www.generations-ahead.org/resources/the-unnecessary-opposition-of-rights.

71. We knew that such a clear statement was necessary because of the long history of disability being used not only to justify specific abortions but to make abortion in general more acceptable. Leslie Reagan describes the process by which middle-class, married, heterosexual white women talking publicly about their own desire for abortion in the wake of the german measles/rubella epidemic "made abortion respectable"; through their stories, abortion came to be seen as a potentially "ethical and responsible" decision. As mentioned in previous chapters, this dynamic is not new; Licia Carlson, among others, details how early twentieth-century feminists deployed eugenic rhetoric about the dangers of "feebleminded offspring" in their battle for women's reproductive rights. Carlson, *Faces of Intellectual Disability*, 175–76; Reagan, *Dangerous Pregnancies*, 104.

72. One of the motivations of this chapter is to honor and name that work. When someone at a feminist studies conference recently lamented to me that "no one is talking about the relationship between disability and abortion," I understood and shared her frustration; I had given a paper making that very point a few years earlier. Certainly on one level we were right—much more open and difficult dialogue is necessary, both within disability studies and beyond it. On another level, though, our concerns reveal an erasure of activist and intellectual histories. We need to gather the stories of those people, primarily but not exclusively disabled women, who pioneered this work.

73. See, for example, Adrienne Asch and Michelle Fine, "Shared Dreams: A Left Perspective on Disability Rights and Reproductive Rights," in *Women with Disabilities: Essays in Psychology, Culture, and Politics*, ed. Michelle Fine and Adrienne Asch (Philadelphia: Temple University Press, 1988): 297–305; Anne Finger, *Past Due: A Story of Disability, Pregnancy, and Birth* (Seattle: Seal Press, 1990); Dorothy Roberts, *Killing the Black Body: Race, Reproduction, and the Meaning of Liberty* (New York: Vintage, 1999); and Saxton, "Disability Rights and Selective Abortion."

74. Hubbard, "Abortion and Disability," 99, 101, 102.

75. Ibid., 102.

76. Asch and Fine, "Shared Dreams," 297.

77. Ibid., 298.

78. Adrienne Asch, "A Disability Equality Critique of Routine Testing and Embryo or Fetus Elimination Based on Disabling Traits," *Political Environments* 11 (2007): 43–47, 78.

79. Silliman et al., *Undivided Rights*, 22n36.

80. Jesudason is the founder and executive director of Generations Ahead. Sujatha Anbuselvi Jesudason, "In the Hot Tub: The Praxis of Building New Alliances for Reprogenetics," *Signs: Journal of Women in Culture and Society* 34, no. 4 (2009): 901–24.

81. Roberts, *Fatal Invention*, 301.

82. Roberts, *Fatal Invention*, 302–6. See also Eli Clare, preface to the 2009 South End Press Classics edition of *Exile and Pride: Disability, Queerness, and Liberation* (Boston: South End Press, 2009), xi.

83. Liat Ben-Moshe, "Disabling Incarceration: Connecting Disability to Divergent Confinements in the USA," *Critical Sociology* (2011): 1–19.

84. Robert McRuer, *Crip Theory: Cultural Signs of Queerness and Disability* (New York: New York University Press, 2006), 36, 57.

85. McRuer makes this point during his reading of Grace Chang's *Disposable Domestics*. Chang writes about immigrant women of color who populate domestic service jobs, such as home health workers, and McRuer urges disability studies scholars to recognize their stories as disability stories. As he explains, "[A] system that wants 'young and strong workers' is always haunted by disability, and the need for surplus profit ensures that a system that generates disability must immediately conjure it away when it appears." McRuer, *Crip Theory*, 204; see also 199–208.

86. For one description of the gaps between these two movements, and of the possibilities for bridging them, see Bob Kafka, "Disability Rights vs. Workers Rights: A Different Perspective," *Znet*, November 14, 2003, http://www.zcommunications.org/disability-rights-vs-workers-rights-a-different-perspective-by-bob-kafka.

References

Abel, Elizabeth. "Bathroom Doors and Drinking Fountains: Jim Crow's Racial Symbolic." *Critical Inquiry* 25 (Spring 1999): 435–81.

Abod, Jennifer. *The Edge of Each Other's Battles: The Vision of Audre Lorde*. Long Beach, CA: Profile Productions, 2002. VHS.

Alaimo, Stacy. *Bodily Natures: Science, Environment, and the Material Self*. Bloomington: Indiana University Press, 2010.

Allen, Vanessa. "Outrage as Agony Aunt Tells TV Audience 'I Would Suffocate a Child to End Its Suffering.'" *Daily Mail*. October 5, 2010. http://www.dailymail.co.uk/news/article-1317400/Virginia-Ironside-sparks-BBC-outrage-Id-suffocate-child-end-suffering.html.

Asch, Adrienne. "A Disability Equality Critique of Routine Testing and Embryo or Fetus Elimination Based on Disabling Traits." *Political Environments* 11 (2007): 43–47, 78.

Asch, Adrienne, and Michelle Fine. "Shared Dreams: A Left Perspective on Disability Rights and Reproductive Rights." In *Women with Disabilities: Essays in Psychology, Culture, and Politics*, ed. Michelle Fine and Adrienne Asch, 297–305. Philadelphia: Temple University Press, 1988.

Banks, Taunya Lovell. "Toilets as a Feminist Issue: A True Story." *Berkeley Women's Law Journal* (1990): 263–89.

Baynton, Douglas C. "Disability and the Justification of Inequality in American History." In *The New Disability History: American Perspectives*, ed. Paul K. Longmore and Lauri Umansky, 33–57. New York: New York University Press, 2001.

Ben-Moshe, Liat. "Disabling Incarceration: Connecting Disability to Divergent Confinements in the USA." *Critical Sociology* (2011): 1–19.

Browne, Kath. "Genderism and the Bathroom Problem: (Re)Materialising Sexed Sites, (Re)Creating Sexed Bodies." *Gender, Place, and Culture* 11, no. 3 (2004): 331–46.

Case, Mary Anne. "Changing Room? A Quick Tour of Men's and Women's Rooms in U.S. Law over the Last Decade, from the U.S. Constitution to Local Ordinances." *Public Culture* 13, no. 2 (2001): 333–36.

Cavanagh, Sheila L. *Queering Bathrooms: Gender, Sexuality, and the Hygienic Imagination*. Toronto: University of Toronto Press, 2010.

Charles, Andrew, and Huw Thomas, "Deafness and Disability—Forgotten Components of Environmental Justice: Illustrated by the Case of Local Agenda 21 in South Wales." *Local Environment* 12, no. 3 (June 2007): 209–21.

Chen, Mel Y. "Toxic Animacies, Inanimate Affections." *GLQ: A Journal of Lesbian and Gay Studies* 17, nos. 2–3 (2011): 265–86.

Chess, Simone, Alison Kafer, Jessi Quizar, and Mattie Udora Richardson. "Calling All Restroom Revolutionaries!" In *That's Revolting! Queer Strategies for Resisting Assimilation*, ed. Matt Bernstein Sycamore, 189–206. New York: Soft Skull, 2004.

Clare, Eli. *Exile and Pride: Disability, Queerness, and Liberation*. Boston: South End Press, 1999.

Cooper, Patricia, and Ruth Oldenziel. "Cherished Classifications: Bathrooms and the Construction of Gender/Race on the Pennsylvania Railroad during World War II." *Feminist Studies* 25, no. 1 (1999): 7–41.

Di Chiro, Giovanna. "Polluted Politics? Confronting Toxic Discourse, Sex Panic, and Eco-Normativity." In *Queer Ecologies: Sex, Nature, Politics, Desire*, ed. Catriona Mortimer-Sandilands and Bruce Erickson, 199–230. Bloomington: Indiana University Press, 2010.

Di Chiro, Giovanna. "Producing 'Roundup Ready®' Communities? Human Genome Research and Environmental Justice Policy." In *New Perspectives on Environmental Justice: Gender, Sexuality, and Activism*, ed. Rachel Stein, 139–60. New Brunswick, NJ: Rutgers University Press, 2004.

Feinberg, Leslie. *Trans Liberation: Beyond Pink or Blue*. Boston: Beacon, 1998.

Finger, Anne. "Hurricane Katrina, Race, Class, Tragedy, and Charity." *DSQ: Disability Studies Quarterly* 25, no. 4 (2005). Accessed from http://www.dsq-sds.org/article/view/630/807.

Finger, Anne. *Past Due: A Story of Disability, Pregnancy, and Birth*. Seattle: Seal Press, 1990.

Gagliardi, Barbara. "West Coast Women's Music Festival." *Big Mama Rag* 9, no. 10 (1981): 3, 22

Garland-Thomson, Rosemarie, ed. *Freakery: Cultural Spectacles of the Extraordinary Body*. New York: New York University Press, 1996.

Generations Ahead. *Bridging the Divide: Disability Rights and Reproductive Rights and Justice Advocates Discussing Genetic Technologies*. 2009. http://www.generations-ahead.org/resources.

Gershenson, Olga. "The Restroom Revolution: Unisex Toilets and Campus Politics." In *Toilet: Public Restrooms and the Politics of Sharing*, ed. Harvey Molotch and Laura Norén, 191–207. New York: New York University Press, 2010.

Gershenson, Olga, and Barbara Penner, eds. *Ladies and Gents: Public Toilets and Gender*. Philadelphia: Temple University Press, 2009.

Hershey, Laura. "Choosing Disability," *Ms*. July/August 1994, 26–32.

Hubbard, Ruth. "Abortion and Disability: Who Should and Who Should Not Inhabit the World?" In *The Disability Studies Reader*, ed. Lennard J. Davis, 93–103. New York: Routledge, 2006.

Hutchins, Loraine. "Trouble and Mediation at Yosemite." *off our backs* 11, no. 10 (1981): 12–13, 25

Jesudason, Sujatha Anbuselvi. "In the Hot Tub: The Praxis of Building New Alliances for Reprogenetics." *Signs: Journal of Women in Culture and Society* 34, no. 4 (2009): 901–24.

Johnson, Valerie Ann. "Bringing Together Feminist Disability Studies and Environmental Justice." *Barbara Faye Waxman Fiduccia Papers on Women and Girls with Disabilities*. Center for Women Policy Studies. February 2011, 5. http://www.centerwomenpolicy.org/programs/waxmanfiduccia/BFWFP_ BringingTogetherFeministDisabilityStudiesandEnvironmentalJustice_ValerieAnnJohnso.pdf.

Kafka, Bob. "Disability Rights vs. Workers Rights: A Different Perspective." *Znet*. November 14, 2003. http://www.zcommunications.org/disability-rights-vs-workers-rights-a-different-perspective-by-bob-kafka.

Kelly, John B. "Incontinence." *Ragged Edge*, no. 1 (2002). http://www.ragged-edge-mag.com/0102/0102ft3.htm.

Kirkland, Anna. "When Transgendered People Sue and Win: Feminist Reflections on Strategy, Activism, and the Legal Process." In *The Fire This Time: Young Activists and the New Feminism*, ed. Vivien Labaton and Dawn Lundy Martin, 181–219. New York: Anchor, 2004.

Kitchin, Rob, and Robin Law. "The Socio-spatial Construction of (In)accessible Public Toilets." *Urban Studies* 38, no. 2 (2001): 287–98.

Levi, Jennifer, and Bennett Klein. "Pursuing Protection for Transgender People through Disability Laws." In *Transgender Rights*, ed. Paisley Currah, Richard M. Juang, and Shannon Price Minter, 74–92. Minneapolis: University of Minnesota, 2006.

McRuer, Robert. *Crip Theory: Cultural Signs of Queerness and Disability*. New York: New York University Press, 2006.

Mog, Ashley, and Amanda Lock Swarr. "Threads of Commonality in Transgender and Disability Studies." *Disability Studies Quarterly* 28, no. 4 (2008). Accessed from http://www.dsq-sds.org.

Mollow, Anna. "No Safe Place." *WSQ: Women's Studies Quarterly* 39, nos. 1–2 (2011): 188–99.

Molotch, Harvey. "Learning from the Loo." Introduction to *Toilet: Public Restrooms and the Politics of Sharing*, ed. Harvey Molotch and Laura Norén, 1–20. New York: New York University Press, 2010.

Molotch, Harvey, and Laura Norén, eds. *Toilet: Public Restrooms and the Politics of Sharing*. New York: New York University Press, 2010.

Mouffe, Chantal. "Feminism, Citizenship, and Radical Democratic Politics." In *Feminists Theorize the Political*, ed. Judith Butler and Joan W. Scott, 369–84. New York: Routledge, 1992.

Munson, Peggy. "Fringe Dweller: Toward an Ecofeminist Politic of Femme." In *Visible: A Femmethology*, vol. 2., ed. Jennifer Clarke Burke, 28–36. Ypsilanti, MI: Homofactus Press, 2009.

Munt, Sally R. "The Butch Body." In *Contested Bodies*, ed. Ruth Holliday and John Hassard, 95–106. London: Routledge, 2001.

Nelson, Jennifer. *Women of Color and the Reproductive Rights Movement*. New York: New York University Press, 2003.

Norén, Laura. "Only Dogs Are Free to Pee: New York Cabbies' Search for Civility." In *Toilet: Public Restrooms and the Politics of Sharing*, ed. Harvey Molotch and Laura Norén, 93–114. New York: New York University Press, 2010.

Oaks, Laury. "What Are Pro-Life Feminists Doing on Campus?" *NWSA Journal* 21, no. 1 (2009): 178–203.

Overall, Christine. "Public Toilets: Sex Segregation Revisited." *Ethics and the Environment* 12, no. 2 (2007): 71–91.

Panzarino, Connie. *The Me in the Mirror*. Seattle: Seal Press, 1994.

Plaskow, Judith. "Embodiment, Elimination, and the Role of Toilets in Struggles for Social Justice." *Cross Currents* (Spring 2008): 51–64.

Reagon, Bernice Johnson. "Coalition Politics: Turning the Century." In *Home Girls: A Black Feminist Anthology*, ed. Barbara Smith, 356–68. New York: Kitchen Table, 1983.

Roberts, Dorothy. *Killing the Black Body: Race, Reproduction, and the Meaning of Liberty*. New York: Vintage, 1999.

Samantrai, Ranu. *AlterNatives: Black Feminism in the Postimperial Nation*. Stanford, CA: Stanford University Press, 2002.

Sandahl, Carrie. "Anarcha Anti-Archive: Depends®." *Liminalities: A Journal of Performance Studies* 4, no. 2 (2008). http://liminalities.net/4-2/anarcha.

Saxton, Marsha. "Disability Rights and Selective Abortion." In *Abortion Wars: A Half-Century of Struggle: 1950–2000*, ed. Rickie Solinger, 374–93. Berkeley: University of California Press, 1998.

Siebers, Tobin. *Disability Theory*. Ann Arbor, MI: University of Michigan, 2008.

Silliman, Jael, Marlene Gerber Fried, Loretta Ross, and Elena R. Gutiérrez. *Undivided Rights: Women of Color Organize for Reproductive Justice*. Boston: South End Press, 2004.

Skotko, Brian. "Prenatally Diagnosed Down Syndrome: Mothers Who Continued Their Pregnancies Evaluate Their Health Care Providers." *American Journal of Obstetrics and Gynecology* 192 (2005): 670–77.

Smith, Andrea. "Beyond Pro-Choice versus Pro-Life: Women of Color and Reproductive Justice." *NWSA Journal* 17, no. 1 (2005): 119–40.

Solinger, Rickie. *Beggars and Choosers: How the Politics of Choice Shapes Adoption, Abortion, and Welfare in the United States*. New York: Hill and Wang, 2001.

Solinger, Rickie. *Pregnancy and Power: A Short History of Reproductive Politics in America*. New York: New York University Press, 2005.

Spade, Dean. "Resisting Medicine, Re/modeling Gender." *Berkeley Women's Law Journal* 18 (2003): 15–37.

Spade, Dean. *Toilet Training: Companion Guide for Activists and Educators*. Sylvia Rivera Law Project. New York: Urban Justice Center, 2004.

Thompson, Becky. *A Promise and a Way of Life: White Antiracist Activism*. Minneapolis: University of Minnesota Press, 2001.

Titchkosky, Tanya. "'To Pee or Not to Pee?': Ordinary Talk about Extraordinary Exclusions in a University Environment." *Canadian Journal of Sociology/Cahiers Canadiens de Sociologie* 33, no. 1 (2008): 37–60.

Tremain, Shelley. "Reproductive Freedom, Self-Regulation, and the Government of Impairment in Utero." *Hypatia* 21, no. 1 (2006): 35–53.

Williams, Zoe. "Abortion and Euthanasia: Was Virginia Ironside Right?" *Guardian*. October 5, 2010. http://www.guardian.co.uk/world/2010/oct/04/virginia-ironside-tv-euthanasia-abortion.

Zwillinger, Rhonda. *The Dispossessed: Living with Multiple Chemical Sensitivities*. Paulden, AZ: The Dispossessed Outreach Project, 1999.

26 Mammies, Matriarchs, and Other Controlling Images

PATRICIA HILL COLLINS

Intersecting oppressions of race, class, gender, and sexuality could not continue without powerful ideological justifications for their existence. As Cheryl Gilkes contends, "Black women's assertiveness and their use of every expression of racism to launch multiple assaults against the entire fabric of inequality have been a consistent, multifaceted threat to the status quo. As punishment, Black women have been assaulted with a variety of negative images" (1983, 294). Portraying African-American women as stereotypical mammies, matriarchs, welfare recipients, and hot mommas helps justify U.S. Black women's oppression. Challenging these controlling images has long been a core theme in Black feminist thought.

As part of a generalized ideology of domination, stereotypical images of Black womanhood take on special meaning. Because the authority to define societal values is a major instrument of power, elite groups, in exercising power, manipulate ideas about Black womanhood. They do so by exploiting already existing symbols, or creating new ones. Hazel Carby suggests that the objective of stereotypes is "not to reflect or represent a reality but to function as a disguise, or mystification, of objective social relations" (1987, 22). These controlling images are designed to make racism, sexism, poverty, and other forms of social injustice appear to be natural, normal, and inevitable parts of everyday life.

Even when the initial conditions that foster controlling images disappear, such images prove remarkably tenacious because they not only subjugate U.S. Black women but are key in maintaining intersecting oppressions (Mullings 1997, 109–30). African-American women's status as outsiders becomes the point from which other groups define their normality. Ruth Shays, a Black inner-city resident, describes how the standpoint of a subordinate group is discredited: "It will not kill people to hear the truth, but they don't like it and they would much rather hear it from one of their own than from a stranger. Now, to white people your colored person is always a stranger. Not only that, we are supposed to be dumb strangers, so we can't tell them anything!" (Gwaltney 1980, 29). As the "Others" of society who can never really belong, strangers threaten the moral and social order. But they are simultaneously essential for its survival because those individuals who stand at the margins of society clarify its boundaries. African-American women, by not belonging, emphasize the significance of belonging.

The Objectification of Black Women as the Other

Black feminist critic Barbara Christian asserts that in the United States, "the enslaved African woman became the basis for the definition of our society's *Other*" (1985, 160). Maintaining images of U.S. Black women as the Other provides ideological justification for race, gender, and class oppression. Certain basic ideas crosscut these and other forms of oppression. One such idea is binary thinking that categorizes people, things, and ideas in terms of their difference from one another (Keller 1985, 8). For example, each term in the binaries white/black, male/female, reason/emotion, culture/nature, fact/opinion, mind/body, and subject/object gains meaning only in *relation* to its counterpart (Halpin 1989).

Another basic idea concerns how binary thinking shapes understandings of human difference. In such thinking, difference is defined in oppositional terms. One part is not simply different from its counterpart; it is inherently opposed to its "other." Whites and Blacks, males and females, thought and feeling are not complementary counterparts—they are fundamentally different entities related only through their definition as opposites. Feeling cannot be incorporated into thought or even function in conjunction with it because in binary oppositional thinking, feeling retards thought and values obscure facts.

Objectification is central to this process of oppositional difference. In binary thinking, one element is objectified as the Other, and is viewed as an object to be manipulated and controlled. Social theorist Dona Richards (1980) suggests that Western thought requires objectification, a process she describes as the "separation of the 'knowing self' from the 'known object'" (p. 72). Intense objectification is a "prerequisite for the despiritualization of the universe," Richards writes, "and through it the Western cosmos was made ready for ever increasing materialization" (p. 72). A Marxist assessment of the culture/nature binary argues that history can be seen as that in which human beings constantly objectify the natural world in order to control and exploit it (Brittan and Maynard 1984, 198). Culture is defined as the opposite of an objectified nature. If undomesticated, this wild and primitive nature might destroy more civilized culture.[1] Feminist scholarship points to the identification of women with nature as being central to women's subsequent objectification and conquest by men (McClintock 1995). Black studies scholarship and postcolonial theory both suggest that defining people of color as less human, animalistic, or more "natural" denies African and Asian people's subjectivity and supports the political economy of domination that characterized slavery, colonialism, and neocolonialism (Torgovnick 1990; Chow 1993, 27–54; Said 1993; Bannerji 1995, 55–95).

Domination always involves attempts to objectify the subordinate group. "As subjects, people have the right to define their own reality, establish their own identities, name their history," asserts bell hooks (1989, 42). "As objects, one's reality is defined by others, one's identity created by others, one's history named only in ways that define one's relationship to those who are subject" (p. 42). The treatment afforded U.S. Black women domestic workers exemplifies the many forms that objectification can take. Making Black women work as if they were animals or "mules uh de world" represents one form of objectification. Deference rituals such as calling Black domestic workers "girls" enable employers to treat their employees like children, as less capable human beings. Objectification can be so severe that the Other simply disappears, as was the case when Judith Rollins's employer treated her as if she were invisible.

Finally, because oppositional binaries rarely represent different but equal relationships, they are inherently unstable. Tension may be temporarily relieved by subordinating one half of the binary to the other. Thus Whites rule Blacks, men dominate women, reason is thought superior to emotion in ascertaining truth, facts supersede opinion in evaluating knowledge, and subjects rule objects. The foundations of intersecting oppressions become grounded in interdependent concepts of binary thinking, oppositional difference, objectification, and social hierarchy. With domination based on difference forming an essential underpinning for this entire system of thought, these concepts invariably imply relationships of superiority and inferiority, hierarchical bonds that mesh with political economies of race, gender, and class oppression.

African-American women occupy a position whereby the inferior half of a series of these binaries converge, and this placement has been central to our subordination. The allegedly emotional, passionate nature of Black women has long been used to justify Black women's sexual exploitation. Similarly, restricting Black women's literacy, then claiming that we lack the facts for sound judgment, relegates African-American women to the inferior side of the fact/opinion binary. Denying Black women status as fully human subjects by treating us as the objectified Other within multiple binaries demonstrates the power that binary thinking, oppositional difference, and objectification wield within intersecting oppressions.

Despite its seeming permanence, this way of thinking, by fostering injustice, can also stimulate resistance. For example, U.S. Black women have long recognized the fundamental injustice of a system that routinely and from one generation to the next relegates U.S. Black women to the bottom of the social hierarchy. When faced with this structural injustice targeted toward the group, many Black women have insisted on our right to define our own reality, establish our own identities, and name our history. One significant contribution of work on domestic workers is that it documents Black women's everyday resistance to this attempted objectification.

Analyzing the particular controlling images applied to African-American women reveals the specific contours of Black women's objectification as well as the ways in which oppressions of race, gender, sexuality, and class intersect. Moreover, since the images themselves are dynamic and changing, each provides a starting point for examining new forms of control that emerge in a transnational context, one where selling images has increased in importance in the global marketplace.

Controlling Images and Black Women's Oppression

"Black women emerged from slavery firmly enshrined in the consciousness of white America as 'Mammy' and the 'bad black woman,'" contends Cheryl Gilkes (1983, 294). The dominant ideology of the slave era fostered the creation of several interrelated, socially constructed controlling images of Black womanhood, each reflecting the dominant group's interest in maintaining Black women's subordination. Moreover, since Black and White women were both important to slavery's continuation, controlling images of Black womanhood also functioned to mask social relations that affected all women.

According to the cult of true womanhood that accompanied the traditional family ideal, "true" women possessed four cardinal virtues: piety, purity, submissiveness, and domesticity. Propertied White women and those of the emerging middle class were encouraged to aspire to these virtues. African-American women encountered a different set of controlling images.

The first controlling image applied to U.S. Black women is that of the mammy—the faithful, obedient domestic servant. Created to justify the economic exploitation of house slaves and sustained to explain Black women's long-standing restriction to domestic service, the mammy image represents the normative yardstick used to evaluate all Black women's behavior. By loving, nurturing, and caring for her White children and "family" better than her own, the mammy symbolizes the dominant group's perceptions of the ideal Black female relationship to elite White male power. Even though she may be well loved and may wield considerable authority in her White "family," the mammy still knows her "place" as obedient servant. She has accepted her subordination.

Black women intellectuals have aggressively criticized the image of African-American women as contented mammies. Literary critic Trudier Harris's (1982) volume *From Mammies to Militants: Domestics in Black American Literature* investigates prominent differences in how Black women have been portrayed by others in literature and how they portray themselves. In her work on the difficulties faced by Black women leaders, Rhetaugh Dumas (1980) describes how Black women executives are hampered by being treated as mammies and penalized if they do not appear warm and nurturing. Striking a similar chord, Barbara Omolade's (1994) description of the "mammification" of Black professional women also takes aim at the imagined Black woman mammy. But despite these works, the mammy image lives on in scholarly and popular culture. Audre Lorde's account of a shopping trip offers a powerful example of its tenacity: "I wheel my two-year-old daughter in a shopping cart through a supermarket in … 1967, and a little white girl riding past in her mother's cart calls out excitedly, 'Oh look, Mommy, a baby maid!'" (1984, 126).[2]

The mammy image is central to intersecting oppressions of race, gender, sexuality, and class. Regarding racial oppression, controlling images like the mammy aim to influence Black maternal behavior. As the members of African-American families who are most familiar with the skills needed for Black accommodation, Black mothers are encouraged to transmit to their own children the deference behavior that many are forced to exhibit in their mammified jobs. By teaching Black children their assigned place in White power structures, Black women who internalize the mammy image potentially become effective conduits for perpetuating racial oppression. Ideas about mammy buttress racial hierarchies in other ways. Employing Black women in mammified occupations supports the racial superiority of White employers, encouraging middle-class White women in particular to identify more closely with the racial and class privilege afforded their fathers, husbands, and sons. In a climate where, as Patricia Williams (1995) puts it, "those blacks who do indeed rise into the middle class end up being figured only as those who were *given* whatever they enjoy, and the black 'underclass' becomes those whose sole life activity is *taking*" (p. 61), no wonder that working-class Whites expect Black women to exhibit deferential behavior, and deeply resent those who do not. Mammy is the public face that Whites expect Black women to assume for them.

The mammy image also serves a symbolic function in maintaining oppressions of gender and sexuality. Black feminist critic Barbara Christian argues that images of Black womanhood serve as a reservoir for the fears of Western culture, "a dumping ground for those female functions a basically Puritan society could not confront" (1985, 2). Juxtaposed against images of White women, the mammy image as the Other symbolizes the oppositional difference of mind/body and culture/nature thought to distinguish Black women from everyone else. Christian comments on the mammy's gender significance: "All the functions of mammy are magnificently physical. They involve the body as sensuous, as funky, the part of woman that white southern America was profoundly afraid of. Mammy, then, harmless in her position of slave, unable because of her all-giving nature to do harm, is needed as an image, a surrogate to contain all those fears of the physical female" (1985, 2). The mammy image buttresses the ideology of the cult of true womanhood, one in which sexuality and fertility are severed. "Good" White mothers are expected to deny their female sexuality. In contrast, the mammy image is one of an asexual woman, a surrogate mother in blackface whose historical devotion to her White family is now giving way to new expectations. Contemporary mammies should be completely committed to their jobs.

No matter how loved they were by their White "families," Black women domestic workers remained poor because they were economically exploited workers in a capitalist political economy. The restructured post–World War II economy, in which African-American women moved from service in private homes to jobs in the low-paid service sector and to jobs in clerical work and mammified professions, has produced similar yet differently organized economic exploitation. Historically, many White families in both the middle class and working class were able to maintain their class position because they used Black women domestic workers as a source of cheap labor (Rollins 1985; Byerly 1986). The mammy image was designed to mask this economic exploitation of social class (King 1973). Currently, while the mammy image becomes more muted as Black women move into better jobs, the basic economic exploitation where U.S. Black women either make less for the same work or work twice as hard for the same pay persists. U.S. Black women and African-American communities pay a price for this exploitation. Removing Black women's labor from African-American families and exploiting it denies Black extended family units the benefits of both decent wages and Black women's emotional labor in their homes. Moreover, as the attention to issues of stress in Black feminist analyses of U.S. Black women's health suggest, participating in this chronically undercompensated and unrecognized labor takes its toll (White 1994, 11–14).

For reasons of economic survival, U.S. Black women may play the mammy role in paid work settings. But within African-American families and neighborhoods these same women often teach their own children something quite different. Bonnie Thornton Dill's (1980) work on child-rearing patterns among Black domestics shows that while the participants in her study showed deference behavior at work, they discouraged their children from believing that they should be deferential to Whites and encouraged their children to avoid domestic work. Barbara Christian's analysis of the mammy in Black slave narratives reveals that, "unlike the white southern image of mammy, she is cunning, prone to poisoning her master, and not at all content with her lot" (1985, 5).

The fact that the mammy image by itself cannot control Black women's behavior is tied to the creation of the second controlling image of Black womanhood. Though a more recent phenomenon, the image of the Black matriarch fulfills similar functions in explaining Black women's placement in intersecting oppressions. Ironically, Black scholars such as William E. B. DuBois (1969) and E. Franklin Frazier (1948) described the connections among higher rates of female-headed households in African-American communities, the importance that women assume in Black family networks, and the persistence of Black poverty. However, neither scholar interpreted Black women's centrality in Black families as a *cause* of African-American social class status. Both saw so-called matriarchal families as an *outcome* of racial oppression and poverty. During the eras when DuBois and Frazier wrote, the political disenfranchisement and economic exploitation of African-Americans was so entrenched that control over Black women could be maintained without the matriarchal stereotype. But what began as a muted theme in the works of these earlier African-American scholars grew into a full-blown racialized image in the 1960s, a time of significant political and economic mobility for African-Americans. Racialization involves attaching racial meaning to a previously racially unclassified relationship, social practice, or group (Omi and Winant 1994). Prior to the 1960s, Black communities contained higher percentages of families maintained by single mothers than White ones, but an ideology that racialized female-headedness as one important cause of Black poverty had not emerged. Interestingly, the insertion of the Black matriarchy thesis into discussions of Black poverty came in the midst of considerable Black activism. Moreover, the public depiction of U.S. Black women as unfeminine matriarchs came at precisely the same moment that the women's movement advanced its critique of U.S. patriarchy (Gilkes 1983, 296).

While the mammy typifies the Black mother figure in White homes, the matriarch symbolizes the mother figure in Black homes. Just as the mammy represents the "good" Black mother, the matriarch symbolizes the "bad" Black mother. Introduced and widely circulated via a government report titled *The Negro Family: The Case for National Action*, the Black matriarchy thesis argued that African-American women who failed to fulfill their traditional "womanly" duties at home contributed to social problems in Black civil society (Moynihan 1965). Spending too much time away from home, these working mothers ostensibly could not properly supervise their children and thus were a major contributing factor to their children's failure at school. As overly aggressive, unfeminine women, Black matriarchs allegedly emasculated their lovers and husbands. These men, understandably, either deserted their partners or refused to marry the mothers of their children. From the dominant group's perspective, the matriarch represented a failed mammy, a negative stigma to be applied to African-American women who dared reject the image of the submissive, hardworking servant.

Black women intellectuals who study African-American families and Black motherhood typically report finding few matriarchs and even fewer mammies (Myers 1980; Sudarkasa 1981; Dill 1988). Instead they portray African-American mothers as complex individuals who often show tremendous strength under adverse conditions, or who become beaten down by the incessant demands of providing for their families. In *A Raisin in the Sun*, the first play presented on Broadway written by a Black woman, Lorraine Hansberry (1959) examines the struggles of widow Lena Younger to actualize her dream of purchasing a home for her family. In *Brown Girl, Brownstones*, novelist Paule Marshall (1959) presents Mrs. Boyce, a Black mother negotiating a series of relationships with her husband, her daughters, the women in her community, and the work she must perform outside her home. Ann Allen Shockley's *Loving Her* (1974) depicts the struggle of a lesbian mother trying to balance her needs for self-actualization with the pressures of child-rearing in a homophobic community.

Like these fictional analyses, Black women's scholarship on Black single mothers also challenges the matriarchy thesis, but finds far fewer Lena Youngers or Mrs. Boyces (Ladner 1972; Brewer 1988; Jarrett 1994; Dickerson 1995; Kaplan 1997). In her study of Black teenage mothers, Elaine Bell Kaplan (1997) learned that the reactions of mothers to their teenaged daughters' pregnancies were far from the image of the superstrong Black mother. Mothers in the new working poor felt their pregnant teenage daughters had failed them. Until their daughters' pregnancies, these mothers hoped that their daughters would do better with their lives. The mothers who came from humble beginnings and who had worked hard to achieve a modicum of middle-class respectability felt cheated when their daughters became pregnant. Among both groups of mothers, adjusting to their daughters' pregnancies brought on much hardship.

Like the mammy, the image of the matriarch is central to intersecting oppressions of class, gender, and race. While at first glance the matriarch may appear far removed from issues in U.S. capitalist development, this image is actually important in explaining the persistence of Black social class outcomes. Assuming that Black poverty in the United States is passed on intergenerationally via the values that parents teach their children, dominant ideology suggests that Black children lack the attention and care allegedly lavished on White, middle-class children. This alleged cultural deficiency seriously retards Black children's achievement. Such a view diverts attention from political and economic inequalities that increasingly characterize global capitalism. It also suggests that anyone can rise from poverty if he or she only received good values at home. Inferior housing, underfunded schools, employment discrimination, and consumer racism all but disappear from Black women's lives. In this sanitized view of American society, those African-Americans who remain poor cause their own victimization. In this context, portraying African-American women as matriarchs allows White men and women to blame Black women for their children's failures in school and with the law, as well as Black children's subsequent poverty. Using images of bad Black mothers to explain Black economic disadvantage links gender ideology to explanations for extreme distributions of wealth that characterize American capitalism.

One source of the matriarch's failure is her inability to model appropriate gender behavior. Thus, labeling Black women unfeminine and too strong works to undercut U.S. Black women's assertiveness. Many U.S. Black women who find themselves maintaining families by themselves often feel that they have done something wrong. If only they were not so strong, some reason, they might have found a male partner, or their sons would not have had so much trouble with the law. This belief masks the culpability of the U.S. criminal justice system, described by Angela Davis (1997) as an "out of control punishment industry" that locks up a disproportionate number of U.S. Blacks. African-Americans are almost eight times more likely to be imprisoned than Whites (p. 267), a social policy that leaves far fewer men for Black women to marry than the proportion of White men available to White women. Moreover, not only does the image of the Black matriarch seek to regulate Black women's behavior, it also seems designed to influence White women's gendered identities. In the post–World War II era, increasing numbers of White women entered the labor market, limited their fertility, and generally challenged their proscribed roles as subordinate helpmates in their families and workplaces. In this context, the image of the Black matriarch serves as a powerful symbol for both Black and White women of what can go wrong if White patriarchal power is challenged. Aggressive, assertive women are penalized—they are abandoned by their men, end up impoverished, and are stigmatized as being unfeminine. The matriarch or overly strong Black woman has also been used to influence Black men's understandings of Black masculinity. Many Black men reject Black women as marital partners, claiming that Black women are less desirable than White ones because we are too assertive.

The image of the matriarch also supports racial oppression. Much social science research implicitly uses gender relations in African-American communities as one seeming measure of Black cultural disadvantage. For example, the Moynihan Report (1965) contends that slavery destroyed Black families by creating reversed roles for men and women. Black family structures are seen as being deviant because they challenge the patriarchal assumptions underpinning the traditional family ideal. Moreover, the absence of Black patriarchy is used as evidence for Black cultural inferiority (Collins 1989). Under scientific racism, Blacks have been construed as inferior, and their inferiority has been attributed either to biological causes or cultural differences. Thus, locating the source of cultural difference in flawed gender relations provides a powerful foundation for U.S. racism. Black women's failure to conform to the cult of true womanhood can then be identified as one fundamental source of Black cultural deficiency. Advancing ideas about Black cultural disadvantage via the matriarchal image worked to counter efforts by African-Americans who identified political and social policies as one important source of Black economic disadvantage. The image of Black women as dangerous, deviant, castrating mothers divided the Black community at a critical period in the Black liberation struggle. Such images fostered a similar reaction within women's political activism and created a wider gap between the worlds of Black and White women at an equally critical period in women's history (Gilkes 1983).

Taken together, images of the mammy and the matriarch place African-American women in an untenable position. For Black women workers in service occupations requiring long hours and/or substantial emotional labor, becoming the ideal mammy means precious time and energy spent away from husbands and children. But being employed when Black men have difficulty finding steady work exposes African-American women to the charge that Black women emasculate Black men by failing to be submissive, dependent, "feminine" women. This image ignores gender-specific patterns of incorporation into the capitalist economy, where Black men have greater difficulty finding work but make higher wages when they do work, and Black women find work with greater ease yet earn much less. Moreover, Black women's financial contributions to Black family well-being have been cited as evidence supporting the matriarchy thesis (Moynihan 1965). Many Black women are the sole support of their families, and labeling these women "matriarchs" erodes their self-confidence and ability to confront oppression. In essence, African-American women who must work encounter pressures to be submissive mammies in one setting, then are stigmatized again as matriarchs for being strong figures in their own homes.

A third, externally defined, controlling image of Black womanhood—that of the welfare mother—appears tied to working-class Black women's increasing access to U.S. welfare state entitlements. At its core, the image of the welfare mother constitutes a class-specific, controlling image developed for poor, working-class Black women who make use of social welfare benefits to which they are entitled by law. As long as poor Black women were denied social welfare benefits, there was no need for this stereotype. But when U.S. Black women gained more political power and demanded equity in access to state services, the need arose for this controlling image.

Essentially an updated version of the breeder woman image created during slavery, this image provides an ideological justification for efforts to harness Black women's fertility to the needs of a changing political economy. During slavery the breeder woman image portrayed Black women as more suitable for having children than White women. By claiming that Black women were able to produce children as easily as animals, this image provided justification for interference in enslaved Africans' reproductive lives. Slave owners wanted enslaved Africans to "breed" because every slave child born represented a valuable unit of property, another unit of labor, and, if female, the prospects for more slaves. The controlling image of the breeder woman served to justify slave owners' intrusion into Black women's decisions about fertility (King 1973; Davis 1981; D. White 1985).

In the post–World War II political economy, African-Americans struggled for and gained rights denied them in former historical periods (Squires 1994). Contrary to popular belief, U.S. Black women were not "given" unearned entitlements, but instead had to struggle for rights routinely offered to other American citizens (Amott 1990; Quadagno 1994). African-Americans successfully acquired basic political and economic protections from a greatly expanded social welfare state, particularly Social Security, unemployment compensation, school feeding programs, fellowships and loans for higher education, affirmative action, voting rights, antidiscrimination legislation, child welfare programs, and the minimum wage. Despite sustained opposition by Republican administrations in the 1980s, these social welfare programs allowed many African-Americans to reject the subsistence-level, exploitative jobs held by their parents and grandparents. However, these Black citizenship rights came at a time of shrinking economic opportunities in U.S. manufacturing and agriculture. Job export, de-skilling, and increased use of illegal immigrants have all been used to replace the cheap, docile labor force that U.S. Blacks used to be (Nash and Fernandez-Kelly 1983; Brewer 1993; Squires 1994). Until the mid-1990s, the large numbers of undereducated, unemployed African-Americans ghettoized in U.S. inner cities, most of whom were women and children, could not be forced to work. This surplus population no longer represented cheap labor but instead, from the perspective of elites, signified a costly threat to political and economic stability. African-American men increasingly became targeted by a growing punishment industry (Davis 1997). In the absence of legitimate jobs, many men worked in the informal sector, serving as low-level employees of a growing, global drug industry that introduced crack cocaine into U.S. Black neighborhoods in the 1980s. For many, becoming entangled with the punishment industry was one cost of doing business.

Controlling Black women's fertility in this political and economic context became important to elite groups. The image of the welfare mother fulfills this function by labeling as unnecessary and even dangerous to the values of the country the fertility of women who are not White and middle class. A closer look at this controlling image reveals that it shares some important features with its mammy and matriarch counterparts. Like the matriarch, the welfare mother is labeled a bad mother. But unlike the matriarch, she is not too aggressive—on the contrary, she is not aggressive enough. While the matriarch's unavailability contributed to her children's poor socialization, the welfare mother's accessibility is deemed the problem. She is portrayed as being content to sit around and collect welfare, shunning work and passing on her bad values to her offspring. The image of the welfare mother represents another failed mammy, one who is unwilling to become "de mule uh de world."

The image of the welfare mother provides ideological justifications for intersecting oppressions of race, gender, and class. African-Americans can be racially stereotyped as being lazy by blaming Black welfare mothers for failing to pass on the work ethic. Moreover, the welfare mother has no male authority figure to assist her. Typically portrayed as an unwed mother, she violates one cardinal tenet of White, male-dominated ideology: She is a woman alone. As a result, her treatment reinforces the dominant gender ideology positing that a woman's true worth and financial security should occur through heterosexual marriage. Finally, on average, in the post–World War II political economy, one of every three African-American families has been officially classified as poor. With such high levels of Black poverty, welfare state policies supporting poor Black mothers and their children have become increasingly expensive. Creating the controlling image of the welfare mother and stigmatizing her as the cause of her own poverty and that of African-American communities shifts the angle of vision away from structural sources of poverty and blames the victims themselves. The image of the welfare mother thus provides ideological justification for the dominant group's interest in limiting the fertility of Black mothers who are seen as producing too many economically unproductive children (Davis 1981).

With the election of the Reagan administration in 1980, the stigmatized welfare mother evolved into the more pernicious image of the welfare queen (Lubiano 1992). To mask the effects of cuts in government spending on social welfare programs that fed children, housed working families, assisted cities in maintaining roads, bridges, and basic infrastructure, and supported other basic public services, media images increasingly identified and blamed Black women for the deterioration of U.S. interests. Thus, poor Black women simultaneously become symbols of what was deemed wrong with America and targets of social policies designed to shrink the government sector. Wahneema Lubiano describes how the image of the welfare queen links Black women with seeming declines in the quality of life:

> "Welfare queen" is a phrase that describes economic dependency—the lack of a job and/or income (which equal degeneracy in the Calvinist United States); the presence of a child or children with no father and/or husband (moral deviance); and, finally, a charge on the collective U.S. treasury—a human debit. The cumulative totality, circulation, and effect of these meanings in a time of scarce resources among the working class and the lower middle class is devastatingly intense. The welfare queen represents moral aberration and an economic drain, but the figure's problematic status becomes all the more threatening once responsibility for the destruction of the American way of life is attributed to it. (Lubiano 1992, 337–38)

In contrast to the welfare mother who draws upon the moral capital attached to American motherhood, the welfare queen constitutes a highly materialistic, domineering, and manless working-class Black woman. Relying on the public dole, Black welfare queens are content to take the hard-earned money of tax-paying Americans and remain married to the state. Thus, the welfare queen image signals efforts to use the situation of working-class Black women as a sign of the deterioration of the state.

During this same period, the welfare queen was joined by another similar yet class-specific image, that of the "Black lady" (Lubiano 1992). Because the Black lady refers to middle-class professional Black women who represent a modern version of the politics of respectability advanced by the club women (Shaw 1996), this image may not appear to be a controlling image, merely a benign one. These are the women who stayed in school, worked hard, and have achieved much. Yet the image of the Black lady builds upon prior images of Black womanhood in many ways. For one thing, this image seems to be yet another version of the modern mammy, namely, the hardworking Black woman professional who works twice as hard as everyone else. The image of the Black lady also resembles aspects of the matriarchy thesis—Black ladies have jobs that are so all-consuming that they have no *time* for men or have forgotten how to treat them. Because they so routinely compete with men and are successful at it, they become less feminine. Highly educated Black ladies are deemed to be *too* assertive—that's why they cannot get men to marry them.

Upon first glance, Black ladies also seem far removed from charges of unearned dependency on the state that are so often leveled at working-class U.S. Black women via the welfare queen image. Yet here, too, parallels abound. Via affirmative action, Black ladies allegedly take jobs that should go to more worthy Whites, especially U.S. White men. Given a political climate in the 1980s and 1990s that reinterpreted antidiscrimination and affirmative action programs as examples of an unfair "reverse racism," no matter how highly educated or demonstrably competent Black ladies may be, their accomplishments remain questionable. Moreover, many Black men erroneously believe that Black ladies are taking jobs reserved for them. In their eyes, being Black, female, and seemingly less threatening to Whites advantages Black ladies.

Wahneema Lubiano points out how images of the welfare queen and the Black lady evolved in tandem with persistent efforts to cut social welfare spending for working-class Blacks and limit affirmative action opportunities for middle-class Blacks: "Whether by virtue of not achieving and thus passing on bad culture as welfare mothers, or by virtue of managing to achieve middle-class success … black women are responsible for the disadvantaged status of African Americans" (Lubiano 1992, 335). Thus, when taken together, the welfare queen and the Black lady constitute class-specific versions of a matriarchy thesis whose fundamental purpose is to discredit Black women's full exercise of citizenship rights. These interconnected images leave U.S. Black women between a rock and a hard place.

A final controlling image—the jezebel, whore, or "hoochie"—is central in this nexus of controlling images of Black womanhood. Because efforts to control Black women's sexuality lie at the heart of Black women's oppression, historical jezebels and contemporary "hoochies" represent a deviant Black female sexuality. The image of jezebel originated under slavery when Black women were portrayed as being, to use Jewelle Gomez's words, "sexually aggressive wet nurses" (Clarke et al. 1983, 99). Jezebel's function was to relegate all Black women to the category of sexually aggressive women, thus providing a powerful rationale for the widespread sexual assaults by White men typically reported by Black slave women (Davis 1981; D. White 1985). Jezebel served yet another function. If Black slave women could be portrayed as having excessive sexual appetites, then increased fertility should be the expected outcome. By suppressing the nurturing that African-American women might give their own children which would strengthen Black family networks, and by forcing Black women to work in the field, "wet nurse" White children, and emotionally nurture their White owners, slave owners effectively tied the controlling images of jezebel and mammy to the economic exploitation inherent in the institution of slavery.

Rooted in the historical legacy of jezebel, the contemporary "hoochie" seems to be cut from an entirely different cloth. For one, whereas images of Black women as sexually aggressive certainly pervade popular culture overall, the image of the hoochie seems to have permeated everyday Black culture in entirely new ways. For example, 2 Live Crew's song "Hoochie Mama" takes Black women bashing to new heights. In this song, the group opens with the rallying cry "big booty hoes hop wit it!" and proceeds to list characteristics of the "hoodrat hoochie mama." The singers are quite clear about the use of such women: "I don't need no confrontation," they sing. "All I want is an ejaculation cos I like them ghetto hoochies." The misogyny in "Hoochie Mama" makes prior portrayals of jezebel seem tame. For example, 2 Live Crew's remedy for "lyin" shows their disdain for women: "Keep runnin ya mouth and I'ma stick my dick in it," they threaten. And for those listeners who remain confused about the difference between good and bad women, 2 Live Crew is willing to help out:

Mama just don't understand
why I love your hoochie ass
Sex is what I need you for
I gotta good girl but I need a whore

In the United States, guarantees of free speech allow 2 Live Crew and similar groups to speak their minds about "hoochies" and anything else that will make them money. The issue here lies in African-American acceptance of such images. African-American men and women alike routinely do not challenge these and other portrayals of Black women as "hoochies" within Black popular culture. For example, despite the offensive nature of much of 2 Live Crew's music, some Blacks argued that such views, while unfortunate, had long been expressed in Black culture (Crenshaw 1993). Not only does such acceptance mask how such images provide financial benefits to both 2 Live Crew and White-controlled media, such tacit acceptance validates this image. The more it circulates among U.S. Blacks, the more credence it is given.

The "hoochie" image certainly seems to have taken on a life of its own. For example, an informal poll of my friends, students, and colleagues revealed a complex taxonomy of "hoochies." Most agreed that one category consisted of "plain hoochie" or sexually assertive women who can be found across social classes. Women who wear sleazy clothes to clubs and dance in a "slutty" fashion constitute "club hoochies." These women aim to attract men with money for a one-night stand. In contrast, the ambition of "gold-digging hoochies" lies in establishing a long-term relationship with a man with money. These gold-digging hoochies often aim to snare a highly paid athlete and can do so by becoming pregnant. Finally, there is the "hoochie mama" popularized by 2 Live Crew, an image that links the hoochie image to poverty. As 2 Live Crew points out, the "hoochie mama" is a "hoodrat," a "ghetto hoochie" whose main purpose is to provide them sexual favors. The fact that she is also a "mama" speaks to the numbers of Black women in poverty who are single parents whose exchange of sexual favors for money is motivated by their children's economic needs.

Within assumptions that normalize heterosexuality, the historical jezebel and her modern "hoochie" counterpart mark a series of boundaries. Heterosexuality itself is constructed via binary thinking that juxtaposes male and female sexuality, with male and female gender roles pivoting on perceptions of appropriate male and female sexual expression. Men are active, and women should be passive. In the context of U.S. society, these become racialized—White men are active, and White women should be passive. Black people and other racialized groups simultaneously stand outside these definitions of normality and mark their boundaries. In this context of a gender-specific, White, heterosexual normality, the jezebel or hoochie becomes a racialized, gendered symbol of deviant female sexuality. Normal female heterosexuality is expressed via the cult of true White womanhood, whereas deviant female heterosexuality is typified by the "hot mommas" of Black womanhood.

Within intersecting oppressions, Black women's allegedly deviant sexuality becomes constructed around jezebel's sexual desires. Jezebel may be a "pretty baby," but her actions as a "hot momma" indicate that she just can't get enough. Because jezebel or the hoochie is constructed as a woman whose sexual appetites are at best inappropriate and, at worst, insatiable, it becomes a short step to imagine her as a "freak." And if she is a freak, her sexual partners become similarly stigmatized. For example, the hypermasculinity often attributed to Black men reflects beliefs about Black men's excessive sexual appetite. Ironically, jezebel's excessive sexual appetite masculinizes her because she desires sex just as a man does. Moreover, jezebel can also be masculinized and once again deemed "freaky" if she desires sex with other women. 2 Live Crew had little difficulty making this conceptual leap when they sing: "Freaky shit is what I like and I love to see two bitches dyke." In a context where feminine women are those who remain submissive yet appropriately flirtatious toward men, women whose sexual aggression resembles that of men become stigmatized.

When it comes to women's sexuality, the controlling image of jezebel and her hoochie counterpart constitute one side of the normal/deviant binary. But broadening this binary thinking that underpins intersecting oppressions of race, class, gender, and sexuality reveals that heterosexuality is juxtaposed to homosexuality as its oppositional, different, and inferior "other." Within this wider oppositional difference, jezebel becomes the freak on the border demarking heterosexuality from homosexuality. Her insatiable sexual desire helps define the boundaries of normal sexuality. Just across the border stand lesbian, bisexual, and transgendered women who are deemed deviant in large part because of their choices of sexual partners. As a sexual freak, jezebel has one foot over the line. On this border, the hoochie participates in a cluster of "deviant female sexualities," some associated with the materialistic ambitions where she sells sex for money, others associated with so-called deviant sexual practices such as sleeping with other women, and still others attached to "freaky" sexual practices such as engaging in oral and anal sex.

Images of sexuality associated with jezebel and the hoochie not only mark the boundaries of deviant sexualities, they weave throughout prevailing conceptualizations of the mammy, matriarch, and the

Janus-faced welfare queen/Black lady. Connecting all is the common theme of Black women's sexuality. Each image transmits distinctive messages about the proper links among female sexuality, desired levels of fertility for working-class and middle-class Black women, and U.S. Black women's placement in social class and citizenship hierarchies. For example, the mammy, one of two somewhat positive figures, is a desexed individual. The mammy is typically portrayed as overweight, dark, and with characteristically African features—in brief, as an unsuitable sexual partner for White men. She is asexual and therefore is free to become a surrogate mother to the children she acquired not through her own sexuality. The mammy represents the clearest example of the split between sexuality and motherhood present in Eurocentric masculinist thought. In contrast, both the matriarch and the welfare mother are sexual beings. But their sexuality is linked to their fertility, and this link forms one fundamental reason they are negative images. The matriarch represents the sexually aggressive woman, one who emasculates Black men because she will not permit them to assume roles as Black patriarchs. She refuses to be passive and thus is stigmatized. Similarly, the welfare mother represents a woman of low morals and uncontrolled sexuality, factors identified as the cause of her impoverished state. In both cases Black female control over sexuality and fertility is conceptualized as antithetical to elite White male interests. The Black lady completes the circle. Like mammy, her hard-earned, middle-class respectability is grounded in her seeming asexuality. Yet fertility is an issue here as well. Despite the fact that the middle-class Black lady is the woman deemed best suited to have children, in actuality, she remains the least likely to do so. She is told that she can reproduce, but no one except her is especially disturbed if she does not.

Taken together, these prevailing images of Black womanhood represent elite White male interests in defining Black women's sexuality and fertility. Moreover, by meshing smoothly with intersecting oppressions of race, class, gender, and sexuality, they help justify the social practices that characterize the matrix of domination in the United States.

Controlling Images and Social Institutions

Schools, the news media, and government agencies constitute important sites for reproducing these controlling images. Whereas schools and the scholarship produced and disseminated by their faculty historically have played an important part in generating these controlling images (Morton 1991), their current significance in reproducing these images is less often noted. Take, for example, how social science research on Black women's sexuality has been influenced by assumptions of the jezebel. Two topics, both deemed as social problems, take the lion's share—Black women's sexuality appears within AIDS research and within scholarship on adolescent pregnancy. Both reference two types of allegedly deviant sexuality with an eye toward altering Black women's behavior. In AIDS research, the focus is on risky sexual practices that might expose women, their unborn children, and their partners to HIV infection. Prostitutes and other sex workers are of special concern. The underlying reason for studying Black adolescent sexuality may lie in helping the girls, but an equally plausible stimulus lies in desires to get these girls off the public dole. Their sexuality is not that of risky sexual practices, but sexuality outside the confines of marriage. Embedding research on Black women's sexuality within social problems frameworks thus fosters its portrayal as a social problem.

The growing influence of television, radio, movies, videos, CDs, and the Internet constitutes new ways of circulating controlling images. Popular culture has become increasingly important in promoting these images, especially with new global technologies that allow U.S. popular culture to be exported throughout the world. Within this new corporate structure, the misogyny in some strands of Black hip-hop music becomes especially troubling. Much of this music is produced by a Black culture industry in which African-American artists have little say in production. On the one hand, Black rap music can be seen as a creative response to racism by Black urban youth who have been written off by U.S. society (Rose 1994; Kelley 1997, 43–77). On the other hand, images of Black women as sexually available hoochies persist in Black music videos. As "freaks," U.S. Black women can now be seen "poppin' that coochie"—yet another term by 2 Live Crew that describes butt shaking—in a global context.

Government agencies also play a part in legitimating these controlling images. Because legislative bodies and, in the case of 2 Live Crew's obscenity trial (see, e.g., Crenshaw 1993), courts determine which narratives are legitimated and which remain censured, government agencies decide which official interpretations of social reality prevail (Van Dijk 1993). The inordinate attention paid to Black adolescent pregnancy and parenting in scholarly research and the kinds of public policy initiatives that target Black girls illustrate the significance of government support for controlling images. Because assumptions of sexual hedonism are routinely applied to Black urban girls, they are more likely to be offered coercive birth control measures, such as Norplant and Depo Provera than their White, suburban, middle-class counterparts (Roberts 1997).

Confronting the controlling images forwarded by institutions external to African-American communities remains essential. But such efforts should not obscure the equally important issue of examining how African-American institutions also perpetuate these same controlling images. Although it may be painful to examine—especially in the context of a racially charged society always vigilant for signs of Black disunity—the question of how the organizations of Black civil society reproduce controlling images of Black womanhood and fail to take a stand against images developed elsewhere is equally important.

Since 1970, U.S. Black women have become increasingly vocal in criticizing sexism in Black civil society (Wallace 1978; E.F. White 1984; Cleage 1993; Crenshaw 1993). For example, Black feminist Pauline Terrelonge confronts the issue of the Black community's role in the subordination of African-American women by asking, "If there is much in the objective condition of black women that warrants the development of a black feminist consciousness, why have so many black women failed to recognize the patterns of sexism that directly impinge on their everyday lives?" (1984, 562). To answer this question, Terrelonge contends that a common view is that African-Americans have withstood the long line of abuses perpetuated against us mainly because of Black women's "fortitude, inner wisdom, and sheer ability to survive." Connected to this emphasis on the strength of Black women is the related argument that African-American women play critical roles in keeping Black families together and in supporting Black men. These activities have been important in preventing the potential annihilation of African-Americans as a "race." As a result, "many blacks regard the role of uniting all blacks to be the primary duty of the black woman, one that should supersede all other roles that she might want to perform, and certainly one that is essentially incompatible with her own individual liberation" (p. 557).

This analysis shifts our understanding of Black community organizations. Rather than seeing family, church, and Black civic organizations through a race-only lens of resisting racism, such institutions may be better understood as complex sites where dominant ideologies are simultaneously resisted and reproduced. Black community organizations can oppose racial oppression yet perpetuate gender oppression, can challenge class exploitation yet foster heterosexism. One might ask where within Black civil society African-American women can openly challenge the hoochie image and other equally controlling images. Institutions controlled by African-Americans can be seen as contradictory sites where Black women learn skills of independence and self-reliance that enable African-American families, churches, and civic organizations to endure. But these same institutions may also be places where Black women learn to subordinate our interests as women to the allegedly greater good of the larger African-American community.

Take, for example, historically Black colleges and universities. In their goal of dispelling the myths about African-American women and making Black women acceptable to wider society, some historically Black colleges may also foster Black women's subordination. In *Meridian* Alice Walker describes an elite college for Black women where "most of the students—timid, imitative, bright enough but never daring, were being ushered nearer to Ladyhood every day" (1976, 39). Confined to campus, Meridian, the heroine, had to leave to find the ordinary Black people who exhibited all of the qualities that her elite institution wished to eliminate. Walker's description of the fence surrounding the campus symbolizes how stultifying the cult of true womanhood was for Black students. But it also describes the problems that African-American institutions create for Black women when they embrace externally defined controlling images:

> The fence that surrounded the campus was hardly noticeable from the street and appeared, from the outside, to be more of an attempt at ornamentation than an effort to contain or exclude. Only the students who lived on campus learned, often painfully, that the beauty of a fence is no guarantee that it will not keep one penned in as securely as one that is ugly. (Walker 1976, 41)

Jacquelyn Grant (1982) identifies the church as one key institution whose centrality to Black community development may have come at the expense of many of the African-American women who constitute the bulk of its membership. Grant asserts, "it is often said that women are the 'backbone' of the church. On the surface, this may appear to be a compliment. ... It has become apparent to me that most of the ministers who use this term are referring to location rather than function. What they really mean is that women are in the 'background' and should be kept there" (1982, 141). At the same time, Black churches have clearly been highly significant in Black political struggle, with U.S. Black women central to those efforts. Historically, Black women's participation in Black Baptist and other Black churches suggests that Black women have been the backbone yet have resisted staying totally in the "background" (Gilkes 1985; Higginbotham 1983). One wonders, however, if contemporary Black churches are equipped to grapple with the new questions raised by the global circulation of the hoochie and comparable images. Denouncing "hoochies" and all they represent from the pulpit with a cautionary warning "don't be one" simply is not enough.

African-American families form another contradictory location where the controlling images of Black womanhood become negotiated. Middle-class White feminists seemingly have had few qualms in criticizing how their families perpetuate women's subordination (see, for example, Chodorow 1978). Until recently, however, because Black families have been so pathologized by the traditional family ideal, Black women have been reluctant to analyze in public the potential culpability of families in Black women's oppression. Black women thinkers have been more uniformly positive when describing Black families, and much more reluctant to criticize Black family organization than their White counterparts. As a result, Black studies emphasizes material that, although it quite rightly demonstrates the strengths of U.S. Black families in a context of intersecting oppressions, skims over problems (see, e.g., Billingsley 1992). But this emphasis on strengths has often come at a cost, and that cost has far too often been paid by African-American women. Thus, within Black feminist scholarship, we are finally hearing not only the long-hidden stories of those strong Black women (Joseph 1981; Collins 1986), but those of women whose gendered family responsibilities cause them trouble (Richie 1996; Kaplan 1997).

Some Black feminist activists claim that relegating Black women to more submissive, supporting roles in African-American organizations has been an obstacle to Black political empowerment. Black nationalist philosophies, in particular, have come under attack for their ideas about Black women's place in political struggle (White 1990; Lubiano 1997; Williams 1997; Collins 1998, 155–86). In describing the 1960s nationalist movement, Pauli Murray contends that many Black men misinterpreted Black women's qualities of self-reliance and independence by tacitly accepting the matriarchy thesis. Such a stance was and is highly problematic for Black women. Murray observes, "The black militant's cry for the retrieval of black manhood suggests an acceptance of this stereotype, an association of masculinity with male dominance and a tendency to treat the values of self-reliance and independence as purely masculine traits" (1970, 89). Echoing Murray, Sheila Radford-Hill (1986) sees Black women's subordination in African-American institutions as a continuing concern. For Radford-Hill the erosion of Black women's traditional power bases in African-American communities which followed nationalist movements is problematic in that "Black macho constituted a betrayal by black men; a psychosexual rejection of black women experienced as the capstone to our fall from cultural power. ... Without the power to influence the purpose and direction of our collective experience, without the power to influence our culture from within, we are increasingly immobilized" (p. 168).

Color, Hair Texture, and Standards of Beauty

Like everyone else, African-American women come to understand the workings of intersecting oppressions without obvious teaching or conscious learning. The controlling images of Black women are not simply grafted onto existing social institutions but are so pervasive that even though the images themselves change in the popular imagination, Black women's portrayal as the Other persists. Particular meanings, stereotypes, and myths can change, but the overall ideology of domination itself seems to be an enduring feature of intersecting oppressions (Omi and Winant 1994).

African-American women encounter this ideology through a range of unquestioned daily experiences. But when the contradictions between Black women's self-definitions and everyday treatment are heightened, controlling images become increasingly visible. Karen Russell, the daughter of basketball great Bill Russell, describes how racial stereotypes affect her:

How am I supposed to react to well-meaning, good, liberal white people who say things like: "You know, Karen, I don't understand what all the fuss is about. You're one of my good friends, and I never think of you as black." Implicit in such a remark is, "I think of you as white," or perhaps just, "I don't think of your race at all." (Russell 1987, 22)

Ms. Russell was perceptive enough to see that remarks intended to compliment her actually insulted African-Americans. As the Others, U.S. Blacks are assigned all of the negative characteristics opposite and inferior to those reserved for Whites. By claiming that Ms. Russell is not really "black," her friends unintentionally validate this system of racial meanings and encourage her to internalize those images.

Although most Black women typically resist being objectified as the Other, these controlling images remain powerful influences on our relationships with Whites, Black men, other racial/ethnic groups, and one another. Dealing with prevailing standards of beauty—particularly skin color, facial features, and hair texture—is one specific example of how controlling images derogate African-American women. A children's rhyme often sung in Black communities proclaims:

Now, if you're white you're all right,
If you're brown, stick around,
But if you're black, Git back! Git back! Git back!

Prevailing standards of beauty claim that no matter how intelligent, educated, or "beautiful" a Black woman may be, those Black women whose features and skin color are most African must "git back." Within the binary thinking that underpins intersecting oppressions, blue-eyed, blonde, thin White women could not be considered beautiful without the Other—Black women with African features of dark skin, broad noses, full lips, and kinky hair.

Race, gender, and sexuality converge on this issue of evaluating beauty. Black men's blackness penalizes them. But because they are not women, valuations of their self-worth do not depend as heavily on their physical attractiveness. In contrast, part of the objectification of all women lies in evaluating how they look. Within binary thinking, White and Black women as collectivities represent two opposing poles, with Latinas, Asian-American women, and Native American women jockeying for positions in between. Judging White women by their physical appearance and attractiveness to men objectifies them. But their White skin and straight hair simultaneously privilege them in a system that elevates whiteness over blackness. In contrast, African-American women experience the pain of never being able to live up to prevailing standards of beauty—standards used by White men, White women, Black men, and, most painfully, one another. Regardless of any individual woman's subjective reality, this is the system of ideas that she encounters. Because controlling images are hegemonic and taken for granted, they become virtually impossible to escape.

In her Preface to *Skin Deep: Women Writing on Color, Culture and Identity*, editor Elena Featherstone suggests that contrary to popular belief, "issues of race and color are *not* as simple as Black and white—or Red, Yellow, or Brown and white" (1994, vi). Featherstone is right, and volumes such as hers remain necessary. Yet at the same time, colorism in the U.S. context operates the way that it does because it is deeply embedded in a distinctly American form of racism grounded in Black/White oppositional differences. Other groups "of color" must negotiate the meanings attached to their "color." All must position themselves within a continually renegotiated color hierarchy where, because they define the top and the bottom, the meanings attached to Whiteness and Blackness change much less than we think. Linked in symbiotic relationship, White and Black gain meaning only in relation to one another. However well-meaning conversations among "women of color" concerning the meaning of color in the United States may be, such conversations require an analysis of how institutionalized racism produces color hierarchies among U.S. women. Without this attention to domination, such conversations can work to flatten bona fide differences in power among White women, Latinas, Asian-American women, Native women, and Black women. Even Featherstone recognizes the fact of Blackness, by pointing out, "color is the ultimate test of 'American-ness,' and black is the most un-American color of all" (1994, iii).

Since U.S. Black women have been most uniformly harmed by the colorism that is a by-product of U.S. racism, it is important to explore how prevailing standards of beauty affect U.S. Black women's treatment in everyday life. The long-standing attention of musicians, writers, and artists to this theme reveals African-American women's conflicted feelings concerning skin color, hair texture, and standards of beauty. In her autobiography, Maya Angelou records her painful realization that the only way she could become truly beautiful was to become white:

> Wouldn't they be surprised when one day I woke out of my black ugly dream, and my real hair, which was long and blond, would take the place of the kinky mass that Momma wouldn't let me straighten? … Then they would understand why I had never picked up a Southern accent, or spoke the common slang, and why I had to be forced to eat pigs' tails and snouts. Because I was really white and because a cruel fairy stepmother … had turned me into a too-big Negro girl, with nappy black hair. (Angelou 1969, 2)

Gwendolyn Brooks also explores the meaning of skin color and hair texture for U.S. Black women. During Brooks's childhood, having African features was so universally denigrated that she writes, "when I was a child, it did not occur to me even once, that the black in which I was encased … would be considered, one day, beautiful" (Brooks 1972, 37). Early on, Brooks learned that a clear pecking order existed among African-Americans, one based on one's closeness to Whiteness. As a member of the "Lesser Blacks," those furthest from White, Brooks saw firsthand the difference in treatment of her group and that of the "Brights":

> One of the first "world" truths revealed to me when I at last became a member of SCHOOL was that, to be socially successful, a little girl must be Bright (of skin). It was better if your hair was curly, too—or at least Good Grade (Good Grade implied, usually, no involvement with the Hot Comb)—but Bright you marvelously *needed* to be. (1972, 37)

This division of African-Americans into two categories—the "Brights" and the "Lesser Blacks"—affects dark-skinned and light-skinned women differently. Darker women face being judged inferior and receiving the treatment afforded "too-big Negro girls with nappy hair." Institutions controlled by Whites clearly show a preference for lighter-skinned Blacks, discriminating against darker ones or against any African-Americans who appear to reject White images of beauty. Sonia Sanchez reports, "Sisters tell me … that when they go out for jobs they straighten their hair because if they go in with their hair natural or braided, they probably won't get the job" (Tate 1983, 141).

Sometimes the pain most deeply felt is the pain that Black women inflict on one another. Marita Golden's mother told her not to play in the sun because "you gonna have to get a light husband anyway, for the sake of your children" (1983, 24). In *Color*, a short film exploring the impact of skin color on Black women's lives, the dark-skinned character's mother tries to get her to sit still for the hot comb, asking "don't you want your hair flowing like your friend Rebecca's?" We see the sadness of a young Black girl sitting in a kitchen, holding her ears so they won't get burned by the hot comb that will straighten her hair. Her mother cannot make her beautiful, only "presentable" for church. Marita Golden's description of a Black beauty salon depicts the internalized oppression that some African-American women feel about African features:

> Between customers, twirling in her chair, white-stockinged legs crossed, my beautician lamented to the hairdresser in the next stall, "I sure hope that Gloria Johnson don't come in here asking for me today. I swear 'fore God her hair is this long." She snapped her fingers to indicate the length. Contempt riding her words, she lit a cigarette and finished, "Barely enough to wash, let alone press and curl." (Golden 1983, 25)

African-American women who are members of the "Brights" fare little better, for they too receive special treatment because of their skin color and hair texture. Harriet Jacobs, an enslaved light-skinned woman, was sexually harassed because of her looks. Her straight hair and fair skin, her appearance as a dusky White woman, made her physically attractive to White men. But the fact that she was Black made her available to White men as no group of White women had been. In describing this situation, Jacobs notes, "if God has bestowed beauty upon her, it will prove her greatest curse. That which commands admiration in the white woman only hastens the degradation of the female slave" (Washington 1987, 17).

This different valuation and treatment of dark-skinned and light-skinned Black women influences the relationships among African-American women. Toni Morrison's (1970) novel *The Bluest Eye* explores this theme of the tension that can exist among Black women grappling with the meaning of prevailing standards of beauty. Frieda, a dark-skinned, "ordinary" Black girl, struggles with the meaning of these standards. She wonders why adults always got so upset when she rejected the White dolls they gave her and why light-skinned Maureen Peal, a child her own age whose two braids hung like "lynch-ropes down her back," got the love and attention of teachers, adults, and Black boys alike. Morrison explores Frieda's attempt not to blame Maureen for the benefits her light skin and long hair afforded her as part of Frieda's growing realization that the "Thing" to fear was not Maureen herself but the "Thing" that made Maureen beautiful.

Gwendolyn Brooks (1953) captures the anger and frustration experienced by dark-skinned women in dealing with the differential treatment they and their lighter-skinned sisters receive. In her novel *Maud Martha*, the dark-skinned heroine ponders actions she could take against a red-headed Black woman whom her husband found so attractive. "I could," considered Maud Martha, "go over there and scratch her upsweep down. I could spit on her back. I could scream. 'Listen,' I could scream, 'I'm making a baby for this man and I mean to do it in peace'" (Washington 1987, 422). But Maud Martha rejects these actions, reasoning, "If the root was sour what business did she have up there hacking at a leaf?"

This "sour root" also creates issues in relationships between African-American women and men. Maud Martha explains:

> It's my color that makes him mad. I try to shut my eyes to that, but it's no good. What I am inside, what is really me, he likes okay. But he keeps looking at my color, which is like a wall. He has to jump over it in order to meet and touch what I've got for him. He has to jump away up high in order to see it. He gets awful tired of all that jumping. (Washington 1987, 421)

Her husband's attraction to light-skinned women hurt Maud Martha because his inability to "jump away up high" over the wall of color limited his ability to see her for who she truly was.

Black Women's Reactions to Controlling Images

In *Their Eyes Were Watching God*, Nanny eloquently expresses her perspective on Black womanhood: "Ah was born back in slavery so it wasn't for me to fulfill my dream of whut a woman oughta be and do. But nothing can't stop you from wishin! You can't beat nobody down so low till you can rob 'em of they will. Ah didn't want to be used for a work-ox and a brood-sow and Ah didn't want mah daughter used dat way neither" (Hurston 1937, 17). Like many African-American women, she resisted the controlling images of "work-ox" and "brood-sow," but her status as a slave prevented her fulfilling her "dreams of whut a woman oughta be and do." She saw the constraints on her own life but managed to keep the will to resist alive. Moreover, she tried to pass on that vision of freedom from controlling images to her granddaughter.

Given the ubiquitous nature of controlling images, it should not be surprising that exploring how Black women construct social realities is a recurring theme in Black feminist thought. Overall, despite the pervasiveness of controlling images, African-American women as a group have resisted these ideological justifications for our oppression (Holloway 1995). Unlike White women who "face the pitfall of being seduced into joining the oppressor under the pretense of sharing power," and for whom "there is a wider range of pretended choices and rewards for identifying with patriarchal power and its tools," Black women are offered fewer possibilities (Lorde 1984, 117–18). In this context, individual women and subgroups of women within the larger collectivity of U.S. Black women have demonstrated diverse reactions to their treatment. Understanding the contours of this heterogeneity generally, and how U.S. Black women can be better equipped to resist this negative treatment, constitutes one important task for U.S. Black feminist thought.

Historically, literature by U.S. Black women writers provides one comprehensive view of Black women's struggles to form positive self-definitions in the face of derogated images of Black womanhood. Portraying the range of ways that African-American women experience internalized oppression has been a prominent theme in Black women's writing. Mary Helen Washington's (1982) discussion of the theme of the suspended woman in Black women's literature describes one dimension of Black women's internalized oppression. Pain, violence, and death form the essential content of these women's lives. They are suspended in time and place; their life choices are so severely limited that the women themselves are often destroyed. Pecola Breedlove, an unloved, "ugly" 11-year-old Black girl in Toni Morrison's novel *The Bluest Eye* (1970), internalizes the negative images of African-American women and believes that the absence of blue eyes is central to her "ugliness." Pecola cannot value her Blackness—she longs to be White so that she can escape the pain of being Black, female, poor, and a child. Her mother, Pauline Breedlove, typifies the internalization of the mammy image. Pauline Breedlove neglects her own children, preferring to lavish her concern and attention on the White charges in her care. Only by accepting this subordinate role to White children could she, as a poor Black woman, see a positive place for herself.

U.S. Black women writers have chronicled other forms of Black women's attempts to escape from a world predicated upon derogated images of Black womanhood. Fictional African-American women characters use drugs, alcohol, excessive religion, and even retreat into madness in an attempt to create other worlds apart from the ones that produced such painful Black female realities. Pauline Breedlove in *The Bluest Eye* and Mrs. Hill in *Meridian* (Walker 1976) both demonstrate an attachment to religion that allows them to ignore their daughters. Eva Medina in Gayl Jones's *Eva's Man* (1976), Merle Kibona in Paule Marshall's *The Chosen Place, the Timeless People* (1969), and Velma Henry in Toni Cade Bambara's *The Salt Eaters* (1980) all experience madness as an escape from pain.

Denial is another characteristic response to the controlling images of Black womanhood and their accompanying conditions. By claiming that they are not like the rest, some African-American women reject connections to other Black women and demand special treatment for themselves. Mary Helen Washington (1982) refers to these characters as assimilated women. They are more aware of their condition than are suspended women, but despite their greater potential for shaping their lives, they still feel thwarted because they see themselves as misplaced by time and circumstances. Light-skinned, middle-class Cleo, a key figure in Dorothy West's novel *The Living Is Easy* (1948), typifies this response. In one scene strong-willed Cleo hustles her daughter past a playground filled with the children of newly arrived Southern Blacks, observing that "she wouldn't want her child to go to school with those niggers." Cleo clings to her social class position, one that she sees as separating her from other African-Americans, and tries to muffle the negative status attached to her Blackness by emphasizing her superior class position. Even though Cleo is more acceptable to the White world, the price she pays for her acceptance is the negation of her racial identity and separation from the sustenance that such an identity might offer.

U.S. Black women writers not only portray the range of responses that individual African-American women express concerning their objectification as the Other: they also document the process of personal growth toward positive self-definitions. The personal growth experienced by Renay, the heroine in Ann Allen Shockley's *Loving Her* (1974), illustrates the process of rejecting externally defined controlling images of Black womanhood. Shockley initially presents Renay as a suspended woman who is trapped in a heterosexual marriage to an abusive husband and who tries to deny her feelings for other women. Renay retreats into music and alcohol as temporary spaces where she can escape having her difference—in this case, her Blackness and lesbianism—judged as inferior and deviant. After taking a White woman lover, Renay is initially quite happy, but she grows to realize that she has replaced one set of controlling images—namely, those she experienced with her abusive husband—with another. She leaves her lover to pursue her own self-definition. By the novel's end Renay has begun to resist all external definitions of herself that stem from controlling images applied to Blacks, women, and lesbians.

Renay's experiences typify how Black women writers explore the theme of Black women's resistance to these controlling images, a resistance typified by the emergent woman in Black women's literature. Sherley Anne Williams's novel *Dessa Rose* (1986) describes a Black slave woman's emerging sense of power after she participates in a slave revolt, runs away, and eventually secures her own freedom. Dorine

Davis, the heroine in Rosa Guy's *A Measure of Time* (1983), is raped at age 10 by her White employer, subsequently sleeps with men for money, yet retains a core of resistance. Bad things happen to Dorine, but Guy does not portray Dorine as a victim. In *The Bluest Eye* (1970), Toni Morrison presents the character of Claudia, a 10-year-old Black girl who, to the chagrin of grown-ups, destroys White dolls by tearing off their heads and who refuses to share her classmates' admiration of light-skinned, long-haired Maureen Peal. Claudia's growing awareness of the "Thing that made her [Maureen Peal] beautiful and us ugly" and her rejection of that Thing—racist images of Black women—represents yet another reaction to negative images of Black womanhood. Like Merle Kibona in Paule Marshall's *The Chosen Place, the Timeless People*, Vyry in Margaret Walker's *Jubilee* (1966), Janie Crawford in Zora Neale Hurston's *Their Eyes Were Watching God* (1937), or Meridian in Alice Walker's *Meridian* (1976), Claudia represents a young version of emergent Black women carving out new definitions of Black womanhood.

Independent Black women heroines populate U.S. Black women's fiction of the 1990s. Many of these Black female fictional characters express varying dimensions of the emergent woman thesis. Just as social class differences have become more prominent in Black women's controlling images overall, images of emergent women in Black women's literature also reflect social class diversity. Working-class women become emergent women by overcoming an array of hardships, many of them financial, that aim to keep them down. In Barbara Neely's novel *Blanche on the Lam* (1992) Blanche evades the law by hiding out as a domestic worker for a rich White family. Another working-class heroine is Valerie Wilson's fictional detective Tamara Hale. A single mother of a teenage son, Hale juggles issues of financial well-being and raising her son in the Newark metropolitan area. Interestingly, in both Neely and Wilson's fiction, working-class women spend little time bemoaning their unmarried, uncoupled status. Neither fictional heroine agonizes over the absence of a Black male husband or lover in their lives. In contrast, middle-class Black women become emergent women by changing their expectations about their femininity and Black men's expectations. Terry McMillan's two volumes, *Waiting to Exhale* (1992) and *How Stella Got Her Groove Back* (1996), can be read as companion pieces that advise Black middle-class women how to emerge. In *Waiting to Exhale*, four Black women friends struggle with issues of having satisfying relationships with Black men. By the end of the book, two of the women have found meaningful relationships with men. More importantly, what they have all learned is that their friendship with one another is as important as their ties to men. In McMillan's subsequent volume, Stella, a Black single mother who is a highly paid, successful professional, takes a trip to Jamaica by herself and meets Winston, a much younger man. By the end of the volume, Stella has shed the limitations of distinctly American controlling images, and decides that true love transcends differences of age and nationality. Whereas racism, sexism, and class exploitation do not preoccupy the emergent women created by Neely, Wilson, and McMillan, the social contexts in which these authors embed their characters are clearly structured by these oppressions.

The many documentaries and feature films where Black women appear as central characters constitute another arena where emergent Black women appear. Not only could Black women read about emergent Black women in Terry McMillan's fiction, audiences could view images of Black women trying to "exhale" and "get their groove" on the big screen. This theme of U.S. Black women coming to know themselves, and often doing so in company of other Black women, wove throughout a cluster of films whose subject matter differed dramatically. Feature films made by Black women directors, such as Julie Dash's *Daughters of the Dust*, Michelle Parkerson's *Gotta Make This Journey: Sweet Honey in the Rock*, and Ayoka Chenzira's *Alma's Rainbow* all illustrate the value Black women filmmakers place on Black women's emerging self-definitions.

Emergent women may have only recently made their appearance in Black women's fiction and film, but such women have long populated everyday lived experience. In her autobiography, Lorene Cary, a working-class African-American woman who helped desegregate a prestigious New England boarding school, tells of what happens when everyday Black women decide to "turn it out":

> My mother, and her mother, who had worked in a factory, and her mother, who had cleaned apartments in Manhattan, had been studying these people all their lives. … And I had studied them. I had studied my mother as she turned out elementary schools and department stores. I always saw it coming. Some white department-store manager would look at my mother and see no more than a modestly dressed young black woman making a tiresome complaint. He'd use that tone of voice they used when they had important work elsewhere. Uh-oh. Then he'd dismiss her with his eyes. I'd feel her body stiffen next to me, and I'd know that he'd set her off. And then it began in earnest, the turning out. She never moved back. It didn't matter how many people were in line. … Turning out, I learned, was not a matter of style; cold indignation worked as well as hot fury. Turning out had to do with will. (Cary 1991, 58–59)

Emergent women have found that one way of surviving the everyday disrespect and outright assaults that accompany controlling images is to "turn it out." This is the moment when silence becomes speech, when stillness becomes action. As Karla Holloway says, "no one wins in that situation, but usually we feel better" (1995, 31).

Notes

1. Donna Richards (1980) offers an insightful analysis of the relationship between Christianity's contributions to an ideology of domination and the culture/nature binary. She notes that European Christianity is predicated on a worldview that sustains the exploitation of nature: "Christian thought provides a view of man, nature, and the universe which supports not only the ascendancy of science, but of the technical order, individualism, and relentless progress. Emphasis within this worldview is placed on humanity's dominance over *all* other beings, which become 'objects' in an 'objectified' universe. There is no emphasis on an awe-inspiring God or cosmos. Being 'made in God's image,' given the European ethos, translates into 'acting *as* God,' recreating the universe. Humanity is separated from nature" (p. 69). For works exploring the connections among Western thought, colonialism, and capitalism, see works by Marianna Torgovnick (1990), Rey Chow (1993), Edward Said (1993), and Anna McClintock (1995).

2. Brittan and Maynard (1984) note that ideology (1) is common sense and obvious; (2) appears natural, inevitable, and universal, (3) shapes lived experience and behavior; (4) is sedimented in people's consciousness; and (5) consists of a system of ideas embedded in the social system as a whole. This example captures all dimensions of how racism and sexism function ideologically. The status of Black woman as servant is so "common sense" that even a child knows it. That the child saw a Black female child as a baby maid speaks to the naturalization dimension and to the persistence of controlling images in individual consciousness and the social system overall.

References

Amott, Teresa L. 1990. "Black Women and AFDC: Making Entitlement Out of Necessity." In *Women, the State, and Welfare*, ed. Linda Gordon, 280–98. Madison: University of Wisconsin Press.

Angelou, Maya. 1969. *I Know Why the Caged Bird Sings*. New York: Bantam.

Bambara, Toni Cade. 1980. *The Salt Eaters*. New York: Vintage.

Bannerji, Himani. 1995. *Thinking Through: Essays on Feminism, Marxism, and Anti-Racism*. Toronto: Women's Press.

Billingsley, Andrew. 1992. *Black Families in White America*. Englewood Cliffs, NJ: Prentice Hall.

Brewer, Rose. 1988. "Black Women in Poverty: Some Comments on Female-Headed Families." *Signs* 13 (2): 331–39.

Brewer, Rose. 1993. "Theorizing Race, Class and Gender: The New Scholarship of Black Feminist Intellectuals and Black Women's Labor." In *Theorizing Black Feminisms: The Visionary Pragmatism of Black Women*, ed. Stanlie M. James and Abena P.A. Busia, 13–30. New York: Routledge.

Brittan, Arthur, and Mary Maynard. 1984. *Sexism, Racism and Oppression*. New York: Basil Blackwell.

Brooks, Gwendolyn. 1953. *Maud Martha*. Boston: Atlantic Press.

Brooks, Gwendolyn. 1972. *Report from Part One: The Autobiography of Gwendolyn Brooks*. Detroit: Broadside Press.

Byerly, Victoria. 1986. *Hard Times Cotton Mills Girls*. Ithaca, NY: Cornell University Press.

Carby, Hazel. 1987. *Reconstructing Womanhood: The Emergence of the Afro-American Woman Novelist*. New York: Oxford University Press.

Cary, Lorene. 1991. *Black Ice*. New York: Knopf.

Chodorow, Nancy. 1978. *The Reproduction of Mothering*. Berkeley: University of California Press.

Chow, Rey. 1993. *Writing Diaspora: Tactics of Intervention in Contemporary Cultural Studies*. Bloomington: Indiana University Press.

Christian, Barbara. 1985. *Black Feminist Criticism, Perspectives on Black Women Writers*. New York: Pergamon.

Clarke, Cheryl, Jewell L. Gomez, Evelyn Hammonds, Bonnie Johnson, and Linda Powell. 1983. "Conversations and Questions: Black Women on Black Women Writers." *Conditions: Nine* 3 (3): 88–137.

Cleage, Pearl. 1993. *Deals With the Devil and Other Reasons to Riot*. New York: Ballantine.

Collins, Patricia Hill. 1986. "Learning from the Outsider Within: The Sociological Significance of Black Feminist Thought." *Social Problems* 33 (6): 14–32.

Collins, Patricia Hill. 1989. "A Comparison of Two Works on Black Family Life." *Signs* 14 (4): 875–84.

Collins, Patricia Hill. 1998. *Fighting Words: Black Women and the Search for Justice*. Minneapolis: University of Minnesota Press.

Crenshaw, Kimberle Williams. 1993. "Beyond Racism and Misogyny: Black Feminism and 2 Live Crew." In *Words That Wound: Critical Race Theory, Assaultive Speech, and the First Amendment*, ed. Mari J. Matsuda, Charles R. Lawrence III, Richard Delgado, and Kimberle Crenshaw, 111–32. Boulder: Westview.

Davis, Angela Y. 1981. *Women, Race and Class*. New York: Random House.

Davis, Angela Y. 1997. "Race and Criminalization: Black Americans and the Punishment Industry." In *The House That Race Built*, ed. Wahneema Lubiano, 264–79. New York: Pantheon.

Dickerson, Bette J., ed. 1995. *African American Single Mothers: Understanding Their Lives and Families*. Thousand Oaks, CA: Sage.

Dill, Bonnie Thornton. 1980. "'The Means to Put My Children Through': Child-Rearing Goals and Strategies among Black Female Domestic Servants." In *The Black Woman*, ed. La Frances Rodgers-Rose, 107–23. Beverly Hills, CA: Sage.

Dill, Bonnie Thornton. 1988. "Our Mothers' Grief: Racial Ethnic Women and the Maintenance of Families." *Journal of Family History* 13 (4): 415–31.

Du Bois, William E. B. 1969. *The Negro American Family*. New York: Negro Universities Press.

Dumas, Rhetaugh Graves. 1980. "Dilemmas of Black Females in Leadership." In *The Black Woman*, ed. La Frances Rodgers-Rose, 203–15. Beverly Hills, CA: Sage.

Featherstone, Elena, ed. 1994. *Skin Deep: Women Writing on Color, Culture and Identity*. Freedom, CA: The Crossing Press.

Frazier, E. Franklin. 1948. *The Negro Family in the United States*. New York: Dryden.

Gilkes, Cheryl Townsend. 1983. "From Slavery to Social Welfare: Racism and the Control of Black Women." In *Class, Race, and Sex: The Dynamics of Control*, ed. Amy Swerdlow and Hanna Lessinger, 288–300. Boston: G. K. Hall.

Gilkes, Cheryl Townsend. 1985. "'Together and in Harness': Women's Traditions in the Sanctified Church." *Signs* 10 (4): 678–99.

Golden, Marita. 1983. *Migrations of the Heart*. New York: Ballantine.

Grant, Jacquelyn. 1982. "Black Women and the Church." In *But Some of Us Are Brave*, ed. Gloria T. Hull, Patricia Bell Scott, and Barbara Smith, 141–52. Old Westbury, NY: Feminist Press.

Guy, Rosa. 1983. *A Measure of Time*. New York: Bantam.

Gwaltney, John Langston. 1980. *Drylongso, A Self Portrait of Black America*. New York: Vintage.

Halpin, Zuleyma Tang. 1989. "Scientific Objectivity and the Concept of 'The Other.'" *Women's Studies International Forum* 12 (3): 285–94.

Hansberry, Lorraine. 1959. *A Raisin in the Sun*. New York: Signet.

Harris, Trudier. 1982. *From Mammies to Militants: Domestics in Black American Literature*. Philadelphia: Temple University Press.

Higginbotham, Elizabeth. 1983. "Laid Bare by the System: Work and Survival for Black and Hispanic Women." In *Class, Race, and Sex: The Dynamics of Control*, ed. Amy Swerdlow and Hanna Lessinger, 200–15. Boston: G. K. Hall.

Holloway, Karla. 1995. "The Body Politic." In *Codes of Conduct: Race, Ethics, and the Color of Our Character*, 15–71. New Brunswick: Rutgers University Press.

hooks, bell. 1989. *Talking Back: Thinking Feminist, Thinking Black*. Boston: South End Press.

Hurston, Zora Neale. [1937] 1969. *Their Eyes Were Watching God*. Greenwich, CT: Fawcett.

Jarrett, Robin. 1994. "Living Poor: Family Life Among Single Parent, African American Women." *Social Problems* 41 (February): 30–49.

Jones, Gayl. 1976. *Eva's Man*. Boston: Beacon.

Joseph, Gloria. 1981. "Black Mothers and Daughters: Their Roles and Functions in American Society." In *Common Differences*, ed. Gloria Joseph and Jill Lewis, 75–126. Garden City, NY: Anchor.

Kaplan, Elaine Bell. 1997. *Not Our Kind of Girl: Unraveling the Myths of Black Teenage Motherhood*. Berkeley, CA: University of California Press.

Keller, Evelyn Fox. 1985. *Reflections on Gender and Science*. New Haven, CT: Yale University Press.

Kelley, Robin D. G. 1997. *Yo Mama's Disfunktional: Fighting the Culture Wars in Urban America*. Boston: Beacon.

King, Mae. 1973. "The Politics of Sexual Stereotypes." *Black Scholar* 4 (6-7): 12–23.

Ladner, Joyce. 1972. *Tomorrow's Tomorrow*. Garden City, NY: Doubleday.

Lorde, Audre. 1984. *Sister Outsider*. Trumansberg, NY: Crossing Press.

Lubiano, Wahneema. 1992. "Black Ladies, Welfare Queens, and State Minstrels: Ideological War by Narrative Means." In *Race-ing Justice, En-Gendering Power*, ed. Toni Morrison, 323–63. New York: Pantheon.

Lubiano, Wahneema. 1997. "Black Nationalism and Black Common Sense: Policing Ourselves." In *The House That Race Built: Black Americans, U.S. Terrain*, ed. Wahneema Lubiano, 232–52. New York: Pantheon.

Marshall, Paule. 1959. *Brown Girl, Brownstones*. New York: Avon.

Marshall, Paule. 1969. *The Chosen Place, the Timeless People*. New York: Vintage.

McClintock, Anne. 1995. *Imperial Leather: Race, Gender and Sexuality in the Colonial Conquest*. New York: Routledge.

McMillan, Terry. 1992. *Waiting to Exhale*. New York: Viking.

McMillan, Terry. 1996. *How Stella Got Her Groove Back*. New York: Viking.

Morrison, Toni. 1970. *The Bluest Eye*. New York: Pocket Books.

Morton, Patricia. 1991. *Disfigured Images: The Historical Assault on Afro-American Women*. New York: Praeger.

Moynihan, Daniel Patrick. 1965. *The Negro Family: The Case for National Action*. Washington, D.C.: Government Printing Office.

Mullings, Leith. 1997. *On Our Own Terms: Race, Class, and Gender in the Lives of African American Women*. New York: Routledge.

Murray, Pauli. 1970. "The Liberation of Black Women." In *Voices of the New Feminism*, ed. Mary Lou Thompson, 87–102. Boston: Beacon.

Myers, Lena Wright. 1980. *Black Women: Do They Cope Better?* Englewood Cliffs, NJ: Prentice-Hall.

Nash, June, and Maria Patricia Fernandez-Kelly, eds. 1983. *Women, Men and the International Division of Labor*. Albany: State University of New York.

Neely, Barbara. 1992. *Blanche on the Lam*. New York: Penguin.

Omi, Michael, and Howard Winant. 1994. *Racial Formation in the United States: From the 1960s to the 1990s, Second Edition*. New York: Routledge.

Omolade, Barbara. 1994. *The Rising Song of African American Women*. New York: Routledge.

Quadagno, Jill. 1994. *The Color of Welfare: How Racism Undermined the War on Poverty*. New York: Oxford University Press.

Radford-Hill, Sheila. 1986. "Considering Feminism as a Model for Social Change." In *Feminist Studies/Critical Studies*, ed. Teresa de Lauretis, 157–72. Bloomington: Indiana University Press.

Richards, Dona. 1980. "European Mythology: The Ideology of 'Progress.'" In *Contemporary Black Thought*, ed. Molefi Kete Asante and Abdulai S. Vandi, 59–79. Beverly Hills, CA: Sage.

Richie, Beth E. 1996. *Compelled to Crime: The Gender Entrapment of Battered Black Women*. New York: Routledge.

Roberts, Dorothy. 1997. *Killing the Black Body: Race, Reproduction, and the Meaning of Liberty*. New York: Pantheon.

Rollins, Judith. 1985. *Between Women, Domestics and Their Employers*. Philadelphia: Temple University Press.

Rose, Tricia. 1994. *Black Noise: Rap Music and Black Culture in Contemporary America*. Hanover, NH: Wesleyan University Press.

Russell, Karen K. 1987. "Growing Up with Privilege and Prejudice." *New York Times Magazine*, June 14, 22–28.

Said, Edward W. 1993. *Culture and Imperialism*. New York: Knopf.

Shaw, Stephanie J. 1996. *What a Woman Ought to Be and to Do: Black Professional Women Workers During the Jim Crow Era*. Chicago: University of Chicago Press.

Shockley, Ann Allen. 1974. *Loving Her*. Tallahassee, FL: Naiad Press.

Squires, Gregory D. 1994. *Capital and Communities in Black and White: The Intersections of Race, Class, and Uneven Development*. Albany: State University of New York Press.

Sudarkasa, Niara. 1981. "Interpreting the African Heritage in Afro-American Family Organization." In *Black Families*, ed. Harriette Pipes McAdoo, 37–53. Beverly Hills, CA: Sage.

Tate, Claudia, ed. 1983. *Black Women Writers at Work*. New York: Continuum Publishing.

Terrelonge, Pauline. 1984. "Feminist Consciousness and Black Women." In *Women: A Feminist Perspective*, 3d ed., ed. Jo Freeman, 557–67. Palo Alto, CA: Mayfield.

Torgovnick, Marianna. 1990. *Gone Primitive: Savage Intellects, Modern Lives*. Chicago: University of Chicago Press.

Van Dijk, Teun A. 1993. *Elite Discourse and Racism*. Newbury Park, CA: Sage.

Walker, Alice. 1976. *Meridian*. New York: Pocket Books.

Walker, Margaret. 1966. *Jubilee*. New York: Bantam.

Wallace, Michele. 1978. *Black Macho and the Myth of the Superwoman*. New York: Dial Press.

Washington, Mary Helen. 1982. "Teaching *Black-Eyed Susans*: An Approach to the Study of Black Women Writers." In *But Some of Us Are Brave*, ed. Gloria T. Hull, Patricia Bell Scott, and Barbara Smith, 208–17. Old Westbury, NY: Feminist Press.

Washington, Mary Helen, ed. 1987. *Invented Lives: Narratives of Black Women 1860–1960*. Garden City, NY: Anchor.

West, Dorothy. 1948. *The Living Is Easy*. New York: Arno Press/New York Times.

White, Deborah Gray. 1985. *Ar'n't I a Woman? Female Slaves in the Plantation South*. New York: W.W. Norton.

White, E. Frances. 1984. "Listening to the Voices of Black Feminism." *Radical America* 18 (2–3): 7–25.

White, E. Frances. 1990. "Africa on My Mind: Gender, Counter Discourse and African-American Nationalism." *Journal of Women's History* 2 (Spring): 73–97.

White, Evelyn, ed. 1994. *The Black Women's Health Book: Speaking for Ourselves*. Seattle: Seal Press.

Williams, Patricia J. 1995. *The Rooster's Egg: On the Persistence of Prejudice*. Cambridge, MA: Harvard University Press.

Williams, Rhonda. 1997. "Living at the Crossroads: Explorations in Race, Nationality, Sexuality, and Gender." In *The House That Race Built: Black Americans, U.S. Terrain*, ed. Wahneema Lubiano, 136–56. New York: Pantheon.

Williams, Sherley A. 1986. *Dessa Rose*. New York: William Morrow.

27 Women and Bugs

CYNTHIA A. FREELAND

Monstrous Mothers: Female Agency in Recent Horror

There's something going on in horror that I call the "women-and-bugs" phenomenon. "Bugs" play a part in some of the most frightening and disturbing images in recent horror movies: Geena Davis's nightmare of giving birth to a slimy maggot in *The Fly*; the six-foot flying cockroaches of *Mimic*; the gruesome metamorphoses of the gorgeous half-alien female in *Species*; the bald green beautiful Borg Queen in *Star Trek: First Contact*; the big fat Brain Bug (Figure 27.1) in *Starship Troopers*. And we must not forget all the horrific scenes in the *Alien* series: the cocooned humans, the slithering brown egg masses, the fierce and fearsome mother Alien.

In the films I will discuss in this chapter, female monsters or "queen bugs," offer new but nasty examples of female agency in horror. Furthermore, the bugs are pitched against female protagonists who lead the human defense against them. I want to consider whether these examples represent a *feminist* development in horror. Can there be feminist horror—and if so, what sorts of monsters and heroines will it offer? To answer these questions, I will focus on two primary examples, the *Alien* series and *Mimic*. I will explore how these films revisit *Frankenstein* to offer new treatments of its themes of good and evil, monsters and mad science, and the relation of women to nature. I will also contextualize this subgenre by tracing some of its roots in 1950s horror classics like *Them!*, with its giant ants. Along the way, I will have more to say about method in film studies. A cognitivist approach helps make clear that even bug films can offer thought-provoking moral messages, about women, evil, and social and political issues.

Background: Male Monsters, Female Victims

In horror classics of the 1930s and 1940s, there are few female agents and many female victims. The paradigm scenario has a male monster attacking a screaming (and preferably nubile) young woman. Dracula, Frankenstein's monster, the Wolfman, King Kong, the Mummy, and the Creature from the Black Lagoon are all typical horror movie villains. Clearly male, their attacks on women have an erotic element. The trend continued into the 1960s, although the supernatural monsters changed to slashers in films like *Peeping Tom* and *Psycho*. In the 1980s and 1990s, the psychopaths shifted into surreal monstrous men like Pinhead and Freddy, lascivious sadists with a crude sense of humor. Other villains like Jason, Leatherface, and Michael Myers may not relish women victims more than men, but they are still male themselves and pretty messed up about sex. I will examine representatives of these sorts of male monsters later on in this book.

There are exceptions, though, to the general rule. Women have sometimes also been monsters and agents of horror.[1] As early as Sheridan le Fanu's *Carmilla*, written in 1872, there was a threatening female

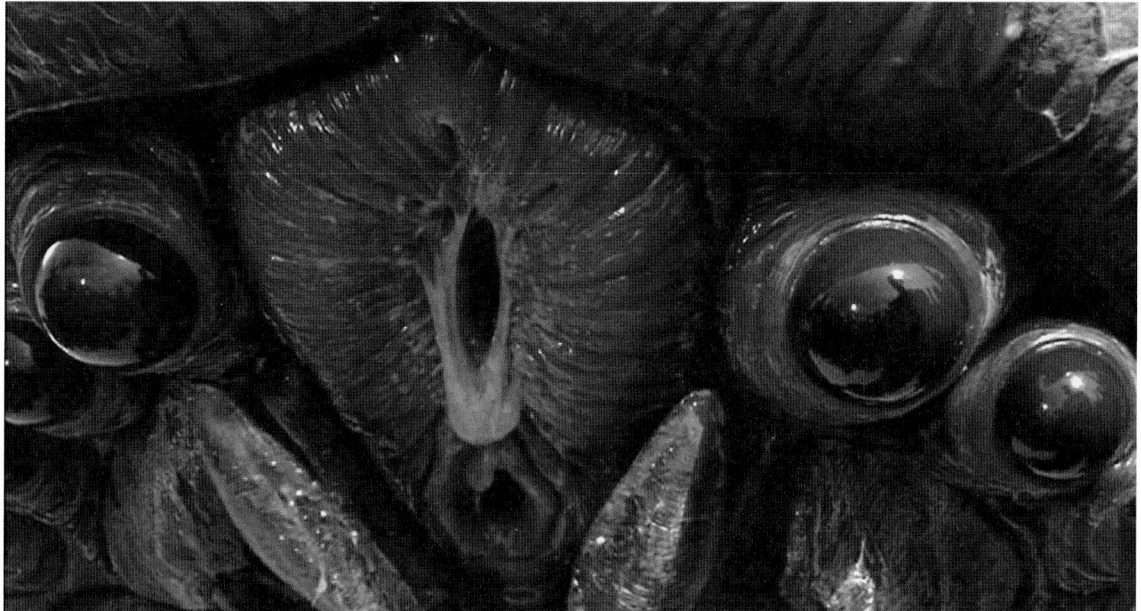

Figure 27.1 The nasty Brain Bug in *Starship Troopers*: A feminized vision of alien evil?

vampire. Hammer Studios brought us lots of buxom and blond fanged females, in movies like *The Vampire Lovers* and *Kiss of the Vampire*. There is a later variant in *The Hunger*, and there are strong female vampires like Claudia in Anne Rice's *Interview with the Vampire*. Witches are another female horror paradigm, with variations like Carrie in the famous Brian De Palma film that bears her name. And we shouldn't forget the miscellaneous female monstrosities in classics like *Attack of the 50-Foot Woman*. (We also should not forget that the gender of the slasher in horror often turns out to be a surprise: "Jason" was really not the boy but his mother in the first *Friday the 13th*, reversing the way Norman Bates turned out to be his own "mother" in *Psycho*. The female slasher of *Dressed to Kill* is really the male psychiatrist played by Michael Caine, and so forth.)

There is something new, though, about the victims in horror since the 1970s. Often a girl or young woman fights back and triumphs over the monster in the end. This is the phenomenon that Carol J. Clover has dubbed the "Final Girl" and has studied in her book, *Men, Women, and Chain Saws: Gender in the Modern Horror Film*.[2] Such "fighting back" was heralded by *Carrie*, where the victim was a sort of witch, whom we paradoxically cheered on in her horrific final rampage. Jamie Lee Curtis in *Halloween* has a different fate from that suffered by her mother, Janet Leigh, in *Psycho*. In *Nightmare on Elm Street* Nancy is smart and gutsy, as is Kirsty in *Hellraiser*. When Kirsty's boyfriend tries to use the magic box to send the hideous Cenobites back to Hell, Kirsty grabs it back and does the job herself. The character Stretch in *The Texas Chainsaw Massacre, Part 2* not only survives the horror of the cannibal family but ends the film atop a small mountain wielding her own chain saw in victory.[3] But in Clover's analysis, the "Final Girl" type of female agency in recent horror is misleading and not particularly feminist. Women and girls are still punished for their sexuality, since the Final Girl survives "because" she stays "pure" and virginal. And further, the "girl" only succeeds by manifesting male, or "boy," types of virtues, like rigging bombs or jump-starting cars.

I want to look in a different direction in recent horror from Clover's "Final Girl" movies. My interest is in films that feature both a female monster and a strong female protagonist. Here femininity or "femaleness" remains an issue right through to the end—for both the monster and the victim/heroine. The women in these movies do not fit Clover's description of the "Final Girl." I admit that my "women-and-bugs" label is loose and not biologically accurate. I use "bugs" in a nontechnical sense that I hope will not cause entomological offense, including in the category lizardlike beings, arachnids, and extraterrestrial crawly things like the Alien. (I remind you that in *Aliens* the Marine Corps grunts ask the lieutenant at their briefing if this is going to be "another bug hunt." He replies, "Yes, a xenomorph is involved," and snickering, they say, "Another bug hunt."[4]) There are plenty of other "critters" in horror: rabbits, cats, dogs, birds, pumas, bats, wolves, alligators, sharks, killer whales, rats, you name it (even tomatoes). So why bugs? They do not invoke the old Adam and Eve story of the snake, nor do they play upon noir-ish tropes of lithe female predatoriness like *Cat People* did. We need to consider why female bugs are so horrible, and why it takes a female hero to defeat them.[5]

Method: Some Options

As I explained in the Introduction, my own approach to film studies is cognitivist. That means that I regard films as complex artifacts that present ideas and prompt various judgments and emotional responses from their audiences. Of course, like other horror films, women-and-bugs films aim especially at evoking fear or dread. But they may inspire other feelings such as elation, sympathy, moral outrage, anger, and even humor. They may also encourage a range of thoughts on various issues, as I shall try to describe further below. Our responses to a scene in a women-and-bugs film may be simple and relatively predictable, like reflex jumping at sudden movement. Probably everyone in the audience recoils during *Mimic* when the baby roach that Dr. Susan Tyler is slowly unwrapping in her dark lab at night suddenly "stings" her or when one of the Alien babies drops on top of the bed Ripley and Newt are sleeping under in *Aliens*. But on the whole, these movies call for more complex responses. Good horror films produce their effects through their narrative structures as well as through other artistic choices. And these films have complex concerns that go beyond the issues often focused on by psychoanalytic theorists, beyond any form of personal psycho-dynamics. As we watch them, we engage in various acts of interpretation and hypothesizing that lead to understanding, prediction, and moral assessment.

For example, we can judge of *Aliens* that the situation of the people in the alien cocoons is dreadful and that the crew should kill them out of pity. They are human, to be sure, but a merciful death is the best one can do for them. Or we can agree that Ripley has been right to warn the corporate military bosses who think they can capture *this* alien to use it as a weapon; only a very evil and nefarious military-technical complex would believe this is a good goal. Again, it is wrong for Bob (the FBI agent) to try to keep Dr. Pat Medford (the ant specialist) from going down into the ants' nests in *Them!*; or we may feel that Dr. Susan Tyler is justified in genetically engineering cockroaches in *Mimic*, despite the risks, because she must stop the horrible plague that is killing children. Finally, the new genetically engineered Ripley in *Alien Resurrection* has a frightening bond to the Alien mother that may make her dangerous and unpredictable to her human friends. And so on. Emotional responses to horror scenes like these, even if they involve an element of almost physical or reflex reaction, can play a part in reaching a rational assessment of a film's narrative components and its overall message. Such responses in fact resemble our reactions to challenging situations or "paradigm scenarios" in real life.[6] Emotions in situations of real danger or fear can cue our actions, reactions, and our moral judgments.

In the Introduction, I explained my disagreement with psychoanalytic feminist approaches to horror. One particular complaint I have is that they tend to ignore or downplay the complexity of the moral messages in horror; they may altogether neglect horror films' political or social dimensions. An account confined to personal psychodynamics, particularly one phrased in terms of neurotic personality processes (such as suture, regression, transference, castration anxiety, fetishism, and the like), is inadequate to plumb the complexity of a movie and discounts the role of the audience's intelligence. To interpret our responses to a film in terms of psychopathology raises doubts about whether any meaningful moral assessment can occur as we view a film. From a psychoanalytic perspective, the audience's interest in a horror movie like *Alien* (whether in the spectacle of the monster or in the vision of the heroine) is always somehow neurotic and dysfunctional. This blocks the possibility of learning a meaningful lesson, evaluating a possible female heroine, or having reasons to be satisfied at the end, say, when Ripley blasts the monster into space and contentedly goes to sleep with her cat. Too often, psychoanalytic feminist accounts of horror films are reductive because they just do not consider that horror films like *Alien* can have interesting visual and technical, let alone social or political, dimensions. Since at least one prominent recent feminist psychoanalytic book on horror addresses *Alien* in detail, I shall take that account up next in order to explain my disagreement with this general approach in more detail.

Feminist Psychoanalysis: Barbara Creed on *Alien*

I want to consider here the construal of *Alien* offered by Barbara Creed in her recent book *The Monstrous-Feminine: Film, Feminism, Psychoanalysis*.[7] According to Creed, "*Alien* presents various representations of the primal scene."[8] This refers to the Freudian claim that all children have memories or fantasies of witnessing a "primal scene" of sex between their parents. Let us assume for the moment that this is so. A further Freudian assumption is that this scene presents an "archaic mother." The child's first view of the mother is shocking because of her absence of a phallus, so the child posits a powerful archaic mother who *does* possess the missing phallus. Here, Creed departs from Freud in a presumably feminist revision involving a third assumption. She argues that the monstrous phallus of the archaic mother does not cover up the mother's missing phallus but rather her *vagina dentata* (toothed vagina). A creature like the Alien monster is horrifying because it confronts us with images of this aggressive, destructive archaic mother, through either the Alien baby's nasty way of insinuating itself down people's throats into their stomachs ("raping" the victim) or the big monster Alien's toothily phallic head.

Creed now has enough laid out to claim that the archaic mother is the "backdrop for the enactment of all the events" in the movie *Alien*.[9] In supporting this statement, however, she switches suddenly away from her *vagina dentata* assumption to introduce yet another claim: "The central characteristic of the archaic mother is her total dedication to the generative, procreative principle."[10] We have now accumulated a significant diversity of hypotheses about the nature of an alleged archaic mother. It (a) possesses the missing phallus, so is castrated; (b) possesses the *vagina dentata*, so is castrating; and (c) is driven by the generative procreative principle.

Creed also spends much of her book describing how horror films illustrate Julia Kristeva's concept of "abjection." This concept is quite complex (and vague), but it basically involves a deep revulsion and aversion toward a mother (or anything else) seen as disgustingly dirty, slimy, putrid, and so on. Abjection concerns our feelings about an earlier primal state of union with the mother before bodily fluids became separate and disgusting or forbidden. So we must add "abjection" as hypothesis (d) to our list, as yet another claim or characteristic about the alleged archaic mother. The Alien as archaic mother is also horrible in the sense of being *abject* because it is slimy, nasty, and creepy-crawly. Its jaws leak fluid, its indeterminate genital parts lay large slimy eggs, and its very form is shifting. When it cocoons a human, the human is trapped in a sticky white substance so as to lack physical independence and to be "bound" back to the mother.

Adding to Freud and Kristeva, Creed also uses Lacanian psychoanalytic theory. She invokes Lacan's account of the mirror stage, or of the way images of the self are constitutive of personal identity. This leads to hypothesis (e), which concerns not simply the archaic mother herself but how a viewer *looks* at her in watching a film. Creed reaches this claim after summarizing five "looks" that a Lacanian theorist maintains are possible in relation to films or the screen.[11] The last of these looks is one Creed adds herself: "The horror film puts the viewing subject's sense of a unified self into crisis, specifically in those moments when the image on the screen becomes too threatening or too horrific to watch." Looking away from the screen in horror is necessary, in other words, to allow for a process of reconstitution of the self, which "is also reaffirmed by the conventional ending of some horror narratives in which the monster is 'named' and destroyed."[12]

Even if we were willing to accept these fundamental and quite disputable psychoanalytic assumptions about the nature of the archaic mother, the role of the mirror stage, or the determinative psychic role of the primal scene, Creed's use of the archaic mother concept is just too vague, general, and reductive: It is so open-ended that it can explain almost anything in a trivial sense. Indeed, Creed seems pleased about this as she writes about the numerous aspects of the archaic mother. This concept conveniently fuses all the distinct theories she employs, even though she admits, "It is difficult to separate out completely the figure of the archaic mother, as defined above, from other aspects of the maternal figure: the maternal authority of Kristeva's semiotic, the mother of Lacan's imaginary, the phallic woman, the castrated and castrating woman."[13]

This convenient assemblage allows Creed to make vast generalizations such as this: "The archaic mother is present in all horror films as the blackness of extinction—death."[14] This claim seems odd, too, given that in her book, the archaic mother is meant to be just one among seven possible types of female monstrousness. It would lead one to doubt, with reason, the claim that the seven are truly distinct. Why else could she generalize like this? The archaic mother hypothesis is especially handy since, as Creed notes, its many aspects can be either positive *or* negative. As a negative force, the archaic mother encompasses horrors such as a bird's mouth, a pulsating womb, the shark's maw in *Jaws*, or the spider in *The Incredible Shrinking Man*. As a positive force, the womb is not empty but full, and it evokes a terrifying female who does not depend for definition on the male.[15]

Notice the extraordinary reduction and leveling of films in Creed's proposed analysis.[16] All horror films are about the same thing, and they all work in the same way. Creed is talking about depth psychology, not about psychology on a more presumably superficial level. Hence, there is no reference to differences among viewers, the effects of marketing and advertising, or the social aspects of film-going. Fears in horror films are always fears not of *things*—however evil and frightening they might be—but fears of what things *represent*. And it turns out that they all represent one thing, the archaic mother. Yet some things are just frightening, and with good reason: Giant ants or spiders or sharks or blobs, and the representation of these things on film, are also frightening as we imagine the characters dealing with them. We do not need to invoke the further, and reductive, hypothesis that they are frightening for some one alleged thing that they *represent*.

Alien: Another Look

Creed's study of *Alien* ignores many significant aspects of its plot and themes. Despite its gut-wrenching power, this is also an intellectual movie of sorts. What does Creed think about the film's revisionist approach to the *Frankenstein* theme of male violation of nature or of its political hints about how an evil corporation in the background is at fault, driving this space expedition for purposes of exploitation, war, and greed? What is the impact of setting the story in outer space on a ship named the *Nostromo* (named after the title of the Joseph Conrad novel), rather than having the aliens invade earth, as they do in so many horror movies, from *Day of the Triffids* to *Independence Day*? Have humans asked for trouble by raiding space for their own greedy ends, like old colonialists in the era of Joseph Conrad?

Also disturbing about Creed's archaic mother hypothesis is the simplistic attitude it manifests toward the art of cinema. Apart from discussing the alleged voyeurism of viewing, Creed's book makes little reference to film technique, style, or cinematography. Any aspects she does notice, for instance, the special effects used to depict the Alien Mother or the stage sets for the ship where the eggs are first encountered, are just grist for her mill, grinding out the same end result repeatedly like a mechanical refrain: archaic mother, archaic mother, archaic mother. But *Alien* is a tremendously exciting and visually spectacular film right from the start—as we meander through space and see the eerie white struts of a spaceship that gradually materialize into angular sans serif letters that spell out the film's title. The opening sequence almost instantly sets the mood for a chilling and adventurous story. As it develops, the movie's timing and pacing are superb. Slow scenes of awakening and of the crew's casual friendly interactions lead on into suspenseful moments of exploration and then into horrific sudden jolting visions of the Alien monster and of deathly fights. There is a marvelous ensemble of actors. Add to all this the magnificent stage sets, stunning special effects, and well-chosen music. All the cinematic components work together with the narrative, plot, and laconic script to give this movie its distinctive impact and meaning. They *all* contribute to our understanding of the role and meaning of the heroine Ripley. I will zero in on just one example to explain more of what I mean. In the sequences near the end of *Alien*, the editing of sights and sounds interacts with acting and plot to create an unforgettable heroine.

Near the end of the film is a notorious scene where Ripley (Sigourney Weaver) undresses after she seems to have defeated the Alien. According to Creed, our views of Ripley's body as she undresses at the end of *Alien* (and her adoption of the little orange cat) can be explained

> by a phallocentric account of female fetishism. … The visually horrifying aspects of the Mother are offset through the display of woman as reassuring and pleasurable sign. … Compared to the horrific sight of the alien as fetish object of the monstrous archaic mother, Ripley's body is pleasurable and reassuring to look at. She signifies the "'acceptable' form and shape of woman."[17]

According to Creed, Ripley has been too masculine in combating the beast and we need to see her nearly naked female body for two reasons: to be reminded that she is female and to make up for our horrific visions of the Alien (a.k.a. archaic mother). Both filmic images speak to an apparently universal audience neurosis and fetishism. There is no reason to deny that these shots of Ripley's body are very voyeuristic. Ripley strips off not one but several layers of clothes. She ends up so skimpily clad that we can see her breasts jiggle and virtually peek into the crack at the top of her buttocks as we eye her from behind and her bikini underpants slip down. But Creed ignores where this scene is placed in the *narrative* of the film, and in so doing, she misses many of its most significant aspects, including its emotional tone and resonance. These make a difference in what the audience can infer and judge, so I shall say more about what has preceded the scene, and then return to it with my own account.

In the scene before this striptease, Ripley has rigged the ship to explode so as to kill off the Alien. She aims to escape in the small shuttlecraft along with the only other remaining members of the ship's seven-person crew. Just as she is throwing all the switches to launch the ten-minute countdown, she hears their screams over the ship's telecom system. She rushes to their aid, to find only their ravaged bleeding bodies. Ripley is now alone with the Alien monster, the only human within millions of miles of empty dark space on a ship about to explode. As she runs toward the shuttle to escape, she encounters the beast—at least, she sees its shadow and glimpses its savage head lurking around one corner. During this entire cat-and-mouse sequence, the film's sounds and sights are enormously effective at building tension. The ship's lights strobe, steam hisses out of ventilators as cooling systems shut down, and alarms screech. A mechanical female voice announces the countdown to Armageddon. The pacing is frenetic and so are the visuals; this part of the film is almost literally a light show. Moments of blurry screen movement as we hear Ripley's panting or screaming are juxtaposed against still moments when her face is caught like a rabbit in headlights by the flashing strobes. We see her at times spotlit in blue and sweating, then we cross-cut to scary glimpses of the Alien's big brutal head. It goes without question that we empathize with her in these scenes. They continue earlier scenes that build a picture of Ripley's distinctive traits. Like Captain Dallas (Tom Skerritt), she is brave; but unlike him, she is cautious. Like the science officer, Ash [Ian Holm], she is smart; but unlike him, she is human and has a conscience. Like the only other woman, Lambert (Veronica Cartwright), Ripley is frightened and can cry, but she does not dissolve into tears when there is grave and imminent danger. Like the enraged Parker (Yaphet Kotto), she is determined to get even with the Alien; but unlike him, she keeps her head when facing the monster. All told, Ripley is an admirable human being and not, like Clover's "Final Girl," merely an amalgam of stereotyped masculine traits in female disguise.

This breathless escape sequence leads into two more scenes that, amazingly enough, raise the levels of tension even higher. Ripley has reached seeming safety on the shuttle, and the film's music signals a momentary respite. But as there is just one minute left for her to move away from the ship before it explodes, a new panic arises about whether she can escape the blast. Now Ripley displays other virtues and skills by working dexterously under extreme pressure. Again she is smart and quick but not stereotypically male: She hits buttons and turns switches with her long graceful fingers. She does manage to get the shuttle free. Then she (and we) watch as the ship detonates. At this point, the film as light show climaxes; it is at its most purely visual and cinematically spectacular (especially when seen in a theater on the large screen and with Dolby sound). There are long yellow-blue lines of light across the full screen followed by wondrous and loud billowy nuclear explosions of reds and yellows. The explosions are punctuated by blinding flashes of white light. The dramas of exterior space are intercut with tight close-ups of Ripley's face as she sits at the shuttle controls. These shots are extraordinary because she looks consumed in ecstasy as she is bathed in white light. Her head is slanted back at a forty-five-degree angle with eyes closed, lips slack. She moans slightly; in short, she looks orgasmic. I propose that the sexuality in these scenes is visual testimony to the prowess of the filmmaker at his movie's climax—he has his most satisfying creative bursts in this sequence! Creed, by isolating and discussing only the very final scenes when Ripley strips off her overalls after this grueling sequence, ignores this entire cinematic tour de force. It may indeed be that the film is sexist, but if so, it is in ways that are more complex and also more intrinsically linked to its artfulness than the Freudian formulaic analysis of voyeurism can capture.

And now I also want to suggest a different reading of Ripley's striptease before the final combat sequence. These scenes set up another bizarre sexual interaction of sorts in her ultimate confrontation with the Alien. We should keep in mind the beast here is clearly *male* in *Alien* (Ripley says on the shuttle, "I got you, you son of a bitch"—it will be a female and a "bitch" in the later films).[18] This scene is thus a variation on the typical horror movie cliché of male monster as erotic threat. But the sexuality in the scene is rather bizarre. In her final fight with the Alien, after she has donned a huge insulating space suit and helmet, Ripley utters small moans and mumbles over a space of several minutes. This part of the script is quite unusual. On the one hand, Ripley does seem "masculine" in that she is brave, heroic, mechanically adept, and a rational, careful planner. But on the other hand, she is also very "female" in her manner. As she plans some sort of action to take against the Alien, it is hard to make out her words. She keeps up a continuous mutter to herself and says things like "lucky lucky" and "oh oh" and even "I want to fuck you"(!) as she plans how to open the airlock and blast the Alien out into space. Thus, her final dance with the beast is a heavily sexualized battle. But I am not sure that femininity is especially marked here. If it is, it is a femininity with deep-reaching historical roots—like that of the martyr in the Roman Circus who becomes almost male as she fights the wild beasts and emerges victorious. The acts and bravery of female martyrs are like the male warrior's vision of the ecstasies of mortal combat.[19] After all, both sex and this kind of fighting are intensely intimate and private physical encounters.

Unlike Creed, then, I would argue that in the context of *the scene I have just described*, the sight of Ripley's body is not reassuring. Quite the contrary, it induces empathic fear on her behalf. Just as she finally feels herself safe and free of the exploded mother ship, the Alien's arm drops down into her face, and we realize that it, too, is on the shuttle. (It has apparently gone to sleep in the wall spaces of the shuttle. We see its jaws snap in a seeming dream.) Now she is the typical female victim of a (probably male) monster—a monster that has already reached out a seductive tentacle to wrap around the legs of the only other female victim, Lambert. But is the scene really only about sex and erotic threats? Beyond the stereotype, we should note that Ripley's flesh is indisputably *human*: pink, soft, natural, jiggling. Such flesh contrasts sharply with the adult Alien's flesh: blue-black, steely, hard, unnatural, almost mechanically designed. This scene thus echoes the film's opening scenes where the vast dark and empty body of the mechanical ship is contrasted with the small, pale, and nearly naked humans. It is relevant to note that Kane (John Hurt), with his pale and somewhat delicately pink body, is also treated in a similar way as Ripley. He is also shown almost naked, clad in a "diaper," tremendously vulnerable and exposed as he is invaded by the Alien baby parasite. Here, too, this human's pinkness is juxtaposed against the monster's unnatural color, at this stage a nasty yellow-green, and his smoothness to its rough scaliness.

Just as this scene brings out Ripley's human vulnerabilities, so in other scenes does she exemplify a human being's best traits, in contrast to those of the Alien, and also in contrast to the "inhuman" people (whether the android science officer Ash or the corrupt corporation representative Burke in *Aliens*). *Alien* is about individuality, survival, and being human. The distinctness of fine actors helps show their separateness. Many of the people who die are too individual: They insist on going alone to do things. It could be described as a Hobbesian movie with a Marxian twist, in that the most sinister threats are posed by the greedy higher-ups within the Company (a military-industrial bureaucracy). Ripley as security officer tries to prevent the alien "infection" by maintaining quarantine, but she is overruled by science officer Ash, who follows his private "eyes-only" Directive #937 from the Company to get aliens back for scientific study at all costs: "All other priorities are rescinded. Crew expendable." Similarly, in *Aliens*, Ripley and her surrogate daughter, Newt, are nearly made victims of the alien parasites because the Company's representative, Burke, wants to profit by smuggling the aliens out through quarantine in their host bodies. Ripley comments to him: "You know, Burke, I don't know which species is worse. You don't see them fucking each other over for a goddamn percentage." As I read at least these first two movies in the *Alien* series, then, they are about what it means to be *human*. Ripley's femininity is relevant to this to be sure, but perhaps even more relevant is her *humanity*.

Ripley is horrified to discover that Ash, the science officer, actually admires the Alien: "I admire its purity … no conscience, remorse, or delusions of morality." This is an important line because it allows the audience to take a different perspective for a moment about this monster: It is indeed terrifying, but it is also intelligent and has its own elegance, awesome power, and force. The visual realizations of H. R. Giger's artistic design are splendid and spectacular.[20] We both want and yet fear to look at this creature more. Its lines are long and elegant, its skin is smooth with the gemlike quality of beautifully tooled metal. But any human sympathy should make plain how immoral such respect is, given the Alien's malignant nature: It destroys all other life forms it encounters. This is confirmed by the film when we realize that the radio signal was a warning note left by the previous Alien victim and when we see Ash revealed to be an android—not a real but a mechanical man. He bleeds white, colorlessly, not the red blood of humans. As the other six members of the *Nostromo* crew are picked off one or two at a time, Ripley by contrast is a superior representative of humanity. She shows both fear and courage (a realistic combination Plato and Aristotle would approve of as true courage). When the only remaining crew members are Ripley, Ash, Lambert, and Parker, she is the most heroic: Ash seems to have given up figuring out a scientific way to kill the Alien (we later learn why); Parker is consumed by rage; Lambert cries and shakes in fear; only Ripley can think things through and plan to carry them out. As senior officer, she can give the orders. To complain that this exemplary human cannot be truly female is to give up the claims of feminism in advance! (I do think that such criticisms are better justified about the latest film in the series, however; see below.)

In the *Alien* series, the heroine herself is not the overreacher, but there are still echoes of *Frankenstein*. Evil science is used in the service of a vast capitalist military-technical machine, and its misguided attempts to control or use a monstrous nature put humans at dire risk. The heroine is the one who must correct the problems that corporate science causes. She is the one who clearly sees the danger of such over-reaching and meddling with nature. By choosing to make the agent of justice a woman, the series offers an interesting continuation (with revisions) of Mary Shelley's thematic opposition between "good" femininity and "evil" masculinity. That is, masculine overreaching must be countered by feminine features aligned with domesticity and sociality. Such a view has its dangers and limitations, as I argued in Chapter 1. And there are the other problems I have remarked upon concerning visual voyeurism and the filmmaker's use of Ripley as an orgasmic respondent to his own art. But we are unfair to Ripley if we view her as either just a reassuring fetish object or a "final girl" who only survives by becoming virtually masculine.

Later films in the series continue the Frankenstein theme as they represent the evil "Company" looking for the latest and best weapon of destruction. As in *Frankenstein* (and in other films like *Species* and *Species II*), the (male) scientists in the military-industrial complex become too enamored of their unnatural monster. In *Aliens*, Burke wants to bring samples of the Alien babies back to earth to study and market them; he is the only evil human in the film, and he betrays all the others. In *Alien Resurrection*, the corporation scientists have not simply encountered the Alien monster out there but have deliberately re-created it from Ripley's DNA (which became blended with it through her impregnation in *Alien*[3] with the larva of a queen Alien). Once again, the scientists are the sleazeballs of the film; one of them remarks: "The animals themselves are wondrous. They'll be invaluable once we've harnessed them." This series "punishes" the male scientists by the most direct means of death at the "hands" of the very monsters they have created or sought to appropriate. Such moments are obviously just retribution (and prove audibly satisfying to audience members).

Why does only Ripley, the strong, smart woman, survive? Why does the Ripley character change as the series evolves? First she adopts a cat and then a small child; next acquires a lover; then progresses to self-immolation and rebirth as a genetically altered half-breed clone of herself. Depth psychology leaves us little room for interesting analysis of how the *Alien* series has developed in the nearly twenty years since it began. In Creed's view, this is all a matter of competing views of maternity and the maternal body. Here is what she says about *Aliens*:

> Throughout, *Aliens* opposes two forms of mothering: Ripley's surrogate mothering in which there is no conception or birth and where the female body is unmarked; and Mother Alien's biological, animalistic, instinctual mothering where the maternal body is open and gaping. … Mother Alien represents Ripley's other self, that is, *woman's*, alien, inner, mysterious powers of reproduction. It is the latter, the female reproductive/mothering capacity *per se*, which is deemed monstrous, horrifying, abject. Like Mother Alien, Ripley also transforms into an indestructible killing machine when her child—even though a surrogate offspring—is threatened.[21]

Further, Creed writes that the heroic, self-sacrificing Ripley at the end of *Alien*[3] "is betrayed by her body, unable finally to preserve her own flesh from contamination by the abject, alien other—the monstrous fecund mother."[22]

Notice how these comments equate all the movies. Yet many viewers feel strongly that these films are very different. Some prefer the first movie as a strikingly original departure in sci-fi horror. Some think James Cameron's direction in *Aliens* made that movie more thrilling; I have heard it called one of the best movie sequels ever made. Most fans of the series will agree that the last two films went downhill. Why are the films different as films, if their horror is the same? Isn't it an insult to the heroism of Ripley to keep saying that she is just an alternative or a parallel to the Alien archaic mother?[23] My questions are ones Creed does not raise and would presumably not find interesting, because they turn away from focusing on the deep psychological truth of the structures that impel us to react as we do to the primal scene of the Alien Mother herself.

What can an audience get out of assessing a strong heroine in a bug movie? As an action hero, Ripley offers interesting possibilities for complex audience identification and empathy. She is simply more human than Arnold Schwarzenegger, Bruce Willis, Steven Segal, or most other male heroes in action films. Sure, Ripley can kick butt, drive a tank, lob grenades, punch computer code, face off with the Alien, or dive suicidally into the flames. Yet she also cries, quakes, has nightmares, trembles, and is sometimes weak and deeply afraid. This emotional vulnerability makes her a more interesting and believable character in many ways than her male action counterparts (some of whom, like Robocop and the Terminator, are ironically enough in search of human emotions!). Moreover, she is a strong advocate of basic human values like companionship, camaraderie, and caring for others. Indeed, her ability to show some sympathy and caring may make her a better combatant and leader than most of the men she outlives. She cares about people enough to think their options through and to never give up on rescuing someone. She berates the inhuman corporation man for aiming only at his own greedy goals—in her book, he is no better than the Alien. She earns the trust of frightened little Newt so she can find out what the girl may know about the space colony and the Aliens.

In my view, then, Ripley's genetic merger with the Alien Queen in the most recent entry in the series was a mistaken step backward, pushing her into the inhuman mold of the android Schwarzenegger plays in *Terminator*. She has an excuse for her inhumanity now as she simply becomes a big bug herself, a strong tough fighter with inhuman abilities of sense and smell. (This is foreshadowed perhaps by the final scenes of *Aliens*, where she dons a giant mechanical body to use in her last fight against the "bitch.") These "male" aspects do not fit with her sudden and literal descent into the maternal realm of the Alien nest, where she wallows voluptuously among the creepy tentacles and eggs (Figure 27.2). *Alien Resurrection* is an unimaginative parody of its predecessors, an emptied-out formulaic genre exercise. This seems to be admitted when the two inhuman female heroes comment knowingly at the end of the film: "So you did it. You saved the Earth." Ripley speaks with such deadpan irony to Call (Winona Ryder) at the end of the movie that is hard to avoid taking the whole thing as a put-on. *Alien Resurrection* offers no truly interesting female characters on the side of either good or evil.

A Different Take on Bugs

I don't think we need or benefit from the archaic mother hypothesis. Bugs in movies, like bugs in the world, can sometimes be very nasty vermin.[24] They can undermine the foundations of our homes, eat our clothes, ruin our food, eviscerate books in our libraries, defoliate our trees, despoil our gardens, spread human diseases, and deliver painful bites or stings. Bugs live in filthy sewers, dark scary tunnels, or wet storm drains. They are unpredictable and nonhuman in their appearance and movements. They are neither soft and cuddly like kittens nor beautifully effective killers like falcons or cheetahs. They fly at you or squiggle past you, they eat putrid things in foul ways, their eggs and cocoons are slimy, brown, and pulsating. Eventually, they will consume our corpses.[25]

But why then *women* and bugs? I will grant this much to the archaic mother hypothesis: A main reason bugs are horrible in the movies is that they are "queens" who are frightening because of their reproductive powers. They combine a primitive instinctual drive to reproduce with a tendency to dominate the male of the species. Like the praying mantis, they destroy or else simply abandon their mate after he has done his duty. Males are only minimally necessary to them. In *Species*, the lizard lady, clothed in the external garb of a blond bombshell, literally rapes and then murders her male lovers if she scents out their genetic inadequacy. In *Mimic*, the cockroach attackers are all females who keep just one fertile male ready to service them in their nest. In *Them!*, the queen ants are twice as large as the males and can live on for years to lay many eggs and prosper long after their mates have fallen from the sky. The Borg Queen is the only interesting member of a species that is nothing more than high-tech futuristic ants. She combines the efficiency of their mass personality with a unique desire for seduction and novelty.

Here is what psychoanalysis misses out on. The bug movies are interesting not because they conjure up bug queens as images of the archaic mother driven by reproduction but because they creatively explore the *consequences* of bugs' revised sexual arrangements. Sexuality is always linked to larger issues about social frameworks. The bug movies are hence also about science and nature, politics, war and weaponry, good and evil.[26] Large-scale bugs are truly frightening monsters because of their alternative social structures, communicative ability, swarm behavior, and amazing physical powers. The old scientist in *Them!* explains to a blue-ribbon panel of military experts at the White House that ants are formidable foes, "ruthless, savage, and courageous fighters … the only other creatures on earth, other than man, who make war." They can lift twenty times their own weight, and they turn captives they do not kill into slave laborers. Chemical weapons and biological warfare are in the bug arsenal, too, as they use stingers to dispense ruinous acids or spit out poisonous sprays. The arachnids in *Starship Troopers* shoot "bug plasma" out across interstellar space like nuclear warheads. Unlike our troops in Operation Desert Storm, the giant ants of *Them!* do very well in harsh desert conditions. The bugs' intelligence operations are phenomenal.

Figure 27.2 The new cloned Ripley (Sigourney Weaver) lolls with her own Alien kind in *Alien Resurrection*.

They perceive through clever radarlike antennae or bulging composite eyes. They communicate through whistles and clicks. Big bugs can emit bad odors, and the roaches of *Mimic* deposit huge mounds of sticky excrement. Bugs come equipped with hard armor on the outside. Their weaponry is vast and varied: fierce slashing mandibles, quick thrusting tongues, lacerating arms, or strong crushing jaws. Their motives are brutal. In *Mimic*, the wise old scientist quotes Hobbes's remark that human life is nasty, brutish, and short. "Ants would put it more succinctly," he says. "Can I eat it, or will it eat me?"

Not all "bugs" or bug films are the same. We can better understand what is unique about films like the *Alien* series by contextualizing these films in the horror tradition, especially in relation to a film like *Them!*, made in 1954. I next go back in time to explore some background of modern women-and-bugs movies by looking at two interesting examples from the 1950s.

Bug Films of the 1950s

The ants of *Them!* are very similar to the Alien in size, shape, and threateningness. They, too, are female, crawl out of dark holes, lay eggs in vast numbers, protect their babies fiercely, crush and kill innocent people (including the entire crew of a naval destroyer), and menace us with their poisonous body acids. But *Them!* is a movie with themes that are characteristic of the 1950s.[27] It is about the indiscriminate victims of war in a thermonuclear age and the threat of communism. Not only are the ants products of nuclear tests, signifying an early awakening of environmentalist consciousness, but they also symbolize the cold and faceless efficiency of the Soviet army and intelligence machine. *Them!* asks if the ants will beat the individualistic Americans, making us extinct within a year, because *they* have a form of perfect communication and cooperation—unlike *us*.

Them! is also striking (and surprising, given our stereotypes about the 1950s) because it presents a female scientist in a prominent role. Spunky women start to appear on the horror scene in these 1950s films. To match the "formicologist" in *Them!* there is an "ichthyologist" in *Revenge of the Creature* (1955). In each film, the female scientist is a smart and sensible character. However, she must be made unusually attractive in order to counteract her anomalous status qua scientist. I want to consider these women to think more about female heroic agency in bug movies.

In the scene of the scientists' arrival in *Them!*, the male heroes, a policeman and an FBI agent, wait to meet a plane and wonder why two Department of Agriculture scientists, "the Doctors Medford," are being flown in to deal with the mysterious tracks they have found after some thefts and murders in New Mexico. First, we see a somewhat paunchy older male scientist descend the plane's ladder. He absently greets the locals and then shouts for "Pat." Expecting another man, the police agents turn and are delighted to see a woman's beautiful legs, her feet clad in high heels, on the ladder. The voyeuristic scene is extended for the audience as well, as she pauses mid-descent and exclaims, "I'm stuck!" with only her elegant legs on view. The men's response is very 1950s: "If she were the kind of doctor that takes care of sick people, I could get a fever real quick."

In *Revenge of the Creature*, the female scientist is introduced as we hear a radio interviewer tell his audience that he is talking about the Gill Man with an expert who is, amazingly enough, "one of the prettiest young women I've ever had the pleasure to meet." We see "Miss Hobson" with her pert blond curls and little hat, smiling as she stands beside the aquarium tank. She patiently explains what ichthyology is and why they are trying to revive the Gill Man by moving his body through the water in the tank. There was also a beautiful heroine in the first *Creature* movie, but she was the usual damsel in distress destined to be a victim. She went along on the Amazon trip with her boyfriend largely as his assistant and was never presented as having scientific credentials. Julie Adams in this role existed largely, we suspect, to tempt the

Creature by swimming languidly in her stunning white suit straight into his watery domain. Like any green-blooded male, he immediately lusted after this lovely human female, and most of the threat and suspense in this film ensues from his pursuit and abduction of her.[28] Similarly in the sequel, the now tank-bound creature spends most of his time mooning with his fishy goggle eyes toward the heroine through the portholes of his tank. Once he escapes, he also ogles her in a shower scene that anticipates the more famous one to come five years later in *Psycho*.

Significantly in both *Creature* movies, the woman is a voice of balance poised between two competing male heroes. She is aligned with the "good" hero who is a scientist out for knowledge, rather than with the "bad" hero who is a mere adventurer out for fame and money.[29] The movies do not seem to acknowledge the fact that both men are exploiting the Creature in similar ways. In the second film, as in the King Kong movies, the heroine does show moments of sympathy for this poor Creature, who has been ripped from his natural habitat, moved thousands of miles, and made into a high-priced zoo spectacle for entertainment in a Florida aquarium. Even beyond this, he has been treated cruelly by the scientist's bizarre educational techniques. We really cannot be sure about his levels of consciousness, but he *looks* intelligent and perceptive. As he reaches for the food the woman offers him, the male scientist tries out operant learning techniques by shocking him painfully with a giant bull prod. Simultaneously, the woman says "no," reinforcing the 1950s message that it is the female role to train male creatures to limit their desires. These painful (and scientifically ill-judged) scenes now seem disturbing, and they make it almost impossible not to cheer later when the Creature escapes. In this movie as well, Helen, like Kay in the first film, is shown as expressing pity for the creature, particularly for his isolation and loneliness.

In *Revenge of the Creature*, the woman's goal of being a scientist will and obviously "should" be subordinated to finding love and marriage. To get married and bear children will require her to give up her scientific ambitions. She lies on the beach mulling over her options with her boyfriend as he explains all this to her. He says: "It's tough on you girls. I'm not saying it should be. Just that it is." Although in this scene she seems undecided and in other scenes she is a strong figure, not just smart but quick on her feet in verbal duels, we later learn that they are engaged. She has obviously made up her mind in a direction the filmmakers expect the audience to consider appropriate.

Them! is a far better movie in almost every respect: plot, pacing, dialogue, cinematography, acting. Its view of the woman scientist will strike us in the 1990s as more contemporary. Joan Weldon, as Dr. Pat Medford in *Them!*, is quite different from the female ichthyologist. Although she is often coded as "feminine" by her attire and attractiveness as she accompanies either her famous father or the male FBI agent (James Arness) like a sidekick, she nevertheless is also a strong, smart, and brave character who is a dedicated scientist. Her knowledge is essential to defeating the giant ants. Even after a romance is hinted at between her and Bob, the FBI agent (she tells him to "call me 'Pat'" if the 'Doctor' bothers you"), she is never compelled to sacrifice her science—and indeed that would appear unlikely, given her clear dedication.

This is all the more surprising, given that the movie includes a conventional scene showing Pat as female victim. She ventures out into the New Mexico sands wearing her inappropriate high-heeled shoes and suit, only to become the typical screaming damsel who spots a giant ant, is attacked by it, and then is rescued by the male hero. However, later she dons fatigues and intrepidly enters the ants' nests alongside the men. Bob tries to prevent her, insisting, "This is no place for you or any other woman!" but she simply silences him with her forceful logic in a brisk no-nonsense voice (Figure 27.3). "Listen, Bob; someone with scientific knowledge has to go down there, and my father is physically unable to. … There's no time to give you a fast course in insect pathology." This Dr. Medford even assumes command in the expedition, since she is the only one who can recognize the queens.[30] Upon finding them in their egg chamber, she gives the orders in no uncertain terms: "Destroy everything in here. Burn it. I said burn it!"

Figure 27.3 Dr. Pat Medford (Joan Weldon) directs Bob (James Arness) in the battle against the giant ants in *Them!*.

I see this increasing respect for the female role as correlated to another important feature of the villains in women-and-bugs movies. *Them!* opens with the specific threat that bugs pose to human children. Its initial and still strikingly suspenseful sequence shows a small girl wandering in a stark desert setting. In his book *Terror and Everyday Life: Singular Moments in the History of the Horror Film*, Jonathan Lake Crane comments that the plane and the flying ants emphasize the indiscriminate threat of nuclear bombs, where no one is spared, however innocent.[31] Children are also central in the climax when troops battle the colony of giant ants in the storm drains under Los Angeles. Two small boys have been cornered there, so the army cannot use gas in their attack. There are frequent cross-cuts from the action and suspense of the search in the tunnels to the mother waiting outside, sobbing and frightened. Much of the fearfulness of the film's final scenes depends on the threat to the boys, and one hero is killed by the ants while saving them.[32]

Them! seems to end, though, with everything put right. The two children who were the focus of the rescue efforts have been restored to their mother, and there is a strong hint that the woman scientist has been provided with a suitable mate of her own. (Mysteriously, though, we never do see the little girl from the beginning again.) By making children seem so central to both women and men, this film seems to assure its audience that "normal" female reproduction and "normal" parenting will replace the abnormal methods of the queen ants.[33] The challenge posed by the group-think ants has been met, as all the relevant American bureaucracies learn to get along, communicate, trust each other, and share control against a common enemy. The fledgling queen ants are all destroyed before any can develop their wings enough to fly away. True, old Dr. Medford concludes the movie with a dire message about the unknown evils that science may have wrought. Even though his words of warning are enforced by "dramatic" music in the score at the end, the film's optimism overall works to undermine this warning and suggests it is merely a formula.

One reason for the strong presence of female figures as heroes in the bug films becomes clear in *Them!*: A specific threat in these movies is directed at *children*. *Them!* sets up a dialectic that reappears thirty-two years later in *Aliens* and forty-three years later in *Mimic*. Women are allowed by the logic of these films to don military garb and behave aggressively for a primal reason: protecting babies. It is no accident that the main threat to children comes from giant queen ants who are mothers; they fly through the air breeding new queens to cover all areas of the country. Similarly, in *Aliens* after Ripley adopts the little girl Newt, she is far more aggressive than in *Alien* (Figure 27.4). She wears heavy weaponry, acts physically tougher and angrier, and fights the "bitch" Alien mother as she and the Alien mother each protect their offspring. This difference is signaled best perhaps by the fact that she wears only a white space suit at the end of *Alien* but dons an entire giant metal robotic body at the conclusion of *Aliens*. And most recently in *Mimic*, Dr. Susan Tyler genetically engineers cockroaches for much the same sort of goal—in order to save human children from a plague spread by normal roaches.

To speak about reproduction as the central issue of women-and-bugs films is, however, to risk another kind of reductiveness. We should not overlook further aspects of femininity that are very significant in these films, aspects that stem from the *Frankenstein* tradition. Like the women in Mary Shelley's novel, women in 1950s horror films often bring humanity to situations that have gotten out of hand due to the impersonal aims of a (male) scientific-military technocracy. The rationality of science in films like *Revenge of the Creature* or *The Day the Earth Stood Still* is excessive, cruel and pitiless—so much so that it is actually bad as science. Mark Jancovich points out that in these movies, "feminine" qualities such as feeling, intuition, interaction, and imagination are often valued. Further, he notes that "women's involvement is often central

Figure 27.4 Ripley (Sigourney Weaver) protects Newt (Carrie Henn) from the Alien Mother in *Aliens*.

to defeat of the menace."[34] This is true as early as *Them!* when Pat Medford must identify the queens. Also noteworthy is that the men, too, at the start of *Them!* show great concern for the little girl in shock and that some of the men near the film's conclusion argue against a utilitarian military leader who wants to gas the tunnels, despite the risk posed to two boys. The heroes point to the children's mother; individual human emotions outweigh the policy of "greatest good for the greatest number."

Despite these hints of a feminist revision of stereotypical male values, we can still criticize the presentation of femaleness in these 1950s films, just as I did for *Frankenstein*. It seems good that women are valued for certain alleged features, yet their treatment in these older horror films is essentializing. That is, though women may not have a biological destiny, certain emotional stereotypes are attributed to the feminine, and women must again serve men by "humanizing" them.[35] Let us move now to my final and very recent example of a women-and-bugs film to see whether this trend continues

The New *Frankensteins*

I have just described some 1950s antecedents of the modern women-and-bugs films and a rationale for their visible female heroes. I pointed out that these movies begin to depict strong women in the context of fights with female monsters over which species' offspring will survive. Their concern for monstrous reproduction and the female socializing of men into true humanity makes these films heirs of an even older horror tradition, the mad-scientist story stemming from *Frankenstein*. In these movies, we also often find the message that a scientist overreacher can violate natural processes only with dire results. But the monsters created here are female, and the particular form that human destruction will take is their monstrous reproduction—leading to an infestation of all-powerful and mostly female bugs. The women-and-bugs movies offer a kind of inverse of *Frankenstein*, since they are about ways of bypassing the masculine role in reproduction.

An interesting recent entry in the women-and-bugs genre is *Mimic*, because here the heroine who fights the bugs is also the scientist overreacher who has created them. She violates nature by genetically manipulating cockroach DNA, combining it with that of the termite and the mantis—surely a recipe for verminous disaster! It does indeed lead to bad effects: unanticipated six-foot monster roaches who can masquerade as people and who see humans as tasty meat. The female scientist who created the bugs must then figure out how to destroy her own monstrous progeny. In *Mimic*, there is even an explicit allusion to the *Frankenstein* theme. A point I want to emphasize in discussing this film is that once again, there are social aspects of the depiction of the monstrous bugs that go beyond the immediate personal or psychodynamic threat they pose as monstrous mothers. We shall also see how the heroine's "femininity," as with Ripley or Dr. Pat Medford, plays a key part in the narrative of combat and victory against the bugs.

Mimic

Mimic (Guillermo del Toro, 1997) starts, like *Them!*, with a threat to human children. This is not shown through graphic attacks but is sketched in the film's brilliant and chilling credit sequence. As the credits roll, we see static, almost Victorian, images of impaled bugs. These are juxtaposed against huge news headlines that scream disaster and death. Next we see a pretty woman (Mira Sorvino) visiting a bizarre hospital ward. Rows of children lie in a chamber that once again, like the credit sequence, has archaic and Victorian overtones. In this vaulted and beehive-like hall, there are rows of beds with floating oxygen tents. Topped by tall white shrouds, they look eerily like insect cocoons. Seen closer up, each cocoon contains a small child who gasps for breath. Some children turn away to die as their relatives plead tearfully with the woman visitor for help. Thus, from the start of the film with this almost wordless mini-narrative, we can infer two things. First, the situation is dire; and second, this woman is someone of importance and power who can act to change things. Further, because of her tears, she is obviously compassionate. Warm and human, she hardly fits our stereotype of the hubristic Victor Frankenstein. Instead, the suffering shown here prompts us to endorse the judgment that this woman must help if she can.

In flashbacks and voice-over narration, we watch as Dr. Tyler releases her genetically engineered "Judas" species of cockroaches into the sewers of New York City. Clearly she does so with the lofty and seemingly supportable moral aim of killing the normal roaches that have been spreading the hideous plague that is killing all the children of the city. The story of this new Frankenstein breeding program is told from the perspective of a seemingly successful outcome, as Dr. Tyler stands and speaks beside her husband, Dr. Peter Mann (Jeremy Northam), a Centers for Disease Control doctor. They are appearing at a news conference to announce their victory over the plague. But the camera zooms in to show the face of a wise-looking older man in the audience who ominously shakes his head, a dire forecasting that all is not well with this solution. This note of warning is cross-cut with scenes depicting the couple's exhilaration as they celebrate together at home. They embrace in the bathtub and imagine having children of their own in the near future. *Mimic* is typified by such swings of mood and also by shifts from light to dark and from public to private settings.

This initial ominous hint is fulfilled when Dr. Tyler's "Judas" insects, which were meant to destroy their fellows and then die off, mutate and reappear as fearsome six-foot variants who "mimic" or disguise themselves as men in overcoats. Now Susan's mentor, the wise older scientist (F. Murray Abraham), says, "So, you think your little Frankensteins have gotten the better of you." She protests, "But they all died in the lab!"—to which he replies, "Yes, Susan, but you let them out in the world. The world's a much bigger lab."

The *Frankenstein* allusion is visually reinforced in various ways, too. Not only do the credits and the bizarre hospital chamber offer filmic references to a scientific past, but Susan's laboratory is anachronistic for a researcher allegedly at the forefront of work on genetic engineering. Like Dr. Frankenstein, Dr. Tyler works alone on a stormy night in a lab that looks like one minimally updated from a Dr. Jekyll and Mr. Hyde movie: It is shadowy, containing wooden furniture and old specimen cases, not the sleek modern white and steel outfittings we might expect. She does not have a cadre of postdocs running experiments under her supervision. The scenes of her working alone late at night, of course, also emphasize her vulnerability as a woman. Susan, like Pat Medford of *Them!* and Ripley in *Alien*, becomes a potential victim of the bugs. The brilliant Mexican horror director Guillermo del Toro choreographs these lab scenes with clever sadism and suspense, as a shadowy and unidentifiable bug figure flits in and around, even across the ceiling, undetected by Susan. There are many more Hitchcockian moments of ghastly humor throughout the movie.

Just as *Them!* began and ended by highlighting threats to children, so do Dr. Tyler's concerns about and relations with children drive much of her action in *Mimic*. Besides aiming to save the lives of all the children of New York City, Susan has an affinity with small children, particularly boys. Her encounters with children emphasize her feminine and maternal side, which she has not lost despite being a top scientist. Two young helpers comb the subways for unusual bug specimens for her. She says to a friend that it is better for them to be occupied in this way than to be in a gang. It is a mark of the change of times that here, unlike in *Them!*, the movie kills off these two children in an unexpectedly horrifying scene when they first encounter the Judas roaches. We cannot see who their attackers are or exactly what happens; but we do see a frighteningly sudden and vicious attack with rapid cuts between their twisted, screaming faces, their spurting blood, and their mangled corpses. Despite this violence, *Mimic*, like both *Them!* and *Aliens*, foregrounds a threatened symbolic child who is ultimately saved. This is Chuy, the apparently autistic grandson of a Latino shoeshine man (Giancarlo Giannini). Chuy rarely speaks except to identify people's shoes, but he is not frightened when Susan questions him. He is the first person to observe the giant mutant roaches, but he can only call them by his own label, "Mr. Funny Shoes." He even seems to communicate with them by clicking spoons.

As I have said, *Them!* dealt with the indiscriminate destruction of atomic weaponry, concerns about nuclear environmental impact, and the need for bureaucratic cooperation to ward off the clonelike Communists in the Cold War. *Alien* and *Aliens* offered cynical analysis of the small person's victimization by the larger forces of amoral corporate greed. *Mimic*, made in 1997 after the fall of communism and the end of the Cold War, focuses on a new set of social issues and a new war, in which the enemies are epidemic disease and social ills brought to the United States by immigration. Set in the urban blight of New York City, *Mimic* takes for granted its many scenes of grim poverty and urban filth. Chuy and his grandfather, Manny, live in a bombed-out area across from a mission for the homeless run by an aged Asian priest. These scenes emphasize that social problems and poverty affect immigrants, the elderly, the lower classes, and non-whites most severely—that is, those who stereotypically live in closer contact with roaches (and who, by implication, are also carriers of disease). The mutant roaches begin their inroads on humans and establish colonies by killing off unnamed and unnoticed homeless people: the mentally ill, alcoholic bums, kids from poor neighborhoods, and bag ladies.

It is surely significant to note, then, that from the threatened heroic small group highlighted in this movie, the heterosexual white couple survives, whereas the savvy black male subway cop (Charles S. Dutton) and the gentle Mexican shoeshine man are hideously massacred and devoured by the Judas roaches. After he realizes Susan is the person who created the mutant bugs, Manny excoriates her as the typical scientist who did not think about the consequences of her acts, and Leonard, the black subway cop, agrees that she did not care about their children. Also significant is that these two men each die sacrificing themselves, Manny for his grandson Chuy, Leonard to save the others. He even goes down singing.[36]

Despite *Mimic*'s dire prognosis about the measures needed to cleanse the world of urban blight, the film does conclude with an optimistic note on the racial-tension front. Several scenes in the movie highlight the white couple's desire to reproduce. As already noted, in the introductory film sequence after their press conference, they are shown embracing in a bathtub and imagining their future children. Later, we see Susan one morning waiting for the results of her home pregnancy test. She happily scans her abdomen's reflection in the mirror while bouncy music plays on the soundtrack. A phone call interrupts with dire news of a sewer bug discovery, and at the same time, Susan learns that the test is negative. She is despondent enough that the film seems to hint she may have fertility problems, though Peter promises her that "we'll keep trying." This suggests that the white race cannot quite live up to its evolutionary imperative—or perhaps that the couple are being punished for Susan's transgressions. Her only "babies" are the monster bugs out in the sewers. The point is highlighted by the visual juxtaposition of her home pregnancy test kit with the two test strips in her lab in the scene that confirms her worst suspicions about the genetic identity of the new giant "baby" bug (Figure 27.5). She remarks when first opening up the box holding the monstrous bug, "You're just a baby!"—right before it viciously stings her.

Concern for children is again brought out in the rather sappy final moments of the film. Trapped alone with Chuy and an immediately threatening roach, Susan cuts her own hand so that the roach will scent her and spare the boy. Like Ripley in *Aliens*, she has become fiercely protective of this one symbolic child, and like Ripley at the end of *Alien*[3], she offers to sacrifice herself instead. But this does not prove necessary; and in the end, a miraculously saved and reunited Peter and Susan embrace. Their horrendous battle with the bugs has ended with a huge explosion, roasting all the subways (and, we presume, all the roaches in them) in one massive fireball. The camera pans down to highlight little Chuy nestled between them. Clearly implied here is that they are the adoptive parents of this now fatherless and homeless

Figure 27.5 Dr. Susan Tyler (Mira Sorvino) studies a baby mutant roach in *Mimic*.

Mexican boy. (No doubt they will also find a special school for autistic children in order to help him realize his full potential.)

I emphasized that in *Them!* the FBI agent must accede to the woman scientist's demand to go down into the ants' nest to destroy the queens. In *Mimic* when the victims are trapped in the subway car and one of them must leave to try to rewire it, Susan volunteers, saying she knows more about what's out there than the others. But her husband goes instead, after pointing out that she is the key person who absolutely must get out of the trap, because she is the one who must put a stop to what's happening. Like Victor Frankenstein, Dr. Tyler bears responsibility for her interventions in nature. Unlike him, she is never shown as mad, excessive, or hubristic—unless we are to take the small hints of disapproval she gets from her mentor figure seriously. But even he confesses that since his own grandchildren are probably alive today because of her, it would be hypocritical of him to chastise her. Rather than trying to create a new human baby in an illicit way like Victor Frankenstein, Susan has worked to save human babies, but in doing so, she has "mothered" a vile species that she cannot control and that must be aborted. Dr. Tyler is just another woman driven by the one primary goal of rescuing children. If she cannot have children of her own, she will take care of the children of others—the sick children she sees at the film's start, the little boys on her bug exploration team, or the small and frightened "special" boy Chuy.

Conclusion

Is female agency in recent horror films, whether of female scientists or of evil female queen bugs, a significant feminist development? My basic hypothesis has been that it is easier for filmmakers to depict females as heroes combating horror if the monsters are also female, especially if they set up a primitive female contest in the reproductive and mothering arena. After all, when is it ever deemed appropriate in our culture for women to exhibit aggression and even ruthless destruction, if not to protect their babies and children? Such movies may reinforce unsavory conservative notions of women's roles and downplay male interests in reproduction and caring for offspring. Through their depiction of the more disgusting biological aspects of creatures that reproduce on a massive scale, these films may reinforce negative images of women's biological nature as primitive and driven by this one chief end. Certainly a film like *Species* would fit into this latter category, with its seductive blond villainess who uses men and then destroys them in her quest for a perfect mate who will help her fulfill her inner, ugly, and nasty drive to reproduce. It is interesting in this regard, though, that back in the 1950s, things were apparently different, in that the men in *Them!* are equally concerned with protecting and salvaging both the girl at the start of the film and then the two children in the tunnel later on.

The depiction of females as agents in these movies could thus be criticized as underscoring a biological and essentialist account of women. The recurring emphasis on childbearing and nurturing reinforces not only a strict biological conception of female nature but also a vision of women's narrow domestic social roles. It is hard to avoid the same kind of ambivalent evaluation of women-and-bugs films that I reached concerning *Frankenstein*. Women and female traits are valued here as the corrective that will balance or make up for male scientific and technological excesses and violations of nature. This suggests that women still play a supportive role as understudies of men.

However, our assessment need not be so completely negative. As a continuation of the *Frankenstein* theme, these movies do highlight significant moral contributions that women can make toward resolving some of the problems of hubristic science. Science in these films is confronted with questions that are legitimate and important ones, and often *women* raise them. In *Revenge of the Creature*, Miss Hobson is doubtful about the value of the scientist's cruel tests of the lonely creature. *Them!* raised warnings about the environmental impact of nuclear testing. The *Alien* series links science (as it has become linked in fact) to broader forces of military technology and capitalism. *Mimic* links science (as it has become linked in fact) to social programs of disease control, economics, demographic study, and population analysis. In each of these films, the women who are the heroes are morally defensible in their behavior. Their femaleness is linked to admirable traits that are, to be sure, worrisome if they are essentialized or seen as women's sole prerogative, but that are nevertheless bona fide human virtues: compassion, caring, planning for a better future, and, even under some conditions (as in *Alien*[3]), self-sacrifice. (Remember that Ripley turns down the promise that she can be operated on so as to be "normal" and even have children because she knows she cannot trust the sickly sweet human version of Bishop.) I have tried to suggest in particular that in the first three *Alien* movies, Ripley is a viable and attractive female agent in a horror film. This does not mean that her treatment in these films is fine or that the development of the Ripley character in the series is without flaws.[37] A major issue to be pondered is whether the films' treatment of social themes and issues is intriguing or rather just simplistic. Perhaps *Aliens* delivers a reductive anti-technology, anti-corporation message that is purely ironic given its big-budget status; and the do-gooder white, individualistic liberalism of *Mimic* speaks for itself. What we are getting here is, at any rate, not the dark vision of uncanny horror that we will see developed in other films that I examine later in this book.

One remaining topic for assessment in my women-and-bugs movies concerns the nature of their female villains. A big problem with bugs in horror movies is that it is very hard to make insects interesting as villains. Think how dull the bugs are, for example, by comparison with the eloquent Pinhead or the metaphysical vampires Lestat and Louis in Anne Rice's novels. It is hard to do much with a monster who doesn't talk and has an altogether alien psychology. *Starship Troopers*, with its inordinate parodies of the war-film tradition, plays upon this very fact: Bugs are perhaps the one enemy we can teach our children to hate without worries about dehumanization, since the inhumanity of bugs is a simple matter of biological fact.

In assessing villains or monsters for feminist purposes, we can pause for a moment to contrast these films with ones with more traditional male monsters and think about how the monsters function in them. Male personalities simply seem to have been more deeply explored in horror, which is probably no accident, given that most of the writers, directors, special effects creators, and producers are men. This may not change until the economic conditions of female participation in the horror-film industry also change. Male monsters have been developed so as to allow them on the whole more internal complexity. They may be inadvertently evil and disgusting, hence a locus of sympathy, like the Wolfman or the Frankenstein monster. Or they may, like Dracula, Hannibal Lecter, Pinhead, or Lestat, be seductive Nietzschean types who violate the usual social norms and offer women victims escape from their humdrum mortal existence. I shall be moving on to discuss such seductive and heroic male monsters in Part 2 of this book.

Horror audiences are usually interested in villains or monsters. Noël Carroll argues in *The Philosophy of Horror* that monsters are central in horror because people want to learn more about them.[38] Monsters are the focus of the cognitive pleasures of horror. In films this is also true, but we must add in the relevant visual pleasures as well. Even if bugs cannot be psychologically interesting, they can be very visually interesting. In these films, we learn about bug behavior and psychology by seeing the bugs, just as we learn more about what they want and how they might be defeated. The Alien monsters have always been fascinating to look at.[39] The fact of their metamorphoses makes them unpredictable, and there is much to get to know about them. *Mimic* is an interesting and different sort of bug movie rooted in the *Frankenstein* tradition. Director del Toro may not provide the bad bugs with a very clear psychology or complex motivations, but it is worth saying that the giant Judas roaches of *Mimic* have an astonishing visual realization, combining eerie beauty with hideous horror. It is hard to believe that a truly revolting cockroach could have a beautiful visage enabling it to conceal itself and mimic its own predator, man. The film's extraordinary verve, pacing, and visual style make it more interesting to consider than the somewhat simplistic social messages in it would suggest. Also, since fire is the common denominator used to destroy the bugs in all the films I have discussed here, the filmmakers have the opportunity to engage in visual pyrotechnics; flames even look impressive in the black and white of *Them!*

Of course it is unclear whether as feminists we should ask for more female villains in movies. There *have* been genres with female villains, notably film noir, with its femmes fatales. Films like *Species*, *Angels and Insects*, or *Star Trek: First Contact* owe much to this tradition, with their very fatal yet seductive insect femmes. I would count the Borg Queen as the most intriguing villain on my list; she seeks novelty and has a complex strategy of seduction that differs according to her intended victim, whether it be Data or Captain Picard. But the Aliens, giant ants, or giant cockroaches are not at all cast in a seductive mold. Their agency is limited to the drive to reproduce and to destroy other species that might get in their way.

Species and *Species II* are perhaps the oddest and most genre-bending entries into the recent women-and-bugs subgenre. Played by supermodel blond beauty Natasha Henstridge, the lizard lady who is a human-alien blend is a bombshell and femme fatale in the most literal sense. The two films do interestingly different things with this basic premise. In the first film, the scientist who has created Sil by combining human and alien DNA (Ben Kingsley) loves her as his daughter and creation; but, like Victor Frankenstein or the scientists of *Alien Resurrection*, he will be destroyed by his offspring when she metamorphoses into her lizard manifestation at the end of the movie. The men who lust after her are also destroyed in gruesome and graphic ways during the sex act. The lizard or alien version of Eve/Sil is another H. R. Giger design, much like the Alien only with a more humanoid shape, including large and pulsating breasts (from which tentacles occasionally emerge). She is simultaneously hideous, seductive, and elegant with her flowing green tentacle locks of hair. Notably, this alien body is prone to developing wavy appendages, phalluses gone wild that can pierce human bodies in any of a variety of alarming ways. On the one hand, *Species* suggests that a woman this beautiful is bound to be dangerous and that in fact such a woman is really bent on just one thing—using men for reproductive ends. But on the other hand, she is also a victim and seems to be in pain when her lizard side emerges foremost.

This victim side is especially brought out in *Species II* when Eve is shown much more like the Creature in *Revenge of the Creature*. This time, she is both pitied and befriended by a female scientist, Dr. Laura Baker (Marge Helgenberger), a woman who is almost a mother or sister figure and who has always cared for her. Eve escapes and finally mates with one of her own kind, but in this film *his* sexual attentions kill *her* off. Indeed, she is just the latest in a vast line of big-breasted female victims who suffer hideous fates after he rapes and instantly impregnates them. Eve helps to save her caretaker doctor/"mother" from him just before she dies. She is thus morally exonerated in the end. *Species II*, I might add, is an unbelievably bad movie with a terrible script, characters who seem to be important but who go nowhere, illogical actions and plot motivations, gratuitously excessive scenes of violation of women's bodies, and an only thinly veiled pornographic aim. But its scenes of lizard sex are so visually extraordinary that they might just (barely) make the movie worth watching.

One thing I have shown here is that a cognitivist approach to women-and-bugs films provides insight by looking beyond the psychological dimensions of horror to consider the themes, messages, and moral dimensions of these movies. Because most of the films I have discussed here present an interesting social issue in the context of effective suspense and have intelligent dialogue, good acting, and beautiful cinematography, they are well worth our attention. They challenge the audience to respond on many levels—emotionally, visually, intellectually—as we form judgments about their messages. *Them!* is about the horror of giant ants but is also about bureaucracy, Cold War efficiency, and caring for our children in an individualistic society. The *Alien* series is about the threat to human values in an era of corporate and individual greed, when science is serving the ends of a vast faceless military bureaucracy. Within this context, once again, individualism is a value, but it must be coordinated with human compassion, caring, and camaraderie. And *Mimic* is about new urban social problems, including poverty and immigration. It unfortunately provides, yet again, a purely pat and individual resolution to a large and complex set of social problems. In sum, not all bug movies are alike, and their themes do range beyond the issues of reproductive success or the threats posed by an alleged archaic mother.

Notes

1. This is a key thesis in Barbara Creed's *The Monstrous-Feminine: Film, Feminism, Psychoanalysis* (London and New York: Routledge, 1993). Creed describes seven variations of the monstrous-feminine in horror films and notes that the prominence of female monsters in horror has been neglected by film theorists and historians; even those accounts that take gender seriously tend to assume that woman is, by nature, a victim (p. 7).

2. Carol J. Clover, *Men, Women, and Chain Saws: Gender in the Modern Horror Film* (Princeton: Princeton University Press, 1992). Clover treats *Alien* as part of her "Final Girl" series of modern horror films (p. 16).

3. I discuss these and other examples of graphic spectacular horror films in Chapter 8.

4. Also, the *Alien* story may have been based on a story by A. E. Van Vogt in *The Voyage of the Spaceship Beagle*, which featured a giant female wasp. It is, after all, wasps that cocoon animals as prey to feed "babies" once

they hatch. Van Vogt won some damages in his suit against the first film. (I am grateful to Justin Leiber for this information.)

5. I will not address films in which female monsters confront *male* heroes, such as *Independence Day* or *Star Trek: First Contact*, though the buglike monsters in them definitely have a female construction. There are more buglike monsters of indeterminate gender in recent movies like *Starship Troopers* and *Naked Lunch*. Another recent film with a significant treatment of women and bugs is *Angels and Insects*, based on A. S. Byatt's acclaimed *Angels and Insects: Two Novellas* (first published 1992; New York: Vintage Books International, 1994).

6. My approach here is somewhat similar to one advocated by Noël Carroll in "The Image of Women in Film: A Defense of a Paradigm," in Peggy Zeglin Brand and Carolyn Korsmeyer, eds., *Feminism and Tradition in Aesthetics* (University Park: Pennsylvania State University Press, 1995), 371–391, originally published in *The Journal of Aesthetics and Art Criticism* 48 (4) (Fall 1990): 349–360. Carroll writes, "The study of the image of women in film might be viewed as the search for paradigm scenarios that are available in our culture and that, by being available, may come to shape emotional responses to women" (p. 386). He refers here to Ronald de Sousa, *The Rationality of Emotions* (Cambridge: MIT Press, 1987), and to Robert Solomon, "Emotion and Choice," in Amélie Oksenberg Rorty, ed., *Explaining Emotions* (Berkeley and Los Angeles: University of California Press, 1980), 251–281.

7. See Creed, *The Monstrous-Feminine*, 16–30. Other films Creed discusses in her book are *The Exorcist*, *The Brood*, *The Hunger*, *Psycho*, *Sisters*, *I Spit on Your Grave*, and *Carrie*. The earliest of these movies is *Psycho*, from 1960, thus one complaint I have about her book is its neglect of the horror tradition; but there are other problems with her explanations, as I shall explain further below.

8. Ibid., 18.

9. Ibid., 19.

10. Ibid., 27.

11. Ibid., 29.

12. Ibid.

13. Ibid., 27.

14. Ibid., 28.

15. Ibid., 27–28.

16. Jonathan Lake Crane says that "to characterize Kristeva's summation as reductionistic is to miss the point of structural/psychoanalytic criticism." Still, he criticizes such approaches for failing to grasp changes in the very nature and operation of the unconscious: "[M]ight terror work on planes other than the extraordinarily vast territory claimed for the unconscious?" I believe there are serious problems with psychoanalytic reductionism, as I explain further here. See Crane, *Terror and Everyday Life: Singular Moments in the History of the Horror Film* (Thousand Oaks, Calif., London, and New Delhi: Sage Publications, 1994), 35.

17. Creed, *The Monstrous-Feminine*, 23; she is alluding to answers given by others to the question of why Ripley strips at the end of the film. Creed says questions are also asked about why Ripley saves the cat and risks violating quarantine laws. This is absurd, since the quarantine laws apply to alien species or microbes only! The cat has a name and has clearly been on board all along as a crew pet. The psychoanalytic account is that Ripley saves it as substitute child (or phallus substitute); I would submit that she saves it because otherwise she would be utterly alone in a vast dark universe.

18. Thomas Doherty comments, "*Vagina dentata* and phallic drill, the alien is a cross-dressing monster from the id whose sexual confusion mirrors the shifting gender dynamics of the series." See Doherty, "Genre, Gender, and the *Aliens* Trilogy," in Barry Keith Grant, ed., *The Dread of Difference: Gender and the Horror Film* (Austin: University of Texas Press 1996), 196.

19. I am thinking of stories like that of the female Christian martyr Perpetua, who was thrown to the beasts in the Roman Circus. See Perpetua, "A Christian Woman's Account of Her Persecution," in Ross S. Kraemer, ed., *Maenads, Martyrs, Matrons, Monastics: Sourcebook on Women's Religions in the Greco-Roman World* (Philadelphia: Fortress Press, 1988), 96–107. (I am grateful to Leslie Marenchin for bringing this text to my attention.) Female martyrs in literature and film often die as male warriors. We can think also of Greek heroines such as Iphigeneia in Euripides' *Iphigenia in Aulis* or of Joan of Arc. Creed notes, brilliantly, Ripley's similarity to Maria Falconetti in Carl Dreyer's film *The Passion of Joan of Arc*, when she appears with her head shorn and dies in the flames at the end of *Alien*[3]; see Creed, *The Monstrous-Feminine*, 52–53.

20. Effects and artist credits on these movies are lengthy, but to give partial credit where credit is due: *Alien* (1979), directed by Ridley Scott, special effects by Carlo Rambaldi, H. R. Giger, Brian Johnson, Rick Allder, Denys Aling; with Bolaji Badejo as the Alien. *Aliens* (1986), directed by James Cameron, special effects by Robert Soktak, Stan Winston, John Richardson, Suzanne Benson. *Alien*[3] (1992), directed by David Fincher (after Vincent Ward, original director), special effects by George Gibbs and Richard Edlund, Alien effects by Alec Gillis and Tom Woodruff Jr. *Alien Resurrection* (1997), directed by Jean-Pierre Jenet, visual effects supervisors Pitof and Erik Henry, alien effects designed and created by Alec Gillis and Tom Woodruff Jr.

21. Creed, *The Monstrous-Feminine*, 51.

22. Ibid., 53.

23. I prefer a reading of the films like that offered by Valerie Gray Hardcastle in "Changing Perspectives of Motherhood: Images from the *Aliens* Trilogy," *Film and Philosophy* 3 (1996):167–175.

24. Even if they are beautiful, like moths or butterflies, bugs can take on other complex metaphorical connotations, as A. S. Byatt's *Angels and Insects* demonstrates.

25. Fears of bugs might be irrational for reasons having nothing to do with the abject or the archaic mother. (1) Some cases of insect phobias have been cured by antipsychotic medications like Risperidone (see Gerard Gallucci and Gary Beard, "Risperidone and the Treatment of Delusions of Parasitosis in an Elderly Patient," *Psychosomatics* 36 (6) (November–December 1995):578–580). (2) Socialization may teach children to fear bugs through confusions that arise as they learn about illness and germs (Simon R. Wilkinson, *The Child's World of Illness: The Development of Health and Illness Behaviour* [Cambridge, England: Cambridge University Press, 1988]). (3) Delusions and fears of bugs are common effects of alcohol or other drug abuse; see Jerry Mitchell and Arlyn D. Vierkant, "Delusions and Hallucinations of Cocaine Abusers and Paranoid Schizophrenics: A Comparative Study," *Journal of Psychology* 125 (3) (1991):301–310. And (4) for an alternative psychoanalytic account of fear of bugs, see Michael Eigen, "A Bug-Free Universe," *Contemporary Psychoanalysis* 33 (1) (1997):19–41. (I am grateful to Anne Jacobson for research providing all these references.)

26. These points are noted by some (nonpsychoanalytic) critics. See especially Mark Jancovich, *Rational Fears: American Horror in the 1950s* (Manchester and New York: Manchester University Press, 1996), 58–61 (on *Them!*) and 176–188 (on *Creature from the Black Lagoon* and its sequel); also Peter Biskind, *Seeing Is Believing: How Hollywood Taught Us to Stop Worrying and Love the Fifties* (London: Pluto, 1983).

27. My reading of *Them!* is much indebted to the account offered by Jonathan Lake Crane in *Terror and Everyday Life*.

28. This is a crude summary; for an account that interestingly argues that there are certain feminist dimensions of the film, see Jancovich, *Rational Fears*, 176–184. He points out that the Creature is shown with sympathy and dignity, that Kay and the Creature share the "pre-phallic pleasures of the watery zone" where they swim, and that Kay keeps insisting on the fact that the Creature has not harmed her and that it should be left alone.

29. Here I am indebted to Jancovich's readings of both films in *Rational Fears*. He mentions yet another interesting female investigator in a 1950s horror film, *It Came From Beneath the Sea* (1955); see 61.

30. Jancovich notes the remarkable treatment of Pat Medford in this film ("*She* controls the gaze") and mentions that "it's the men who have problems"; *Rational Fears*, 61.

31. See Crane, *Terror and Everyday Life*, 100–131; he also points out that this movie was a real shocker at the time with its emphatic threat to children.

32. Crane comments: "*Them!* cannot go so far as to have the children eaten or trampled by the beast. As a compromise measure, the film will threaten children but not kill them" (*Terror and Everyday Life*, 126). Crane also comments, "The end of the crew is really extraordinary: in *Them!*, more people die than were probably killed in all horror films preceding the arrival of nuclear power" (p. 124).

33. Crane says that *Them!* "rapidly devolves from a relatively innovative horror picture into a routine war movie" (*Terror and Everyday Life*, 127).

34. Jancovich, *Rational Fears*, 28.

35. Per Schelde in *Androids, Humanoids, and Other Science Fiction Monsters: Science and Soul in Science Fiction Films* (New York and London: New York University Press, 1993) notes it is common for women in science fiction films to exemplify one or more of five key stereotypes: nurturers, producers of children, sex objects, earthy and homebound beings, and socializers; see 71–76.

36. Something should be said about the presence of large, emotionally expressive, and self-sacrificing black men in these movies: Parker (Yaphet Kotto) in *Alien*; Dillon (Charles S. Dutton) in *Alien*[3]; Leonard (Charles S. Dutton once more) in *Mimic*; and Dan Smithson (Forrest Whittaker) as the psychic in *Species* (1995). These men pose no sexual threats or erotic attraction to the (white) heroine; they die for or serve others; and there are no black women in the movies. I am not sure what to make of these facts, beyond the obvious stereotyping. Perhaps these heroic black men, like the strong white women in the films, reinforce the message that something has gone wrong with white masculinity. We might also note that the black character Dennis Gamble (Mykelti Williamson) in *Species II* (1998) is the one member of the crew on the Mars voyage who does not become infected by the alien parasite—due to, of all things, his carrying the sickle-cell trait! This proves the key to killing the alien, and he, too, must shed his blood (a lot of it, painfully!) to destroy the monster. (*Them!* of course, as a typical example of 1950s representation of the U.S. citizenry, had no black people in it at all.)

37. For a far more negative assessment, see Thomas Doherty, "Genre, Gender, and the *Aliens* Trilogy": "Her alert intelligence and active initiative cannot be contained in marriage, the conventional wrap-up for female-centered narratives, yet neither can she be unleashed to roam free in an uncharted feminist galaxy" (p. 198). It is possible that some of my own assessment stems from the fact that I am writing after the release of *Alien Resurrection*, so I "know" that Ripley is not truly dead and perhaps is now roaming free in a far more uncharted galaxy with her new half-Alien DNA—not to mention her new inhuman daughter, Call (Winona Ryder), a pleasant enough substitute for the lost Newt. Even without knowing of this later "resurrection," I would be tempted to point out that martyrdom is, after all, a strong criticism of the status quo rather than an endorsement of it.

38. Noël Carroll, *The Philosophy of Horror, or Paradoxes of the Heart* (New York and London: Routledge, 1990).

39. I would except the monster in *Alien*[3] from this claim; to make it mobile, the artistic designer and special effects director have placed its familiar outsized head on a scrawny body. This results in a disproportionate and almost gawky beast rather than the elegant, massively impressive one of the earlier films. This is "Teen Alien," with disgusting table manners as it smacks while consuming its ghastly meals of human flesh.

References

Biskind, Peter. *Seeing Is Believing: How Hollywood Taught Us to Stop Worrying and Love the Fifties*. London: Pluto, 1983.

Carroll, Noël. "The Image of Women in Film: A Defense of a Paradigm." *Journal of Aesthetics and Art Criticism* 48:4 (Fall 1990): 349–360.

Carroll, Noël. *The Philosophy of Horror, or Paradoxes of the Heart*. New York and London: Routledge, 1990.

Clover, Carol J. *Men, Women, and Chain Saws: Gender in the Modern Horror Film*. Princeton: Princeton University Press, 1992.

Crane, Jonathan Lake. *Terror and Everyday Life: Singular Moments in the History of the Horror Film*. Thousand Oaks, Calif., London, and New Delhi: Sage Publications, 1994.

Creed, Barbara. *The Monstrous-Feminine: Film, Feminism, Psychoanalysis*. London and New York: Routledge, 1993.

de Sousa, Ronald. *The Rationality of Emotions*. Cambridge, Mass., and London: MIT Press, 1987.

Doherty, Thomas. "Genre, Gender, and the *Aliens* Trilogy." In *The Dread of Difference: Gender and the Horror Film*, edited by Barry Keith Grant, 181–199. Austin: University of Texas Press 1996.

Hardcastle, Valerie Gray. "Changing Perspectives of Motherhood: Images from the *Aliens* Trilogy." *Film and Philosophy* 3 (1996):167–175.

Jancovich, Mark. *Rational Fears: American Horror in the 1950s*. Manchester and New York: Manchester University Press, 1996.

Schelde, Per. *Androids, Humanoids, and Other Science Fiction Monsters: Science and Soul in Science Fiction Films*. New York and London: New York University Press, 1993.

Solomon, Robert C. "Emotion and Choice." In *Explaining Emotions*, edited by Amélie Oksenberg Rorty, 251–281. Berkeley and Los Angeles: University of California Press, 1980.

Concluding Thoughts

Following on from the challenges to dominant imagery included in Part 6, and before I echo So Mayer's entreaty and say 'over to you', I'd like to draw attention to some other stereotypical and oppressive images in film and visual culture that feminist scholars have tackled and unpacked but that demand more attention from feminist film philosophers. Work on ageing women by scholars including Deborah Jermyn and Su Holmes (2015), Sally Chivers (2019), and Aagje Swinnen (2015), has changed the academic discourse on representation, celebrity and stardom. The critique has given rise to the discussion of assumptions about 'ageing well' and the cultural characteristics associated with middle-aged, menopausal, and older women. Sally Chivers (2019) has challenged the conflation of ageing and disability in the sub-genre now justifiably named 'Alzheimer's movies', many of which feature a female protagonist played by a female star (Bolton 2015). The way in which these scholars interrogate and expose the assumptions about stages in women's lives is a philosophical endeavour in its own right but also indicates a field of film philosophy that calls for more film thinking.

Anne Dufourmantelle wrote that 'philosophy has used its hatred of emotion to avoid thinking about sex' ([2003] 2007: 22). She expands, it is 'not frightened by the mechanics of sex, only by its emotional charge, its power to seduce, a power that would undo the workings of philosophical concepts one by one and tilt them gently toward the incomprehensible' ([2003] 2007: 22–23). This intriguing perspective does prompt the question of how film philosophy has approached cinematic sex. The work of Linda Williams on body genres and pornography studies (1989; 2008) and Vivian Sobchack's on bodies (2004) was groundbreaking in its study of unruly and misbehaving bodies. The emotional power of sex that Dufourmantelle refers to, however, needs to be thought about in relation to philosophies of intimacy and love, as film philosophers are beginning to do (Coulthard 2010; Wheatley 2019; Rushton 2023). It is remarkable that the topics of eroticism, seduction, and sexual intimacy – so integral to cinema – have not received more attention already from feminist film philosophy.

An area of representation and depiction that urgently requires attention is that of the suffering and death of women, images and stories of which are omnipresent in the history of cinema. Work on women and healthcare, such as that of Elinor Cleghorn's *Unwell Women: A Journey Through Medicine and Myth in a Man-Made World* (2021), has systematically demonstrated the ignorance and prejudice against women as narrators of their own health experience. The array of films collected by Kier-La Janisse in *House of Psychotic Women* demonstrates how cinema provides a welcoming platform for 'crippling paranoia, desperate loneliness, masochistic death-wishes, dangerous obsessiveness, apocalyptic hysteria' (2022). Film philosophy has so far failed to interrogate the prevalence of suffering, dying and dead women in films, and consequently has yet to forge the significant insights that it could undoubtedly bring, similar to those so powerfully argued by scholars in feminist film studies (Clarke Dillman 2014), art history (Pollock 2022) and literature (Bronfen 1992).

In *On Being Ill* Woolf described how little record there is of the 'daily drama of the body' in philosophy and literature, and saw the inadequacy of language as one of the main drawbacks of illness as a topic for writers. English, she wrote, 'has no words for the shiver and the headache' ([1926] 1930: 5, 6). What we need to express how we feel when we are ill, Woolf suggests, is not only 'a new language … primitive, subtle, sensual, obscene' but also 'a new hierarchy of the passions' ([1926] 1930: 7), so that illness is favoured as a topic above love, jealousy, villainy or heroism. Perhaps a phenomenological encounter with illness in a film such as *Safe* (1995) or *Electricity* (2014) might meet the needs that Woolf expressed.

To end, I turn to Joanna Zylinska's prophetically titled *The End of Man*, and her call for 'a feminist counterapocalypse' (2018). Zylinska wants to challenge 'the widespread belief that salvation from the current planetary apocalypse will come from a secularized yet godlike elsewhere: an escape to the heavens in the form of planetary revolution, or an actual upgrade of humans to the status of gods via Artificial Intelligence' (2018: 1). Identifying the political nature of these technocratic solutions, Zylinska's 'feminist counterapocalypse' would adopt precarity as the fundamental condition of living in the global postindustrial world, and contest many of the masculinist and technicist solutions to the global crisis (2018: 2). Zylinska's proposal is this:

> The feminist counterapocalypse framework creates a space for an ethical opening onto the precarious lives and bodies of human and non-human others – including the male bodies and minds that have been discarded in the downsizing process of disruptive semiocapitalism. In doing so, it promises liberation from the form of subjectivity pinned to a competitive, overachieving, and overreaching masculinity. It also prompts us all to ask: If unbridled progress is no longer an option, what kinds of coexistence and collaborations do we want to create in its aftermath? (2018: 59)

Zylinska calls for a consideration of Gaia according to Isabelle Stengers (2015: 58). That is, a Gaia who intrudes – shifting the emphasis on humans from the centre to the margins – in a move of philosophical humility which is linked essentially to a political drive for justice. Zylinska accompanies her treatise with a short photo-film – *Exit Man* – and declares that it has been her ambition for a while to outline a theoretical argument with media 'other than just words' (2018: 63). *Exit Man* uses her own photographs and voiceover. This film is designed to pick up the themes from her book, *The End of Man*, and it 'aims to help us rethink and resense both the Anthropocene and ourselves as humans *in* and *with* the Anthropocene. It also hopes to make us see ourselves on the ground and hear a different – less stern, even if not less serious – story of our planet and its various species' (67). Zylinska's use of Stengers and Gaia is creative feminist philosophy, and she expresses her argument through visual art as well as the written word. This is similar to the type of inventive, creative and mould-breaking feminist film philosophy that this collection is designed to inspire. It may not be as colossal a concept as a feminist counterapocalypse, but it has the potential to be monumental.

Rosi Braidotti recalls the moment when she realized the importance of art and theory while at a Laurie Anderson concert in the late 1980s (Chapter 21). Braidotti describes Anderson as 'one of those conceptual artists who seamlessly unfolds into a public intellectual, creating acoustic and aesthetic expressions for the transformations of our times'. Braidotti's description of the current changes and threats to universities and the arts recalls Iris Murdoch's analysis in *Metaphysics as a Guide to Morals* (1992), where she writes, 'Art is informative and entertaining, it condenses and clarifies the world, directing attention upon particular things. This intense showing, this bearing witness, of which it is capable is detested by tyrants who always persecute or demoralize their artists' (1992: 8). Murdoch clarifies the power of art to illuminate life, 'so as to enable us to survey complex or horrible things which would otherwise appal us' (1992: 8). It is this drive to create reflective and illuminating work that has propelled the curation of this anthology, which bursts with provocative and generative ideas. I hope that it will enable others to survey, reflect, and create.

References

Bolton, L. (2015), 'Winslet, Dench, Murdoch and Alzheimer's Disease: Intertextual Stardom in *Iris*', in L. Mulvey and A. Backman Rogers (eds), *Feminisms*, Amsterdam: University of Amsterdam Press.

Bronfen, E. (1992), *Over Her Dead Body: Death, Femininity and the Aesthetic*, Manchester: Manchester University Press.

Chivers, S. (2019), 'Still Julianne: Projecting Dementia on the Silvering Screen', in K. Ellis, G. Goggin, B. Haller and R. Curtis (eds), *The Routledge Companion to Disability and Media*, London: Routledge.

Clarke Dillman, J. (2014), *Women and Death in Film, Television, and News: Dead but Not Gone*, New York and Basingstoke: Palgrave Macmillan.

Cleghorn, E. (2021), *Unwell Women: A Journey Through Medicine and Myth in a Man-Made World*, London: Weidenfeld and Nicolson.

Coulthard, L. (2010), 'Desublimating Desire: Courtly Love and Catherine Breillat', *Journal for Cultural Research*, 14 (1): 57–69.

Dufourmantelle, A. ([2003] 2007), *Blind Date: Sex and Philosophy*, Trans. C. Porter, Urbana, Chicago and Springfield: University of Illinois Press.

Janisse, K. (2022), *House of Psychotic Women (Expanded Edition)*, Godalming: FAB Press.

Jermyn, D. and S. Holmes, eds (2015), *Women, Celebrity and Cultures of Ageing: Freeze Frame*, Basingstoke, Hampshire: Palgrave Macmillan.

Murdoch, I. (1992), *Metaphysics as a Guide to Morals*, London: Chatto & Windus.

Pollock, G. (2022), *Killing Men and Dying Women*: *Imagining Difference in 1950s New York Painting*, Manchester: Manchester University Press.

Rushton, R. (2023), *Modern European Cinema and Love*, Manchester: Manchester University Press.

Sobchack, V. (2004), *Carnal Thoughts: Embodiment and Moving Image Culture*, Berkeley, CA and London: University of California Press.

Stengers, I. (2015), *In Catastrophic Times: Resisting the Coming Barbarism*, Trans. A. Goffy, London: Open Humanities Press.

Swinnen, A. (2015), 'Ageing in Film', in J. Twigg and W. Martin (eds), *The Routledge Handbook of Cultural Gerontology*, London: Routledge.

Wheatley, C. (2019), *Stanley Cavell and Film: Scepticism and Self-Reliance at the Cinema*, London: Bloomsbury Academic.

Williams, L. (1989), *Hard Core: Power, Pleasure and the Frenzy of the Visible*, Berkeley: University of California Press.

Williams, L. (2008), *Screening Sex*, Durham, NC: Duke University Press.

Woolf, V. ([1926] 1930), *On Being Ill*, London: L. & V. Woolf.

Zylinska, J. (2018), *The End of Man: A Feminist Counterapocalypse*, Minneapolis: University of Minnesota Press.

Filmography

2 Seconds (1998), Dir. Manon Briand, Canada: Cable Distribution Fund.

52 Tuesdays (2013), Dir. Sophie Hyde, Australia: Closer Productions.

A Nightmare on Elm Street (1984), Dir. Wes Craven, USA: New Line Cinema.

A Study in Choreography for the Camera (1945), Dir. Maya Deren, USA.

Albert Nobbs (2011), Dir. Rodrigo Garcia, USA: Mockingbird Pictures.

Alien (1979), Dir. Ridley Scott, UK and USA: Twentieth Century Fox.

$Alien^3$ (1992), Dir. David Fincher, UK and USA: Twentieth Century Fox.

Alien Resurrection (1997), Dir. Jean-Pierre Jeunet, USA: Twentieth Century Fox.

Aliens (1986), Dir. James Cameron, UK and USA: Twentieth Century Fox.

Alma's Rainbow (1994), Dir. Ayoka Chenzira, USA: Red Carnelian Films.

Angels and Insects (1995), Dir. Philip Haas, UK and USA: Playhouse International Pictures.

At Land (1944), Dir. Maya Deren, USA.

Attack of the 50-foot Woman (1958), Dir. Nathan Juran, USA: Woolner Brothers Pictures.

Avatar (2009), Dir. James Cameron, US and UK: Twentieth Century Fox.

Black Swan (2010), Dir. Darren Aronofsky, USA: Searchlight Pictures.

Boyhood (2014), Dir. Richard Linklater, USA: IFC Productions.

Boys Don't Cry (1999), Dir. Kimberly Peirce, USA: Searchlight Pictures.

Calamity Jane (1953), Dir. David Butler, USA: Warner Bros.

Carrie (1976), Dir. Brian De Palma, USA: Red Bank Films.

Cat People (1982), Dir. Paul Schrader, USA: RKO Pictures.

Clash of the Titans (1981), Dir. Desmond Davis, UK and USA: Charles H. Schneer Productions.

Clash of the Titans (2010), Dir. Louise Leterrier, USA: Warner Bros.

Coal Miner's Granddaughter (1991), Dir. Cecilia Dougherty, USA: Video Data Bank.

Color (1983), Dir. Warrington Hudlin, USA: New York Black Filmmaker Foundation.

Contact (1997), Dir. Robert Zemeckis, USA: Warner Bros.

Creature from the Black Lagoon (1954), Dir. Jack Arnold, USA: Universal International Pictures.

Dallas Buyers Club (2013), Dir. Jean-Marc Vallée, USA: Truth Entertainment (II).

Daughters of the Dust (1991), Dir. Julie Dash, USA: Geechee Girls.

Dead Man Walking (1995), Dir. Tim Robbins, UK and USA: Havoc and Polygram Filmed Entertainment.

Dressed to Kill (1980), Dir. Brian De Palma, USA: Filmways Pictures.

Electricity (2014), Dir. Bryn Higgins, UK: Soda Pictures.

Eternal Sunshine of the Spotless Mind (2004), Dir. Michel Gondry, USA: Focus Features.

Frankenstein (1931), Dir. James Whale, USA: Universal Pictures.

Frankenstein (1994), Dir. Kenneth Branagh, USA: TriStar Pictures.

Frida (2002), Dir. Julie Taymor, USA: Handprint Entertainment.

Friday the 13th (1980), Dir. Sean S. Cunningham, USA: Paramount Pictures.

Fried Green Tomatoes at the Whistle Stop Café (1991), Dir. Jon Avnet, USA: Universal Pictures.

Girlhood/Bande de filles (2014), Dir. Céline Sciamma, France: Hold Up Films.

Gotta Make This Journey: Sweet Honey In The Rock (1983), [Television Special] Dir. Joseph Camp, USA: produced by Michelle Parkerson.

Halloween (1978), Dir. John Carpenter, USA: Compass International Pictures.

Hellraiser (1987), Dir. Clive Barker, UK: Film Futures.

How Stella Got Her Groove Back (1998), Dir. Kevin Rodney Sullivan, USA: Twentieth Century Fox.

I Am Not a Witch (2017), Dir. Rungano Nyoni, UK: Arte Prize.

Independence Day (1996), Dir. Roland Emmerich, USA: Twentieth Century Fox.

Innocence (2004), Dir. Lucile Hadžihalilović, France: Ex Nihilo.

Interview with the Vampire (1994), Dir. Neil Jordan, USA: Geffen Pictures.

I Spit on Your Grave (1978), Dir. Meir Zarchi, USA: Déjà vu.

It Came from Beneath the Sea (1955), Dir. Robert Gordon, USA: Clover Productions.

Jaws (1975), Dir. Steven Spielberg, USA: Zanuck/Brown Productions.

Jeanne Dielman, 23, quai du Commerce, 1080 Bruxelles (1975), Dir. Chantal Akerman, Belgium: Paradise Films.

Jurassic Park (1993), Dir. Steven Spielberg, USA: Universal Pictures.

La Haine (1995), Dir. Mathieu Kassovitz, France: Les Productions Lazennec.

Lawrence of Arabia (1962), Dir. David Lean, UK and USA: Horizon Pictures (II).

Losing Ground (1982), Dir. Kathleen Collins, USA: produced by Eleanor Charles.

Lost Highway (1997), Dir. David Lynch, France and USA: CiBy 2000.

Meshes of the Afternoon (1943), Dirs. Maya Deren and Alexander Hammid, USA.

Mimic (1997), Dir. Guillermo del Toro, USA: Dimension Films.

Mona Lisa (1986), Dir. Neil Jordan, UK: HandMade Films.

Naked Lunch (1991), Dir. David Cronenberg, Canada: Recorded Picture Company.

Nil by Mouth (1997), Dir. Gary Oldman, UK and France: SE8 Group and EuropaCorp.

October: Ten Days that Shook the World (1927), Dirs. Grigori Aleksandrov and Sergei Eisenstein, Soviet Union: Sovkino.

Once Were Warriors (1994), Dir. Lee Tamahori, New Zealand: Communicado Productions.

Orlando (1992), Dir. Sally Potter, UK: Adventure Pictures.

Paris, Texas (1984), Dir. Wim Wenders, West Germany: Road Movies Filmproduktion.

Peeping Tom (1960), Dir. Michael Powell, UK: Michael Powell (Theatre).

Psycho (1960), Dir. Alfred Hitchcock, USA: Alfred J. Hitchcock Productions.

Raintree County (1957), Dir. Edward Dmytryk, USA: Loew's.

Revenge of the Creature (1955), Dir. Jack Arnold, USA: Universal International Pictures (UI).

Safe (1995), Dir. Todd Haynes, US: American Playhouse Theatrical Films.

Saint Maud (2019), Dir. Rose Glass, UK: Escape Plan Productions.

She's Gotta Have It (1986), Dir. Spike Lee, USA: 40 Acres & A Mule Filmworks.

Showboat (1951), Dir. George Sidney, USA: Metro-Goldwyn-Mayer.

Showing Up (2022), Dir. Kelly Reichardt, USA: A24.

Shulie (1967), Dirs. Jerry Blumenthal, Sheppard Ferguson, James Leahy and Alan Rettig, USA.

Shulie (1998), Dir. Elisabeth Subrin, USA: Video Data Bank.

Sisters (1972), Dir. Brian De Palma, USA: Pressman-Williams Enterprises.

Something Must Break/Nånting måste gå sönder (2014), Dir. Ester Martin Bergsmark, Sweden: Garagefilm International.

Species (1995), Dir. Roger Donaldson, USA: Metro-Goldwyn-Mayer.

Species II (1998), Dir. Peter Medak, USA: Metro-Goldwyn-Mayer.

Starship Troopers (1997), Dir. Paul Verhoeven, USA: TriStar Pictures.

Star Trek: First Contact (1996), Dir. Jonathan Frakes, USA: Paramount Pictures.

The Boys (1998), Dir. Rowan Woods, Australia: Arenafilm.

The Brood (1979), Dir. David Cronenberg, Canada: Canadian Film Development Corporation.

The Cabinet of Dr Caligari/Das Cabinet des Dr Caligari (1920), Dir. Robert Wiene, Germany: Decla-Bioscop AG.

The Color Purple (1985). Dir. Steven Spielberg, USA: Warner Bros.

The Danish Girl (2015), Dir. Tom Hooper, UK: Working Title Films.

The Day of the Triffids (1963), Dirs. Steve Sekely and Freddie Francis, UK: Allied Artists Pictures.

The Day the Earth Stood Still (1951), Dir. Robert Wise, USA: Twentieth Century Fox.

The Edge of Heaven/Auf der anderen Seite (2007), Dir. Fatih Akın, Germany, Turkey, Italy: Anka Film.

The Exorcist (1973), Dir. William Friedkin, USA: Warner Bros.

The Fly (1986), Dir. David Cronenberg, USA: SLM Production Group.

The Hunger (1983), Dir. Tony Scott, UK: Peerford.

The Incredible Shrinking Man (1957), Dir. Jack Arnold, USA: Universal International Pictures.

The Kiss of the Vampire (1963), Dir. Don Sharp, UK: Hammer Films.

The Lord of the Rings: The Fellowship of the Ring (2001), Dir. Peter Jackson, New Zealand and USA: New Line Cinema, WingNut Films.

The Lord of the Rings: The Return of the King (2003), Dir. Peter Jackson, New Zealand and USA: New Line Cinema, WingNut Films.

The Lord of the Rings: The Two Towers (2002), Dir. Peter Jackson, New Zealand and USA: New Line Cinema, WingNut Films.

The Outlaw (1943), Dir. Howard Hughes and Howard Hawks, USA: Howard Hughes Productions.

The Passion of Joan of Arc/La passion de Jeanne d'Arc (1923), Dir. Carl Theodor Dreyer, France: Société générale des films.

The Physics of Love (1998), Dir. Diane Bonder, USA.

The Sticky Fingers of Time (1997), Dir. Hilary Brougher, USA: Crystal Pictures.

The Terminator (1984), Dir. James Cameron, UK and USA: Helmdale.

The Texas Chainsaw Massacre 2 (1986), Dir. Tobe Hooper, USA: Cannon Films.

The Unforgiven (1960), Dir. John Huston, USA: Hecht-Hill-Lancaster Productions.

The Vampire Lovers (1970), Dir. Roy Ward Baker, UK: Hammer Films.

Them! (1954), Dir. Gordon Douglas, USA: Warner Bros.

Tomboy (2011), Dir. Céline Sciamma, France: Hold Up Films.

Troy (2004), Dir. Wolfgang Petersen, USA: Warner Bros.

Waiting to Exhale (1995), Dir. Forest Whitaker, USA: Twentieth Century Fox.

Water Lilies/Naissance des pieuvres (2007), Dir. Céline Sciamma, France: Balthazar Productions.

Wrath of the Titans (2012), Dir. Jonathan Liebesman, USA: Warner Bros.

Appendix: Study Material

These are suggested topics and resources for teaching Feminist Film Philosophy. I have taught all these topics, films, and readings on my undergraduate and postgraduate modules over the years, and hope they can be drawn upon when planning teaching sessions and as a study resource for students.

This study material is split into twelve Sections. Each Section contains sufficient material for a week's tuition/study. I am particularly grateful to Giulia Rho for identifying and planning the topics and resources for Sections Four, Five and Eight.

Section One: Introduction to Feminism, Film and Film Philosophy

Essential Viewing

The Watermelon Woman (1996), Dir. Cheryl Dunye, USA: Dancing Girl.
Thriller (1979), Dir Sally Potter, UK: Adventure Pictures.

Essential Reading

Bolton, L. (2015), '"Frozen in Showcases": Feminist Film Theory and the Abstraction of Woman', in L. Bolton, *Film and Female Consciousness: Irigaray, Cinema and Thinking Women*, 8–28, London: Palgrave Macmillan.
Mayer, S. (2009), '*Thriller*', in S. Mayer, *The Cinema of Sally Potter: A Poetics of Love*, 27–39, London: Wallflower.
Zimmer, C. (2008), 'Histories of *The Watermelon Woman*: Reflexivity Between Race and Gender', in *Camera Obscura*, 23 (2 (68)): 41–66. https://doi.org/10.1215/02705346-2008-002 (accessed 3 May 2025).

Further Viewing

A Question of Silence/De stilte rond Christine M. (1982), Dir. Marleen Gorris, Netherlands: Sigma Film Productions.
Orlando (1992), Dir. Sally Potter, UK: Adventure Pictures.

Further Reading

Kuhn, Annette (1994), *Women's Pictures: Feminism and Cinema*, London: Verso.
Mayer, S. (2009), *The Cinema of Sally Potter: A Poetics of Love*, London: Wallflower.
Shaw, D. (2008), *Film and Philosophy: Taking Movies Seriously*, London: Wallflower.
Sinnerbrink, R. (2011), *New Philosophies of Film: Thinking Images*, London: Bloomsbury.
Tay, S. L. (2009), 'On the Edges of Art Cinema: Sally Potter and the Feminist Response', in S. L. Tay, *Women on the Edge: Twelve Political Practices*, 84–107, Palgrave Macmillan: London.

Section Two: Feminist Film Phenomenology

Essential Viewing

Innocence (2004), Dir. Lucile Hadžihalilović, France: Ex Nihilo.

Essential Reading

Bakewell, S. (2016), *At the Existentialist Café: Freedom, Being and Apricot Cocktails*, 40–43, London: Chatto & Windus.

Quinlivan, D. (2009), 'Material Hauntings: The Kinaesthesia of Sound in *Innocence*', *Studies in French Cinema* 9 (3): 215–24.

Sobchack, V. (1991), *The Address of the Eye: A Phenomenology of Film Experience*, 1–26, Princeton, NJ and Oxford, Princeton University Press.

Further Viewing

Fish Tank (2009), Dir. Andrea Arnold, UK: BBC Film.

How to Have Sex (2023), Dir. Molly Manning-Walker, UK: MUBI.

The Hours (2002), Dir. Stephen Daldry, USA: Paramount Pictures.

The Piano (1993), Dir. Jane Campion, New Zealand: CiBy 2000.

Wuthering Heights (2011), Dir. Andrea Arnold, UK: Film4.

Further Reading

Bolton, L. (2015), 'Mia in *Fish Tank*: Being a Modern Girl in Modern Britain', in F. Handyside and K. Taylor (eds), *International Cinema and the Girl*: *Local Issues, Transnational Contexts*, 75–84, London: Palgrave Macmillan.

Bolton, L. (2015), 'Solving Suicide: Facing the Complexity of *The Hours*', in W. Buckland (ed.), *Hollywood Puzzle Films*, 265–78, London and New York: Routledge.

Ince, K. (2012), 'Feminist Phenomenology and the Films of Sally Potter', in J. Boulé and U. Tidd (eds), *Existentialism and Contemporary Cinema: A Beauvoirian Perspective*, 161–74, New York and Oxford: Berghahn Books.

Ince, K. (2017), 'Female Subjectivity in Philosophy and Theory', in K. Ince, *The Body and the Screen: Female Subjectivities in Contemporary Women's Cinema*, London and Oxford: Bloomsbury.

Wilson, E. (2012), 'Girlhood in *Innocence*', in J. Boulé and U. Tidd (eds), *Existentialism and Contemporary Cinema: A Beauvoirian Perspective*, 17–32, New York and Oxford: Berghahn Books.

Woolf, V. (1926), 'The Cinema', in *The Nation and Athenaeum*, 3 July 1926, pp. 381–3. Reproduced in full in this volume.

Young, I. M. ([1990] 2005), 'Throwing Like a Girl: A Phenomenology of Feminine Body Comportment, Motility, and Spatiality', in *On Female Body Experience: 'Throwing Like a Girl' and Other Essays in Feminist Philosophy and Social Theory*, 27–45, Oxford: Oxford University Press.

Section Three: The Existentialist Heroine

Essential Viewing

Morvern Callar (2002), Dir. Lynne Ramsay, UK: Alliance Atlantis Motion Picture Production.

Essential Reading

Beauvoir, S. de (2015), *The Second Sex*, London: Vintage Classics. (Extracts from Part IV Chapter 1, 'Childhood' and Part VIII Chapter 1, 'The Independent Woman').

Bolton, L. (2009), 'Remembering Flesh: Morvern Callar as an Irigarayan Alice', in J. Chamarette and J. Higgins (eds), *Guilt and Shame : Essays in French Literature, Thought and Visual Culture*, 189–200, Bern and Oxford: Peter Lang.

Sartre, J. P. (2007), 'Existentialism is a Humanism', New Haven, CT and London: Yale University Press.

Further Viewing

Clouds of Sils Maria (2014), Dir. Olivier Assayas, France: CG Cinéma.

Priest (1994), Dir. Antonia Bird, UK: BBC Film.

Things to Come/L'avenir (2016), Dir. Mia Hansen-Løve, France: CG Cinéma.

Further Reading

Bakewell, S., (2016), *At the Existentialist Café: Freedom, Being and Apricot Cocktails*, Chatto & Windus.

Boulé, J. and U. Tidd, eds, (2012), *Existentialism and Contemporary Cinema: A Beauvoirian Perspective*, New York and Oxford: Berghahn Books.

duGraf, L. (2018), 'Cinema in the Eyes of Simone de Beauvoir', *Screen* 59 (3): 381–90.

Fuery, K. (2022), *Ambiguous Cinema: from Simone de Beauvoir to Feminist Film-Phenomenology*, Edinburgh: Edinburgh University Press.

Marso, L. (2016), 'Perverse Protests: Simone de Beauvoir on Pleasure and Danger, Resistance, and Female Violence in Film', *Signs* 41 (4): 869–94.

Williams, L. R. (2002), 'Escape Artist: Lynne Ramsay's *Morvern Callar*', *Sight & Sound*, 12 (10): 22–5.

Section Four: Queer Time as New Historiography

Essential Viewing

Far from Heaven (2022), Dir. Todd Haynes, USA: Focus Features.

Essential Reading

Freeman, E. (2010), 'Introduction: Queer and Not Now', in E. Freeman, *Time Binds: Queer Temporalities, Queer Histories*, 1–20, Durham, NC: Duke University Press.

Luciano, D. (2007), 'Coming Around Again: The Queer Momentum of *Far from Heaven*', *GLQ* 13 (2–3): 249–72.

Rich, R. B. (1992), 'New Queer Cinema', *Sight and Sound*, 2 (5): 30–4.

Further Viewing

All that Heaven Allows (1955), Dir. Douglas Sirk, USA: Universal International Pictures.

Petite Maman (2021), Dir. Céline Sciamma, France: Lilies Films.

Further Reading

Colebrook, C. (2009), 'Stratigraphic Time, Women's Time', *Australian Feminist Studies*, 24 (59): 11–16, https://doi.org/10.1080/08164640802645125 (accessed 3 May 2025).

Derrida, J. (1995), 'The Time is Out of Joint' in Anselm Haverkamp (ed.), *Deconstruction Is/In America: A New Sense of the Political*, New York: NYU Press.

Dinshaw, C., L. Edelman, R. A. Ferguson, C. Freccero, E. Freeman, J. Halberstam, A. Jagose, C. S. Nealon and T. H. Nguyen (2007), 'Theorizing Queer Temporalities: A Roundtable Discussion', *GLQ*, 13 (2–3): 177–95.

Grosz, E. (1999), 'Becoming … an Introduction', in E. Grosz (ed.), *Becomings: Explorations in Time, Memory and Futures*, 1–11, New York: Cornell University Press.

Hilderbrand, L. (2006), 'Retroactivism', *GLQ*, 12 (2): 303–17.

Keeling, K. (2019), *Queer Times, Black Futures*, New York: NYU Press.

Munoz, J. E. (2009), *Cruising Utopia*, New York: NYU Press.

Section Five: Myth and Fable

Essential Viewing

Daughters of the Dust (1991), Dir. Julie Dash, USA: Geechee Girls.

Essential Reading

Keeling, K. (2007), 'In the Interval', in *The Witch's Flight: The Cinematic, the Black Femme, and the Image of Common Sense*, 27–44, Durham, NC: Duke University Press.

Sudhinaraset, P. (2018), '"We Are Not an Organically City People": Black Modernity and the Afterimages of Julie Dash's *Daughters of the Dust*', *Black Scholar*, 48 (3): 46–60.

Further Viewing

Lemonade visual album (2015), Dir. Beyoncé et al., USA: Good Company.
Meshes of the Afternoon (1943), Dirs. Maya Deren and Alexander Hammid, USA.
The Future (2011), Dir. Miranda July, USA: GNK Productions.
Water Ritual #1: An Urban Rite of Purification (1979), Dir. Barbara McCullough, USA.

Further Reading

Dash, J. (1993), *Daughters of the Dust: The Making of an African American Woman's Film*, New York: The New Press.

Field, A. N., Horak, J.-C., and Stewart, J. N., eds, (2015), *L.A. Rebellion: Creating a New Black Cinema* (1st ed.). Berkeley, CA: University of California Press.

hooks, b. (2016), 'Moving Beyond Pain', *bell hook's Books*. https://bellhooksbooks.com/blog/moving-beyond-pain/ (accessed 25 August 2025).

Irigaray, L. (1994), *Thinking the Difference*, trans. Karin Montin, London: The Athlone Press.

Keeling, K. (2011), 'School of Life: On the LA Rebellion', *Artforum* 50 (2): 294–7.

Keeling, K. (2019), 'Introduction: Black Futures and the Queer Times of Life: Finance, Flesh, and the Imagination', in *Queer Times, Black Futures*, 1–40, New York: NYU Press.

Kelley, R. D. G. (2002), *Freedom Dreams: Black Radical Imagination*, Boston, MA: Beacon Press.

Machiorlatti, J. A. (2005), 'Revisiting Julie Dash's "Daughters of the Dust": Black Feminist Narrative and Diasporic Recollection', *South Atlantic Review*, 70 (1): 97–116. http://www.jstor.org/stable/20462733 (accessed 3 May 2025).

Mayer, S. (2016), 'Mirror Mirror: Fairy Tales of the Feminist Fantastic', in S. Mayer, *Political Animals*, 118–32, New York: I. B. Tauris.

Moten, F. (2003), *In the Break: The Aesthetics of the Black Radical Tradition*, Minneapolis, MN: Minnesota University Press.

Phillips, S. (2017), 'Beyoncé vs Daughters of the Dust: How an American Indie Classic Inspired Lemonade', London: BFI Features and Reviews.

Quan, H. L. T., (2017), 'It's Hard to Stop Rebels That Time Travel: Democratic Living and the Radical Reimagining of Old Worlds' in G. T. Johnson (ed.), *Futures of Black Radicalism*, 205–23, London, UK: Verso.

Section Six: Women and Horror

Essential Viewing

Dark Water (2002), Dir. Hideo Nakata, Japan: Kadokawa Shoten Publishing Co.

Essential Reading

Creed, B. (2001), 'Horror and the Monstrous-Feminine', in Mark Jancovich (ed.), *Horror, the Film Reader*, London: Routledge.

Martin, N. K. (2008), 'Dread of Mothering: Plumbing the Depths of *Dark Water*', *Jump Cut*, 50, Spring 2008, np https://www.ejumpcut.org/archive/jc50.2008/darkWater/ (accessed 3 May 2025).

Further Viewing

Carrie (1976), Dir. Brian DePalma, USA: Red Bank Films.
Prevenge (2016), Dir. Alice Lowe, UK: Western Edge Pictures.
Rosemary's Baby (1968), Dir. Roman Polanski, USA: William Castle Productions.
The Babadook (2014), Dir. Jennifer Kent, Australia: Screen Australia.

Further Reading

Arnold, S. (2013), *Maternal Horror Film: Motherhood and Melodrama*, London: Palgrave Macmillan.

Buerger, S. (2017), 'The Beak that Grips: Maternal Indifference, Ambivalence and the Abject in *The Babadook*', *Studies in Australasian Cinema*, 11 (1): 33–44.

Clover, C. ([1992] 2015), *Men, Women and Chainsaws: Gender in the Modern Horror Film*, London: BFI.

Creed, B. (1993), *The Monstrous Feminine: Film, Feminism, and Psychoanalysis*, London: Routledge.

Gillmor, A. (2015), 'Feminist Horror: Plotting Against Patriarchy', in *Herizons Women's News and Feminist Views*, 2015, np.

Jacobsen, P. (2016), 'Eye on Fiction: *The Babadook and Maternal Depression*', *The Psychologist*, 29 (11): 840–41.

Kristeva, J. (1982), *Powers of Horror: An Essay on Abjection*, trans. L. S. Roudiez, New York: Columbia University Press.

Williams, L. (2001), 'When the Woman Looks', in M. Jancovich (ed.), *Horror, the Film Reader*, London: Routledge.

Section Seven: Gender Non-Conforming Bodies and Phenomenologies

Essential Viewing

Tomboy (2011), Dir. Céline Sciamma, France: Hold Up Films.

Essential Reading

Lindner, K. (2018), 'Céline Sciamma's "Queer" Cinema: Affirming Gestures of Refusal in *Tomboy* and *Girlhood*', in K. Lindner, *Film Bodies: Queer Feminist Encounters with Gender and Sexuality in Cinema*, 194–245, London: I. B. Tauris. Reproduced in full in the volume.

Further Viewing

Disclosure (2020), Dir. Sam Feder, USA: Disclosure Films.
Ma vie en rose (1997), Dir. Alain Berliner, Belgium: Haut et Court.
Tangerine, (2015), Dir. Sean Baker, USA: Freestyle Picture Company.

Further Reading

Steinbock, E. (2019), *Shimmering Images: Trans Cinema, Embodiment, and the Aesthetics of Change*, Durham, NC: Duke University Press.
Waldron, D. (2013), 'Embodying Gender Nonconformity in "Girls": Céline Sciamma's *Tomboy*', *Esprit Createur*, 53 (1): 60–73.
Wilson, E. (2021), *Céline Sciamma: Portraits*, Edinburgh: Edinburgh University Press.

Section Eight: Eco-Feminism, Posthuman Feminism

Essential Viewing

Wendy and Lucy (2008), Dir. Kelly Reichardt, USA: Field Guide Films.

Essential Reading

Braidotti, R. (2015), 'Four Theses on Posthuman Feminism' in R. Grusin (ed.), *Anthropocene Feminism*, 21–48, Minneapolis, MN: University of Minnesota Press.
Haraway, D. J. (2008), 'Introductions' in *When Species Meet*, 3–44, Minneapolis, MN: University of Minnesota Press.
Pick, A. (2011), 'Creaturely Bodies' in *Creaturely Poetics: Animality and Vulnerability in Literature and Film*, 1–20, New York: Columbia University Press.

Further Viewing

Nausicaä of the Valley of the Wind (1984), Dir. Hayao Miyazaki, Japan: Nibariki.
The Turin Horse (2011), Dir. Béla Tarr and Ágnes Hranitzky, Hungary: TT Filmmûhely.

Further Reading

Derrida, J. (2008), *The Animal That Therefore I Am*, New York: Fordham University Press.
Hall, D. E. (2018), 'Breakthrough: *Wendy and Lucy*' in *ReFocus: The Films of Kelly Reichardt*, 64–85, Edinburgh: Edinburgh University Press.
Haraway, D. (2003), *The Companion Species Manifesto: Dogs, People, and Significant Otherness*, Chicago, IL: Prickly Paradigm Press.

Mayer, S. (2016), 'Not in Kansas: Animal Selves and Becoming-Girls', in S. Mayer, *Political Animals: The New Feminist Cinema*, 29–33, London: I. B. Tauris.

McMahon, L. (2018), 'Film' in *The Edinburgh Companion to Animal Studies*, 215–31, Edinburgh: Edinburgh University Press.

Section Nine: Women and Madness

Essential Viewing

Saint Maud (2019), Dir. Rose Glass, UK: Escape Plan Productions.

Essential Reading

Appignanesi, L. (2008), *Mad, Bad & Sad: A History of Women and the Mind Doctors*, 368–77, London and New York: W. N. Norton.

Russo, J. (2016), 'Towards our Own Framework, or Reclaiming Madness Part Two', in *Searching for a Rose Garden: Challenging Psychiatry, Fostering Mad Studies*, 59–67, Exeter: Imprint Digital.

Williams, M. (2020), 'The Gospel of Rose Glass', *Sight & Sound*, 30 (9): 26–30.

Further Viewing

Girl, Interrupted (1999), Dir. James Mangold, USA: Columbia Pictures.
Suddenly, Last Summer (1959), Dir. Joseph L. Mankiewicz, USA: Columbia Pictures.
The French Lieutenant's Woman (1981), Dir. Karel Reisz, UK: Juniper Films.
Tom & Viv (1994), Dir. Brian Gilbert, UK: British Screen Productions.

Further Reading

Janisse, K. (2022), *House of Psychotic Women (Expanded Edition)*, Godalming: FAB Press.

Section Ten: Girlhood

Essential Viewing

Girlhood/Bande de filles (2014), Dir. Céline Sciamma, France: Hold Up Films.

Essential Reading

Handyside, F. and K. Taylor, eds, (2016), *International Cinema and the Girl*: *Local Issues, Transnational Contexts*, London: Palgrave Macmillan.

Pember, A. (2020). 'Visions of Ecstasy': Resilience and Melancholy in the Musical Moments of *Bande de filles* (Céline Sciamma, 2014), *French Screen Studies*, 20 (3–4): 298–316.

Further Viewing

Anatomy of Violence (2016), Dir. Deepa Mehta, Canada and India: Hamilton-Mehta Productions.
Fish Tank (2009), Dir. Andrea Arnold, UK: BBC Film.

Ginger and Rosa (2012), Dir. Sally Potter, UK: Adventure Pictures.
I Am Not a Witch (2017), Dir. Rungano Nyoni, UK: Arte Prize.
Mustang (2015), Dir. Deniz Gamze Erguven, France: CG Cinéma.
The Falling (2014), Dir. Carol Morley, UK: Cannon and Morley Productions.
Water Lillies (2007), Dir. Céline Sciamma, France:Balthazar Productions.

Further Reading

Boyle, K. (2019), *#MeToo, Weinstein and Feminism*, Cham, Switzerland: Palgrave Pivot.
Hill, S. (2021), *Young Women, Girls and Postfeminism in Contemporary British Film*, London: Bloomsbury Academic.

Section Eleven: Public Discourses of Dementia

Essential Viewing

Still Alice (2014), Dir. Richard Glatzer, Wash Westmoreland, USA: BSM Studio.

Essential Reading

Chivers, S. (2019), 'Still Julianne: Projecting Dementia on the Silvering Screen', in *The Routledge Companion to Disability and Media*, London and New York: Routledge.
Haskell, M. (2014), 'Review: *Still Alice*', *Film Comment*, 51 (1): 62–3.

Further Viewing

Away from Her (2006), Dir. Sarah Polley, Canada: Foundry Films.
Elizabeth is Missing (2019), [TV Movie] Dir. Aisling Walsh, UK: STV Productions.
Iris (2001), Dir. Richard Eyre, UK: BBC.

Further Reading

Bolton, L. (2015), 'Winslet, Dench, Murdoch and Alzheimer's Disease: Intertextual Stardom in *Iris*', in L. Mulvey and A. Backman Rogers (eds), *Feminisms*, Amsterdam: University of Amsterdam Press.
Deng, M. (2023), *Ageing, Dementia and Time in Film: Temporal Performances*, Edinburgh: Edinburgh University Press.

Section Twelve: Film Phenomenology and the Sick Body

Essential Viewing

Electricity (2014), Dir. Bryn Higgins, UK: Soda Pictures.

Essential Reading

Baxendale, S. (2015), 'Electricity Crackles with Authenticity', *The Lancet*, 14 (5): 467. https://www.thelancet.com/journals/laneur/article/PIIS1474-4422(14)70269-8/fulltext (accessed 3 May 2025).

Beesley, R. (2014), 'Alternate Perspective' *Aesthetica*, https://aestheticamagazine.com/alternate-perspective/ (accessed 3 May 2025).

Sobchack, V. (1992), 'Chapter One, Phenomenology and Film Experience', in *The Address of the Eye: a Phenomenology of Film Experience*, 3–26, Princeton, NJ: Princeton University Press.

Further Viewing

Cake (2014), Dir. Daniel Barnz, USA: Cinelou Films.

Safe (1995), Dir. Todd Haynes, USA: American Playhouse Theatrical Films.

Further Reading

Collins, S., trans. (2022), *On Being Ill: Virginia Woolf, Audre Lorde*, Amsterdam: Uitgeverij HetMoet.

Quinlivan, D. (2015), *Filming the Body in Crisis: Trauma, Healing and Hopefulness*, Basingstoke, Hampshire: Palgrave Macmillan.

Wohlmann, A. (2022), *Metaphor in Illness Writing: Fight and Battle Reused*, Edinburgh: Edinburgh University Press.

Index

embodiment
    queer cinema 95, 98, 102, 107, 110, 112, 113, 117, 125
    Tomboy (Sciamma) 98–115, *110, 112, 113*
    trans 72
    transformative 71–2
    see also bodies; breasts; pregnant bodies
emotion(s) 13–14, 86, 391
The End of Man (Zylinska) 392
environmental ethics 2
environmental harm 167
environmental justice, disability and 319–22
eroticism 151, 213, 219, 224, 229, 233, 256, 391
erotic power
    excellence, internal requirement towards 232–3
    fear of 234
    functions of 234
    as kernel within ourselves 234
    living in touch with 234–5
    meaning of 233
    sharing/recognizing feelings of 235
    spiritual/political separation 233
    suppression and mistrust of 232
    as true knowledge 234
    of work 233
erotics 205, 207, 209
erotohistoriography
    antigenealogical, *Frankenstein* as 199–201
    defined 199
    dialectics of feeling 216–21, *220*
    erotic relations to history in *Frankenstein* 205
    femme/bottom historiography 214
    Frankenstein (Shelley) 199–205
    history, *Frankenstein* and 201–2
    lesbian 208
    noir 221–4, *223*
    Orlando (Woolf) 205–8
    queerly hybrid in time, Frankenstein's monster as 200–1
    The Sticky Fingers of Time (Brougher) 209–24, *212, 220, 223*
    sympathy, emphasis on in *Frankenstein* 202–3
    temporally out of joint, families in *Frankenstein* as 200–1
    see also time
ethical attention
    camera work 279–80
    camera work and editing 274
    characters, film's engagement with 274
    close-ups and 272
    detachment 272–4
    filmic attention 277–83, *278, 279, 281, 282*
    inscription of attention in film texts 268

inscription of vision as movement 268
    lack of criteria 267–8
    length of scenes 275
    moral vision 268, 271–6
    Nil by Mouth (Oldman) 268, 269–70, 272, 274–6, 280–3, *282,* 284, 286
    objective of 267
    Once Were Warriors (Tamahori) 268, 271–3, 274, 275, 276, *281,* 282–3
    perception and attention 268–71, *270*
    realist filmic conventions 271–2
    requirements of 267
    spectatorship 283–6
    theory of attention 268
ethics 35, 38, 39, 40, 47
    behaviourist 32
    of care 2
    of the duel 257
    environmental 2
    film philosophy and 4
    posthuman 242, 243
    see also ethical attention
Exit Man (Zylinska) 392
The Expression of the Emotions in Man and Animals (Darwin) 85, 165

fables
    morality and 35–6, 37, 40–1, 43–4
    universal rules and 40–1
families, Black, controlling images of Black women and 352
Faulkner, William
    Absalom, Absalom! 255–60, 262
    Light in August 253–5, 262, 265 n.7
Featherstone, Elena 354
Feeling and Form (Langer) 87
Felski, Rita 71
female sexuality
    She's Gotta Have It (Lee) 236–41
    see also Black female sexuality; lesbianism
feminism
    black 221, 229, 237
    as critique of past conditions 180
    disability, issues of and 315–16, 323
    as spectralized 177
    see also dominant imaginary, challenging
feminist aesthetics 2
    destruction, aesthetics of 33
    Innocence (Hadžihalilović) 31–2, *32*
feminist counterapocalypse 392
feminist ethics of care 2
feminist film philosophy
    cinematic sex and 391

still photography comparison 171
unshared horizons, (dis)abled-people and 187
utopian thinking 180–3
vertical time 83
see also erotohistoriography
Time Binds: Queer Temporalities, Queer Histories (Freeman) 181
Titchkosky, Tanya 319
toilets, public, accessible futures and 316–19
Tomboy (Sciamma)
bathroom scene 107, 109–11, *110*
casting of Héran 107
disclosure of Laure's gender 107, 113–14
dress, Laure forced to wear 107–8, 113, *113*
final scene with Lisa 114–15
football sequences 108–9, 111–13, *112*
phenomenological analysis 98
sensory opening moments 104–6
tools/weapons 141–5
Torok, Maria 213, 214, 215, 217, 218
torture 68–9, 134, 145, 146
tragic mulatto/a, figure of
Absalom, Absalom! (Faulkner) 255–60
alterity, problematics of 254
blood 262–3
Christmas (character) in *Light in August* (Faulkner) 253–5
fictional/historical, comparison of 253
fictional texts 264 n.2
origin of mulatto/a-ness 261
others, existing for 253
paternity of 253
phallus, naming and celebrating 254
retrieval of as topic, reasons for 252
self-reference 253, 265 n.5
sexuality and 254, 256–68, 266 n.14
shadow of 261–2
slavery *260*, 260–1, 266 n.18
TransBrandeis 318
trans people
access to public restrooms 314, 317–18, 330 n.19
Barbin, Herculine 75–6
cinema and 76
cultural series, phantasmagoria as 74–5
disability access to public restrooms 318
identity 72, 73, 76
illusory stereotype 72
modern/postmodern formation 72–3
phantasmagoria and 71–2
photographic images 73
shimmering 33
see also Girlhood (Sciamma); *Tomboy* (Sciamma)

traumatic content in art 89–90
turning out 359

unconscious inference 84
unconscious kinesthetic memories 85
unconsciousness of animals, belief in 163–4
unfinished, the 5, 180, 183
universal rules, fables and 40–1
universities
Black, controlling images of Black women and 351–2
changes in 244–7
cities and 247–8
civic dimension of 248
financial precarity 249
global era and 247–8
as multi-versities 247, 250
posthuman theory and 247–8
unreliable memories 84
unshared horizons, (dis)abled-people and 187
utopian thinking 180–3

vaginas 295
ventral streams 85
vertical time 83
Vincendeau, Ginette 116
violence
bodily response to 92
domestic 271, 279, 282, 288 n.12
against the helpless 67–9
impact of 284
Judith Decapitatiing Holofernes (Gentileschi) 90–1
news and documentaries 90
paintings 33
rape scene in *She's Gotta Have It* (Lee) 239–40
war 327
Virility School of Creativity 19–21
visibility/invisibility 176, 177
visibility machines 74
visible representation of thoughts and emotions 13–14
vision
filmic attention 277–8
morality and 37, 38, 40, 44, 46, 231, 271–6, 282–3
pain and imagining 137
pathways in the brain 85
prior experience and 84
relation to the earth 167
as sight 84–5
stereotyping and 84
technologically mediated 285–6
Visionaries book series 4
vital materialism 243
vulnerable/helpless as not synonymous 67–9